TARANTO
AND NAVAL AIR WARFARE IN THE MEDITERRANEAN, 1940–1945

Two 899 NAS pilots pose by a Seafire IIC for a press photo call on *Indomitable* just before she sailed for Operation Husky. (*Author's collection*)

TARANTO

AND NAVAL AIR WARFARE IN THE MEDITERRANEAN, 1940–1945

DAVID HOBBS

Seaforth
PUBLISHING

Copyright © David Hobbs 2020

First published in Great Britain in 2020 by
Seaforth Publishing
An imprint of Pen & Sword Books Ltd
47 Church Street, Barnsley
S Yorkshire S70 2AS

www.seaforthpublishing.com
Email info@seaforthpublishing.com

British Library Cataloguing in Publication Data
A CIP data record for this book is available from the British Library

ISBN 978-1-5267-9383-6 (HARDBACK)
ISBN 978-1-5267-9384-3 (EPUB)
ISBN 978-1-5267-9385-0 (KINDLE)

All rights reserved. No part of this publication may be reproduced or transmitted in any form or by any means, electronic or mechanical, including photocopying, recording, or any information storage and retrieval system, without prior permission in writing of both the copyright owner and the above publisher.

The right of David Hobbs to be identified as the author of this work has been asserted in accordance with the Copyright, Designs and Patents Act 1988

Pen & Sword Books Limited incorporates the imprints of Atlas, Archaeology, Aviation, Discovery, Family History, Fiction, History, Maritime, Military, Military Classics, Politics, Select, Transport, True Crime, Air World, Frontline Publishing, Leo Cooper, Remember When, Seaforth Publishing, The Praetorian Press, Wharncliffe Local History, Wharncliffe Transport, Wharncliffe True Crime and White Owl.

Typeset and designed by Mac Style
Printed and bound in Great Britain by T J Books Limited, Padstow

The men of the Royal Navy's Fleet Air Arm fought against considerable odds in the Mediterranean conflict. They set standards that continue to define the determination and capability of naval aviation in modern conflict and did so with minimal, often obsolescent, resources and great gallantry against numbers that should, in theory, have overwhelmed them. Their success in a wide range of operations, many of them never envisaged before 1940, is all the more memorable for that. This book is dedicated to all the Fleet Air Arm personnel who fought in the Mediterranean and especially those who never came home.

Contents

Foreword		ix
Acknowledgements		xi
Glossary		xii
1	Introduction	1
2	War spreads to the Mediterranean in 1940	10
3	Operation Judgement – the Taranto Strike	48
4	Fleet operations up to the Battle of Matapan	89
5	Operations in 1941 after the Battle of Matapan	138
6	Disembarked operations by naval air squadrons in 1941	163
7	Force H and the reinforcement of Malta	192
8	Operations in North Africa, Malta and with Force H in 1942	223
9	The Pedestal Convoy	248
10	Operation Torch	281
11	The Allied invasions of Sicily and Italy in 1943	314
12	Operation Dragoon	351
13	The final series of carrier operations in the Mediterranean	375
14	Retrospection	395

Appendices
A	Royal Navy aircraft operated in the Mediterranean Theatre 1940–44	404
B	Royal Navy fighter weapons	408
C	Aircraft reinforcements flown to Malta from aircraft carriers	410

D	RN and RAF aircraft reinforcements for the Eastern Mediterranean ferried by or flown off aircraft carriers to Takoradi for onward flight across Africa to Egypt	411
E	Royal Navy planned and actual front-line aircraft strengths 1939–44	412
F	Aircraft carrier flight deck, hangar and lift statistics	413

Notes 414
Bibliography 423
Index 427

Foreword

With the end of the Norwegian campaign in June 1940, the focus of naval warfare shifted to the Mediterranean. Sadly, the first operations were against a fleet that had been Britain's ally until only days earlier when Marshal Petain's French Government signed a separate peace treaty with Germany. Operations against Vichy French capital ships were intended to prevent them from falling into German hands and involved several aircraft carriers and their aircraft. The declaration of war on the British Empire by Italy began a campaign in which the Royal Navy's aircraft were to play a significant part operating from both ships and airfields ashore. Some of the latter were of a temporary nature with only a cluster of tents and vehicles marking them out from the surrounding desert.

Although every service had its part to play and many new weapons and tactics were to prove vital components of the Allied forces that eventually gained victory, it must be said that without the Royal Navy's carrier force and its aircraft, Malta might well have fallen and its loss may well have led to a very different outcome to the conflict in which Allied victory in North Africa and even the Middle East with its vital oil supplies could not have been taken for granted.

Many books have been written about the war in the Mediterranean but I believe that this is the first to concentrate on the Fleet Air Arm's important role as part of the Royal Navy's contribution to that conflict. In doing so I have sought to emphasise the fact that it was not a separate force fighting a war in the clouds that was divorced from what went on below. The Fleet Air Arm was an integral part of the Royal Navy that contributed to its operations above, on and under the surface of the sea and which also extended the reach of sea power over the land. It fought a naval war against an enemy fleet that suffered from the fact that it had no similar organisation of its own and was very much the worse for it. This book is the result of many years of fascinating research and is drawn in part from material that has never, previously, been published. As in the

Norwegian campaign, naval aircraft did many things for the first time in history, not least the night attack on the Italian battle fleet in its base at Taranto on 11 November 1940. In addition to describing what happened, I have tried to explain why it happened and to analyse the results. Where I have made criticisms, these usually reflect opinions that were expressed in the Admiralty at the time or my belief after studying contemporary documents that things that were done well at the time could actually have been even better. I accept that hindsight gives a wider perspective on events than was available to men at the time but I have made full use of my own experience as a carrier pilot, including periods spent in the Mediterranean in a variety of aircraft carriers.

In the years of the divided control of naval aviation prior to 1939, a succession of British politicians including Winston Churchill had stated that the relationship between the RAF and RN with regard to air operations would be that of teacher and pupil. The so-called 'indivisibility' of air power meant that a reserve of aircraft and aircrew would be retained by the RAF to support the other services when it deemed them to be needed. Reality in 1940, after the Admiralty regained full control of the Fleet Air Arm, proved to be very different. There was no reserve of aircraft or airmen, in fact the RN had to support the RAF, which was woefully short of both in the Mediterranean at first. It was the RN that developed both fighter direction and strike tactics, including the use of torpedoes at night against ships in harbour and at sea and the development of the pathfinder role by Albacore squadrons that found targets in the desert for RAF bombers. Importantly, the RAF learnt what the word 'joint' really meant in joint operations. That said, it was clear that as the war progressed co-operation between the forces grew rapidly with the RN Fighter Wing within the Desert Air Force, partially equipped with Hurricanes from RAF stocks, setting a good example.

Apart from the skills displayed by both naval aircrew and maintenance personnel, the aircraft that equipped the Fleet Air Arm in the Mediterranean must be mentioned. The Swordfish, Albacore, Skua and Fulmar were all markedly inferior to the aircraft operated by the German and Italian air forces and this makes the achievements of the men who flew them shine all the more brightly. The Martlet/Wildcat, Sea Hurricane and Seafire were all better fighters but still had their drawbacks. The Hellcat was outstanding.

David Hobbs MBE
Commander Royal Navy (Retired)
Alnwick
March 2020

Acknowledgements

My research projects and the books that follow from them have been encouraged and helped as always by my wife Jandy together with my son Andrew and his wife Lucyelle. Compiling and analysing the material that forms the basis of this book has taken many years in the Naval Historical Branch at its various locations in Empress State Building and New Scotland Yard in London and, to a limited extent, at its present location in Portsmouth Naval Base. I also carried out research at the MOD Archive when it was at Hayes and was also able to study a vast amount of material while I was the curator of the Fleet Air Arm Museum at Yeovilton. I am indebted to David Brown, Christopher Page and Stephen Prince, Heads of the Naval Historical Branch at various times, for their unstinted support for my projects, and to Jenny Wraight, the Admiralty Librarian. I would also like to thank Barbara Gilbert at the National Museum of the Royal Navy for her help.

I was able to draw on my archive for most of the photographs in this book but I am grateful to Philip Jarrett, the Sea Power Centre – Australia and Erminio Bagnasco, who made some of their own extensive collections available. This publication contains Public Sector information licensed under the Open Government Licence v 1.0 in the UK. I am also grateful to John Jordan, who provided me with the drawing of the Mark XII torpedo and the diagrams of the Italian battleships as they lay grounded on the seabed at Taranto. My thanks also go to Anthony Cowland, who painted the cover illustration, and Peter Wilkinson, who drew the maps.

Over decades of historical research in the margins of my naval career and full time after it I have been fortunate to discuss the development of naval aviation within the Commonwealth with many friends at historical symposia and other events in the UK, Australia, France and the USA. These have stimulated my own thought processes and helped me to look at events from differing perspectives. Norman Friedman in the USA and David Stevens in Australia are among these, together with fellow Society for Nautical Research members Eric Grove and Derek Law. That said, of course, all errors or omissions in the text are entirely my own.

I continue to be very grateful to Rob Gardiner of Seaforth Publishing for his continued support for my writings. This book is the ninth in our successful publishing partnership and I have already started work on the tenth.

Glossary

1SL	First Sea Lord
2SL	Second Sea Lord
3SL	Third Sea Lord
5SL	Fifth Sea Lord
(A)	Air Branch Officer not qualified for executive duties
AA	Anti-Aircraft
AAA	Anti-Aircraft Artillery
ACNS	Assistant Chief of the Naval Staff
ADDL	Airfield Dummy Deck Landing
AED	Air Engineering Department
AEO	Air Engineering Officer
AFO	Admiralty Fleet Order
AIO	Action Information Organisation
AOC	Air Officer Commanding (RAF)
AOC-in-C	Air Officer Commanding-in-Chief
AP(N)	Air Publication (Naval)
AS	Anti-Submarine
ASV	Air-to-Surface Vessel
Asdic	RN term for sonar before and during the Second World War
Avgas	Aviation Gasoline
BR	Book of Reference
CAFO	Confidential Admiralty Fleet Order
CAP	Combat Air Patrol
CB	Confidential Book
C-in-C	Commander-in-Chief
CO	Commanding Officer
COS	Chiefs of Staff
CPO	Chief Petty Officer
CS	Cruiser Squadron
CV	USN type designation for a fleet aircraft carrier

CVE	USN type designation for an escort aircraft carrier
DAD	Director of the Admiralty Air Department
DAM	Director of Air Material within the Admiralty
DCNS	Deputy Chief of the Naval Staff
DF	Destroyer Flotilla
DLCO	Deck Landing Control Officer (batsman)
DSC	Distinguished Service Cross
DSO	Distinguished Service Order
GP	General Purpose (bomb)
FDO	Fighter Direction Officer
FO	Flag Officer
FFO	Furnace Fuel Oil
HE	High Effect (bomb)
HF	High Frequency
HMS	His Majesty's Ship
HMAS	His Majesty's Australian Ship
hp	Horsepower
IFF	Identification Friend or Foe
kc/s	Kilocycles per Second
LA	Leading Airman
lb	pound
LG	Landing Ground
MAP	Ministry of Aircraft Production
MATMU	Mobile Air Torpedo Maintenance Unit
MBE	Member of the Order of the British Empire
MLA	Mean Line of Advance
MPA	Maritime Patrol Aircraft
MTB	Motor Torpedo Boat
NA	Naval Airman
NAD	Naval Air Division (within the Admiralty)
NAS	Naval Air Squadron
NCEF	Naval Commander Expeditionary Force
nm	nautical mile
OBE	Officer of the Order of the British Empire
PO	Petty Officer
PPI	Plan Position Indicator
RAF	Royal Air Force
RAAF	Royal Australian Air Force
RAN	Royal Australian Navy
RANAS	Rear Admiral Naval Air Stations
RCN	Royal Canadian Navy

RCNVR	Royal Canadian Naval Volunteer Reserve
RFA	Royal Fleet Auxiliary
RM	Royal Marines
RN	Royal Navy
RNAS	Royal Naval Air Station
RNAY	Royal Naval Air Yard
RNR	Royal Naval Reserve
RNVR	Royal Naval Volunteer Reserve
R/T	Radio Telephone
SAP	Semi-Armour Piercing (bomb)
shp	shaft horsepower
SNOPG	Senior Naval Officer Persian Gulf
SS	Steam Ship
TAC-R	Tactical Reconnaissance
TAG	Telegraphist Air Gunner
TBR	Torpedo Bomber Reconnaissance (aircraft)
Torpex	Torpedo explosive
TNT	Tri-Nitro Toluene (explosive)
TSR	Torpedo Spotter Reconnaissance (aircraft)
UK	United Kingdom
USA	United States of America
USAAF	United States Army Air Force
USN	United States Navy
USS	United States Ship
VA	Vice Admiral
VF	USN designation for a fighter squadron
VHF	Very High Frequency
VO	USN designation for an observation squadron
WS	'Winston Special' Convoy
W/T	Wireless telegraphy

1

Introduction

This book is intended to follow logically from my previous title *The Dawn of Carrier Strike* published in 2019 and to describe events as the focus of the Royal Navy's Fleet Air Arm operations moved from the North Sea to the Mediterranean in the second half of 1940. Operations against the Vichy French in the north and west African littoral have been included together with those in the Persian Gulf for the sake of completeness. It is now more than fifty years since the Admiralty ceased to control the Royal Navy's technological development, administration and operational command; readers may, therefore, find a brief description of the part it played in the period from 1940 to 1945 both interesting and enlightening.

The Admiralty

The Admiralty was directly responsible for every aspect of the naval service from the recruiting, training and appointment or drafting of all uniformed personnel, to the design and procurement of warships and their weapons systems. It managed the Royal Dockyards, both in the UK and overseas, as well as stores, armament and victualling depots. Some 127,000 men and women worked in the UK Dockyards in 1941, together with a further 45,000 in Gibraltar, Malta, Simonstown and Singapore.[1] A system of Admiralty overseers was maintained in every commercial shipyard and factory that fulfilled Admiralty contracts to ensure that their work met specifications and Admiralty Standards. The development of surface weapons, radar, Asdic (sonar), underwater weapons, guns and other material was carried out in Admiralty research establishments but the procurement of aircraft was complicated by the creation of a Ministry of Aircraft Production, MAP, which failed to recognise the importance of naval aviation. During the Second World War the Admiralty was also responsible for the control of merchant shipping and all aspects of shipbuilding, both naval and civilian.

The original Admiralty Building was completed in 1726 and until its use was changed by Government reforms in the 1990s it was the oldest

Designed by Thomas Ripley and completed in 1726, the original Admiralty building is seen here as it was in 1730. Today this Grade 1 listed building is known as Ripley Block. Note the foul-anchor device above the Palladian-style entrance. (*Author's collection*)

government office in the world still used for its original purpose. It is now listed as an ancient monument and the Admiralty Board Room has been preserved as it was. Other Admiralty offices were situated across London and in Bath.

The Board met frequently in the Admiralty Board Room and comprised both uniformed and civilian members who were able to focus on many aspects of the naval war and ensure their co-relation. The Board of Admiralty had been charged by the Admiralty Act of 1832 with 'full power and authority to do everything which belongs to the Office of Our High Admiral'.[2] In the period covered by this book the Board comprised two members of the government, six senior naval officers and one permanent civil servant organised thus:

    First Lord
    First Sea Lord and Chief of Naval Staff
    Second Sea Lord and Chief of Naval Personnel
    Third Sea Lord and Controller of the Navy
    Fourth Sea Lord – Chief of Naval Supplies and Transport
    Fifth Sea Lord and Deputy Chief of Naval Staff – responsible for Air Matters

Vice Chief of Naval Staff
Civil Lord
Permanent Secretary

Of these, the First Lord was a politician and member of the War Cabinet. All other Board members were responsible to him for the discharge of their specific duties.

Unlike the War Office and Air Ministry, which had no operational control over the Army and RAF respectively, the Admiralty controlled the operations of naval forces deployed around the world. During both world wars the Commonwealth navies of Australia, Canada, New Zealand, India and South Africa were placed under Admiralty control by their respective governments. The First Sea Lord, 1SL, was responsible for the operational direction of all the various fleets and forces, taking instructions from the War Cabinet and advice as necessary from the Naval Staff. His unique position was recognised by the rule that 'in any matter of great importance 1SL is always to be consulted' by the other Board members. 1SL had three key responsibilities; the first was joint as a member of the Board and the second individual as Chief of the Naval Staff when issuing orders to the fleet affecting war operations and the dispositions of ships and aircraft. The third was also individual when he acted as principal adviser to the Prime Minister and the War Cabinet on naval matters.

Under 1SL's direction the Deputy Chief of Naval Staff, DCNS, was responsible for naval air policy, technical development, tactics, the operational training of ships and naval air squadrons as well as all matters related to the ships, aircraft, weapons and fighting efficiency of the RN. To support him he had a number of Divisions within the Naval Staff, each headed by a senior Captain RN. These included, among others, the Naval Air Division, NAD, which was responsible for the organisation and training of the Fleet Air Arm; liaison with the MAP on the procurement of new types of naval aircraft and with the Air Ministry on the development of air weapons. All reports of proceedings, combat, action and damage reports were forwarded to one or more relevant Admiralty Divisions, which used them to understand the 'state of the art' in the fleet at sea and to make recommendations on possible improvements. Their surviving comments have proved a valuable source of information when researching the various operations I describe later. The Vice Chief of Naval Staff, VCNS, was responsible for operational policy, planning and direction, a range of subjects that covered naval intelligence and security, which were covered within the Naval Intelligence Division.

In 1939 the Admiralty was an excellent administrative organisation but was not fortunate enough to have an operational leadership capable of making the best use of the new technology available to it.³ When he became First Lord for the second time in September 1939, Churchill consistently interfered with operations in a way that historian Nicholas Rodger has described as 'more characteristic of intrigue than command'. To make matters worse, Pound arguably continued to demonstrate the same faults that had been such a negative influence on the conduct of war at sea between 1914 and 1918. He was an obsessive centraliser who worked himself too hard and Rodger described him as a humourless, narrow man, 'a driver rather than a leader' who suffered from several serious and painful illnesses, including a brain tumour, which affected his power of concentration. He had little of the breadth of intellect and experience that might have helped him stand up to Churchill on the one hand or leave commanders at sea to make their own decisions on the other.⁴

The foul-anchor device over the Palladian entrance as it appears today. It presents an interesting technological contrast with the communications aerials that once connected the operations rooms under the citadel with fleets across the world and which can still be seen rigged over the building. (*Andrew Hobbs collection*)

When Churchill left the Admiralty to become Prime Minister in May 1940 he continued, as Minister of Defence, to use the Admiralty War Registry and Pound failed to prevent him doing so. The new First Lord, A V Alexander, was carefully chosen to provide administrative efficiency and political balance⁵ with little risk that he might challenge Churchill over any naval matter. The War Cabinet was dominated by the new Prime Minister and dealt directly with the Joint Chiefs of Staff, leaving the First Lord out of the war's innermost council. Direction of the war effort came from the former Committee of Imperial Defence Secretariat at Storey's Gate, which now filled the triple role of Cabinet Office, Ministry of Defence and Prime Minister's Office to connect Churchill through Admiral Pound and the other Chiefs of Staff to the Naval Staff. The Board of Admiralty remained central to the vast organisation of supply and administrative matters but had less operational input than it should have done.

Thus the Naval Staff, which actually directed the war at sea and the Operational Intelligence Centre, which formed the 'brain' of the whole organisation, was faced with both opportunities and problems that were unparalleled. Intelligence information was provided by the Government Code & Cypher School, GC & CS, to the select group able to receive Ultra messages once enemy codes were broken and a vast quantity of information by teleprinter came into the Admiralty's communications centre from units in contact with the enemy across the globe. This was all assimilated in the bomb-proof operations rooms beneath the Admiralty citadel, known to the men and women who worked in them as 'Lenin's Tomb'. One room covered operations in the Home/Atlantic theatre and the other the rest of the world including the Mediterranean. Teams in both were led by senior captains RN. Pound had more information about his opponents' fleet activities at his fingertips than any previous 1SL and historians have reproached him for interfering excessively with task force commanders who were in contact with the enemy. On reflection, eighty years later, it can be appreciated that the real fault lay not with the concept of centralised direction from the Admiralty but in allowing a sick man to do so who was unable to use his staff properly. When Pound died in 1943[6] the First Lord insisted that Admiral of the Fleet Sir Andrew Cunningham, a man who Churchill had grown to respect, was the best choice to replace him.

Admiralty direction of fleets and forces

The Admiralty gave directions that controlled the activities of the Commonwealth navies through senior flag officers.[7] These were usually the RN Commanders-in-Chief of the fleets deployed in the geographical stations across the world's oceans, of which the Mediterranean Fleet was one.[8] When the occasion demanded, a flag officer who was not a C-in-C was given an improvised task force for which he was responsible directly to the Admiralty and this is what happened when Force H was created in 1940. Communication between the Admiralty and senior flag officers was carried out in a number of ways depending on urgency and the need for secrecy. Only a very small number of very senior officers were allowed access to Ultra messages from the GC & CS. Pains were taken when Ultra messages were acted upon to make it appear that that there was a plausible non-intelligence reason for enemy forces to be intercepted and engaged to prevent the enemy from realising that codes had been broken. Air reconnaissance was one such. Messages could be sent by telegraph to fleet bases using a worldwide web of secure undersea cables controlled by the British firm Cable & Wireless Ltd or by W/T, which could be intercepted, or by post, usually in the hands of a King's Messenger for important material.

Broad principles were communicated by the Admiralty in the Fighting Instructions, which gave advice on the latest tactics. Detailed information on specific topics such as the Fleet Air Arm, gunnery, torpedoes, navigation and direction were produced by the relevant Admiralty Divisions and published as confidential documents that were used to spread experience and knowledge of the latest operations and tactics. Administrative orders were distributed as numbered Confidential Admiralty Fleet Orders, CAFOs, and Admiralty Fleet Orders, AFOs. These covered a wealth of detail, some of which impacted on combat operations, for instance the colour schemes in which ships and aircraft were to be painted and the variations in tool kit content to be made when air mechanics were drafted to a squadron that was equipped with American rather than British-built aircraft.[9] Both orders had a 'life' of two years, at the end of which they had to be incorporated into the Kings Regulations and Admiralty Instructions, other standing order books or reissued.

Some senior officers, for instance the Rear Admiral Naval Air Stations, Flag Officer Submarines and the Commandant General Royal Marines, had appointments that were based on function and not a specific geographical area. Cs-in-C and Force Flag Officers controlled their fleets through subordinate force and group commanders. They also controlled subordinate commanders in charge of ports, naval bases and naval air stations. The Mediterranean Fleet and others had a Flag Officer (Air), who had specific responsibility for the employment of aircraft carriers

The men and women who worked in the operations rooms under the citadel built alongside the Admiralty during the Second World War referred to it as 'Lenin's Tomb'. It contrasts starkly with the older red brick building but today ivy has mellowed its external appearance. The monument in the right foreground is the Great War Royal Naval Division Memorial designed for the Admiralty by Sir Edwin Lutyens. (*Andrew Hobbs collection*)

and their air groups. However, some naval air squadrons, NAS, that were disembarked ashore might be put under the command of the local senior RAF officer so that their operations could be co-ordinated with other aircraft. The Admiralty could give orders and instructions to any unit directly but experience was to show that such a move should be considered carefully before being taken. Cases did arise where the Admiralty operations room had better and more up-to-date information than the commander on the spot, or when units from different fleets were engaged in a concerted but impromptu action together but even then advice might be more appropriate than the remote assumption of control. The need for worldwide communications and for a staff large enough to assimilate the whole intelligence picture and plan the best use of it coupled with the need for radio silence at sea gradually forced Cs-in-C to command their forces from shore bases. Both Admiral Cunningham and Admiral Somerville commanded their forces from their flagships in 1940 but by 1942 Cunningham had moved ashore with his staff. Senior officers encapsulated their orders to ships and units under their command in books of standing orders, which were constantly updated.

The state of the Fleet Air Arm

The Admiralty had only resumed full control of its air arm in May 1939 after the recommendation made in the Inskip Award of 1937.[10] It was still short of the number of aircraft artificers and mechanics required and measures had been taken to recruit and train the men required. The Admiralty calculated in 1937 that 4,000 new aircraft technicians would be needed by 1939 but this number had not been reached. Generously, the Air Ministry agreed to leave 1,460 men on extended loan to the RN until the gaps were filled and by 1943 the RN had recruited and trained over 12,000 air technical ratings. The situation with air engineering officers was similar and numbers were only just sufficient to fill front-line appointments in 1940.

Aircrew numbers, already low, were significantly reduced by the losses sustained during the defence of Norway in 1940 but by then hundreds of young men were in training, most of them members of the RNVR Air Branch. A number of air stations were being built in the UK to house disembarked front-line squadrons, raise and commission new ones and to act as parent units for training squadrons and schools. By mid-1940 the carriers *Courageous* and *Glorious* had been lost, leaving *Furious* and the new *Ark Royal* as the only fleet carriers capable of embarking viable air groups. The prototype carriers *Hermes* and *Eagle* were really too small but had to operate to the best of their ability and even the elderly training

The British Chiefs of Staff in 1939. From the left: Sir Cyril Newall of the RAF, Sir Dudley Pound, First Sea Lord, and Sir Edmond Ironside, Chief of the Imperial General Staff. (*Author's collection*)

carrier *Argus*[11] had to be used as an operational carrier from 1940, limiting her availability as a deck landing training ship. *Illustrious*, the first of the armoured carriers, was completed on 25 May 1940 with five sister-ships in various stages of construction. At the time they represented the largest aircraft carrier construction programme in the world.

The RN had aircraft such as the Swordfish, Albacore and Fulmar in production during 1940 and others, including the Martlet, were being procured from the USA but none were available in the numbers required or at the pace of production the RN needed. In its first year the MAP failed to understand the RN's need for aircraft and this had the unfortunate effects of slowing down, rather than increasing, the deliveries of aircraft to the RN's front-line squadrons and actually stopping the development of new naval types. In terms of ships, aircraft and manpower, the striking feature of the Fleet Air Arm in 1940/41 is how very small it was and this fact makes its achievements all the more remarkable. To give a single example, the twenty-one Swordfish that carried out the attack on Taranto in November 1940 represented 15 per cent of the total front-line Swordfish force. The following tables show just how small the Royal Navy's air resources were.

Aircrew

	Sept 1939	Sept 1940	July 1941	July 1942	July 1943	July 1944
Trained pilots	406	764	939	1,632	2,357	3,933
Under training	332	635	936	1,400	2,563	2,607

	Sept 1939	Sept 1940	July 1941	July 1942	July 1943	July 1944
Trained observers	260	350	383	740	1,181	1,620
Under training	248	252	427	586	925	750

	Sept 1939	Sept 1940	July 1941	July 1942	July 1943	July 1944
TAG	350	554	668	910	1,232	1,730
Under training	210	192	310	429	863	805[12]

Total numbers of aircraft on the strength of RN front-line units

	Sept 1939	Sept 1940	Sept 1941	Sept 1942	Sept 1943	Sept 1944
Swordfish	140	139	129	114	156	201
Walrus	45	58	51	72	15	2
Skua	18	33	–	–	–	–
Sea Gladiator	12	15	–	–	–	–
Albacore	–	30	69	95	35	–
Fulmar	–	30	58	64	3	–
Sea Hurricane	–	–	34	42	17	6
Martlet/Wildcat	–	–	32	87	117	108
Seafire	–	–	–	59	98	173
Hellcat	–	–	–	–	28	92[13]

Note these numbers show aircraft serving in front-line naval air squadrons throughout the world, not just those serving in the Mediterranean theatre of operations. They do not include the aircraft allocated to second-line or training squadrons.

2

War spreads to the Mediterranean in 1940

On 10 June 1940 the Italian Government declared war on the British Empire and France, a cynical move that followed the French collapse and the withdrawal of the largest element of the British Expeditionary Force, BEF, from the continent of Europe through Dunkirk. It must have seemed to the Italian dictator Benito Mussolini that the conflict was about to end with an armistice on terms that would be favourable to Germany and its Axis partner Italy. He could not have been more wrong. Churchill's new government had anticipated the declaration and, as far as possible given the grave situation at home, the Mediterranean Fleet had been maintained with sufficient strength to defend British interests.

Some of the first British moves in the Mediterranean, however, were not against Italy but against France after it abandoned its former ally to sign an armistice with Germany. Most French battleships and cruisers had left their home ports before the completion of the negotiations between Marshal Petain and the Germans and Churchill recognised at once that the use of force against these warships might be necessary to prevent them falling into German hands.[1] The battlecruisers *Dunkerque* and *Strasbourg* were at Mers-el-Kébir, a French naval base close to the port of Oran. Also present in this base were the older but modernised battleships *Provence* and *Bretagne*, the seaplane tender *Commandant Teste* and several modern cruisers and destroyers. The War

Admiral Somerville, Flag Officer Force H, photographed in flying kit before a flight in a Swordfish from *Formidable* in 1942. (*Author's collection*)

Cabinet decided, therefore, that Marshal Petain's Vichy Government must conform to certain conditions about the disposal of its fleet that were to be presented to the French Admiral at Mers-el-Kébir. A British task force, designated Force H, was assembled at Gibraltar under Vice Admiral Sir James Somerville with instructions to negotiate and, ultimately, to use force if the talks failed. Force H comprised the battlecruiser *Hood* as Somerville's flagship, the aircraft carrier *Ark Royal* flying the flag of the Vice Admiral Aircraft carriers, Vice Admiral Wells,[2] the battleships *Valiant* and *Resolution*, two cruisers and eleven destroyers.

Action against the French Fleet at Mers-el-Kébir

There was little enthusiasm in Force H for the task it had been given but the vital necessity to use force if negotiations failed was obvious. Somerville and his staff planned to neutralise the French ships with long-range gunfire, bombing and torpedo attack by carrier-borne aircraft in that order. They were fortunate that there was no French minefield in the

Mers-el-Kébir harbour photographed from one of *Ark Royal*'s Swordfish after the first strike on 6 July 1940. It shows the battlecruiser *Dunkerque* damaged and beached in shallow water. (*Author's collection*)

waters adjacent to the naval base and after the French Admiral refused to accept British terms, offensive action began on 3 July 1940. *Ark Royal*'s Swordfish spotted for the capital ships' gunfire and this task proved to be of critical importance when the harbour was shrouded in smoke from explosions and fires after the first salvoes hit and fire-control directors could no longer see their targets. After ten minutes' bombardment at a range of 17,500yds the battleship *Bretagne* and a destroyer were seen to have blown up and both the *Dunkerque* and *Provence* were damaged and aground. A second phase began after *Strasbourg* was seen to have sailed, heading east with several destroyers at high speed. A strike force of six Swordfish was airborne on its way to attack ships in harbour. It was retasked in flight to attack *Strasbourg* and did so despite heavy and accurate anti-aircraft fire. Each aircraft was armed with four 250lb SAP and four 20lb Cooper bombs,[3] a choice of weapons subsequently described as 'curious' by NAD. The 20lb bombs could do little, if any, structural damage to a warship and were intended for use as anti-personnel weapons but in this operation the object had been 'to do as much damage as possible while imposing the fewest possible casualties'. In any case, the correct load to be carried in a strike against a capital ship should have been six 250lb SAP bombs.[4] Two Swordfish were shot down by *Strasbourg*'s anti-aircraft fire but their crews were located and rescued by Force H destroyers. The loss of two Swordfish out of six showed the type's vulnerability in a daylight dive-bombing attack against well-armed opposition.

A further strike force of six Swordfish, this time armed with torpedoes, was prepared and flown off ninety minutes after the first attack. In his report, quoted in the Naval Staff History,[5] Captain C S Holland RN, *Ark Royal*'s commanding officer, explained that this strike took longer than he would have wished to prepare because of the disruptions to the planned flying programme caused by repeated postponements of the original bombardment to allow the prolongation of negotiations. To an extent, however, the ship was limited by the narrow flight deck and the excessively large round-down aft, which limited the number of aircraft that could be ranged for take-off. Better flight deck design and more flexible operating techniques would improve matters in later carriers. The strike leader astutely delayed his attack until just after sunset, by which time he had led his force into a position ahead of and to the east of *Strasbourg* with the distant, darkening, shore as a background.[6] He was thus able to take advantage of the light conditions with the ship well lit by the afterglow of sunset while his aircraft attacked at low level out of a dark background, achieving complete surprise. One hit was observed and there may have been another; a creditable achievement given the pilots' lack of recent night or dusk torpedo attack practice and the target's high speed. Mark XII torpedoes were the best ship-killing weapon available and they were fitted with duplex pistols and a depth setting of 20ft. Apparently this depth was selected so that the pistol would function non-contact if it passed under a destroyer on the battle cruiser's screen but NAD felt that this reasoning indicated confused thinking. The object had been to destroy or cripple *Strasbourg* but a depth setting of only 20ft ruled out the possibility of obtaining a non-contact hit under her hull that would have had the best chance of causing critical damage. At 20ft, the torpedo would have detonated against the side armour, causing damage that would probably not be fatal. Set to run deeper, the magnetic pistol would have detonated under the keel and probably broken the ship's back.

Air reconnaissance by Swordfish subsequently showed *Dunkerque* to be aground but no serious damage was visible and it was decided to complete her immobilisation with a strike by torpedo-armed aircraft. On 6 July three waves of Swordfish from *Ark Royal* attacked her, starting at sunrise. The first comprised six aircraft of 820 NAS, which approached the harbour at 7,000ft and carried out a shallow diving attack in line ahead from directly up sun. Their torpedoes were fitted with duplex pistols and set to run at only 12ft because of the shallow water in which the ship was grounded. This attack achieved complete surprise with five hits on *Dunkerque* and an ammunition barge alongside her, which exploded and caused considerable damage to the battlecruiser. The sixth torpedo probably failed to detonate against the target because it was dropped inside the safety range of the pistol but it did explode on hitting a jetty. There was no anti-aircraft fire before the attack and very little as the aircraft withdrew. No aircraft were damaged.

Two further attacks, each by a sub-flight of three Swordfish from 810 NAS, followed at intervals but surprise had been lost and they encountered heavy anti-aircraft fire. The second attack achieved two hits but the third torpedo was not dropped as the pilot had failed to select his armament master switch to the 'on' position. Minor damage was suffered by one aircraft. The third attack obtained two hits but the torpedoes failed to detonate as they were probably dropped inside the safety range of the duplex pistols. The third torpedo exploded under a tug that was, unfortunately, in the line of fire and it was seen to disintegrate. This attack was heavily engaged by anti-aircraft fire from defences that were now thoroughly alert and all three aircraft were damaged, one of them severely, but they all managed to return and land on safely. The aircrews' reports convinced Admiral Somerville that the ship had been satisfactorily immobilised. The second and third waves had been escorted by Skuas and

Swordfish ranged on *Ark Royal* in 1939. Note the large, sloping area of deck on the after round-down that could not be used to range aircraft. (*Author's collection*)

those of the third wave were intercepted by Vichy French Morane-Saulnier 406 and Curtiss Hawk 75 fighters.[7] These were described as 'easily out-manoeuvring' the Skuas but did not appear to press home their attacks. One Skua was damaged and forced to ditch but its crew was rescued by a destroyer. There were no other casualties.

Attack on the Richelieu *at Dakar*

The new battleship *Richelieu* had sailed from Brest on 18 June 1940 for Dakar in the French West African colony of Senegal. A British task force, which included the aircraft carrier *Hermes* and the seaplane carrier *Albatross*, was assembled off west Africa to deal with it and their activities are worthy of description for the sake of completeness. With the hardening of Vichy French attitudes against its former ally, the Admiralty gave orders that the French battleship was to be given an ultimatum similar to that given to the Admiral in Mers-el-Kébir. Captain R J F Onslow MVO

DSC RN, the commanding officer of *Hermes*, was temporarily promoted to Rear Admiral to act as senior officer of the task force, which included the heavy cruisers *Dorsetshire* and *Australia*. The ultimatum was rejected on the evening of 7 July and, because *Richelieu* was protected by nets and surrounded by merchant ships, an unusual form of attack was devised to immobilise her that would hopefully not cause heavy loss of life.[8] A fast motor boat from *Hermes* was armed with four depth charges and carried out a hazardous approach at night, passing over an anti-submarine boom, avoiding torpedo nets and using merchant ships as cover. It dropped its charges within 30yds of the battleship's stern but, disappointingly, they all failed to detonate because the water was too shallow for them to arm properly.

A strike force comprising six torpedo-armed Swordfish of 814 NAS was flown off *Hermes* to attack at dawn on 8 July 1940. The awkward position in which *Richelieu* was lying, together with the proximity of merchant ships and an inner torpedo net boom, limited their options and the aircraft attacked along a narrow lane between anchored ships on a south-westerly heading in line astern with torpedoes dropped in succession, a plan that proved to be well conceived and well executed. Half had a depth setting of 38ft and were armed with duplex pistols, used by 814 NAS for the first time, and, as insurance against any malfunction, the other half had a depth setting of 24ft and were fitted with well-proven contact pistols. The attack was successful, even though only one torpedo was actually confirmed as a hit. The other torpedoes were difficult to assess and some of those set to run deep may have stuck in mud on the seabed close to the target. Heavy anti-aircraft fire had been opened from a number of French ships and shore batteries but all aircraft returned safely with only slight damage. Reconnaissance after the attack showed *Richelieu* to have a slight list and a considerable amount of oil was seen around her. The Admiralty did not learn until later that at least one torpedo had hit and had caused considerable damage. Repairs to make her seaworthy took over a year to complete at Dakar. In its analysis NAD minuted that the setting put on the torpedoes intended to run under the target should not have exceeded 33ft; that is, 6ft greater than the ship's known draught, in order to decrease the risk of their grounding in the seabed. The torpedoes intended to explode on contact should have been set to run at 21ft, or 6ft less than the ship's known draught. They also criticised the use of the high-speed, 40 knot, setting used on the torpedoes when the charted depth of water at the dropping position was only 7 fathoms (42ft). Admiralty policy[9] was that only the lower-speed, 27-knot, setting should be used for attacks in shallow water.

Anxiety about *Richelieu* led the British Government to approve a plan for the occupation of French West Africa, which included Dakar, by a Free French force under General de Gaulle, one of the objects of which was to ensure the immobilisation of the battleship. A large task force, including the aircraft carrier *Ark Royal* and the battleships *Barham* and *Resolution* with five cruisers and six troop transports, two of which were French, was assembled off Dakar during August with Vice Admiral J H D Cunningham in command. It was hoped that the landings, designated Operation Menace, would succeed without resistance but if this proved not to be the case, force was to be used. In addition to *Richelieu*, Vichy French forces included two cruisers, at least six destroyers and three submarines. Gun batteries ashore were known to be strong and efficiently manned, and there were a number of fighters at several airfields around Dakar. It was hoped to win over the Vichy French aircrew, however, by landing Free French pilots in light aircraft that had been embarked in *Ark Royal* for the purpose.

The task force arrived off Dakar on 22 September and a Skua from *Ark Royal* began the operation with a long-range photographic reconnaissance of the harbour and its surrounding area. It was not detected because the pilot glided over the target area from 15,000ft with his engine throttled back and was neither seen nor heard by the defenders; the mission was a complete success. At dawn on 23 September two Free French Caudron Luciole biplanes with French pilots and two Swordfish carrying French envoys were flown off *Ark Royal*; The French aircraft landed at the Vichy airfield at Oukam but the Swordfish were intercepted by Vichy Curtiss fighters and anti-aircraft batteries opened fire on them, forcing them to return to the carrier. Similar hostile receptions were given to Free French emissaries who landed from sloops, and gunfire from shore batteries left no doubt about the Vichy garrison's intention not to join the Free French cause.

On 24 September Dakar was attacked at dawn but an attempted landing proved to be a failure. Bad visibility hampered bombardment but strikes were carried out by *Ark Royal*'s aircraft. These began with a dive-bombing attack on *Richelieu* by six Swordfish originally flown off to attack gun emplacements on Gorée Island, each armed with four 250lb SAP and eight 20lb bombs. They were rebriefed to attack the battleship after take-off, notwithstanding the fact that their light bombs would be useless against its armoured hull.[10] They were intercepted by fighters and heavy anti-aircraft fire, which brought down three Swordfish before they could begin their attacks, but the remaining three attacked successfully and reported that they had observed hits on the target's forecastle. It was

French Caudron Luciole biplanes on *Ark Royal*'s flight deck being prepared to fly Free French officers ashore in an attempt to negotiate the surrender of Dakar on 23 September 1940. (*Author's collection*)

not known if they were by the larger or smaller bombs but, either way, the effect was negligible. This was followed by another attack by six Swordfish that had been flown off to attack the French General Staff Office and a W/T station, each armed with four 250lb GP bombs, fused NDT, and eight 20lb bombs, but again their orders were changed after take-off and they were instructed to attack a gun battery at Cape Manuel. SAP rather than GP bombs would undoubtedly have been more effective against this target and the changes of plan resulting in the use of inappropriate weapons was but one of many negative aspects in a campaign that did not go well.

The use of aircraft to spot the fall of shot for bombardments became indispensable after ground mist and a smokescreen laid by Vichy cruisers obscured every target. The battleships had not undergone recent training in the relevant techniques and events underlined the importance of this in preparation for operations of this nature. After about half an hour Vichy bombers attacked the task force from high level but made no hits and it withdrew to seaward. A reconnaissance by one of *Ark Royal*'s aircraft revealed that there had been a possible 15in shell hit on *Richelieu*, another on a fort and a fire was observed in a cruiser. The bombardment was resumed in the afternoon but return fire from *Richelieu* was well

A range of Skuas starting up on *Ark Royal* in 1940. The wingtip just visible to their right marked 5F is a Swordfish. (*Author's collection*)

directed, hitting *Barham* several times. Vichy fighters eventually drove off the spotting aircraft and the bombardment was terminated.

A torpedo attack followed, for which nine Swordfish escorted by three Skuas were flown off *Ark Royal* to attack two *Gloire*-class cruisers seen getting under way. Unfortunately the Swordfish leader ditched following an engine failure on take-off and only eight aircraft carried out the attack.[11] Some measure of surprise was achieved and the aircraft dropped their torpedoes from positions inside the anti-submarine netting in the only place possible given the close proximity of the land and the depth of water. The Skuas reported that two torpedoes appeared to have hit the leading cruiser and a possible third hit the rear ship. Both ships were in action the next day, however, and NAD took the view after examining the evidence that there had been no hits. It was thought possible that the torpedoes may have hit obstructions on the seabed and the explosions seen by the fighters might, therefore, have been close to the leading cruiser without damaging it. The attacking Swordfish had approached their targets at 8,000ft and dived into their attack in loose line astern as anti-aircraft fire became intense. They had no visible horizon beyond their targets and little sea room between the nets in which to manoeuvre. The torpedoes were fitted with duplex pistols and were set to run at 20ft at the low-speed setting; *Gloire*'s standard draught was known to be 16.5ft.

By 25 September Vichy fighter opposition was preventing Swordfish from maintaining patrols or flying reconnaissance in the port area. Vichy gunfire had increased in both intensity and accuracy and further attacks were made on the task force by bombers but Skuas prevented them from bombing accurately. On the other hand, they lacked the speed to destroy any of the bombers[12] and Admiralty analysis of the operation noted that Skuas 'could achieve no decisive results owing to their inferior speed'.[13] Operation Menace was abandoned a day later as it had become clear that serious damage was being inflicted on the task force for no very obvious gain.

Three important points emerge from the Admiralty analysis of Operation Menace. As in the Norwegian campaign, a task force had operated close to a hostile shore for an extended period and relied on its own aircraft not only for its own protection but for the whole conduct of the operation. Also, as in Norway, it was recognised that the aircraft embarked in *Ark Royal* were no match for the fighters and bombers that opposed them. Operation Menace exposed the weakness of attempting to carry out an amphibious assault with a hastily prepared plan and forces with no specialised training in this form of warfare.

Initial operations against Italian sea and air forces

As soon as he learnt of the Italian declaration of war, the Commander-in-Chief of the Mediterranean Fleet, Admiral Sir Andrew Cunningham, sailed from Alexandria with a force that included the aircraft carrier *Eagle*, which had arrived in May after a long refit in Singapore. She had 813 and 824 NAS embarked, each with nine Swordfish plus three Sea Gladiators that had been held in reserve for *Glorious*' 802 NAS at RNAS Dekheila.[14] They formed a fighter flight of 813 NAS flown by Commander Charles Keighly-Peach DSO RN, the ship's Commander 'Air'. He had previously flown Hawker Nimrod fighters and was assisted by Swordfish pilots, some of whom had fighter experience.

In his report Cunningham wrote that 'this initial cruise had as its primary object the attack on enemy forces at sea and it also provided a means of assessing the enemy's surface, submarine and air effort'.[15] No enemy forces were encountered but the C-in-C was able to confirm beyond doubt that the few RAF reconnaissance aircraft available in the Mediterranean were inadequate to meet his fleet's needs. As far back as 1921, the then C-in-C Mediterranean, Admiral Sir John de Robeck, had written to the Admiralty expressing his dissatisfaction at the failure of the RAF to meet the aviation requirements of his fleet.[16] Despite the passage of two decades in which politicians had urged the RN to accept that the RAF would know best what was required, little had changed by June 1940. The pernicious impact of an air policy that concentrated on a continental bombing strategy was to cost the British Commonwealth dearly and its influence was felt in many ways. In both the USA and Japan navies operated their own shore-based reconnaissance aircraft trained to search for enemy surface forces, shadow and attack them in concert with the surface fleet but, even after the Inskip Award, the UK lacked this capability. The few aircraft the RAF did deploy on maritime reconnaissance had crews that were not trained to operate as part of a fleet. Their signals were sent to RAF command centres at first and then, after delays that might be considerable, forwarded to the Admiralty for onward transmission to the relevant fleet. For time-sensitive targets such as warships at sea this tactic had little value and, lacking shore-based maritime patrol aircraft under its own command, the RN had to rely on carrier-borne aircraft to search for the enemy as well as provide strike forces and airborne anti-submarine patrols.

Admiral Sir Andrew Cunningham, Commander-in-Chief Mediterranean Fleet. (*Author's collection*)

As Cunningham now realised, the small carrier *Eagle* was stretched to its limit providing extensive reconnaissance and anti-submarine patrols as well keeping a viable strike force ready during daylight hours.

Another lesson learnt the hard way by the British Government was the paradoxical position of Malta, for over a century the dockyard and base for the Mediterranean Fleet. It was ideally placed to operate air and sea forces that could intercept convoys from mainland Italy to its colonies in North Africa but since no attempt had been made to bolster its defences before the war it had been considered too vulnerable to function as a base in 1940. That was the principal reason for redeploying the fleet to Alexandria and for retaining Force H in Gibraltar. The Italian battle fleet was larger than the British and had ships that were both more modern and faster. However, Cunningham was determined to maintain an aggressive posture and decided that rather than use his forces piecemeal, he would sail his whole fleet including the carrier on every possible occasion to achieve a broad range of aims. This policy had the advantages of concentrated force and economy of effort but it also meant that whenever the fleet was at sea some objectives were given a higher priority than others. At this time the Mediterranean Fleet lacked the ability to replenish its warships at sea and was limited to sorties of finite length from bases where ships could be refuelled and rearmed in relative safety. Neither Gibraltar nor Alexandria was close enough to the Central Mediterranean basin to allow the maintenance of surface patrols strong enough to blockade Italian North Africa permanently.

Action off Calabria

Operation MA 5 began on 7 July 1940 with the aim of covering the passage of both fast and slow convoys from Malta to Alexandria. To divert enemy attention from it, Force H sailed and Swordfish from *Ark Royal* were to carry out attacks on the Italian base at Cagliari in Sardinia on 9 July. Unfortunately it was located by the enemy and bombed while it was still more than 250nm west of Sardinia. These attacks caused no damage but Somerville felt the risk to *Ark Royal* was too great and decided to return to Gibraltar. The Mediterranean Fleet also suffered high-level bombing attacks but Cunningham took heart from the fact that no serious damage had been done. His staff calculated that, statistically, Italian bombers flying at 12,000ft using a level bombing technique against fast, manoeuvring targets ought to achieve 1 per cent hits, rising to 2 per cent as they gained experience. However, the bombers only succeeded in hitting the cruiser *Gloucester*, destroying her compass platform and killing her commanding officer Captain F R Garside RN, six other officers and eleven ratings. However, she was able to remain with the fleet.

On 6 July 1940 an Italian task force sailed to cover a convoy of five merchant ships from Naples carrying supplies to the Italian army in Libya.[17] From the outset, the British war effort in the Mediterranean concentrated on the protection of vital logistic supplies to its own forces in North Africa and the destruction of Axis convoys performing a similar function for their own forces. Victory was likely to go to the side that succeeded in this contest and carrier-borne aircraft had a considerable part to play, indeed it would be fair to say that without carriers, the British could not have succeeded. Their ability to concentrate force where and when it was needed became a critical factor that the Axis powers could not match. By coincidence, the Italian convoy coincided with MA 5, initiating a war of logistic dominance. The Italian covering force included the battleships *Giulio Cesare* and *Cavour* and was commanded by Admiral Campioni.

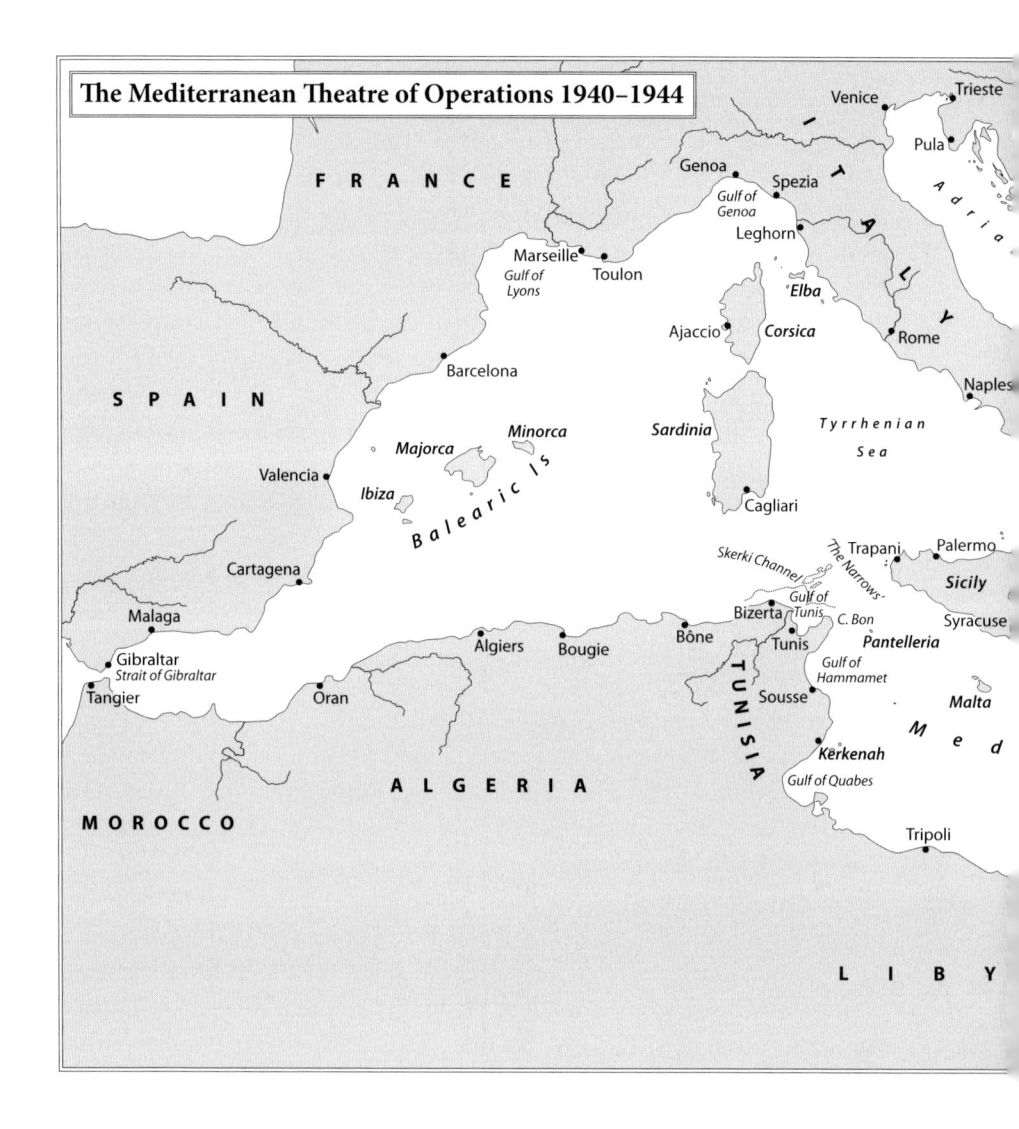

Cunningham was not aware that this force was at sea until 8 July when the submarine *Phoenix* and an RAF Sunderland both reported it 220 miles north of Benghazi as it headed north after completing its mission. Cunningham calculated that he could not bring it to action unless he could place himself between the Italian warships and their base at Taranto. He proceeded, therefore, directly towards Taranto but the Italians were able to read some RN signal traffic and when it became aware of Cunningham's intention the Italian Naval Command ordered Campioni to avoid battle until at least noon on 9 July when the British fleet would be within range of Italian bombers.

Early on 9 July the Italian force was located by a Swordfish from *Eagle* 145nm west of Cunningham's flagship, the battleship *Warspite*. It shadowed the enemy force, sending a series of reports that gave Cunningham situational awareness but, in contrast, Campioni lacked certainty of the British fleet's position until the two fleets were within

80nm of each other and a seaplane catapulted from his flagship, *Giulio Cesare*, located the British force. Despite requests from the Naval Command, the Italian Air Force had failed either to fly searches for the British or to attack them but Campioni was still in a strong position. His two battleships were faster than their three British opponents and their main armament could outrange *Royal Sovereign* and *Malaya* but not the modernised *Warspite*. His six heavy and ten light cruisers and thirty-two destroyers should have been more than a match for the five light cruisers, one of them damaged, and eleven destroyers with Cunningham. The damaged *Gloucester* had in fact been detached from the main force to support *Eagle*. The Mediterranean Fleet's only aircraft carrier might be small with only a limited number of obsolescent aircraft embarked but her aircrew were nearly all experienced men who could be relied upon to do their best in difficult circumstances.

Eagle's 813 NAS was tasked with reconnaissance and shadowing missions, while 824 NAS armed its nine Swordfish with torpedoes ready for a strike.[18] They were briefed to approach the enemy force at 8,000ft in three sub-flights, making steep dives to attack the target indicated by the leader from three different angles 120 degrees apart. No. 824 NAS launched at 1145 under a brilliant, cloudless sky with unlimited visibility and flew towards the last reported position of the enemy fleet but unfortunately the shadowing aircraft had lost contact. At 1252, however, they located the rear elements of the Italian fleet, two heavy cruiser divisions and their escorting destroyers. The cruisers, later identified as the *Fiume*, *Pola*, *Trieste* and *Zara*, were misidentified as battleships and the flights worked their way into attacking positions[19] but with no recent practice the attack was not well executed. Instead of concentrating on a single target, the flights launched their torpedoes against different ships and none hit. The Italian ships put up a heavy barrage once they penetrated the destroyer screen and the cruisers even fired their main armament into the water ahead of the aircraft to confuse the pilots' aim.

After their recovery, these nine Swordfish were rearmed, refuelled and flown off to arrive over the enemy force again at 1545. Once again they mistook heavy cruisers for battleships, this time those at the head of the force, and worked their way into an attacking position on their starboard bow. They were in action against the British fleet by this stage and firing salvoes over their starboard quarter. At the last moment, as the Swordfish released their torpedoes, one target was identified as a *Bolzano*-class heavy cruiser; in fact it was the *Bolzano* herself. She manoeuvred hard to evade them and succeeded but splashes and spray as she turned convinced

Eagle launching Swordfish of 813 and 824 NAS, photographed by the observer of an aircraft that has just taken off. Returning aircraft orbiting the ship await their time to land on when the launch is complete. (*Author's collection*)

pilots that there had been at least one hit. Nine Swordfish had been too small a striking force to guarantee success.

The two fleets' cruisers sighted each other at about 1500 and the Italians were the first to open fire. *Warspite* was faster than the other British battleships and had drawn ahead of them; at 1553 *Warspite*'s gun direction team saw the Italian battleships and opened fire on them at a range of 26,000yds. Straddles were observed almost at once and at 1600 Cunningham saw the orange flash of a heavy explosion at the base of the enemy flagship's funnels. This hit caused a fire below decks and other damage, and Campioni ordered his fleet to retire behind a smokescreen to the south-west and the safety of his own protected waters in the Messina Strait. Cunningham was reluctant to enter the smoke in case he was being lured into a submarine trap and decided to work his fleet round it to the north. When he got to windward of it, however, the enemy was no longer visible. He lacked the speed for a continued chase but held his course and closed to within 25 miles of the Italian coast at Calabria before turning away.

Campioni's willingness to accept battle, which had ended with *Warspite*'s impressive long-range shooting, was actually contrary to

Italian strategic policy, which saw nothing to be gained from a naval battle for its own sake.[20] The Italian battle fleet's aim had been the protection of a military convoy to Libya and this had been achieved successfully. Campioni knew nothing of the British convoy movements and had tried to draw the British force within range of Italian bombers but had been let down by his own air force. It was not until nearly forty minutes after his flagship had been hit that the first bombers appeared, and then not only did they fail to hit any British ships but a number attacked their own fleet by mistake. No hits were achieved on either fleet but attacks on the British fleet continued intermittently for the next four days.

On 12 July *Warspite* was attacked twenty-two times and in one attack thirty-six bombs fell together within 200yds of her, twenty-four to port and twelve to starboard. *Eagle* was near-missed on a number of occasions and suffered an accumulation of minor defects. The fleet's anti-aircraft fire proved to be as ineffective as the bombers' attacks but *Eagle*'s Sea Gladiator pilots did well. During the latter part of 1940 they shot down a confirmed total of seven enemy bombers and damaged another three but their main value lay in the number of enemy formations they broke up. Commander Charles Keighly-Peach was credited with three enemy aircraft shot down, plus one shared with another pilot and one damaged,[21] an impressive performance in its own right but also one that demonstrated what could have been achieved by a well-equipped force of carrier-borne fighters.

Operation MA 5 ended with the safe arrival of the British convoys at Alexandria and, even including the action off Calabria, material losses had been minor on both sides. Neither fleet commander had fully understood the lessons of this first encounter but the pattern for the immediate future had been set. A British fleet operating from Alexandria could not prevent the Italians from running convoys to Africa and from an Italian perspective this supported the view that there was nothing to be gained from seeking a battle as an end in itself. However, the Italian supreme command failed to draw the conclusion that this situation must force the British into strengthening Malta into a base from which Italian convoys to Libya could be interdicted by submarines, aircraft and light surface forces. The British Chiefs of Staff now accepted that Malta's strategic value was so great that it must be held and reinforced at all costs. The only certain way to deny it to the British would have been to invade and capture it immediately after the Axis declaration of war while it lay virtually defenceless. The Italian Navy actually recommended doing so but the Supreme Command rejected the idea as unnecessary since both the Italian and German air forces boasted that the island could be

Ark Royal operating aircraft in the Mediterranean with *Argus* astern. (*Author's collection*)

neutralised by air attacks alone. This was to prove a fatal mistake for the Axis powers.

The British appreciation of the action off Calabria was that the Italian fleet was unwilling to stand and fight. However, since the Mediterranean Fleet's battleships were all slower than their Italian contemporaries, the only prospect of forcing an action was to use carrier-borne strike aircraft with torpedoes to hit and slow the enemy force so that battleships could engage and destroy them.[22] This was a lot to ask of *Eagle* and her small air group and Cunningham asked 1SL for a second carrier and a another battleship. Despite the immediate danger to the UK itself in the autumn of 1940, the new armoured carrier *Illustrious* and the modernised battleship *Valiant* were sent to join the Mediterranean Fleet in August. No matter what strategic reasons the Italian fleet had for avoiding battle, the action off Calabria had left the RN with a moral ascendancy, which was highlighted on 19 July when the light cruiser HMAS *Sydney*, commanded by Captain J S Collins RAN, with five destroyers sank the Italian cruiser *Bartolomeo Colleoni* in a running fight off the north coast of Crete.

Naval aviation was evolving quickly. The first torpedo strike flown off by *Eagle* had failed to find its intended target because the continuity of shadowing had been broken at a critical moment. The Rear Admiral Naval Air Stations, RANAS, minuted on the Admiralty copy of Cunningham's report that 'continuous shadowing might well have influenced the whole action'[23] and surprisingly little use had been made of spotting aircraft from the battleships and cruisers. NAD minuted that their lack might have adversely affected the results gained by long-range gunfire with the obvious exception of *Warspite*'s outstanding hit. Too little use had been made of spotting aircraft; sometimes this was due to the aircraft being damaged before they could be catapulted. This was caused by the blast of the ship's own guns in the case of *Warspite* and splinter damage from enemy fire in the case of the cruiser *Neptune*. *Sydney*'s success was achieved without her Walrus embarked because of previous damage and no replacement aircraft had been available.

On the need for fighter protection against the incessant Italian air attacks while the fleet was at sea, NAD noted that, whilst the lack of fighters together with an adequate fighter direction system was keenly felt, the excellent results gained by *Eagle*'s Sea Gladiators, without loss to themselves, was a happy augury for the future. Cunningham wrote that 'this obsolescent aircraft carrier with only seventeen Swordfish found and kept touch with the enemy fleet, flew off two striking forces of nine torpedo aircraft within the space of four hours, both of which attacked and all aircraft returned. Throughout the five days' operations *Eagle* maintained anti-submarine patrols in daylight and carried out several searches. Most of *Eagle*'s flying operations were carried out in the fleeting intervals between, and even during, the bombing attacks.'

Reinforcing Malta

The realisation that Malta must be held at all costs led to measures being taken to bolster the island's defences as quickly as possible. Italian air raids against the island had begun on 12 June 1940 and four Sea Gladiators, originally held in reserve for *Glorious*' 802 NAS at Hal Far, were assembled for use by the RAF.[24] Three of them were put into service, popularly known as Faith, Hope and Charity, and before the French collapse five RAF Hurricanes were flown across France to reach Malta.

During November 1939, aircraft from 767 and 770 NAS including Swordfish, Skuas, Sea Gladiators and de Havilland Tiger Moths had been embarked in *Argus* and deployed to the French naval air station at Hyères le Palyvestre, near Toulon. The ship then operated in the local area as a deck landing training carrier. Student pilots travelled by train across France for courses, which usually lasted one week.[25] Part of 767 NAS had remained in the UK but in March 1940 it flew out, via RNAS Lee-on-Solent and Nantes, to Hyères and 770 NAS was absorbed into it, the

A Fairey Swordfish armed with a Type A Mark I mine. The absence of an observer, TAG or internal fuel tank show that this aircraft was probably photographed on a training sortie. (*Author's collection*)

whole detachment being commanded by the Senior Naval Officer, Hyères, Commander G C Dickins RN.

As France collapsed and Italy emerged as a threat, the Admiralty considered ways to use 767 NAS operationally. As a training unit it had limitations that needed to be overcome first; few of the squadron's aircraft had full blind-flying instrument panels, torpedo crutches, bomb racks or machine guns, and these had to be sent out from the UK. Commander Dickens was instructed to study the possibility of attacking Genoa if Italy came into the war using as many Swordfish as possible flown by instructor pilots and the best students available at Hyères. The unit had no observers and so the Admiralty appointed Lieutenant Commander F D Howie RN to the squadron. He was at RNAS Hatston in Orkney and, on being told to get to Hyères as quickly as possible, he flew to Wick in Caithness on 21 May 1940 and then on to London. After a briefing at the Admiralty he caught a train to Southampton on 24 May and then travelled to Jersey in the Channel Island ferry *Isle of Sark*. From there he got on one of the last ferries to St Malo on 26 May and was in Paris a day later. A train journey to Marseilles followed and by 28 May he was at Hyères.

After a brief docking in Malta, *Argus* arrived in Toulon on 31 May and her commanding officer, Captain H C Bovell RN, reported to the Prefecture Maritime, where he was informed that in the event of war with Italy the French did not want his ship in Toulon or the adjacent sea areas. He reported this to the Admiralty and on 3 June the ship was ordered to sail for Gibraltar, taking all RN fighter aircraft from Hyères and those Swordfish for which no pilots were available. Nine Swordfish were to be prepared as a striking force with the resources available from *Argus*. Dickens telegraphed the Admiralty that the force, commanded by Howie, was 'prepared to carry out any bombing operation required of them'. The nine pilots were given as much night flying practice as possible since it was appreciated that Swordfish would be too vulnerable to interception by Italian fighters in daylight.

Argus left Toulon on 4 June and landed on the aircraft listed by the Admiralty after 1330. Tugs and lighters promised by the French Navy were late and time was wasted waiting before stores could be landed for 767 NAS and those not wanted ashore taken on board. However, at 1730 a further Admiralty signal ordered *Argus* to disembark all available Swordfish to Hyères and this meant landing more stores, some of which had only just been taken on board. She sailed for Gibraltar at 1230 on 5 June after flying off the Swordfish. That night Howie led his aircraft on a rehearsal for a potential attack on Genoa.

There was a change of plan after Italy declared war when the Admiralty ordered Howie to be ready to drop magnetic mines off Spezia. The weapons were being transported by rail across France, but although a technical expert arrived to explain how to prepare and load them, the mines themselves never arrived, lost in the chaos that had overwhelmed the country. The only weapons available were bombs improvised from French 12in naval shells converted for the purpose by RN armourers and

A Swordfish cockpit interior fitted with the blind-flying panel with its artificial horizon, direction indicator and altimeter. (*Author's collection*)

fitted with improvised fuses. There was no wiring from the bomb carriers to the cockpit so they were fused ready to detonate on impact after being loaded onto the aircraft. The Admiralty ordered the attack on Genoa to take place on 13 June but, although the aircraft took off, the mission was aborted because there was no moon and the aircraft still lacked blind-flying instruments. It was carried out on the next night, 14 June. Howie flew with the squadron's senior pilot, Lieutenant Commander J N Garnett RN, and, in the absence of any definite intelligence, he briefed pilots to attack the docks. Howie managed to fix his position accurately fifteen minutes before arrival over the target and Garnett led the Swordfish down through cloud and drizzle at sunset. With anti-aircraft fire bursting around them, they dropped their bombs on targets of opportunity, believed to be a dry dock and gun batteries, then returned to Hyères. On 16 June a dive-bombing and strafing attack was carried out on the Italian fighter base at Albenga and, again, results were uncertain but all nine aircraft returned safely. The attitude of the French towards them was now awkward and becoming more hostile by the hour. On 17 June the French Government under Marshal Petain began armistice negotiations with the Germans.

At 0300 on 18 June an Admiralty signal ordered 767 NAS to 'fly to England via Bordeaux but if fog precludes proceed to Bone in French North Africa' and by dawn fog at Bordeaux was forecast to be a problem. When Dickins telephoned the airfield to ask about the actual weather conditions he was answered by a man speaking German. Eighteen Swordfish were prepared for take-off and a route planned for Bone, hoping that French North Africa might hold out for long enough for them to fly on to Malta or Gibraltar. Kit was crammed into the aircraft, Lieutenant Charles Ashburner RN strapping his BSA motorbike onto the torpedo crutches of his aircraft. Swordfish that lacked pilots were burnt together with stores that might be useful to the enemy. It took four hours twenty minutes to fly to Annaba airfield near Bone, close to the limit of the aircraft's endurance, and two days were spent awaiting Admiralty instructions, during which Howie was anxious to get away. At last, on 20 June the Admiralty instructed him to split the squadron in two with six Swordfish flying to Gibraltar via Rabat. The other twelve were to fly to Hal Far in Malta, where they were to re-form as 830 NAS with Howie as commanding officer.

The aircraft for Malta left a day later at 0740, landing at Medjez-el-Bab in Tunisia to refuel by hand pump from fuel drums. Once ready, they flew on to Malta. The embryo squadron's twelve pilots on this day were Lieutenant Commander Garnett, the senior pilot; Lieutenants Ashburner, Cambell, Hall and Waters; Sub Lieutenants Thompson and

Lieutenant Commander F D Howie RN. (*Author's collection*)

Thornton; Midshipmen Edmonson, Elwell and Smith and Petty Officers Parr and Wines.[26] The new squadron was to attack Italian shipping, especially convoys to North Africa, together with attacks on ports and airfields. Most operations were to be flown at night since the Swordfish would be vulnerable to Italian fighters operating from Sicily in daylight. The squadron formed officially on 1 July 1940 and in addition to its original Swordfish it absorbed several more from an RAF anti-aircraft co-operation unit already based at Hal Far,[27] although none of these aircraft were fitted with operational equipment. Initially 830 NAS was limited by a lack of ground crew and weapons but it made up for these shortcomings with its determination to take the fight to the enemy. A dive-bombing attack was carried out against oil storage tanks in Sicily on 30 June 1940 and a U-boat was attacked on 19 July.

An attack on an airfield at Catania in Sicily on 5 July was typical of the early operations. The target was 100nm from Hal Far and nine Swordfish arrived over it at dusk armed with bombs. As they withdrew, fires were seen in hangars and on their return journey they carried out a reconnaissance of the harbour at Augusta, where they saw the harbour was 'full of Italian warships that were perfect targets for torpedo attack',[28] but the opportunity to do had been lost by the choice of target and weapon on RAF advice. On 13 August an attack on Augusta harbour was carried out by nine Swordfish, six of which were armed with bombs and three with torpedoes. A dive-bombing attack by the former on a merchant ship resulted in it being damaged but flares were not used to illuminate targets for the torpedo aircraft and all three of them were lost. The limited use of torpedoes, again on RAF advice, showed a lack of conviction that they were the best weapon and the lack of flares was probably instrumental in the loss of the torpedo aircraft. No. 830 NAS carried out its final operation of 1940 with an attack on Tripoli harbour on 21 December in which six Swordfish laid mines and a further four carried out a successful dive-bombing attack on buildings with 250lb bombs.

The only way of deploying single-engined fighters to Malta was to ferry them part of the way in aircraft carriers, flying them off as soon as the island was within their range. Two ferry operations, 'Hurry' and 'White', were carried out in 1940, the first on 2 August and the second on 17 November. In the first *Argus* was loaded with twelve RAF Hurricanes on her arrival back in the UK, which she ferried to Gibraltar with two RN Skuas to lead them to Malta from a launch position in the western Mediterranean. She was the only carrier immediately available but had the advantage that her cruciform lift allowed Hurricanes to be struck down into the hangar. Hurry was a success, the aircraft being launched from a position to the south of Sardinia 300nm from Malta. There was no interference from the enemy, the observers in the Skuas made perfect landfall but one of the Hurricanes was slightly damaged on landing. RAF mechanics and stores to support the Hurricanes were shipped to Malta in the submarines *Proteus* and *Pandora* from Gibraltar.

Force H acted as cover and Swordfish from *Ark Royal* carried out a diversionary strike in daylight on the enemy airfield at Cagliari. Nine Swordfish from 810, 818 and 820 NAS achieved hits on hangars and destroyed four enemy aircraft on the ground in successful dive-bombing attacks. A further three Swordfish laid mines off Cagliari harbour and the last aircraft to attack machine-gunned an enemy seaplane on the water. The strike aircraft were escorted by Skuas

Lieutenant Wellham's Swordfish being repaired after the Bomba strike. (*Author's collection*)

from 800 and 803 NAS, which had several combats with enemy aircraft and successfully kept them away from the Swordfish. No enemy aircraft attempted to attack *Argus* and no enemy warships were detected at sea. In the latter part of 1940, *Ark Royal*'s Skuas engaged in fifteen combats in which six Italian aircraft were claimed as destroyed and eight damaged for the loss of two Skuas.[29]

In August, *Argus* pioneered a second route, carrying a shipment of thirty disassembled Hurricanes from the UK to Takoradi in the Gold Coast, now Ghana. After assembly they were flown across Africa in stages to Egypt. A second operation using *Argus* to ferry fighters within range of Malta, Operation White on 17 November, was less successful than the first. Once more twelve Hurricanes and two Skuas for their navigational guidance were craned on board the ship in the UK and Force H sailed to give cover after she returned to Gibraltar. The weather was not good, however, and Admiral Somerville cancelled a bombing attack by *Ark Royal*'s Swordfish on the airfield at Alghero, to which Italian aircraft had moved after the attack on Cagliari. However, the bad weather led Somerville to consider the chances of enemy interference with Force H or the Hurricanes' flight to be minimal. The chosen flying off position was further from Malta than in Hurry but was calculated to be comfortably inside the Hurricane's range, which was understood to be identical to that of the aircraft in August. There was one important difference, however; these aircraft were fitted with constant-speed propellers.[30] None of the RAF pilots had flown with this device before, or even been instructed in its proper handling to obtain the maximum fuel economy. Consequently, many of them used fuel at too high a rate and eight Hurricanes and one of the two Skuas failed to reach Malta. Four Hurricanes and the other Skua arrived safely.[31] Such operations came to be known within Force H as 'Club Runs' and they were usually timed to fit in with a wider range of objectives to achieve economy of force.

Operations by Swordfish disembarked from Eagle

When *Eagle* was in Alexandria her squadrons usually disembarked to RNAS Dekheila. They were there when 202 Group RAF requested suitable aircraft to cover operations off the North African coast and Swordfish detachments were sent to landing grounds in the desert. Nine Swordfish of 813 NAS were deployed to Ma'aten Bagush, 100nm west of Alexandria, in early July,[32] all armed with torpedoes. Next they deployed even further forward to the airstrip at Sidi Barrani, from where they carried out a dusk torpedo attack on warships and shipping in the port of Tobruk, 100nm west of the airstrip, while RAF Blenheim bombers

4H of 824 NAS from *Eagle* was one of the four Swordfish shot down on 4 September 1940 and it made a forced landing on Kasos Island. It is seen here standing on a jetty surrounded by Italian naval and military personnel while being prepared for shipment to Rhodes, where it was to be examined. (*Author's collection*)

attacked enemy installations ashore. The attack was to have been at dusk on 5 July; the weather was cloudless, there was no moon and sunset was at 1942. Accurate timing was important but delays caused by a burst tail wheel tyre at Ma'aten Bagush and slow refuelling at Sidi Barrani[33] meant that the first sub-flight was not ready to take off at the pre-arranged time. Lieutenant Commander N Kennedy DSC RN, the squadron's commanding officer, decided to send on the other two sub-flights at 1855 with his own following as soon as it was ready at 1925. The approach to the target was made from the east with Swordfish flying just above the sea surface with the after-glow of sunset ahead of them to give a horizon while the enemy would be unable to see the aircraft against the dark, eastern skyline. This stealthy approach was intended to achieve surprise but in the event it failed to do so, possibly because the sub-flight that had taken off late flew closer to the coast to make up time and may have been seen or heard before it reached Tobruk. A heavy anti-aircraft barrage began as the first two sub-flights approached the target and all aircraft came under fire as they crossed the boom at the entrance to the harbour. The attack was driven home with determination but the sub-flight that arrived late found the target to be in complete darkness and Lieutenant Commander Kennedy was the only one to locate it. The earlier flights had achieved success, however, sinking the destroyer *Zeffiro*,[34] the 15,000-ton liner *Liguria* and damaging the destroyer *Euro*, which had its bow blown off. A small freighter, the *Manzoni*, was also sunk with two others damaged and beached.[35] All the aircraft returned safely, one of them having strafed the nearby airstrip at El Gubbi.

By 10 July *Eagle* was at sea again when intelligence was received that three enemy cruisers were anchored in Augusta harbour in Sicily. Nine swordfish of 813 NAS were flown off to attack them from a position 40nm south of Malta at 1815. Sunset on that day was at 2023. At 2115 they approached the harbour at low level[36] but found the intelligence stale. The harbour only contained the destroyer *Leone Pancaldo*[37] moored to a buoy with an oil tanker nearby. The destroyer was hit by two torpedoes, one of them Lieutenant Commander Kennedy's, and sank in shallow water at 2140. Another torpedo hit the tanker but a fourth, aimed at the tanker, apparently turned to starboard after starting to run true and missed. The remaining Swordfish returned with their torpedoes to the carrier. There had been no enemy reaction until the first torpedo was dropped and all nine aircraft returned safely.

Later in July 824 NAS deployed six torpedo-armed Swordfish to Sidi Barrani and at 0145 on 20 July they carried out an attack on Tobruk where an enemy cruiser was believed to be sheltering. It was not there but the attackers did locate and attack two Italian destroyers. *Nembo* was hit in the boiler room and *Ostro* in the after magazine; both exploded and sank quickly. Another attack by aircraft of 824 NAS operating from Sidi Barrani was carried out on 22 August that proved to be even more successful. On 21 August an RAF reconnaissance Blenheim flying along the coast located an enemy submarine depot ship in Ain-el-Gazala, a small port in Bomba Bay. The Air Officer Commanding the RAF in the Western Desert, Air Commodore Raymond Collishaw CB DSO OBE DSC DFC RAF, a former RNAS fighter pilot, asked for naval aircraft to carry out a torpedo attack on it. The target was about 300nm west of Sidi Barrani, well beyond the normal range of a Swordfish. Long-range tanks for Swordfish had not yet arrived from the UK and so squadron engineers modified 44-gallon oil drums to fit as overload tanks into the observers' cockpits of three swordfish.[38] This defined the size of the strike force and the observers flew in the TAG's cockpit, the TAGs themselves being left behind. They had to navigate, work the radio and, if necessary, operate the Lewis gun while surrounded by avgas fumes from the overload tank air vent. At the last moment one of the pilots developed severe bronchitis and was replaced by Captain Ollie Patch RM, the senior pilot, who was flown to Ma'aten Bagush next morning in an RAF transport aircraft.

The three Swordfish deployed to Sidi Barrani at 0700 on 22 August. Captain Patch flew with Midshipman (A) C J Woodley as his observer and the other two aircraft were flown by Lieutenant (A) N A F Cheeseman RN with Sub Lieutenant (A) F Stovin-Bradford and Lieutenant (A) J Wellham RN with Petty Officer A H Marsh RN. Woodley was suffering from tonsillitis but was determined not to be left out and insisted with a dreadful croak that he was all right. Sidi Barrani was a rough strip with a surface like a ploughed field and every movement by aircraft or vehicles caused a sandstorm that reduced visibility to almost nothing. After landing, the aircraft were refuelled, avgas having to be pumped by hand from drums through a muslin cloth to prevent sand getting into the tanks. The officers' mess, which doubled as an operations room, was made out of sand-filled petrol tins with a tarpaulin as a roof. Two wooden benches and a few camp stools were the only furniture. Breakfast was generously provided by its RAF inhabitants, consisting of tinned sausages, baked beans and bread with marmalade scoured from a tin with the bread knife. As the aircrew were eating, an RAF Bombay transport aircraft arrived with a squadron maintenance team with their tools and essential spare

Commander C L Keighly-Peach DSO RN, *Eagle*'s Commander 'Air', unstrapping from Sea Gladiator N5507 of 813 NAS Fighter Flight after landing on in 1940. All five of his 'kills' were made flying this aircraft, which is being pushed back by handlers to the clear the hook from the arrester wire. (*Author's collection*)

parts. Among them was Leading Torpedoman Arthey, who always did a superb job keeping his torpedoes serviceable. A report from another Blenheim arrived at 1000 to say that the enemy ships were still in Bomba Bay so the aircraft took off after a quick briefing. They flew out sea for 50nm, no higher than 50ft in loose 'vic' formation and then turned onto a westerly heading. Loose formation meant fewer throttle movements and, therefore, less fuel used to keep together. After two hours, Patch indicated by hand signal that they were to turn south to close Bomba Bay and a few minutes later land was seen in the distance with ships' masts just visible.

Minutes later, Marsh and Wellham saw a submarine on the surface moving very slowly, presumably charging its batteries. Washing was hung on lines from stem to stern and many of the crew were sunbathing on deck. On seeing three aircraft armed with torpedoes coming straight at them several crew dived overboard but a machine gun opened fire from the conning tower. Wellham pulled away to port and Cheeseman to starboard in order to go for the depot ship from different sides. Patch continued straight at the submarine and dropped his torpedo from a few hundred yards on its beam. It hit amidships and all three Swordfish crews saw a big explosion, after which the boat split in two and sank. It was later identified as the Italian *Iride*.

As Wellham continued towards the big depot ship he noticed a destroyer and another submarine tied up alongside her. Alerted by the *Iride*'s destruction, the enemy ships opened fire with both tracer and heavier guns but the two Swordfish were not hit before they released their torpedoes from opposite sides of the stationary target, Wellham on its starboard beam, Cheeseman on its port. As he broke away, Wellham saw a cloud of black smoke issuing from the far side of the target a second before his own torpedo hit and caused a tremendous explosion. He learnt later that just as Cheeseman had been about to release his torpedo, Stovin Bradford saw that they were over shoal water and called for the drop to be delayed.[39] They flew in to 350yds from the target and released their weapon, watching as it hit the submarine alongside the depot ship, amidships. Three seconds later Wellham's torpedo hit the depot ship below its bridge. Both crews saw a terrific explosion where the ships had been as they flew out of the bay, possibly caused by a magazine explosion in the depot ship. All three ships disappeared from sight in a cloud of steam and smoke while large pieces of metal fell into the sea around them. The depot ship was subsequently identified as the *Monte Gargano*.[40]

The three Swordfish returned to Sidi Barrani, where Wellham's Swordfish was found to have been too badly damaged to fly back to Ma'aten Bagush and so he and his observer flew back crammed into the rear cockpits of the other aircraft. Wellham's ankle had been grazed by an enemy bullet as it exited the fuselage. Admiral Cunningham was delighted with this demonstration of the airborne torpedoes' effectiveness but, inevitably, there was some scepticism about the aircrews' claim to have sunk four ships with three torpedoes. Confirmation arrived that evening, however, after photographs taken by a reconnaissance Blenheim were analysed and proved that all four ships had indeed been sunk and the harbour was littered with oil and debris. At 0311 the next day a signal was received from the Admiralty marked IMMEDIATE and addressed to the C-in-C Mediterranean repeated to HQ Middle East. It stated 'Submarine broke in two. Some of the crew jumped overboard when torpedo was running... subsequent recce confirms two submarines, one destroyer and one depot ship destroyed. Wreckage and heavy oil smear visible on the sea'.

In Cunningham's despatch he wrote that 'this attack which achieved the phenomenal result of the destruction of four enemy ships with three torpedoes was brilliantly conceived and most gallantly executed. The dash, initiative and co-operation displayed by the sub-flight concerned are typical of the spirit which animates the Fleet Air Arm squadrons of HMS *Eagle* under the inspired leadership of her commanding officer.' Patch was subsequently awarded the DSO, the other officers the DSC and Marsh the DSM.

Reinforcements for the Mediterranean Fleet

Apart from the urgent need to reinforce the Mediterranean Fleet in the latter part of 1940, there was also a requirement to reinforce the Malta garrison and to build up British forces in the Middle East to defend the Suez Canal against a potential Italian attack from Libya. At the end of August 1940 the new aircraft carrier *Illustrious*, the battleship *Valiant* and the anti-aircraft cruisers *Coventry* and *Calcutta* made their way through the Mediterranean to join the Mediterranean Fleet in Alexandria. Until then only one of the fleet's warships had been equipped with radar but all the reinforcements except *Calcutta* had Type 79 air warning radar. *Illustrious*, flagship of Rear Admiral A L St G Lyster, Rear Admiral Aircraft Carriers Mediterranean, who had commanded *Glorious* during the Abyssinian Crisis, was the first aircraft carrier to be fitted with radar. Her air group comprised the Swordfish of 815 and 819 NAS and the new eight-gun Fairey Fulmar fighters of 806 NAS, and her arrival in the Mediterranean fleet with both air warning radar and an effective fighter marked a significant improvement in the fleet's operational capability.

A Fairey Fulmar Mark II of 759 NAS, part of the RN Fighter School at RNAS Yeovilton. (*Author's collection*)

Valiant had been modernised to the same standard as *Warspite* and had recently served with Force H. The other ships had sailed from the UK to join her in Gibraltar, from where Operation Hats[41] began on 29 August 1940. Once more, several aims were brought together to achieve economy of force and ships carrying Army and RAF reinforcements for Malta and the Middle east sailed east from Gibraltar at the same time as part of the first all-through eastbound convoy since war with Italy had begun. There was no contact with the Italian fleet but a number of high-level bombing attacks were carried out by Italian aircraft. During the short stay in Gibraltar, *Illustrious*' operations officer, Commander G Beale RN, had been briefed on the intercept techniques used by *Ark Royal* and her fighters.[42] *Ark Royal* had no radar and the cruiser *Sheffield*, fitted with Type 79, passed plot information to her by flag signals, which were then relayed to fighters by radio. A midshipman on the flagship *Renown*'s bridge read the signals and used them to maintain an air plot for Admiral Somerville on a chalk board.[43]

Admiral Cunningham's Mediterranean Fleet was less radar aware than Force H or the Home Fleet because it had lacked the means to test it in action. Fortunately, *Illustrious*' arrival allowed a sharper focus and both Admiral Lyster and her commanding Officer, Captain D W Boyd RN, took an intelligent and enthusiastic interest in the advancement of fighter direction techniques. Her fighter direction officer sat in front of a vertically mounted clear perspex 'spider's-web' plot showing the air picture derived from radar contacts and 'told' to plotters by telephone from radar operators. It was updated every five minutes and to allow direction officers to see the picture without obstruction, plotters wrote with grease pencils from behind, writing backwards. *Illustrious* soon established control over the air space above the fleet whenever it was at sea.

On 1 September nine Swordfish of 810 and 820 NAS from *Ark Royal* carried out a diversionary dive-bombing attack on Elmas airfield near Cagliari from a launch position 155nm away as part of Operation Hats. They were armed with 250lb GP bombs, 25lb incendiary bombs and flares and flew off the carrier at 0340.[44] The night was moonless but clear and the weather was perfect; the nine aircraft set heading in company but three became detached while manoeuvring over the land and attacked before the remainder. Unfortunately they bombed what proved to be a decoy airfield, a field north-west of Elmas on which the enemy had lit a line of flares to simulate a runway. The remaining six aircraft located the airfield successfully after dropping flares, although their leader reported that they were hardly necessary because of the illumination provided by the volume of enemy anti-aircraft fire. They hit barracks, airfield buildings and dispersed aircraft. Structures hit and damaged included a W/T station and what the Italian Air Force described as a 'Headquarters Room'. Damage to this may be the reason why the Italian Air Force allowed the considerable British naval force taking part in this operation to pass south of Sardinia without being attacked and the diversionary attack was an undoubted success. All nine Swordfish returned safely to *Ark Royal*. On the evening of 2 September, a further nine Swordfish were flown off *Ark Royal* with the same armament as on the night before. Their objectives were a power station at Cagliari and a re-strike at Elmas airfield but the weather on this occasion was bad. Layers of cloud at 4,000 and 5,000ft over the target area prevented them from being located, although the force spent forty-five minutes searching for them. Finally, two aircraft saw and attacked what they took to be a flare path but which turned out to be the decoy attacked in error earlier. Four aircraft attacked searchlights, one of which was put out, and the remaining aircraft jettisoned their bombs into the sea. Despite a barrage fired through the clouds, directed by sound locators, at the aircraft while they searched, none were hit and all returned safely to the carrier.

Once the reinforcements and convoy were close to Malta they were joined by the Mediterranean fleet, which accompanied them to Alexandria while Force H returned to Gibraltar. On 4 September, eight Swordfish from *Illustrious*' 815 and 819 NAS attacked Calato airfield on Rhodes from a launch position 100nm away. The plan had been to fly off twelve but, due to a crash on deck, only eight took off at 0345. They were each armed with six 250lb GP bombs and eight 25lb incendiary bombs. Six attacked the airfield and the other two barracks a mile south of Calato village using a dive-bombing technique involving a 50 degree dive and a release height of 1,500ft. Surprise was achieved and there was no anti-aircraft fire until after the attack had started.[45] Six or seven enemy aircraft were seen to be destroyed on the ground and fires and explosions were seen in the buildings at the south end of the airfield. Fires and explosions were also seen in the barrack area, and in one instance flames were seen to reach as high as 150ft. No aircraft were damaged and they all returned safely to the carrier.

On the same day, thirteen Swordfish from *Eagle*'s 813 and 824 NAS were flown off in two ranges to attack Maritza airfield on Rhodes. It had been intended to attack at dawn, 0557 on that day, but low wind conditions slowed the launch and the attack was not delivered until 0616. Five aircraft were armed with four 250lb GP bombs and four 25lb incendiary bombs; three were armed with thirty-two 25lb incendiary bombs and the remaining five with two 500lb SAP and four 25lb incendiary bombs. Some aircraft became detached on the flight to the target and one of these successfully attacked a gun battery near the town of Lindos. The remainder attacked the airfield and saw a petrol dump blow up and a large fire break out on a hangar apron that was probably used as a refuelling point. The Swordfish pilots also saw three aircraft blow up on the ground; one hangar destroyed by fire and explosions; workshop and store buildings burning and a large fire in the barrack area. However, the delayed launch meant that the attack began in daylight, surprise was not achieved and enemy fighters intercepted the Swordfish as they withdrew; four were lost. In another diversionary operation, the cruisers *Sydney* and *Orion* bombarded Makri Yalo airfield on the island of Scarpanto, the former using her Walrus for spotting.

On 17 September, Swordfish from *Illustrious* attacked shipping in Benghazi at night under a full moon. Nine aircraft of 815 NAS carried out a bombing attack, each of them armed with six 250lb GP bombs fitted with tail fuses set for instantaneous detonation. Six of the aircraft also carried eight 25lb incendiary bombs. A further nine Swordfish of 819 NAS were each armed with Type A Mark 1 mines to be laid off the harbour entrance. The attack took place at 0150 with the bombers throttling back to glide down from 7,000 to 4,000ft in order to minimise the possibility of engine noise being detected by Italian sound locators. They were engaged by erratic and ineffective anti-aircraft fire but two aircraft suffered bomb release failures, one only dropping two bombs.[46] The minelayers approached at 50ft with aircraft in line astern and sub-flights in echelon. They were not engaged and were probably not observed, dropping their mines on signals from each section leader. The bombers succeeded in sinking the destroyer *Borea* and two merchant ships.[47] Daylight reconnaissance by the RAF subsequently showed oil spreading from the wrecks many miles out to sea. The mines were believed subsequently to have sunk the destroyer *Aquilone* and two small patrol vessels, besides causing considerable disruption to Italian shipping.

Ark Royal surrounded by near misses from a high-level attack by Italian bombers. (*Author's collection*)

Another night attack on 17 September was carried out by a single Swordfish of 813 NAS disembarked to Ma'aten Bagush. The target was an Italian Air Force supply ship in Derna; it was attacked with bombs and intelligence sources later confirmed that it had been severely damaged. On 29 September there was a further night attack from this airstrip, this time by two Swordfish of 813 NAS armed with torpedoes against an enemy convoy of five ships reported off Bomba. It was attacked in failing light and it was learnt later that one or possibly two ships had been hit, although one Swordfish was hit by a South African gun battery in a regrettable 'friendly fire' incident as it returned and had to carry out a forced landing but the crew were unharmed.[48]

On 12 October, following a night action between the cruiser *Ajax* and several Italian destroyers, an aircraft from *Eagle* sighted two enemy destroyers, one of which was on fire and stopped with the other standing by it. A torpedo striking force of three Swordfish from *Illustrious* was flown off to attack them and saw the undamaged destroyer clearing off at high speed making smoke. The attack was set up from its starboard bow but only the first two dropped. The enemy took avoiding action by turning 90 degrees to starboard into the attack and both torpedoes missed. The third aircraft had not dropped and attacked again from the starboard bow, but again the destroyer evaded by a hard turn to starboard. The C-in-C's staff minuted on the carrier's report of this attack that it 'illustrated the difficulty of attacking a fast-moving target with complete freedom to manoeuvre. Had the third aircraft been able to drop during its first attack, it would have been in a good position to take advantage of the target's first turn to starboard.'

Attacks on shipping and Italian ports began to have a serious impact on the Italian Army's operations. On 15 October fifteen Swordfish of 815 and 819 NAS from *Illustrious* carried out a dive-bombing attack with 250lb GP bombs and incendiaries against installations on Leros from a launch position 95nm away. Each was armed with six 250lb GP bombs with tail fuses set for instantaneous detonation and eight 25lb incendiary bombs. After forming up, they took departure from the carrier at 2220 and sighted Leros at 2330 in clear moonlit conditions. There was no opposition until the leader began his attack, then a good deal of erratic light anti-aircraft fire was experienced but none of the Swordfish was hit. The first briefed target comprised workshops at San Giorgio and these were hit by several bombs, which started fires and a column of black smoke was seen. The second target was a group of hangars at Lepida Cove. Three aircraft attacked them and two hangars were left on fire. The third target was a barrack complex at Gonia Cove, which was attacked by eight aircraft and considerable damage was seen as they withdrew. One aircraft attacked what the pilot believed to be three destroyers off Brachos Point; hits were claimed but could not be substantiated despite a large explosion seen on the southern shore of the bay ten minutes after the attack as the aircraft withdrew.

On 24 October an attack on Tobruk was carried out by fourteen Swordfish disembarked from both *Eagle* and *Illustrious*, operating from Fuka, a satellite airstrip to the east of Mersa Matruh in Egypt. The distance to the target was 225nm, close to the Swordfish's maximum radius of action. The strike force comprised four Swordfish of 824 NAS armed with bombs and flares to create a diversion; six Swordfish of 819 NAS and four Swordfish of 815 NAS all armed with Type A Mark 1 mines. All aircraft were fitted with internal auxiliary fuel tanks and had to fly without their TAGs. The operation was originally planned to take place on the night of 22/23 October[49] but blown sand on the airstrip as the aircraft attempted to taxi into position for take-off obscured visibility to the extent that the operation had to be postponed at 0045. On the next night the aircraft were pushed into position on the airstrip before dark and they took off successfully at 2350, climbing initially to 3,000ft. During the second half of the outbound flight the bombing force climbed to 8,000ft after passing their expected time of arrival over the target to the minelayers by flashing light. The latter remained at 3,000ft to make their approach. The bombers started their run over the target at 0305, met by heavy and accurate anti-aircraft fire as the first bombs were dropped at 0311. Synchronisation was excellent and all the mines were laid between 0313 and 0316 without apparently having been seen by the enemy. Searchlights were locked on the bombers and while some anti-aircraft guns fired in the direction of the minelayers, their shells burst far above them. All fourteen Swordfish returned safely.

On 27 October a dive-bombing attack on Port Maltezana on Stampalia Island was carried out by eight Swordfish of 813 and 824 NAS from *Eagle*, which were flown off 100nm from the target. They were each armed with six 250lb GP bombs and incendiaries and, after taking off, they set heading towards the target at 0417. They attacked at 0553, approaching from the north-west over the land. Their briefed targets were not detailed in the action report but pilots believed that all bombs had been well placed on fuel installations, hangars and buildings, which were left on fire. Anti-aircraft fire was intense and one Swordfish was slightly damaged.

Ark Royal's 810, 818 and 820 NAS carried out a further strike on Elmas airfield near Cagliari on 9 November 1940, an attack intended to divert Italian attention away from *Illustrious*' strike on the Italian battle fleet in Taranto. Nine Swordfish from the three squadrons flew off from 0435 and while the leader was climbing, he entered a cloud layer that had appeared to be thin but proved to be much extensive. The force became split up and aircraft proceeded independently to the objective but arrived at the same time. At 0615 the leader dropped a semicircular line of flares, illuminating the target,[50] before he dived into the attack followed by five other aircraft. Two hangars and their adjacent buildings were hit and fires were seen

The Supermarine Seagull V was closely similar to the RN Walrus, the most widely used spotter-reconnaissance aircraft carried on battleships and cruisers in the early years of the Second World War. This Seagull, A2-2/076, is loaded onto HMAS *Sydney*'s EIIH catapult ready to be launched. (*Sea Power Centre – Australia*)

to break out. One heavy explosion was seen. The other three Swordfish failed to locate the airfield but one attacked and hit a factory near a power station and the other two attacked anti-aircraft gun batteries. Anti-aircraft fire had been slight until after the attacks were completed and then it became intense. Thirty-four 250lb GP bombs, twenty-eight 40lb bombs and thirty-six incendiaries were dropped; twelve of the 250lb bombs were fitted with Number 17 long-delay fuses intended to detonate after clearance operations had begun in order to stop or slow them. Delayed action fuses could only be fitted to certain types of bomb that were not in general naval use at this time and fifty fitted with Number 17 fuses were supplied to *Ark Royal* from RAF stores in Gibraltar as a special measure for this operation, illustrating the importance that was placed on this diversionary attack. The Admiralty took prompt steps to procure this type of fuse in quantity for issue to carriers now that it was clear that attacks on land targets such as airfields were becoming commonplace.

By the autumn of 1940 Admiral Cunningham believed that the addition of the radar-equipped *Illustrious* and her Fulmar fighters together with the effective strikes by Swordfish from *Ark Royal* in Force H were giving the British the upper hand in the Mediterranean. It was clear that although RN aircraft might be obsolescent, the aircrew were of the highest quality. The RAF Air Officer Commanding in the Mediterranean had taken up with the Air Ministry the urgent need to provide an air striking force and reconnaissance aircraft in Malta as soon as the fighter requirement had been met. He stated that he could not meet the Mediterranean Fleet's calls for air support[51] and that the embryo 830 NAS represented the only air striking force available on the island. This squadron would go on to achieve a remarkable degree of success but much more was needed to fully interdict the passage of Italian convoys to Libya. This was, of course, a joint-service problem since without adequate air defence, naval surface forces could not be stationed in Malta and even submarines would find it difficult to operate effectively. Senior RAF officers had to concede that, contrary to the Air Ministry's pre-war theories, they relied on sea power to bring fighters and everything else to the beleaguered island.

In Italy, Admiral Campioni noted that the absence of fighter aircraft operating as an integral part of his own fleet was a weakness that could be exploited by the British aircraft carriers, which could use their own aircraft to search for and shadow his fleet unopposed and to attack his capital ships with torpedoes. The ineffectiveness of Italian pattern bombing from high level against manoeuvring warships had given the Mediterranean Fleet the impression that the bomber threat had been exaggerated pre-war but in reality they had yet to encounter the more dangerous threats of specialised dive and torpedo bombing carried out by specially trained

HMAS *Sydney* returning to Alexandria after the action off Cape Spada on 19 July 1940 when she sank the Italian cruiser *Bartolomeo Colleoni*. (*Sea Power Centre – Australia*)

pilots. Unfortunately for the British, this over-sanguine view was soon to change when the Luftwaffe deployed Junkers Ju 87 dive bombers and other attack aircraft to the theatre to bolster its Italian ally. Despite Cunningham's feeling of optimism that his fleet demonstrated a moral ascendancy over the Italians, it was clear that a British fleet based as far east as Alexandria could not prevent the safe passage of Italian supply convoys to Africa.[52] Only the expansion of forces based in Malta could do that on a regular basis. The remoteness of the British battle fleet in Alexandria reinforced the Italian Naval High Command's view that there was nothing to be gained from sending out its own battle fleet to seek action as an end in itself.

From the British perspective, Cunningham's belief that moral ascendancy would allow him freedom of manoeuvre and hence control of the central Mediterranean, and that his fleet's determination would overcome the menace from high-level bombers, was soon shown to be over-optimistic. For those with eyes to see, the balance of power had already moved from battleships to aircraft carriers and their embarked air groups in 1940, and it was the small air groups of three carriers with their gallant aircrew who allowed Cunningham to achieve such localised dominance as he had in 1940 even though his fleet was surrounded by well-equipped enemy airfields. That said, the enemy battle fleet clearly continued to pose a threat as a fleet in being and it was superior to the British in both quantity and quality. It was based at Taranto and by October 1940 included the impressive new battleships *Littorio* and *Vittorio Veneto* as well as four older but extensively modernised battleships. The only way the British could eliminate the enemy battleships' latent danger was to attack it at source, in its heavily protected harbour with carrier-borne aircraft.

3

Operation Judgement – The Taranto Strike

The destruction of warships in a protected harbour by a fleet that dominates its sea approaches is a tactic that has been used by the RN for centuries. Naval aircraft had already sunk the German cruiser *Konigsberg* in Bergen[1] but it was the strike on the Italian battle fleet at Taranto in November 1940 by Swordfish of 813, 815, 819 and 824 NAS embarked in *Illustrious* that defined the capability and importance of the Royal Navy's Fleet Air Arm.

Origins

An early example of attack at source was Sir Francis Drake's attack on the Spanish Armada with fire-ships at the Battle of Gravelines in August 1588.[2] Admiral Lord Nelson demonstrated at the battles of Aboukir Bay and Copenhagen that a bold commander could take his fleet into a defended anchorage to engage ships at anchor given the right conditions of wind and tide but the advent of defences comprising large-calibre, rifled guns, torpedoes, mines, submarines and torpedo boats had greatly increased the risk of such tactics by 1900.

In 1912 a torpedo specialist, Lieutenant D H Hyde-Thomson RN, wrote a service paper describing the potential importance of aircraft in attacks on enemy warships both at sea and in harbour. At the time there was no aircraft engine powerful enough to allow an aircraft with its pilot and a meaningful load of fuel to get airborne with even a lightweight torpedo but he was appointed to HMS *Vernon*, the torpedo school at Portsmouth, to work on airborne torpedo design. In July 1914 a prototype 14in torpedo weighing 900lb was carried a few feet into the air and dropped from a Short Type 166 seaplane powered by a 200hp Salmson engine and piloted by Squadron Commander A M Longmore RNAS. However, the aircraft had only just managed to get airborne with the weapon and could not yet be considered a viable weapon system. In 1915 the seaplane carrier *Ben-my Chree* took three improved 14in

Sopwith T.1s carrying out their successful demonstration torpedo attack against the RN Atlantic Fleet anchored in Portland Harbour during 1919. (*Author's collection*)

torpedoes to the Dardanelles and they were used with modest success against Turkish shipping by her Short Type 184 seaplanes[3] fitted with 225hp Sunbeam engines.

By 1917 an improved torpedo had been developed and Sopwith was contracted to design an aircraft capable of operation from the flight decks of specially modified ships to carry it. The result was the Sopwith T.1[4] and Admiral Sir David Beatty, the C-in-C of the Grand Fleet, and his staff believed that it was the weapon most likely to be effective against the German capital ships, which remained for most of the time in their harbours behind extensive minefields and coastal defences. At first they envisaged a single 'knock-out' blow with 121 Sopwith T.1s launched from eight carrier ships in three waves of forty. The odd one was a strike co-ordinator in a brightly painted aircraft with extra fuel but no torpedo.[5] Each carrier ship was to embark fifteen T.1s with the strike co-ordinator embarked additionally in the task force commander's ship. Additionally, each carrier was to embark two Sopwith 2F.1 fighters for fleet air defence duties and RNAS flying boats from air stations on the east coast of the UK were to attack lock gates and other targets under the strike co-ordinator's direction. Each forty-aircraft wave was to comprise eight flights of five aircraft; each flight briefed to find, identify and attack specific capital ships. The strike co-ordinator was to be the first airborne and he was to remain overhead while all three waves attacked before returning, the last of all, to his carrier ship. Flights of five were deemed to be the most practical number of aircraft that could be launched in a single range and subsequently operate cohesively together to locate their targets and attack them. A single hit by a lightweight torpedo was considered unlikely to sink a capital ship but five aircraft engaging the same target were statistically more likely to cause severe or even fatal damage, especially if surprise was achieved and the ships did not have their watertight doors closed.

The T.1's weapon was the 18in Mark IX torpedo, which weighed 1,000lb and had a warhead comprising 170lb of TNT. The pilot had a control that allowed him to alter the torpedo's running depth after release. A larger torpedo for use by aircraft was also designed during the war and designated the Mark VIII, which weighed 1,423lb.[6] It could not be carried by the T.1 but became the standard aircraft weapon in the 1920s. The T.1 had a single pilot and was powered by a 200hp Sunbeam Arab engine. With full fuel it had an endurance of four hours and a maximum speed of 90 knots, giving it a radius of action of over 100nm with sufficient fuel for several minutes' at full power during the attack and time to loiter waiting for the carrier to be ready to recover its aircraft.

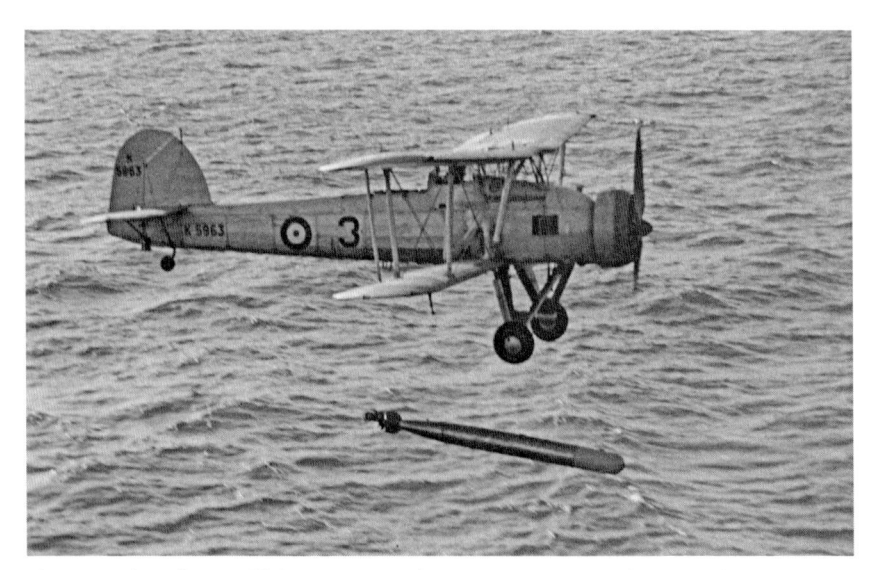

Photographs of Swordfish in action during 1940 are, unfortunately, very rare. However, this pre-war image shows a Swordfish of the Torpedo Trials Unit at Gosport dropping a Mark XII, like those used at Taranto, under ideal conditions in daylight. Note how the torpedo has adopted a nose-down attitude before entering the water. (*Philip Jarrett collection*)

Mk XII Torpedo

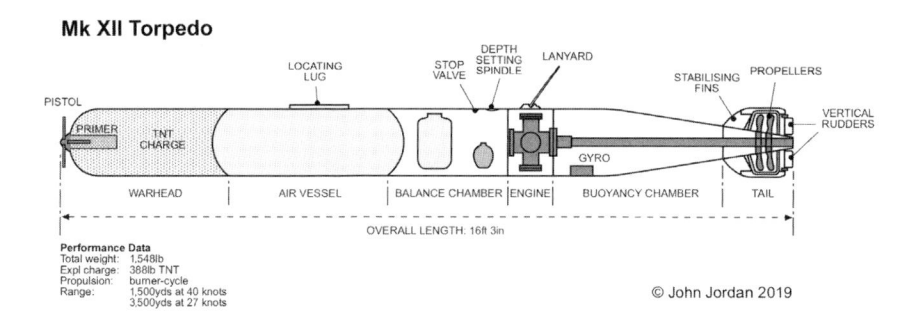

[Diagram of Mk XII Torpedo with labels: PISTOL, PRIMER, TNT CHARGE, LOCATING LUG, STOP VALVE, DEPTH SETTING SPINDLE, LANYARD, GYRO, STABILISING FINS, PROPELLERS, VERTICAL RUDDERS, WARHEAD, AIR VESSEL, BALANCE CHAMBER, ENGINE, BUOYANCY CHAMBER, TAIL. OVERALL LENGTH: 16ft 3in]

Performance Data
Total weight: 1,548lb
Expl charge: 388lb TNT
Propulsion: burner-cycle
Range: 1,500yds at 40 knots
3,500yds at 27 knots

© John Jordan 2019

No. 185 Squadron was formed at RNAS East Fortune in 1918 to operate the Sopwith T.1 and work up the skills and tactics necessary to attack the German fleet in harbour. The Admiralty had not agreed the conversion of armed merchant cruisers into carrier ships so the strike by the full 121-aircraft strike force would not have been possible. The actual strike in 1918 would, therefore, have been carried out using the maximum number of T.1s that could be embarked in the first true aircraft carrier, *Argus*, and the semi-carriers *Furious* and *Vindictive*.[7] The latter two had after landing decks but suffered severe turbulence from the residual superstructure amidships, which made landing on them dangerous in any but the most benign conditions. It is likely, therefore, that after the strike as many aircraft as possible would have landed on *Argus* and the remainder would have had to ditch close to the fleet like the 2F.1 Camels that had attacked Tondern from *Furious* in July 1918. *Argus* and 185 Squadron were ready to carry out the attack in early November 1918 but the Armistice that came into effect on 11 November ended the war before it could take place.

Of interest, the 1918 East Fortune Christmas Card illustrated their frustration with the statement 'Would that we two had met'. On the right there was a photograph of the German battle fleet steaming into captivity with the caption '*Our Objective* – BUT THE HUNS SURRENDERED'. The idea had been born, however, and in 1919 the squadron was given the chance to demonstrate its potential.

A demonstration of what torpedo attack could achieve

On Saturday, 6 September 1919 the 2nd Battle Squadron was moored in Portland Harbour and Admiral Madden the C-in-C Atlantic Fleet had given permission for 185 Squadron to carry out a demonstration attack at a pre-arranged time. Eleven aircraft took part, eight of which were armed with running torpedoes fitted with inert warheads and the remaining three with smoke bombs, intended to mask the attacking aircraft as they approached and to confuse the defenders. Since it was a demonstration, the attack was carried out in daylight rather than at dawn or dusk in conditions that would have made the aircraft more difficult to detect and engage with anti-aircraft fire. The attack was made by two groups of aircraft, the larger comprising five aircraft with torpedoes and two with smoke bombs, which approached low over the land to the north. The smaller group comprised the remaining three torpedo-armed aircraft and a single smoke bomber and it attacked from the sea to the south slightly later than the northern group.

The shallow water in Portland Harbour presented a technical challenge, as the seabed at Taranto would do in 1940, because torpedoes that dived below their set running depth on release ran the risk of hitting the bottom. In his report, Admiral Madden wrote that the attack was both well-planned and executed. He had no doubt that even under the clear conditions that prevailed and with the exact hour of the attack by a relatively small number of aircraft known beforehand, anti-aircraft gunnery could not have brought down more than a small proportion of the attackers, if any. The attack from the south, while all attention was focused on the aircraft to the north, would have been pressed home unopposed. Some of the smoke bombs failed to ignite but those that did formed an effective screen against the simulation of aimed fire from the target ships at critical moments.

Madden and his staff were convinced that this method of attack was effective and easily adapted to awkward conditions such as the shallow water found in fleet anchorages. The five northern torpedo aircraft scored one hit each on two battleships and two on a third but the fifth torpedo had dived into the seabed. The three southern torpedo aircraft scored two hits on the flagship *Queen Elizabeth* and the third weapon hit the seabed. Despite its shortcomings, the T.1 was now considered to be operationally effective and the technical difficulties of dropping torpedoes in shallow water had clearly been overcome since only two out of eight weapons had hit the bottom in water that was known to be about the minimum depth in which a battle fleet could be expected to anchor safely. Aircraft had become the most effective platform for launching torpedo attacks against capital ships.

It is clear from the subsequent correspondence that both Beatty, now 1SL, and Madden both believed that in the carrier-borne torpedo aircraft the RN had developed its most devastating anti-surface ship weapon system. Even the conservative Admiral Jellicoe recognised their immediate value. In only six years the air-dropped torpedo had developed from a bright idea beyond the capability of existing technology into a practical and effective weapon with even greater potential for the future.

Glorious pre-war with Swordfish of 825 NAS overhead. This squadron was the first to re-equip with the type in July 1936. Note the aircraft about to land on close to the ideal position on the flight deck marked by a white circle. (*Author's collection*)

However, problems followed the creation an independent air force directed by an Air Ministry that regarded all naval operations as obsolete and concentrated on bombers with free-fall weapons that could not be aimed with any accuracy against moving targets. Despite considerable opposition, the Admiralty fought to retain and improve the torpedo-carrying aircraft in its carrier air groups throughout the inter-war years with the evolution of new aircraft, weapons and tactics. From 1936 the front-line squadrons began to be re-equipped with the torpedo-spotter-reconnaissance, TSR, the Fairey Swordfish; the aircraft that carried out the Taranto strike.

Influences

The Italian dictator, Benito Mussolini, created a border incident on 5 December 1934 that was intended to carry forward his aim of seizing part of Abyssinia and adding it to his African Empire. Abyssinia sought arbitration under the auspices of the League of Nations but further border incidents were followed by an Italian invasion on 3 October 1935. The Council of the League condemned the Italian attack and called for sanctions against Italy. At the time the only force capable of implementing sanctions on the scale that would be required was the British Mediterranean Fleet and war with Italy seemed possible.[8] The aircraft carrier *Glorious* worked up to a high standard of efficiency in both night flying and torpedo attack, becoming arguably the most efficient carrier in any navy during this period. She was still in the Mediterranean in September 1938 at the time of the Munich Crisis when war again seemed likely, this time against Germany with Italy as its potential ally.

During this crisis, the C-in-C Mediterranean, Admiral Sir Dudley Pound who was soon to become 1SL, ordered Captain A L St G Lyster CVO DSO ADC RN, the captain of *Glorious*, to formulate a plan if war broke out 'to hit the Italian Fleet at once as hard…as we can'.[9] A plan for a torpedo attack on the Italian fleet in Taranto, originally prepared by *Glorious* in 1935, had been retained on board and Lyster brought it up to date with Commander 'Air', Commander G Willoughby RN and Operations Officer, Commander L D Mackintosh DSC RN. By then her TSR squadrons, 812, 823 and 825 NAS, were equipped with Swordfish and the plan was of immediate value when war did come.

Vice Admiral Lyster and Captain Robertson photographed later in the war after both had been promoted. (*Author's collection*)

Other indicators came from the early weeks of war in the North Sea. Attempts in 1939 by aircraft of RAF Bomber Command to attack German warships there had proved disastrous. They were ill-prepared, one Wellington finding that his aircraft had no bombs loaded and another found that none of his machine guns worked when he ordered his gunners to test them.[10] These attacks had been flown by poorly trained airmen using ill-considered tactics but there were some lessons that had to be taken into account by the naval officers who planned the attack on Taranto. Details of enemy defences must be gathered by timely photographic reconnaissance and the results used to brief the aircrew. The attack would have to be carried out at night under the best conditions of moon and light over the targets, after which the survivors had to face a long flight back to the carrier in the dark and, having located it, land on in the dark. When the time came, the planners believed implicitly in the skill and determination of the pilots and observers who would carry out the attack but must have reflected, after the losses suffered by Bomber Command in 1939, that casualties might be very heavy.

However, the operation that probably had the most influence on the Taranto strike planners was the torpedo attack by six Swordfish of 814 NAS on *Richelieu* in Dakar harbour on 8 July 1940.[11] Three torpedoes had been armed with the new duplex pistols and three with contact pistols, all six set to run at their maximum speed of 40 knots. French sources analysed by the Admiralty's intelligence experts revealed that *Richelieu* had been hit by a single torpedo that caused a hole 25 by 20ft in the hull. Its detonation fractured the sternpost, distorted the starboard inboard propeller shaft and flooded three compartments. Repairs to the ship away from a French dockyard port took over a year to complete. NAD's analysis was critical to the success of the Taranto strike. Taking into account the shallowness of the water at Dakar and the fact that the target had been at anchor, experts warned that the high-speed setting should not have been used as it caused Mark XII torpedoes to dive excessively on entering the water. At the slower speed setting the dive was appreciably less. Also, the running depth of the duplex-pistol torpedoes at Dakar was assessed as having been set too deep and, since the conditions at Taranto would be similar with ships at anchor in roughly 40ft of water, these recommendations formed the basis for the planned attack; all torpedoes used were to be set to run at 27 knots at a depth of 33ft and be fitted with duplex pistols.

The evolution of the Taranto strike operation

By November 1940 Admiral Cunningham's fleet had carried out sixteen sweeps into the Central Mediterranean but the Italian battle fleet was encountered on only three of these. Nevertheless it remained a dominant factor and the situation had been made worse on 28 October by the Italian invasion of Greece since the Italian fleet in its heavily defended base at Taranto was able to dominate the waters around the country. The Greek Government appealed to the UK for assistance and steps were taken to assist its defences with naval, military and air forces[12] at the expense of Britain's own operations in North Africa. Like his predecessor, Cunningham considered an air strike to be an effective form of attack but he did not consider *Eagle* to be capable of carrying it out, not least because her three Sea Gladiator fighters were inadequate to destroy or drive off persistent reconnaissance aircraft that could detect the carrier's approach to a flying off position within range of Taranto. The arrival of

Illustrious in September allowed plans to be made to use both carriers in a set-piece strike.

The former captain of *Glorious*, now Rear Admiral Lumley Lyster, was now flying his flag in *Illustrious* as Flag Officer Aircraft Carriers (Mediterranean) and he assumed all responsibilities with regard to naval air operations.[13] At his first meeting with the C-in-C, Lyster raised the question of an air attack on the Italian fleet in Taranto harbour and Cunningham 'gave him every encouragement to develop the idea'. Pound had thought of the operation as 'the last dying kick of the Mediterranean carrier before it was sent to the bottom' and had not been impressed by the Swordfish as a strike aircraft but Cunningham thought the strike no more dangerous than other fleet operations. To succeed the Swordfish aircrew would need practise to reach and maintain efficiency in night operations and it was an obvious requirement to know that the enemy battleships were actually in Taranto on the night chosen for the strike. Cunningham therefore requested photographic surveillance of the target area to be carried out with the results communicated quickly to his staff in Alexandria. At first these were flown by Short Sunderland flying boats that were unsuited to the dangerous task but by October a flight of four Glenn Martin reconnaissance aircraft that had been procured from the USA took over the task. Designated as 431 Flight, it was ably commanded by an Australian officer, Flight Lieutenant E A Whitely RAF. These aircraft, later named Marylands, flew at up to 26,000ft at 250 knots, making them difficult for Italian fighters to intercept, and they brought back good photographs.

Lyster's planning staff saw the Swordfish positively. A biplane with open cockpits, it was, by 1939, the torpedo aircraft in the most widespread use in the RN, although it was gradually being replaced by the Albacore. Considered by some to be obsolete, it was actually robust, very manoeuvrable and capable of carrying a heavy weapon load of up to 2,000lb, twice that of an RAF Blenheim bomber. Some historians, who ought to know better, have referred to the Swordfish that took part in the Taranto attack as 'ancient biplanes'. This is far from true and Ray Sturtivant managed to identify several of the aircraft and their delivery dates. P4011 (L4K), for instance, was delivered to the RN in February 1939 and P4205 (L5K) in September 1939. While their design might have been dated, they were mostly new airframes.[14] The Swordfish's primary weapon in 1940 was the Mark XII torpedo, a genuine 'ship-killing' development of the earlier British airborne marks. It had a warhead containing 388lb of TNT and its total weight was 1,610lb. Running depth could be adjusted in flight but was more usually set before take-off when the nature of the target and its environment were known and speeds of either 27 or 40 knots could be set, allowing maximum runs of 3,500 or 1,500yds. The higher speed was almost always used in open water as the longer run associated with the lower speed gave moving targets more time to evade the weapon.[15]

It was propelled by a semi-diesel 'burner-cycle' engine that developed 140hp. When the pilot released the weapon a lanyard activated a valve that allowed high-pressure air from a chamber within the torpedo to be released into an igniter. There it mixed with a small amount of atomised kerosene to produce a pressurised air/gas mixture at 1,000° Centigrade, which was fed into the engine cylinders via poppet valves. More fuel was injected into the cylinders themselves, which ignited spontaneously to run the engine. As the compressed air supply ran down, the engine slowed and would eventually stop. A second compressed air bottle provided a high-pressure air jet that span the weapon's gyros, signals from which kept the weapon running straight and level. Heading was controlled by rudders and depth by elevators, both set behind the propellers to give maximum effect. Like all torpedoes, airborne versions had two contra-rotating propellers driven by concentric shafts from a gearbox behind the engine; if there had been only one propeller, the torque as it tried to spin against the pressure of the water would have rotated the smooth-surfaced torpedo rather than propelled it. The two propellers cancelled out this effect. For the Taranto strike the torpedo crutches under the aircraft were rigged so that the weapons dropped with their noses just below level to minimise the plunge after they entered the water before the depth control system became effective. The limits for a Mark XII drop were 200ft and 200 knots with no yaw on the aircraft.

Illustrious and *Eagle* were originally to have attacked Taranto together on 21 October, Trafalgar Day, the first opportunity with a suitable moon. Success was expected to depend on three factors – accurate and timely reconnaissance to confirm that enemy battleships were in Taranto; an undetected approach from the greatest range, which meant fitting Swordfish with long-range tanks brought from the UK in *Illustrious*, and

Captain Dennis Boyd in 1940. (*Author's collection*)

a sufficient standard of night flying skill. However, *Illustrious* suffered a hangar fire shortly before sailing and the attack had to be postponed. Mechanics had been fitting a long-range fuel tank into one of the Swordfish when there was a spark from a short-circuiting battery that ignited avgas dripping from the tank.[16] Two Swordfish were destroyed, five others were damaged and the salt water hangar sprays that extinguished the fire caused some damage that had to be repaired. It was then hoped to carry out the raid on the night of 30/31 October when the fleet was expected to be operating off Greece but it had to be deferred again as there was no moon and the aircrew were still thought to have had insufficient practice in the use of flares. The delay proved valuable, however, as reconnaissance photographs showed that the Italians had installed a balloon barrage and anti-torpedo net defences around the battleship anchorages.

It was eventually decided that the attack would form part of a number of concurrent operations throughout the whole Mediterranean designated Operation MB 8. These included the passage through the Sicilian narrows from the west of reinforcements for the Mediterranean Fleet as well as Operation Coat, the movement of ships carrying military reinforcements for Malta. They were escorted in the Western basin by Force H and in the east by Cunningham's battle fleet comprising *Warspite*, *Malaya* and *Valiant* after it had covered the passage of convoys to and from Malta and to Souda Bay in Crete. The attack on Taranto was to take place after *Illustrious* and her consorts detached from the battle fleet and this part of the overall MB 8 was designated as Operation Judgement. Finally, a raid by cruisers was to be made into the Straits of Otranto but one final change was made before the fleet sailed on 6 November; *Eagle* had suffered what were described severe defects in her avgas system,[17] 'caused undoubtedly by the many bomb near misses she had experienced in the early days of the Italian war', which were said to prevent her from accompanying the fleet and so she remained in Alexandria.

Admiral Lyster's Plan for Operation Judgement

Admiral Lyster's plan was for a night attack on Italian warships in Taranto expected to comprise between four and six battleships, five cruisers and twenty destroyers. He was ably assisted by *Illustrious*' captain, Captain D W Boyd RN, his Commander 'Air', Commander J Robertson RN, known as 'Streamline Robertson' in the Fleet Air Arm for his remarkable ability to speed up any operation connected with the handling of aircraft, and Commander C G Thompson RN, the Operations Officer. The assistant Operations Officer was Lieutenant D Pollock RNVR, a former solicitor who had specialised in photographic interpretation on joining the RNVR[18] and made a careful study of 431 Flight's images. He saw lines of white blobs annotated by the RAF as blemishes but which he believed to be barrage balloons. Surprisingly, considering it was the C-in-C Mediterranean Fleet who had requested the photographs in the first place, the RAF intelligence headquarters in Cairo to which they had been taken considered them to be exclusively RAF property. Pollock was allowed to look at them but when he asked to take them back to Alexandria to show Admiral Lyster, he was not allowed to remove them from the building. His solution was to sit at a desk and plot the positions of gun emplacements and anti-torpedo nets but, when the flight lieutenant in charge of the headquarters went out of the room, he did what one would hope an operations officer determined to acquire the best briefing material for his aircrew would do under the circumstances; he stole the photographs. Overnight he had them copied by *Illustrious*' photographic section, showed them to his admiral and then returned the originals to the RAF. Their temporary absence had not been noticed. The carefully detailed plan included the following main points:

(a) A moonlight torpedo attack against battleships and cruisers in the outer harbour, the Mare Grande. At the same time there was to be a dive-bombing attack on warships in the inner harbour, the Mare Piccolo. The dive-bombing attacks were intended to confuse the defences by making it difficult to determine the height, direction and tactics being used by the main attacking force.

(b) The torpedo attack was to be made from the west towards the moon so that targets would stand out in the sheen of moonlit water.

(c) The carrier task force was not to proceed north of the line Malta–Kithera before dark and the run to the north was to be made before moonrise to avoid detection. Aircraft of the first wave were to be

Illustrious in June 1940 only weeks after her completion. (*Author's collection*)

flown off as soon as possible after 2100 on 11 November 1940 but were to be no further than 200nm from the target. None were to be expected to fly a total of more than 400nm out and back to the carrier.

The carrier force was to reach a flying off position 60 miles west-south-west of Cephalonia and was to be in a position 20 miles west of Cephalonia for the recovery. *Illustrious* had a significant after round-down intended to smooth airflow over the deck and this limited the deck-load range to twelve armed Swordfish at most.[19] Fulmars were expected be directed by the ship's fighter direction officers to drive off or destroy enemy aircraft attempting to locate the fleet. It was anticipated that consecutive strikes on successive nights might be required and so the ship's magazine stowage capacity had to be taken into account. It was:[20]

Illustrious air weapons magazine capacity in 1940
45 × 18in torpedoes
250 × 500lb SAP bombs
650 × 250lb SAP/GP bombs
100 × 100lb AS bombs
600 x 20lb bombs
4.5in flares
Considerable quantities of .303in machine gun ammunition.

There was slight doubt among the planners about the wisdom of using the new magnetic duplex pistols (Duplex Coil Rod or DCR pistols) to detonate the torpedoes in restricted waters despite NAD being firmly in favour of their use. In the event it was decided to run off 100yds of the Mark XII torpedo's safety range and to remove the battery resistance, making them remain dangerous and capable of detonation at the end of their run. It was also estimated that the positions of the balloons and anti-torpedo nets limited the number of torpedo aircraft to only six in each wave because of the limited space for effective weapon release.

Surface or submarine attacks by the enemy were to be countered by a strong surface escort comprising the 3rd Cruiser Squadron, 3CS, with *Gloucester* (flag CS3), *Berwick*, *Glasgow* and *York* together with four destroyers, *Hyperion* (Captain D2), *Ilex*, *Hasty* and *Havock*, which were to provide an anti-submarine screen and, if necessary, contribute to a surface action group. Anti-aircraft fire from shore batteries was not expected to be a serious deterrent to the strike aircraft attacking out of darkness but several elements of the plan were intended to limit their

Illustrious landing on Swordfish in August 1940. Two have taxied into Fly 1, the parking area forward of the barrier, after landing and had their wings folded. The third has just been stopped by an arrester wire and the after barrier is still raised ahead of it. The barrier will be lowered, like the forward one, when the aircraft begins to taxi forward. (*Author's collection*)

effectiveness. Searchlights could dazzle pilots at low level as they aimed their torpedoes and the bombing aircraft were intended to keep them pointing upwards as the torpedo aircraft attacked. A mix of high and low attackers was intended to cause confusion about the exact nature of the strike. Lyster requested RAF reconnaissance sorties to cover the Ionian Sea, the Straits of Otranto and the Gulfs of Taranto and Messina up to midnight on 11 November and confirm that the area was clear as the *Illustrious* task force made its run to the launch position.

The removal of *Eagle* inevitably led to last-minute changes, as did the discovery that defences included barrage balloons and anti-torpedo nets, although the latest reconnaissance revealed that part of the balloon barrage had been blown away in a recent storm. The Italians lacked sufficient hydrogen in the Taranto area to replace it quickly and the net defences had not yet been completed. In order to provide the most experienced strike force options, six Swordfish and eight crews were transferred from *Eagle* to *Illustrious* before she sailed.[21] Two Sea Gladiators of 813 NAS' fighter flight were also transferred.[22]

Illustrious *embarked aircraft November 1940*

806 NAS	15 Fairey Fulmar
815 NAS	9 Fairey Swordfish
819 NAS	9 Fairey Swordfish
813 NAS	4 Fairey Swordfish and 2 Gloster Sea Gladiator detached from *Eagle*
824 NAS	2 Fairey Swordfish detached from *Eagle*

There was no time to rehearse the revised plan and the pilots from *Eagle*'s squadrons deserve credit for operating from a carrier in which they had only embarked on the day before it sailed. The final plan called for the attack to be carried out from *Illustrious* in two waves of twelve but even this modest number had to be reduced after three Swordfish ditched while carrying out anti-submarine patrols on 10 November. Fortunately all three crews were recovered. Commander Robertson ordered an investigation, which found that all three were from 819 NAS and had been refuelled at the same point in the hangar. Overnight the squadron fitters had to drain and completely flush out the tanks and engines of the remaining six aircraft and then refuel them from a different ship's tank. The offending tank was found, like the aircraft, to have contained avgas contaminated with sand and water together with a peculiar fungal growth, later found to have been embarked from the tanker *Toneline* in Alexandria. Had these aircraft not been used for anti-submarine patrols, it is possible that all nine of 819 NAS' aircraft might have taken off for the attack with contaminated fuel and the results would have been disastrous. Their loss must, therefore, be considered fortunate. The long-planned attack on the Italian fleet in its harbour was now to be carried out on 11 November 1940 by just twenty-one Fairey Swordfish in two waves, the first of twelve aircraft and the second of nine. Modest as this force was, it actually represented 15 per cent of the RN front-line Swordfish force.

In the final version of the plan that was explained at the aircrew briefing, *Illustrious* and her task force were to be in position X, 270 degrees 40nm from Kabbo Point,[23] Cephalonia, 200nm south-east of Taranto at 2000 on 11 November 1940 when the first range of twelve aircraft were to fly off, to be followed by the second range at 2100. As it evolved it had retained all the elements essential for success; it was practical and achievable but above all else it offered flexibility. Difficulties over the ownership of reconnaissance photographs having been resolved at a higher level, a Swordfish was flown to Malta on 10 November, flown by Lieutenant (A) C B Lamb RN, which returned the next morning with the latest photographs.

The passage to the launch position

The intensive fleet operations prior to 11 November allowed no rehearsal and the reduction of aircraft due to *Eagle*'s withdrawal and *Illustrious*' avgas contamination had complicated matters. There was, however, an atmosphere of 'zeal and enthusiasm...to carry out this great enterprise'.[24] After the Royal Navy's years of struggle to regain full control of its own air arm there was a distinct sense that this operation would vindicate the faith of those who had struggled so hard and for so long to achieve it. In his memoirs[25] John Wellham, one of the pilots who had been transferred from *Eagle*, said that 'we were in a different world... *Illustrious* was huge and full of equipment that we had never seen or even heard of... we also appreciated the atmosphere on board. Every member of the ship's company was dedicated to the operation of the aircraft and proud and enthusiastic about her.'

Wellham spent the hours before the attack with other pilots in the hangar watching the aircraft being loaded with torpedoes, 250lb SAP bombs and 4.5in flares. He described how the bombing aircraft carried cigar-shaped, long-range fuel tanks, which were fixed to the torpedo crutches, but the torpedo-armed aircraft carried long-range tanks that fitted into the observers' cockpit, the observers themselves flying in the TAG's cockpit. There was little else to do but 'have some food and wait'.

For others, however, the daylight period before the attack was more exciting. At noon, Lieutenant George Going DSO RN was the observer in a Swordfish on anti-submarine patrol piloted by Sub Lieutenant (A) A Keith RN when it suffered an engine failure on climbing through 1,500ft after take-off. After ditching they were rescued from their dinghy by a boat from

Flying from an aircraft carrier's deck was dangerous in 1940 with the ever-present risk of fire after a crash on deck. Teams of aircraft handlers dressed in fire-resistant 'Fearnought' suits like this one on *Illustrious* were always ready to get the aircrew out of a burning wreck if necessary whenever the ship was at flying stations. The aircraft that can be seen landing on is a Swordfish. Note the buckets of sand to the firesuitman's left, which were used to cover an avgas spillage after a crash to prevent it from igniting or to smother small fires in the era before fire-fighting foam became widely available. (*Author's collection*)

Swordfish were started by an inertia unit rotated by a handle, which was inserted into an aperture in the fairing behind the Pegasus engine on the port side. This engaged with a chain and sprocket drive that, in turn, rotated a balanced flywheel and when this was spun up to high speed it would be clutched into the engine to turn the crank shaft. As seen here, two ground crew were needed to rotate the handle up to the speed required. To gain the best leverage, one had to stand on the lower centre section of the wing and the other with one foot on the bracing strut of the port undercarriage and the other on top of the tyre. As can be imagined, start-up on a wet deck at night with the ship pitching, especially as the nearby propeller began to turn, could be a dangerous process that required considerable skill and nerve. (*Philip Jarrett collection*)

Gloucester[26] and, on climbing onto the cruiser's deck, Going realised that unless he could get back to *Illustrious* he would miss the attack on Taranto and immediately made his way to the bridge to seek the captain's help. Captain H S Rowley RN proved sympathetic and ordered the ship's Walrus to be catapulted off to return the two aircrew to their ship. In his book *The Attack on Taranto*, Vice Admiral B B Schofield wrote that Going had been described by an officer who knew him well as the bravest man he had ever met. Going's actions on 11 November bear out that assessment.

The photographs collected from Malta were studied by Lieutenant Commander K W Williamson RN, the commanding officer of 815 NAS, who was to lead the first wave, and Lieutenant Commander J W Hale RN, the commanding officer of 819 NAS, who was to lead the second. They showed five Italian battleships in the harbour and fears that some of these might sail before the attack could commence were allayed when a patrolling Sunderland reported not only that none had sailed but a sixth had arrived to join them. On the evening of 11 November 1940[27] all of Italy's six battleships were moored in Taranto's outer harbour, the Mar Grande; the two new 15in gunned *Vittorio Veneto* and *Littorio* together with the 12.6in gunned *Cavour*, *Giulio Cesare*, *Caio Duilio* and *Andrea Doria*. Also present in the outer harbour were the heavy cruisers *Zara*, *Fiume* and *Gorizia* and eight destroyers. In the inner harbour, the Mar

Piccolo, the heavy cruisers *Trieste* and *Bolzano* were moored to buoys, with *Pola* and *Trento* secured stern on to the jetty. The light cruisers *Garibaldi* and *Abruzzi* were secured in the same way close to them, together with seventeen destroyers, five torpedo boats, sixteen submarines and minesweepers, oil tankers, supply ships and a hospital ship. There were also a number of merchant ships alongside the civilian dock areas.

Illustrious' Fulmars made a considerable contribution to Operation Judgement.[28] In the period between the ship's arrival with the Mediterranean Fleet and the strike they achieved air dominance whenever the fleet was at sea and David Brown, Head of the Naval Historical Branch, calculated that 806 NAS destroyed or damaged over forty enemy aircraft, preventing the Italians from gaining any clear idea of the fleet's movements or intentions by air reconnaissance. On 8 November one reconnaissance aircraft was shot down and a formation of seven S-79 bombers was intercepted and turned back 35nm from the fleet with one destroyed and another damaged. On 9 November a reconnaissance aircraft was shot down and on 10 November another reconnaissance aircraft was shot down and a bomber formation broken up. After Operation Judgement, on 12 November, three reconnaissance aircraft were shot down before they could make reports about the fleet's position. During the whole course of Operations MB 8 and Judgement only one enemy air attack had been made on ships of the Mediterranean Fleet, a success ascribed by Admiral Cunningham to the work of 806 NAS.

Williamson decided to approach the harbour at between 8,000 and 10,000ft and then split up. He and one other torpedo aircraft would descend to approach from the west while the remainder would descend and attack from the north-west. He hoped that by attacking from two directions they would confuse the enemy defences but he briefed his pilots to act independently if necessary. Hale decided to approach with all six of his torpedo aircraft in line astern from the north-west to give each a good run in as well as a better chance of hitting since from that angle the battleships appeared to overlap each other. The disadvantages of this approach were that it would take his aircraft dangerously close to the anti-aircraft gun batteries positioned on either side of the canal that linked the inner and outer harbours and they would have to cross a line of balloons moored to lighters on the north-western side of their targets. The balloons were measured as being roughly 300yds apart and the wingspan of a Swordfish was 45ft 6 in, so the chance of flying between them was favourable. The average depth of the anchorage where the battleships lay was 49ft, not greatly affected by tides.

The Italians were aware from the constant reconnaissance flights that an air attack was likely and on the evening of 11 November the ships

Fulmars of 806 NAS and a single Swordfish ranged aft on *Illustrious* in November 1940. The two Sea Gladiators of 813 NAS Fighter Flight can be seen parked aft of the island clear of the runway's starboard wingtip safety line. They could be pushed out onto the centreline quickly if they needed to be launched in a hurry. (*Author's collection*)

were at a high state of readiness with anti-aircraft guns fully manned and their main armament half manned. That said, senior Italian officers expected that an aircraft carrier approaching to within flying off distance would almost certainly be detected by air reconnaissance before it could do so. It is also probable that the wide-ranging operations just carried out by both the Mediterranean Fleet and Force H had confused the Italians and they lacked the situational awareness needed to know exactly where the carrier task force was or what its intentions were.

Taranto strike aircraft and their aircrew

First striking force

Aircraft	Squadron	Pilot/Observer	Weapon
L4A	815	Lt Cdr K Williamson RN Lt N J Scarlett RN	1 × torpedo
L4C	815	Sub Lt (A) P D J Sparke DSC RN Sub Lt (A) A L O Neale RN	1 × torpedo
L4R	815	Sub Lt (A) A S D Macauley RN Sub Lt (A) A L O Wray RN	1 × torpedo
L4K	815	Lt N McI Kemp RN Sub Lt (A) R A Bailey RN	1 × torpedo

Aircraft	Squadron	Pilot/Observer	Weapon
L4M	815	Lt (A) H A I Swayne RN Sub Lt (A) J Buscall RNVR	1 × torpedo
E4F	813	Lt M R Maund RN* Sub Lt (A) W A Bull RN*	1 × torpedo
L4P	815	Lt (A) L J Kiggell RN Lt H R B Janvrin RN	4 × 250lb bombs 16 × 4.5in flares
L4B	815 813	Lt (A) C B Lamb RN Lt K G Grieve RN*	4 × 250lb bombs 16 × 4.5in flares
E5A	824	Capt O Patch RM* Lt D G Goodwin RN*	6 × 250lb bombs
L4L	815	Sub Lt (A) W C Sarra RN Mid (A) J Bowker RN	6 × 250lb bombs
L4H	815	Sub Lt (A) A J Forde RN Sub Lt (A) A Mardel-Ferreira RNVR	6 × 250lb bombs
E5Q	824	Lt (A) J B Murray RN* Sub Lt (A) S M Paine RN*	6 × 250lb bombs

Second striking force

Aircraft	Squadron	Pilot/Observer	Weapon
L5A	819	Lt Cdr J W Hale RN Lt G A Carline RN	1 × torpedo
E4H	813	Lt G W L A Bayly RN* Lt H J Slaughter RN*	1 × torpedo
L5H	819	Lt (A) C S C Lea RN Sub Lt (A) P D Jones RN	1 × torpedo
L5K	819	Lt F M A Torrens-Spence RN Lt A W F Sutton RN	1 × torpedo
E5H	824	Lt (A) J W G Wellham RN* Lt P Humphreys RN*	1 × torpedo
L5B	819	Lt R W V Hamilton RN Sub Lt (A) J R Weekes RN	2 × 250lb bombs 16 × 4.5in flares
L4F	815	Lt (A) R G Skelton RN Sub Lt (A) E A Perkins RNVR	2 × 250lb bombs 16 × 4.5in flares
L5F	819	Lt E W Clifford RN Lt G R M Going RN	6 × 250lb bombs
L5Q	819	Lt (A) W D Morford RN Sub Lt (A) R A F Green RN	1 × torpedo

In this list aircraft with the first side-letter L belonged to *Illustrious*, while those with the letter E were from *Eagle*. The subsequent number indicates the squadron, 4 for 815 NAS, 5 for 819 NAS from *Illustrious*, and 4 for 813 NAS and 5 for 824 NAS from *Eagle*. Letters after the squadron numbers indicate the individual aircraft. Thus L4A is aircraft A from 815 NAS embarked in *Illustrious*. Aircrew marked * transferred from *Eagle* to *Illustrious* for this operation.

The First Wave

At 1800 on 11 November *Illustrious* and her escorts were detached by Admiral Cunningham to proceed in accordance with their previous instructions while the battle fleet remained in support to the south. The weather at position X was fine with a light and variable wind at the surface and at higher altitude it was westerly at about 10 knots. There was a thin layer of cloud giving almost total cover at 8,000ft and the moon was three-quarters full bearing south. Observers were given a last-minute briefing while pilots checked their aircraft; once all twelve aircraft in the first range were manned and running, Commander Robertson shone a dim green light from Flyco that indicated the captain's permission to launch; chocks were pulled clear and the leading aircraft marshalled onto the flight deck centreline. The first wave commenced flying off at 2035 and all twelve were airborne by 2040.

They formed up in a position 015 degrees 8nm from *Illustrious* and when all were in loose formation they set heading towards Taranto, 170nm away, at 2057.[29] At 2115, flying at a height of 4,500ft, they entered cloud and several aircraft became separated, with the result that they did not all arrive over the target simultaneously. Williamson continued with eight aircraft in company with him, five with torpedoes, one with bombs and the two flare-droppers. Every observer maintained his own plot so that he could take over his own aircraft's navigation if it became separated from the others in darkness or cloud and in fact there proved to be no problem as the aircraft that had become detached all attacked individually when they arrived at Taranto. Their task was made slightly easier by the dark

A Martin Maryland taking off from Malta for a reconnaissance flight. (*Author's collection*)

mass of Cephalonia to the east and on the return, after four hours in the air, there was the comforting thought that they should be able to pick up the carrier's homing beacon once they approached to within 50nm of it.

At 1955, shortly before *Illustrious* began launching her aircraft, an Italian sound location device at Taranto detected aircraft engines to the south. Ten minutes later other locators reported suspicious noises and alarms were sounded in and around the harbour. Guns were manned and the civilian population moved into air raid shelters. One battery even began firing a precautionary box barrage but ceased when the sound of engine noises faded. The intruder had apparently turned away and was almost certainly the RAF Sunderland of 228 Squadron searching the Gulf of Taranto for enemy surface forces. Three-quarters of an hour later further engine noises were detected and a second alert was sounded but, as before, they faded and the all clear was sounded. At 2250 the sound locators began to detect the first wave of Swordfish as they approached from the south-east and a third alarm was sounded. Again some shore batteries began firing a box barrage and the flash from gunfire and exploding shells acted as a beacon to guide Williamson towards the target. The weather at the target was fine and clear like that in position X, with a light surface wind below a thin overcast. The moon was three-quarters full to the south at an elevation of 52 degrees at 2300. By then the missing torpedo aircraft, L4M, had re-joined the strike force, having made straight for the target to await the others and it was probably this aircraft that was responsible for the second alert. The strike aircraft found the six Italian battleships moored roughly three-quarters of a mile from the eastern shore of the Mar Grande and partially protected by the Diga di Tarantola breakwater, encircling lines of barrage balloons and a zareba of anti-torpedo nets.

At 2256 Williamson detached the flare-droppers L4P and L4B to seaward of Cape San Vito and they came under fire from several batteries as searchlights probed for them. Both were at 7,500ft and at 2302 Kiggell in L4P began dropping a line of 4.5in magnesium flares at half-mile intervals in a north-easterly direction to the south-eastward of the line of barrage balloons that protected the landward side of the anchorage. They were set to fall by parachute and ignite to burn from 4,500ft downwards. Having dropped his flares and waited for fifteen minutes to see that they illuminated the target area correctly, Kiggell carried out a dive-bombing attack on the oil storage tanks a quarter of a mile inland from the anchorage. Lamb, in L4B, was briefed as the standby flare-dropper and after checking that L4P's flares were functioning correctly, he too bombed the oil storage tanks before turning for the return journey to the carrier.

At 2315 the flares began to illuminate the harbour and Williamson led his torpedo aircraft down from the west over San Pietro Island, levelled off 30ft above the water and headed for the southerly group of battleships. As they were seen flying through the box barrage they were engaged individually by a number of close-range automatic weapons firing tracer from ships, anchored barges and shore batteries. Williamson took a more southerly route before turning north-east to fly through the balloon barrage to aim at *Cavour*, the most southerly battleship. He allowed himself time to aim steadily at his target and released his torpedo at 700yds. It hit and a large explosion was seen on the ship's port side. Unfortunately, his line of attack took him between the destroyers *Lampo* and *Fulmine*, which engaged him at almost point-blank range. After weapon release he broke away to starboard across the stern of *Fulmine* and was shot down, ditching near a floating dock. Both Williamson and Scarlett, his observer, were picked up by a boat from the dock and made prisoners of war. They were both well treated by the Italian Navy and Williamson later recounted that they were regarded almost as heroes. Two nights after the strike there was an RAF air raid and they were taken to an air raid shelter full of Italian sailors; cigarettes were pressed on them

Illustrious' two lifts were situated one forward and one aft of the armoured area of flight deck but they were still designed to be small in order to minimise the extent of openings in the steel deck that could be a cause of weakness. Consequently, even folded Swordfish were a tight fit as they were ranged from the hangar and struck down into it. (*Author's collection*)

and towards the end of the raid about twenty men sang 'It's a long way to Tipperary' for their benefit.

The next two Swordfish, Sparke in L4C and Macauley in L4R, took a slightly more northerly line across the Mar Grande. They passed through the balloon barrage on an easterly heading and turned hard once through to aim at *Cavour*. They seem not to have had time to gain a good sight picture and released at less than 700yds. Both torpedoes missed ahead of *Cavour* but continued to run and eventually detonated about 200yds short of *Andrea Doria* without causing damage. *Andrea Doria* reported what it thought were two bombs exploding near her at about 2315 but no bombs had been dropped in this part of the harbour.

The next two aircraft, L4K and L4M, split up over the submerged breakwater just to the north of San Pietro Island. Swayne, in L4M, flew across the centre of the Mar Grande; past the northern tip of the Diga di Tarantola and turned north, to the east of the anti-torpedo nets, to aim at *Littorio*. The torpedo was released at 400yds and hit the battleship on the port quarter. Kemp, in L4K, meanwhile crossed the submerged breakwater somewhat higher and continued to dive across the northern arc of the harbour, passing across the northernmost balloon of the northern barrage and turning onto a southerly heading to the east of the nets to aim at *Littorio*. He released at 1,000yds and hit the battleship on the starboard bow. The last of the torpedo aircraft in the first wave was Maund in E4F. He coasted in just north of Cape Rondinella and flew round the northern shore of the harbour under heavy fire until he reached a point just south of the canal into the Mar Piccolo, where he turned onto a heading just east of south to aim at *Vittorio Veneto*, releasing his torpedo at 1,300yds. It probably hit the bottom and detonated short of its target.

The bombing attacks lasted slightly longer. The two flare-droppers had bombed the oil storage depot inland to the south-east of the harbour. Patch, in E5A, passed over San Pietro Island at 2306 at a height of 8,500ft and headed for the warships moored stern-to along the jetty in the Mar Piccolo. It took him a few minutes to identify targets amid the smoke and flash of the anti-aircraft barrage bursting around him but he dive-bombed them without, unfortunately, achieving any hits. Sarra, in L4L, crossed the enemy coast west of Taranto at 8,000ft and dived to 1,500ft over the Mar Piccolo. He too found target identification difficult and flew over the dockyard before seeing the seaplane base ahead of him. Deciding that this would be an excellent target, he descended to 500ft and released his bombs, noting a large explosion and subsequent fires in the hangars.

Forde, in L4H, crossed the coast just east of Cape San Vito and quickly saw the ships lying stern-to in the dockyard, which he described as looking like sardines in a tin. He bombed them from a height of 1,500ft but saw

The Taranto Strike 11 November 1940

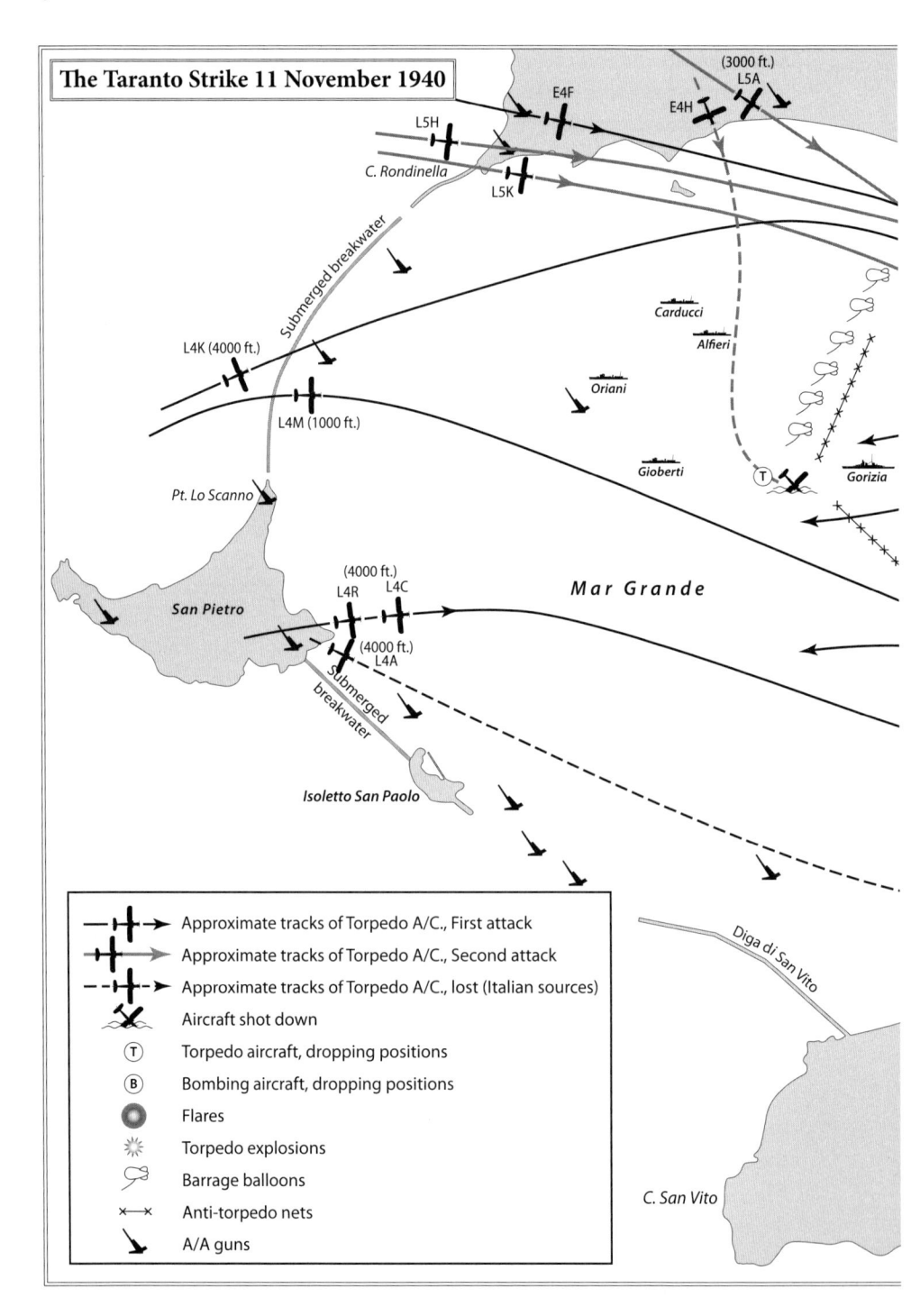

OPERATION JUDGEMENT – THE TARANTO STRIKE

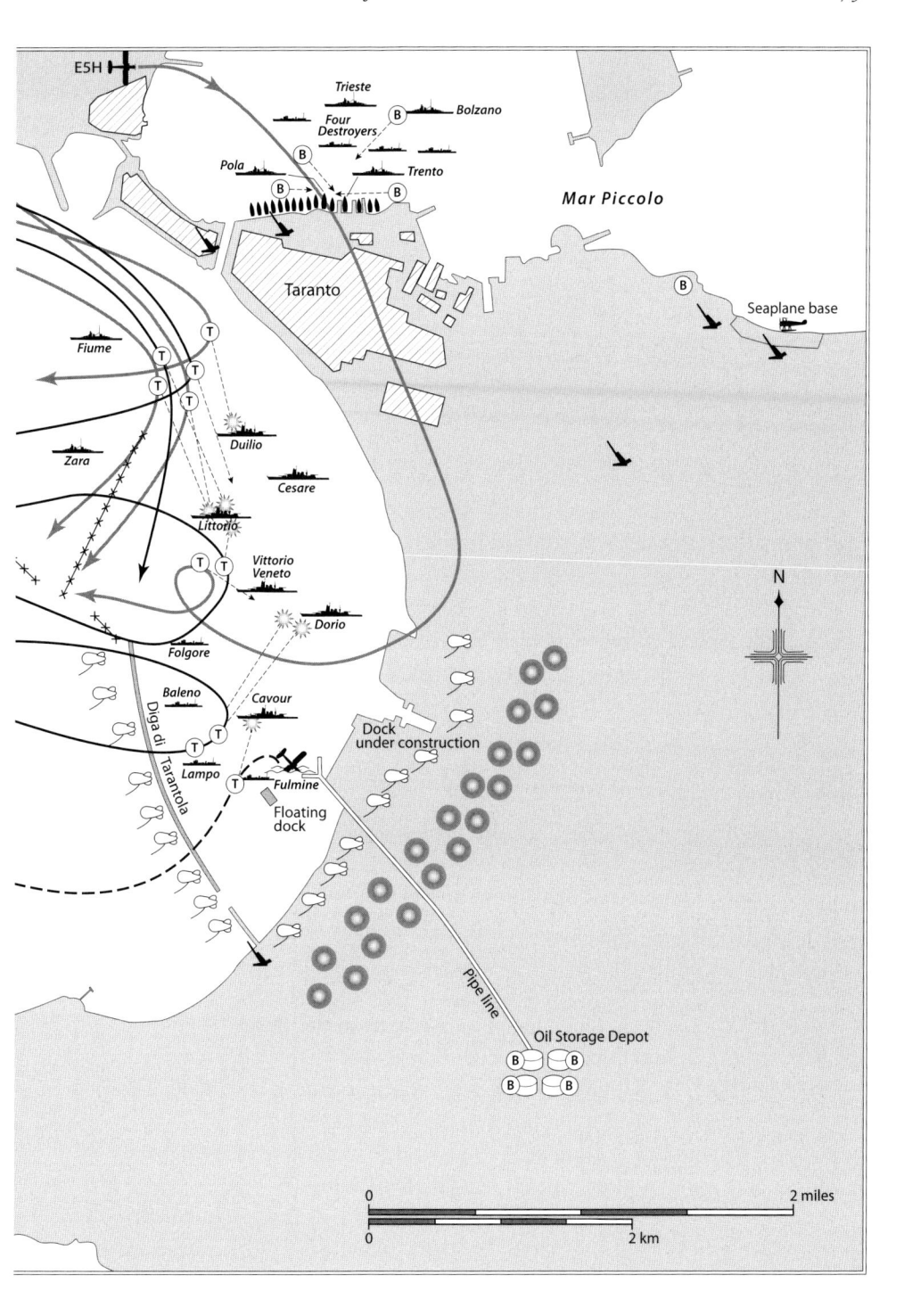

no hits. Unsure that all his bombs had released, he circled and repeated his attacking run before breaking away to the north-west and then turning to the south for the return flight. The last bombing aircraft in the first wave was Murray in E5Q. He followed L4H to the east of Cape San Vito and attacked the line of moored ships in the Mar Piccolo on westerly heading at 3,000ft. One bomb hit the destroyer *Libeccio* but failed to detonate.

By 2335 the first wave had completed its attack but the Italian box barrage continued because sound-locating devices had picked up the approaching engine noises of the second wave to the south. Half the torpedoes dropped had hit their targets and large fires had been started at the oil storage depot and the seaplane base. On the other hand, the bombers had apparently not succeeded in damaging warships in the inner harbour. Despite the intense anti-aircraft fire aimed at all the aircraft only one Swordfish had been brought down. Fears that there would be heavy losses had proved unfounded and the good news that Williamson and Scarlett had survived and been taken prisoner was received in the fleet several days later.[30]

The Second Wave

At 2120 the second wave led by Hale began to take-off but this launch was not completed as efficiently as its predecessor. The first seven aircraft were airborne and beginning to form up as the eighth, L5F, was marshalled onto the centreline. Inexplicably the ninth, L5Q, began to move forward at the same time into the same part of the deck and their wingtips struck each other.[31] Both engines had to be shut down as they were pulled apart but L5Q was thought to be undamaged and, after a brief discussion between Captain Boyd and Commander Robertson, it was ordered to restart and take-off to join the others. L5F, crewed by Clifford and Going, was found to have two broken wing ribs and torn fabric. It was optimistically struck down into the hangar for riggers to carry out rapid repairs and for the second time that day Going made his way to the bridge of a warship, this time his own, to plead with senior officers for a chance to take part in the attack. Supported by Robertson, Captain Boyd agreed to let him go and he made his way back to the flight deck as the repaired L5F was ranged for the second time. The first eight aircraft formed up in position 130 degrees 8nm from *Illustrious* and took departure for Taranto at 2145 just as L5F was being ranged. It was airborne only minutes after Hale set heading for Taranto.[32]

At 2205 one of the bombing aircraft, Morford in L5Q, had to turn back when its external fuel tank detached, leaving it with insufficient fuel to complete the mission. This was the other aircraft involved in the collision on deck and it is possible that its external tank attachment was damaged in the incident but not noticed in the rush to get it airborne. This was the only failure of a long-range tank.

At 2355 Hale detached the two flare-droppers to illuminate the harbour from a line to the east of the eastern shore, after which he led the torpedo aircraft down into attacking positions from the north-west. He crossed the coast at 5,000ft well north of Cape Rondinella and followed the north shore to a position south of the canal, where he turned south and aimed at the *Littorio*. After aiming steadily, he released his torpedo at 700yds and turned onto south to get away. At very much the same time, Torrens-Spence in L5K passed over Cape Rondinella and followed a similar track to Hale. He turned onto an attacking heading just south of the canal and released his torpedo about 700yds from *Littorio*. The battleship was hit by a single torpedo on her starboard bow, which detonated at 0001. This may have been L5A's or L5K's since both were released on similar headings within seconds of each other. The Italians subsequently found an unexploded torpedo stuck in the mud under *Littorio*'s keel. From the records available it has not proved possible to discover which was which.

E4H dived over the harbour on a southerly heading from a position halfway between Cape Rondinella and the town of Taranto. The Italians believed that it was aiming for a gap in the anti-torpedo nets at the southern end of the northern balloon barrage and was turning onto east to aim at the cruiser *Gorizia* when it was shot down into the harbour. Lieutenants Bayly and Slaughter were both killed. Lea, in L5H, crossed over Cape Rondinella and dived along the northern shore line. At a position only 2.5 cables south of the canal he turned onto south and aimed at *Duilio*, releasing his torpedo at 800yds. It hit her on the starboard side abreast 'B' turret and Lea got away to the west. Wellham, in E5H, coasted in over Cape Rondinella and then flew furthest to the north, crossing over the Mar Piccolo and the town of Taranto at low level. He narrowly missed the northernmost balloon in the eastern barrier before attacking *Vittorio Veneto* from the east. He temporarily lost control of the aircraft when an outer aileron rod was hit but managed to regain control and launch his torpedo without a steady tracking run from a position 500yds fine on the battleship's starboard bow. Unfortunately it missed but Wellham got away despite the damage to his Swordfish.

Hamilton, in L5B, dropped his line of flares from 5,000ft at fifteen-second intervals on a line south-west to north-east and then, like his predecessors in the first wave, bombed the oil storage depot. Skelton, in L4F, followed suit. The last aircraft to attack was Clifford in L5F, who had departed *Illustrious* twenty-four minutes after his colleagues. He arrived as the other aircraft completed their attacks and flew over the ships moored stern-to in the Mar Piccolo at 2,500ft. He hit the cruiser *Trento* and narrowly missed other ships but sadly after all Going's gallant efforts that day none of their bombs detonated. They flew on over the

Battleship Grounding Positions

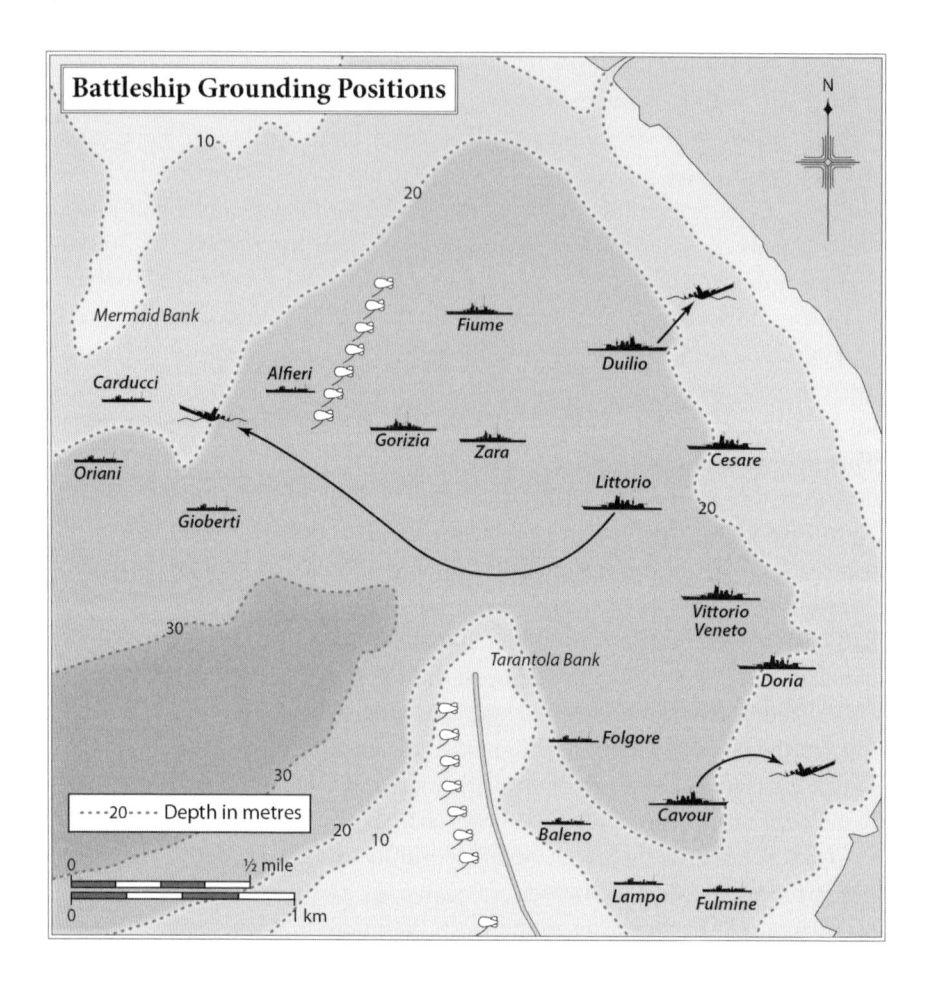

[Map showing Taranto harbour with ship positions: Mermaid Bank, Carducci, Alfieri, Fiume, Duilio, Oriani, Gorizia, Zara, Cesare, Gioberti, Littorio, Vittorio Veneto, Doria, Tarantola Bank, Folgore, Baleno, Cavour, Lampo, Fulmine. Depth contours at 10, 20, 30 metres.]

land to coast out 5 miles east of the harbour entrance. By 0250 on 12 November 1940 all the surviving aircraft had landed on and *Illustrious* and her task force headed to re-join the commander-in-chief's battle group in its covering position 90nm to the south. She was greeted by a signal hoist from the flagship that read 'Illustrious manoeuvre well executed'.

Individual recollections

None of the men of Taranto are alive in 2020 but several left accounts of the attack in their books. In *War in a Stringbag*, Charles Lamb described his view of the attack:[33]

> Blood Scarlett's dimmed Aldis light flashed the break-away signal to Kiggell and me, telling us to start adding to the illuminations over the crowded harbour and…for an unforgettable half hour I had a

bird's eye view of history in the making... The arrival of the first aircraft at the harbour entrance coincided exactly with Kiggell's first flare bursting into a yellow orb of light which seemed to be hanging quite stationary in the still night air... the shells of... tracer bursts illuminated the first Swordfish so brightly that from above, instead of appearing bluey-grey, it seemed to be a gleaming white... the anti-aircraft high-angle guns were concentrating on Kiggell's flares... following each flare in turn wasting all their ammunition trying to hit these small, elusive bundles of incandescent flame.

John Wellham described his recollection of the attack in his book *With Naval Wings*.[34] As they arrived over Taranto he:

followed the leader as he lost height... suddenly there was a burst of light to the eastward as the first flare ignited, followed by others until they hung in the sky like a necklace of sparkling diamonds... ahead there seemed to be a partial hole in the flak just where I wanted to be... the slip-stream was screaming through the struts and bracing wires and past my ears; my nose was filled with the stench of cordite; there was tracer above us, tracer below us and tracer seemingly passing between the wings... there was a tremendous jar, the whole aircraft juddered and the stick flew out of my hand... we were completely out of control. It was no time for finesse. I applied brute force and ignorance. It moved most of its travel to the right but only partially to the left... Buildings, cranes and factory chimneys were streaking past below us then we shot over the eastern shore of the harbour and were level over a black mirror speckled with the reflection of flames and bursting shells... A quick glance round: to my right and slightly behind me was a massive black object covering most of the horizon... a battleship... I levelled out after turning 180 degrees and pointing towards the great black hulk of the ship. Height OK, judging from the level of her deck – air speed dropping nicely – angle of attack not ideal but the best I could do – aircraft attitude for dropping rotten. The only way that I could achieve a straight line was skidding with some left rudder and the right wing slightly down... Strings of lights prickled along her decks and multiple bridges and grew into long, coloured pencil lines drawn across the sky above us... she seemed unable to depress her guns low enough to hit us. Closer and closer we came... I pressed the button on my throttle lever, felt the torpedo release.'

The Italian Battleships Following the Attack

Littorio

starboard side

water level

port side

harbour bottom

torpedo hit no 1 at 23.15: breach 10m x 7.5m

torpedo hit no 3 at 23.59: breach 11m x 9m

torpedo hit no 2 at 23.15: breach 7m x 1.5m

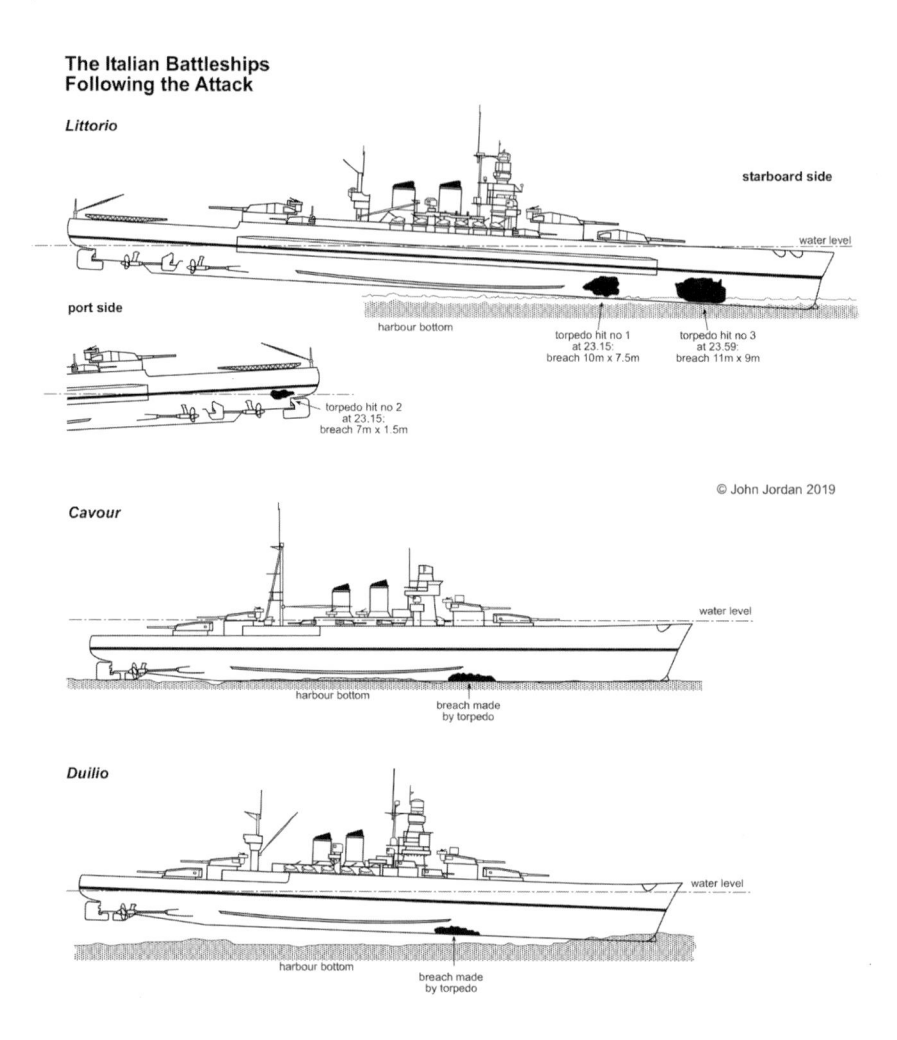

© John Jordan 2019

Cavour

water level

harbour bottom

breach made by torpedo

Duilio

water level

harbour bottom

breach made by torpedo

The scale of the defences

The scale of the Italian defences was formidable. There were twenty-one gun batteries armed with 4in guns, sixty-eight machine gun mountings with a total of eighty-four guns in positions ashore and afloat and 109 light machine guns ashore and afloat.[35] These were supported by thirteen sound locators, known to the Italians as airphonic stations, two of which were linked to searchlights, and twenty-two other searchlight positions. Each ship was instructed to contribute two searchlights to the overall base system. Only 4,200m of anti-torpedo netting had had been laid to protect ships in the Mare Grande, a further 2,900m were in stores at the base to be placed in position shortly and the remainder of the 12,800m required had still to be manufactured. There were twenty-seven barrage balloons arranged in rows to the west of the Diga di Tarantola, another north-west of it and a third along the eastern shore of the anchorage.

Persistent bad weather in the previous days had, however, destroyed a number of balloons and it had not been possible to replace them.

Surprise had not been achieved. The base and all the warships within it were at a state of complete readiness and there had already been two air raid warnings that evening before the first wave arrived. Anti-aircraft guns were fully manned and many were already firing the box barrage that Williamson saw in the distance before he arrived over the target area.

Results of the Swordfish strike

The aircrew were able to state with confidence at their debriefing that the strike had been a success with torpedo hits scored on battleships and bomb hits that started fires at the seaplane base and oil storage depot. Admiral Lyster's force re-joined the battle fleet on 12 November and preparations were made for a second strike on the night of 12/13 November while the fleet maintained its position. A striking force of fifteen Swordfish was prepared, of which six were to be armed with torpedoes, seven with bombs and two with a mix of flares and bombs. The weather deteriorated, however, and was forecast to deteriorate even further after nightfall and so, after consulting Rear Admiral Lyster by signal, Cunningham decided to cancel the second strike. Many aircrew were relieved to hear this after the stress and emotion of the previous night; one observer who had been selected to stand by for the second strike was said to have remarked that 'after all they had only asked the Light Brigade to charge once'.[36]

The true scale of the success achieved became apparent as the Vice Admiral Malta, Vice Admiral Sir Wilbraham Ford, and his staff examined reconnaissance photographs on 12 November. In his signal to Admiral Cunningham, date/time group 2031/12,[37] Ford said:

> Have examined Taranto photographs carefully and until enlarged I do not wish unduly to raise your hopes but it definitely appears that:
>
> (a) One *Littorio* class is down by the bows with forecastle awash and a heavy list to starboard. Numerous auxiliaries alongside.
> (b) One *Cavour* class beached opposite entrance to graving dock under construction. Stern including 'Y' turret is under water. Ship is heavily listed to starboard.
> (c) Inner harbour; 2 cruisers are listed to starboard and are surrounded by oil fuel.
> (d) Two auxiliaries off commercial basin appear to have stern underwater.
>
> Hearty congratulations on a great effort.

Later in the same day he sent an amplifying signal, 2345/12 in which he said:

> My 2301/12. The stern only of northern *Cavour* class battleship shows on photograph but by fix from entrance of Passagio Picolo (sic) which also just shows the bow is in about 4 fathoms. There is oil round the stem and it seems certain that the ship has been beached. The remaining one *Littorio* and two *Cavour* class battleships appear undamaged.

The one drawback with attacking ships in harbour, of course, is that it is difficult to destroy them completely since they settle in shallow water from which they can be raised and refurbished;[38] ships damaged to the same extent in the open ocean would be irretrievably lost. By early morning on 12 November, *Littorio*'s bow was resting on the bottom; between 0400 and 0627 she had been towed through gaps in the torpedo nets across the Mar Grande to the west and grounded on the Mermaid Bank in a position with a water depth of about 45ft.

By 14 November she had two auxiliaries, a tanker, several small craft and a submarine alongside her, the latter to provide electrical power. She had been hit by three torpedoes and the Italians later reported that the first had blown a hole 49ft by 32ft in the bulge abreast number one 6in turret. The second blew a hole 23ft by 5ft abreast the tiller flat on the port quarter and the third exploded on the starboard side, forward of the first

Cavour photographed on 12 November 1940. (*E Bagnasco collection*)

at very low level in the bulge, blowing a hole 40ft by 30ft. Subsequently raised and docked for repairs, she was not made operational again until March 1941.[39] A dent in her starboard quarter may have been due to the fourth torpedo, which was found unexploded in the mud beneath her.

Cavour to the south of her was in a worse state.[40] Flooding was causing her bow to sink lower in the water by about 2ft every thirty minutes and by 0155 her draught forward had reached 46ft and it was clear that she could not be kept afloat.

By 0330 it was finally accepted that counter-flooding measures in all three battleships were not stabilising them and orders were given to beach them. *Cavour* was towed for about 100yds from her anchor position to the east and grounded at 0445 in about 50ft of water with a sandy bottom on the eastern side of the Mar Grande. She was abandoned at 0600 but as her keel settled fully onto the bottom she came to rest at 0800 with her upper deck underwater. She had been hit under the foremost turret by a torpedo that blew a hole 40ft by 27ft. Two oil fuel tanks were flooded and flooding in adjacent compartments could not be checked. She was refloated in July 1941 and towed to Trieste but was not repaired in time to play any further part in the war.

Duilio, north of *Littorio*, moved under her own power with the assistance of a tug and grounded in shallow water about 40ft deep 150yds north of her anchor position. She was attended by small craft and belatedly enclosed by nets. The single hit on the starboard side abreast number one 5.25in mounting blew a hole 36ft by 23ft and caused the flooding of two magazines. She was raised and towed to Genoa, where repairs were carried out which were completed in July 1941.

Italian reports also stated the bombs that had hit *Trento* and *Libeccio* failed to explode, a disappointing outcome after the gallantry with which the attacks had been executed but if this is the case, it is difficult to explain the amount of oil fuel on the surface seen on the reconnaissance photographs taken after the attack. It is possible that bombs that did not detonate caused some damage in the vicinity of FFO tanks, which subsequently leaked. In the days after the strike the Italian battleships that had survived were moved to more northerly bases, away from the focal point of operations in the central Mediterranean and the Greek littoral.

The cruiser raid into the Strait of Otranto began as the Swordfish attacked Taranto and also achieved success. The force comprised the cruisers *Orion*, *Sydney* and *Ajax* together with the destroyers *Nubian* and *Mohawk* under Vice Admiral Pridham-Wippell. They encountered an Italian convoy at 0115 on 12 November 1940 and engaged it minutes later. Four merchant ships were sunk and their escorts driven off in an action described by Admiral Cunningham as 'a boldly executed operation into narrow waters.'

Overall, the Italian Navy had suffered a devastating night and the British fleet returned to Alexandria unscathed at 0700 on 14 November.

Taranto is rightly remembered as the battle in which the Fleet Air Arm demonstrated what it could achieve, even with the obsolescent aircraft with which it was equipped in 1940. It showed that carrier aircraft had become the dominant factor in naval warfare, not only providing aircraft as the third dimension of a modern naval task force but as a mobile striking force of strategic importance, able to take the fight to enemy fleets in harbour and even to oppose land and air forces beyond the littoral. By striking at an enemy fleet in its supposedly well-defended base, *Illustrious* and her aircraft had revealed to the world that a radical change in naval warfare had occurred. In his report Captain Boyd wrote unequivocally that:

> …it has been demonstrated before and repeated in no uncertain fashion by this success that the ability to strike unexpectedly is conferred by the Fleet Air Arm. It is often felt that this arm which has had a long struggle with adverse opinions[41] and its unspectacular aircraft is underestimated in its power. It is hoped that this victory will be considered a suitable reward to those whose work and faith in the Fleet Air Arm has made it possible.

Admiral Cunningham remarked in his own covering words that the attack was:

> …admirably planned and the determined and gallant manner in which it was carried out reflects the highest credit on all concerned… There can be little doubt that the crippling of half the Italian battle fleet is having, and will continue to have, a marked effect on the course of the war. Without indulging in speculation as to the political repercussions, it is already evident that this successful attack has greatly increased our freedom of movement in the Mediterranean and has thus strengthened our control over the central area of this sea. It has enabled two battleships to be released for operations elsewhere while the effect on the morale of the Italians must be considerable.

His Majesty King George VI signalled a message to Admiral Cunningham, which was received on 18 November. It said:

> The recent successful operations of the Fleet under your command have been a source of pride and gratification to all at home. Please

Amidships detail of *Cavour* after she had settled on the seabed, 12 November 1940. (*E Bagnasco collection*)

convey my warm congratulations to the Mediterranean Fleet, and in particular to the Fleet Air Arm on their brilliant exploit against the Italian warships at Taranto.

The relative strength of the fleets contesting control of the Mediterranean had certainly changed and the defeat was undoubtedly a blow to Italian morale and a boost to that of the British. It allowed *Malaya* and *Ramillies* to be redeployed, bringing some relief to the destroyer force that had to screen them, but Cunningham's belief that the enemy battle fleet represented his greatest threat is open to doubt. In reality, sea control now rested on the deployment of naval air strength, both offensive and defensive, and the Royal Navy had been able to make effective use of its carrier-borne aircraft.[42] The Italian Navy had been forced to rely entirely upon an independent air force that was poorly trained and badly equipped for war over the sea and had, even prior to Taranto, been neutralised in the battle space where it mattered by the fighters embarked in *Illustrious* in the eastern basin and those in *Ark Royal* of Force H in the western basin. The few Fulmars in these two carriers were sufficient to take much of the 'sting' out of the efforts of Italian high-level bombers, and RN torpedo aircraft had demonstrated their ability to compensate most effectively for the Italian superiority in capital ships.

Honours and Awards

After the glowing terms in which the attack on Taranto was described in the days following Operation Judgement, it might be supposed that immediate gallantry awards would have been commensurate[43] but they were not. Cunningham's initial list published in the Supplement to the *London Gazette* dated 20 December 1940 announced the award of the DSO to the leaders of the two Swordfish strike forces, Lieutenant Commanders Williamson and Hale. Their observers, Lieutenants Scarlett and Carline, were awarded the DSC, as was Captain Patch and his observer Lieutenant Goodwin. That was all. It may be that the delay was administrative because less than two weeks later in the New Year's Honours List of January 1941 Rear Admiral Lyster received a CB and Captains Boyd of *Illustrious* and Bridge of *Eagle* were each awarded a CBE. In *The Attack on Taranto*, Vice Admiral Schofield observed that 'the meagreness of the awards caused considerable ill-feeling amongst the ship's company of the *Illustrious*, especially on account of the absence of recognition for the magnificent work done by the fitters and riggers in carrying out repairs after the disastrous fire just before the attack was due to take place and ensuring that the aircraft were ready for service when required'.[44] The matter was drawn to the attention of those in authority and a supplementary list of awards was issued in May 1941, but by then several of those listed were dead. In this list Lieutenant Going was awarded the DSO and Lieutenants Torrens-Spence, Lea, Kiggell, Hamilton, Janvrin and Sutton together with Sub Lieutenants Macauley, Bailey, Jones, Neale and Weekes the DSC. Lieutenants Swayne, Maund, Bayly, Slaughter and Sub Lieutenants Sarra and Forde together with eight members of the ship's company were Mentioned in Despatches.

The reason for the initial lack of recognition is not easy to explain. It is unlikely to have originated in the Admiralty because Pound had added a handwritten minute to the report on the *Konigsberg* strike in April that instructed 5SL to 'confirm that awards to the Fleet Air Arm are got out as quickly as those to the RAF'.[45] He is unlikely, therefore, to have taken a less positive view of the Taranto strike. Cunningham makes no mention of the issue in his biography and it seems most likely that even after the event he had still not fully appreciated its true significance and the exceptional nature of the effort that had made it possible. As Thomas Lowry and John Wellham pointed out in *The Attack on Taranto*,[46] however, 'whatever ribbons and medals a government may or may not award, the bravery and skill of those fliers, and all those who provided for their needs and tended their machines, cannot be diminished'. That seems to me to be fair comment.

Analysis

For those able to comprehend what had happened, the oily wreckage-strewn surface of the Mar Grande on the morning of 12 November 1940 marked the eclipse of the battleship as the dominant factor in naval warfare and the arrival of carrier-borne aircraft as the fighting core of the fleet. RN aviators had succeeded in doing what they had always believed to be possible despite opposition from the Air Ministry and a lack of complete understanding by some politicians. The Imperial Japanese Navy certainly took note. A potential attack on the US Pacific battle fleet at Pearl Harbor had been war-gamed as a 'classroom exercise'[47] by the Japanese naval staff college prior to 1940. An air strike on the US Pacific Fleet in Pearl Harbor would have been considered a viable plan since the British Mission to Japan in the 1920s led by William Forbes-Sempill had revealed plans for the Grand Fleet attack on the German fleet in 1918 with Sopwith T.1s. However, the Japanese naval staff believed that the harbour's shallow water would make a torpedo attack too uncertain and had, therefore, limited their conjectural plans to high-level bombing. Taranto showed the Japanese that, with careful planning and carefully prepared weapons, a torpedo attack on capital ships in harbour was not only feasible but represented the best method of achieving decisive results. As with the Italian ships, however, they were to discover that ships sunk in shallow water can be raised and repaired to fight again. Taranto taught the

Littorio with her forecastle awash and salvage vessels alongside photographed on 12 November 1940. (*E Bagnasco collection*)

Imperial Japanese Navy another lesson, perhaps just as valuable, the need for the largest possible strike force – mass. The RN had only used one of its three Mediterranean-based carriers for the Taranto strike and had not armed the largest possible number of aircraft with torpedoes. The small force that carried out the strike had sent three battleships to the bottom, which were out of action for the immediate future but further attacks carried out through the hours of darkness, even if the later crews were less well trained, could have caused even more decisive results. To me, the fact that the Japanese committed six fleet carriers to strike a decisive blow at Pearl Harbor shows that they understood the need for numbers.

The obvious success of the attack on Taranto has masked the fact that it could, potentially, have been even more decisive if Cunningham had given it the priority it deserved. Viewed objectively eighty years after the event, it is difficult to understand why *Eagle* was left behind. The stated reason was the need to repair damage caused to the avgas system by concussion from near-miss bombs but surely she could have sailed with one or two avgas bowsers on deck to provide her aircraft with fuel. Requirements would have been minimal if her Swordfish were kept fully fuelled ready for the strike while *Illustrious* carried out airborne anti-submarine patrols, as she had to do without *Eagle* in any case. If bowsers were in limited supply from RNAS Dekheila or RAF sources in Egypt, sufficient avgas could even have been embarked in the sort of fuel drums used at desert air strips to top up *Eagle*'s aircraft for a deck load strike. Lieutenant Going had begged two captains to give him the chance to take part in the operation because he believed in it so much. Did the captain of *Eagle* beg to have his ship included at all costs? If he did the fact has not emerged in any extant Taranto papers. Lyster certainly regretted the absence of *Eagle* deeply, writing in a private letter that 'her fine squadrons would have increased the weight of the attack considerably and I believe would have made it devastating'.[48] Perhaps Cunningham really thought, like Pound, that the carrier that carried out the strike was likely to be overwhelmed by surface forces and destroyed? If so, he did not say so in his autobiography and nor has such a view emerged in any previous study of Operation Judgement. Why then did Cunningham not make the attack on Taranto as devastating as possible, getting every available Swordfish into the air even if one of his two carriers had to sail with temporary avgas facilities?

A possible answer is that Admiral Cunningham only envisaged the air strike against Taranto as a diversion, part of the wider picture of MB 8 until after its outstanding success became clear to him. At the end of November he wrote in his diary[49] that the large measure of control his fleet now had over the Mediterranean east of Malta was due to three factors: the arrival of powerful reinforcements including a new aircraft carrier and other ships fitted with radar; the use of Souda Bay in Crete as an advanced refuelling base; 'and last but by no means least the crippling of the Italian battle fleet by the Fleet Air Arm attack on Taranto'.[50] The fact that he wrote of the air strike as one of a number of factors, and then not the first, would seem to indicate that he had not thought initially in terms of a decisive blow but subsequently recognised success when he saw it.

There was a third carrier in the Mediterranean in November 1940, *Ark Royal*, which had thirty Swordfish, twelve Fulmars and twelve Skuas embarked. There had already been close co-ordination between Force H and the Mediterranean Fleet as part of the complex series of convoy operations that preceded Operation Judgement. On 9 November her aircraft had even delivered a diversionary attack on Sardinian airfields to draw enemy attention away from Taranto. She was, thus, frustratingly close to a position from which she could have joined *Illustrious* and *Eagle* to create a concentrated striking force. The two fleets had operated close to each other before. *Ark Royal*'s air group included some new squadrons that were not as well worked up as those in *Illustrious* and *Eagle* but if they had followed the first waves in the early hours of 12 November her aircrews could have been briefed to attack what they saw and would probably have achieved a measure of both surprise and success against the damaged battleships as they were run aground and the undamaged ships still at anchor. By then the Italian defences would have been tired, uncertain what was coming next and perhaps even low on ammunition since it had been used at a prodigious rate. Cunningham probably still thought at this stage in pre-war terms of aircraft operated as adjuncts to the battle fleet, not as strike forces with strategic capability in their own right. If this was in fact the case, he missed the ideal opportunity to destroy completely the enemy battle fleet that he regarded as the primary threat to control of the central Mediterranean.

What was Admiral Cunningham's primary objective, therefore? Did he see Operation Judgement as a 'hit and run' raid intended to gain temporary tactical advantage from any damage inflicted on the Italian Fleet or did he envisage it as a means of eliminating the Italian battle fleet?[51] The plan that was actually carried out contained elements of both but lacked the mass needed to achieve maximum destruction of the Italian battleships. If annihilation of the enemy battle fleet was Cunningham's aim, why did he not seek to strike with the largest number of aircraft possible? Did he see Judgement merely as a sideshow in a wider, complicated series of inter-linked operations or, like Pound, did he think that the strike carrier was so vulnerable that it must be lost to air or surface attack while carrying out such an attack, in which case he might have sought to limit his losses by only deploying one. The plan itself placed too much emphasis on

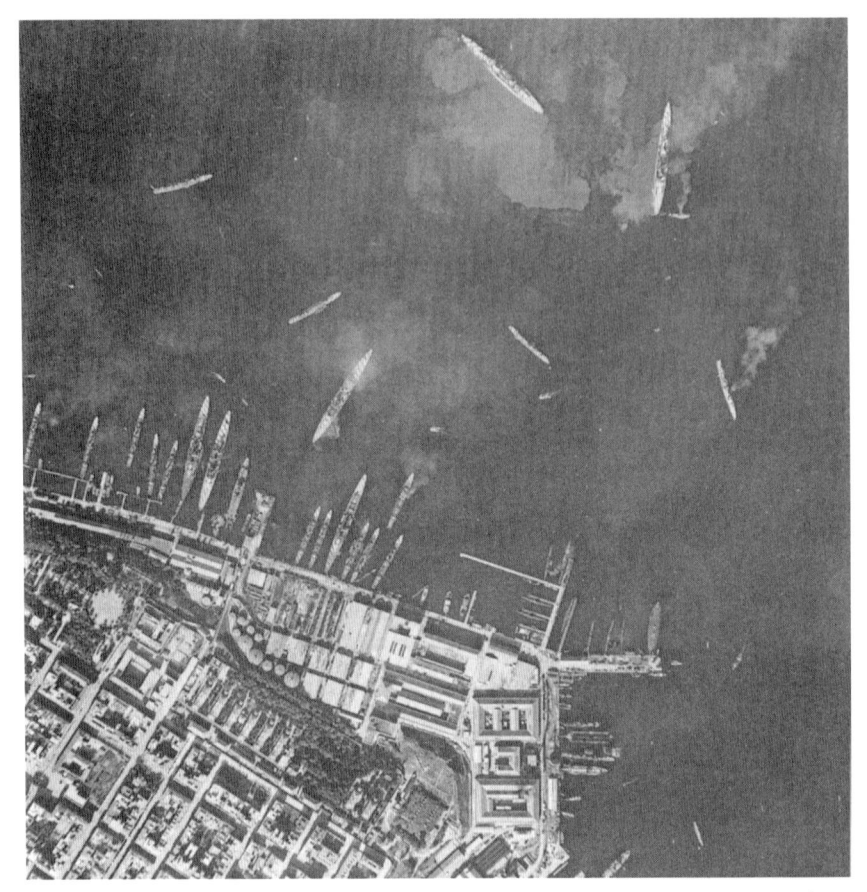

An overhead view of the Mar Piccolo taken by an RAF reconnaissance aircraft on 12 November 1940. The leaking fuel oil seems to indicate that some damage must have been inflicted on the cruisers anchored away from the dockside despite the failure of many bombs to detonate. (*Author's collection*)

distracting the defences with dive bombers and more aircraft should have been armed with torpedoes. The two flare-droppers were essential parts of each wave but more aircraft could have been armed with torpedoes, using time to limit the number attacking at one time. Separations of five to ten minutes would have been possible and effective. Two token bombers to distract the anti-aircraft defences would have sufficed.

The attack on Taranto was an outstanding success, carried out by dedicated and determined aircrew flying the remarkable Fairey Swordfish and planned by men such as Lyster and Boyd who believed in what they could achieve. They grasped a victory that demonstrated that in its Fleet Air Arm the Royal Navy had its most powerful weapon and the imperishable memory of the men who carried it out continues to be celebrated every year on 11 November.

4

Fleet operations up to the Battle of Matapan

After Taranto naval aircraft carried out a series of strike operations involving carrier task forces, cruisers and the Swordfish based in Malta. At the end of November Operation Collar provided protection for a convoy carrying supplies through the Mediterranean to Egypt. It was co-ordinated with the passage of the cruisers *Manchester* and *Southampton* from west to east and the battleship *Ramillies* together with the cruisers *Newcastle* and *Berwick* from Alexandria to Gibraltar. RAF personnel were embarked in *Manchester* and *Southampton*, deemed the ships most likely to get them safely to Malta.

Both Force H and the Mediterranean Fleet sailed on 25 November and on 27 November one of *Ark Royal*'s reconnaissance aircraft located an Italian force at 0906 off Cape Spartivento, the southernmost tip of Sardinia. The report was not received in *Ark Royal*, however, and the fact that an Italian battle fleet was at sea had not been revealed by intelligence sources or air reconnaissance from Malta. It posed a serious threat as defects had prevented *Royal Sovereign* from sailing with Force H, leaving *Ark Royal*'s Swordfish, *Renown* and five light cruisers, two of which were crowded with RAF personnel, to oppose an enemy surface force. Further support from the westbound force including *Ramillies* was 100nm to the east. A steady flow of reports from the shadowing Swordfish described the Italian force as two battleships with destroyers and two groups of cruisers to the westward of them. These reports were received in some ships but not in *Renown*, Somerville's flagship, which missed the first eleven reports because of a faulty W/T receiver. After being made aware of the enemy by a visual signal from *Ark Royal*, however, Somerville decided to concentrate his force with *Ramillies* and close the enemy. The convoy was ordered to alter course to the south-east, clear of immediate danger.

British and Italian cruisers gained visual contact and exchanged fire but the Italians turned away, following the Italian policy of avoiding action unless the circumstances favoured a successful outcome. Since *Ramillies*

A Fulmar of 808 NAS taking off from *Ark Royal* with another Fulmar and Skuas of 800 NAS running in the range behind it. Note the lowered barrier lying flat across the deck. (Author's collection)

was only capable of 20 knots and the Italians could easily outrun her, an air strike was ordered to slow their withdrawal. Eleven Swordfish armed with torpedoes were flown off *Ark Royal* at 1125 when the enemy was only 35nm from *Renown* on a north-easterly course heading for Cagliari. The carrier was some 25nm further west. The attack achieved surprise, there was no defensive manoeuvring by the enemy capital ships and at first it was thought that two hits had been achieved but no reduction in speed became evident. Somerville knew he was drawing rapidly away from the convoy and that its protection was his aim but at 1315 he ordered a second strike. To get the maximum number of aircraft, this would have to include aircraft that had just returned from routine patrols, quickly armed and refuelled. Nine Swordfish took off for this strike but as they joined up at 1410 the enemy capital ships were less than 25nm from their own coast and the strike leader decided to attack one of the cruiser squadrons further to the west, not the battleships. In his report, he said that they were reached first and the capital ships were already within the effective protection of an enemy airfield from which aircraft were seen approaching. The attack itself was not well executed; instead of attacking one ship with sub-flights from different angles, the leader chose to attack hastily in line astern from the same direction.[1] A possible hit was claimed but not confirmed.

Somerville had already decided to turn his force south-east to close the convoy but a third strike comprising seven Skuas armed with 500lb SAP bombs was flown off *Ark Royal* to attack one of the cruiser squadrons as he did so. Three *Condottieri*-class cruisers were taken by surprise and attacked with one ship estimated as damaged by near misses. As the surface forces separated, sporadic Italian bombing attacks developed, most of which were directed against *Ark Royal* but there were no hits. Despite their inferior speed, three Fulmars attacked an enemy force comprising ten Savoia-Marchetti SM.79 bombers escorted by six Fiat CR.42 fighters, causing most of the former to jettison their bombs and all of them to fail in their briefed mission. A single Skua attacked a further five SM.79s and achieved a similar result. Two enemy aircraft including a three-engined Cant bomber were shot down.

The Admiralty asked the senior RN aviator, Rear Admiral Bell-Davies, Rear Admiral Naval Air Stations or RANAS, for comment and, after reading action reports of what became known as the Battle of Cape Spartivento in English language histories, he noted the fleet's surprising lack of interest in air spotting for its long-range gunfire:

> Air spotting would have been invaluable to our ships owing to the enemy's effective use of smoke and the urgent need of reports for line but, unfortunately, the spotting aircraft were given no opportunity of proving their worth. Out of the 5 cruiser aircraft available only 3 were flown off, and one of these after the ship had ceased fire; the remaining 2 were unable to establish communication with *Renown* and *Manchester* as neither ship had a transmitter available. The presence of a carrier meant that there were no problems of recovery of catapult aircraft during the action.[2]

Ramillies subsequently reported that she 'did not establish communication with the spotting aircraft' because it was not known whether it had been flown off by *Ark Royal*. *Southampton*'s action report typified the overall failure. Her captain reported that direct spotting of fire from the gunnery director control tower was difficult, resulting in salvoes that were 'somewhat ragged for deflection and the long range and smoke produced by the enemy made spotting most difficult. The rate of fire depended entirely on the difficulties of spotting...'. The solution had lain with the Supermarine Walrus that sat ready to launch on his ship's catapult but it never seems to have occurred to him to use it. His report concluded with the rather inept statement that 'the aircraft was ready but was not flown off as it could have served no useful purpose'.

Admiral Somerville wrote in his own report that several lessons about the operation of a carrier within a task force had been learnt from this encounter with the enemy. He believed that 'shadowing or action observation aircraft are probably in the best position to report the results of air striking force attacks, based on the subsequent behaviour of the target. This is rarely observed by the striking force since the latter retire at low altitude to avoid anti-aircraft fire and fighter interception.' He had not been informed of the observed result of the first strike until after the action had been broken off and to emphasise his general opinions on the handling of a carrier he stated that:

> Provided the commanding officer of the carrier is fully aware of the admiral's views on how his aircraft are to be employed it is most desirable that the carrier should act independently. Signalled instructions concerning striking forces, reconnaissance etc add to wireless congestion and may be impractical to execute precisely without dislocating the intricate flying on and off programme.

Ark Royal's flying programme was certainly congested because she was the only carrier in Force H. She had to provide aircraft for reconnaissance, CAP and shadowing sorties, all of which had to be relieved at specific intervals, The largest possible torpedo-armed striking forces had to be launched, often at short notice, and each type of sortie had its own specific requirements for fuel, maintenance and arming. The captain and his commander 'air' were focused on estimating the enemy's position, disposition, course and speed from shadowing reports, the assessment of strike requirements and aircrew briefing. Returning aircrew had to be debriefed and the need for intelligence specialists soon became evident.

A torpedo-armed SM.79 bomber of the Italian Air Force. (*Author's collection*)

Senior officers literally lacked sufficient time to absorb information and make use of it.

The Italian admiral's appreciation, quoted in the Naval Staff History, was that 'the British aircraft will damage our ships, the Italian aircraft will not damage theirs', further commenting that the failure of Italian air reconnaissance had forced his fleet to engage an enemy force without any clear idea of its position or composition. Cunningham saw the action as 'intensifying our hold on the Eastern Mediterranean...whilst a beginning has been made in our establishing the through-Mediterranean route'. The growing number of radar-fitted ships and a modern aircraft carrier 'enabled the air menace to be largely overcome'. He was concerned, however, by the growing menace of torpedo bombers capable of attacking his fleet at dusk or in moonlight. 'The problem was,' he said, 'receiving earnest attention for if the enemy increase their scale of attack by this method the danger to convoys as well as to warships will become serious.'

Another action, which involved a Walrus embarked in the cruiser *Leander*, was carried out in the Red Sea at this time. On 29 November it was launched twice to attack a direction-finding station with its attached hutments at Bandar Alula in Italian Somaliland. On both occasions it was armed with two 250lb GP bombs, nose-fused for instantaneous detonation. No obvious damage to the huts was seen after these attacks but all the bombs had detonated among them and it was hoped that they had caused some splinter damage at least.[3]

On the same day, aircraft from *Illustrious* disembarked to Heraklion in Crete to carry out strike operations against Italian forces in the Dodecanese Islands. Bad weather became a factor, however, and only one attack proved possible. Early on the morning of 1 December two Swordfish, both armed with four 250lb GP bombs and four 25lb incendiary bombs, took off at 0330 and headed for Stampalia, where they dropped three 250lb bombs, three incendiaries and a single flare, opposed by light anti-aircraft fire. At 0500 they carried out a diversion over Pisleopi and at 0515 another over Niseros; both without encountering opposition. At 0525 they dropped a further three 250lbs and a single flare on Kos, again without opposition. At 0535 they set heading for Rhodes but were forced to turn back by thunderstorms and so they dropped their remaining weapons on Stampalia at 0603, watching anti-aircraft fire directed at flares rather than themselves. They returned to Heraklion at 0720 after an eventful sortie, although they were unable to say for certain what their bombing had achieved.[4]

Admiral Cunningham used the highly trained air groups in *Illustrious* and *Eagle* in a series of pinprick attacks against targets in the Eastern

A Ju 87 dive bomber. Note the arm between the undercarriage legs, which swung the bomb carried under the aircraft's centreline clear of the propeller disc when it was dropped in a steep dive. This aircraft has dropped its bomb. (*Philip Jarrett collection*)

Mediterranean rather than another attack on capital ships in harbour. On 12 December Swordfish from *Illustrious* carried out a dive-bombing attack on military installations at Bardia with results that were not recorded in the Mediterranean War Diary.[5] A day later eight Swordfish from Malta dive-bombed shipping in Port Tripoli, obtaining hits on three ships and on 17 December five Swordfish from *Illustrious*' 819 NAS were flown off to dive-bomb shipping in Stampalia from a position 120nm away. A further six from 815 NAS attacked Rhodes. Both groups were armed with six 250lb GP bombs, tail-fused for instantaneous detonation, and eight 25lb incendiary bombs. The weather at the position in which they were flown off was described as fairly good but the Rhodes strike force encountered bad weather and only one of its aircraft found the briefed target, obtaining a hit on what was described as a headquarters building.[6] The Stampalia strike force also encountered bad weather but four aircraft managed to attack the naval base at Maltesana and dropped their bombs among buildings with unseen results. A fifth aircraft loitered for twenty-five minutes hoping that the weather would clear, but when it did not the pilot attacked barracks on Condronisi Island without obtaining any observed results. In retrospect these attacks seem to have made poor use of an important resource.

Greater success was achieved after an RAF reconnaissance aircraft located an Italian convoy off the north-west coast of Sicily on 20 December. *Illustrious* flew off three Swordfish at 1015 on 21 December to search for it after receiving the report and the convoy was located at 1300. It was found to consist of two merchant vessels, one of 6,000 and one of 3,000 tons, escorted by a destroyer and a trawler. At 1400 nine Swordfish armed with torpedoes were flown off and they reached the convoy at 1542. Three aircraft attacked the leading ship, the 3,000-ton vessel, which blew up and sank within two minutes of being hit. Five aircraft then attacked the second, 6,000-ton, ship, which was also hit and sank within ten minutes. The ninth Swordfish attacked the trawler but failed to hit it. Complete surprise had been achieved and none of the Swordfish sustained any damage. The destroyer did not open fire until the attack was over. On the same day, six Swordfish from 830 NAS laid a minefield off Tripoli while a further four dive-bombed buildings to draw away enemy attention.

The last carrier strike operation of 1940 took place on 22 December when fifteen Swordfish from 815 and 819 NAS dive-bombed Tripoli from a flying off position 125nm away. They were flown off in two ranges, all armed with six 250lb GP bombs with tail fuses set for instantaneous detonation together with eight incendiary bombs. The first range attacked at 0515 and the second at 0615, both in moonlight. Ten aircraft attacked Spanish Quay, where a warehouse was seen to explode and others set on fire. Three aircraft attacked a stores depot west of the town, leaving it on fire and the other two attacked the army headquarters and an anti-aircraft gun battery respectively. There was heavy anti-aircraft fire but no aircraft were hit and there were no casualties.[7] This strike significantly damaged the Italian supply chain and the Mediterranean War Diary stated that other opportunities for carrier-borne torpedo aircraft to attack warships and convoys at sea could have been taken if the number of Swordfish

The core of Force H: *Renown*, *Ark Royal* and *Sheffield*. (Author's collection)

available in the fleet had been adequate to fulfil this task as well as reconnaissance and anti-submarine patrols. *Eagle*'s squadrons spent the last weeks of 1940 operating from shore bases, flying at least seventeen sorties in support of the Army, which was driving the Italians back into Cyrenaica. A total of ninety 250lb GP bombs was dropped on retreating forces in a series of night attacks.

German intervention in the Mediterranean

The Fuehrer Conference papers quoted in the Naval Staff History[8] revealed anxiety about the lack of Italian success within the German High Command. The staff view was that the early capture of Gibraltar offered the best solution. On 14 November this was seen as being of decisive importance but on 10 December Hitler issued a directive to the Luftwaffe that instructed it to 'operate as soon as possible from the south of Italy in the battle in the Mediterranean…their most important task is to attack the British Navy'. On 11 December the mooted capture of Gibraltar was postponed indefinitely and elements of the Luftwaffe's X Fliegerkorps commanded by General Geisler were deployed to Sicily. By January 1941 there were 330 aircraft spread between airfields at Catania, Comiso, Trapani, Palermo and Reggio Calabria.[9] The Korps included some aircrew and aircraft originally intended for service in the aborted German aircraft carrier *Graf Zeppelin* and, after the importance of British carrier operations had been recognised in the Norwegian campaign, it had undergone intensive training in the anti-surface vessel role with particular emphasis on the tactics for attacking aircraft carriers.[10] Its equipment included both Junkers Ju 87 dive bombers and Ju 88 high-speed medium bombers, together with Messerschmitt Bf 110 long-range fighters and Arado 196 reconnaissance aircraft. Unfortunately, British intelligence sources failed to identify either the scale or intended purpose of X Fliegerkorps' deployment.

Mediterranean Fleet priorities after Taranto included support for Greece after the Italian invasion, hence the strikes in the Dodecanese Islands. In January 1941 a convoy designated Operation Excess was to pass through the Mediterranean from west to east that included three ships loaded with equipment for the Greek Army to be landed at Piraeus. Another ship was loaded with stores for Malta and Force H was to escort the convoy as far east as the narrows between Sicily and Tunisia. The Mediterranean Fleet was to cover it beyond that and Cunningham organised three subsidiary convoys transiting both ways between Malta and Alexandria under the same cover. Two of Cunningham's cruisers, *Gloucester* and *Southampton*, were sent west of the narrows to strengthen the convoy's close escort as

Force H turned away and it then had to cover 150nm under the threat of air, submarine and torpedo boat attack through the narrows before coming under the protection of the Mediterranean Fleet from a position 15nm south-east of the island of Pantelleria. At the core of Cunningham's battle force were what he referred to as his 'first eleven', the aircraft carrier *Illustrious* together with the battleships *Warspite*, which flew his flag, and *Valiant*.

The rendezvous between the convoy and the Mediterranean Fleet took place at 0800 on 10 January 1940, by which time the fleet had been seen and reported by enemy reconnaissance aircraft and four torpedo-carrying aircraft made unco-ordinated and unsuccessful attacks. The last of these happened at 1223 when two aircraft dropped their torpedoes 2,500yds from the battleships, which had no difficulty avoiding them. Unfortunately these attacks had the effect of drawing *Illustrious'* four CAP Fulmars down to sea level as they chased them out to 20nm from the fleet, damaging them both. As the three capital ships regained formation, a large formation of aircraft was detected on radar closing the force at high level. Fighter direction officers ordered the CAP to resume station but two reported that they had fired out all their ammunition and the others had very little left. At 1234, therefore, *Illustrious* turned into wind and flew off four Fulmars and two Swordfish as replacements for the airborne CAP and anti-submarine patrols respectively. Two groups of enemy aircraft were already visible and identified as Junkers Ju 87 dive bombers, which took up a position astern of the carrier at 12,000ft. The attack began at 1238 and it was immediately obvious that the carrier was their target. Sub flights of three aircraft peeled off to make perfectly co-ordinated attacks from astern and each beam, diving straight down to release their bombs at about 1,500ft. Later aircraft spiralled down to about 5,000ft before

Illustrious under attack on 10 January 1941. (*Author's collection*)

tipping into a vertical dive and releasing their weapons in some cases as low as 800ft. In his autobiography, Admiral Cunningham wrote that:

> One was too interested in this new form of dive-bombing attack really to be frightened and there was no doubt we were watching complete experts. Formed roughly in a large circle over the fleet, they peeled off one by one when reaching the attacking position. We could not but admire the skill and precision of it all. The attacks were pressed home to point-blank range and as they pulled out of their dives some of them were seen to fly along the flight deck of the Illustrious below the level of her funnel.[11]

Captain Boyd made drastic alterations of course but only a large number of fighters in a position to break up the attackers' formations before individual aircraft began their dives would have been effective at this point since the fleet's anti-aircraft fire proved to be ineffective against the dive bombers' steep-diving attack profile. Almost immediately, a 500kg bomb passed through the loading platform of *Illustrious*' P1 pom-pom, damaging the gun and killing two of its crew. It then passed

Illustrious' flight deck on 10 January 1941 showing the bomb hit forward of the after lift, on the centreline, that penetrated the armoured flight deck. The wreckage of the after lift is visible projecting above the deck aft of it and the amount of steam and smoke give an indication of the heat being generated by the fire in 'C' hangar. (*Author's collection*)

down through the sponson and bounced off the side armour into the sea, fortunately without detonating. Seconds later a second bomb hit the flight deck, forward of the armoured area between the lifts, and passed down through the ratings' recreation space on the port side and out through the flare above the bows before detonating 10ft above the water, causing splinter damage to the hull that led to flooding in forward compartments. At the same time a bomb, assessed to be a 60kg anti-personnel device, hit S2 pom-pom just forward of the island, killing most of the gun's crew and setting fire to ammunition in the loading trays. 'Jumbo', the mobile flight deck crane, was parked nearby and the blast caused its jib to collapse across S1 pom-pom. Electric power to both starboard forward pom-pom mountings was severed by splinter damage and blast.

Two bombs of at least 250kg hit the after lift well almost simultaneously. One hit in its starboard forward corner, penetrated the lift platform and detonated at the base of the lift well. The other hit the lift platform on its port side and detonated. The lift platform itself was at the halfway point, being raised from the hangar deck to range a Fulmar, which disintegrated and set fire to four other Fulmars and several Swordfish in 'C' hangar, the aftermost one of three. Fire spread out of control, gutting the ship between frames 162 and 166 right down to the armour over the steering compartment and all electrical leads in this area were severed by splinters, cutting power to both the after ammunition hoists and the steering motors. A near miss off the starboard quarter caused shock damage to the steering gear and splinters penetrated its compartment to cause flooding. Without steering the ship was now out of control with the rudder jammed hard to port. Fire parties tried to suppress the fire in 'C' hangar and lowered the fire curtains that divided 'A', 'B' and 'C' hangars. Lieutenant Janvrin, who had flown in L4P on the Taranto strike, remembered climbing into his Swordfish to collect a first-aid kit when he felt a blast ripping the aircraft free of its lashings to be blown sideways and wrecked.

At 1242 a seventh bomb, estimated to be 500kg, hit the flight deck near the runway centreline halfway between the island and the after lift. It penetrated the 3in armoured deck[12] and detonated about 2ft above the hangar deck, causing considerable damage. Blast buckled the forward lift platform and caused it to arch upwards, allowing air to be sucked into the hangar and this fanned the fire in 'C' hangar into even greater intensity. The after lift platform was blown out and came to rest at a crazy angle amid the flames. Blast also tore the recently deployed metal fire screens to shreds and splinters from them wrought terrible execution among the fire-fighting parties and spray operators in 'C' hangar and its access lobbies. Collateral damage was inflicted on 4.5in gun ammunition hoists and one round exploded in its tray. Lieutenant Going, who had begged to be allowed to take part in the Taranto strike, had been watching the attack from the starboard catwalk and made his way into 'C' hangar. He found that the officer in charge of the damage control party there had been killed and immediately took charge, helped by other pilots and observers. Another near miss on the port side produced splinters, which started a fire in the senior ratings' mess and damaged both lighting and power leads. One large splinter from this bomb penetrated as far as the island and cut through power lines to the radar, gyro compass repeaters and 20in signal lanterns. A further near miss on the starboard side started a fire in the Royal Marines' barracks.

Amidst the explosions from this succession of bomb hits, a Ju 87 that had been hit by anti-aircraft fire crashed into the after lift well, its burning fuselage adding to the uncontrolled fire. The engine and boiler rooms under the hangar deck armour remained undamaged through all this carnage but smoke and fumes from chemicals used to try to cut down the fire in 'C' hangar were drawn into the boiler rooms by their intake fans. Gallantly the stokers all remained at their posts despite the deck above them glowing red hot. They had to breathe through wet rags tied over their mouths and noses. In his report, Captain Boyd wrote that 'the courage and devotion to duty of the boiler room crew was magnificent'.[13] By 1303 the emergency steam steering system had been connected, the rudder was again usable and the ship was under control, although the fire aft continued to rage. At 1313 speed was increased to 26 knots and by 1330 *Illustrious* was 10nm north-eastward of the battleships, which were themselves 10nm south of the 'Excess' convoy, when a high-level bombing attack by Italian aircraft began. Seven aircraft attacked the battleships, three the convoy and a further seven *Illustrious*, but none scored any hits. Taking stock of his crippled ship and noting the flames still emanating from the after lift well, Captain Boyd signalled his intention to head for Malta at his best speed, an action with which Cunningham fully concurred and two destroyers were detached to act as escort. However, at 1335 the steering gear failed again and for the next hour *Illustrious* was only able to make erratic progress. By 1448 she was steering using main engines and making good a speed of 14 knots. Heroic damage control efforts continued under the direction of her executive officer, Commander G S Tuck RN, but at 1610 there was another attack, this time by fifteen dive bombers and five escorting fighters of X Fliegerkorps. They were detected by the fleet's radar, however, and the Fulmars that had been airborne at the time of the first attack had been able to fly to Malta, now less than 60nm to the east, where they had been refuelled and rearmed. They were

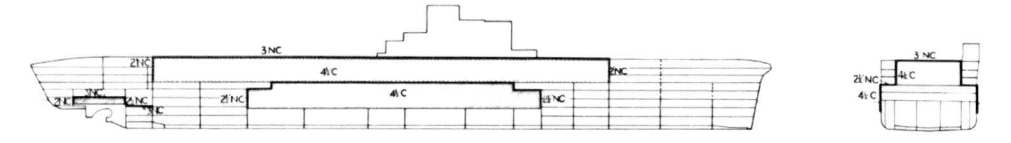

Illustrious' armour design. The numbers show the thickness of the armour in inches; C indicates 'cemented' armour plate and NC 'non-cemented'. (*Author's collection*)

now on CAP above their carrier and managed to prevent six of the dive bombers from attacking. Repairs in the ship had got the forward 4.5in guns and five of the six pom-pom mountings back into action; power to the after 4.5in turrets could not be restored.

As before, the attacks were made from astern and from either beam, but Captain Boyd noted that 'this attack was neither so well synchronised nor so determined as the previous one'. Nevertheless, a 500kg bomb penetrated the after lift well and detonated on impacting the after ammunition conveyor, killing or severely wounding everyone in the wardroom flat. Officers snatching a hasty cup of tea in the wardroom were killed, the after part of the ship lost power and was plunged into darkness. Many of the men fighting the fires were also killed but the blast did blow some of them out. One of the casualties in this attack was Going, who received injuries that necessitated the amputation of one of his legs. Seconds later, a near miss close to the stern added to the flooding in the steering compartment and killed everyone in the temporary sick bay that had been set up on the quarterdeck. Another near miss exploded in the sea abreast the island but caused only minor splinter damage.

By 1631 the last enemy aircraft was flying away but the fight to get *Illustrious'* fires under control continued; they were not to be extinguished until well after the ship arrived in Malta Dockyard. At about this time the fires threatened one of the after magazines and Captain Boyd was asked for permission to flood it. The possibility of further attacks made it a difficult decision but Boyd decided to accept the risk of not flooding. Ammunition was, therefore, available for the guns when a further attack developed at 1920, fully justifying his decision. By then the ship was only 5nm off the entrance to Grand Harbour when two torpedo bombers were seen approaching an hour after sunset in clear moonlight. They were met by a barrage of fire from the carrier and her two escorts, which kept them at a safe distance. If torpedoes were dropped, their tracks were not seen and *Illustrious* passed St Elmo light on the breakwater at 2104 aided by three tugs. Still on fire, she secured to Parlatorio Wharf at 2215.

In all, *Illustrious* suffered seven bombs hits on that fateful day, with further damage caused by five near misses and a crashed enemy aircraft. The four bombs that caused such devastation aft had all hit unarmoured surfaces and the one bomb that penetrated the flight deck armour did so aft of the machinery spaces. The damage control organisation had functioned magnificently throughout the action and the devotion to duty of the boiler room personnel was worthy of the highest praise.

Illustrious' losses on 10 January 1941 were heavy. Eighty-three officers and men were killed with a further sixty seriously and forty slightly wounded. Several of the officers who had flown in the Taranto strike were among the dead. They included Lieutenant N McI Kemp RN, Lieutenant (A) R G Skelton RN, Sub Lieutenant (A) E A Perkins RNVR, the former dying of wounds two days later. Lieutenant E W Clifford RN, Going's pilot was killed and so, too, were Sub Lieutenant (A) A Mardel-Ferreira RNVR and Sub Lieutenant (A) A L O Wray RNVR.

A day after *Illustrious*' arrival in Malta the fires were eventually extinguished but desperate work had to be carried out to make her seaworthy because she remained vulnerable to air raids. Surprisingly, there were no further enemy attacks until 16 January, when there was

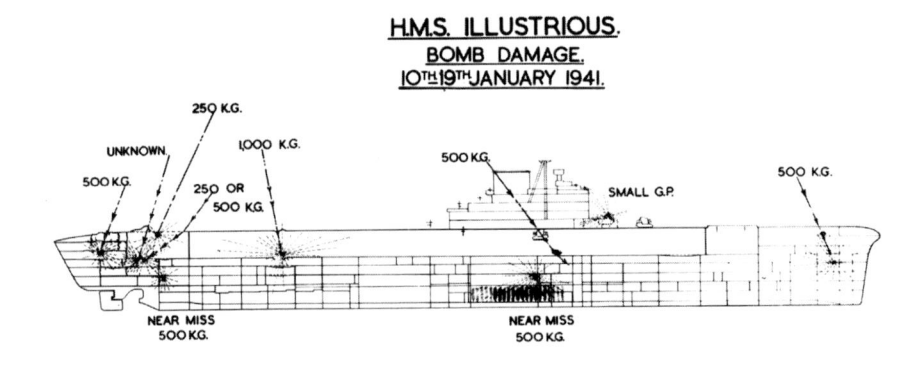

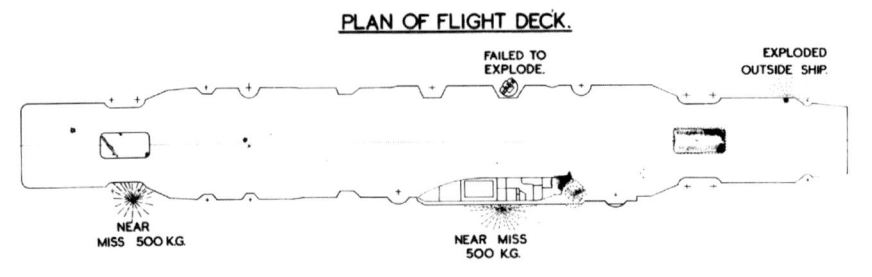

The damage suffered by *Illustrious* on 10 January 1941 and the subsequent near miss while she was in Malta Dockyard. (*Author's collection*)

a raid by between sixty and seventy high-level bombers during which a single bomb hit right aft and passed through the flight deck and captain's quarters before detonating on the quarterdeck, where it added to the structural weakness in that part of the hull. Fortunately it caused no casualties. Further raids followed on 18 and 19 January and on the latter a near miss burst on the harbour bottom, causing a mining effect on the hull that fractured the sliding feet of the port turbines and damaged piping and brickwork in the port boiler room. The ship's side below the port armour belt was dented inwards by about 5ft over an area about 75ft in length. Any success these attacks might have achieved was limited by the efforts of RAF Hurricanes reinforced by the surviving Fulmars of 806 NAS. The gallantry of the Malta Dockyard employees who continued to work on *Illustrious* through the air raids was praised by a number of senior officers.

Illustrious was ready to sail on 23 January and slipped her moorings at 1746, making her escape in darkness at 24 knots as soon as she was clear of Grand Harbour. She reached Alexandria at 1330 on 25 January and was accorded a tremendous welcome by ships in harbour. Further repairs were carried out and she sailed south through the Suez Canal on 10 March under the command of the newly promoted Captain Tuck, her former executive officer. Captain Boyd was promoted to rear admiral and appointed to replace Admiral Lyster as Rear Admiral Aircraft Carriers (Mediterranean). *Illustrious* was docked in Durban to have her underwater damage assessed while arrangements were made for her to be repaired in the USA at Norfolk Navy Yard in Virginia, where she arrived on 12 May.

Lessons from 10 January were quickly absorbed by the Admiralty. The fleet's anti-aircraft gunnery was not of a high enough standard and clearly suffered from the lack of practice against realistic targets. Short-range guns, especially the 2pdr pom-pom, had worked well but their method of control was described in reports as being useless. Extra fighter squadrons and the need to embark them for operations that required the maximum CAP were now seen to be important but most important of all, an interceptor fighter with a good rate of climb was now recognised as being essential for fleet work. Only a single-seater could meet this requirement and it is worth noting that nearly all future Fleet Air Arm fighters including Martlets/Wildcats, Sea Hurricanes, Seafires, Hellcats and Corsairs were to be single-seaters. The two-seater Firefly was to be a fighter reconnaissance/night fighter type. From mid-1941 carriers' aircraft complements varied from operation to operation, with the ratio of fighters to TBR aircraft gradually increasing.

While *Illustrious* was in Malta, the German Embassy in Lisbon reported: 'Naval Attaché Lisbon reports that the British Naval Attaché there has expressed the view that *Illustrious* has been so severely damaged that it will not be possible to repair her at Malta. He is deeply concerned about the future of the carrier.'[14]

Swordfish from Ark Royal *attack the Tirso dam*

After Operation Excess, plans were prepared by Force H for a bombardment of Genoa and, as a diversion, designated Operation Picket, torpedo-armed Swordfish from *Ark Royal* were to attempt to breach the San Chiara Ula Dam on Lake Tirso in central Sardinia. Its hydro-electric generators provided a large proportion of Sardinia's power and although the lake was situated amid hills, its approaches were not thought be difficult. The bombardment of Genoa, Operation Result, was given priority by the Admiralty after intelligence reports claimed that German forces were assembling an expeditionary force there. Somerville thought that this might be directed against Spanish east coast ports with the objective of neutralising Gibraltar but the Admiralty thought the Balearic Islands were the more likely objective. The bombardment of an enemy port 850nm from Gibraltar involved high risk, especially as RAF reconnaissance assets were insufficient to search for widely separated Italian fleet units. Briefly the two operations were to comprise:

a. An attack on the Tirso dam at dawn on 2 February 1941, after which Force H was to move towards the central Mediterranean as a feint.
b. Weather permitting, a high-speed approach towards Genoa was to be made that night with *Ark Royal* and her screen detached about 40nm from the objective to bomb the oil refinery at Leghorn and lay mines off Spezia.
c. *Renown*, *Malaya*, *Sheffield* and screening destroyers to carry out the bombardment at dawn on 3 February 1941, afterwards withdrawing with *Ark Royal* at high speed to the westward of the Balearic Islands.
d. Vice Admiral, Malta, Vice Admiral Sir Wilbraham T R Ford, was to arrange the bombing of Elmas airfield near Cagliari, Sardinia, on the nights of 1/2 February and 2/3 February 1941 as well as air reconnaissance of Genoa and weather reports immediately prior to both operations. (In the event, bad weather and the loss of an aircraft prevented this air reconnaissance.)

e. C-in-C Mediterranean with *Warspite*, *Valiant*, *Eagle* and their screen to stage a diversionary operation off the south-west corner of Crete while Vice Admiral Light Forces, VALF, carried out a sweep in the southern Aegean with two cruisers and three destroyers.

The plans were approved by the Admiralty, which forwarded the latest maps and plans of the Tirso dam to Gibraltar. Force H sailed on 31 January and at 0550 on Sunday, 2 February *Ark Royal* reached the briefed flying off position 80nm west of the Tirso dam. Eight Swordfish from 810 NAS led by its commanding officer, Lieutenant Commander M Johnstone RN, were flown off, all armed with Mark XII torpedoes fitted with contact pistols and set to run at 44ft and 40 knots. The weather was bad, however, with almost complete cloud cover at 1,500ft and intermittent rain showers. It was dark with no moon and the icing level in cloud was briefed at 5,000ft.

In these conditions the form-up went badly and after several attempts aircraft set heading in separate groups towards the Sardinian coast at Cape Mannu. The weather deteriorated still further with heavy rain and low cloud, delaying the onset of daylight, and one by one the aircraft turned back out to sea to await better light conditions, except for the last, which pressed on at 5,000ft. When ice was seen to be forming on his aircraft's wings, the pilot could not see land beneath him, let alone

Illustrious' progress towards Malta temporarily stopped at about 1400 on 10 January 1941 while repairs were made to her steering gear. She is still on fire with flames and smoke pouring from her after lift. Ships of the 'Excess' convoy are just visible on the horizon. (*Author's collection*)

the target, and decided to jettison his torpedo and return to *Ark Royal*. Another pilot jettisoned his torpedo from 1,500ft when he encountered intense anti-aircraft fire near the target and a third returned to *Ark Royal* with his torpedo when he failed to locate the target.

The remaining five Swordfish acted independently and approached the dam from different directions, some of them in better conditions low down and some through gaps in the clouds. They all came under heavy anti-aircraft fire, which surprised them because the intelligence briefing before the sortie had said that the target was undefended. One pilot reported that the gunfire appeared to track his aircraft through cloud. Eventually four aircraft managed to attack the target. One made a bad drop, which probably caused the torpedo to break up, and two made drops described as 'indifferent' in their reports, both of which apparently failed to hit. However, Swordfish 2L, flown by Sub Lieutenant (A) R S Charlier RN with Sub Lieutenant (A) D M Beattie RN as observer and Leading Airman D R B Evans as TAG, made a well-aimed release after approaching the dam flying low over the lake for several miles. He was probably the first to drop as he reported no anti-aircraft fire until after his attack and he almost certainly scored a hit. Intelligence sources confirmed a single hit on the dam. Sub Lieutenant Charlier and his crew were commended by the Captain of *Ark Royal*, Captain C S Holland RN, for carrying out their attack under difficult conditions.[15] Unfortunately this single hit did not breach the dam. One of the eight aircraft was never seen

Illustrious under attack while she was alongside Parlatorio Wharf in Malta Dockyard. She is noticeably down by the stern. (*Author's collection*)

again after taking departure from the ship and an Italian radio broadcast on 3 February announced that it had been shot down with Lieutenant M H A O'Sullivan RN, Sub Lieutenant R B Knight RN and Petty Officer (A) E Hall taken prisoner. At about 0900 the seven returning Swordfish landed on after a desperate venture in very bad weather with the enemy apparently well aware of what was happening.

Operation Picket analysed

At the Chiefs of Staff Meeting held on 6 February 1941, Churchill tasked the Naval and Air Staffs to re-examine the data on which Operation Picket had been based and to report on whether any more effective means of carrying it out could be devised. The letter covering the response was signed by General Ismay, Churchill's Military Assistant, and dated 18 February 1941. In it he wrote:

1. The Air Ministry Bombing Committee investigated, at a meeting held on the 26th July 1938, the problem of attacking reservoir dams. In addition to the Service members of the Committee, representative dam engineers and authorities were present.
2. Their conclusions can be summarised as follows:-
   i) The destruction of reservoir dams from the air to be a feasible operation.
   ii) The most suitable weapons for use against single arch dams (the type most commonly met with) were, in order of priority:-
      a) A number of 18 inch torpedoes.
      b) Large G P bombs (1,000lb and upwards).
      c) 500lb bombs if neither (a) nor (b) were available.
   iii) That multiple arch dams were probably more vulnerable than the single arch type.
      (Note: The Tirso Dam is of this type of construction).
   iv) That the attack should be developed primarily against the high water side of the dam.
3. Very complete technical data was available from both the British and Italian technical press concerning the Tirso dam. It is close to the sea in comparatively open surroundings and the reservoir it forms is the largest artificial lake in Europe. Its construction is of the type which is probably the most vulnerable to air attack, and, so far as was known, only a very light scale of defence was to be expected. For the above reasons it was considered, when proposing the operation, that this dam provided a suitable target for attack by Force H and furthermore that it was the most suitable dam against which to carry

out the full scale experiment required to confirm the opinion of the Bombing Committee.

4. It was not anticipated that, even if the attack was completely successful, the dam would collapse immediately. What was hoped for was that the face of the dam would be cracked and that the resultant seepage would cause either the ultimate destruction of the dam or that, to avoid such a catastrophe, the reservoir would have to be emptied. For this reason, the torpedoes were set to hit the dam well below the surface, but where the construction was not too massive. Moreover, it was estimated that 6 torpedoes would be required to obtain 2 hits on one of the compression arches of the dam.

5. The fact that no damage was visible to the attacking aircraft is no guarantee that the dam has not been damaged. Further confirmation may be obtainable from air photographs.

6. As regards the actual execution of the attack:-
   a) The weather conditions were bad.
   b) An unexpectedly heavy scale of defence was encountered.

7. As a result of the above, the attack could be carried out neither on the scale intended nor as deliberately as was required to obtain the necessary number of hits. It is therefore considered that until confirmation by reconnaissance is obtained the results of this 'full scale experiment' must be considered to be inconclusive.

8. The water level in the reservoir, unless damage has occurred, will remain very much at its present level until the end of the rainy season in April. It will then fall steadily until, by midsummer, it is too low to allow this dam to be attacked with much prospect of success.

9. This interval is too short to allow of the development of any new weapons.

10. Of the existing weapons, the torpedo remains the most suitable, in the absence of any evidence to the contrary, because of its large explosive charge and of the high percentage of hits likely to be obtained on a target of this type, and the fact that it is the only known weapon that can produce an explosion underwater in contact with the face of the dam.

11. It is considered that, if such an operation were to be repeated, a heavy scale of torpedo attack offers the best prospect of success. Any possibility of tactical surprise had now been forfeited and the carrier must expect to be subjected to a heavy scale of dive-bombing attack from aerodromes in Sardinia. It is therefore considered that the risk to such a valuable ship by a repetition of this operation cannot be justified by the importance of the target.

12. If the disposition of the enemy dive bombers is changed, the matter may be worth re-consideration in the light of the new conditions.
13. Recommendations.
    It is recommended that:-
    a) The operation is not repeated under present conditions.
    b) If future developments make the operation desirable, the same method of attack should be employed but on a heavier scale.

17 February 1941

The immediate lessons drawn from Operation Picket had not been new. The essential element of surprise had been lost waiting for daylight and there was no recent intelligence about the target's defences. There were also no recent aerial photographs and the form up after take-off had not met the required standard, admittedly under difficult conditions at night and in poor weather. Reading through the Force H reports all these years after the event it is difficult to escape the conclusion that Somerville thought of the attack only as a diversion and probably failed to realise either the importance of the dam or the impact its destruction would have

The impact point of the bomb that penetrated *Illustrious*' after lift well and detonated on striking the after ammunition conveyor in the wardroom flat below. (*Author's collection*)

had on Italian morale. In reality it was important enough to merit an attack on a larger scale by squadrons that had practised the techniques required. General Ismay's report was exactly right when it noted that the possibility of a successful outcome was 'forfeited' on 2 February by a small-scale diversionary strike on a night of appalling weather. Given the conditions encountered it would have been wiser to abort it and carry out a larger strike, retaining an element of surprise, that was not linked to another operation.

After the strike force's return the weather deteriorated further and at 1730 Captain Holland informed Somerville that he considered it too bad for *Ark Royal* to range or fly off aircraft in the dark. By dawn only nine aircraft could be ranged and handled at one time and, with the amount of low cloud forecast, he did not hold out much hope for the next day's planned attack. If the bombardment went ahead, moreover, he would be unable to recover the capital ships' Walrus amphibians after their bombardment spotting sorties. At 1910, therefore, Somerville aborted Result and at 0400 Force H altered course for Gibraltar. At dawn on 3 February *Ark Royal* was ordered to fly off Swordfish for surface patrols up to 50nm from the Spanish coast with the intention of sending a destroyer to board and search any ship located but nothing was sighted. Force H returned to Gibraltar on the evening of 4 February.

The bombardment of Genoa

Somerville was urged by the Admiralty to replan the bombardment of Genoa as quickly as possible. His staff were concerned by rumours circulating in Gibraltar on 30 January that Force H was to bombard Genoa but, lacking any substantiated evidence of compromise, new bombardment plans went ahead, this time with elaborate deception measures including the issue of orders for a different but fictitious operation. The orders for the genuine operation, renamed Operation Grog and due to take place on 9 February, were sealed and not to be opened until Force H was at sea. The new objectives were:

   a. to destroy Italian battleships and/or cruisers if present in Genoa.
   b. to lower Italian morale.
   c. to divert Italian naval and air resources to North Italy.
   d. To damage industry, shipping and supplies.

Force H sailed from Gibraltar in three groups, the first comprising *Renown* (flag), *Malaya*, *Ark Royal* and *Sheffield*. The second comprised six destroyers and the third a further four destroyers to act as a screen for

Swordfish 'R' of 830 NAS fitted with a long-range fuel tank in the observer's cockpit. The store under the starboard wing rack is a 4.5in flare. (*Author's collection*)

the big ships. After dark they all joined up and *Ark Royal* flew routine anti-submarine patrols from 7 February and maintained a CAP with Fulmars and Skuas from 8 February. At 1900 the whole force was in a position 80nm off Cape St Sebastian near the Spanish–French border and turned on a heading of 050 degrees for Genoa at 21 knots. During the day it was thought that the force had been sighted by six aircraft, four of which were probably French, but none was shot down. The Italians were aware that Force H had sailed and Admiral Iachino was actually at sea with the battleships *Vittorio Veneto*, *Cesare* and *Doria*, intending to rendezvous with the cruisers *Trieste*, *Trento* and *Bolzano* in the Bonifacio Strait between Sardinia and Corsica but he had no idea of Force H's exact position or intentions.

At 0230 on 9 February Force H fixed its position using the Porquerolles Light on a fine, moonlit night and, had they known it, the Italian battleships were only 30nm to the south. At 0400 *Ark Royal* and three destroyers detached to launch aircraft for a diversionary strike against the oil refinery at Azienda near Leghorn and to lay a minefield off Spezia harbour as the remainder of Force H began its run towards the target area. Seven Swordfish of 810 NAS and seven of 820 NAS led by Lieutenant Commander M Johnstone RN flew off *Ark Royal* from 0500 at a launch position 70nm south-west of Leghorn, each armed with four 250lb GP bombs and fourteen incendiary bombs. Moonset was at 0517 but sunrise was not until 0733. A further range of four Swordfish from 818 NAS led by Lieutenant (A) L R Tivy RN followed, all armed with a single Type A Mark 1 magnetic mine. Finally, just after 0600, three Swordfish were flown off to stand by as spotting aircraft for the three bombarding ships and forty-five minutes later three Fulmars were flown off as fighter escorts for them. The weather was fine with no wind but a slight haze up to 2,000ft.

The Swordfish formed up in two groups initially over flame floats 5nm apart, later joining up to form a single strike force. The procedure was cumbersome and slow, taking thirty minutes before they set off, a reflection of the large number of new aircrew in *Ark Royal*'s squadrons. They crossed the coast at 0625, having climbed to 8,000ft, but Lieutenant Commander Johnstone mistook his landfall in the half light and turned north. After following him for about 5nm, 820 NAS' leader realised that they were already too far north and turned south-eastward, followed by the two sub-flights of 810 NAS. This group attacked the briefed target in dives, releasing their bombs from 2,000 to 3,500ft at 0645. The target was well covered with hits, which caused a great deal of smoke and dust within which several small fires were seen to break out. No anti-aircraft fire was encountered until after the second sub-flight had attacked. One of 820 NAS' pilots attacked the nearby railway station because the main target was obscured. Johnstone, attacked Pisa airfield but the other two of his sub-flight returned to attack the refinery sometime after the first attack. One aircraft failed to return but had been seen carrying out its attack.[16] Anti-aircraft fire was intense over the target area and there was an unexpected balloon barrage along the shore to the west of the refinery. The mine layers arrived off the Spezia peninsula at 0540 but found it too dark. They loitered for fifteen minutes then two aircraft laid their mines in the western entrance abreast the end of the breakwater. The third was helped in its landfall by lights from the poorly blacked out town and also laid its mine in the western entrance. The fourth Swordfish chose the eastern entrance but was met by heavy anti-aircraft fire and placed its mine slightly outside the breakwater end. One aircraft of 820 NAS was lost, presumed to have hit a balloon cable at Leghorn. Its crew, Sub Lieutenant (A) N G Attenborough RN, Midshipman (A) S W Foote RNVR and Leading Airman G W Halifax, were all killed.

The bombardment of Genoa began with *Renown*, *Malaya* and *Sheffield* flying off their own aircraft for spotting from 0630 and tuning them in on the correct frequency together with the standby spotters from *Ark Royal*. At 0655 the ships turned onto the bombardment course after obtaining a good position fix. Gunfire in the direction of Spezia showed that the minelaying operation was in progress, and at 0714 *Renown* fired the first salvo using the indirect fire technique since Genoa could not be seen in the early morning haze. The opening salvoes from each ship were deliberately short so that the air spotters could see them easily and correct onto the specified targets, for which purpose the observers had been issued with special gridded maps of the area. Ranges varied between 18,000 and 23,000yds. The spotting aircraft reported that there were no battleships or cruisers alongside but the battleship *Duilio* was in dry dock in the eastern part of the docks. A scale model of Genoa had been made in *Renown* and passed to *Ark Royal*, where it was used to brief observers. They reported that it had allowed them to identify each objective, a view borne out by the ease and speed with which target changes were carried out. Fire was checked at 0745 and all spotting aircraft were recovered on *Ark Royal*, about 35nm away, by 0848. The aircraft spotting for *Renown* signalled 'magnificent' to Admiral Somerville, from which it was concluded the bombardment had been a success.

Force H then withdrew to the southwest at 22 knots, maintaining a CAP overhead as heavy air attacks were expected. The light easterly wind meant large alterations of course for *Ark Royal* to launch or recover aircraft, which caused a considerable reduction in the force's speed of advance but, still unaware of the proximity of a superior Italian force, Somerville was not unduly worried. No large air attacks developed but two Fiat BR.20s attempted to bomb *Ark Royal* at 1120, their bombs missing well astern. CAP fighters shot down two shadowing aircraft; Skuas of 800 NAS a Cant Z.506 floatplane at 1110 and Fulmars of 808 NAS a Cant Z.1007 at 1350. Of interest, the first interception was at sea level and the Skuas' windscreens misted up as they dived from 17,000ft so badly that the pilots had to aim by 'hosing' their tracer ammunition onto the target.

Mark XII torpedoes on their loading trolleys in a protective stone revetment at Hal Far. While protected against blast from the side, there was no overhead cover and keeping them ready for action under these conditions was a remarkable achievement. (*Author's collection*)

The Italian force under Admiral Iachino had rendezvoused west of the Bonifacio Strait and was aware that Force H was at sea but had no idea of its intentions. It might be repeating the attack on the Tirso dam, covering a reinforcement operation to Malta or raiding targets on the Italian coast. He was not informed of the bombardment of Genoa until two hours after it was over and conflicting reports from the Italian naval staff confused his tactical picture. The indifferent result of his own air searches and poor communications added to the Italian failure to turn the situation to their advantage and Force H returned to Gibraltar unscathed on the afternoon of 11 February.

Immediately after the operation, Somerville's staff believed that the material damage to Genoa had been considerable but post-war analysis of Italian records showed that it had been somewhat more limited. The morale effect on the Italians, however, had been significant. The Italian Captain Bragadin was on duty in the operations room in Rome during the bombardment and wrote in his book *Che Ha Fatto La Marina*[17] that:

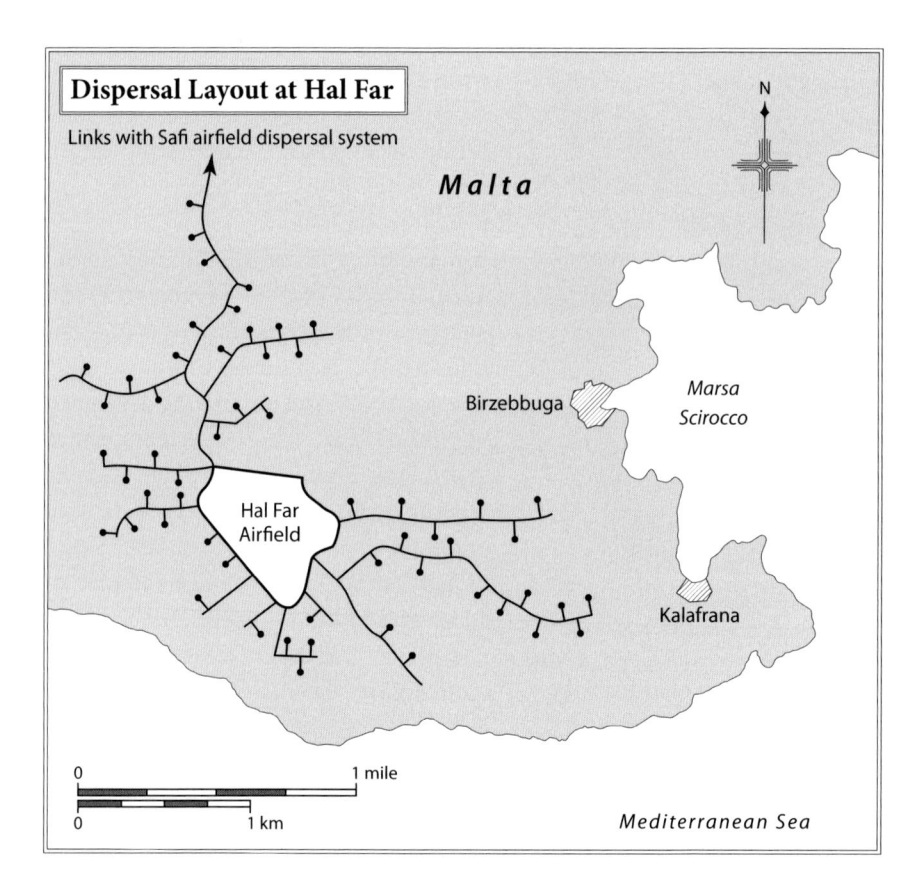

the bombardment of Genoa inflicted serious damage to the city. In the harbour four steamers and the old training ship Garaventa were sunk. Fortunately the most important target, the Duilio, which was still under repair after Taranto, was not hit. There were grave morale effects throughout Italy, all the more because while the effects of our aircraft were appreciated not a word was said about the search made by our naval squadron. As a result of such silence the Italian people thought in so many words that the Navy had run away. This was very far from being true.

In his own report Somerville commented that Force H had benefitted from deteriorating weather on 9 February, having learnt that seventy bombers of X Fliegerkorps had sortied from Sicily and Sardinia to search for it but failed to find it. That they came close to doing so was evident from the fact that several formations of enemy aircraft had appeared on radar at about 1400 but had got no closer than 30nm before fading. Had either the German or Italian bombers been equipped with radar the outcome of Operation Grog might have been different. Intelligence sources had been wrong about the preparation of an Axis invasion force in Genoa. Taken together, the bombardment, the subsidiary attacks on the Tirso dam and the refinery at Leghorn showed a fine aggressive spirit but the handful of Swordfish available did not yet constitute a large enough or, it has to be said, sufficiently experienced force to do significant damage to their targets.

830 NAS operations from Malta
Operations by 830 NAS from Hal Far in Malta had established a good reputation for teamwork in attacking enemy ports, airfields and shipping by day, but it was not until the spring of 1941 when its aircraft had been fitted with full instrument-flying panels and long-range fuel tanks that the squadron began to increase its ability to carry out night operations against Axis convoys. Torpedoes were its main weapons, although a proportion of its aircraft were armed with bombs to act as diversions to its primary attacks. The squadron also carried out a number of minelaying sorties, mainly off Tripoli. A classic daylight attack was carried out on 27 January after an RAF Sunderland flying boat located two merchant ships escorted by a destroyer 28nm north-east of the Kerkenah Bank off the Tunisian coast steering 170 degrees at 15 knots. The Sunderland continued to shadow and within fifty minutes 830 NAS had a strike force of six Swordfish, in two sub-flights of three, armed with torpedoes airborne following a strike leader armed with four 250lb GP bombs. They set

heading to intercept the convoy in a position 180nm south-west of Malta and it was seen at 1315. The weather was clear and the strike leader led his force into a position up sun from the enemy at 10,000ft. Before commencing their attack they were joined by two Fulmars of 806 NAS disembarked from the damaged *Illustrious*, which acted as escort. One of the merchant ships, estimated at 7,200 tons, was believed to have been hit by the first sub-flight and emitted clouds of smoke and steam but did not sink. Italian records do not confirm this hit but record that it was hit by Lieutenant Commander M D Wanklin RN's submarine *Upholder* later in the day. The second sub-flight hit the other merchant ship, later learnt to be the 3,950-ton SS *Inga*, which broke in two and sank within ten minutes. All the aircraft returned safely to Hal Far at 1540.

Co-operation with RAF reconnaissance aircraft based in Malta was good and they often flew with an RN observer on board if there was thought to be any likelihood of a Swordfish strike after a sighting. In December the RAF's 148 Squadron had re-formed in Malta with Wellington bombers and frequently flew diversion sorties over Tripoli to draw enemy fire while Swordfish laid mines outside the harbour entrance. Malta suffered its first 'blitz' period in the first five months of 1941, making both the operation and maintenance of aircraft at the various airfields difficult and dangerous. Frequent bombing attacks meant night-flying crews at Hal Far had to get what sleep they could during forenoons as far away from the airfields as practicable. Aircraft maintenance was carried out between air raids but the squadron's serviceability remained remarkably good and the Vice Admiral Malta made frequent reference to this in his despatches. He also mentioned the high percentage of good runs by torpedoes, which showed their efficient preparation and the fine devotion to duty of the torpedo maintenance parties. Other points that emerge from a study of the operational reports are the high standard of night navigation and the fact that the majority of torpedo attacks were driven home at close range to ensure that torpedoes hit their targets. The number of attacks in which surprise was achieved are also noteworthy, often brought about by ruses such as the shadowing aircraft flying low across convoys several times to draw attention away from the flanks or by a diversionary bombing attack by one or more aircraft before the torpedo aircraft began their run-in. Whatever the means, an element of surprise was always important as it limited the escort's ability to lay a smokescreen around the convoy. The enemy's lack of success in shooting down 830 NAS Swordfish was rather surprising but the Italian Navy was not yet equipped with fire control radar or gyro gunsights and relied entirely on visually trained weapons. During the whole of 1941 only nine of 830's aircraft failed to return from operations but many others were damaged by

Even when parked in sandbagged revetments outside Hal Far's perimeter, 830 NAS aircraft were still vulnerable as this Swordfish, which was destroyed in an air raid, demonstrates. It could, however, still be a valuable source of spare parts. (*Author's collection*)

anti-aircraft fire and many aircrew displayed great fortitude getting their aircraft back to Hal Far. Other aircraft were damaged on the ground during enemy bombing. Between 11 February 1941 and 10 June for instance, two Swordfish were destroyed and a number of others damaged, while almost all the buildings and hangars had been hit. It was only by camouflage, dispersal and by the construction of stone pens for the aircraft that the squadron was kept in action.[18]

An attack on an Italian convoy was carried out on the night of 13/14 February 1941. Three of 830 NAS' Swordfish and a leader armed with flares took off at 2220 and took departure from Delimara Point, Malta, for an armed reconnaissance of the Tunisian coast.[19] At 0120 a convoy was sighted ahead at a range of 2nm, which was found to consist of four merchant vessels between 2,000 and 6,000 tons escorted by two destroyers, heading north. The weather was hazy and the moon obscured by clouds but the enemy ships were well illuminated by the leader's flares dropped to the west of the convoy. The torpedo aircraft attacked from the east and released their weapons at 600yds with results that were difficult to see but one torpedo was thought to have definitely hit and possibly a second. They were all fitted with duplex pistols and set to run at 40 knots at a depth of 22ft. Once the attack was over the torpedo droppers returned to Malta but the leader remained to shadow the convoy. The rear destroyer was seen to drop astern and make what appeared to be a smokescreen and a large 'whitish' patch was visible astern of the convoy that persisted for at least half an hour but no wreckage was seen.

On the night of 15/16 February 1941 two striking forces from 830 NAS, each consisting of three torpedo aircraft and a leader armed with flares, took departure from Filfola Island, Malta, at 2225 and 2325 respectively. They, too, were briefed to carry out an armed reconnaissance of the Tunisian coast. The first strike force was searching from Kuriat Island to Kerkenah Bank when it sighted a southbound supply ship estimated at 7,000 tons at 0006. The weather was hazy with maximum visibility assessed at 7nm when the leader dropped flares to the east of the vessel. The three torpedo aircraft made their attack from the west at two-minute intervals, dropping at ranges between 600 and 700yds. One torpedo struck the target right aft and the ship immediately stopped and settled by the stern. The second striking force was searching to the south of the Kerkenah Bank at the time but saw the first force's flares about 40nm away. They continued their search initially as they had not received a sighting signal or enemy report but at 0106 they received the signal and turned north. The leader of the first force had continued to shadow the target and at 0200 he dropped the remainder of his flares before turning to return to Hal Far. These guided the second force towards the vessel and they sighted it at 0207. The visibility had by then deteriorated and despite the leader dropping flares, only two of the strike aircraft saw the target. One of these did not attack as he considered that the ship was already sinking but the other did attack and hit the vessel amidships, after which it promptly sank.

Naval air squadrons ashore in Greece and Crete up to April 1941

After the German intervention in the Balkans in early 1941, a forward RN base was established at Souda Bay in north-west Crete, reflecting the War Cabinet's decision to hold the island irrespective of what happened on the Greek mainland. The RAF took steps to improve the primitive landing ground at Heraklion but this was too far from Souda Bay to provide adequate fighter protection for the fleet anchorage and so another airfield was developed at Maleme, 8nm west of the naval base. However, shortages of labour, materials and equipment meant that its development was only carried forward in a desultory manner and it was turned over to the RN in January 1941 in an unfinished state. Limited operations began when four Swordfish of 815 NAS commanded by Lieutenant Commander J de F Jago RN arrived from Egypt and began reconnaissance patrols over the Kithera Channel on 31 January. A fortnight later the rest of the squadron arrived, having been operating under the control of 202 Group RAF during General Wavell's advance into Cyrenaica. For Maleme's own protection, three Fulmars from 806 NAS arrived in mid-February, both squadrons from the damaged *Illustrious'* air group. Enemy attacks on Souda Bay and Maleme proved to be rare but on 24 February a Heinkel He 111 was destroyed and another damaged. However, 815 NAS was hard pressed to cope with all the calls made on it. Small but frequent night armed reconnaissance and strike missions were carried out against the enemy-occupied airfields on Scarpanto and Stampalia, roughly 150nm to the east and north-east respectively, as well as on other targets in the Dodecanese Islands. Routine armed reconnaissance patrols over the Kithera Channel were continued, and while the attacks on Scarpanto were not particularly effective in terms of destroying enemy aircraft on the ground, they had nuisance value and capitalised on the lack of enemy night fighters in the area.

The deteriorating situation in the Balkans led the Greek Government to ask for military assistance from Britain and on 5 March 1941 the first convoy of British and Commonwealth troops from Egypt to Greece set out, a deployment designated Operation Lustre. In anticipation of enemy air attacks on the troop transports, 805 NAS was deployed to Maleme from Egypt to relieve the Fulmars, which were due to embark in *Formidable*. No. 805 NAS had re-formed at Aboukir under Lieutenant Commander A F Black RN on 1 January with a mixed force of Fulmars, Gladiators and American Brewster Buffaloes. The latter suffered from incessant

An Axis merchant ship torpedoed during an 830 NAS strike off North Africa. (*Author's collection*)

engine problems and were soon discarded. In early March Lieutenant A H Sutton RN was sent to Athens as liaison officer to the RAF headquarters there. He took with him instructions from Admiral Cunningham that part of 815 NAS was to move from Maleme to Eleusis airfield near Athens to carry out strike operations against the Italian supply line to Valona, the offloading port in Albania about 40nm behind the Italian front line.

After consultation with the Greek authorities, six Swordfish of 815 NAS fitted with full instrument panels but without ASV radar deployed to Eleusis on 11 March, taking on charge six torpedoes from the Greek Navy. On the next day they were to fly to a small landing strip in the mountains of north-west Greece that was only 45nm south of the Greco–Italian front line at Paramythia. It was about 30nm east-south-east of Corfu in a valley between two mountain ranges and closed by them at its northern end. It was already being used as a clandestine forward refuelling site by RAF Blenheim bombers of 211 Squadron and great importance was attached by the Air Headquarters to keeping knowledge of its use from the enemy. For this reason the Swordfish at Eleusis were always to land after sunset at Paramythia, refuel and then take off in the dark for their strike. On their return, they were to refuel again and be airborne for Eleusis before first light. Rearming would take place at Eleusis and the cycle of operations started again after the next sunset. The night flying arrangements at Paramythia were, unsurprisingly, primitive and take-off fully loaded with torpedoes or, on one occasion, mines was always downhill from north to south between glim lamps that marked the clear area. Landing was usually made uphill from south to north towards a cul-de-sac formed by the mountains. A further eighteen torpedoes were sent to Athens, where they were stored by the Greek Navy and then transported when necessary to Eleusis in trucks provided by the British Royal Army Service Corps. They were maintained and prepared at Athens by an RN mobile airborne torpedo maintenance unit, MATMU.[20]

The results obtained by 815 NAS were good. Previous attempts by the RAF to bomb Italian supply dumps had lacked accuracy and failed to produce positive results. The decision to concentrate on the shipping carrying the material into theatre, therefore, proved to be the best option and it was the original intention to attack with every aircraft on alternate nights. After the first strike, however, the policy was changed to one of attacking every night with whatever aircraft 815 NAS had available.[21] This meant running a shuttle service with some aircraft at Paramythia ready to attack and some at Eleusis reloading. It was also decided to limit strikes to four aircraft as larger numbers were more difficult to control and were more easily detected by the defences. The first reconnaissance revealed a

Formidable in 1941. (*Author's collection*)

quantity of enemy shipping at Valona and only a few ships at Durazzo, and so it was decided to attack the Valona shipping exclusively until ships were forced to use Durazzo, after which attacks would concentrate on the latter.

An attack was planned for the night of 12/13 March in which RAF Blenheims were to provide a diversion but RAF HQ refused to allow them to land at Paramythia by night and so timing had to be altered and it was carried out just before dawn with the moon to the west. This was not a good direction for the attack profile the aircraft were forced to fly but, nevertheless, six Swordfish took off armed with torpedoes and they carried out their attack at 0530 on 13 March. Lieutenant Commander Jago hit the water while lining his aircraft up for an attack on shipping in Valona and both he and his observer Lieutenant J A Caldecott-Smith RN became prisoners of war. In spite of well-synchronised diversionary attacks by the Blenheims, no enemy ships were sunk that night. Lieutenant F M A Torrens-Spence RN assumed command of the squadron and led a further attack on 14 March. This proved to be more successful and the 7,289-ton merchant ship *Po* was sunk. The Italians subsequently claimed that she was being used as a hospital ship but the Mediterranean War Diary noted that several ships claimed to be hospital ships had been seen operating in a suspicious manner in the Mediterranean.[22] No. 815 NAS continued to operate with Paramythia as its forward base until 23 April without, as far as was known, the Italians ever becoming aware of the airstrip's importance. The Swordfish were then forced to withdraw to Maleme as the evacuation of British and Commonwealth forces from Greece had begun a week earlier, a process designated Operation Demon.

In all, seven strikes had been made against shipping at Valona and two at Durazzo. There had also been a minelaying sortie off Brindisi and an armed reconnaissance on the night of 5 April when, unfortunately no enemy ships were encountered. No. 815 NAS' operations during its six weeks in Greece were recognised by letters of congratulation from the

Admiralty and Admiral Cunningham. The squadron had dropped twenty-one torpedoes and laid five mines. Seven certain torpedo hits were recorded together with six probables and two that were possible. Post-war Italian records revealed that three merchant ships had been sunk with six more damaged. One small warship had been sunk. Against this two Swordfish had been lost due to enemy action or mishap, another one crashed and two were damaged sufficiently to warrant minor repairs by the RAF personnel at Paramythia. The Admiralty subsequently discovered that Italian records of ships damaged in the area were incomplete and the figures quoted above may not accurately represent the full extent of 815 NAS' achievement.

Formidable relieves Illustrious in the Mediterranean Fleet
Formidable, commanded by Captain A W La T Bisset RN, arrived in Alexandria on 10 March 1941 to relieve *Illustrious*. Rear Admiral Lyster returned to the UK to become 5SL from 14 April 1941. *Formidable*'s air group comprised 826 NAS with twelve Fairey Albacores commanded by Lieutenant Commander W H G Saunt RN; 829 NAS with nine Albacores commanded by Lieutenant Commander J Dalyell-Stead RN and 803 NAS with twelve Fulmars commanded by Lieutenant Commander G M Bruen RN. Admiral Boyd transferred his flag to her from *Eagle* on the day she arrived.

Formidable had headed for the Suez Canal around the Cape of Good Hope and her squadrons had played a part in the East African Campaign by carrying out a series of attacks on Italian-held ports. The first was on 2 February 1941 when the ship was 100nm east of Mogadishu in Italian Somaliland. Nine Albacores of 826 and 829 NAS were all armed with six 250lb GP bombs fitted with both nose and tail fuses set for instantaneous detonation and some also carried incendiaries. A second strike force of Albacores was armed with Type A Mark 1 mines.[23] The minelaying preceded the bombing attack by ten minutes, with the latter taking place between 1855 and 1915. Targets included an ordnance depot, airfield workshops, a railway station, a power station, petrol storage tanks and a barracks. Hits resulted in a very large fire being seen on the airfield and a fire followed by an explosion at the petrol storage area. One Albacore was slightly damaged by small arms fire.

The next operation was on 13 February from a position 135nm off the Eritrean port of Massawa. This strike comprised seven Albacores armed with torpedoes and a further seven armed with six 250lb SAP and eight 25lb incendiary bombs. Their targets were Italian destroyers and submarines but because of low cloud and bad weather the operation did not go as planned. A navigational error led to landfall being made 25nm north of

Massawa but the error was not immediately appreciated because of the cloud cover. The seven torpedo aircraft were all from 829 NAS, briefed to attack submarines alongside and at anchor, and they were the first to realise the navigational error. Their leader attacked through the harbour entrance under heavy anti-aircraft fire but released his torpedo inside the safety range of its pistol. The second aircraft of his sub-flight approached over land and carried out a good attack on the submarines lying alongside; the third aircraft did not return. The other four attacked merchant ships anchored off the harbour and one, the Italian SS *Moncalini*, was claimed to have been sunk but it was later learnt that it had only been damaged. The bombing aircraft lost contact with each other in cloud and three of them failed to find Massawa. One had to carry out a forced landing in enemy territory but three found the harbour after the torpedo attack had

Fulmars of 803 NAS parked aft of *Formidable*'s island. (*Author's collection*)

started. Their dive-bombing profile was hampered by low cloud but two eventually attacked merchant vessels with no observed result. The third carried out a shallow dive attack against a destroyer and straddled it but no hits could be confirmed. The attack was repeated a week later on 21 February by seven Albacores from the two squadrons, which took off at 0415 armed with six 250lb SAP bombs each from a launch position 100nm east-north-east of Massawa. It was still dark when they arrived over the town, however, and considerable searchlight and anti-aircraft opposition made shallow dive-bombing difficult. A single hit or near miss was claimed but four aircraft were damaged. All returned to the carrier, however. The lack of success achieved by these strikes reflected the inexperience of these squadrons.

Formidable arrived at Suez on 23 February but her passage through the canal was blocked by mines that had been laid by X Fliegerkorps until 7 March and she finally arrived at Port Said on 9 March. *Eagle*'s passage south was delayed by the need to clear a wreck but *Illustrious* was able to get through and she entered the canal on 15 March. X Fliegerkorps carried out further minelaying, however, and her passage eventually took six days. *Formidable* embarked 806 NAS, now commanded by Lieutenant Commander J N Garnett DSC RN after he relieved Lieutenant Commander C L G Evans DSC RN. After *Illustrious*' damage, 806 NAS had been employed in support of operations in the Western Desert in addition to its period in Crete. During the ten days that elapsed before *Formidable* sailed for her first operation with the Mediterranean Fleet, 826 NAS was disembarked to RNAS Dekheila to carry out a night torpedo attack on a target described by an RAF reconnaissance aircraft as a 'considerable concentration of enemy shipping' off Burat el Sun, 240nm west of Benghazi across the Gulf of Sirte. On 16 March six Albacores armed with torpedoes left Dekheila for the RAF airstrip at Benina, 480nm away, where three aircraft were found to be temporarily unserviceable. After refuelling the other three flew on to Burat el Sun at midnight in bright moonlight where they only found four small vessels at anchor, all in very shallow water. One torpedo was dropped but no hit was claimed. A repeat attack by all six aircraft a day later only found a single ship at El Araar and none at Burat. A hit was claimed but Italian post-war records show no sinking on that date. One Albacore piloted by Sub Lieutenant (A) C P Bailey RN with Sub Lieutenant (A) J J C Coe RN as his observer failed to return to Benina and they were listed as killed on 19 March 1941.[24] The remaining five returned to Dekheila on 19 March. The distances flown by this detachment were the longest so far accomplished by RN aircraft on anti-shipping strikes and it was disappointing for those who took part that they found no worthwhile targets.

Aircraft handlers pushing a Fulmar of 803 NAS aft into *Formidable*'s range. The arrester wire under their feet appears to be badly kinked and may have been left unreset so that it can be replaced. (Author's collection)

On 20 March the Mediterranean Fleet sailed for Operation MC 9, the passage of an important convoy from Haifa and Alexandria to Malta. *Formidable* re-embarked 826 NAS and flew routine CAP and Albacore patrols. One shadower was damaged by fighters and then shot down by the fleet's anti-aircraft fire. No enemy reconnaissance aircraft found the convoy and it arrived safely but within a few hours Malta was subjected to intense bombing when the enemy learnt that the ships had arrived. The fleet returned to Alexandria on 24 March but was at sea again three days later.

Operation Lustre had, by then, begun with over 58,000 Commonwealth troops transported to Greece with their vehicles and equipment. However, German troops were known to be arriving in Libya and a counter-offensive under General Rommel was anticipated. The British Government's decision to send aid to Greece was, therefore, courageous but dangerous in the extreme but with hindsight it can be argued that the intervention significantly delayed German plans to invade Russia. The movements of convoys during Lustre were inevitably observed by the enemy and since the Germans had neither surface ships nor U-boats in the Mediterranean at that time, the Italian Navy was urged to make further efforts and the Battle of Matapan was the immediate result.

The part played by the Fleet Air Arm in the Battle of Matapan

On 26 March intense enemy air activity over the Aegean was reported to Admiral Cunningham and attacks were carried out on Lustre convoys. His staff deduced that a sortie by a powerful Italian task force might be imminent and 201 Group RAF was requested to increase the scale of reconnaissance over the Ionian Sea to within visibility distance of the Greek coast. At 1220 on 27 March a Sunderland flying boat operating from Scaramanga in Greece reported three Italian cruisers and a destroyer 80nm east of Cape Passero in south-east Sicily heading east-south-east. Bad weather prevented it from shadowing despite urgent requests from Cunningham's staff and no further signals were heard from it. Later, Cunningham learnt from intelligence sources that *Vittorio Veneto* was at sea, probably following astern of the reported cruiser force. He delayed sailing until the evening of 27 March, however, knowing that it had been reported in harbour by enemy reconnaissance aircraft earlier in the day. He departed Alexandria at 1900 with *Warspite*, *Barham*, *Formidable* and a destroyer screen. The Vice Admiral Light Forces, VALF, Vice Admiral Sir Henry Pridham-Wippell KCB CVO, in the cruiser *Orion* with *Ajax*, *Perth*, *Gloucester* and three destroyers in company, was already at sea west of Crete and he was ordered to rendezvous with the battle fleet south of Gavdo Island by daylight on 28 March.

Formidable's air group comprised thirteen Fulmars of 803 and 806 NAS commanded by Lieutenant J M Bruen RN and Lieutenant Commander J N Garnett DSC RN respectively with ten Albacores and four swordfish of 826 and 829 NAS commanded by Lieutenant Commanders W H G Saunt and J Dalyell-Stead RN. The number embarked was well below the ship's designed maximum and demonstrates the growing impact of MAP restrictions on the production of naval aircraft. *Eagle*'s Swordfish had flown south to Port Sudan on that day as part of a previously arranged plan to destroy Italian naval units in Massawa. *Warspite* had two Swordfish seaplanes embarked, *Valiant* had another two and the cruiser *Gloucester* had a single Walrus. At RNAS Maleme in Crete, 815 NAS had five Swordfish and its commanding officer, Lieutenant Torrens-Spence, had been commuting between Athens and Paramythia. He was determined not to miss a fleet action, however, and flew back to Maleme late on 28 March with the last serviceable Swordfish and torpedo from Greece. At Cunningham's request, the senior RAF officer in Greece held twenty-four Blenheims of 84 and 113 squadrons at readiness to support the Mediterranean Fleet, all of which could be armed with two 500lb or 250lb GP bombs.

The Italian force comprised four separate elements, with the first consisting of *Vittorio Veneto*, Admiral Iachino's flagship, with a screen of four destroyers. The second comprised the cruisers *Zara*, *Fiume*, *Pola* and four destroyers. The third comprised the cruisers *Trento*, *Trieste*, *Bolzano* and three destroyers and the fourth comprised the cruisers

Giuseppe Garibaldi and *Duca Degli Abruzzi* and two destroyers. Cruisers in the second and third groups had catapult aircraft embarked. Admiral Iachino's objective was to attack British shipping between Alexandria and Greece and to sink on sight anything encountered to the west and south of Crete. British warships, however, were only to be engaged if the relative strength of the forces in contact favoured his force. The Italian naval staff requested support from X Fliegerkorps and Marshal Goering agreed to give it but stipulated that the protection of German convoys to North Africa must be given precedence. As events unfolded, however, Axis aircraft had little or no effect on the battle and the Italian staff doubted whether the Germans had actually carried out their share of the plan.

At 0400 on 28 March Cunningham's battle group was heading 310 degrees at 16 knots with 200nm to run to the rendezvous with VALF. At 0600 the latter's force sighted an Italian Ro.43 aircraft, the type embarked in capital ships and cruisers. It had been catapulted by the *Vittorio Veneto* with instructions to search the line Gavdo Island to Alexandria out to 100nm. To the south-east, *Formidable* flew off four Albacores and a Swordfish of 826 NAS at 0555 to search between Crete and Cyrenaica as far as 23 degrees east. Additional Swordfish and Fulmars had also been launched for anti-submarine patrols and CAP.

Commander Beale at Maleme was given instructions for the participation of his aircraft on 27 and 28 March in a signal from Admiral Boyd received at 0200 on 27 March. This warned of probable enemy air attacks on Cretan airfields and tasked 805 NAS fighters be airborne before dawn on 27 March, after which the Fulmars were to patrol over Scarpanto for three-quarters of an hour to catch enemy bombers returning from operations. The Sea Gladiators were to maintain a CAP over Maleme on both days. Swordfish were instructed to spend 27 March at Eleusis, returning to Maleme by nightfall. On 28 March, four Swordfish of 815 NAS took off armed with torpedoes at 0445 tasked with searching for shipping between

A sailor standing guard by RNAS Maleme's quarterdeck. (*Author's collection*)

the north-west tip of Crete and the Greek coast for enemy shipping. They found nothing, however, and returned four hours later.

Formidable's search aircraft had better fortune and at 0720 on 28 March 5B, the most northerly Albacore, located and reported four enemy cruisers and four destroyers and at 0739 search Albacore 5F made an initial report of four cruisers. 5F's report was 15nm in error and VALF thought that one of the groups reported might even be his own force. 5B's report was three *Zara* and two *Abruzzi*-class cruisers and 5F's three *Trieste*-class cruisers. Doubts were dismissed at 0745, however, when smoke was seen to the north of VALF's flagship, *Orion*, and minutes later enemy cruisers were identified. At 0812 the Italian cruisers opened fire. Surface visibility on 28 March was good but from the air it was patchy and never more than about 10nm. Winds were variable but sometimes strong enough to affect accurate air navigation and introduce inaccuracies in both side's reporting.

As the first Italian salvoes fell short, 5F reported three battleships but no verification followed as a Junkers Ju 88 chose that moment to attack and the Albacore was forced to take evasive action. Pridham-Wippell discounted this report, knowing that *Garibaldi*-class cruisers had similar silhouettes to *Cavour*-class battleships. He was closing Cunningham's force but the enemy ships were faster than his and drawing nearer. He did not yet know that an enemy battleship was only 16nm away on his port quarter. Cunningham was receiving conflicting reports from both naval and RAF aircraft and, as a precaution, he ordered *Formidable* to range a striking force armed with torpedoes at 0833. Fifteen minutes later he instructed Maleme to launch 815 NAS to attack the enemy cruisers but his signal did not reach Commander Beale until 1005. Signals for Maleme had been passed through the cruiser *York* in Souda Bay but she had been beached after being damaged by Italian explosive motor boats. Alternative signal routing caused delays.

At 0830 *Gloucester* catapulted her Walrus to spot her gunfire as opposing cruiser groups exchanged long-range fire and as her salvoes found the range the enemy turned away and at 0855 firing ceased. The Walrus remained airborne and transmitted enemy reports but did so on the spotting wavelength and none of them got any further than the ship's gun direction team, who failed to pass them to the command. This was particularly unfortunate because they included the first sighting of the third cruiser group, north of the group, which had just ceased fire. Had VALF or Cunningham received them, they would have helped clarify an otherwise obscure position, although the proximity of the enemy battleship would still have been unknown to them.

At 0900 Admiral Iachino ordered his cruisers to withdraw because of the danger from attacks by carrier-borne aircraft. As they turned away,

Moving torpedoes aft on *Formidable*. This is probably a posed photograph but it does show the Admiralty-designed loading trolleys to good effect. They contained a jack that allowed the weapon to be elevated from the trolley into the aircraft crutches and secured. (*Author's collection*)

VALF followed and maintained contact heading north-west at 28 knots. At 0922 Cunningham decided to delay *Formidable*'s strike force until the situation was clarified and requested 201 Group RAF to send flying boats to locate and shadow the enemy fleet.[25] Reading through the action reports many years later it is not clear how he thought 201 Group could provide any assistance in the short-term but doubt about the possible presence of enemy battleships was probably uppermost in his mind. Worryingly, *Formidable*'s observers were omitting their duty letters and even their own positions from some shadowing reports and this added to the confusion in the flagship. The C-in-C's staff was never made aware of the patchy visibility from the air.

At 0939 Cunningham decided to order *Formidable* to fly off its torpedo strike force and seventeen minutes later six Albacores from 826 and 829 NAS took off with two Fulmars of 803 NAS as escort. A single Swordfish of 826 NAS followed to undertake action observation Duty J. They were led by Lieutenant Commander Saunt and briefed to attack enemy cruisers. Torpedoes were set to run at 34ft but three observers reset their weapons to 28ft while they were in flight and it is unclear why the deeper setting was ordered in the first place since cruisers were the intended targets but, as it turned out, the deeper proved the better option. *Formidable*'s action narrative[26] stated that at 1100 the strike leader 'first sighted, to the southward, a force of cruisers and destroyers steering to the west which fired a few salvoes at them. Subsequently this proved to be VALF, although at the time there was some doubt in the leader's mind.' He then saw a large ship with four destroyers heading east at high speed and, working his way around it to the north and then the west, he saw a second force of cruisers and destroyers to the south-west. The large ship was engaging VALF's force, which had now turned onto south, and it was confirmed as a battleship at 1125. This was the *Vittorio Venetto*. Saunt attacked immediately on the enemy's engaged side. The first sub-flight of three dropped their torpedoes from the inner bow as she started to turn to starboard and the second sub-flight crossed over and dropped from a good position on the outer bow. A hit was claimed and reported on the *Vittorio Veneto*'s stern but all six torpedoes had in fact missed, passing astern of her as she turned onto west and broke off her engagement with the British cruisers. Before the Albacores began their attack, two Ju 88s attempted to intercept them but the escorting Fulmars shot one down and drove the other off.

The Italian battleship had been seen to the north from *Orion* at 1058 and *Vittorio Veneto* had opened fire on *Orion* at 32,000yds, achieving a near miss that caused some damage but did not affect her speed as VALF turned towards Cunningham. At 1135 it was estimated that VALF was 65nm west of *Warspite*. Three Swordfish from Maleme arrived over the enemy cruisers at 1200, having taken off at 1050 armed with torpedoes set to run at 20ft. They attacked out of the sun from 9,000ft at 1205, selecting *Bolzano* as their target. Two Swordfish dropped their torpedoes on her port bow and beam while the third attacked from the port bow. *Bolzano* turned hard and all the torpedoes missed. Anti-aircraft fire during both attacks had been intense.

Formidable appreciated that a second striking force was required but was hard pressed to achieve it. It was hoped that some search aircraft could be recovered and turned around in time and one of these, a Swordfish, landed on at 1130 and was refuelled, armed with a torpedo and ready by 1155, when Boyd signalled that a strike force of three Albacores and two Swordfish was ready. It was a remarkable achievement to have got it ready at all but its small size hardly offered the best chance of success.

At 1225 Cunningham ordered his battleships to fly off their spotting aircraft, indicating that he considered surface action to be imminent, and at 1230 he ordered *Formidable* to fly off her second strike. She altered course away from the battleships to launch it and recover the first strike, and as before two Fulmars were launched as escort. This strike was led by Lieutenant Commander Dalyell-Stead, who was briefed to remain over the carrier until the two battle fleets were engaged or, if no further instructions were received, to proceed towards the enemy at 1330. *Formidable* was attacked at this stage by two SM.79 torpedo bombers, which approached at low level to avoid radar detection and were seen too late for the CAP to be directed onto them. Their attack was unsynchronised and they dropped their weapons at long range so both tracks were easily combed and the torpedoes exploded harmlessly astern at the end of their run.

Despite his preparations Cunningham was still not certain of the enemy's exact position. Three Albacores from the first strike were, therefore, refuelled and flown off to locate and shadow the enemy battleship towards which Dalyell-Stead's strike force was heading after its hour's wait. There seemed little chance by then of bringing the Italian force to action unless its speed could be reduced by air attack, the classic role envisaged pre-war for RN torpedo aircraft. The first strike had the beneficial effect of causing the Italian battleship to break off its engagement with VALF's cruisers but from Cunningham's perspective it had frustrated his attempt to force a surface action. In his report[27] he wrote that 'few things could have been more timely than their intervention but it had the effect I always feared...the enemy turned for home with a lead which could not be closed to gun range in daylight'.

At 1330 Dalyell-Stead set heading for *Vittorio Veneto* using a position estimated at 1307. This was corrected by the C-in-C's staff at 1350 and passed to the strike leader, who saw her at 1430 fine to starboard. Dalyell-Stead moved into a position up sun from the target and, as he did so the Italian force was distracted by a medium-level bombing attack by RAF Blenheims from Greece. There had been no pre-arranged plan to synchronise it with the torpedo attack but it forced the Italians to divide their anti-aircraft fire. The

Torpedo-armed Albacores setting off on a strike. (*Author's collection*)

Blenheims failed to score any hits but in his account of the battle[28] Admiral Iachino admitted that 'the attention of the lookouts and anti-aircraft gunners was thus diverted by the approach of the bombers'.

Once he was in an ideal attacking position at 1510 Dalyell-Stead led the three Albacores into a dive, which was unobserved until the leading destroyer opened fire as they passed 5,000ft. The two escorting Fulmars then strafed this destroyer in a classic Fleet Air Arm strike tactic. After their dive, Albacores 5F, 5G and 5H released torpedoes on *Veneto*'s port bow and she took drastic avoiding action by altering course through 180 degrees to starboard. The depth and safety range settings applied to the torpedoes before launch were 34ft and 400yds, and all were fitted with duplex pistols. Admiral Iachino's account is quite clear that it was 5G, the leader's aircraft, which dropped a torpedo that hit *Veneto*'s port quarter in an attack that was pressed home so closely that a miss was unlikely. Seconds before it hit, Dalyell-Stead, with his observer Lieutenant R H Cooke RN and TAG Petty Officer G L Blenkhorn, were shot down and none of them survived. They were, therefore, sadly unaware that their gallant attack had been a success. Dalyell-Stead was posthumously awarded the DSO, Cooke the DSC and Blenkhorn the DSM. Lieutenant A S Whitworth RN, the pilot of 5F, said in a post-war interview that all three torpedoes entered the water within seconds of each other, making it difficult to determine exactly which one hit and it is possible that there was at least one more hit, or 'run-under' with a failure of the duplex pistol. The pilot of 5H was Lieutenant (A) R E Bibby RN. The torpedo struck *Veneto* abreast the port outer propeller, 16ft below the waterline, fracturing the shaft and reducing the ship's speed to 16 knots.

The second sub-flight of two swordfish, 5K and 4B, led by Lieutenant G M T Osborn RN got into a position up sun as *Veneto* finished her turn. Like the Albacores, both had torpedoes set to run at 34ft with a safety range of 400yds and they attacked their target from the starboard side just forward of the beam. As *Veneto* had slowed to about 14 knots by then, a fairly easy full deflection shot was presented but neither torpedo appeared to hit, although it is possible that their duplex pistols failed to detonate. Some 4,000 tons of water flooded *Veneto* aft, her rudder jammed and she lost all way until about 1530. After that she gradually got under way again, steering by hand wheel, and used her starboard engines to work up to 16 then 19 knots. While she was stopped, further RAF Blenheims attacked the Italian cruisers, again without scoring any hits. At 1649 Cunningham received the welcome signal from Boyd that hits on *Veneto* had been made by Dalyell-Stead's strike.

He replied 'Well done' and instructed *Formidable* to prepare the largest possible strike against *Veneto* at dusk; sunset was at 1840. Eight Albacores and Swordfish led by Saunt with Lieutenant F H E Hopkins RN as his observer, were armed with torpedoes set to run at 34ft and they took off at 1735 with their target 53nm to the west.

Torrens-Spence at Maleme was determined to carry out another strike but only two Swordfish could be made ready in time. A Fulmar was flown off at 1500 to locate the enemy and returned an hour later with last-minute details that were used to brief the strike before it took off at 1655, forty minutes ahead of *Formidable*'s third strike. Cunningham was still uncertain of the enemy's dispositions and ordered *Warspite*'s to catapult its Swordfish seaplane with the very experienced observer, Lieutenant Commander A S Bolt RN, to obtain information that he could use to decide what action to take after sunset. Given his obvious lack of situational awareness throughout the day one has to wonder why he had not done so before. Bolt's pilot was the experienced Petty Officer F C Rice and the TAG was

The Italian battleship *Vittorio Veneto*. (*Author's collection*)

The Italian cruiser *Garibaldi*. These images show the similarity between these two types, which made them difficult to tell apart under action conditions. (*Author's collection*)

Petty Officer M G Pacey. Their sortie proved to be the outstanding example of how shadowing sorties should be conducted and Bolt made a series of lucid reports from 1831 that clarified enemy positions, courses and speeds.

The enemy battleship, three cruisers and seven destroyers bore 292 degrees from *Warspite* at 50nm. They were heading 300 degrees at 12 knots and by 1912 Bolt had reported that five further cruisers had joined *Vittorio Veneto*, which was at the centre of a concentrated group of warships disposed in five columns. The British battle squadron was gaining on them but with no chance of reaching gun range before nightfall. Bolt then took up a position 5nm astern of the enemy at 2,000ft and watched the next torpedo attack by aircraft from *Formidable* and Maleme. After that he returned to *Warspite* to report and have his aircraft refuelled once it had been hoisted in.

Saunt found the enemy just before sunset and decided to wait until it was dark before attacking, taking up a waiting position at low level astern out of anti-aircraft gun range. Whilst orbiting he was joined by Torrens-Spence and Lieutenant (A) L J Kiggell RN from Maleme, who had located the Italians an hour earlier. Iachino knew another attack was imminent through intercepted signal traffic and his force was, thus, aware and fully prepared, even catching glimpses of aircraft in their waiting position. In Saunt's action report[29] he wrote that at 1925 when dusk had fallen:

> the striking force made its approach just above the water in single line ahead. When they still had 2 miles to run the enemy laid a smokescreen followed by an intense anti-aircraft barrage of all calibres which the aircraft were unable to penetrate. They withdrew, therefore, split up and carried out individual attacks on the battleship from different bearings...the results were difficult to assess in the light conditions prevailing but one hit on a cruiser was observed.

The two 815 NAS aircraft followed the *Formidable* aircraft's attack so as not to confuse it. Torrens-Spence reported that 'almost all the ships started to emit black or white smoke-screens which, combined with the dazzling effect of gunfire, searchlights and tracers, made it very difficult to pick anything out'. He and Kiggell made independent attacks, Torrens-Spence on a cruiser inside the screen and Kiggell 'into the brown', out of which emerged a 'large ship' as he turned away after dropping his torpedo.

The last air strike of the day had not hit *Veneto* but left the cruiser *Pola* stopped in the water. None of the aircraft had been shot down immediately but Torrens-Spence's had been damaged and was forced to ditch about 30nm west of Crete, where he and his crew were rescued by the destroyer *Juno*. Bolt had returned to his shadowing position in semi-darkness, after which he flew back to Crete and, after releasing three flame-floats, landed safely alongside them in Souda Bay.

The hit on *Pola* struck the starboard side between the engine and boiler rooms. Boyd attributed it at the time to either Sub Lieutenant Williams from *Formidable* in 5A or the second aircraft from Maleme. Since the latter, Kiggell, attacked an unknown type of ship from the port side this is probably incorrect but Torrens-Spence had attacked a cruiser from the starboard side at 1950 from a range of only 450yds. As *Pola* was hit between 1946 and 1950 it must have been either Torrens-Spence or Williams who achieved it. Whoever did so, the explosion cut off all steam to the main engines, she stopped and lost all lighting. About thirty minutes later Iachino ordered *Zara* and *Fiume* to return to her assistance, completely unaware of the British fleet's position. The Italians lacked radar but *Valiant* detected *Pola* by this means at 2203 at a range of 9nm. The turrets of the Italian cruisers were still trained fore and aft when fire was opened on them by the British battleships at close range at 2230. *Fiume*, disabled by gunfire and possibly hit by a torpedo from *Stuart*, sank at 2300. *Zara*, also disabled by gunfire, was sunk at 0240 by a torpedo from *Jervis* and *Pola*, disabled in the Fleet Air Arm attack, was sunk by torpedoes from *Jervis* and *Nubian* at 0340. Two Italian destroyers were also sunk, *Giosue Carducci* and *Vittorio Alfieri*. The other two destroyers, *Oriani* and *Gioberti*, escaped although the former had been damaged.[30]

Before the battleships opened fire, *Formidable* moved away as she was of little value in a night surface action. She re-joined at 2325 and made preparations to fly off a dawn search with the few remaining Albacores augmented by Fulmars. These flew off at 0430 on 29 March but located nothing of importance and Cunningham decided to return to Alexandria since the enemy would soon be under cover from X Fliegerkorps aircraft based in Sicily. During the afternoon a dive-bombing attack was carried out on the British fleet by Ju 88s. It was directed at *Formidable* but her radar gave adequate warning and the Fulmar CAP was directed onto the bombers in time to break up the attack partially. Several bombers jettisoned their bombs but some near misses were achieved that caused her hull to whiplash and damaged gunnery directors. Two enemy aircraft were shot down. At dawn on 30 March a shadowing SM.79 was shot down by Fulmars, an action described in the ship's action narrative as 'a very just reward for the fighters and for the fighter-direction and RDF [radar] personnel who had all put in a lot of hard work during the operation'.

While the failure to destroy the Italian battleship was disappointing, destruction of three heavy cruisers and two large destroyers for a loss to the RN of one Albacore and its crew, one swordfish and one Fulmar was a good result. It deterred the enemy from trying to interfere with Lustre convoys, which resumed immediately after the battle, and no attempt was made to disrupt the eventual evacuation of British and Commonwealth forces from Greece and later Crete by enemy surface forces.

From a Fleet Air Arm perspective, the low numbers of TSR aircraft available in *Formidable* and at Maleme limited the size of every torpedo attack, all of which were carried out with numbers too small to produce decisive results. Taking this limitation into account, the strikes had been as successful as could be expected. The hit on *Pola* in the last attack brought about her own destruction and that of two other heavy cruisers. On 28 March F*ormidable*'s little force of fourteen Albacores and Swordfish had carried out two air searches and three torpedo attacks in addition to several shadowing sorties which had had extended the capabilities of such a small air group to the limit.

Until the launch of *Warspite*'s Swordfish as Duty Q for the second time at 1745 air reconnaissance and shadowing had not been satisfactory since neither had presented the C-in-C with a clear picture of the tactical situation. The visibility from the air was variable, as was the wind direction, but the presence of three separate enemy forces in the area had caused confusion. The silhouette and appearance from the air of the Italian *Garibaldi*-class

Photographs of Fleet Air Arm aircraft in action during the Battle of Matapan are rare, for obvious reasons. This Italian image shows an Albacore breaking away after dropping its torpedo; the splash from its water entry can be seen at the bottom left. (*Author's collection*)

cruisers and their *Cavour*-class battleships were similar and enemy aircraft occasionally attacked the shadowers. All these factors limited the value of early sighting reports. Another factor that needed to be addressed was that the aircraft reconnaissance frequency was not the same as the one used by surface units and aircrew were, therefore, not aware which ships were in contact with the enemy. Iachino, on the other hand, received a number of translated intercepts of RN aircraft sighting and shadowing reports, although the extent to which his own forces were being reported probably gave him little comfort as he wrote in his account of the battle:

> Truly there was a striking contrast between the information situation in which we found ourselves and that of the English who, in fact, had an exact idea not only of the composition and formation of our naval force, but also of their course and speed; whereas we knew absolutely nothing of the enemy forces at sea which were following us at a short distance.[31]

At the time of Matapan, *Formidable* had the most advanced radar-directed aircraft control facilities at sea. Commander P Yorke RN was described in the ship's action narrative as 'directing fighters with great skill' and he went on to play an important part in establishing the Fighter Direction School at RNAS Yeovilton. The lack of identification friend or foe, IFF, equipment on some RN and RAF aircraft that took part in the battle caused considerable difficulty and its more widespread use would have simplified fighter direction and thus added to the efficiency of the fleet's protection against air attack.

The value of having RNAS Maleme as a diversion within aircraft range of the battle area was emphasised by the ability of 815 NAS to augment both searches and strikes and by its ability to recover the dusk strike aircraft after their attack. The attacks by the much-reduced 815 NAS were carried out in the exemplary style that, by now, was associated with it and because of the difficult communications between the flagship and Maleme, independent searches for the enemy had been instituted when its position was in doubt and before its strike force was allowed to take off. Cunningham spoke highly of the initiative shown by Torrens-Spence throughout the battle and he was awarded the DSO to add to the DSC awarded for the Taranto attack.

The failure of the Italian and German land-based air forces to provide efficient fighter cover or reconnaissance led to orders being given for the conversion of two Italian liners, the *Roma* and *Augusta*, into aircraft carriers. They were to be renamed *Aquila* and *Sparviero* respectively. *Aquila* was nearly complete in 1943 when the Italians asked for an armistice.

5

Operations in 1941 after the Battle of Matapan

After the Battle of Matapan the Axis commands recognised the threat from British carrier-borne aircraft and placed restrictions on operations in which they might be encountered. Despite all their limitations, however, naval air squadrons afloat and ashore continued to do remarkably well despite their small numbers.

830 and 828 NAS operations from Malta from April 1941 onwards
The tactic of using a leader with flares and torpedo-armed Swordfish to form a night striking force was used to good effect on 12 May when 830 NAS despatched aircraft to attack an enemy convoy located off the Tunisian coast by an RAF Maryland reconnaissance aircraft from Malta. Four torpedo-armed aircraft had taken off but one returned after a cockpit lighting failure that prevented the pilot from seeing his instruments. The convoy was an important one with seven merchant vessels escorted by two cruisers and seven destroyers but, unfortunately, casualties and sickness prevented a larger striking force from being sent out. The convoy was seen in the path of the moon at 2030 and the three torpedo aircraft attacked the three merchant ships in the starboard column, passing low over the destroyer screen.[1] Their attack was made up moon without flares and one torpedo was seen to miss a merchant vessel but hit a destroyer and a second hit a merchant vessel. The attack had achieved complete surprise and there was no enemy anti-aircraft fire; the Swordfish all returned safely to Malta.

A bombing attack on Tripoli harbour was carried out by Swordfish from Malta on 8 June. Its object was to set fire to oil reported as covering the water surface in the harbour. Seven aircraft left Malta at 1930 each armed with two 250lb GP bombs with nose fuses and rod attachments set for instantaneous detonation, the intention being for them to burst just above the water surface as the rod hit it. They also carried four Mark II

An 830 NAS Swordfish armed with bombs. (*Author's collection*)

flame floats and twenty Mark I flame floats. The bombs were released by aircraft in their dives at 4,000ft and two hit Spanish Quay. The aircraft continued their dives to release the flame floats and the majority were seen to fall in the harbour as planned. The oil did not ignite, however, and NAD observed that it was notoriously difficult to ignite oil on water.

A further bombing attack on Tripoli harbour was carried out on 12 June for which six Swordfish took off at 2012. All except the leader were armed with six 250lb GP bombs and four 25lb incendiaries; the leader carried four 250lb GP bombs and eight flares. Two had to return with engine problems but the remaining four carried out dive-bombing attacks with sticks of bombs seen to fall across Spanish Quay. One aircraft's bombs failed to release but were later jettisoned. The enemy started a smokescreen as the attack began so the full impact damage could not be assessed but a large glow was observed through the smoke as the aircraft withdrew.

NAD assessed that by the end of 1941 830 NAS had attacked about eighty enemy ships with torpedoes, of which at least forty were sunk or seriously damaged. Some others were damaged by bombs and it was estimated that some 200,000 tons of Axis shipping was either sunk or disabled by this one squadron. Additionally, at least four of their escorting destroyers were sunk or damaged. In addition to bombing and torpedo sorties, 830 NAS had shown its versatility between February and October 1941 by carrying out minelaying operations, dropping seventy mines in the vicinity of Tripoli,[2] which continued to be effective even though their results were not immediately apparent. Aircrew often logged over eight hours flying in a single night, a remarkable achievement, but by the middle of 1941 many were in desperate need of rest. Given the intensity of enemy air attacks, this was hardly possible on Malta itself and the Admiralty set in train a programme of reliefs.

As its aircraft were fitted with ASV radar from June, 830 NAS aircrew's skill in using it increased, gradually reducing their dependence on moonlight for the location of enemy convoys at night. Flare dropping for the final illumination was increasingly timed and positioned using ASV.[3] Convoys to North Africa usually had a ratio of one warship to every merchant ship and the latter were usually limited to four, the maximum that Libyan ports could handle. On nights with no moon when Swordfish leaders used flares to illuminate targets the enemy either stopped engines or altered onto divergent courses and increased speed. In both cases escorts increased speed and made smoke while turning in wide circles to divert attention from the merchant ships. Stopping engines was often effective as with no moon a ship's wake was the only means by which aircraft could finally identify a target.

Enemy anti-aircraft fire was only occasionally accurate but when tracer was used it helped strike aircraft locate targets on dark nights. No. 830 NAS achieved surprise in its attacks more often than not and a formation of Swordfish could sometimes pass safely over a convoy between 3,000 and 5,000ft without being detected. Even if the aircraft were heard the Italians often did not open fire until the attack developed in the hope that they would not be seen in the dark but this allowed the first few aircraft to attack unmolested.

Ultra decrypts sometimes gave warning that a convoy was imminent but they were usually located by RAF aircraft from Malta. However, interceptions of their sighting reports could warn a convoy in time for it to make a drastic alteration of course. If the reconnaissance aircraft delayed its contact report, however, there was often a good chance of interception after sunset. As 830 NAS became fully proficient in the use of ASV the interception of convoys became a probability, not a possibility. On an enemy report being received, its track was plotted in an operations room at Hal Far and the best attack position was calculated. The state of the moon and its bearing were taken into account, together with the distance of the convoy from Malta and experience of the enemy's convoy routing history, the latter factor being considered of the greatest importance. It became common practice to send out one ASV-fitted aircraft from one to two hours ahead of the strike force to locate and then shadow a convoy. This aircraft, which on several occasions even located convoys hugging the North African coastline where ASV conditions were most difficult, made sighting and amplifying reports coded by a SYKO device and then remained in contact to shadow. The striking force, whose leader also flew in an ASV-fitted aircraft, then picked up the convoy at a distance of anything up to 30nm. The advent of ASV meant that it was no longer necessary for the shadowing aircraft to indicate the convoy's position to the strike force with flares, although they were still needed to illuminate targets for the actual attack on dark nights. Finally, fuel state permitting, the shadowing aircraft would carry out a post-attack visual damage assessment before returning to Malta.

A typical anti-shipping strike force comprised six Swordfish armed with torpedoes and an ASV-fitted leader armed with two 250lb GP bombs and flares. The flight leader carried an external long-range fuel tank on its torpedo crutches, while the remaining torpedo-armed aircraft were

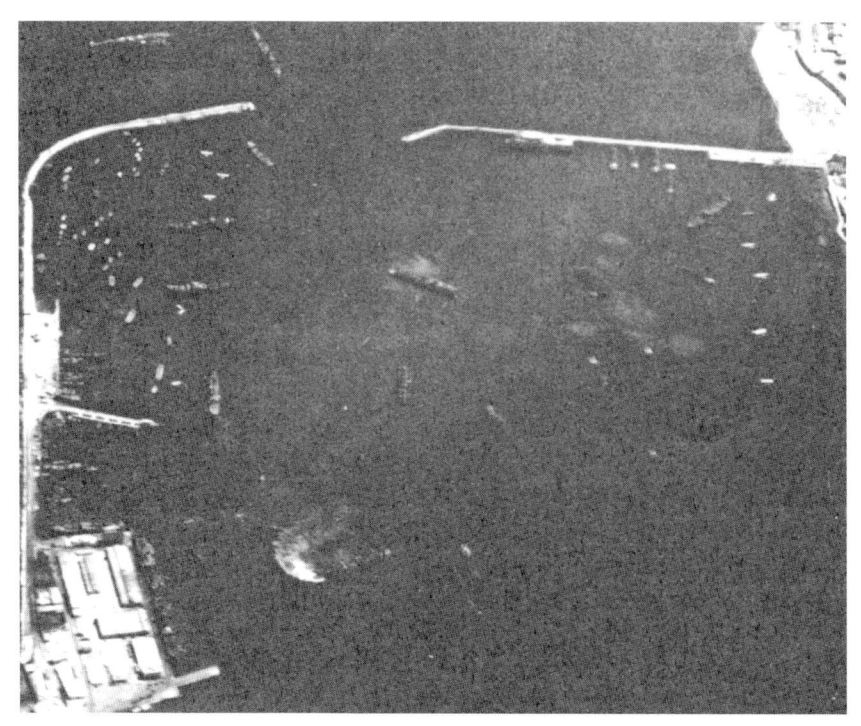

Tripoli harbour photographed by an RAF reconnaissance aircraft in 1941. Spanish Quay is at the bottom left of the picture and the vulnerability of the narrow entrance to mining is evident. (*Author's collection*)

fitted with internal overload tanks. Flights usually flew at 3,000ft and if the convoy was a particularly attractive target and more aircraft were available, the attack would be made in two waves 10nm apart, the rear one keeping station using its ASV, so that there was no congestion in the target area. Time was a critical factor in an attack and varied with the incidence of moonlight or its absence. In good moonlight conditions the striking force could take its time delivering the attack. With no moon when illumination by flares was necessary, the attack had to be carried out while the ships were still illuminated and before the escort's smokescreen had time to become effective. If there was low cloud cover the flares were dropped through the cloud on ASV bearings. In moonlit conditions the strike leader led the force round into a position in which the convoy was in the path of the moon and then gave the signal to attack. The sub-flights dived in a pre-arranged order, leaving time for the preceding one to get clear. The leader himself usually remained at reconnaissance height, made a quick estimate of the effect of the attack and then dive-bombed any surviving ship before leaving the area. On dark, moonless nights, once the leader's observer had calculated the enemy to be within 2 to 3nm on his ASV screen or, more rarely, had been seen, the striking aircraft were instructed to turn away and position themselves for the attack based on a pre-arranged bearing of the leader's flares once they were dropped. They were usually dropped in a line at 1 to 1½ nm from the convoy in a pre-arranged relative position. It was absolutely essential that the striking force aircraft should have no doubt as to the position of the flares in relation to the target and this knowledge had to be thoroughly understood before the aircraft took departure from Malta. If necessary, the shadowing aircraft used its own flares to increase the period of illumination given by those of the leader.

There were outstanding examples of 830 NAS' skill in September. On 2 September an Axis convoy comprising five supply ships and six destroyers was located in daylight and at 2010 a strike comprising a leader and eight Swordfish armed with torpedoes took off and formed into four sub-flights of two aircraft each. At 2205 ASV contact was gained at 25nm and the strike used ASV bearings to manoeuvre into a position where the convoy was visible in the path of the moon. Complete surprise was achieved and the first four aircraft gained a confirmed hit on an 8,000-ton merchant ship. The convoy broke up in confusion as the fifth aircraft gained a hit and an explosion was seen where the leading ship had been. The remaining three Swordfish attacked under heavy fire and the leader remained overhead to assess results. He only saw four of the five ships, of which one appeared undamaged, one was circling at low speed and one

The Axis convoy attacked on 17 January 1941 by 830 NAS, photographed by one of the Swordfish observers. The ship in the distance was assessed as stopped, on fire and emitting steam and smoke but it could, perhaps, have been laying a smokescreen. The nearer ship has clearly been broken in two by a torpedo hit and is sinking rapidly. (*Author's collection*)

was stopped with a heavy list and smoke pouring from it amidships. The other was moving slowly to the north.

On 18 September a convoy was located in daylight by an RAF Wellington and shadowed. A Swordfish strike comprising a leader and four torpedo-armed aircraft took off at 1940 and made ASV contact at 25nm. The convoy contained four merchant vessels and four destroyers and the first two aircraft attacked by the light of flares; two ships were hit and one was seen to be on fire. The second pair attacked after the flares had gone out but had sufficient light from the burning ship. One torpedo hit it but the other track was not seen. Despite fire from the destroyers no Swordfish were hit and they returned safely.

Post-war searches of Italian records showed that not all the ships assessed as sunk had actually gone down but 830 NAS' operations undoubtedly had considerable impact. Neither Italian ships nor aircraft had radar, giving the Swordfish an advantage. Since the Italian Navy had neither its own Fleet Air Arm nor anything like an escort carrier they could not adequately defend their convoys against air attack and had to rely on shore-based air escort by day only, and even then for only part of their passage.

No. 828 NAS Albacores arrived in Malta on 18 October 1941, ferried to the flying off position by *Ark Royal* in Operation Callboy. By the end of 1941 it had carried out twenty-six operations, mainly night bombing enemy airfields and the U-boat base at Augusta in Sicily. Mines were laid off Tripoli and Suara harbours but only two night torpedo attacks were made against enemy convoys before the end of 1941. In one of these, on 18 December, an Italian merchant ship was hit off Tripoli, but the commanding officer, Lieutenant Commander D E Langmore DSC RN, and his pilot, Lieutenant E A Greenwood DSC RN, were lost. Lieutenant G M Haynes RAN took over command a day later.

During this period 828 NAS had carried out ninety sorties, dropping 20 tons of bombs on a variety of targets and twenty-seven minelaying sorties off Sicily and Tripolitania. An aircraft was lost on 28 November 1941 from which Sub Lieutenant (A) E H Walshe RNVR and Sub Lieutenant (A) J H Lewis RNVR survived but became prisoners of war.

Operations Winch and Dunlop and the bombardment of Tripoli

At the end of March the Afrika Korps began an offensive against British Commonwealth forces in Cyrenaica and within two weeks they were forced back to the Egyptian frontier. Tobruk remained in British hands but was isolated and besieged. Rommel's offensive might have continued into Egypt if he had not been hampered by the actions of Malta-based aircraft against Axis convoys, it was lack of supplies that caused him to stop. During the British retreat three Albacores of 826 NAS were deployed forward to the airfield at El Adem near Tobruk, tasked with attacking any enemy ships that approached the coast. No targets appeared, however, and the aircraft were used to co-operate with RAF bombers attacking targets inland since the observers' navigational skills were found to be particularly useful over the featureless North African desert.

Light surface forces and more aircraft and submarines had, by then, been based in Malta and in March Axis shipping losses amounted to 30,000 tons, By April this had risen to 41,000 tons. The Mediterranean War Diary,[4] described April as 'a month of disasters only relieved by two or three satisfactory incidents'. Rommel's counter-offensive and the German invasion of Greece and Yugoslavia on 6 April, followed by the hazardous evacuation of the Commonwealth expeditionary Force from Greece, were grievous blows but Italian forces in East Africa and Eritrea were defeated. There were only sixteen Hurricanes left to defend Malta and Axis bombing was relentless so *Ark Royal* was in Operation Winch to ferry twelve RAF Hurricanes to a flying-off position 420nm from Malta on 3 April. They were guided by two Skuas of 800 NAS with a Sunderland and a Maryland in company. On the return passage to Gibraltar, *Ark Royal*'s CAP shot down a Cant Z.506 shadower.

On 13 and 14 April 1941 Axis bombers made nine attacks on Malta and Hurricane attrition led to another ferry mission by *Ark Royal* designated Operation Dunlop. This time twenty-three Hurricanes were flown off on 27 April and guided to Malta by three Fulmars of 807 NAS, which had relieved 800 NAS with its Skuas in *Ark Royal* on 5 April. Between 18 and 23 April the Mediterranean Fleet was also at sea to cover the movement of the fast transport *Breconshire* to Malta with aviation fuel and oil and the passage of four other large merchant ships from Malta to Alexandria. During these operations, designated MD 2 and MD 3, *Formidable* maintained constant CAP from an air group that comprised nineteen Fulmars, nine Albacores and six Swordfish. On 20 April the fighter CAPs shot down a Cant Z.1007 shadower and four Junkers Ju 52 transport aircraft but two Fulmars and their crews were lost.

In the early hours of 21 April RAF Wellingtons followed by Swordfish of 830 NAS bombed Tripoli and from 0503 the port was bombarded by *Warspite*, *Barham*, *Valiant* and *Gloucester*. *Formidable* launched six Albacores and Swordfish to illuminate the target area with flares and spotting aircraft for each of the bombarding warships. This was the first time that flares had been used for a bombardment and the results were not successful. Too few flares were used, leaving three-quarters of the target area in darkness and smoke and dust from by early shell bursts made the spotters' task impossible. No enemy air attacks followed the withdrawal but Fulmars shot down a Cant Z.1007 and a Dornier Do 24 that were attempting to shadow the fleet. On 22 April three Ju 88s were intercepted by Fulmars as they tried to attack the fleet; one was shot down and the other two made off after being damaged. The fleet returned to Alexandria unscathed on 23 April. The bombardment was thought to have caused damage but intelligence sources revealed that only a single ammunition ship had been sunk.

The evacuation from Greece – Operation Demon

On 24 April the Greek Government surrendered and about 51,000 British Commonwealth troops were evacuated from ports and beaches to Crete and Egypt, leaving about 8,000 behind. The Luftwaffe was virtually unopposed and two destroyers, three troop transports and three lighters were sunk by air attack. However, since the RAF had only seven Hurricanes left and the situation ashore was out of control with a well-equipped enemy in close contact with the retreating British force, the evacuation went better than it might have done. RAF Sunderlands and BOAC flying boats evacuated 1,529 people from Greece.

Formidable sailed from Alexandria on 29 April with Admiral Boyd embarked in company with *Barham*, *Valiant* and six destroyers to cover a convoy carrying 11,000 troops from Souda Bay. The fleet's sailing was delayed by a shortage of screening destroyers and the bay had become badly congested with ships arriving from Greece. On 30 April two air attacks on the convoy were defeated by *Formidable*'s fighters and anti-aircraft gunfire, allowing Alexandria to be reached on 1 May. However, entry was delayed by seven enemy aircraft, which dropped mines between

A torpedo-armed Albacore of 828 NAS protected by its stone revetment in the complex of dispersals clear of the runway at Hal Far. Aircraft were parked folded to reduce their dimensions. Note the notched bar in front of the pilot's cockpit, this was the torpedo sight, which was fitted to enable the pilot to estimate aim-off when attacking a moving ship. Each notch represented 5 knots of ship speed when it was at right angles to the line of flight. (Philip Jarrett collection)

the harbour entrance and the Great Pass at 2234. *Formidable* and the battleships could not enter the harbour until the afternoon of 3 May.

Passage of the 'Tiger' convoy – Operation MD 4

In two weeks of fighting the British 2nd Armoured Division had lost nearly all its tanks and Churchill directed that they must be replaced. He did not know at the time that German supply position was inadequate and it was only learnt after the war that on 7 May Rommel had reported to Berlin that there would be 'grave consequences if further delay in sea-borne supplies. Troops have less than one issue of ammunition. Stocks in Cyrenaica negligible.'[5]

After the forceful urging from the Prime Minister, the Defence Committee accepted that a fast convoy run through the Mediterranean to Alexandria with replacement tanks was the best solution.[6] It was fully realised that with the loss of the Cyranaican airfields Axis air forces could attack the convoy in both its middle and late stages. The Admiralty accepted it as a vital strategic necessity and designated the convoy Operation MD 4 with the code name Tiger.

The Tiger convoy comprised five diesel-powered fast merchant ships and the carriers' fighter squadrons were to be a major factor in its defence. These included 807 NAS commanded by Lieutenant Commander (A) J S Douglas RN and 808 NAS commanded by Lieutenant Commander R C Tillard RN, both equipped with Fulmars in *Ark Royal*. *Formidable* had 803 and 806 NAS embarked, both equipped with Fulmars and commanded by Lieutenants K M Bruen and G J R Nichols RN respectively. The RAF Beaufighters of 252 Squadron at Malta were to give long-range cover through the narrows directed by *Naiad* but without any training or experience of operating under naval control. This squadron also carried out low-level strafing raids on enemy airfields at Comiso and Catania in Sicily.

The full escort for the Tiger convoy amounted to two aircraft carriers, four battleships and one battlecruiser, ten cruisers, twenty-five destroyers, a minelayer and a fast RN-manned supply ship. They were divided into task forces as follows:

Force B   *Renown, Ark Royal, Sheffield* and three destroyers
Force F   *Queen Elizabeth, Naiad, Fiji* and eight destroyers
Force D   *Gloucester* and two destroyers
Force A   *Warspite, Barham, Valiant, Formidable, Orion, Ajax, Perth, Calcutta, Carlisle, Coventry, Dido, Phoebe, Abdiel,* twelve destroyers and the supply ship *Breconshire*

Forces B, F and D sailed from Gibraltar on 5 May. Force A left Alexandria in time to meet the Tiger convoy and Force F near Malta and covered two small convoys to Malta. The Tiger convoy passed through the Straits of Gibraltar in the early hours of 6 May, having been met to the west of the Rock by Forces B, F and D. The Mediterranean Fleet also sailed on 6 May during a sand storm that hid its movement from enemy air reconnaissance. *Formidable* flew on eight TSRs and seven fighters from RNAS Dekheila which brought her air group up to nineteen Fulmars, six Albacores and six Swordfish, significantly fewer than the numbers she was designed to embark.

The enemy was aware that Force H had sailed east but had no idea why. This changed at 0800 on 8 May when it was reported by a reconnaissance aircraft. *Ark Royal* had already flown off a dawn reconnaissance of three ASV-fitted Swordfish to the east, south and west of Sardinia to search for Italian surface forces with orders not to break W/T silence unless the fleet was immediately threatened. They returned at 0800 with negative results and Somerville moved closer to the convoy and ordered *Ark Royal*

Dispersal was essential but with the lack of fuel for vehicles considerable improvisation was needed. This donkey cart has just been used to carry a torpedo to an 828 NAS Albacore and it has been lifted into place by muscle-power not a jack. (*Philip Jarrett collection*)

to fly off CAPs. These were also instructed to maintain W/T silence until contact was made with the enemy. At the time only twelve Fulmars from the two squadrons were fully serviceable and at 1143 a large floatplane was seen from *Naiad* and engaged but made off into cloud, where fighters proved unable to intercept it. Transmissions from it were heard accurately reporting the composition of the British force.

Ark Royal kept the CAP fighters close to the force and replaced one section every hour so that a section with more than ninety minutes' fuel would be airborne constantly. At 1338 enemy aircraft were detected on radar to the north-east at 32nm and fighters were vectored to intercept them. They intercepted twelve CR.42 fighters escorting eight SM.79 torpedo bombers and a melee ensued during which one enemy fighter was damaged but Tillard, the commanding officer of 808 NAS and his observer, Lieutenant M F Somerville DSC RN, both described as gallant and capable officers in Force H's report of the action, were shot down and not seen again, leaving only five serviceable Fulmars. The torpedo-armed SM.79s' attack was opposed by heavy but poorly directed anti-aircraft fire and each aircraft dropped two torpedoes outside the destroyer screen. Three torpedoes narrowly missed *Renown* and four, two each side, passed *Ark Royal* after skilful avoiding action. Three SM.79s were believed to have been shot down by the fleet's gunfire.

At 1530 one of two shadowing SM.79s was shot down by Blue Section of 807 NAS, Lieutenant (A) R E Gardner RNVR and his observer Petty Officer R Carlyle leading with Lieutenant (A) K Firth RNVR and his TAG Leading Airman Godfrey as number two. One of the Fulmars was forced to ditch but its crew were rescued. At 1620 a high-level bombing attack was made by three SM.79s escorted by CR.42 fighters and the intercepting Fulmars became involved in a series of dogfights in and out of cloud. *Ark Royal* was narrowly missed by a group of small bombs and one of the SM.79s was seen to crash. Another shadower was detected at 1710; Lieutenant R C Hay RM of 808 NAS was directed onto it and shot it down. At 1730 a further high-level bombing attack by five SM.79s was carried out and bombs were seen to fall into the sea near the destroyer screen. Another attack at 1800 was equally unsuccessful.

Somerville wrote in his report that CAP fighter numbers were limited by the few serviceable aircraft left in *Ark Royal*; several had returned with damage and whenever radar screens cleared CAP Fulmars were recovered, refuelled and rearmed. Sometimes there were only two airborne but whenever an attack seemed imminent every serviceable fighter was flown off. At 1910 a large attacking force was detected by radar at 70nm coming from Sicily. Only three Fulmars were airborne but four others had been made serviceable and they were flown off at 1920 as the convoy neared Bizerta. The fighters grouped into three sections as they climbed above the cloud layer, where they saw three separate formations of German aircraft identified as one group of sixteen Ju 87 dive bombers, a second group of twelve Ju 87s and a third group of six Bf 110 long-range fighters. Somerville wrote that:[7]

Albacores of 828 NAS climbing away from Malta for an anti-shipping strike. Hal Far's runway and extensive dispersal pattern can be seen in the foreground, under the aircraft, and Valletta can just be made out in the distance. (*Philip Jarrett collection*)

The seven Fulmars, although greatly outnumbered, fought several vigorous and gallant actions resulting in the certain destruction of one Ju 87 and damage to several others including at least one Bf 110. These attacks disorganised the enemy and forced them to the northward with the result that they probably missed sighting the fleet. They then entered thick cloud and it is possible that the group became separated and all cohesion in the attack disappeared. This was precisely what naval fighters were intended to do, not so much to shoot down individual enemy aircraft but to break up attacks and stop the enemy from co-ordinating set-piece attacks on the fleet.

There was, however, one further attack as Force B was leaving the convoy and Force F to return to Gibraltar. Three torpedo-armed SM.79s attacked *Renown* and *Ark Royal* as they turned west. A radar warning had been given and a CAP Fulmar saw them but could not get into a firing position. All four torpedoes were avoided successfully and the last fighter landed on at 2140, ending a day in which several had flown more than four sorties to prevent the enemy from making any serious bombing attack on the convoy. Fog enveloped the convoy on 9 May and although enemy aircraft were detected on radar, none attacked.

Fears that Italian CR.42 biplane fighters could outperform Fulmars led to a trial by the Naval Air Fighting Development Unit, commanded by Lieutenant Commander B Kendall RN. A captured CR.42 was flown against a Fulmar, confirming the CR.42's greater manoeuvrability and rate of climb, and Kendall advised the Admiralty that unless the Fulmar started with an advantage in height, combat with the CR.42 should be avoided. Writing after the war, however, the outstanding RN test pilot, Captain E M Brown CBE DSC AFC RN, was more positive about the Fulmar,[8] having flown both types. He agreed with Kendall that the CR.42 had superior handling qualities but it lacked speed in a dive. The best tactic for the Fulmar, therefore, was to seek height advantage and bring its heavier armament to bear in the high speed gained in a dive. He also believed that the CR.42 was so under-armed that its chances against a robust aircraft like the Fulmar were poor and it often ended up on the defensive. A short burst from the Fulmar's eight-gun armament was sufficient to cause catastrophic damage to the light and unarmoured CR.42.

The scale of attack on the convoy while Force H was escorting it had been less than anticipated, probably because the enemy lacked knowledge of its exact position, but the interceptions carried out by the small number of Fulmars had undoubtedly been a factor.

Attacks on the Mediterranean Fleet had also begun on 8 May and *Formidable*'s fighters engaged a number of He 111s and Ju 88s in poor visibility and intermittent heavy rainstorms. Two Cant Z.1007 flying boats were shot down by Fulmars flown by Lieutenant C W R Peever RN, with Petty Officer F Coston DSM, and Sub Lieutenant (A) A C Wallace RNVR, with Leading Airman Dooley. Lieutenant Peever's aircraft was seen to ditch shortly after the engagement but a search failed to find any trace of the crew. An hour later two He 111s were shot down by Fulmars flown by Lieutenant (A) P S Touchbourne RN with Leading Airman C H Thompson and Lieutenant (A) L S Hill RNVR. Three He 111s were intercepted at 1100 and one of them was shot down by the commanding officer of 803 NAS, Lieutenant J M Bruen RN and his wing-man Lieutenant (A) L S Hill RNVR. All these successes were achieved by sections from 803 NAS but in the afternoon a section from 806 NAS flown by Lieutenant R S Henley RN and his wing-man Sub Lieutenant (A) P D J Sparke DSC**RN intercepted and badly damaged a Ju 88, which was seen to have one of its engines stopped. These successful combats discouraged the enemy but, as in *Ark Royal*, *Formidable* found it difficult to keep sufficient Fulmars serviceable. Many of the nineteen embarked at the outset needed minor repairs or battle damage rectification and her captain wrote that during the bombardment of Tripoli forty sorties had been achieved in a day with the same number of aircraft but now only twenty-four had been achieved.

On 9 May Brown Section of 806 NAS, flown by Lieutenant Henley and Sub Lieutenant Sparke, shot down a Ju 88 and in the afternoon three additional Fulmars were landed on from Malta, collected by *Formidable* pilots flown ashore to fetch them. These were the aircraft flown to Malta as guides for the RAF Hurricanes in Operation Dunlop. Unfortunately, one of them was damaged by crashing into the barrier on landing and another ditched whilst on CAP. At 1515 Force F and the convoy were met by Force A 40nm south of Gozo Island and the force headed east. At 1600 they were reported by a shadower but no air attacks developed until 10 May.

At 1440 on 10 May a Fulmar went over the side while being catapulted and both it and its aircrew, Lieutenant (A) P S Touchbourne RN and Leading Airman C H Thompson, were lost. Shortly afterwards, Khaki Section of 803 NAS, comprising Petty Officer Gardner and Sub Lieutenant (A) Simpson RN, returned having damaged a Ju 88 that was last seen with its undercarriage down and port engine smoking. A second Ju 88 had fled after being attacked. As the afternoon wore on, small numbers of enemy aircraft were detected holding off at heights above the Fulmars' maximum altitude of 16,000ft.[9] When attempts were made to intercept, the enemy withdrew and the two frustrated fighter squadrons ceased flying when night fell at 2130. Almost immediately afterwards enemy aircraft were detected and these split into small groups and singles and flew towards

A Fairey Swordfish parked at a shore base. (*Philip Jarrett collection*)

the convoy to the south-east of Force A. They were turned away by the fleet's box barrage, however, with some bombs seen in the moonlight to fall outside the destroyer screen and there were no hits. This had been the first night attack on the Mediterranean Fleet and Cunningham described it as interesting[10] but by holding Force A down moon from the convoy the enemy's attention had been held by the warships and no harm had been done except a prodigious expenditure of ammunition.

Further south, the 5th Destroyer Flotilla had been detached to bombard Benghazi and was attacked by dive bombers in full moonlight while returning to the fleet. The flotilla escaped damage by adopting a loose formation, zig-zagging drastically and dropping smoke floats as a ruse to mislead the enemy into thinking that they had obtained hits. It was now clear that X Fliegerkorps posed a threat by night as well as day but the lack of further attacks probably showed that the number of enemy pilots capable of night operations was limited.

The enemy's final attack on the convoy happened on the afternoon of 11 May just before it reached X Fliegerkorps's limiting radius of action. Several groups appeared on *Formidable*'s radar and at 1335 Brown Section of 806 NAS, flown once again by Lieutenant Henley and Sub Lieutenant Sparke, the latter with Leading Airman A S Rush, intercepted seven Ju 88s. Sub Lieutenant Sparke closed in to about 20yds from the rearmost enemy aircraft, which burst into flames and crashed. Unfortunately half Sparke's port wing was shot away and although two parachutes were seen from the fleet and the destroyer *Janus* searched the area, nothing

RAF Hurricanes being loaded onto *Ark Royal* by the ship's starboard crane while she is alongside in Gibraltar during March 1941. (*Author's collection*)

but aircraft wreckage was found. The Tiger convoy had emphasised the importance of the embarked fighter squadrons, with many fighter pilots flying for more than four hours on 8 May and a few for more than six, for much of the time in contact with the enemy.

Estimated enemy aircraft losses in air combat during the 'Tiger' convoy were ten destroyed and seven damaged, numbers that were confirmed by a study of German records after the war, although they were actually found to be too low when losses from all causes were included. Against these four Fulmars were lost but gunfire accounted for a further six enemy aircraft certainly destroyed and probably three more that failed to return to their bases. The total enemy casualties were, thus, sixteen aircraft destroyed, three probables and seven damaged. The Tiger convoy only lost one merchant ship, *Empire Song*, carrying fifty-seven tanks, which was sunk by a mine in the Skerki Channel. The remaining ships brought 238 tanks and forty-three RAF Hurricanes to Egypt, a result that vindicated the decision to risk the venture.

Formidable's *part in the Battle for Crete on 26 May*

Formidable's fighter squadrons were significantly under strength by May and this shortage was felt keenly in the battle for Crete. The island was strategically significant. The British had a naval base in Souda Bay and two airfields; its capture would give the Germans a tighter grip on the Eastern Mediterranean that could ease the Afrika Korps' supply problems. *Formidable* had undergone a short refit in Alexandria with virtually all her Fulmars unserviceable and she was unfit for sea until 25 May but by then it was too late for her to have any significant influence on the battle for Crete.

During the fighting ashore on Crete the Mediterranean Fleet was tasked with preventing the enemy from landing troops on the island by sea and, despite the complete lack of air cover, this was accomplished, albeit with a number of ships lost and damaged. Enemy air strikes had, by then, precluded the use of Souda Bay as a forward base and the fleet had to operate from Alexandria 400nm away. Heavy units of the Mediterranean Fleet left Alexandria at noon on 25 May; they included *Queen Elizabeth*, flagship of Vice Admiral H D Pridham-Wippell, now Flag Officer 1 BS, together with *Formidable*, *Barham* and eight destroyers. The plan was to use *Formidable*'s aircraft to strike aircraft on an airfield at Scarpanto and for this she embarked seven Albacores, eight Swordfish and thirteen Fulmars, an air group considerably smaller than her designed maximum and reflecting the desperate shortage of naval aircraft at the time. A CAP was maintained from 1800 until dusk.

At dawn on 26 May the seven Albacores of 826 and 829 NAS were ranged, each armed with four 250lb GP bombs and twelve 40lb GP bombs, for a strike led by Lieutenant Commander Saunt. Three aircraft

RAF Hurricanes ranged on *Ark Royal* ready to be flown off to Malta. They could not be struck down into the hangar and the ship's own fighters could not be operated until they had flown off. Unlike Sea Hurricanes, they have long-range fuel tanks under their wings and tropical filters on the carburettor air intakes under their noses to limit sand and dust ingestion when they are ashore. Unfortunately, this photograph has been folded at some time but it still gives a rare insight into what was involved in a 'club run'. (*Author's collection*)

suffered malfunctions and so only four arrived over the target in semi-darkness at 0505 to dive-bomb the southern side of the airfield. At 0535 four Fulmars of 803 NAS carried out a strafing attack led by the recently promoted Lieutenant Commander Bruen. Two other Fulmars had failed to start. Both attacks achieved surprise, a large fire was started and at least ten aircraft were thought to have been damaged among the thirty-odd Ju 87s and CR.42s on the airfield, although *Formidable* paid a heavy price for this 'pinprick' operation and the wisdom of ordering it has to questioned. The strike aircraft were recovered by 0700, an hour after the first CAP had flown off, and throughout the forenoon enemy reconnaissance aircraft were driven off by interceptions at distances up to 55nm. At 0830 White Section shot down a Ju 88 and a He 111 was shot down by Sub Lieutenant (A) A J Sewell RNVR at 0940. Another Ju 88 was damaged by 806 NAS' new commanding officer, Lieutenant Commander J N Garnett DSC RN, but his engine cooling system was hit by return fire and he was forced to ditch. Another shadower was driven off, apparently damaged. Until 1000 all approaching enemy aircraft had been shot down or driven off, but at 1015 one slipped past the Fulmars, sighted the fleet and reported it.

At 1240 a large group of aircraft was detected by *Formidable*'s radar approaching the task force from the North African coast and other groups continued to appear. Detection ranges showed the enemy to be at high level but there was only one section of Fulmars to counter them and it was too low to gain sufficient height before the fleet opened fire at 1321. They caught some as they withdrew after the attack, one being shot down and two others damaged, but by then it was too late.

At 1324 the first of several waves of Ju 87s carried out a set-piece dive-bombing attack on *Formidable* and she was hit at 1327 by a large bomb that passed through four decks and detonated in the capstan machinery room, starting a fire and forcing the ship to reduce speed to prevent it from spreading aft. Two minutes later a second bomb hit near

HMAS *Perth*, one of the cruisers damaged in the desperate battle for Crete. Note the Walrus stowed on its catapult; it had no hangar and was always exposed to the elements, a factor that complicated its maintenance. (*Sea Power Centre – Australia*)

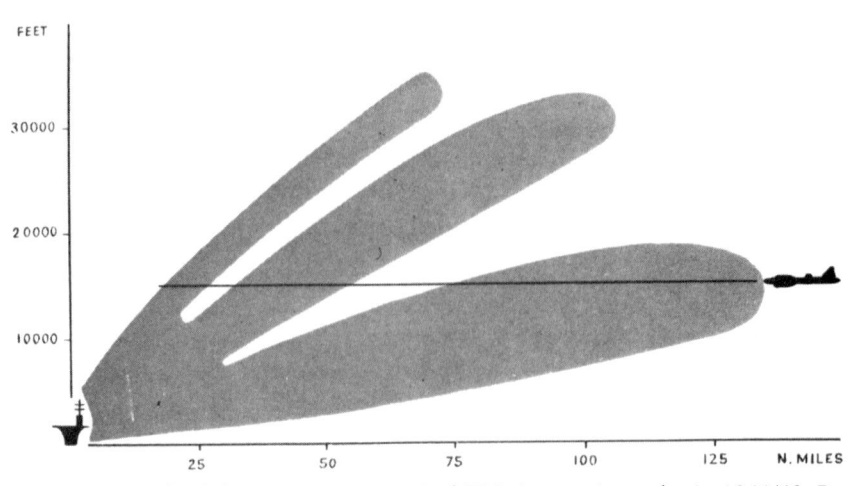

The vertical radar lobe patterns on a typical RN air warning radar in 1941/42. By plotting the ranges at which contacts were first detected then faded and reappeared, fighter direction officers could estimate their altitude with a fair degree of accuracy and position their CAP fighters to intercept them accordingly. (*Author's collection*)

X1 gun turret, passed through the gun bay and out over the side, where it detonated under water close to the starboard propeller, shaking the ship badly. Eleven men were killed and six wounded by these hits. More enemy aircraft attacked but were driven off by the ship's gunfire and in the afternoon high-level bombers attacked the destroyer screen without result. At 0715 on 27 May *Formidable* flew off the few remaining aircraft capable of flying to RNAS Dekheila and entered Alexandria.

Damage to her hull was considerable, particularly aft where the underwater explosion had buckled her side plates, started rivets and bent internal frames and stiffeners, but good damage control arrangements had extinguished the fires in the forward part of the hull promptly. The forward lift was out of alignment, the foremost ammunition conveyor strained and other structural damage made it advisable not to fire the forward 4.5in guns. A large amount of electrical wiring was destroyed and the damage was found to be too serious to repair in Alexandria. Like her sister-ship *Illustrious*, she had to be sent to the USA for repairs and in his covering letter to the action report, Admiral Boyd wrote that:

> the ship was handled admirably during the attack and the defence put up by the gun armament was spirited. The attack was successful because conditions favoured dive-bombing and...aircraft were very difficult to see against a misty blue background...the behaviour of the fighter aircraft was, as usual, beyond praise and their direction by Commander Yorke was admirable.[11]

Fiat CR.42 fighters of the Italian Air Force. (*Author's collection*)

Formidable remained in Alexandria while temporary repairs were effected until 24 July, when she sailed for Norfolk, Virginia, via the Suez Canal with only six Swordfish of 829 NAS embarked for protection on passage. She arrived in Norfolk on 26 August and eventually returned to the Clyde in December.

On 27 May General Freyberg ordered Crete to be evacuated and on the night of 28/29 May 4,000 Commonwealth troops that had been defending the airfield and port at Heraklion were evacuated by warships under Rear Admiral H B Rawlings. All told, operations off Crete during these days cost the Mediterranean Fleet the loss of the cruisers *Gloucester*, *Fiji*, *Calcutta* and the destroyers *Juno*, *Greyhound*, *Kelly*, *Kashmir*, *Imperial* and *Hereward*.[12] *Warspite*, *Barham*, *Formidable*, *Orion*, *Dido*, *Kelvin* and *Nubian* were damaged beyond the capability of repair facilities available in the Mediterranean and *Perth*, *Naiad*, *Carlisle*, *Napier*, *Kipling* and *Decoy* would take some weeks to repair.[13]

The largest evacuation was from Sphakia on the south coast of Crete. It began on the night of 29/30 May and continued for three long and anxious nights. The Luftwaffe failed to intervene by night, however, and it proceeded relatively smoothly. Unfortunately a number of troops arrived too late for the last night's operation and had to be left behind. Some 11,500 troops were evacuated from Sphakia and a grand total of 18,000 reached Egypt out of the 32,000 Commonwealth personnel who had defended Crete.

Formidable being bombed on 26 May 1941. (*Author's collection*)

The loss of Crete was seen at the time as a very severe blow and indeed it was. However, it must not be overlooked that the Germans also learnt a bitter lesson. Of the 23,000 elite troops they had committed to the conquest of Crete, over 5,000 had been killed and at least 2,500 wounded. The actual numbers drowned trying to reach the island by sea may actually have been far greater and were considerably in excess of anything the German High Command had anticipated. Over 370 transport aircraft, gliders and combat aircraft were also lost and Crete proved to be a Pyrrhic victory for the Germans, who proved unable to make full use of the island.

Luftwaffe Ju 87 dive bombers; the type that inflicted considerable damage on both *Illustrious* and *Formidable*. They were actually extremely vulnerable to fighter interception but to break up their attacks successfully the Fleet Air Arm needed numbers of aircraft and in 1941, for a variety of reasons that had been beyond the Admiralty's control, it simply did not have them. (*Philip Jarrett collection*)

The urgent need for more and better naval fighter aircraft

Since the earliest months of the war[14] the need for more and better embarked fighters had been recognised. In January 1941 Somerville forwarded a paper entitled 'Notes on Carrier-Borne Fighter Aircraft' to the Admiralty[15] written by the commanding officer of 800 NAS, Lieutenant R M Smeeton RN. He made the case for a high-performance, single-seat fighter able to fight on more equal terms than the two-seat Skua and Fulmar. Somerville supported Smeeton's argument and drew particular attention to the need for a high rate of climb to eliminate the need for standing fighter patrols.[16] Smeeton stressed that with radar-equipped ships, homing beacons and stable R/T sets, observers were no longer needed in fighters and only detracted from their performance, pointing out that the Fulmar was more manoeuvrable with the rear seat empty.

The Admiralty reply dated 1 May 1941,[17] explained that orders had been placed for the single-seat Blackburn N11/40, later named the Firebrand. This might have been the case but the aircraft proved to be a failure after a protracted period of development.[18] Its designers referred to it as rugged but Captain Eric Brown described it as 'a formidably large aeroplane of extraordinarily robust construction'.[19] In reply, Somerville wrote a second letter[20] saying that N11/40 was not what he and his fighter pilots wanted but by then NAD had published a general memorandum[21] intended to allay what it referred to as 'misgiving in the Fleet concerning the programme of future naval fighter aircraft'. The slow development of naval types led to the interim introduction of the USN F4F

Stills from a gun camera film sequence showing the left-hand aircraft of a pair of Italian SM.79 bombers being hit by fire from a Fulmar of 808 NAS from *Ark Royal*. It catches fire and was subsequently seen to crash into the sea. (*Author's collection*)

Martlet (renamed Wildcat to give commonality with the USN in 1944), followed by the Sea Hurricane and Seafire into service, the latter two adapted from existing RAF fighter designs to hasten their introduction.

Three Sea Hurricanes, which had arrester hooks but non-folding wings, were disembarked from *Furious* to North Front airfield on 1 July 1941 and prepared for sea trials. Two were embarked in *Ark Royal* but Somerville's report was less enthusiastic than one might imagine. He admitted that they were markedly superior to the Fulmar above 12,000ft and could be safely operated from the carrier deck but the fact that their non-folding wings prevented them from being struck down into *Ark Royal*'s hangars because of her small lifts coloured the whole report. Reading the report, it appears that the ship's air department lacked the imagination to use outriggers to park aircraft with their tail wheels well outboard and most of the airframe clear of the deck. This technique was used in *Illustrious*, many USN carriers and by RN carriers in the Home Fleet. The lack of spares for the trials aircraft also drew adverse comment, giving the impression that the ship was mainly concerned with the negative aspects of the new fighter. Under the desperate circumstances in which the RN found itself fighting in mid-1941, this was disappointing.

The first squadron to be equipped with the Grumman F4F Martlet/Wildcat was 802 NAS,[22] commissioned in November 1940. It was to prove itself in the latter half of 1941 during a short but brilliant period of embarked service in the first British escort carrier *Audacity* on the Gibraltar Convoy run. The short-term prospects for a more satisfactory naval fighter were, thus, not quite as black as Admiral Somerville had thought, although there were only 210 aircraft in the first batch of Sea Hurricanes and Martlet/Wildcat deliveries were initially slow to build up. As the war continued, however, British industry had insufficient capacity to meet both RAF and RN aircraft requirements and the RN had to look

A Fairey Fulmar parked at an unknown shore base. (*Philip Jarrett collection*)

increasingly towards USN aircraft types to meet its needs; at first from contract purchases and then from Lend-Lease allocations.

Before 1939 the RAF had rejected the need for long-range fighters, the Air Ministry stating emphatically that there was no requirement for such a type since bombers could defend themselves and the air defence of the UK could be carried out by short-range interceptor fighters. By mid-1941 the lack of British long-range fighters to protect the fleet when no carrier was present had become obvious. The heavy losses suffered by the RN off Crete with no air cover provided by the RAF brought the problem into sharp focus within the Admiralty and in June the Air Ministry was asked to increase the number of long-range fighters in the Eastern Mediterranean where '…our need for long-range fighters remains acute and until they are provided in sufficient numbers, we must continue to expect losses and damage on the present scale when the fleet is at sea'. It will be recalled by those who have read my earlier book *The Dawn of Carrier Strike*[23] that before 1939 the Air Ministry had claimed that carrier-borne aircraft would never need to oppose land-based aircraft and that the RAF would provide whatever aircraft were needed to fight land-based air opposition. The actual experience of war had shown how fatuous this claim had been but no one in Government had thought to question it at the time. Now the Admiralty suggested that fighters could achieve greater range by using external drop tanks or, perhaps, that consideration should be given to developing a composite aircraft that could carry a fighter on the lines of the pre-war Mayo flying boat.[24] Finally, the Admiralty suggested that an immediate joint investigation by naval and air staff officers should be made. One was held in the Air Ministry on 10 July 1941 with ACNS and 5SL, Rear Admiral Lyster present and chaired by the Vice Chief of the

Flown without a rear-seat crew member like this example, the Fulmar was lighter and more manoeuvrable. From 1941 an increasing number were flown in the fighter role without an observer. (*Author's collection*)

Hawker Sea Hurricanes. The type was a basic adaptation of the standard RAF fighter but gave RN fighter squadrons equipped with it a welcome increase in performance. (*Author's collection*)

Air Staff, VCAS. It achieved little to improve an unsatisfactory situation but clarified the positions of the two service ministries. It was agreed that the RAF would do everything in its power to provide long-range fighter support during operations in which the fleet might be in grave danger of enemy air attack from nearby shore bases. The MAP programme was to be re-examined by naval and air staff officers and the Air Ministry undertook to initiate trials in co-operation with Fighter Command and the Home Fleet aimed at improving the technique of RAF fighters being controlled by HM Ships.

A Grumman Martlet taking off. The first examples were purchased from the USA; later aircraft were supplied under Lend-Lease arrangements. (*Philip Jarrett collection*)

6

Disembarked operations by naval air squadrons in 1941

The operations of 830 and 828 NAS from Hal Far in Malta were carried out on a long-term basis and are described in other chapters. Other disembarked squadrons operated on a more temporary basis, often against targets on land.

Disembarked operations by Eagle's *squadrons in the Red Sea*
Nos 813 and 824 NAS had left RNAS Dekheila for Port Sudan in late March led by Commander C L Keighly-Peach DSO OBE RN, *Eagle*'s Commander 'Air', with sixteen Swordfish. Their directive was to search the Red Sea in the vicinity of Massawa and attack any enemy destroyers that were encountered. Cunningham understood from intelligence sources that these warships might attempt a 'do or die' attack on Port Sudan or Suez as soon as their base appeared likely to fall to advancing British forces and on 31 March three of the six Italian destroyers in Massawa sailed to attack Suez. However, one of their number, *Leone*, ran aground on 1 April and its loss so discouraged the others that they returned to harbour.

On 2 April two Swordfish from Port Sudan carrying out an armed reconnaissance bombed an armed trawler and a large merchant ship in Nakra anchorage, hitting the latter. RAF Blenheims of 203 Squadron based in Aden carried out a daily reconnaissance of Massawa and at 1630 on the same day one of its aircraft reported that five destroyers had left Massawa at 1430 heading north. Unfortunately the message was delayed by its passage through the RAF chain of command before it could be acted upon. The destroyers were deemed too distant to ensure a reasonable chance of intercepting them before sunset and it was decided to relocate and attack them at dawn the next morning. By then, the enemy could be close to Port Sudan if this was their objective and it was appreciated that although the plan was logical, it was not risk free.

A Fairey Swordfish at RNAY Fayid. This aircraft, L2818, was at the air yard in October 1941, after which it was issued to 815 NAS. (*Philip Jarrett collection*)

At 0430 on 3 April, half an hour before first light, six Swordfish took off from Port Sudan on a diverging step-aside search designed to cover the possibilities of the enemy either hugging the eastern shore of the Red Sea on passage direct to Suez or avoiding the reefs on an approach to bombard Port Sudan. An additional reconnaissance of Port Sudan's approaches was flown by Commander Keighley-Peach himself and all seven aircraft were armed with six 250lb GP or SAP bombs,[1] as were all subsequent striking forces on that day. At 0511 two destroyers were sighted and reported 28nm east of Port Sudan by one of the search aircraft and its report was decoded in the Fleet Air Arm operations room at Port Sudan within thirty minutes. At about the same time another search aircraft reported four destroyers, all of which had altered from a south-westerly course to a northerly one as soon as they realised that they had been seen. Four Swordfish, including one flown by Keighley-Peach, attacked the group of two destroyers but only achieved several near misses. Another aircraft shadowed the group of four sending constant reports, which enabled a second striking force of seven Swordfish led by Lieutenant A G Leatham RN to attack this group at 0813 using a briefed method in which aircraft attacked targets from either beam and astern with the dive starting at 5,000ft and bombs released at 1,000ft. Aircraft 4H piloted by Midshipman (A) E Sergeant RNVR scored a direct hit on the *Nazario Sauro*, which sank in less than a minute. Other pilots scored near misses on the three other destroyers.

While the remaining three enemy destroyers drew away to the north-east of Port Sudan, a further strike force of five Swordfish led by Lieutenant (E) J L Sedgwick RN found and attacked them at 1010 about 100nm away from the port. The first aircraft to attack was 5C piloted by Sub Lieutenant (A) S H Suthers RN with Midshipman (A) S S Laurie

RNVR as observer and Leading Airman C P H Baldwin as TAG. A hit was achieved on *Danielle Manin*, which was stopped and abandoned, sinking shortly afterwards. Three other aircraft achieved near misses but the fifth aircraft's bombs failed to release. *Cesare Battisti*, which had been damaged, was scuttled off the Arabian coast later in the day.[2] The strike leader remained to shadow the surviving two destroyers, *Pantera* and *Tigre*, until 1100, by which time they were heading 070 degrees at 34 knots, their maximum speed. A further strike force was ready to take off from Port Sudan but it was appreciated that since the enemy's range was opening so rapidly and they appeared to be heading for Jeddah in Saudi Arabia, long-range RAF bombers would be a more appropriate striking force.[3] Both these destroyers were later discovered run ashore and abandoned south of Jeddah by an RAF Wellesley bomber carrying an RN observer. They were bombed by a Blenheim and the destroyer *Kingston* finished them off with gunfire and torpedoes later in the day. *Giovanni Acerdia* was subsequently found sunk across the harbour entrance in Massawa and *Vincenzo Orsini* was bombed by Swordfish in Massawa and later found to have been scuttled there. This small but well-executed operation ended the potential threat posed by Italian destroyers in the Red Sea and on 13 April the two squadrons re-embarked in *Eagle*, which proceeded round the Cape to Freetown.

The Iraq rebellion – 814 NAS disembarked from Hermes

Events in Iraq began to unfold on 31 March 1941 when the Regent was forced to take refuge in the British gunboat *Cockchafer* at Basra. A coup d'état in Baghdad followed on 4 April, staged by the recently superseded pro-Axis Prime Minister Rashid Ali who wanted Axis forces to enter the country to eliminate British influence. On 18 April 1941 a convoy of Indian Army troops arrived in Basra under the terms of a 1930 treaty between the United Kingdom and Iraq that had also allowed the RAF to maintain two air bases, one at Habbaniya, 50nm west of Baghdad, and the other at Shaibah near Basra. The Senior Naval Officer Persian Gulf, SNOPG, had under his command in addition to *Cockchafer* the sloops *Falmouth* and HMAS *Yarra* and these were quickly reinforced by the cruisers *Emerald* and *Enterprise*. The elderly aircraft carrier *Hermes* arrived on 29 April with twelve Swordfish of 814 NAS embarked. These were kept ready on deck to counter any opposition that might be directed at Convoy BP on its passage up river to Basra, while *Hermes* patrolled 80nm south of the Shatt al-Arab.

On 2 May SNOPG ordered *Hermes* to be prepared to disembark her aircraft at short notice for operations from RAF Shaibah if necessary and

Hermes photographed in 1942. The first aircraft carrier to be laid down as such, she was too small and too slow for fleet operations by 1941. (*Author's collection*)

a day later six Swordfish armed with 100lb bombs were flown off to fly over Basra. It was completed without incident and the aircraft landed on with their bombs still in place. On the same day the RAF's Number 4 Flying Training School at RAF Habbaniya, equipped with a miscellaneous collection of aircraft was ordered to commence hostilities against Iraqi forces.

No. 814 NAS flew six Swordfish off *Hermes* at 0510 on 4 May for a transit to Shaibah, where they were refuelled before flying on to attack the Sumana railway bridge over the Euphrates, armed with six 250lb SAP bombs and eight 20lb Cooper bombs. The weather was good and each aircraft made two dive-bombing attacks, dropping the 250lb bombs against the bridge on the first and the 20lb bombs on the guard house at the end of it on the second. No direct hits by 250lb bombs were observed but several of the 20lb bombs hit the bridge. The only opposition came from accurate small-arms fire, which hit every aircraft, although none in any vital spot. After the attack the aircraft refuelled at Shaibah and landed on *Hermes* at 1610. Bridges and railway lines are notoriously difficult targets to destroy and after studying reports NAD minuted that the negligible results from this strike operation were hardly surprising due to the squadron's lack of practice.[4]

Hermes remained 50nm off the Shatt al-Arab but found navigation difficult due to the lack of objects ashore on which to fix a position and sand haze that prevented star sights. It was decided, therefore, that if Swordfish were needed to answer emergency calls for strikes on military objectives, they would be better disembarked to Shaibah. The ship's Air Staff Officer,

Lieutenant Commander H C N Rolfe RN, took six Swordfish, their aircrew and the minimum necessary number of maintenance ratings ashore on 8 and 9 May where, with Admiralty approval, they were placed under the orders of the AOC Iraq. The only bombs available were old, some dating back to the First World War, and Swordfish were armed with a variety of weapons ranging from six 112lb GP and eight 20lb bombs to two 520lb bombs.[5] On 10 May they began offensive operations, disembarking further aircraft from *Hermes* as replacements when inspections fell due and any other maintenance work arose beyond the capacity of the Petty Officer and seven air mechanics who had been taken ashore. On 10 May three Swordfish attacked barracks at Nasariyah, dropping eighteen 112lb and twenty-four 20lb bombs. Another Swordfish patrolled over convoy BP2 as it proceeded upriver. On 11 May three similarly armed Swordfish attacked barracks at Samawa in the morning, and three bombed barracks at Nasariyah in the afternoon. The latter target was attacked again on 12 May by three Swordfish.

On 13 May five Swordfish dropped twenty-seven 112lb, three 100lb AS and forty 20lb bombs on barracks at Amara and on 14 May four Swordfish attacked it again, dropping a total of four 520lb, six 112lb, thirty-two 20lb and six 100lb AS bombs. Samawa Barracks was the target on 15 May with three Swordfish dropping a total of eighteen 250lb and twenty-four 20lb bombs, and on 16 May, in 814 NAS' last strike, twenty-four 250lb and thirty-two 20lb bombs were dropped on petrol and oil tanks in Amara.

The Swordfish had flown 253 hours but the standard of bombing had not been good, over half the bombs falling outside 100yds from their

HMAS *Yarra* in the Persian Gulf. (*Sea Power Centre – Australia*)

intended target, although this was partly due to the different ballistic characteristics of the bombs. Hits were obtained on barrack buildings but on 16 May the AOC decided that there were no important targets left that the Swordfish could reach and they re-embarked on 19 May. Dust storms around Shaibah prevented their flight before that date. Only one aircraft had been lost and the gallant rescue of its aircrew by another Swordfish is worthy of mention.

On 15 May Swordfish H3A was piloted by Lieutenant J H Dundas RN with Sub Lieutenant (A) G R Coy RN as his observer and Leading Airman L E Lasson as TAG. After completing a bombing run over barracks at Samawa they saw a red flare fired by H3B ahead of them. It then made a forced landing close to some shepherds and Dundas carried out a trial approach, which satisfied him that a safe landing was possible on a flat piece of ground near the damaged aircraft. After landing he came under fire from the barracks and the aircraft was hit in the fuel tank. Lasson engaged the approaching Iraqi troops with his Lewis gun and Coy helped the pilot and TAG from H3B into their aircraft. Within two minutes

Lieutenant D C E F Gibson RN standing by the wreckage of a Vichy French MS.406 he shot down during the Syrian Campaign while he was serving in 803 NAS. (*Vice Admiral Gibson via Author*)

of landing, Dundas was airborne again with five people on board, the cloud of dust thrown up by his slipstream helping to confuse the enemy's fire. Fortunately the bullet holes in the fuel tank were above the level of the liquid and there was sufficient fuel to fly back to Shaibah. The C-in-C's report observed that this exploit 'called for skill and courage of a high order'. In the First World War Squadron Commander R Bell-Davies RNAS had rescued a fellow pilot in a similar manner and had been awarded the VC'.[6] Dundas was awarded the DSC and both his crew were mentioned in despatches.

No. 814 NAS's disembarked operations highlighted the need for reliable communications with their parent carrier and at first Rolfe used one of the aircraft's W/T sets to communicate with the ship on 274kc/s, having stretched out its aerial on the ground. Later an RAF mule-pack radio was installed in the squadron office. Both arrangements worked and allowed two-way communications with *Hermes* 120nm away. Shade temperatures had often reached 48° Centigrade and running engine oil temperatures often reached 90°, giving rise to leaks over the fabric that caused the dope to peel off and filters were choked by dust clouds. The service ceiling with a bomb load in these conditions was only 6,500ft. The re-embarkation in *Hermes* on 19 May marked the end of the Fleet Air Arm's contribution to the Iraqi campaign.

Fleet Air Arm involvement ashore in the battle for Crete
Apart from *Formidable*'s brief sortie, Fleet Air Arm involvement in the defence of Crete centred on the activities of personnel from 805 and 815 NAS. Lieutenant Sutton became the second in command on 23 April and did his best to get the airfield and its defences completed by the limited labour force allowed. After the collapse of Greece it was expected that an airborne attack would follow but the speed with which the Germans prepared it came as a surprise. It took them just three weeks to concentrate over 1,300 aircraft and 16,000 airborne troops ready to be dropped or landed in gliders onto Crete. The total naval and RAF fighter strength on 1 May was thirty-six aircraft including 805 NAS' remaining Fulmars, and the squadron's pilots took a share in flying RAF Hurricanes. On 16 May three of them shot down three Bf 109 fighters and a Ju 87 out of an attack on Souda Bay by thirty German bombers escorted by fifteen fighters. Two naval pilots were lost in this encounter, Lieutenant A H M Ash RN and Lieutenant (E) H J C Richardson RN. A third pilot, Lieutenant P F Scott RN, had been lost a day earlier.

Between 16 and 19 May all but seven Hurricanes and Gladiators had been lost in the air or on the ground, despite a reinforcement of ten having

Sub Lieutenant (A) G Denison RNVR of 806 NAS, part of the RN Fighter Squadron, in November 1941 watching an RAF fitter at work on a Hurricane after the unit's re-equipment with the type. (*Author's collection*)

been flown in from Egypt. Fulmars had fought from Maleme and then Heraklion until none were left fit to fly and, with the concurrence of the Prime Minister, the AOC-in-C Middle East[7] ordered the remaining three Hurricanes and four Gladiators to be evacuated to Egypt. There were, therefore, no serviceable British aircraft left in Crete after dawn on 19 May. The German and Italian naval staffs had opposed the operation, which was entrusted to Goering's Luftflotte IV in southern Greece, and they only learned that it had begun when they read decrypted British signals. It was the first time the British Army had opposed an airborne landing on this scale and Maleme's defenders were both short of weapons and only recently evacuated from Greece. Preparations to oppose the landings were incomplete as Commonwealth forces on the island had had seven commanders in the seven months since November 1940. The latest, Major General B C Freyberg VC,[8] had only arrived from Greece three weeks before the battle started.

In a letter to Admiral Boyd written soon after the battle,[9] Lieutenant Sutton described the first few minutes at Maleme after dawn on Sunday, 20 May 1941:

> On the morning of the 20th... an air raid developed at about 0730. This was of great intensity and consisted of machine-gunning and

bombing of defence positions, of the camps (mainly anti-personnel bombs), coastal defence and anti-aircraft gun positions...and then the troop carriers were seen to be over us and swarms of parachutists were dropping...the parachutists were dropping in crowds.

The gliders were the first aircraft to touch down, many crash landed, killing or wounding their occupants, but from those that made reasonably good landings troops sprang out armed with mortars, hand grenades, machine guns and machine pistols ready for immediate action against people in the airfield gun positions. All that day the members of 805 and 815 NAS fought alongside Royal Marines, RAF mechanics and soldiers from New Zealand but more enemy troops arrived in Ju 52 transport aircraft and the turning point came that night when the defenders were ordered to withdraw and regroup with the remaining New Zealand forces to the east.

Sutton wrote that ammunition, stores and undergrowth were set alight by enemy fire and evening came on slowly because of this giant bonfire. He led a group that defended the left flank on foothills of the White Mountains and groups on the seashore were led by Lieutenants (A) A R Ramsay and L K Keith RN. On 24 May a general British withdrawal was ordered and Sutton's group found itself cut off. Ramsay and Keith led their groups to Souda Bay, from where they were evacuated to Egypt in the destroyers *Defender* and *Hero*. Helped by local Cretans, Sutton's group made a gruelling march across the mountains, during which they ate bread and honey, wild cherries, oranges and mulberries. Strict march discipline was kept, stopping for only ten minutes in every hour, and they crossed two separate 7,000ft mountain passes before reaching Sphakia, from where they were picked up by a British warship and taken to Egypt.

Naval aircraft in the Syrian Campaign during June/July 1941
The Vichy French administration in Syria concerned the British Chiefs of Staff because it was feared that they might allow the territory to be used for a German offensive against Egypt and the Suez Canal. As a result, notwithstanding all the other British commitments in the Middle East, they instructed General Wavell, C-in-C Middle East, to prepare an expeditionary force by the first week in June in order to forestall any German attempt to seize Syria. At the time Wavell was primarily concerned with Operation Battleaxe, a British advance intended to relieve Tobruk in which 826 NAS was playing a part.[10] The Mediterranean Fleet had no aircraft carrier operational after the damage inflicted on *Formidable* and so all the available naval air squadrons were disembarked. The Fleet Air

Arm's largest base in Egypt was RNAS Dekheila, commanded by Captain C B Tidd RN, but an air yard for deep maintenance, aircraft assembly and repair was under construction at Fayid. No. 815 NAS had returned to the former with its six remaining Swordfish after withdrawal from Maleme but on 29 May it deployed to Nicosia in Cyprus to support operations in Syria, which were given the overall designation Operation Exporter.

The advance into Syria was due to start on 8 June but 815 NAS was tasked to commence armed patrols to the north of Cyprus and along the Turkish coast immediately with the aim of preventing Vichy French reinforcements being deployed into Syria by sea. On 5 June 803 NAS was deployed from Dekheila to Haifa in order to fly CAP over warships operating along the coast in support of the Army. Two other RN fighter squadrons, 805 and 806 NAS, were not immediately available as they were being re-equipped with Hawker Hurricanes drawn from RAF stocks in Egypt.

On 31 May 1941 an 815 NAS Swordfish located and attacked a small motor vessel off the Syrian coast and daily reconnaissance flights were shared between Swordfish and RAF Blenheims and Beaufighters operating from Lydda in Palestine. Nicosia airfield was described as primitive, maintenance work having to be carried out in the open. Only two torpedo trolleys were available and the weapons were dispersed singly around the perimeter with whatever protection could be improvised. Transport was borrowed from the Royal Army Service Corps and a crane capable

RN air mechanics swinging the propeller of a Hurricane to get its Merlin engine primed ready for start-up as the pilot, dressed in blue reefer jacket and khaki shorts, runs to man it. The aircraft is armed with 250lb GP bombs under the wings and a starter trolley is just visible under the fuselage. (*Author's collection*)

of lifting torpedoes was borrowed from an Australian cavalry unit.[11] Communication with aircraft were carried out using Army W/T pack sets tuned to 6,540k/cs.

The Allied expeditionary force met unexpectedly bitter opposition in June and it was apparent that Vichy French forces had been underestimated, especially with regard to aircraft, and they were supported by a much-depleted X Fliegerkorps and some Italian aircraft based in Dodecanese islands.

Two cruisers, *Phoebe*, flagship of Vice Admiral E L S King, CS 15, and *Ajax*, with four destroyers, left Alexandria on 6 June and were escorted by 803 NAS Fulmars on 9 June when they were attacked by Vichy French Morane-Saulnier M.S.406 fighters. The Fulmars were outmatched, three were shot down and two badly damaged and so immediate arrangements were made re-equip the squadron with Hurricanes with which it returned to Haifa three weeks later. On 10 June 829 NAS deployed six Albacores from Dekheila to Lydda.

Both 829 and 815 NAS operated under the orders of CS 15 and began a series of night strikes against shipping. They were specifically briefed not to attack ships in Beirut harbour, however, as Cunningham hoped to use it soon after its capture. No. 815 NAS also carried out its daily reconnaissance, usually at dawn, to the north and west of Cyprus with occasional searches along the Syrian coast. Strikes never amounted to more than five aircraft armed with either torpedoes or 250lb bombs. The first success came on the night of 12/13 June when five aircraft were dispatched to attack Vichy ships reported off Beirut. Nothing was found in the given position but a sweep to the north located three ships anchored off Djuneh Bay. The largest of these was hit by a torpedo dropped by Swordfish L9733, piloted by Sub Lieutenant (A) A S D Macaulay RN with Sub Lieutenant (A) P A Hall as his observer.[12]

On the evening of 15 June an RAF Sunderland flying boat located the Vichy French destroyer *Chevalier Paul* 75nm north-west of Cape Kormakiti. Unfortunately, there was an air raid on Nicosia airfield when the report was received, delaying the despatch of a Swordfish shadower. A strike force of three torpedo-armed Swordfish took off at 2010 but failed to make contact and returned to Nicosia. While they were away, two Swordfish arrived from Palestine[13] and a further torpedo strike, this time with six aircraft, was made ready by 0100. They took off at intervals from 0130 on 16 June and at 0300 Swordfish L2818, piloted by Sub Lieutenant (A) D A Wise RNVR with Sub Lieutenant (A) J W Neale RN as his observer and Leading Airman S L Boosey as TAG, located *Chevalier Paul* west of Rouad Island, 60nm north of Beirut. Wise carried

Desert air force fighters returned to their landing grounds low and fast to fly their landing patterns inside the anti-aircraft gun defences on the perimeter. This RN Fighter Squadron Hurricane is returning low over the camouflaged operations tent at its landing ground. (*Author's collection*)

out a textbook torpedo attack despite intense anti-aircraft fire and hit his target amidships. He then dropped flares to illuminate it and attracted the attention of three other Swordfish, one of which gained another hit. It was shot down in the process, however, and its crew, Lieutenant (A) M G W Clifford RN and Sub Lieutenant (A) P W Winter RN, were recovered by the Vichy French to became prisoners of war. The loss of the destroyer was subsequently admitted by the Vichy authorities.

Lacking any air cover of its own after 803 NAS' mauling, CS 15's force was open to enemy air attack and on 16 June eight Ju 88s based on Rhodes attacked it and damaged the destroyers *Isis* and *Ilex*. Inadequate fighter resources forced the Allies to choose between fighter cover over the expeditionary force or the naval support on the seaward flank. Unsurprisingly, the former was chosen.

From 16 June shore-based naval air squadrons allocated to Exporter came under the operational control of the HQ RAF Palestine and Transjordan. A day later the dawn Swordfish patrol from Nicosia found that two Vichy French ships seen in the Turkish port of Alanya three days earlier had sailed. One, SS *St Didier*, was believed to be loaded with war materials and it seemed certain that Vichy ships were using Turkish territorial waters to reach Syria. On 20 June an RAF Blenheim north-west of Cyprus sighted the Vichy French destroyer *Vauquelin* and reported it heading east near Castelorizo. A second report an hour later was plotted in the Nicosia HQ and showed a speed of only 12 knots. Seven Swordfish armed with torpedoes took off at 1900 but failed to find anything and returned at 2330.

One of these had to ditch off the coast of Cyprus having run out of fuel. Its crew, Lieutenant (A) M W Rudorf RN, Lieutenant M M Dunlop RN and Leading Airman L W Smith, were all slightly injured but the aircraft was a write-off. At 0840 the next morning *Vauquelin* was relocated approaching Beirut with a strong air escort, too late to be intercepted.[14]

After the German invasion of the Soviet Union it was clear that the Germans had no intention of staging an offensive in Syria but some Luftwaffe assistance to the Vichy French continued. For this reason, Operation Exporter was continued. 806 NAS, now re-equipped with Hurricanes, redeployed from Amariya, near Alexandria to Lydda to provide air defence for CS 15 on 23 June. On 27 June 806 NAS moved to Ramat David airfield in Palestine and on 30 June the Fleet Air Arm squadrons were reorganised to form part of an enhanced effort to stop Vichy reinforcements reaching Syria. Five Albacores of 826 NAS moved to Lydda via Dekheila from the Western Desert and, together with 829 NAS, it moved to Nicosia to augment 815 NAS. Between them the three squadrons had only thirteen serviceable aircraft. At the same time, one flight each from 803 and 806 NAS with their Hurricanes moved from Haifa to Nicosia. They took up residence with the TSR squadrons in a small satellite landing ground 3nm from the main airfield, constructed by the Royal Engineers in only ten days from levelled and rolled agricultural land. A temporary operations room was established in the Police Headquarters at Nicosia and telephone lines were run from it to both the main and satellite airfields. The HQ staff consisted of one RN aircraft controller, one RAF aircraft controller and three cypher officers. Reconnaissance sorties continued to be shared between RN and RAF aircraft and the different types of aircraft employed – Swordfish, Albacores, Blenheims and Beaufighters – were found to complement each other well. Lieutenant Commander J W S Corbett RN,

A pairs take-off by Grumman Martlet IIIs of 805 NAS at Mersa Matruh in late 1941. (*Author's collection*)

the commanding officer of 826 NAS, was placed in overall charge of the satellite field and its activities.

Lieutenant Commander Bolt, who had distinguished himself during the Battle of Matapan, was placed in charge of naval air operations in Cyprus, tasked with preventing Vichy reinforcements and supplies from reaching Syria. Rules of engagement now allowed Vichy vessels in neutral territorial waters to be attacked and on 3 July a patrolling 815 NAS Swordfish attacked an armed trawler in Castelorizo harbour. Its torpedo missed but hit a yacht and fishing vessel nearby and sank them. On 4 July the SS *St Didier* was relocated in Adalia harbour with a deck-load of motor transport and was torpedoed and sunk by aircraft of 829 NAS. At 0815 on 7 July a patrolling 815 NAS Swordfish attacked a Vichy merchant ship west of Cape Khelidonia escorted by three destroyers. Its torpedo narrowly missed but the ship turned away to the west and never reached Syria. Bolt wrote in his report that it would have been preferable for the aircraft that gained contact to shadow the enemy force as it moved east into closer strike range, where a larger striking force could have been homed onto it.

On 11 July 1941 the Vichy authorities asked for a ceasefire and allowed British forces to occupy the whole of Syria. The concentration in Cyprus of all armed sea reconnaissance aircraft had effectively sealed off Syria from all hope of Vichy reinforcement. Nevertheless, Cunningham noted[15] that its success had not been achieved without risk:

it is of interest to note that this comparatively petty campaign absorbed the entire effort of all the reconnaissance aircraft available for naval

A wrecked 805 NAS Martlet III in the desert in August 1941. Like all desert Martlets, it is painted in an overall sand colour. This example was one of the batch of aircraft originally intended for Greece and still bears its original USN BuAir number rather than a British airframe identity. It was later repaired for further service and given the airframe number AX733. (*Author's collection*)

co-operation in the Eastern Mediterranean [ie 201 Group RAF] with the exception of those based on Malta. To achieve the requisite number of aircraft for the Syrian Campaign, all reconnaissance to the west of Alexandria had to be stopped and Tobruk left wide open to surprise. Even so, the available aircraft were insufficient and reliance for coastal reconnaissance had to be placed on the untrained aircraft of the [RAF] Palestine and Transjordan Command.

Operation Exporter had demonstrated that naval air squadrons had inherent mobility and were capable of operating from small, makeshift landing grounds but the lack of fighter cover had limited the movement of naval forces to the hours of darkness and given an enemy of modest size an unacceptable advantage.

Overview of Fleet Air Arm squadrons ashore in late 1941

After operations in Greek and Cretan waters there was a period of comparative calm and the Mediterranean Fleet's main adversary, the Luftwaffe, had become heavily engaged in the German attack on the Soviet Union. The first Malta 'Blitz' period had ended, leaving the Italian Air Force to carry out infrequent raids on the island. There was little activity from the Italian fleet. The position in the Western Desert after Operation Battleaxe remained static, with the Afrika Korps holding a front line just inside the Egyptian border. The logistic supply route around the Cape to Suez was reliable and, for the moment, free from enemy interference, allowing both the big liners to ferry troops and American merchant ships to carry material in addition to British and Allied merchant shipping. Convoys began to build up vast quantities of men and material in Egypt in preparation for a new land offensive, Operation Crusader, being planned for the autumn.

Further west, the Vichy French authorities in Tunisia and Algeria denied the Germans the use of North African ports to offload supplies from Italy, mainly as a result of the considerable pressure brought to bear on them by the US Government. This helped the British offensive from Malta against Axis shipping, which was becoming more effective as the year progressed. Naval air squadrons in the Eastern Mediterranean continued to operate ashore. Nos 803 and 806 NAS with their Hurricanes moved from Palestine to Sidi Heneish to operate over the front line in the desert and gave protection for coastal shipping. No. 805 NAS' Martlets were based at RNAS Dekheila on duties similar to 803 and 806 NAS and these three units were reorganised as a Naval Fighter Squadron in August 1941 under the command of Lieutenant Commander A F Black RN of 805 NAS, although each squadron preserved its own identity. Other

Lieutenant Commander A F Black DSC RN, the commanding officer of 805 NAS, in early 1941. (*Author's collection*)

squadrons ashore included 815 NAS with detachments at Nicosia and Dekheila commanded by the recently promoted Lieutenant Commander Torrens-Spence, and 826 NAS at Ma'aten Bagush using its Albacores as pathfinders and flare-droppers for the RAF Wellington bomber force. No. 775 NAS operated Fulmars at Dekheila and at Hurghada in the Gulf of Suez as a fleet requirements unit and to protect shipping in the Red Sea.

Creation of a naval co-operation group

Admiral Cunningham had complained about the lack of capability displayed by RAF units operating in support of his fleet since the outbreak of war with Italy[16] and his continued requests for a specially trained air force capable of operating effectively over the sea led to a protracted exchange of views between the Admiralty and the Air Ministry. A compromise solution was reached in which 201 Group RAF with its HQ at Alexandria was to be re-formed as 201 (Naval Co-operation) Group with effect from 20 October. The primary function of this group was to operate alongside the Mediterranean Fleet. All disembarked naval air squadrons were placed under the operational control of this group and the group's terms of reference stipulated that, as far as the general situation allowed, as many air units as possible in the Middle East Command were to be trained to operate over the sea in co-operation with the RN. A pool of RN observers was formed to fly in RAF aircraft and, in his autobiography,[17] Cunningham praised the commander of 201 Group, Air Commodore Slatter RAF, who had pre-war Fleet Air Arm experience, for the work of the group.

Naval air squadron operations in the Western Desert

Axis material that reached North Africa was attacked in supply dumps and forward bases by RAF bombers. Their aircrew were not skilled at navigation over the desert, however, and the responsibility for target location and illumination in these raids devolved onto naval TBR squadrons working from forward airfields in the Western Desert, who excelled at the task.[18] Their Albacores were particularly well-suited to the task because they were quiet in the dive with the propeller in coarse pitch, the crew had good all-round visibility and the observers' skills in wind-finding and over-sea navigation proved particularly relevant. The desert was very akin to the sea in this respect and the ability to navigate accurately, together with skill in flare dropping, acquired during intense training, led to a remarkable ability to find, identify and illuminate assigned targets at a pre-arranged time for the RAF night bomber force. That force came to rely more and more on naval squadrons for this task, especially 826 NAS, commanded by Lieutenant Commander J W S Corbett RN, which has a fair claim to be the initiator of the 'Pathfinder' techniques used later in the war by RAF Bomber Command over Germany. Its Albacores had their under surfaces painted matt black and in most sorties anti-aircraft fire only started after attacks had been completed. After recognising the Albacore crews' skills, the AOC-in-C Middle East issued orders to the Wellington squadrons that they were only to attack targets when naval aircraft were available to find and illuminate the target for them.

A Fulmar being prepared for flight from an airfield ashore. (*Author's collection*)

British warships and supply vessels running stores to the besieged garrison of Tobruk were vulnerable to enemy air attack and a proportion of the sorties flown by 803, 805 and 806 NAS provided CAP over coastal movements. The three squadrons were based at Sidi Heneish landing ground 20nm south-east of Mersa Matruh, operating alongside 73 and 274 RAF Squadrons and 1 Squadron South African Air Force as part of 201 Group. No. 805 NAS' Martlets were part of a batch of thirty bought by the Greek Government but transferred to the RN when Greece fell. They were similar to the USN F4F-3 with fixed, rather than folding, wings, which made them less suitable for embarked operation. They were brought from Greece in crates to RNAY Fayid, where they were assembled and an American pilot, Lieutenant Commander Cooper USN, was sent to assist with flight testing. Apparently he flew one operational sortie with 805 NAS on 23 July 1941, four and a half months before the USA entered the war. RN fighter pilots had very little time to convert onto these aircraft and on the day that Lieutenant Commander Cooper flew his operational sortie, 805 NAS had been working up at Fayid but was ordered to fly to Sidi Heneish with the utmost urgency, refuel and then proceed to provide CAP over the fleet under the control of fighter direction officers in *Valiant*. Great credit is due to Cooper for playing his part in getting the squadron into action. Several aircraft were vectored to intercept radar contacts on unidentified aircraft, known as 'bogeys', but none were engaged. Inexperience and high fuel consumption at full throttle led two pilots to run out of fuel and ditch before reaching land. One of them, Lieutenant (A) P R E Woods RN, was lost; the other, Sub Lieutenant (A) R Bryant RNVR was located the following morning in his dinghy and rescued.

The RN Fulmar Flight's aircraft were no match for the Luftwaffe Bf 109F and Italian Fiat G.50s operated by the enemy in Cyrenaica and so they

Images of RN Fighter Squadron Hurricanes in flight are rare so this photograph is worthy of inclusion even though it is of poor quality. Note the tropical sand filters under their noses. (*Author's collection*)

were deployed to Burghada, where they operated as night fighters against long-range bomber attacks on Allied shipping in the Gulf of Suez. On the opening of the Crusader offensive in November, however, the flight moved to Fuka, one of a group of airfields south-east of Mersa Matruh, to give day and moonlight night cover to shipping. As well as shipping CAP, the Naval Fighter Squadron assisted RAF fighters in defending the desert air bases at Fuka, Sidi Barrani, Mersa Matruh and Ma'aten Bagush. Cover was also given to British tactical reconnaissance aircraft operating over the desert and for occasional day bombing raids. Periodical offensive fighter sweeps were also carried out but due to the superior performance of enemy fighters these had to be at least at squadron strength. In general the cover given to shipping was effective but the fighters were sometimes hard pressed. On 21 August eighteen RN, RAF and SAAF Hurricanes and Tomahawks on CAP over shipping near Sidi Barrani saw nineteen Bf 110s and ten Ju 87s together with a formation of He 111 bombers escorted by twenty-five Bf 109F fighters. None of the ships were hit by bombs but two Hurricanes and a Tomahawk were lost for the destruction of a single Bf 110. The aim had been achieved but clearly a more effective fighter was urgently needed.

The RN Fighter Squadron was involved in a number of air combats. In one of these on 28 September Sub Lieutenant (A) R W M Walsh RNVR, in a Martlet of 805 NAS, was escorting a force of eighteen Maryland bombers when he had three separate fights with a formation of Fiat G.50s. In the first of these he shot down his opponent, which broke up in the air and was later confirmed as a 'kill'. When 201 Group was re-formed in October the RN Fighter Squadron came under its control whenever it was engaged in the protection of shipping. On 14 November, 803 and 806 NAS Hurricanes advanced with other elements of what was now designated the Desert Air Force. These two naval air squadrons moved first to Landing Ground LG 109 at Bit Khasa, then on 19 November to LG 123 5nm north-west of Fort Maddalena. On 11 December they moved to Tobruk.

The TSR squadrons needed mobile logistic support for their desert operations and by the Autumn of 1941, 826 NAS had acquired twenty-five 3-ton lorries for the general transport of personnel, tents and stores; three petrol bowser lorries, three radio vans, one van that acted as a mobile HQ and three workshop lorries. A collection of Army, RAF and RN vehicles brought up bombs, flares, ammunition and other consumable stores. As an example of the operations undertaken, the squadron's 'X' Flight with six new Albacores had arrived at Ma'aten Bagush on 31 July together with its vehicles and baggage. In the next two weeks it undertook thirty-four night bombing sorties in which 18 tons of bombs were dropped on targets, mostly in the Bardia area and including barracks, MT workshops, supply dumps and dispersed aircraft on forward landing grounds. It worked sometimes in co-operation with the RAF Blenheims of 113 Squadron and on three occasions carried out torpedo attacks on shipping in Bardia harbour, having received good warning of their presence from intelligence sources. On 15 August an Italian supply submarine was expected to berth at Bardia and so five more Albacores of 'Y' Flight joined the other half of the squadron at Ma'aten Bagush. Three of these carried torpedoes and the remainder sixteen flares and two 500lb bombs each. Two RAF Blenheims joined this small strike force. A large explosion from the one torpedo dropped against a vessel alongside was observed but enemy records did not reveal any loss that night. In fact the submarine in question, *Atrope*, had been delayed and did not arrive until twenty-four hours later. This could have been deliberate as it was later discovered that the enemy[19] had taken note of the regularity with which attacks on the Bardia harbour coincided with the arrival of anxiously awaited supply ships. Attacks on Bardia were always dangerous because enemy searchlight control was good and anti-aircraft fire both heavy and accurate. No. 826 NAS thought afterwards that the shiny torpedoes under its Albacores had been of assistance to the enemy in holding searchlight beams onto aircraft as they attacked; the matt black of their lower fuselages was much more difficult for them to detect and track.

On 18 August the whole squadron moved back to RNAS Dekheila but one flight returned to Ma'aten Bagush two days later to co-operate with 113 Squadron in bombing attacks on enemy aircraft on their landing grounds behind the front line at Sollum. By 26 August 826 NAS was operating with twelve aircraft again with most of its promised new transport, but it was still

An 826 NAS Albacore being loaded with 250lb bombs at a desert landing ground. (*Author's collection*)

dependent on the RAF for domestic services and communications. Between 17 August and 16 September a further seventy-seven sorties were flown. Most were of four-and-half to six-and-a-half hours' duration and 47 tons of bombs together with over 400 parachute flares were dropped. Intelligence sources subsequently assessed that considerable damage had been done to enemy aircraft on the ground at Tmimi, Gazala, Martuba, Gambut and Menastir landing grounds, which were respectively 170, 150, 200, 85 and 55 miles from Sidi Barrani, the forward refuelling base. Altogether thirty-six enemy landing grounds were 'visited' by 826 NAS' Albacores, although only two aircraft were fitted with the long-range tanks that allowed them to reach the more distant ones. Modestly, Lieutenant Commander Corbett described these operations as 'reasonably successful' in his action report. He ascribed success to his squadron's previous knowledge of Cyrenaican territory, the development of flare-dropping skills and the suitability of the Albacore for night flying and bombing. He also drew attention to the experienced aircrew in the squadron and added that the moon helped aircraft to find the rough position of selected targets but that flares were the only means of identifying them positively.

The first 'pathfinder' mission was carried out on 6 September 1941 when two Albacores, each carrying twenty-four flares, successfully illuminated Martuba landing ground for an attack by six RAF Wellington bombers. On another night a target search with flares was successfully carried out. Torpedo attacks were rare, but could still be ordered at short notice and half the RN Mobile Aircraft Torpedo Maintenance Unit, MATMU, based in Egypt was attached to the squadron in September. Aircraft serviceability averaged 75 per cent, a high figure given the circumstances, and Lieutenant Commander Corbett put this down to the fact that the Albacores were new, the ground crews were experienced and excellent assistance was provided by Mr Mossman, the representative of the Bristol Aeroplane Company that made their Taurus engines. Maintenance was also helped by the fact that it was carried out in the day, most flying being done at night. No. 826 NAS usually operated in two flights; an operational one in the desert and one in maintenance at RNAS Dekheila. After every sixty hours flying, each aircraft was flown back to Dekheila for an inspection and crew rest while a replacement was flown forward.

Dive-bombing was practised intensely by day to determine the correct angles of dive, pull-out and height of release for operational sorties carried out at night. On average, aircrew flew about thirty-five to forty operational hours a month, with another five in training. Time was still found, however, to coach squadron ratings in subjects they needed for their advancement to higher rates. It is very clear that high morale and a

An Albacore of 821 NAS at RNAS Dekheila. (*Author's collection*)

keen offensive spirit motivated 826 NAS and added to the effectiveness of its operations. By the time the Crusader offensive began on 18 November the squadron could genuinely be described as ready for anything.

By then it had flown 249 sorties in the desert campaign, dropped 127 tons of bombs, 1,389 parachute flares and eight torpedoes, all in night operations. It had also illuminated targets for bombardment by warships, spotted their fall of shot and carried out trials of the effectiveness of dive-bombing for the destruction of minefields in the desert. The 250lb GP bomb fitted with an N.1 fuse and rod adaptor was used for the latter and was found to be 50 per cent effective in detonating mined areas. The only casualty had been Leading Airman L P E Porter, a TAG, who was killed by anti-aircraft fire on 27 September 1941. No aircraft were lost but four were damaged by anti-aircraft fire, one of which had to be sent back to RNAY Fayid for repair. On a lighter note, 826 NAS had been forced to borrow two marquees, tables, chairs, cooking utensils and galley stores from the RAF, but had brought RN cooks and stewards with it from Dekheila. Their cooking and meal preparation skills were much better than those to which the RAF aircrew had been accustomed and a deal was therefore struck; the RAF did not want its equipment back if it could eat RN food! No. 826 NAS was also noted for preserving naval customs and traditions, even in the harshest desert environment.

No. 815 NAS continued to provide anti-submarine patrols from Cyprus after the Syrian Campaign but by September only one flight continued with this task while the other returned to Dekheila to re-equip with Albacores for operations in the Western Desert alongside 826 NAS. Once converted, they flew anti-submarine patrols in the Alexandria area together with the disembarked catapult flights from the battleships *Queen Elizabeth* and *Valiant*. At the end of September the disembarked naval air squadrons in the Middle East comprised six Swordfish of 815 NAS in Cyprus and eight Albacores at Dekheila; twelve Albacores of 826 NAS at Ma'aten Bagush; the RN Fighter Squadron with twenty-four Hurricanes and ten Martlets at Sidi Heneish and the RN Fulmar Flight at Burghada in the Gulf of Suez.

Logistics remained critical to both sides in the desert war and British efforts to cut off the Axis forces had been increasingly successful in September and October. In the latter month alone, 60 per cent of all enemy shipping destined for ports in Tripolitania and Cyrenaica was sunk or damaged in attacks by submarines, aircraft and surface warships. Only 18,000 tons out of 50,000 tons shipped by the enemy reached a Libyan port and on 18 October all Axis sea transport to North Africa was suspended. It resumed in November and an attempt was made to run a heavily escorted convoy of seven merchant ships to Tripoli and a smaller one from Brindisi to Benghazi. A reconnaissance Maryland sighted the first of these 150nm east of Malta and Force K, comprising the cruisers *Penelope* and *Aurora* together with the destroyers *Lance* and *Lively*, successfully intercepted it on 9 November, sinking every merchant ship and one of the escorting destroyers. The second convoy was attacked by Malta-based aircraft just as it was leaving the Adriatic and it turned back to Navarino. Unfortunately, these disasters for the Axis were apparently the catalyst that led Hitler to order more U-boats to be transferred to the Mediterranean. He also ordered the transfer of an entire additional Fliegerkorps from the Russian front to Sicily, Greece and Crete where, together with X Fliegerkorps, it formed Luftflotte 2. A second blitz on Malta began in December intended to neutralise the island's offensive capability. Hitler declared that the Mediterranean was 'the decisive area for the future conduct of the war'.

British bombing attacks were made on the small port of Derna and its outlying petrol, ammunition and stores dumps. The weather in late 1941 was often bad with low cloud making bombing conditions difficult for both Albacores and Wellingtons. No. 826 NAS operated under the direct control of HQ Middle East, which instructed it to attack specific, small targets at, or near, Baria, Gambut, Gazala, which was the main German fighter base, and Tmimi, which was the main German dive bomber base. The latter was about 170nm west-north-west of Sidi Barrani. From 13 November air strikes began to shift from attacks on logistics to exerting pressure on the enemy's land and air forces to divert attention from the imminent offensive. Enemy bombers and transport landing grounds at Benina, Derna, Barce and Berka as well as Tmimi were attacked by Wellingtons in daylight, as well as Martuba, Gazala and Gambut landing grounds. The Albacores continued the strikes after dark, allowing the enemy no respite.

Two days before Operation Crusader started, on 16 November, ten Albacores concentrated on illuminating Tmimi and Gazala airfields for attacks by Wellingtons. These operations proved so successful that the enemy was taken completely by surprise when Crusader began. The secondary aim had been to entice German fighters into action but they mostly stayed on the ground, probably due to their shortage of fuel. When Crusader began the British 8th Army attacked on a broad front but confused fighting followed and by 24 November the issue hung in the balance. The Mediterranean Fleet played a part with bombardments on the Halfaya area and was at sea on 20 November to divert the attention of enemy air forces from the land battle. At 1700 it was attacked by five He 111 bombers, which were driven off by the RN Fulmar Flight, which was now based at Fuka. On 24 November the fleet was at sea again searching for enemy convoys when the battleship *Barham* was hit by torpedoes fired by U-331 at 1630. She capsized and blew up in less than five minutes, with 862 men lost and 450 rescued.[20]

During the critical first weeks of Crusader naval air squadrons were heavily committed to a number of tasks. No. 826 and one flight of 815 NAS at Ma'aten Bagush spotted for cruiser bombardments and attacked targets by night that were designated by the Western Desert Air HQ. The second flight of 815 NAS redeployed to Dekheila, where its six Swordfish flew day and night anti-submarine patrols and the RN Fighter Squadron escorted day bombers besides flying CAP over airfields. The RN Fulmar Flight's six aircraft protected shipping between Alexandria and Tobruk and the Walrus, Fulmars and Swordfish of 700 NAS at Dekheila and Aboukir flew protection missions over shipping between Egypt, Cyprus, Syria and Palestine.

In addition to their attacks on airfields, 815 and 826 NAS flew thirty-seven sorties against enemy units located at landing grounds at Sidi-Omar, Sollum, Bardia and Gambut; squadron flying programmes were integrated as they both used the same landing ground. No. 805 NAS moved to Ma'aten Bagush in December to protect shipping on the Alexandria to Tobruk run. It also provided fighter cover for the fleet while it was within the Martlets' radius of action.

No. 803 and 806 NAS became completely integrated into the desert fighter force, carrying out fighter sweeps, close support for Blenheim and Maryland bombers, ground strafing and searches for German armoured columns, whose identification always proved difficult and movements uncertain. This was apparently because they often used captured British tanks that had been abandoned when they ran out of fuel.[21] Both squadrons operated from LG 109 at Bir Khamaa and LG 123 near Fort Maddalena and occasionally they were intercepted by enemy Bf 109F fighters, whose

An Albacore dropping a torpedo under ideal conditions. (Philip Jarrett collection)

superior dive and zoom tactics made them difficult to fight. Mutual support proved effective, however, and only one Hurricane was lost while giving close cover to Maryland bombers. It was flown by Lieutenant Cox RN, who was subsequently learnt to have been taken prisoner.

Periods at LG 123 were liable to sudden interruption by enemy armoured battle groups, which forced a hurried departure to the east. This happened on 24 November when enemy tanks moving towards Fort Maddalena forced all the fighter squadrons using LG 123 to move back to LG 128, 20nm to the east, in the half light of a desert evening. The two naval air squadrons, among others, failed to find 128 but managed to land successfully on a salt pan near a RASC Officers' Mess,[22] where it was reported that 'the hospitality extended was of a very high order and the pilots had their best meal for 10 days'.

On the next day the squadrons returned to LG 123 and on their arrival Lieutenant R L Johnston RN, the commanding officer of 806 NAS, was ordered to take off immediately to locate the German armoured column responsible for the sudden exodus on the previous evening. When flying low over tanks 20nm to the north of the landing ground that he had thought to be friendly, his aircraft was hit by anti-aircraft fire and he was forced to land nearby. He was taken prisoner but three hours later he escaped during a bombing attack by RAF Blenheims. He was soon joined by a British Army officer who had also been taken prisoner and managed to return to 806 NAS later in the day, only to find it on the point of evacuating LG 123 once again after a report that it was about to be overrun.

This time 803 and 806 NAS moved back to Sidi Heneish, where they stayed the night. Only five of their Hurricanes were serviceable but three more were made fit for action before daylight. For the next five days every

Airfields used by RN aircraft ashore

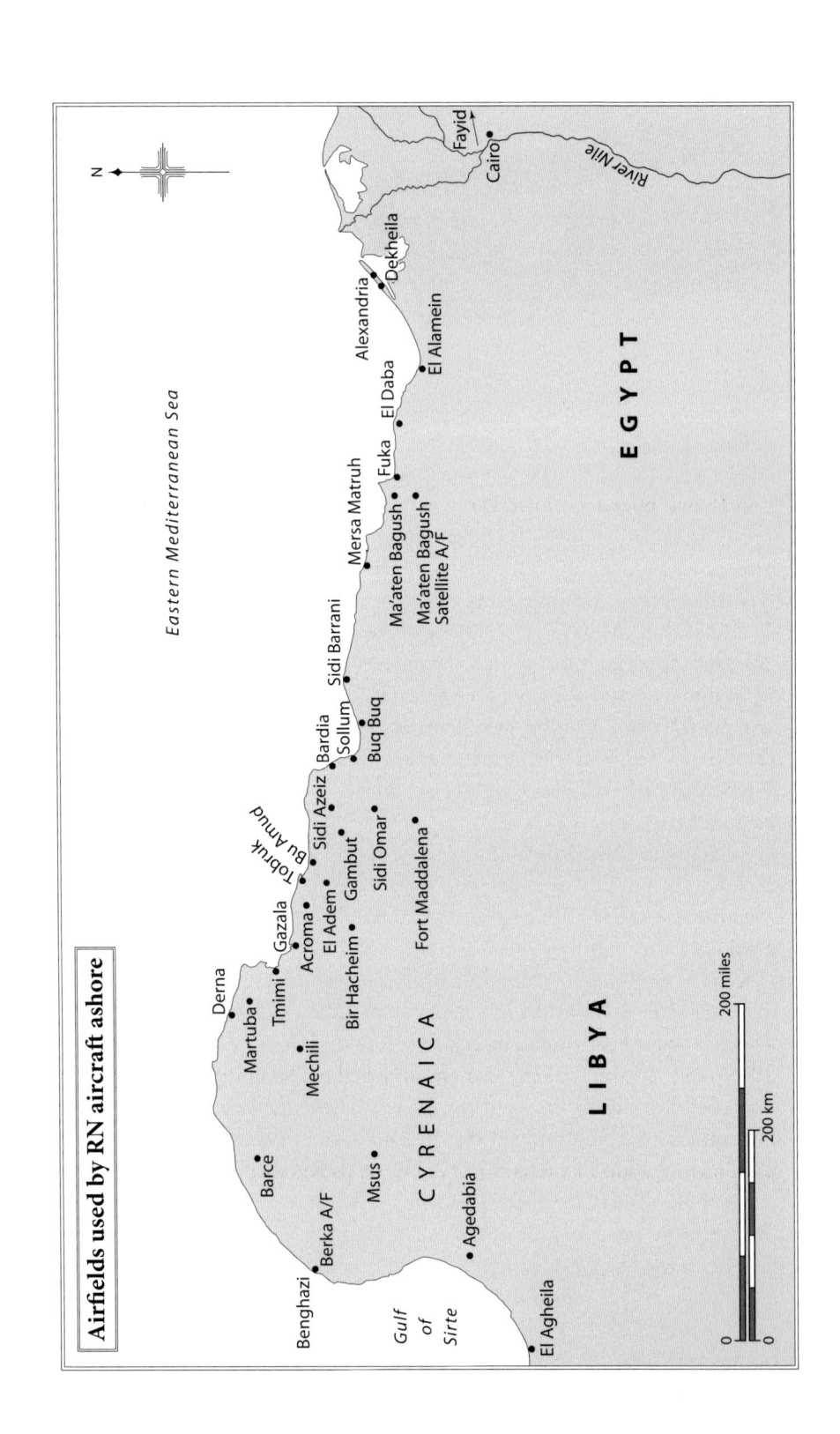

available aircraft was pressed into service and the squadrons returned to LG 123. They provided escorts for RAF bombers attacking Sidi Rezegh, which had changed hands five times during three weeks' fighting. Fort Capuzzo was also attacked and patrols were flown over the Gambut/Tobruk area. On all these missions RAAF Tomahawk fighters flew top cover and in a typical mission twelve Hurricanes of 803 and 806 NAS operating from LG 123, with a squadron of Tomahawks providing top cover on a sweep east of El Adem, encountered a squadron of Ju 87s escorted by Bf 109Fs. Two Hurricanes were shot down, the pilot of one of which, Lieutenant (A) W J Pangbourne RNVR of 806 NAS, was killed. The pilot of the other, Sub Lieutenant (A) P N Charlton RN, got back to the landing ground a day later, where he was able to report that he had shot down two or possibly three Ju 87s and had been about to attack a fourth when he was shot down by a Tomahawk pilot who mistakenly identified him as an enemy. After baling out he was rescued by a British tank crew and, since he was operating as part of the Desert Air Force, he was subsequently awarded the DFC.

At 0815 on 1 December eight naval Hurricanes were on patrol in the El Duda area with twelve RAAF Tomahawks as top cover when nine Ju 88s with a close escort of Fiat G.50s and Bf 109Fs were encountered. The Ju 88s immediately jettisoned their bombs, dived with their escort to ground level and made off to the west. They were followed down by the Hurricanes while the Tomahawks engaged their escort. In the low-level chase that ensued, Lieutenant H P Allingham RNR shot down a Ju 88 and was then attacked himself by a G.50, which he also shot down, seeing it crash in flames. Sub Lieutenant (A) G Dennison RN closed in on another G.50 and saw it spin into the ground during a steep turn before he could fire a round at it. Sub Lieutenant (A) H S Diggins RN claimed to have chased and shot down a third G.50.[23] Three other enemy aircraft were considered to have been damaged in this very successful action. Later in the day news was received that a Bf 109F claimed as damaged by Sub Lieutenant (A) A R Astin RNVR a week earlier had now been confirmed as destroyed. Altogether, between 22 November and 1 December the RN Fighter Squadron had flown 148 operational sorties, resulting in five enemy aircraft destroyed, three probably destroyed and four damaged for the loss of four Hurricanes but only one pilot missing, Sub Lieutenant (A) A J C Willis RNVR.

From 18 December, however, the naval Hurricane squadrons were employed on convoy protection operations, a task that had grown in proportion to the lengthening British advance towards the west. They had fought a total of at least twenty-two individual air combats during Crusader. On 7 December 1941[24] General Rommel, faced with a possible disaster because of his lack of supplies, especially fuel, withdrew the Afrika Korps to Gazala, where it could take up a defensive position of some strength.

The relief of Tobruk and the withdrawal to the west by the Afrika Korps allowed landing grounds that had been captured to be operated by the Desert Air Force. The RN Fighter Squadron moved to Tobruk on 11 December and on 17 December 815 and 826 NAS moved to Bu Amud from Ma'aten Bagush. No. 805 NAS moved from Sidi Heneish to Ma'aten Bagush. On 18 December, operational control of the naval fighter squadrons was transferred to 201 Group and they concentrated on protecting convoys to Tobruk.

On 28 December a single Martlet of 805 NAS flown by Sub Lieutenant (A) R Griffin RNVR was on CAP over Convoy ME 8 when it was attacked by four Italian torpedo-armed SM.79s. He shot down one, forced two more to jettison their torpedoes and drove off the fourth. Sadly, he was killed in this last combat, probably by the rear gunner of the enemy aircraft as he broke away. His aircraft was one of the thirty ex-Greek F4F-3 Martlets that still carried its original USN BuAer[25] number 3895 and it was last seen diving vertically into the sea 50nm north of Ras el Milh. In the *London Gazette* of 10 March 1942 it was announced that Griffin had been posthumously mentioned in despatches for his gallant defence of the convoy.[26]

Albacores attacked retreating enemy columns and armoured formations by night, bombed enemy airfields, harbours, road junctions and, on two occasions, assisted the gunboat *Aphis* in coastal bombardments by illuminating her targets and spotting the fall of shot. When 803 and 806 NAS had arrived at Tobruk they had found the airfield covered in shell splinters, a serious menace to aircraft tyres. Anti-aircraft gunfire almost every night added to the problem but the solution was to employ Italian

No. 826 NAS aircrew preparing for a sortie as dusk approaches. Note the officer wearing a khaki bush jacket who has a Fleet Air Arm scarf around his neck. Days in the desert were hot, while flying at night could be cold. (*Author's collection*)

prisoners of war from a camp near El Adem to pick up the splinters by hand every day. Military Police required a squadron representative to sign for them every morning and on one occasion the number returned exceeded by one the number signed for. The Squadron Diary noted that this was the only time that it had taken a prisoner of war! After four months of desert warfare, during which water had been in short supply, most officers and ratings had grown beards and their staple diet had been bully beef eaten with hard ship's biscuits. The relief of Tobruk meant that they could go on board warships in the harbour to have a shower and their menu was relieved by the arrival at the airfield of a quantity of tins of Maconochie Army ration beef and vegetable stew. These had enjoyed a colourful history, having been captured by the Germans in Crete, shipped to the Afrika Korps in North Africa and recaptured by the 8th Army at a desert supply dump during the Crusader offensive.[27]

In early December the Swordfish flight of 815 NAS had ASV radar fitted at Dekheila, after which it moved to Fuka and Burg-el-Arab later in the month to fly twenty-five night anti-submarine patrols. The Albacore flight flew thirty-three operational sorties in December from Sidi Barrani and Ma'aten Bagush, bombing targets at night and spotting for bombardments. It dropped 14 tons of bombs. Aircraft of 826 NAS flew 133 operational sorties totalling 867 flying hours from Sidi Barrani and Ma'aten Bagush, dropping 93.5 tons of bombs and 1,307 flares.

The RN Fighter Squadron flew 160 sorties from LG 123 and Fort Maddalena in the first half of December and 177 sorties from Tobruk in the second half. No. 805 NAS operated from Sidi Heneish in the first half of the month and Ma'aten Bagush in the second.

Officers of 826 NAS outside their desert accommodation. (*Author's collection*)

7

Force H and the reinforcement of Malta

During June 1941 four ferrying operations to reinforce Malta with RAF Hurricanes were carried out, bringing the island's fighter defences to a level never previously achieved. *Victorious* delivered crated RAF Hurricanes to Gibraltar and then, after they had been assembled, joined *Ark Royal* in ferrying them to Malta in Operation Tracer. She had also brought out 825 NAS with ASV-fitted Swordfish to replace 820 NAS in *Ark Royal* and took the latter unit back to the UK. Later in June *Ark Royal*'s 818 NAS was replaced by 816 NAS, also equipped with ASV Swordfish, which was ferried out in *Furious*.

By this time the enemy was well aware of 'club run' methods and so Somerville considered that for the intensive ferrying programme due to be carried out in June on the orders of the Prime Minister, a change should be devised to allow the aircraft to be flown off from a position as far to the west as possible. The use of RAF Blenheims, staged through Gibraltar, as guides was suggested to both the Admiralty and Air Ministry, approved and the requisite aircraft promised. Dismantled Hurricanes in crates were

Ark Royal flying off Hurricanes. One of their guiding Blenheim bombers can just be seen in the top right of the photograph above *Renown*. (Author's collection)

taken to Gibraltar in one carrier and assembled by a special working party, which started during the latter stages of the voyage. Assembly on a metal ship meant that the aircraft compasses could not be set to work and they could not, therefore, fly an accurate course. The delivery carrier and the ferry carrier were connected by a wooden ramp laid between their flight decks while they lay alongside in the dockyard, across which the assembled fighters were wheeled by handling parties.

Ferry operations to Malta in May and June 1941

Date	Operation	Carriers	nm to Malta	Guides	Hurricanes
21.05.41	Splice	Furious Ark Royal	420	5 Fulmars	47 1 crashed
06.06.41	Rocket	Furious Ark Royal	550	8 Blenheims	43 1 lost
14.06.41	Tracer	Victorious Ark Royal	570	4 Hudsons	43 1 lost*, 3 crashed
27.06.41	Railway I	Ark Royal	480	4 Blenheims	21 1 crashed landing
30.06.41	Railway II	Furious Ark Royal	560	6 Blenheims	35 1 crashed

* The pilot of this aircraft was described at the time as having deserted.[1]

While it was undoubtedly a practical idea, the introduction of RAF aircraft flying from Gibraltar as guides complicated the ferry operations since the multi-engined guide aircraft had to fly up to 500 miles over the sea in darkness before reaching the carriers' briefed position ready for the Hurricanes' take-off at first light. This meant homing them by radar or by the use of transmissions from the aircraft that were picked up by the fleet's direction finders. Both methods gave enemy listeners a good idea of the force's position and what was happening but, overall, the scheme worked as intended. However, given the unprecedented distances flown over the sea by single-seat Hurricanes following an unfamiliar carrier take-off at first light, it is hardly surprising that losses and accidents occurred.

Operation Railway II showed the serious consequences that could follow a take-off error. As the second aircraft in *Furious'* accelerated down the deck, the pilot failed to correct a swing to port and his overload tank hit the ship's port navigating position, detached and burst into flames among the personnel in it. The aircraft crashed over the side and a destroyer recovered the pilot, who was unharmed but not named in the

An 808 NAS Fulmar taking off from *Ark Royal* with a partially spread Swordfish in the background. (*Author's collection*)

ship's action report. Among those enveloped in flames were all the RAF pilots who, while waiting for their own aircraft to be ranged, had decided to watch the first range fly off. Several of these, together with a number of RN and RAF officers and ratings, were very badly burned. A total of fourteen men died, among them several RN aircrew who had also been watching the Hurricanes take off. These included Sub Lieutenant (A) J G Biddle RN, Sub Lieutenant (A) A F Hallett RNVR, Sub Lieutenant (A) C D Livingstone RN and Sub Lieutenant F W Follows RN of 816 NAS, together with Sub Lieutenant (A) O M Wightman RN of 807 NAS.[2] The fire was quickly extinguished and *Furious* was then able to launch the remainder of the first range. The carrier's sea-going and flying efficiency were not affected but the last range of six Hurricanes could not be flown off as their pilots were among those injured by the fire. In his report Somerville wrote that 'the promptness with which the flying-off of the first flight of Hurricanes was re-commenced and successfully completed after the accident reflects great credit on the ship and especially on Commander M Cursham RN, her Commander "Air" who was himself suffering from burns and shock'.

There were other instances of exceptional courage in these June operations, among them Pilot Officer Barnes RAF, who suffered a burst oil pipe in his Hurricane after taking off from *Ark Royal* and who then made, at his second attempt, a successful emergency landing on *Furious* despite having no arrester hook or prior deck landing training.

During June *Ark Royal* usually disembarked some of her Fulmars to the airfield at North Front for the protection of Gibraltar. On 7 June, the day before the British invasion of Syria, the Admiralty ordered Somerville to disembark ten Fulmars to North Front to counter possible retaliatory action by the Vichy French forces in Morocco. In the event there were none. For all ferry operations Force H embarked sufficient TSR aircraft to provide daylight anti-submarine patrols and contacts were made that were assessed as probable Italian boats. Several attacks were carried out but none resulted in any confirmed kills. With the flying off positions for the Hurricanes now moved significantly further to the west, the threat from shadowing and bomber aircraft based in Sicily was reduced and the CAP fighters had no requirement to carry out interceptions during the June operations.

Convoys to Malta

From July Force H protected convoys that were vital to the preservation of Malta as an offensive base. The first was Operation Substance, which began on 21 July and comprised six fast merchant ships carrying stores and motor transport to reinforce and re-store Malta. It also included the troopship *Leinster*, which had 900 Army and RAF personnel on board.

A Fulmar retracting its undercarriage seconds after leaving the flight deck. (*Author's collection*)

A further 3,000 troops were carried in warships. At the same time six empty merchant ships and HMS *Breconshire* escorted by a single destroyer were to make the passage west to Gibraltar from Malta. Force H was reinforced by units of the Home Fleet that had escorted the outbound convoy from the UK. In addition to *Ark Royal*, the force that sailed to cover the convoy included *Renown*, *Nelson*, the radar-equipped light cruiser *Hermione*, which had replaced *Sheffield*, together with *Edinburgh*, *Manchester*, *Arethusa*, *Manxman* and sixteen destroyers. Unfortunately, *Leinster* ran aground near Tarifa in thick fog on sailing from Gibraltar and was unable to join the convoy.

Steps were taken to confuse the enemy as Substance began but enemy aircraft located it having flown below the fleet's radar cover and began shadowing on the morning of 22 July. *Ark Royal*'s Fulmars failed to intercept them and the first enemy air attack began at 0945 on 23 July in a position 105nm south-south-west of Cagliari. It consisted of synchronised high-level bombing and low-level torpedo attacks by groups of nine and seven Italian Air Force SM.79s respectively. The former were detected by radar at 60nm but the latter approached below the radar coverage and were not detected until seen by visual lookouts dead ahead. The bombers failed to score any hits but the cruiser *Manchester* and the destroyer *Fearless* were both hit by torpedoes in the low-level attack, which was completed in less than four minutes. *Manchester* had to return to Gibraltar with only one propeller shaft operable but *Fearless* was stopped in the water and on fire aft with twenty-seven men killed. She had to be scuttled by *Forester* as the fleet could not risk leaving ships to take her in tow whilst under air attack.[3] Two of the SM.79s were shot down by the Fulmar CAP and three others by ships' gunfire but three Fulmars were damaged and forced to ditch, although all their crews were rescued. Another high-level bombing attack half an hour later was broken up by the Fulmar CAP. Despite being unable to climb within 1,000ft of the bombers' ceiling, the Fulmars' aggressive tactics scared them into dropping their bombs outside the destroyer screen. A second torpedo attack by five SM.79s developed during the dog watches of 23 July. This time they flew sufficiently high to be detected by radar and they were intercepted by the Fulmar CAP 20nm away from the force. Two enemy aircraft were shot down and the remainder driven off.

The narrows were approached at 1700 on 23 July and Force H reversed course to the west, leaving a CAP over the convoy and a surface escort designated Force X to escort the convoy closer to Malta. Force X comprised *Edinburgh*, flagship of Rear Admiral E W Syfret, *Arethusa*, *Manxman* and seven destroyers. Beaufighters from Malta arrived to relieve the Fulmars

A damaged Fulmar hung over *Ark Royal*'s port deck edge to clear the flight deck for the recovery of other aircraft; an ingenious solution to the problem of removing a damaged aircraft quickly. The patches over three of the starboard wing guns have been shot away, indicating that this Fulmar has recently been in combat. (*Author's collection*)

on CAP at 1830 but they failed to identify themselves correctly, probably because of their lack of experience in operating with the fleet. Their twin-engine layout was similar to that of enemy aircraft and, when they failed to give the correct recognition signals, the fleet opened fire on them. To complicate matters still further, another torpedo attack, this time by four SM.79s, began at 1900 followed by unusually accurate high-level bombing by seven SM.79s at 1945. The Beaufighters failed to engage either attack and nor did they respond to any instructions given by the fleet's fighter direction officers. The convoy survived a night torpedo attack by six Italian motor torpedo boats (MTBs) off Pantelleria, in which SS *Sydney Star* was hit but only damaged, and a rather half-hearted air attack at 0700 on 24 July before it reached Malta intact that afternoon. Force X entered Malta for just long enough to land the troops and then withdrew at high speed. At the same time, Admiral Somerville turned Force H back to the east to meet it and at 0100 on 25 July *Ark Royal* flew off six Swordfish to Malta as replacements for aircraft lost by 830 NAS.

After the two forces had re-joined company, the combined force headed west and an enemy shadower was shot down by the CAP but one Fulmar was lost in the process. Unfortunately, a second enemy reconnaissance aircraft at low level had already reported the force and attacks by both high-level bombers and torpedo aircraft began at 1100. The CAP of four Fulmars had been reinforced by a further six after the earlier interception and three out of the eight bombers were shot down and the rest driven off. Two Fulmars were unfortunately lost in the brief engagement. Although the torpedo attack was not intercepted by fighters, its pilots were disheartened by the savaging inflicted on the bombers. They failed to drive home their attack effectively and they retired without causing any damage. By noon *Ark Royal* had only twelve serviceable Fulmars left but there were no more air attacks and the force returned safely to Gibraltar on 27 July. *Ark Royal*'s fighters had destroyed seven enemy aircraft with another three probables and three damaged but had lost six Fulmars in doing so, from which only four crews had been saved. The aircrew killed in action were Sub Lieutenant (A) K G Grant RNVR and Leading Airman H McCloud of 807 NAS and Lieutenant A T J Kindersley RN and Petty Officer F A Barnes of 808 NAS. Several of the Italian aircrew that had been shot down were also rescued from the sea and in his action report Somerville remarked that the Fulmar squadrons had contributed a great deal to the safe arrival of the convoy. He added that 'one Italian officer survivor stated that he had been shot down by a Hurricane. It is evident that the enemy hold our Fleet Air Arm fighters in higher esteem than do our own Fulmar pilots.'[4]

Admiral Somerville also commented that the failure of the Beaufighters to give effective fighter cover on 23 July had revealed their lack of experience working with ships and the absolute necessity for them to be briefed to switch their IFF[5] equipment on before closing the fleet. These points were signalled to Malta, where an enquiry was conducted and, as a result, operations in support of the next convoy were greatly improved. All seven of the Substance Convoy merchant ships arrived in Malta and brought a total of 4,500 military personnel and 50,000 tons of stores to the island. The seven empty ships had arrived safely in Gibraltar without loss, having survived both high-level and torpedo attacks during their passage. Other than the MTB attack on 24 July there had been no interference from enemy surface ships and several reconnaissance patrols had been flown by *Ark Royal* to confirm that the Italian battle fleet was not at sea in a position to threaten the convoy.

The grounding of *Leinster* and the return of the damaged *Manchester* to Gibraltar during Substance meant that there were ninety Army and RAF officers and some 1,700 men on the Rock still awaiting passage to Malta and it was decided to carry them to the island at high speed in the cruisers *Hermione* and *Arethusa* together with the minelayer *Manxman*.

Force H carried out a diversionary operation off north-west Sardinia with *Renown*, *Nelson*, *Ark Royal* and five destroyers. Designated as Operation Style, the two forces left Gibraltar on 29 July 1941 and Force H carried out its diversion on 1 August. The passengers were duly delivered to Malta on 2 August, *Hermione* having rammed and sunk the surfaced Italian submarine *Tembien* at 28 knots when it was encountered just west of the island. Force H had meanwhile gained the enemy's attention by showing itself off the Balearic Islands and then at 0310 on 1 August *Ark Royal* flew off a diversionary strike force of nine Swordfish, each armed with four 250lb GP bombs, 40lb bombs and incendiaries. The launch position was 80nm west of Alghero and, having already practised the ranging, arming and flying off of a similar Swordfish strike in daylight, the night strike went exactly to plan. The first flare was dropped a little early, about 2nm short of the airfield but enough illumination was given by the second to reveal that no enemy aircraft were parked on it. The strike aircraft had, therefore, to be content with dive-bombing and setting on fire an equipment shop, a hangar and living quarters. Despite considerable light anti-aircraft fire, no Swordfish was seriously damaged but one thing did go wrong. At 0615, the third aircraft to land on had returned inadvertently with a 40lb bomb hung up on one of its racks. This detached and exploded as soon as the aircraft caught a wire, killing its crew, Lieutenant (A) C M Jewell RN and Sub Lieutenant L A Royall RN of 810 NAS. Lieutenant D G Bowker RN and Leading Airman H F Huxley DSM, also of 810 NAS, were on deck nearby and were also killed.

This is *Furious*' port, flying control, position. It was hit on two separate occasions by Hurricanes that drifted to left of the centreline on take-off. (*Author's collection*)

The aircraft was completely burnt out, the arrester gear was damaged and a hole was blown in the flight deck. Temporary repairs were hastily carried out, however, and the remaining aircraft were recovered by 0715.

An hour later an enemy Cant Z.506B shadowing aircraft was seen briefly as it emerged from low cloud but the CAP, which had been airborne since dawn, failed to intercept it in the murky conditions and it got away. There was little better success against two other shadowers later in the day but on the other hand there were no significant air attacks on the fleet. A solitary low-flying torpedo aircraft attempted to attack *Hermione* after dark but missed. The Italians had clearly believed that the diversion marked the beginning of a larger, slower convoy passage to Malta and after the successful outcome of Operation Style, Somerville signalled the Admiralty saying that 'the enemy in fact appeared bothered, beggared and bewildered'. Force H was employed in a diversionary role again for Operation Mincemeat on 21 August. By then *Renown* had left for a refit in the UK and the force comprised *Nelson* as flagship, *Ark Royal* and *Hermione* with five destroyers. This time it was intended to take enemy attention away from a fast minelaying sortie off Leghorn by *Manxman*, commanded by Captain R K Dickson RN, which was disguised as a French *Tigre*-class destroyer with a false bow, stern, funnels and even French naval uniforms worn by men on the upper deck. *Ark Royal*'s aircraft were briefed to attack cork and olive woods at Tempio in northern Sardinia where, at this time of year, all vegetation was believed to be tinder dry. As was the case with all Somerville's sorties into the Mediterranean, a number of distractions were staged, intended to fool enemy agents watching the Gibraltar Dockyard from Algeciras in Spain. In this instance a tug was sailed to the east towing two Pattern VI targets to give the impression that gunnery exercises were to be carried out to the east of Gibraltar on 21 August. The admiral enjoyed scheming these ploys and they often served their purpose by delaying and, sometimes even preventing, the Italian naval staff in Rome from gathering a true appreciation of what Force H was doing.

At 0800 on 23 August Force H was 80nm north-north-east of Algiers when it was detected by an enemy Cant Z.506B reconnaissance aircraft. It was intercepted by the CAP Fulmars but they failed to shoot it down despite firing out all their ammunition. *Ark Royal* reported that the aircraft might have been fitted with extra armour around the pilot's cockpit since the rear gunner had been silenced quickly during the first attack. However, when the combat reports were analysed in the Admiralty, NAD put the failure down to pilots opening fire at too great a range, a common failing even with experienced fighter pilots, and this certainly seems the more likely explanation. One Fulmar had been forced to ditch after being hit by return

There could be moments of relaxation during a Malta convoy operation, as shown by this photograph of *Ark Royal* taken across *Hermione*'s quarterdeck. (*Author's collection*)

fire but its crew were picked up by a Sunderland flying from Gibraltar. That evening an aircraft was detected on radar and shot down by the CAP, identified as a German Ju 52 transport aircraft. At 0250 on 24 August *Ark Royal* reached a flying off position 100nm west of Tempio on a clear, star-lit night. The strike comprised ten Swordfish armed with incendiary bombs; its navigation to the target area was aided by a poor blackout in Tempio itself and they bombed woods to the south-east and west of the town without any anti-aircraft fire being directed at them. A number of large fires were started, which might have been even more spectacular if there had been any wind to fan them but as it was the glare could be seen by Force H 75nm away. All ten aircraft were safely recovered by 0700.

At 0920 on 24 August a signal from a Malta-based reconnaissance aircraft reported two enemy battleships, four cruisers and eighteen destroyers 30nm south of Cagliari at 0810 heading 240 degrees at 15 knots. Somerville altered course at once to the south-east with the intention of launching an air striking force. At 1615 Force H was 180nm west of Cagliari and had heard nothing more about the enemy's movements since the submarine *Upholder* had reported at 1250 that three battleships, six cruisers and twenty-five destroyers were 30nm south of Sardinia. Somerville had been loath to commit his own aircraft to a surface search because he wanted to have the largest possible strike force ready for action but now felt compelled to order an eastward search to a depth of 110nm. Nothing was encountered, however, because the enemy force had altered course to the east and was now 200nm away from Force H. The failure of Malta-based aircraft to follow up sightings with amplified shadowing reports was a common occurrence at this time but since the Italian fleet kept within the cover of shore-based fighters, it was understandable. However, while *Ark Royal*'s Swordfish were seeking the enemy, Force H was itself being shadowed and reported upon. Fulmars were directed onto the aircraft and made no fewer than sixteen attacks but failed to shoot it down.

After a disappointing day Somerville gave up any hope of attacking the enemy force and at 2230 on 24 August he turned Force H to pass between Ibiza and Majorca with the object of staging a demonstration off Valencia that was intended to impress upon the Spanish that the Western Mediterranean was still under British control. Accordingly, at 0930 on 25 August seventeen Swordfish and fourteen Fulmars were flown off and orbited Force H while it steamed down the Spanish coast between Sagunto and Valencia with the shore about 7nm to starboard. The British Ambassador later reported that the demonstration greatly impressed the Spanish authorities. Flying was completed by noon and after the usual exercises the ships entered Gibraltar on the afternoon of 26 August.

Further aircraft ferrying operations

In mid-August Somerville was informed that *Furious* was on her way to Gibraltar with sixty crated Hurricanes for Malta and nine Swordfish of 812 NAS for *Ark Royal*. She also had a detachment of 880 NAS embarked, the first Sea Hurricane squadron, and its mechanics were able to help erect Hurricanes when the flight deck was no longer required for routine anti-submarine patrols and CAP. The 'club run' to get the Hurricanes into a flying off position west of Malta followed the established routine but because of the number involved, it was divided into two phases designated Operation

Ark Royal with Fulmars ready for take-off during Operation Halberd with ships of the convoy on the horizon. (*Author's collection*)

Status I and II. When the first twenty-four Hurricanes had been erected they were transferred from *Furious* to *Ark Royal* after dark on 7 September. RAF Blenheims were briefed to meet *Ark Royal* 40nm north-east of Algiers at sunrise on 9 September, homed onto *Ark Royal* by *Hermione*'s direction officers using radar. They had no fuel to loiter and so the Hurricanes had to be flown off quickly as soon as the Blenheims were in sight.

Somerville embarked in *Ark Royal* late on 7 September and *Hermione* had sailed to the west earlier in the day to mislead agents in Algeciras. Early on the morning of 8 September, *Ark Royal* sailed but a strong westerly wind made it difficult to move her off the dockside and it took three tugs over an hour to pull her clear. Difficulty was experienced communicating with the Blenheims because of bad W/T conditions on 9 September and only one was successfully homed to the pre-arranged rendezvous, where it picked up the first range of fourteen Hurricanes. All arrived safely at Malta but their small margin of endurance meant that the remaining Blenheims had no time to loiter looking for the carrier and so she had to return to Gibraltar with the remaining twelve Hurricanes still on board, arriving at 0915 on 10 September. Fourteen more Hurricanes were promptly transferred from *Furious* to *Ark Royal* and at 1900 Operation Status II began with *Furious* and her escort sailing to the west as a blind and Somerville, having transferred his flag back to *Nelson*, sailing to the east with the whole of Force H at 2130. On the morning of 11 September *Furious* joined company, having passed through the Straits during the night, and the whole force proceeded to the flying off position at 17 knots. During the night, however, W/T communications with Gibraltar failed completely between 0100 and 0600. The flying off position was reached at 0530 but there had been no news of the departure of the Blenheims or even a weather forecast from Gibraltar. Two hours later, at 0730, a signal was received from Gibraltar, with a time of origin at 0320, which postponed the operation for twenty-four hours, leaving Force H in a dangerous position with *Ark Royal*'s deck full of Hurricanes that could not be struck down into the hangar because of their non-folding wings and unable to operate her own aircraft. *Furious* had cruciform lifts and was able to strike down the RAF Hurricanes into her hangars and range the three Sea Hurricanes of 880 NAS. Force H altered course to the west and by 0930 was 77nm north of Algiers when enemy shadowers were detected on radar and a sighting report from one of them intercepted. Nothing further happened until 1655, when another enemy sighting report was intercepted, but the Sea Hurricanes were held on deck in case an attack developed. In the event none did and Force H was lucky to be able to return to the flying off position at sunrise on 13 September without being attacked.

Argus with Fulmars of 807 NAS ranged aft operating close to the Spanish coast. (*Author's collection*)

A signal was received to confirm that the first three Blenheims had left Gibraltar at 0310 and expected to reach Force H at 0635. At 0623 they were detected on radar at 68nm and then sighted from *Ark Royal*'s bridge at 0648. The light surface wind meant that *Ark Royal* had to increase speed to 28 knots to fly the Hurricanes off and *Furious* was limited to ranging only seven Hurricanes at a time to give the furthest forward enough flight deck to take off safely. A further batch of four Blenheims was directed into the overhead at 0800 and overall it proved possible to fly off forty-six Hurricanes to follow the Blenheims to Malta. There was one loss, the third Hurricane to take off from *Furious*, flown by Sergeant W R Findlay RCAF, which hit the port navigation position having swung to port on take-off and crashed into the sea, killing the pilot. Fortunately this time there was no fire. The remaining forty-five Hurricanes reached Malta, where two of their number were damaged on landing.

As soon as the launch was complete, Force H turned onto west and headed for Gibraltar at 20 knots. Shadowing aircraft were detected at 1615 but no air attacks followed despite the fact that they appeared to remain in contact, risking the possibility of interception by *Ark Royal*'s Fulmars now that her flight deck was clear. When she was within range, *Ark Royal* flew on 812 NAS, commanded by Lieutenant Commander W E Waters RN, from North Front to replace 810 NAS before going alongside in Gibraltar on the evening of 14 September. The nine Swordfish that had been brought to Gibraltar were augmented by a further three from 810 to bring the new squadron strength up to twelve aircraft. On 18 September the remaining six aircraft of 810 NAS were embarked in *Furious* for her passage to the USA, via Jamaica, for refit.

Operation Halberd

This was a repetition of Operation Substance but on a larger scale[6] with nine merchant ships carrying 2,600 troops to Malta together with ammunition and stores. *Ark Royal* sailed with Force H at 2300 on

An 807 NAS Fulmar landing on *Argus* photographed from her quarterdeck. (Author's collection)

24 September with twenty-seven Fulmars of 807 and 808 NAS and the twenty-seven Swordfish of 812, 816 and 825 NAS, a total of fifty-four aircraft embarked, well below her maximum capacity. As before, Force H was reinforced by ships from the Home Fleet and in addition to *Ark Royal*, the Halberd force comprised *Nelson* (flag), *Rodney*, *Prince of Wales*, *Hermione*, *Edinburgh*, *Euryalus*, *Kenya* and *Sheffield*. Swordfish were flown off on anti-submarine patrols from 25 September between dawn and dusk. The first German U-boat to enter the Mediterranean, *U-371*, had passed eastward at night through the Strait of Gibraltar on the surface on 23 September and after the war German records revealed that three more had done so before the conclusion of Halberd. There were six U-boats in the Mediterranean by 10 October but their presence was not yet known to the British.

Six Fulmars were flown around the fleet on 25 September in the hope that gunners would be able to recognise them but despite this sensible precaution the fleet's anti-aircraft fire shot down two Fulmars during Halberd. The first shadower, a Cant Z.506, was detected visually from *Nelson* on 26 September; it was flying very low and had not been detected by radar. From then onwards the force was shadowed continually and a number of enemy reports were intercepted. A CAP comprising a single section of Fulmars was airborne from dawn on 26 September but they were hampered by poor slant visibility at altitude despite the horizontal visibility at sea level being assessed as excellent. One Swordfish was maintained on anti-submarine patrol, the remainder were struck down into the hangars with their petrol tanks drained in the expectation of heavy air attacks.

Visibility on 27 September remained poor at altitude and atmospheric anomalies were so bad that communication between direction officers and the fighters was impossible at times. Enemy sighting reports were intercepted from 0810 onwards, ten minutes after the first section of four fighters arrived at its CAP station. No interceptions at all were made despite the CAP being increased to ten aircraft at 1000, twelve at 1100 and sixteen by noon. The first attack came at 1300 when two formations of enemy aircraft were detected by radar, one to the north and one to the east, both at 30nm. Shortly afterwards the enemy were assessed as diving towards sea level and CAP fighters vectored onto them. The force to the north was identified as twelve BR.20 and Cant Z.1007 torpedo bomber aircraft with six CR.42 fighters 7,000ft above them. Two Fulmar sections engaged four torpedo aircraft 12nm north of the fleet and shot one of them down. Another section dived through a gap in the cloud onto the CR.42s but failed to splash any and one of these Fulmars failed to return to *Ark Royal*. Meanwhile, six of the BR.20s were approaching the fleet between its port beam and bow but were deterred by the barrage fire from the destroyer screen as well as the battleships and cruisers. They dropped their torpedoes about 5,000yds from the heavy ships, giving them a chance to comb the tracks, but several, including *Rodney*, had very narrow escapes. Three of these aircraft were shot down by ships' gunfire and another by fighters, making a total of five, but it was at this stage that two Fulmars were shot down by barrage fire from *Rodney* and *Prince of Wales*. One crew was subsequently rescued but the other, comprising Lieutenant M W Watson RN of 807 NAS and Sub Lieutenant (A) T Couch RN of 808 NAS, was lost.[7] The fact that these two were flying together shows that the two fighter squadrons had pooled their resources.

The second group began their attack at 1327 when six or seven BR.20s, which had been detected by radar, were seen approaching at low level between the starboard beam and bow. One of them was splashed by fighters before it could release its torpedo but three others pressed on through the destroyer barrage with great gallantry and one of these dropped its weapon only 450yds from *Nelson* as she took evasive action. She was hit on the port bow at frame 60 about 10ft below the water line and her speed was reduced at first to 18 and eventually 12 knots. Two of this group of enemy aircraft were shot down by ships' gunfire, taking the total for the day to eight out of eighteen or nineteen torpedo

Ark Royal and *Argus* photographed from *Malaya* returning from Operation Perpetual. (*Author's collection*)

aircraft; a percentage loss that the Italian Air Force could not hope to sustain for long. At 1345 another formation, this time of SM.79 torpedo aircraft, was sighted at very low level to the south. It split into two groups as they approached the barrage; one comprising three aircraft continued although dropped their torpedoes out of range of the convoy but close enough to the destroyer screen to force them to evade. One of these was shot down by fighters after it had dropped its torpedo but the other group retired for the time being. After taking stock, three of these closed the barrage again but only one pressed on, aiming for *Ark Royal*. It was shot down by concentrated fire from the carrier and *Nelson* before it could drop its torpedo. At this stage an Italian CR.42 fighter attempted to divert the fleet's gunfire by performing deliberate aerobatics over the force but it dived into the sea, taking the total number of aircraft lost by the enemy to eleven. During the remainder of the day a succession of less resolute enemy formations were held at bay by the CAP fighters and it was finally estimated that of the thirty torpedo aircraft that had attempted to attack the fleet only eighteen had got within torpedo range.

Writing in his report about safety of his own aircraft, Somerville said that no practical form of aircraft recognition could prevent friendly aircraft being fired on 'if they approached the fleet in the same manner as enemy torpedo aircraft when an attack is in progress'. He suggested that damaged aircraft losing height should be ditched clear of the fleet and preferably ahead of it, although he made no comment about how pilots with a dead or dying engine might accomplish this feat.

While this attack had been in progress, Somerville received a report of an Italian surface force south-east of Sardinia originated by a Malta-based reconnaissance aircraft, which put the enemy about 75nm to the north-east of *Nelson*. If it continued to head south at 20 knots, as reported by the aircraft, a fleet action within two hours was now a possibility. *Ark Royal* was instructed to prepare two Swordfish as shadowers as quickly as possible, to be followed by a torpedo strike. The shadowers were flown off at 1448 but the preparation of the strike force was delayed by having to refuel all the Swordfish, having had their tanks drained. A strike force of twelve Swordfish from 816 and 825 NAS, ten of which were fitted with ASV radar, escorted by four Fulmars was eventually flown off at 1540. In the meantime, further RAF reports of the enemy force, now believed to include two battleships, five cruisers and fourteen destroyers, had been received, which indicated that it had altered course and might not intend to force an action. In fact, Admiral Iachino had not received the fighter cover he had been promised and, having been instructed not to engage a British surface force except in conditions of decisive superiority, he had taken his force out of harm's way. Admiral Somerville hoped that the strike force might damage the Italian capital ships and force them to reduce speed sufficiently for *Prince of Wales* and *Rodney*, which he had detached as a surface action group, to intercept them before dark and bring them to action.

By 1650 there was still no report from the two Swordfish shadowers and the last RAF report had been timed at 1503. Uncertain of the enemy's position, therefore, Admiral Somerville ordered the shadowers to return at 1700. At 1750 the strike force leader reported that he had been unable to locate the enemy and this force was also recalled. The reason why neither the shadowers nor the strike force had been able to gain ASV contact was at first attributed to equipment failures and to the fact that no contact had been received timed later than 1503. It later emerged, however, that a signal timed at 1515 from the RAF shadowing aircraft had reported that the Italian force had altered course onto north but it had not been received in Malta or in any ship of Force H. This alteration meant that the enemy force had already passed out of ASV range by the time the Swordfish closed its last known position.

Ark Royal and her air group had been hard pressed on this day but she had kept fighters on CAP and launched a significant strike force. She had launched Fulmars downwind in order to stay within the main body of the fleet and share the protection of its barrage fire. Some of the strike force Swordfish landed on just after sunset and the remainder in the dark, all with very little fuel remaining. One of the shadowers landed on at 2000 after more than five hours in the air; the other shadower had been damaged after running into seven CR.42 fighters but it also managed to return safely.

Just before 1900 on 27 September the convoy reached the entrance to the Skerki Channel and, in accordance with the plan, Force H turned away to the west. The convoy with its escort of five cruisers and nine destroyers, comprising Force X under Rear Admiral H M Burrough, continued towards Malta and their day was far from over. There were four torpedo bomber attacks after dark, the last of which hit SS *Imperial Star* aft with a torpedo that destroyed her rudder and propellers. Attempts were made to tow her but it was found impossible to hold her on a steady heading and she was scuttled at 0340 on 28 September. As a diversion, *Hermione* had been detached at about the time *Imperial Star* was hit to bombard Pantelleria Island and this ploy proved effective. The convoy and escort altered course to the north and proceeded unmolested throughout the remainder of the night close to the Sicilian coast. After sunrise Fulmars together with Beaufighters and Hurricanes from Malta directed by *Edinburgh* prevented any further air attacks on the convoy despite several formations being detected on radar, showing that earlier lessons about command, control and communications had been acted upon. The force arrived off Malta on the afternoon of 28 September to cheers from the population, many of whom lined the walls of Grand Harbour as ships entered it. Force H continued to be shadowed on its passage west on 28 September but it was not attacked again, although Fulmars shot down a Cant Z.506 after a long chase 55nm from the fleet.

Operation Halberd had been a success but Somerville made the point that had the critical 1515 signal from the shadowing aircraft been received it might have been possible for the Swordfish strike to have made contact. We will never know. He commended *Ark Royal*'s commanding officer, Captain L E H Maund RN, for acting with great judgement and a well-balanced appreciation of the situation in concentrating and maintaining strong fighter patrols despite light variable winds and poor R/T conditions. He ended his report on the operation by observing that:

Ark Royal photographed from *Malaya* a minute after being torpedoed. (*Author's collection*)

It cannot be emphasised too strongly that if operations of this type are carried out during moonlight, the hazards are increased to a very considerable extent. Had the enemy concentrated his torpedo bomber aircraft in attacking from dark onward he might well have succeeded in torpedoing a large proportion of the convoy.

Neither the Air Ministry nor the Admiralty had placed sufficient emphasis on night fighters before 1939 but it was obvious that they were needed urgently for both fleet and trade defence operations.

Operations leading to the loss of Ark Royal

The next 'club run' designated Operation Callboy began on 16 October. Its object was to ferry the twelve Albacores of 828 NAS, commanded by Lieutenant Commander D E Langmore RN, to a flying off position within range of Malta together with two replacement Swordfish for 830 NAS. The aircraft destined for Malta had been brought to Gibraltar in *Argus* a week earlier and *Ark Royal* disembarked 812 and 825 NAS to North Front airfield to make space for them.[8] Force H was also to support the passage of the cruisers *Aurora* and *Penelope* together with the destroyers *Lance* and *Lively*, which were to form a surface strike force based in Malta designated Force K. Force H comprising *Rodney* (flag) with *Ark Royal*, *Hermione* and seven destroyers sailed from Gibraltar at 1100 on 16 October.

As the force headed east around Europa Point, several sonar contacts[9] were gained by the surface escorts that were subsequently assessed as marine life or 'non-sub' but on the afternoon of 17 October a Cant Z.506 shadower was sighted from *Ark Royal* and CAP fighters were vectored to intercept it. They chased it for 20nm and eventually shot it down but not before it was heard to transmit a report. At 0130 on 18 October the two Swordfish and eleven Albacores were flown off from a position 30nm north-west of Cape Bougaroni and all except one Swordfish arrived safely in Malta. The twelfth Albacore suffered an engine starter failure but no reason for the loss of the Swordfish was ever discovered; its pilot was Sub Lieutenant (A) D M Muller RNVR and his observer was Sub Lieutenant (A) A S Denby RNVR, both of whom had recently joined 828 NAS after completing their training.

Force H turned back to the west after flying the aircraft off and continued to maintain CAP and anti-submarine patrols. At 1000 an Italian BR.20 was sighted by one of the screen. It was intercepted by a section of CAP Fulmars and chased 45nm to the south-east, where it was shot down 10nm north of Cape Bengut by Sub Lieutenant (A) J F Underwood RNVR. In order to overtake the fleeing enemy, both Fulmars had exceeded their permitted engine RPM and made what were described as emergency landings on their return to the carrier, although both arrived safely on deck. Other shadowers were detected briefly later in the day but none were intercepted. There was a possible submarine contact at midnight but the next day *Ark Royal* landed on 812 and 825 NAS before returning to Gibraltar, after taking part in the usual exercises. Force K sailed from Gibraltar early on the morning of 19 September and passed Force H as it carried out its exercises. It arrived safely in Malta, after a fast passage, during the forenoon of 21 September and within a fortnight it achieved considerable success by sinking an Italian destroyer and all seven merchant ships of an Axis convoy on its way to North Africa.

The next ferry operation, designated Operation Perpetual, began on 10 November. In the interval between Callboy and Perpetual, Somerville had flown to the UK for consultations with the Admiralty on future operations. HRH the Duke of Gloucester,[10] who had been visiting the Gibraltar Command, travelled with him in the same RAF Sunderland. Shortly after the admiral's return to Gibraltar he was informed by Admiralty signal 2116A dated 5 November 1941 that German U-boats had moved into the Mediterranean and by then there were eight U-boats based at Spezia with orders to occupy an attack area in the Western Mediterranean. Another group of U-boats had been deployed to Salamis in Greece for operations in the Eastern Mediterranean and it was within this greatly increased underwater threat that both Force H and the Mediterranean Fleet would now have to operate.

Argus and the aircraft transport *Athene* arrived in Gibraltar on 7 and 8 November respectively, bringing a total of thirty-seven crated RAF Hurricanes for Malta. Perpetual was intended to use both *Ark Royal* and *Argus* to fly off the aircraft in two sorties and Somerville, now flying his flag in *Malaya*, sailed to the east from Gibraltar for Perpetual I in the early hours of 10 November in company with *Ark Royal*, *Argus*, *Hermione* and seven destroyers. Anti-submarine patrols were flown by RAF aircraft from Gibraltar from 0800 on 10 November and the increased underwater threat level was reflected in instructions from Somerville to the destroyers that they were to keep an especially careful watch for U-boats.

That night the Air Commander Gibraltar signalled that the four Blenheim aircraft intended to lead the Hurricanes to Malta had been delayed by twenty-four hours because of forecast bad weather. This placed Somerville and his force in an even more dangerous position than earlier delays because of the heightened U-boat threat but the admiral counted on conditions improving and decided to continue to the east. *Ark Royal*'s flight deck was full of RAF Hurricanes and she was unable to operate her own fighters until they had been flown off. *Argus* was able to move Hurricanes between her hangar and flight deck and actually had two Sea

Legion coming alongside *Ark Royal* on 13 November 1941. (*Author's collection*)

Hurricanes embarked but, for some unaccountable reason, these had not been placed at alert at dawn on 11 November. The weather between Force H and Malta was fine but without the Blenheims there was little the admiral could do so he retired to the west to await developments. At 0935 two aircraft were detected by radar to the south and a little later they were seen flying along the Algerian coast and were, therefore, presumed to be French. However, an enemy sighting report was intercepted that showed the aircraft to be Italian but with no fighters on standby there was nothing that could be done. Other radar contacts were detected, which were presumed at first to be hostile but they proved to be RAF Catalinas from Gibraltar that had forgotten to switch on their IFF.

At 1910 on 11 November Admiral Somerville had heard nothing further from Gibraltar and signalled to say that if the Hurricanes could not be flown off next morning, 12 November, he intended to return to Gibraltar. He added that if the Air Commander wanted the Blenheims to take off in daylight, he was prepared to wait until 1000 on 12 November at the latest. A return signal was received at midnight to say that the Blenheims would arrive over *Ark Royal* at that time. Conditions were still favourable at dawn on 12 November and both carriers had their decks filled by ranges of RAF Hurricanes when at 0907 two more enemy shadowing aircraft were detected on radar, which proceeded to report Force H's position, course and speed without interruption. At about 1000 the four Blenheims arrived over Force H without having needed to be homed into the overhead and shortly afterwards they disappeared to the east leading nineteen Hurricanes organised into two flights. By 1050 four further Blenheims had collected the eighteen remaining Hurricanes, thirteen from *Ark Royal* and five from *Argus*. Of these, only thirty-four arrived safely in Malta and the force had no news about the missing aircraft's fate. Two had been seen turning towards Tunisia with apparent engine trouble and the third attempted to reverse its course towards the carriers. One of the Blenheims suffered engine trouble and had to return to Gibraltar but the remaining seven arrived safely in Malta.

With some relief, Admiral Somerville turned his force to the west from a position 65nm north-east of Algiers and set course for Gibraltar, zig-zagging at 16 knots. *Ark Royal* was now able to range and recover her own aircraft and both CAP and anti-submarine patrols were flown off in deteriorating weather. Later in the day speed was increased to 18 knots, the maximum that *Argus* was able to achieve. Shadowers were again in evidence and attempts were made to intercept a BR.20 but it evaded into cloud and escaped. Speed had to be reduced to 17 knots when weather deteriorated still further but at dawn on 13 November *Ark Royal* flew off six Swordfish for an ASV search for surfaced U-boats out to 70nm between bearings of 261 and 287 degrees from the force. Inner and outer anti-submarine patrols were flown off in the same launch. The base course between zig-zags had been shaped to give the impression that Force H would pass to the south of Alboran Island but at 0900, after the dawn search had returned without detecting anything, course was altered to pass to the north of it and then directly towards Gibraltar. This was an unusual approach since Force H normally returned along the Spanish or Moroccan coasts. Since the enemy was probably aware of these normal return routes it was thought that any U-boats in the vicinity would be more likely to be patrolling areas near either shore.

At 0955 and 1157 destroyers on the screen reported sonar contacts, although the later one was quickly reclassified as 'non-sub'. Force H then did what it usually did on returning from operations and carried out exercises to the east of Gibraltar. Whether this was wise is open to question.

Legion alongside *Ark Royal* taking off the bulk of her ship's company. She took on over 1,000 men before casting off at 1648. (Author's collection)

An aerial view of *Ark Royal* stopped in the water with smoke coming from her port boiler room intakes and the list to starboard gradually increasing. (*Author's collection*)

In *Ark Royal*'s case, she carried out deck landing training and other air exercises during the afternoon with strict instructions to remain within the destroyer screen. At 1529 she altered course onto 286 degrees to fly off six Swordfish and two Fulmars and then to land on five others. At 1535 the recovery had been completed, the carrier was 4 cables to starboard of the force's 270 degree line of advance but in the act of turning to port to resume her station. Force H had temporarily ceased using zig-zag number 11 and the events that followed were summarised in his report by Admiral Somerville, who witnessed them himself.[11] The original paragraph numbers from his 18 November letter are retained for the sake of clarity:

16. Legion, the starboard wing destroyer, turned to 290 degrees at this time to cover Ark Royal, turning back to port when Ark Royal moved in to regain station. Just before turning to the course of the fleet, hydrophone effect, HE, was reported on the starboard bow but as this coincided with the approximate bearing of Gurkha, the next ahead, and faded out when Legion turned to the course of the fleet, it was disregarded and not reported by Legion. The operator subsequently stated that the HE on this occasion was louder than any he had heard previously. This suggests that the HE heard was in fact the torpedo fired at the Ark Royal.

17. At 1536 zig-zag number 11 was ordered and at 1538 Ark Royal who had practically regained station again, altered course to 286 degrees to complete flying on. At 1540 the force altered course to 290 degrees in accordance with the zig-zag plan and as it appeared that Malaya might close Ark Royal unduly, I ordered the commanding officer of Malaya to keep clear as requisite to

port until flying on had been completed. At this time a number of aircraft were circling the force, either having just taken off or being just about to land on.
18. At 1541 in position 36 degrees 03 minutes N: 04 degrees 40 minutes W, Ark Royal who was bearing 077 degrees 4 cables [800yds] from Malaya was struck by a torpedo on the starboard side [at frame 78]. I observed an explosion apparently abreast the island and noted that it was so severe that the aircraft ranged before the barrier were thrown clear of the deck and bounced once or twice owing to the whip of the flying deck. Malaya altered course...'

After being hit *Ark Royal* rapidly listed 10 degrees to starboard and this increased to 18 degrees after ten minutes with indications that this was increasing.[12] The fact that the aircraft were thrown clear of the deck indicates that they had not been lashed down after recovery. She had been hit by a single torpedo fired by *U-81* about 30nm east of Gibraltar while steaming at 22 knots with starboard wheel on. The area of maximum damage appeared to be between the keel and the starboard side abreast the island, but some of the blast was vented up the bomb lift forward of the island and many of the ship's company described how the ship whipped violently after the explosion. Subsequent analysis calculated that a hole approximately 130ft by 30ft had been blown in the bottom and lower side plating, indicating a failure of the internal anti-torpedo structure. The hole was larger than might have been expected from a single hit but it took some time for the ship to stop and her speed may have exacerbated the damage.

After the explosion the starboard boiler room, air spaces, oil tanks and watertight compartments began to flood, together with the main switchboard room and the lower steering position. The port and centreline boilers continued to steam but the centreline slowly flooded from below. The engine rooms lost all communications, which is why it took so long to stop the ship, and the immediate flooding of the main switchboard room and telephone exchange caused the failure of all the ship's lighting, electrical power and telephones. On the compass platform the situation appeared critical and half an hour after the explosion the captain decided to bring destroyers alongside to evacuate the ship but leave the steam generators in the port and centre boiler rooms running. At 1600 *Legion* came alongside her port quarter and took off over 1,000 men, casting off at 1648. By then, however, Captain Maund had changed his mind and he ordered damage control parties to save the ship. Unfortunately, by then a number of key men had already left but counter-flooding reduced the list to 14 degrees. Electric power, feed-water for the boilers and portable discharge pumps were provided by *Laforey*, which came alongside but she was slipped at 2224 when it appeared that *Ark Royal* had sufficient power of her own once more. The flooding also appeared to be under control following valiant efforts in extremely difficult conditions by a repair party of sailors from *Hermione* and *Legion* led by *Ark Royal*'s Gunner (T).[13]

The ship was being towed by then at 2 knots by the tug *Thames*, sent out from Gibraltar. Steam had been raised in the port boiler room and lighting restored but the starboard engine room continued to flood, slowly increasing the list and lowering the hull in the water. Eventually the water level reached the boiler uptakes at the starboard side where they were taken up into the funnel. With nowhere for the exhaust gas from the port boilers to go, fire broke out in the casing and this led to the boiler room having to be evacuated again and a further total loss of power. The senior engineer and two of his men collapsed while attempting to keep the boilers in operation and had to be given artificial respiration. Viewed in hindsight, it seems extraordinary that *Laforey* was not kept alongside to guarantee an electrical power supply to keep *Ark Royal* afloat. She was brought alongside again 0245 on 14 November but by then it was too late as, even with the pumps restarted, the heel increased to 27 degrees by 0400, at which point the order was given to abandon ship again. By 0430 everyone had been taken off except for the one casualty who had been in the main switchboard room during the initial impact and was presumed to be dead. The heel continued to increase, reaching 35 degrees as the evacuation was completed. The steaming party and Captain Maund left her just in time and, after pausing for a few minutes at 45 degrees, she rolled over and sank at 0613, having been towed to within 25nm of Gibraltar. The last 250 men off had crossed from the tug *St Day* to

Ark Royal photographed at 1700 on 13 November 1941. (*Author's collection*)

Laforey. The ten Swordfish and four Fulmars airborne at the time the ship was torpedoed diverted to North Front, where they landed safely after the former had carried out anti-submarine searches. The remaining aircraft of 808, 816 and 825 NAS went down with the ship.

The major vulnerability had been the position of the boiler uptake trunking but the steady spread of flooding into the centre and then the port boiler rooms through the fan trunking was also a factor. The lack of any diesel generators to provide electrical power if steam was lost was also a critical shortcoming, as was the initial hurried evacuation ordered by the captain at 1600, during which men left open manhole covers and armoured doors in their haste to get off a ship they thought must be about to sink. These openings allowed an unchecked and widespread rate of flooding that had the effect of lowering the hull in the water until the point was reached where the funnel uptakes were submerged on the starboard side. Since the bow and stern sections remained buoyant, the flooded centre section imposed a terrific 'sagging' strain on the hull, which may have exceeded its design limit. Subsequent analysis showed that immediate damage control measures, resolutely taken, could have saved the ship.[14] If the port engine and boiler rooms had been flooded, even after power failed, she could have been brought to an even keel and retained enough buoyancy to be towed into Gibraltar.

A Naval Board of Enquiry was set up to investigate the circumstances attending the loss of the *Ark Royal* and it made the point[15] that the ship might have been saved if:

a) It had not been for the lack of electrical power due to the loss of steam between 1615 and 1815 (when *Laforey* started to supply electrical power).
b) The manhole in the main deck hatch over the switchboard room had been closed instead of left open by a rating who had evacuated this or an adjacent compartment since this had led to the flooding of the Stoker Petty Officers', the Chief Stokers' and the Mechanicians' dressing rooms and wash-places.
c) The boiler room had not been evacuated there was no apparent reason why steam should not have been maintained for as long as it was possible to provide feed water from the drinking tanks – feed suction being maintained by means of the extractor pump which was used when the boiler room was re-occupied.
d) Whatever steps were taken to remove a large proportion of the ship's company, the steaming watch and both damage control and repair parties should not have been brought up from below when they were.

The Board was not impressed with the efficiency and organisation of the electrical repair parties and the ship's supply of secondary lighting appeared to them to be quite insufficient. However, the Board minuted that the behaviour of all on board between 1648 on 13 November and 0430 on 14 November was beyond all praise and particularly drew Their Lordships' attention to the work performed in the port boiler room under conditions that were hardly imaginable. The Board considered the anti-submarine measures taken for the protection of Force H to be adequate except that the outer patrol might have been carried out to a greater depth, but they recognised that this was a matter of opinion. The actual patrols flown on the afternoon of 13 November were an inner patrol of one Swordfish over an arc of 120 degrees between 1 and 2nm ahead of the destroyer screen and an outer patrol of one Swordfish over an arc of 90 degrees between 10 and 15nm ahead of the screen. The Board further noted that it considered it to be essential that the training and organisation of damage control personnel should, in future, be of the highest standard in order to deal satisfactorily with an emergency of this type. Counter-flooding should be carried out quickly to correct any list over 6 degrees.

The wreck of *Ark Royal* was located on the seabed at a depth of 3,497ft in 2002 by an expedition funded by the BBC. They carried out a side-scan sonar survey and filmed the wreckage using an unmanned underwater vehicle, which found that the forward 200ft of the hull and the island had become detached, with the former lying about 500yds from the main part of the hull. This discovery enabled experts to speculate on exactly what happened as the ship sank. The hull planed to the north and broke up close to the surface as it continued to roll during its initial dive to the bottom. The island and a large part of the flight deck tore away like the lid of a sardine can as she turned keel up and at about the same time the bow section broke away and spiralled to the bottom on its own, scattering debris as it did so. The break was exactly at the bulkhead that separated the hangars from the accommodation areas forward of them. The larger after part of the hull continued to roll slowly as it plunged downwards, eventually righting itself before crashing into the seabed still heading in a northerly direction. The main debris field lies between the main hull and the bow section and includes aircraft, gun mountings and lift platforms. The state of the wreck raises questions about the integrity of *Ark Royal*'s largely welded hull,[16] given the unusual severity of the damage resulting from a single torpedo hit and the catastrophic failure of the hull as it sank.

Argus was now attached to Force H until May 1942 and embarked 812 NAS with nine Swordfish commanded by Lieutenant Commander G A L Woods RN and 807 NAS with eight Fulmars and two Sea

Hurricanes commanded by Lieutenant Commander (A) J S Douglas RN. Both squadrons had been re-formed at North Front on the day after *Ark Royal* sank. The twenty-three RAF Hurricanes that were to have been ferried in Operation Perpetual II were dismantled at Gibraltar and reloaded into *Athene*, which transported them to Takoradi a month later for onward flight across Africa to Egypt.

Prior to *Ark Royal*'s loss, some of her squadrons had been disembarked to North Front to make space for the RAF Hurricanes during ferry trips. While ashore they had flown anti-submarine patrols under the nominal control of 200 Group RAF.[17] The number of naval aircraft available varied with the carrier's programme and the exact numbers that were disembarked but there were usually sufficient Fulmars from 807 NAS to provide coastal reconnaissance up to Cape St Vincent. They were also used to photograph the North African ports and coastline within their radius of action and occasionally they sighted U-boats on the surface and strafed them but no conclusive results were achieved. From 27 November 812 NAS was disembarked from *Argus* on a longer-term basis and four of its Swordfish were fitted with ASV Mark II radar, Types R.3039/T.3040. The RAF maintenance facilities at North Front declared themselves unable to cope with the added burden of supporting 812 NAS and so a Naval Air Section was established at the airfield to provide the squadron with deep maintenance support.

The Ship's Company of *Ark Royal* scrambling onto the destroyer *Legion*. (*Author's collection*)

At first the small number of Swordfish available limited the squadron to dawn and dusk patrols but from 27 November it set itself the task of maintaining continuous anti-submarine patrols over the Straits of Gibraltar throughout the night hours from 1900 to 0900 and until the third week in December, 812 NAS spent an exciting and successful time harassing U-boats. The morale of the squadron was high, the aircrew had confidence and skill in the use of their ASV radar and the aircraft were extremely well maintained between sorties. This was an outstanding achievement with only four radar-fitted aircraft. Aircraft frequently had to be flown on two sorties in a single night and one Swordfish flew for 120 hours in a month, a remarkable intensity of operation that could only have been achieved with faultless maintenance back-up. In his report,[18] Woods wrote that the use of ASV made these anti-submarine patrols at least twice as effective as a visual search and the excellent work of his unit illustrated what could be accomplished against U-boats by well-drilled aircrew using an easily flown, slow but handy and comparatively quiet aircraft that possessed really good visibility for both pilot and observer. The Swordfish could only carry a maximum of three Mark VII depth charges and two parachute flares, and had it not been for this limitation, 812 NAS might have done even better and scored more than the one 'kill' it did.

In the period of 1941 between 30 November and 31 December 812 NAS flew 121 hours by day and 323 hours by night. During this period they made two sightings and attacks in daylight; one at dusk and nine at night. When Mark XIII pistols were available for depth charges they were both set to detonate at 25ft when only two were carried. When weather allowed the Swordfish to get airborne from North Front at maximum weight and three depth charges were carried, their pistols were set to detonate at 25, 25 and 50ft. This squadron's success was confirmed after the war by a study of German records carried out by the Naval Historical Branch.

The first contact was on 30 November when *U-96* was detected by radar at 6nm on a clear night with a three-quarter moon. It was seen on

A cross section of *Ark Royal* through her boiler rooms showing how a list to starboard combined with the hull sinking lower in the water would immerse the point on the starboard side from where the exhaust gas from all three boiler rooms was trunked up into the funnel. (*Author's collection*)

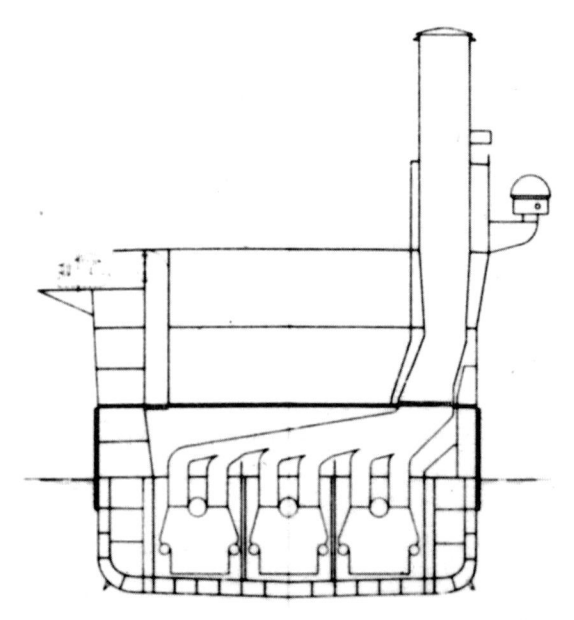

the surface at 2nm proceeding at 16 knots and the attack that followed damaged it. On 1 December *U-558* was detected by radar at 6nm in similar weather conditions and seen at 1.5nm. It, too, was making 16 knots and it was damaged. On 15 December *U-432* was detected by radar at 5.5nm on a dark night with no moon and a sea surface described as choppy. It was seen at 0.5nm and attacked while making 16 knots and assessed as damaged. A day later, on 16 December, *U-569* was detected by radar at 2.5nm on a dark night with no moon and a smooth sea surface. Like its predecessors, it was making 16 knots but was not seen until 0.25nm, although an attack was carried out that was assessed to have damaged the boat. *U 202* was detected by radar at 4nm on 19 December on a clear dark night with no moon and a slight sea. It was seen at 0.5nm and estimated as making 10 to 12 knots. It too was assessed as damaged.

Greater success was achieved on 21 December, when *U-451* was sunk 13nm north-west of Cape Spartel after being detected by radar at 3.5nm on a dark night with no moon and a choppy sea, and seen on the surface making 18 knots at only 0.25nm. The attack sank it, leaving only one survivor. Experience and experimentation led to patrols being flown at 800ft to give the best compromise between the maximum ASV contact range, the visual sighting that was necessary to carry out a depth-charge attack and the time taken to lose height before weapons release. The ideal time on task was two hours, which meant that seven sorties totalling three hours each[19] had to be flown every night. To keep his aircrew efficient, Woods instituted a maximum of two nights' flying out of three and this regime worked well.

No. 812 NAS continued to operate similar patrols up to April 1942 but no more detections were made since the U-boats had been withdrawn to more productive areas off the eastern coast of the USA. In January 1942 the RAF withdrew all its Sunderlands and Hudsons from Gibraltar, leaving 812 NAS as the only anti-submarine unit there. It was placed under the operational control of the Flag Officer North Atlantic.[20]

Lessons learned in 1941

Admiralty analysis of naval air operations in the Mediterranean[21] emphasised the value of aircraft carriers, even in comparatively narrow waters such as the Mediterranean where fleet and convoy operations could be attacked by enemy aircraft from a number of bases. They could launch, deploy and then control fighters by day more or less continuously for long periods as well as providing a base for their repair and maintenance. There was, however, a clear need for more fighter squadrons to alter the balance between fighters and TSR aircraft in carrier air groups and for a practical night fighter to be developed. By 1942 the Admiralty planned to have sufficient resources to embark at least two fighter squadrons of

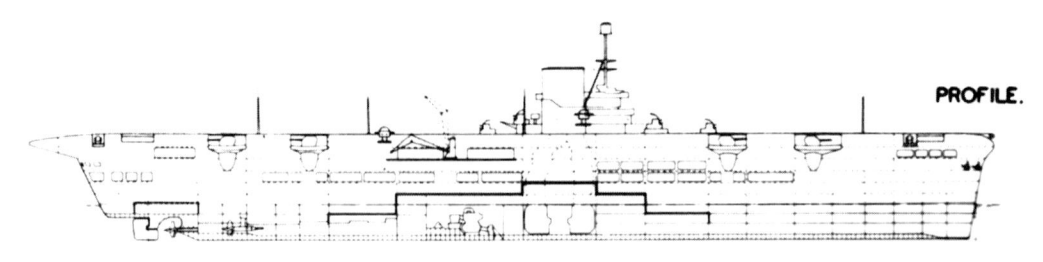

A profile view of *Ark Royal* showing the position of the three boiler rooms sited abreast each other amidships. (*Author's collection*)

twelve aircraft each in fleet carriers with 25 per cent spare aircraft and pilots. The type of fighter embarked should possess a performance equal to or only slightly below that of the enemy's strike aircraft and escort if the average[22] fighter pilot was to have a chance of holding his own. Radar detection of enemy air raids was recognised as a vital factor in the successful fighter protection of fleet operations and convoy escort, considerably increasing the chances of successful interceptions.

In spite of these results justifying optimism for the future, the vulnerability of carriers in confined waters could not be denied. The chief threat was assessed to be a determined attack by dive bombers in visibility conditions favourable to them and, to a lesser extent, low-flying torpedo bomber strikes in bad visibility or below radar cover. In the latter case the risk could be reduced by placing a circular destroyer screen beyond torpedo range from the main body. Against either dive bombers or torpedo attack a high standard of barrage fire from all ships could be very effective but the Admiralty took note that this standard was usually low against initial attacks but rapidly increased in effectiveness against subsequent attacks. The reason for this was undoubtedly the gunners' lack of practice against radio-controlled target aircraft with a realistic performance. Recognition of friendly aircraft was never sure in the heat of action but continued losses to this cause were unacceptable. Apart from the human tragedy involved, any reduction in the already limited number of embarked fighters weakened the defence.

It had not been anticipated that RN squadrons would spend long periods ashore as they did in North Africa. The fact was, however, that they did like many RNAS units before them and some standard provision for equipping a limited proportion for service as independent, mobile units was shown to be necessary.[23] The need for naval aircraft designs that were easy to maintain was never more apparent than in the Western Desert, where aircraft had to be serviced in the open under conditions of heat, sandstorms and humidity and often at night. These conditions were daunting enough without the added handicap of inaccessibility in airframes and engines.

8

Operations in North Africa, Malta and with Force H in 1942

By January 1942 the 8th Army controlled Cyrenaica but was exhausted after months of hard fighting. So too was the Afrika Korps and logistical resupply was the critical issue for both armies. The balance had swung in favour of the enemy, however, and both *Queen Elizabeth* and *Valiant* had been badly damaged by Italian frogmen in Alexandria on 19 December, leaving the fleet with no battleships, no aircraft carriers and only five light cruisers. Against this small force the Italian Navy had four capital ships, three heavy and seven light cruisers, and the newly augmented Luftflotte 2 deployed about 500 aircraft based in Sicily, Sardinia, Crete and Tripolitania. A new series of air attacks on Malta began on New Year's Eve, the opening moves in a second and more devastating blitz intended to destroy the island as an operational base from which Axis convoys could be interdicted. German plans to capture Malta with airborne forces were also set in train.

Reinforcing Malta again

By 1 January the RAF had only eighty-six Hurricanes left in Malta, only half being serviceable at any one time and no more were expected until March. The most intense period of bombing was in April, when the island was largely neutralised. Shipping strikes by RN and RAF aircraft gradually decreased until April, when no enemy ship was sunk by air attack; the first blank month since October 1940. Nos 830 and 828 NAS had fleeting successes in January, February and March.[1] In January they sank SS *Perla* of 5,741 tons in ballast off Pantelleria Island and damaged *San Giovanni Battista* in Tripoli harbour. On the night of 2/3 February they shared the destruction of SS *Napoli* of 6,142 tons with HM Submarine *P.35* off Suss, and also shared in the destruction of SS *Ariosto* of 4,115 tons with *P.38* north of Kerkenah Island on the night of 14/15 February. On the night of 17/18 March the German SS *Achaia* was attacked and damaged

Lieutenant Commander F H E Hopkins DSO DSC RN, who assumed command of 830 NAS in December 1941, seated among his aircrew by the stone wall of an aircraft dispersal near Hal Far. After 1945 he rose to the rank of admiral and served as Flag Officer Naval Flying Training, Flag Officer Aircraft Carriers and 5SL/DCNS. (*Author's collection*)

east of Tripoli in bad weather. It sank shortly afterwards when it hit a mine. In every case the aircraft had been armed with torpedoes and flares. No more victims were sunk until July, by which time bomb damage and the lack of spares had reduced the two squadrons to only four aircraft between them. They had to remain in this state until November, when reinforcements were flown to Malta from Cyrenaica after the 8th Army began its final advance to the west after the Battle of El Alamein.

Ominously, on 5 January eight enemy merchant ships in two heavily escorted convoys had reached Tripoli intact without having suffered any form of attack. These were the first of several that brought relief to the Afrika Korps and there was an obvious correlation between Malta's ability to function as a base for offensive operations and the quantity of stores reaching the enemy in North Africa. By 14 January sufficient stores had reached the Afrika Korps for it to launch an offensive, which made rapid eastward progress supported by newly delivered aircraft and 170 tanks. Benghazi was recaptured by 29 January but the 8th Army held a strong defensive line between Gazala and Bir Hakeim. The two armies then held positions about 30nm apart while they built up strength for renewed operations.

The German advance denied the British Desert Air Force the use of airfields in Western Cyrenaica and it was now considered impossible to give fighter protection for convoys from Alexandria to Malta as they transited the 'bomb alley' between Crete and the North African coast. The desert fighter force still included 803 and 806 NAS, which were now based at El Adem and Gambut with the bombers further east at Sidi Barrani and Ma'aten Bagush. Nos 805, 815 and 826 NAS were also based at Ma'aten Bagush or its satellite airstrips. No. 826 NAS was being used mainly as a torpedo striking force and on 23 January, while temporarily based at Berka near Benghazi, four of its aircraft made a determined dusk torpedo attack against a heavily defended enemy convoy together with several RAF aircraft. One Albacore flown by Lieutenant (A) H M Ellis RN, Sub Lieutenant (A) J F Powell RN and Leading Airman Leslie singled out the 13,000-ton Italian troopship *Victoria* and hit it. Another Albacore flown by Sub Lieutenant (A) J M Brown RNVR, Sub Lieutenant (A) Rushworth-Lund RNVR and Leading Airman Saunders hit and damaged one of the escorting destroyers. Lieutenant Commander Corbett, the commanding officer, with his observer Lieutenant J D Jackson RN and TAG Leading Airman W H Bugden, had intended to attack a *Cavour*-class battleship, which formed part of the escort, but shifted target to the *Victoria*, which they also hit and which subsequently sank. Unfortunately, their Albacore, T9241, was hit by anti-aircraft fire from the troopship's destroyer screen and shot down. The whole crew survived the ditching and were picked up from their dinghy after twenty-four hours in the water by an Italian hospital ship and made prisoners of war.[2] A total of fifty-three RN and RAF aircraft from Egypt and Libya and a further sixteen from Malta including aircraft from 828 and 830 NAS had attacked this convoy but *Victoria* was the only one of ten merchant ships to be sunk.

After this operation 826 NAS moved back to RNAS Dekheila to refit and train replacement aircrew under its new commanding officer Lieutenant C W B Smith DFC RN, formerly of 821 NAS. Unfortunately, on 5 March he was shot down in Albacore T9238 by a Ju 88 at 300ft in bad weather on a communications flight between Fuka and Dekheila.[3] The aircraft crashed near Fuka and Smith was killed together with Leading Airman W Stuttle, Leading Airman N Leslie DSM, AM (1) F C Lockyer and AM (E) G H Halls.[4] Some of them were on the books of 821 NAS at the time but their documentation may not have caught up with reappointment to 826 NAS at Dekheila. Lieutenant P W Compton RN was appointed as the third CO in two months on 5 March. After April 826 NAS flew day anti-submarine patrols from Egyptian airfields but also continued to provide aircraft to drop flares and identify targets for the RAF bomber force during the 8th Army's gradual retreat to El Alamein. In May, 826 NAS was joined in this work by a reconstituted 821 NAS, commanded by Captain A C Newson RM.

The Fulmar Flight, like 805 NAS' Martlets at Ma'aten Bagush, was still working from Fuka to cover Allied shipping between Port Said and Tobruk. One of its Fulmars was shot down by a Cant Z.1007 in early February and on 16 March the unit was recommissioned as 889 NAS. When the front line stabilised for a time at Gazala, 803 and 806 NAS were withdrawn to Dekheila on 6 February 1942. Once there, they exchanged their Hurricanes for twelve Fulmars each, after which they played no further part in the North African Campaign and redeployed to Ceylon.

No. 815 NAS was now commanded by Lieutenant P D Gick RN and its ASV-fitted Swordfish carried out night anti-submarine patrols, an important task as it was estimated that there were twenty German U-boats and sixty Italian submarines operating in the Mediterranean, most of them in the eastern basin. Radar contacts sometimes led to visual sightings and depth charge attacks but none were assessed to have caused more than minor damage. On 2 June, however, *U-652* was sunk off Sollum; a 'kill'

Lieutenant Commander Hopkins briefing 830 NAS aircrew amid the ruins of Hal Far prior to a strike operation. The combination of khaki shorts and fur-lined flying boots indicate the variety of conditions under which they operated, briefing by day and flying at night. (*Author's collection*)

shared between an 815 NAS Swordfish and a Blenheim of 203 Squadron RAF. German records[5] analysed after the war showed that 815 NAS had actually been more successful than the Admiralty had realised at the time. Between January and April 1942 *U-453*, *U-372* and *U-77* had all been badly damaged and forced to return to base for repairs in refits that lasted from two to five months. *U-77*, attacked while surfaced on 1 April off Sidi Barrani, had not even heard the Swordfish approach over the noise of their diesels and both its periscopes were put out of action by depth charge explosions. The exhaust muffler valves could not be closed, both batteries, the after hydroplane and two tanks were damaged and three watertight doors were lifted off their hinges. These defects prevented the boat from diving and it retired on the surface to Crete, where it was unsuccessfully attacked by a German Ju 88. A day later *U-77* was narrowly missed by three torpedoes from what was described as 'an Allied submarine'[6] and she finally arrived at Salamis on 3 April. After temporary repairs, *U-77* went to Spezia for major work to be carried out. No. 815 NAS' accurate night attack took this U-boat out of operations for three months.[7]

Accurate use of ASV radar and good co-ordination between the pilot, observer and the TAG who was responsible for the illumination of the target were essential and the records of this period show that 815 NAS had reached a very high standard. On the night of 4 August 1942, *U-97* was attacked by Swordfish 'A' north-east of Alexandria and was so badly damaged that it could not dive. Five hours later Swordfish 'L' attacked it and caused further damage, including putting all its compasses out of action, but the U-boat managed to reach Salamis for temporary repairs. A long refit was then carried out at Spezia and she did not return to sea until April 1943.[8] In his action report,[9] Lieutenant Gick wrote about the strain imposed on his aircrew by ASV searches, which often lasted up to six hours, and noted that efficiency started to deteriorate if they flew on alternate nights for more than ten days.

The Malta squadrons and further 'Club Runs'

Air attacks on Malta were expected by the Axis general staffs to be the precursor to an airborne assault on the island but Hitler decreed that an invasion must wait until July when he expected Tobruk to have been taken, Cyrenaica to be in Axis hands and the Afrika Korps waiting only for the fall of Malta to advance into the Nile Delta. In the event the Germans took Cyrenaica earlier than anticipated but got no further than El Alamein before running out of supplies. Had the enemy invaded Malta, the war in the Mediterranean and Near East might well have evolved in a very different way but, for whatever reason, the fact is that they did not.[10]

By February there were only twelve serviceable Hurricanes left in Malta and the two naval squadrons had only six aircraft between them. Against them, the enemy had about 320 fighters and 250 other warplanes in Sicily and the resumption of ferry operations had become a clear priority. *Eagle* landed 813 and 824 NAS at Gibraltar in February and embarked sixteen RAF Spitfires, brought out from the UK in SS *Clan Hawke*.[11] To increase their range naval air mechanics fitted the Spitfires with drop tanks but difficulty was encountered with one aircraft and it was 'cannibalised' to provide spare parts. *Eagle* sailed for Operation Spotter on 6 March and flew off eight Spitfires from a first range on 7 March. They were met at 1020 by two Blenheims from Gibraltar and landed safely in Malta. The remaining seven Spitfires were flown off at 1100 and met by a single Blenheim, which led them on. These were the first Spitfires to arrive in Malta but the first batch was almost wiped out by air attack within minutes of their arrival. Plans evolved to taxi aircraft away from the airfield along tracks that led out into widely dispersed revetments in the countryside. Men sat on the wings to guide pilots through swirling dust to their parking places and in this way heavy losses immediately after arrival were avoided. On 20 March *Eagle* sailed from Gibraltar with *Argus*, which acted as a fighter carrier for Operation Picket I. She had embarked a further seventeen Spitfires transferred from SS *Queen Victoria* a day earlier. Nine Spitfires were flown off at 0824 on 21 March but their Blenheim escort was late and that for the second range did not arrive. The weather over Malta was reported as having deteriorated and so *Eagle* returned to Gibraltar with the remaining Spitfires still on board.

On 27 March *Eagle* embarked six Albacores in addition to the remaining Spitfires for Malta and sailed with *Argus* for Operation Picket II. The Albacore launch was postponed on 28 March because of poor weather conditions over Malta but seven Spitfires were flown off on 29 March and picked up by two Blenheims and a Beaufort. An eighth Spitfire was found to be unserviceable and was not launched. On this day enemy shadowing aircraft closed the force but were driven off by a series of running fights that developed after they were intercepted by Fulmars from *Argus*. The danger from enemy aircraft caused the Albacore launch to be cancelled again and *Eagle* returned to Gibraltar on 30 March.

By mid-April, nearly all the Spitfires had been destroyed by bombing or in air combat but some long-range Hurricanes had been flown in from the Western Desert. It was clear that a small carrier like *Eagle* could not keep pace with the ferry requirement but the USN had deployed the USS *Wasp* to the European theatre and agreed to her use for ferry operations. *Wasp* was slightly smaller than *Ark Royal* both in terms of tonnage and

Torpedo-armed Albacores taking off from Hal Far before sunset for a strike against Axis shipping. Note the small stone-walled fields that would have made any German attempt to launch an airborne assault on Malta so difficult. (*Author's collection*)

dimensions[12] but was built to a significantly better design from the point of view of aircraft operations. Her usable flight deck covered the whole length of the hull without the aerodynamic round-downs forward and aft fitted in *Ark Royal* that had limited the number of aircraft that could be ranged and flown off. Most importantly, *Wasp* had large aircraft lifts 48ft long by 45ft (the largest of *Ark Royal*'s was 45ft long by only 25ft wide). These allowed Spitfires to be struck down into her hangar, leaving deck space for some of her own fighters to operate as CAP or lead the RAF fighters towards Malta. Her own air group contained a mix of F4F-3 (non-folding) and F4F-4 (folding-wing) Wildcats, similar to the Martlets in RN service.

Wasp had been lent to the RN Home Fleet based at Scapa Flow and her use allowed ferry operations to be carried out in a more effective way. She had a radius of action of 8,000nm at 20 knots, which allowed her to embark fully assembled RAF Spitfire Vs in Glasgow and carry them directly to the launch position north of Algiers. Importantly, the Spitfires had their compasses set to work before loading, allowing them to navigate themselves to Malta after launch. *Ark Royal* had a similar radius of action but could not be spared from Force H for long enough to make the journey to the UK and back. Her less-effective design would also have reduced the number of Spitfires ferried and she could not have operated her own fighters with them on deck. Having landed some of her own aircraft to RNAS Hatston, *Wasp* loaded forty-seven Spitfires and sailed for the launch position in the Mediterranean 550nm from Malta and on 20 April 1942 all the Spitfires and eleven of *Wasp*'s own fighters were flown off in sixty-one minutes, the latter returning once the RAF aircraft were safely on their way. One of the Spitfires was lost but the remaining forty-six landed in Malta, although that day proved to be one of the worst of the blitz and several were destroyed as they were being refuelled. On her return voyage to the UK, *Wasp* embarked 812 NAS Swordfish from North Front to provide anti-submarine protection, one of the few instances in which RN aircraft have operated from a USN carrier.

After studying *Wasp* the Admiralty realised that its own carriers incorporated too many design restrictions on aircraft operation and its Future Fleet Working Party decided that more carriers with better and bigger flight decks, lifts and catapults were an urgent necessity. British carriers were modified to improve their aircraft operating characteristics and new designs such as the 1942 Light Fleet Carriers and the aborted *Malta* class incorporated the best design features possible in the straight flight deck era. *Wasp* had contributed more than just two very successful ferry operations.

Axis aircraft flew 325 bomber sorties against Malta on 20 April 1942. Some flew from North Africa to avoid overcrowding on the Sicilian airfields and many flew multiple sorties. Attacks on this scale continued over the next two days and in addition to the RAF fighters destroyed, a number were damaged. During April the RAF lost forty-one fighters destroyed and eighty-seven damaged. Ammunition shortage limited anti-aircraft guns to fourteen rounds each per day. On 15 April His Majesty King George VI awarded the George Cross to the population of what he described as the 'Island Fortress of Malta'. It was estimated that 993 tons of bombs were dropped in February; 2,174 tons in March and 6,728 tons in April. Of the April tonnage, 750 tons fell on Hal Far and 3,156 tons fell on the dockyard.

By 30 April only two Albacores and a single Swordfish were assessed as fully serviceable. Malta's position was desperate but after April the enemy's air attacks were reduced because the Germans thought that it had effectively been neutralised. Luftflotte 2 was ordered to transfer its aircraft to other areas, particularly Cyrenaica. They had completely underestimated Malta's power of recovery.

On 9 May Operation Bowery was carried out by Force W, which comprised *Wasp*, *Renown*, *Eagle*, *Charybdis*, eleven British and two American destroyers. It was the largest ferry mission to date and the two

An Albacore of 815 NAS in its sandbagged revetment at RNAS Dekheila, armed with a torpedo and ready for a strike against enemy shipping. (*Author's collection*)

carriers flew off sixty-four Spitfires from a launch position 60nm north of Algiers. They flew unescorted to Malta, where sixty of them arrived safely. *Wasp* launched forty-seven and *Eagle* a further seventeen in fifty-seven minutes. One Spitfire crashed on take-off, its sergeant pilot unfortunately being lost. Another developed a defect in its drop tank after leaving *Wasp* but returned to land on safely. Two others were lost in transit through unknown causes. Force W was not shadowed or attacked and the enemy seemed to be unaware of its existence. This time the Spitfires' arrival was carefully planned and effectively handled; aircraft were taxied to dispersals around the three airfields, refuelled, armed and launched with fresh pilots. Some of them were airborne again within six minutes and Axis bombers were intercepted and driven off.

On 10 May the fast minelayer *Welshman* arrived and unloaded a valuable cargo that included 80,000 rounds of 40mm Bofors anti-aircraft ammunition in only five hours. Twenty-four enemy aircraft were claimed destroyed with another nineteen probables by fighters and anti-aircraft guns. Only six Spitfires were lost and enemy attacks on Malta began to decline. There was no more dive-bombing because the Ju 87s were too vulnerable to interception by Spitfires and heavy bomber attacks were reduced in number. By 25 May on the eve of the Afrika Korps' renewed offensive, Malta's second blitz can be said to have ended. The possibility that the enemy might attempt an airborne invasion was now becoming remote.

A summary of the Malta squadrons' achievements

CB 3053 was NAD's confidential account of worldwide RN air operations and it contained a frank Admiralty view of events for information and study by senior officers. Number 6 published in February 1943 listed, inter alia, the work of 830 and 828 NAS in the latter part of 1942. During that period the Admiralty credited these two squadrons with sinking or severely damaging at least thirty-five Axis supply ships totalling 185,000 tons together with a cruiser and six destroyers or large escorts despite the squadrons being short of nearly every resource they needed. In the reserved words of an officer in the naval staff 'these results were most creditable, especially taking into account the severe restrictions resulting from the heavy and continuous enemy air raids at Malta and the difficulties of maintenance, supply and reinforcement'.[13] The following summaries illustrate some of the squadrons' achievements in 1942.

15 June Four Albacores made daylight attacks on two Italian cruisers and destroyers escorted by fighters, obtaining probable torpedo hits on a cruiser and a destroyer. One Albacore was shot down and another was damaged but able to return to Hal Far. Sub Lieutenant (A) C R Casey RNVR of 830 NAS and his observer Lieutenant W N Paton DSC RNVR of 828 NAS were killed in the aircraft that was shot down.

2/3 September One Swordfish and two Albacores located and attacked a ship of 5,000 tons at night off Cape Spartivento. Two torpedoes were dropped, obtaining one certain and one probable hit. Later reconnaissance found the ship beached.

4/5 September Two Albacores, one armed with bombs and another with a torpedo, attacked the beached 5,000-ton ship. One torpedo and one bomb hit were obtained and a further bomb hit a destroyer nearby.

28/29 September Two Swordfish and two Albacores located and attacked an Italian destroyer at night off Cape Spartivento. Two torpedoes were released, one of which was seen to hit amidships.

14/15 October A Swordfish and two Albacores located an escorted ship of 7,000 tons off the coast of Tripoli during the night. One Albacore attacked with its torpedo and hit the target amidships and it was seen to stop. This aircraft was damaged by anti-aircraft fire but managed to return to Malta. The other Albacore was unable to get into a suitable dropping position and did not attack.

18/19 October One Swordfish and three Albacores attacked a southbound enemy convoy at night north-east of Pantelleria. One torpedo hit was obtained on a 4,000 to 6,000-ton supply vessel.

19/20 October Two Swordfish and two Albacores found and attacked an enemy southbound escorted oil tanker of 8,000 tons at night and attacked it. Two torpedoes were released and resulted in a single hit, which caused a large explosion.

17/18 November Two Albacores with an RAF Wellington flare-dropper located and attacked an 8,000-ton oil tanker 46nm north-east of Homs. Both torpedoes hit and caused a large explosion. The tanker was seen to heel over blazing furiously and the fire was visible 80nm away.

1/2 December Two Albacores located and attacked an escorted oil tanker of 7,000 tons 20nm west of Marettimo. One of the Albacores dropped flares for an attack by the second, which obtained a torpedo hit amidships that caused sparks to rise up to over 60ft. Later the ship was seen to have stopped.

2/3 December Eight Albacores made two successive night attacks on a convoy consisting of at least two ships of 5,000 tons escorted by destroyers and an escort vessel 36nm east of Melita. Five torpedoes were released, obtaining three certain and one probable hits. Later reconnaissance found one ship to have sunk and another on fire.

3/4 December Albacores located and attacked two southbound ships, each of 3,000 tons, off Tripoli. Three torpedoes were released, one ship was blown up and the other set on fire with a heavy list.

12/13 December Albacores laid mines off Sousse harbour.

13/14 December Four Albacores located and attacked an enemy ship of 5,000 tons escorted by four destroyers and E-boats 14nm south of Marettimo. One torpedo was released and obtained a hit, which was followed by a violent explosion aft. The whole ship became enveloped in flames visible 80nm away.

14/15 December Four Albacores located and attacked a ship of 2,000 tons beached north of Sousse at night. They obtained a single torpedo hit and a large patch of oil was seen around the ship.

21/22 December Albacores located and attacked a 4,000-ton ship escorted by three escort vessels and E-boats 22nm north-west of Marettimo. Three torpedoes were released, obtaining one hit on the supply ship abaft the funnel that resulted in a large cloud of smoke followed by fire. Another hit one of the escort vessels and sank it.

28/29 December Four Albacores located and attacked an escorted ship of 4,000 tons 28nm north-west of Pantelleria. One torpedo was released and it hit the ship, which was probably carrying ammunition. It exploded and disintegrated with a mass of flames that rose to 1,000ft.

30/31 December Three Albacores located and attacked one of two escorted 3,000-ton ships 33nm south-west of Marsala. One torpedo was released and hit one of the ships forward, resulting in a brilliant flash and column of smoke. The ship was seen to be down by the bows and later a large fire was reported in this area. Night fighters were successfully evaded after this attack.

It is noticeable how quickly the number of sorties and successful attacks increased after the arrival of the Pedestal convoy in August.

Naval air squadrons in the retreat to El Alamein

The British 8th Army had been ordered to prepare for another offensive in June that was to coincide with, and hopefully act as a distraction for, two convoys that were to carry vital supplies to Malta. One was from the UK via Gibraltar and the other westbound from Alexandria and designated Operations Harpoon and Vigorous respectively. In the event the Germans struck first on 26 May 1942 when Afrika Korps armoured columns carried out an enveloping move around the end of the Gazala line at Bir Hakeim, where there was fierce fighting. By mid June the 8th Army was forced to retreat to the Egyptian frontier, leaving Tobruk open to attack

No. 805 NAS' aircraft serviceability board photographed on 7 June 1942 while it was based at RNAS Dekheila. Although the image is of poor quality, it shows all the unit's aircraft ready for operations. (*Author's collection*)

and its garrison surrendered on 21 June. With it, the Germans captured vast quantities of fuel, stores and provisions that had been stockpiled by the British.[14]

The British air policy during this retreat was to disorganise the enemy air force on the ground and Wellingtons, Baltimores and Hurricane night fighter-bombers kept up a steady programme of attacks on enemy forward airfields and landing grounds. Albacores of 821 and 826 NAS provided target location and illumination for Wellington bombs. No. 826 NAS had retained sufficient 'old hands' among its aircrew to retain skill levels in this difficult form of warfare but 821 NAS was new to it. For the next five months, however, the two units co-operated as a single cohesive force, although each retained its own commanding officer and administration. Since its formation in March, 821 NAS had flown day anti-submarine patrols interspersed with torpedo attacks on Axis shipping. It had also carried out bombardment spotting exercises with the monitor *Roberts*. After the German offensive began both squadrons deployed a detached flight to work in the desert under the orders of the Desert Air Force HQ. Standard operating procedures were devised for use by both squadrons and the Wellington force that were based on 826 NAS' experience to date.

All Albacore aircrew were carefully briefed with local area details and daily photographic reconnaissance and came to know their operating area intimately. These briefings were essential because some targets, including the Martuba landing ground complex, were very difficult to find at night even for 826 NAS' experienced crews. Each Albacore carried thirty-two flares, which, with two aircraft dropping sticks of two flares in turn, were sufficient to illuminate targets for an hour continuously. To pinpoint the target in the first instance, an initial stick of four flares was usually required. All were dropped from 6,000 to 7,000ft above target level with a maximum delay setting that gave illumination at about 3,300ft. As enemy anti-aircraft fire increased in intensity three aircraft were used, each doing a twenty-minute stint over the target and carrying four 250lb GP bombs fitted with rod attachments to ensure a burst above ground level and so serve to 'quieten' the gun batteries. The Albacores normally arrived over the target a quarter of an hour before zero-hour for the Wellingtons' first bombing wave, which usually consisted of ten aircraft. The whole strike force numbered thirty Wellingtons on most nights and the bombing was completed within an hour from heights between 6,000 and 10,000ft. This technique made night bomber operations in North Africa extremely accurate and facilitated 'round-the-clock' attacks on enemy forces that materially influenced the course of the land fighting up to and including the Battle of El Alamein. It is surprising to learn that when the tactic

Officers of 826 NAS photographed in front of one of their Albacores at RNAS Dekheila in August 1942. The commanding officer, Lieutenant P W Compton DSC RN, is seated at the centre of the front row (with a beard). The others are named on my copy but with no indication of whether they were (A), RN or RNVR in most cases. They were: *Front row left to right:* Sub Lieutenant A Brunt RNZNVR, Sub Lieutenant L P Dunne, Sub Lieutenant P D T Stevens, Lieutenant D K McIntosh, Lieutenant G H Gunner (Senior Observer), Commanding officer, Sub Lieutenant (A) R E Bradshaw DSC RN, Sub Lieutenant B F Sutton DSC, Sub Lieutenant S L Revett, Sub Lieutenant R P Barker, Sub Lieutenant W D Orwin. *Centre row left to right:* Sub Lieutenant J Hodgson, Surgeon Lieutenant N B Mundy (Squadron Medical Officer), Sub Lieutenant G P Greenaway, Sub Lieutenant P D B Wise, Sub Lieutenant J A Wall, Sub Lieutenant T J McClister, Sub Lieutenant (A) J D Murricane RNVR, Sub Lieutenant F Cooper, Sub Lieutenant G F Arnold, Lieutenant D E Balme DSC, Lieutenant R G Hunt, Sub Lieutenant A G Clook, Sub Lieutenant J S Graham (Staff Officer). *Back row left to right:* Sub Lieutenant J D Watson, Warrant officer Dobson, Sub Lieutenant D M Judd, Sub Lieutenant O S E Lloyd, Sub Lieutenant C R Neville, Pilot Officer Robertson RAAF (Communications Liaison Officer). (*Author's collection*)

was explained to the AOC-in-C of RAF Bomber Command he showed absolutely no interest in it.[15]

On 26 May the detached flights of 821 and 826 NAS were using the forward airfields at El Adem and Gambut but as the German advance gathered momentum they moved back first to Sidi Barrani and then even further east. Immediately after the fall of Tobruk every available Albacore based at Ma'aten Bagush was redeployed to join their detached flights at LG 05 and used to lay mines in Tobruk harbour. LG 05 was by then the most advanced of all those left in British hands and the two naval air squadrons were the last to leave before the enemy overran it. At this critical phase their chain of command seems to have broken down and they had been left to act independently. Once back at Ma'aten Bagush they combined the tasks of moonlight bombing sorties against enemy motor transport, now nose-to-tail along the desert roads, with the minelaying in enemy harbours and anti-submarine work. By 27 June the 8th Army was moving steadily eastwards with the enemy hard on its heels but suffering considerable losses from air attacks. There was virtually no opposition from the Luftwaffe because of the losses it had suffered in the fighting around Bir Hakeim and Tobruk and also the distraction caused by Operation Vigorous. It had very few aircraft left. From Ma'aten Bagush the Albacores moved to LG 104 near El Daba on 28 June for one night's operations before returning to Dekheila.

Albacores continued their work with the bomber force up to the end of November 1942 from Dekheila; by then the final, victorious, British advance westward from El Alamein into Cyrenaica and Tripolitania had begun. Neither squadron received the recognition it deserved in the official communiqués of the period and, surprisingly, the Admiralty itself seemed to have no very clear idea of their achievements. In signal 0100A/22/November 1SL, asked Cunningham how these squadrons were being employed. Cunningham's reply stated simply that they had 'been used throughout the El Alamein battle and were a vital factor in the whole night bombing operation'. By then 889 NAS had moved back to the Gulf of Suez, where it recommenced its convoy escort task, and 700 NAS Walrus Flight, which had flown anti-submarine missions from Aboukir, moved at first to Haifa and then Beirut in April, where its aircraft were fitted with ASV radar and it undertook night anti-submarine patrols in addition to day convoy escort. On 11 July it obtained its first confirmed success when it shared in the sinking of the Italian submarine *Ondina* with the South African sloop *Protea*. In August 1942 it was recommissioned as 701 NAS.

Operations LB, Style, Salient, Harpoon and Vigorous
The British Chiefs of Staff directed that Malta must be restocked with fighters before any attempt was made to run the two planned convoys. This was to be carried out by *Eagle* and *Argus*[16] in three ferrying operations designated LB, Style and Salient on 19 May, 3 June and 9 June respectively, which resulted in seventy-six more Spitfires arriving in Malta safely. *Argus* only took part in the first of these. The force carrying out LB was attacked inconclusively by Italian torpedo bombers from Sardinia and Vichy French Dewoitine fighters on 18 May, one of which was shot

down by one of 807 NAS' Fulmars from *Argus*. One Fulmar was shot down; its pilot was rescued but the observer, Petty Officer H W Nuttall, was lost. It had been the intention to fly off six Albacores to Malta as reinforcements for 828 NAS and they were actually on their way when, inexplicably, an engine defect caused the whole formation to return to *Eagle*, which, together with *Argus* was already heading west towards Gibraltar. All seventeen Spitfires flown off reached Malta safely.

In Operation Style the last batch of Spitfires to leave *Eagle* were attacked by Bf 109F fighters as they passed Pantelleria Island and four of them failed to reach Malta. This was the first ferry mission to suffer this kind of attack and it gave rise to concern that the enemy had installed a radar station on Pantelleria as well as in Sicily. Twenty-seven Spitfires did reach Malta safely, however, where they were quickly taken in hand by the new rapid dispersal techniques. In the last of these three operations, Salient, there were no incidents and all thirty-two Spitfires arrived safely over Malta. One unfortunately crash-landed but its pilot was unhurt.

While these two operations were in progress, *Argus* had returned to the UK to bring out 801 NAS with twelve Sea Hurricanes commanded by Lieutenant Commander R A Brabner MP RNVR for embarkation in *Eagle*. She arrived back in Gibraltar on 7 June and the squadron transferred to *Eagle* two days later. No. 813 NAS, commanded by Lieutenant Commander A V Lyle RN, had been disembarked to North Front during the ferry operations. It remained based there carrying out

Aircrew of 821 NAS photographed informally at a desert landing ground. (*Author's collection*)

Albacore 4G of 826 NAS in soft sand at Mersa Matruh after suffering damage from anti-aircraft fire when attacking shipping at Bardia. (*Author's collection*)

anti-submarine patrols until November, when it moved to Algiers during Operation Torch, the North African landings.

Operation Harpoon

The next attempt to fight a convoy through to Malta from the west was Operation Harpoon. All hope of the enemy being distracted by operations on land was lost when the 8th Army began its long retreat and the convoy relied on two groups of warships and their embarked aircraft for its defence. The convoy itself comprised six large merchant ships, which carried 40,000 tons of cargo between them. Its close defence was provided by Force X comprising the anti-aircraft cruiser *Cairo* commanded by Captain C Hardy RN, the destroyers *Bedouin*, *Marne*, *Matchless*, *Ithuriel*, *Partridge*, *Blankney*, *Middleton*, *Badsworth* and the Polish *Kujawiak*, the minesweepers *Speedy*, *Hebe*, *Rye* and *Hythe* plus six minesweeping motor launches, all of which were to carry on to Malta with the convoy. Heavy support was provided by Force W under Vice Admiral A T B Curteis and it comprised *Eagle* commanded by Captain E G N Rushbrooke RN, *Argus* commanded by Captain G T Philip RN, *Malaya*, *Kenya* (flag), *Liverpool*, *Charybdis* and the destroyers *Onslow*, *Icarus*, *Escapade*, *Wishart*, *Westcott*, *Wrestler*, *Vidette* and *Antelope*. Neither carrier was the best example of its type but they were all that was available. Between them they embarked the sixteen Sea Hurricanes of 801 NAS and 813 NAS Fighter Flight, six Fulmars of 807 NAS and eighteen Swordfish of 813 and 824 NAS. The comparatively large number of TSRs embarked reflected the intention to provide a torpedo strike force

Albacore X 8980 photographed when newly arrived at RNAY Fayid with its undersides sprayed matt black ready for night operations. It was allocated to 826 NAS in 1942. (*Philip Jarrett collection*)

against Italian surface forces if they attempted to attack the convoy and to provide anti-submarine patrols. The convoy passed through the Straits of Gibraltar at 12 knots on the night of 11/12 June.[17]

On 14 June *Eagle*'s Sea Hurricanes provided high cover while *Argus*' Fulmars flew as low cover and the twenty-two RN fighters available put up a brave fight against continuous attacks by heavily escorted groups of high-level bombers, dive bombers and torpedo aircraft that approached from both Sardinia and Sicily. By that evening only eight Sea Hurricanes remained serviceable in *Eagle* and *Argus* had lost four of her six Fulmars. During the day's fighting, the achievements of 801 NAS White Section, Lieutenant F R A Turnbull RN and Sub Lieutenant (A) H E Duthie RNVR, stood out. These two pilots in combination shot down three SM.79 torpedo bombers and damaged a further three. A day later, on 15 June, after Force W had turned west to return to Gibraltar, they shot down a further SM.79 but by then the two old carriers could only keep four Sea Hurricanes and two Fulmars in the air at any one time and their primitive fighter direction arrangements had been stretched to the limit.

Against what Captain Rushbrooke rather bitterly described as his own fleet's 'most inadequate measures' on 14 June, successive waves of enemy bombers each had an escort of twenty or more fighters and despite the naval pilots' gallant efforts, the cruiser *Liverpool* was hit and damaged and one of the convoy's merchant ships was sunk. At times there were up to seventy enemy aircraft in the vicinity of the convoy and the carriers' flying operations were complicated by the fact that the light wind was from the west. In order to save time *Eagle* kept all her Sea Hurricanes on deck, having found it possible to park six abaft the island to be refuelled and rearmed while still leaving a clear landing strip to port. Sea Hurricanes were launched downwind to prevent the ship from wasting time manoeuvring into wind. Another factor was inexperience among the Sea Hurricane pilots, only one of whom had previous combat experience. Surprisingly, seven others had never landed on a carrier deck before because *Argus*, the only deck landing training carrier, had to be used operationally after the loss of *Ark Royal*. The Admiralty had been unable to make any other carrier available on a regular basis for the task because of worldwide operational commitments, this inability to provide even basic deck landing training for newly qualified pilots demonstrating how stretched the Fleet Air Arm had become by this stage of the war. Casualties on 14 June included Lieutenant P R Hall RN, Sub Lieutenant (A) J T D Ceeley RNVR, Sub Lieutenant (A) P E Palmer RNVR, Sub Lieutenant (A) G Spalding RNVR and Leading Airman J B Duncan from 807 NAS in *Argus* together with Lieutenant L F Tickner RN of 801 NAS in *Eagle*.[18]

Once the convoy reached the narrows, Force W turned away to the west at 2130 on 14 June for Gibraltar, arriving on 17 June. When the convoy got within 140nm of Malta RAF fighters began to defend them. They were directed by two fighter direction officers in *Cairo*, one RNVR and one RAF, communications were good and interceptions developed into more than forty air combats.

On 15 June reconnaissance aircraft located two Italian cruisers, *Montecuccoli* and *di Savoia*, in a position to menace the convoy after it passed through the narrows. They engaged the escort briefly south-west of Pantelleria Island and damaged the destroyer *Bedouin* at 0700. She was

A pristine new Albacore, X9521, allocated to 821 NAS at RNAY Fayid. As yet its undersides have not yet been painted black. Note the long-range fuel tank fitted on the centreline in the torpedo stowage position. (*Philip Jarrett collection*)

subsequently hit and sunk by Italian torpedo aircraft at 1200. Two small strike forces from 828 and 830 NAS were launched against the Italian cruisers from Malta, one in the forenoon and one in the afternoon, each escorted by two RAF Beaufighters. The first strike was led by Lieutenant Commander A J T Roe RN and the second by Lieutenant M E Lashmore RN. Both attacks were made in daylight in the face of strong enemy fighter cover. Neither attack gained any torpedo hits and one Albacore was shot down and both its pilot, Sub Lieutenant (A) C R Casey RNVR, and observer, Lieutenant (A) W N Paton DSC RNVR, were lost. The strikes had the effect of discouraging enemy surface forces from taking any further action against the convoy and they withdrew.

Only two of the six merchant ships reached Malta; of the others, one had been sunk by torpedo bomber attack, one by bombing and two so badly damaged by bombing that they had to be scuttled. The Polish destroyer *Kuzawiak* struck a mine off Grand Harbour at 0100 on 16 June and sank in less than three minutes.[19] Unfortunately, one of the ships that were scuttled had been the new American fast oil tanker *Kentucky*, which carried 14,100 tons of fuel oil and kerosene. She had been lent to the British Ministry of War Transport by Texaco on the direct instructions of President Roosevelt but was largely British manned.[20] She had suffered a

Aircrew stand next to their 889 NAS Fulmar at a shore base. Unfortunately it has not proved possible to identify them. (*Author's collection*)

fractured steam pipe that had immobilised her but was otherwise intact. By 1030 on 16 June there were further heavy air attacks and the threat that the Italian cruisers might return and overwhelm the escort. Towing *Kentucky* had tied up three of Captain Hardy's escorts out of a force that could already be described as inadequate and so he decided to scuttle her with another damaged merchant ship, *Burdwan*, in order to get the two undamaged ships into Malta. It was a terrible decision to have to make and the loss of *Kentucky*'s cargo of oil had a severe impact on Malta's defences.

Enemy losses included sixteen aircraft shot down by ships' gunfire, thirteen shot down by carrier-borne fighters and a further six shot down by RAF fighters from Malta. Given that the Axis forces had committed about 200 combat aircraft to attacks on the Harpoon convoy, this was a scale of loss the enemy could not sustain. The RN had lost seven fighters, one of them shot down by the fleet's anti-aircraft fire.

In its analysis of Operation Harpoon, the Admiralty felt that three factors stood out. First was the need to embark as many fighters as possible, even at the expense of strike and anti-submarine aircraft. Once more it stressed that better recognition training of anti-aircraft gunners was needed to prevent 'blue-on-blue' incidents. This problem was never solved during the remainder of the Second World War.[21] Lastly, the advantage of altering the force's course before enemy torpedo release was stressed because it gave the enemy a more difficult target.[22]

Operation Vigorous

Vigorous began at the same time under the direction of Admiral Sir Henry Harwood, who had relieved Cunningham as C-in-C Mediterranean on 20 May. No naval aircraft were directly involved as the critical phases took place outside their radius of action from Malta and Egypt. It was, however, an indication of the growing RAF strength in the Middle East and the first deployment of USAAF bombers to the Canal Zone that long-range strike and fighter missions were flown in support of Vigorous from Egypt. However, instead of the land fighting drawing enemy air resources away from the westward-bound convoy as had been expected, the opposite happened, an indication of the importance the Germans placed on preventing the resupply of Malta. At least 170 enemy aircraft from North Africa and Crete were employed against the convoy rather than giving air support to the Afrika Korps' advance. During the passage of the convoy along the Egyptian coast on 12, 13 and 14 June continuous day fighter cover was provided by Desert Air Force Hurricanes, Tomahawks, Kittyhawks and Beaufighters. Seven Beaufighters, two Kittyhawks and two Tomahawks were lost in action.

A Spitfire being prepared on *Eagle*'s flight deck for its flight to Malta. The two drum-shaped objects under the port wingtip are ammunition drums for the aircraft's 20mm cannon waiting to be loaded. (*Author's collection*)

The Italian fleet was reported leaving Taranto at 1845 on 14 June and a series of strikes by Wellingtons and Beauforts from Malta hit and disabled the cruiser *Trento*, which was subsequently torpedoed and sunk by the British submarine *P 35*. The Italian force included the battleships *Littorio* and *Vittorio Veneto*, and at 1345 on 15 June they were seen by a Malta-based reconnaissance aircraft to be continuing to head south, drawing closer to the convoy, but at 1515 they turned away towards Taranto. The convoy was by then only 100nm to the south but it had been under continuous synchronised air attack for two hours and the escort's anti-aircraft ammunition had by then been largely expended and it was decided, reluctantly, to order the convoy back to Alexandria. A final strike against the Italian fleet by five torpedo-armed Wellingtons was launched from Malta and located the enemy 100nm west of Cape Matapan and nearly 300nm from Malta. One Wellington, more determined than the others, pressed home its attack and hit the *Littorio*, which had already been hit by a 500lb bomb dropped by a USAAF B-24 Liberator bomber. She was put out of action for several months.

During Harpoon and Vigorous the Italian fleet used over 15,000 tons of its dwindling stock of furnace fuel oil, FFO. This limited future operations significantly and had an impact on the protection of the Afrika Korps' supply chain. The overall British losses had been heavy though.

Swordfish of 813 NAS parked at North front airfield in Gibraltar. (*Author's collection*)

For the safe arrival of two merchant ships in Malta out of the seventeen that started in the two convoys, the RN had lost *Hermione* torpedoed by *U-205*, *Liverpool* badly damaged and both *Birmingham* and *Arethusa* less so. Five destroyers had been sunk and several others damaged. Malta had been relieved for the short-term future, although fuel supplies remained critically short after the loss of the *Kentucky*.

El Alamein

By the last week in June the British position in North Africa looked grim and Churchill exhorted the 8th Army that 'Egypt must be held at all costs'.[23] Hitler and Mussolini, on the other hand, were elated with the magnitude of Rommel's apparent success and made their fatal mistake; they decided not to invade Malta.

From 25 June the Desert Air Force attacked the advancing German forces with every available aircraft and both 821 and 826 NAS played a full part. The 8th Army was able to move behind the El Alamein Line on the night of 29/30 June and, once there, it had time to make preparations. Fleet Air Arm aircraft at Dekheila were at short notice to evacuate but the line at El Alamein was held and Albacores continued to fly their missions every day. RAF reports recorded that:

> the Albacores of the Fleet Air Arm which accompanied the Wellingtons on the raid on the night of 1/2 July not only performed their usual task of flare dropping but dive-bombed the enemy, wrecking vehicles and causing a considerable number of fires.
>
> Fleet Air Arm Albacores of 821 and 826 NAS, with their accumulated experience of operating over the desert by night and of recognising landmarks, worked in close co-operation with the ground forces for the dive-bombing of enemy armour in the battle area.[24]

A Swordfish of 813 NAS off the eastern coast of Gibraltar. (*Author's collection*)

A note in the Mediterranean War Diary[25] says that on 10 July nine Albacores of 826 NAS flew to a desert landing ground on salt flats 44nm south of Sollum and at least 200nm behind enemy lines. With the assistance of an RAF Bombay aircraft that brought fuel, stores and maintenance ratings, they took off again hoping to attack an enemy supply convoy reported to be near Tobruk. Unfortunately they were unable to locate it but the mission demonstrated what the Albacore force was capable of doing at this stage of the desert war. No. 815 NAS left one flight at Dekheila and the other moved to Gamil airfield near Port Said. The Dekheila flight stopped flying anti-submarine patrols and began a series of night armed reconnaissance missions, using their ASV radar to detect enemy supply ships, barges and landing craft, known locally as 'F' boats, off the enemy-held coast. Several successes were achieved against them and the threat of such attacks limited the number of enemy vessels that sailed. No. 805 NAS also moved to Gamil to give fighter cover to convoys running between Alexandria, Port Said and the Levant. Successes included two SM.79s shot down in July but in August it left Egypt for Kenya. No. 889 NAS moved from Dekheila to Hurghada on the Gulf of Suez in July but there was very little enemy air activity against Allied shipping in the Gulf and supplies for the 8th Army continued to arrive through the Red Sea without any serious interruption.

By 7 July the front line at El Alamein stabilised and it became clear that the enemy's supply position was precarious. Luftflotte 2 was ordered to carry out another blitz against Malta but the defence was spirited and the Germans suffered heavy losses they could ill afford.

Rommel launched another offensive at the end of August but the Afrika Korps was defeated on 2 September in the Battle of Alam el Halfa by a rejuvenated 8th Army now commanded by General Bernard Montgomery. General Alexander had taken over as C-in-C Middle East from General Auchinleck and air attacks helped to drive the enemy back to his starting point by 6 September. As ever, 821 and 826 NAS played a valuable part and carried out nightly reconnaissance over the enemy front line as well as their location and illumination tasks for the bombers. Their work drew a tribute from Air Marshal Tedder, AOC-in-C Middle East:[26]

> Please convey to 826 and 821 [Naval Air] Squadrons my sincere congratulations on their magnificent work with and for the Wellingtons. There is no doubt that these continuous night attacks were one of the decisive factors in crushing the enemy's attack.

The turning point came at the Battle of El Alamein, when a better-trained and equipped 8th Army decisively defeated Rommel's forces and forced them into a retreat the Afrika Korps was never able to stop. Naval air squadrons had played a significant part in the land campaign's eventual victory in North Africa and their outstanding achievements in a role for which they had never been trained or even expected to perform before the war deserve to be remembered with pride.

Crowds of sailors on the USS *Wasp*'s island watch an RAF Spitfire Vc fitted with a 90-gallon jettisonable ferry tank take off for Malta. (*Author's collection*)

9

The Pedestal Convoy

The 15,000 tons of stores unloaded from the Harpoon convoy amounted to less than a month's rations, remained critical but, with the loss of *Kentucky*, oil and avgas reserves were desperately low. The Governor, General Lord Gort, had brought a team of food experts to Malta and he asked them for a frank appraisal of how long the island could survive. Their answer was based on how long the supply of bread could last. The flour ration could not be reduced so the calculation was straightforward and gave a target date after which the island and its garrison must starve or surrender. Other consumables must be made to last as long as bread. Lord Gort never announced the target date publically but he knew that the Admiralty was planning a heavily escorted convoy in August intended to fight its way through to the island at all costs. Bread would last for fourteen days after it was due in mid-August. If the convoy failed, Malta and both its brave population and garrison were lost.

Designated Operation Pedestal, the August convoy drew on the hard-won experience of Harpoon but was meticulously planned on a larger scale. It comprised fourteen fast merchant ships and there was to be a larger close escort and a heavy covering force that included, most importantly, a considerably larger number of embarked fighters. However, the geography of the Western Mediterranean basin allowed little variation in the course the convoy would have to follow. The heavy escort, Force Z, was to stay in close proximity until it reached the Skerki Bank, the last position in which the larger warships would have the freedom to manoeuvre with safety,[1] and then turn back to Gibraltar. The close escort, Force X, was to fight the convoy through the last 300nm to Malta. While they remained in close proximity to the convoy, the two forces were combined as Force F under Vice Admiral E N Syfret. Having turned away, Force Z was to loiter in the longitude of Algiers to await the return of Force X after it had delivered the convoy.[2] Cruisers were included in Force X to defend the merchant ships against enemy surface units if necessary as well as adding their considerable batteries of anti-aircraft guns to the convoy's barrage fire.

Force F, split into Forces Z and X comprised:

Force Z

Nelson	Flagship of Vice Admiral Syfret
Rodney	

Victorious	Flagship of Rear Admiral (Air) Home Fleet – Rear Admiral
Indomitable	L St G Lyster
Eagle	

Sirius
Phoebe
Charybdis

The 19th Destroyer Flotilla commanded by Captain R M J Hutton RN, D19, in *Laforey* with *Antelope, Eskimo, Ithuriel, Lightning, Lookout, Quentin, Tartar, Vansittart, Westcott, Wilton, Wishart, Wrestler* and *Zetland*.

Force X

Nigeria	Flagship of Rear Admiral H M Burrough
Kenya	
Manchester	
Cairo	

The 6th Destroyer Flotilla commanded by Captain R G Onslow RN, D6, in *Ashanti* with *Bicester, Bramham, Derwent, Foresight, Fury, Icarus, Intrepid, Ledbury, Pathfinder* and *Penn*.

The merchant ships were *Ohio*,[3] *Almeria Lykes, Brisbane Star, Clan Ferguson, Deucalion, Dorset, Empire Hope, Glenorchy, Melbourne Star, Port Chalmers, Rochester Castle, Santa Elisa, Waimarama* and *Wairangi*, several of which were to earn immortal fame. They had sailed initially as Convoy WS 21S from the UK to Gibraltar.

Concerns that Spitfire numbers in Malta were reduced caused the Admiralty to plan another, concurrent, operation, designated Operation Bellows, within Pedestal to ferry more RAF Spitfires to the island. *Furious* was to ferry them and *Argus* was used to ferry Sea Hurricanes to Gibraltar but took no direct part in either Pedestal or Bellows. After the experience gained in Harpoon, the air groups of the three aircraft carriers in Force Z

Operation Berserk, the preparatory work up for the Pedestal convoy. All five aircraft carriers, *Indomitable*, *Victorious*, *Eagle*, *Furious* and *Argus*, together with the battleships *Nelson* and *Rodney*, are visible in this photograph taken by the observer of an Albacore. (*Author's collection*)

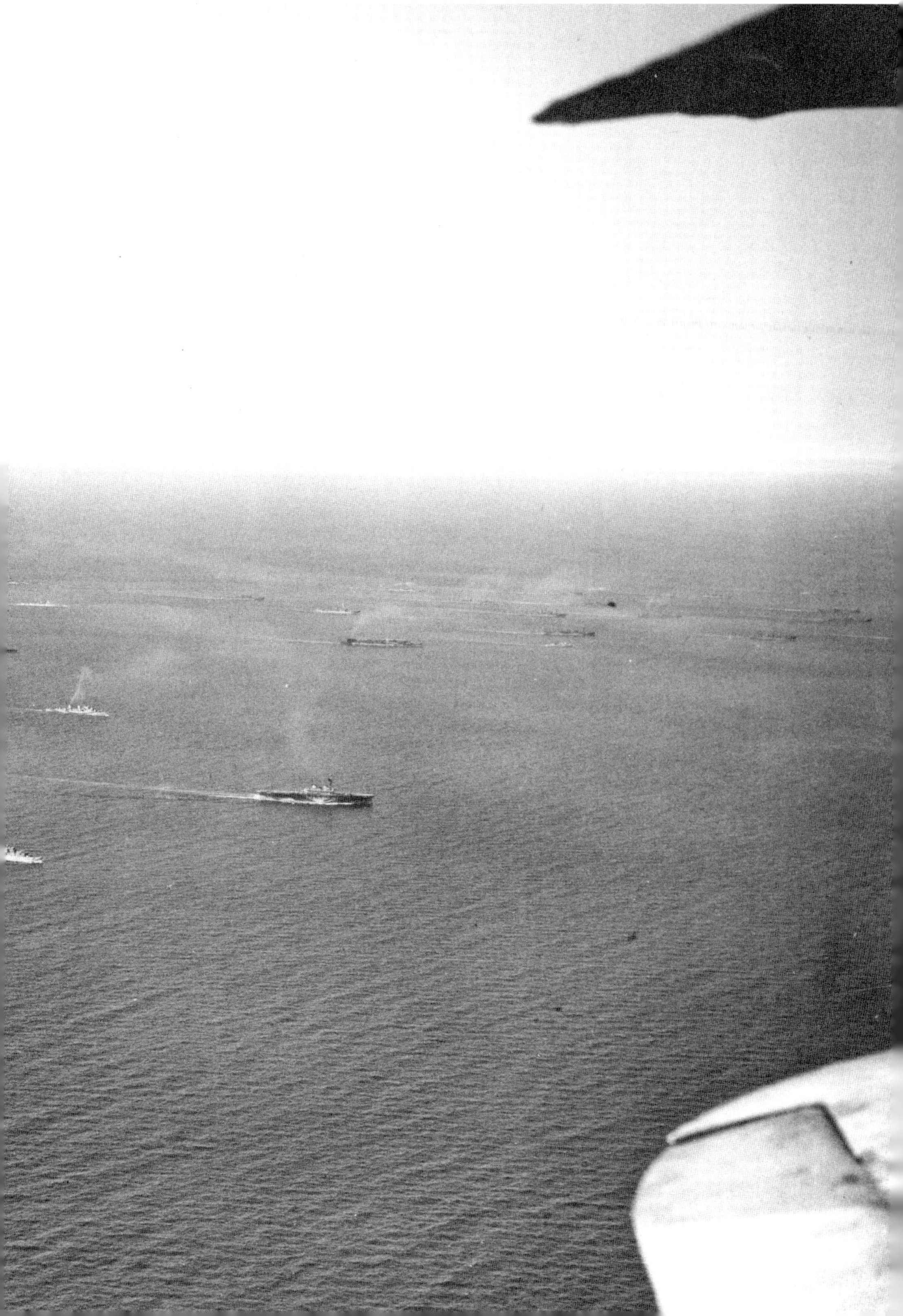

were adjusted to give a preponderance of fighters. The air groups of the escorting and ferrying forces were the largest yet deployed by the RN and were as follows:

Victorious	Captain H C Bovell RN	
809 NAS	12 Fulmars	Lieutenant E G Savage RN
884 NAS	6 Fulmars	Lieutenant N G Hallett RN
885 NAS	6 Sea Hurricanes	Lieutenant R H P Carver RN
817 NAS	2 Albacores (9 disembarked)	Lieutenant L E D Walthal DSC RN
832 NAS	12 Albacores	Lieutenant Commander W J Lucas RN
Indomitable	Captain T H Troubridge RN	
806 NAS	6 Martlets	Lieutenant R L Johnston RN
800 NAS	12 Sea Hurricanes	Lieutenant Commander J M Bruen RN
880 NAS	12 Sea Hurricanes	Lieutenant Commander F E C Judd RN
827 NAS	12 Albacores	Lieutenant Commander D K Buchanan-Dunlop RN
831 NAS	12 Albacores	Lieutenant Commander A G Leatham RN
Eagle	Captain L D Mackintosh RN	
801 NAS	16 Sea Hurricanes	Lieutenant Commander (A) R Brabner MP RNVR
813 NAS	4 Sea Hurricanes	Lieutenant Commander C L Hutchinson RN
Furious	Captain T O Bulteel RN	
822 NAS	4 Albacores	Lieutenant H A L Tibbetts RCNVR

38 RAF Spitfires to be flown off to Malta

Argus	Captain G T Philip RN	
804 NAS	6 Sea Hurricanes	Captain A E Marsh RM

Prior to Pedestal/Bellows, *Eagle* and *Argus* were in Gibraltar, the latter having ferried 804 NAS from the UK, while *Indomitable* was in Freetown, having steamed around southern Africa after taking part in Operation

Ironclad, the British landings in Madagascar. *Victorious* deployed from the Home Fleet and Pedestal was a classic demonstration of the ability of aircraft carriers to concentrate aircraft, with their logistic support, where and when they are needed. Between 6 and 8 August 1942 the five aircraft carriers concentrated in the Atlantic to the west of Gibraltar and carried out fighter direction and inter-carrier exercises designated Operation Berserk. These were great value since they gave the different fighter squadrons and direction teams the experience of working together. Several amendments were made to the operational plans after Berserk. *Victorious*' Type 79B radar had better height-finding characteristics than *Indomitable*'s Type 281 but the latter had better low-level capability. Because of this, she and the similarly fitted *Sirius* were to maintain an all-round search while *Victorious* and the other cruisers concentrated on height finding, which was vital for accurate fighter direction. For the first time VHF radio was fitted in all ships for the rapid exchange of information on a common air-raid reporting net and the practice in using it was invaluable. All fighters were fitted with both VHF R/T and IFF[4] and considerable thought was given to identifying aircraft as friendly or hostile but these did not work as well in practice as expected. Fighters returning from CAP were briefed to fly in stepped up line-astern formation, coming in from the opposite side to the sun. When 5nm from the centre of the convoy, they were to turn a complete circle to permit both radar and visual 'de-lousing' to

The three fleet carriers, *Victorious* (top), *Indomitable* (centre) and *Eagle* (nearest), each with its attendant anti-aircraft cruiser, turn together at the end of Operation Berserk. (*Author's collection*)

ensure that they were neither being followed by hostile aircraft nor an enemy formation approaching in an unusual way. As a further measure to help over-eager gunners identify carrier fighters, aircraft tail fins and the wing leading edges were painted yellow as a high-visibility, visual identification feature. These ideas worked in daylight but they did not work in the dusk after an evening air attack, when gunners tended to fire at anything that flew. On 9 August all five aircraft carriers joined Admiral Syfret's flag west of the Straits of Gibraltar for a further series of work-up exercises that included radar reporting, fighter direction and simulated air attacks on the fleet. This was the first time that the RN had operated five carriers together, although *Argus* left at the end of this day.

Admiral Syfret's staff planned enhanced roles for RAF aircraft based in Gibraltar and Malta. Shore-based aircraft were to locate, report and shadow enemy surface forces and carry out photographic reconnaissance of Italian ports and airfields in Sicily and Sardinia as well as providing both long- and short-range fighter cover for Force X and the convoy as they approached Malta. Beaufighters were to disconcert Axis air forces with strafing and low-level bombing attacks on airfields and Consolidated Liberator bombers from Malta were to attack airfields in Sardinia. The USAAF agreed that Liberators based in Egypt would attack the Italian fleet, ports in Sicily and Southern Italy as well as airfields in Sicily and Pantelleria Island on the night of 12 August. Disappointingly, however, its support was withdrawn on 8 August on the grounds that ranges were too great and that 'other considerations had rendered the project impracticable'.[5] By August the RAF had the largest establishment of aircraft in Malta yet achieved, including, with aircraft ferried in Bellows, 100 Spitfires, some of which could be fitted with drop tanks, thirty-six Beaufighters, thirty Beauforts, three Wellington torpedo bombers, two Baltimores and five Liberators. There were also three Fleet Air Arm Swordfish and Albacores, the survivors of 828 and 830 NAS. Reconnaissance could be carried out by six photographic reconnaissance Spitfires, five ASV-fitted Wellingtons and five Baltimores. The operation of these aircraft on anything but the most limited scale, however, depended on the arrival of *Ohio* with the Pedestal convoy.

Unsurprisingly, Axis staff planners gave thought to ways in which a relief convoy from the west could be prevented from reaching Malta and when news of the Pedestal convoy's passage into the Mediterranean reached the Italian naval staff on the afternoon of 10 August it activated a prepared plan. Eighteen Italian and three German U-boats were at sea with twenty-three motor torpedo boats on standby. There were 600 Axis aircraft in Sardinia, Sicily and Pantellaria including 247 fighters,

Vice Admiral Sir Neville Syfret GCB KBE. (*Author's collection*)

of which seventy-two were German; 224 bombers and ninety torpedo bombers, of which overall total 147 were German. The remainder were reconnaissance aircraft. To defend the convoy, the RN had seventy-four embarked fighters.

A Hudson of 233 Squadron RAF located and bombed *U-331* on the evening of 8 August east-south-east of Formentera Island, leaving only two German boats, *U-73* and *U-205*, on patrol across Force Z's line of advance. The enemy had developed new tactics after Harpoon including the synchronisation of attacks by high-level and torpedo bombers and the use of a circling torpedo known to the Italians as the Motobomba FF. Axis fighter patrols were flown over their airfields and anti-sabotage measures were taken along the southern coast of Sardinia and Sicily. Enemy air reconnaissance was flown over the Western Mediterranean from 11 August and five Italian cruisers were ordered to rendezvous on the evening of 12 August off Pantelleria but, most emphatically, only if Axis fighters were provided to protect them. The Italian shortage of fuel oil meant that no battleships could be included in the Italian plan but this significant fact was not discovered by British intelligence sources. As the convoy passed close to Sardinia on 12 August Axis fighters had sufficient range to escort bombers throughout the day.

By 1600 on 10 August 1942 the Pedestal Convoy and its escort, together with *Furious* and her thirty-eight RAF Spitfires, were heading east at 13.5 knots. Fighters were launched from deck alert on several occasions to intercept aircraft detected by radar but they all turned out to be RAF aircraft from Gibraltar that had forgotten to switch on their IFF. Soon after dawn on 11 August enemy shadowers were detected and by 1000 the Italian naval staff knew the convoy's position, composition, course and speed. *Victorious* and *Indomitable* both had sections of fighters airborne from first light; the former's Fulmars at 2,000ft and the latter's Sea Hurricanes at 12,000ft. Both carried out interceptions and one enemy shadower was damaged. The speed of the shadowing Ju 88s made them difficult for even the Sea Hurricane to intercept, leading Syfret to comment in his report that 'it will be a happy day when the Fleet is equipped with modern fighter aircraft'[6]. The first report of the convoy's movement to reach the enemy, however, came from Vichy French Algeria.[7] Early on 11 August, *Indomitable*'s Sea Hurricanes shepherded an Air France civilian aircraft away from the convoy. On landing at Algiers the crew informed the authorities who, in turn, passed on the intelligence to the Italian Armistice Commission.

At 1040 and again at 1235 large formations of enemy aircraft were detected on radar. The first, comprising Ju 88s, was broken up by *Indomitable*'s Sea Hurricanes but the later force was not seen despite *Eagle* vectoring the four Sea Hurricanes of 801 NAS Red Section to intercept it. These four aircraft never saw their ship again because at 1315 she was hit on the port side by three, or possibly four torpedoes fired by *U-73*, which had managed to pass under the destroyer screen about 65nm south of Majorca,[8] 584nm west of Malta. Seventeen other Sea Hurricanes went down with the ship. *Eagle*'s outdated underwater protection system was defeated by these major explosions and she sank in only eight minutes. Fortuitously, her ship's company was changing from action to defence stations and a considerable proportion were able to escape. Thirteen officers and 158 of her company were lost but 789 survivors,

Rear Admiral Sir Harold Burrough GCB KBE DSO. (*Author's collection*)

including Captain Mackintosh, were picked up by *Laforey* and *Lookout* with the rescue tug *Jaunty*. Red Section, led by 801 NAS' commanding officer Lieutenant Commander Brabner, landed on the other carriers,[9] two on *Victorious* and two on *Indomitable* since space on both ships was at a premium. *Furious* was flying off Spitfires when *Eagle* was hit but all thirty-eight were successfully flown off. One developed a defect and returned to land on *Indomitable* but the remaining thirty-seven all landed in Malta. The loss of *Eagle* meant that the other two carriers' Fulmars had to be employed to carry out interceptions at any altitude they could reach, not just at low level.[10]

At 1430 a Ju 88 shadower was intercepted and shot down by *Indomitable*'s CAP but its return fire hit the second Sea Hurricane and forced it to ditch. A lull followed although shadowers still appeared on radar. It was anticipated that a major enemy attack might be made at dusk and, as the sun sank below the western horizon, a large force was detected on radar heading towards the convoy. Extra Sea Hurricane sections were flown off to back up the airborne CAP but, with daylight fading interception proved difficult and most of the thirty-six attacking Ju 88s and He 111s were actually driven off by the gun barrage, which appeared 'most spectacular' in the twilight. Three enemy aircraft were confirmed as shot down by anti-aircraft fire but in the gathering gloom the returning Sea Hurricane and Fulmar pilots were fired on every time they tried to return to their carriers. By the time the enemy bombers had gone it was pitch dark and some of the fighters were almost out of fuel. Lieutenant Savage, commanding officer of 809 NAS, wrote in his report that:

> I now became very anxious about my 3 companions as they had done very few day [deck] landings, about an hour and a half night flying in the last year, and only 3 dusk landings to prepare them for the coming ordeal. Moreover we had all become separated in the darkness... and I doubted their capacity to find their way home. It was a little misty and the darkness soon became that of [the inside of] a cupboard with neither sea, horizon or stars, and flying had to be done by instruments. The fighter direction staff were, however, still vectoring us cheerfully from place to place, only to be met in each locality with a fresh barrage from the Fleet.

Sporadic firing at the fleet's own fighters continued[11] as they circled to land on. Lieutenant Savage's 809 NAS Fulmars eventually managed to find *Victorious* but several of *Indomitable*'s fighters also landed on *Victorious*. Two Sea Hurricanes hit others that had been parked on deck and a third

Indomitable with a solitary Sea Hurricane ranged aft ready for take-off. (*Author's collection*)

hit the island and burst into flames. A fourth hit a pom-pom mounting and was so badly damaged that it had to be jettisoned immediately to make space on deck. Fortunately none of the pilots were injured.

The Sea Hurricane pilot that hit the island was Sub Lieutenant H Popham RNVR of 880 NAS, who gave a vivid word picture of the evening's events from a carrier pilot's perspective in his outstanding book *Sea Flight*:[12]

> The day wore on. At 2000 Brian [Lieutenant D B M Fiddes RN] and I were back on standby... We hung about on the flight deck, Mae Wests[13] on, helmets around our necks, gloves in sticky hands... the Tannoy crackled. 'Scramble the Hurricanes! Scramble the Hurricanes!' The fitters[14] in the cockpits pressed the starter-buttons and the 4 Merlins opened up with a blast of sound and a gust of blue smoke. As we scrambled up the wings, the crews hopped out on the other side, fixing our straps with urgent fingers... the ship was under full helm, racing up into wind and we were off and climbing at full boost on a northerly vector to 20,000ft, heads swivelling... there they were, a big formation of Ju 88s below us. They broke formation as they saw us coming and Brian and I picked one and went after him. He turned and dived away and we stuffed the nose down, full bore, willing our aircraft to make up on him. At extreme range we gave him a long burst; bits came off and smoke poured out of one

engine and then he vanished into the thickening twilight. We hadn't a hope of catching him and making sure... and so, cursing our lack of speed, we re-formed, joined up with Steve Harris and Paddy Brownlee, the other members of the flight, and started to climb back to base.

The sight we saw took our breath away. The light was slowly dying and the ships were no more than a pattern on the grey steel plate of the sea... but they were enclosed in a sparkling net of tracer and bursting shells, a mesh of fire... We had already been in the air for an hour, most of it with the throttle wide open. There was no sign of the Ju 88s which had started it all and it was not clear at first what the ships were still firing at. Then we saw the tracer coming nosing up towards us and one or two black puffs of smoke burst uncomfortably close. We moved around the fleet and the bursts followed us; the truth could no longer be disregarded. They were firing at anything that flew.

We pulled away out of range, called up the ship and asked for instructions... 'Stand by Yellow Flight. Will pancake[15] you as soon as possible.'... Worlds seemed to divide the dark cockpit and its glowing instruments from the dark Air Direction Room with its glowing screens, worlds of twilight sky and sea, as black now as well-water, and the spasmodic blurts of fire... I tested the gauges of the three tanks and found I had less than twenty gallons left, a bare half-hour's flying. On my own now, I throttled right back, cut the revs, went into fully weak mixture. It looked as if those eighteen gallons were going to have to last a long time. Every now and then I approached the ships, still just visible below and each time the guns opened up. At last I dropped down to 50ft and ploughed slowly up and down between the screen and the convoy, waiting for a chance to find the ship and hoping to find her into wind. From time to time one of the merchant ships on one side – they had thoughtfully been provided with 4 Bofors guns each against just such an opportunity – or the destroyers on the other side would spot me and the red dots of their tracer would come drifting up at me.

I was down to ten gallons and began to go over in my mind the procedure for ditching, for if I wasn't shot down, and if I didn't find a deck to land on very soon, I should surely have to land in the sea. I jettisoned the hood and released my parachute harness and kept ducking the gusts of gunfire and came, all at once, to the sudden, stabbing realisation that this might be the end of me... Automatically I checked the tanks. Five gallons. The time had come for desperate measures unless I was going to accept without an effort my own approaching death ... I just managed to make out what looked like a carrier astern of the convoy. I made for it, dropping hook, wheels and flaps on the way. It was difficult to see what she was doing: then I caught the glimmer of her wake and began my approach. There wasn't a light showing but I could see by the wake that she was under helm. Would she be into wind in time?

I steadied into the approach and a pair of lighted bats materialised on her deck and began mechanically to wave me around. I checked my petrol for the last time. All the tanks were reading zero. There was a slight chance I might get down in one piece, even with the deck swinging: there was no chance of my getting round again ... It was my last chance. I crammed the nose down, cut the throttle and with the last bit of extra speed tried to kick the aircraft into a turn to match the ship's ... the skid wiped off the undercarriage and the aircraft hit the deck and went slithering and screeching up towards the island on its belly ... for a fraction of a second I was too relieved

Sea Hurricanes, Martlets and Albacores ranged on *Indomitable*'s flight deck while both watches of aircraft handlers and air mechanics are being mustered during a brief refuelling stop in Freetown, Sierra Leone, as the ship made its way from the Indian Ocean to join the Pedestal task force. (*Author's collection*)

Eagle in her final paint scheme as she appeared during Operation Pedestal. (*Author's collection*)

to move. And then, out of the corner of my eye, I saw a tongue of blue flame flicker across the bottom of the cockpit and I yanked the pin out of the straps and was over the side. An instant later the wreck went up in a haze of flame.

Indomitable's batsman, Lieutenant Commander G M Pares RN, was badly wounded by the premature explosion of a round from one of the after 4.5in guns, which also smashed his illuminated bats. His deputy, Lieutenant A P Boddam-Whetham RN, immediately took over, holding

A Sea Hurricane and Fulmar ranged at immediate readiness on *Victorious* with *Indomitable* and then *Eagle* astern of her. (*Author's collection*)

Unlike *Victorious*, *Indomitable*'s forward lift was large enough to strike down Sea Hurricanes into her upper hangar but they had to go down sideways and be fitted onto trolleys with castors that allowed them to be moved fore and aft. (*Author's collection*)

one electric torch in his mouth and one in each hand. With this temporary arrangement he was able to bring on seven of his own fighters and one from *Victorious*. The day's flying finally ended at about 2200 with roughly fifty fighters left, not all of which were serviceable.

The force had not done well after the dusk attack by Ju 88s and the loss of fighters and unnecessary wastage of ammunition had weakened the convoy and its escort on the eve of the critical day, 12 August, when the heaviest enemy air attacks were expected, every one of them likely to be escorted by fighters superior to those embarked in the two remaining carriers. During the night of 11/12 August, RAF Beaufighters based in Malta attacked Elmas and Decimomannu airfields in Sardinia and Sicily, where their bombs destroyed five SM.79 torpedo bombers, an enemy reconnaissance aircraft and damaged seventeen others as well as disturbing the enemy's sleep.[16]

12 August 1942

Wednesday, 12 August dawned fine with an easterly wind, which allowed the carriers to operate aircraft while remaining inside the screen. Mechanics had been working all night to get aircraft serviceable and at first light, 0610,[17] *Indomitable* and *Victorious* exchanged the fighters that had landed on the wrong carrier the night before.[18] Lyster ordered off a section of Sea Hurricanes to provide CAP at 12,000ft and shadowers were detected on radar soon afterwards. The convoy was shadowed continuously from all points of the compass and sometimes from a great height. It was suspected, and later confirmed from intelligence reports, that vertical photographs had been taken of Force Z on the previous two days to help the enemy plan their attacks. *Victorious*' Fulmars of 884 NAS led by Lieutenant R A F Churchill RN intercepted a Cant Z.1007 and shot it down in flames after a long chase. *Indomitable*'s fighters destroyed another. The CAP was increased to twelve aircraft and all of them were in combat as the day progressed. At no time did the number of naval fighters airborne exceed twenty-four, of which up to eight were obsolescent Fulmars. Against them, the enemy launched attacks by nearly 200 bombers escorted by over 100 fighters.

At 0900 the first attack appeared on radar 65nm from Force Z. It consisted of nineteen Ju 88s from Sicily escorted by sixteen Bf 109Fs. Eight Sea Hurricanes of 800 and 880 NAS were on CAP at 20,000ft with a pair of 884 NAS Fulmars at low level. Another eleven Sea Hurricanes and four

An Albacore being flown off *Indomitable*, photographed from *Victorious*, which has a deck alert Sea Hurricane with its pilot strapped into the cockpit in the foreground. *Eagle* is the third carrier in line. (*Author's collection*)

Fulmars were at deck alert and these were flown off immediately. The two fighter divisions on CAP intercepted the enemy at 25nm and shot down four with four others dropping out of their formation damaged. One of the enemy bombers had been hit by 880 NAS' senior pilot Lieutenant W H Martyn RN, who saw his bullets impact the starboard engine. It was then taken under fire by his number two, Sub Lieutenant Hastings, who saw it crash into the sea.[19] The Bf 109F escort failed to prevent the interception before the Ju 88s began their shallow gliding attacks and even then they only accounted for one 880 NAS Sea Hurricane. The bombers were intercepted in the midst of their attack profile by the fighters that had just taken off and more were shot down, damaged or forced to turn away. Only four got through to attack the ships but an 801 NAS Sea Hurricane was shot down and three other fighters damaged in this fight at low level. Nine Ju 88s were destroyed and six damaged.

One of 880 NAS' pilots was Lieutenant (A) R J Cork DFC RN, who had been one of the fifty-six RN pilots lent to RAF Fighter Command in 1940. He was the top-scoring RN pilot on 12 August and gave a press interview after Pedestal in which he explained that:

> the sky at first sight seemed to be filled with aircraft. The enemy kept in tight formation and our fighters snapped at their heels, forcing them to break in all directions. One Junkers turned away from the main group and I led my section down towards it. I was well ahead and fired when it filled my sights. Smoke poured from its wings and it disappeared below me into the sea. A few minutes later I saw another Ju 88 out of the corner of my eye heading along the coast

Most photographs of Sea Hurricane operations from *Eagle*'s flight deck went down with the ship. This photograph is, unfortunately, of poor quality but it shows the last aircraft to land on before she was torpedoed. (*Author's collection*)

The Pedestal convoy steams on as *Eagle* rolls to port and sinks. (*Author's collection*)

of North Africa, so I set off in pursuit by myself. At 1000ft I came within range and fired. It seemed to stagger in the air, then dropped into the sea with a big splash.

Nos 809 and 884 NAS Fulmars continued to destroy shadowers throughout the day but sufficient enemy aircraft were available to replace them on task, with Cant Z.1007s at low level and Ju 88s unmolested at 30,000ft. The second major attack was detected on radar shortly before noon when the convoy was only 70nm south of Cagliari. Enemy formations were plotted as they moved to the east to begin their approach and when they began to close the convoy they were estimated at ninety-eight bombers with a forty-strong fighter escort. The CAP at this stage comprised four Martlets of 806 NAS led by Johnston, the commanding officer; four Sea Hurricanes of 801 NAS led by Brabner, their commanding officer, at 20,000ft and two Fulmars of 884 NAS led by 'Buster' Hallett, their commanding officer, at 10,000ft. Six Sea Hurricanes led by Bruen and four Fulmars on deck alert were flown off to back up the CAP and *Indomitable* continued to refuel and rearm fighters on the flight deck to maintain the flow of available fighters. The attack began with ten SM.84s dropping Motobomba FF circling torpedoes in the grain of the convoy intended to force the ships to break up their formidable defensive formation and take evasive action. They were escorted by eight CR.42 fighter-bombers, which were briefed to attack the screen in order to open a gap for forty-three SM.79 and SM.84 torpedo bombers. Thirty-seven Ju 88s were to deliver a shallow diving attack as the torpedo bombers ran in and there was to be a special attack by two Reggiane Re.2001 fighter-bombers, which were to drop 1,400lb armour-piercing bombs on the carriers' decks, and a radio-controlled SM.79 packed with explosive.

This complicated attack plan needed a high degree of co-ordination, which was not achieved. The first eighteen Ju 88s lost one of their number to the Martlets and the SM.84s carrying the circling torpedoes were intercepted 40nm out by Fulmars and subsequently harried by other fighters. The CR.42s only managed to attack one destroyer, which they missed. Combat with the escorting fighters tied up some of the carriers' fighters but sufficient broke free to engage and demoralise the SM.79 torpedo bombers as they began their approach. At least twelve were shot down or forced to jettison their torpedoes and evade, three of them credited to 'Buster' Hallett and Lieutenant F Pennington RN; those that continued on released their torpedoes at long range from outside the screen and no hits were achieved. The final element of this attack consisted of the remaining nineteen Ju 88s which were intercepted by 809 NAS Fulmars at 19,000ft. Several were damaged and forced to jettison their bombs but as the bombers began their dives the Fulmars were unable to keep pace with them and the one damaging hit of this attack was achieved by one of these Ju 88s on the freighter *Deucalion*, which lost speed and had to drop out of the convoy formation. She made for the Tunisian coast but later in the day she was hit by attacking SM.79s and blew up. The special attack by Reggiane Re.2001s came to nothing and frustratingly, given Hugh Popham's experience the night before, the fleet's gunners mistook these Italian fighters for Sea Hurricanes and did not fire at them

A Sea Hurricane taking off from *Indomitable*. (*Author's collection*)

A Sea Hurricane landing on *Indomitable* well aft of the ideal touch-down point and even short of number 1 wire. The batsman is behind the small screen just forward of the 4.5in gun turrets with his bats lowered in the 'cut' position, and the handlers in the port catwalk are craning forward ready to run out and remove the aircraft's hook from the arrester wire when it stops moving. (*Author's collection*)

despite their lack of yellow markings. The guided bomb SM.79 went out of control and crashed in Algeria, much to the annoyance of the Vichy French authorities.

There was a lull in enemy air activity after the midday attacks but destroyers on the screen continued to gain submarine contacts and attacked them with depth charges, which kept the boats down. None attacked the convoy. Another lull allowed damaged fighters to be repaired and made ready for action but *Victorious* experienced problems with her aircraft lifts and the forward one was out of action for over two hours. It was found that the shock from continuous anti-aircraft gunfire had severed a number of electrical connections. At 1600 *Ithuriel* forced the Italian submarine *Cobalto* to the surface after several depth charge attacks and rammed it. The submarine sank but *Ithuriel* suffered a damaged bow.

The next attack came after 1700 and, as in the earlier attack, the enemy gave over an hour's warning by forming up within the fleet's radar coverage. This raid was smaller than the earlier efforts, comprising fourteen SM.79s, twenty-nine Ju 87 dive bombers, seventeen of which were flown by Italian crews, and eighteen Ju 88s, with about forty escorting fighters. A Martlet section on CAP was vectored 30nm out to intercept the first enemy group to close the convoy but it was found to comprise six bombers escorted by over twenty fighters and the Martlets were ordered back to Force Z. At 1800, having formed up, the enemy headed towards the force from two different directions with eleven separate groups tracked on radar at

Air mechanics preparing a Sea Hurricane for flight. Armourers on top of the wings are reloading the eight Browning 0.303in machine guns in the wings and a photographer in a white T-shirt is putting a new film into the gun camera in the starboard wing root. The Sea Hurricane's fixed wings were not always a disadvantage since they made it easier to reload the guns' ammunition trays than was the case with folding-wing fighters such as the Fulmar and Martlet, in which access could be cramped and at awkward angles. (*Author's collection*)

heights between 10,000 and 20,000ft and ranges between 50 and 69nm from the convoy. By then there were three Martlets, twelve Sea Hurricanes and six Fulmars on CAP. By 1830, as the attack developed, *Victorious* was launching four Fulmars and two Sea Hurricanes, and *Indomitable* was preparing to catapult four Sea Hurricanes. Force Z turned away to the west at 1900 in accordance with the plan but it had taken the full weight of the evening attack; the enemy had ignored the convoy and its close escort completely.

Only eight fighters were vectored out to intercept the enemy groups closing from the south-east and north-east, the remainder were held in reserve to fight a close-in battle. All the former were engaged by enemy fighters, which were handled on this occasion in a far more determined manner. Relatively few of the naval fighters were able to get at the bombers and as *Indomitable* was completing her launch and was in the process of ranging four more Sea Hurricanes, she was attacked by the twelve Luftwaffe Ju 87s. Their attack was well pressed home from a position up sun on an after bearing where funnel gases masked their approach. At 1850, before her guns could fire effectively, *Indomitable* was hit three times on the flight deck and near-missed by several other bombs, one of which blew a hole in the ship's side and bottom abreast the wardroom. The hits put the flight deck and both lifts out of action, wrecked the two after gun turrets manned by Royal Marines and killed six officers and forty-four men. A further fifty-nine were wounded. Two big fires were started but fortunately these were in positions where they could be tackled from several directions by large numbers of men backing up the initial fire parties. Neither fire mains in the vicinity nor the avgas plumbing had been damaged and within half an hour the situation was well in hand. *Indomitable* could play no further part in flying activities but as darkness approached the enemy's air effort was spent, at least temporarily, and damage to the carrier was not followed up despite shadowing aircraft having seen and reported it. The Sea Hurricane division that had just taken off destroyed five of the Ju 87s after the attack together with one

The near-contemporary aircraft direction room, ADR, in a 1945 light fleet carrier. The equipment visible in this tightly packed space was typical of those fitted in aircraft carriers, battleships and cruisers by this stage of the war and included: 1. Ship's head indicator. 2. Ship's speed indicator. 3. General air plot, kept up to date from behind so that the plotter did not obscure the direction officers' view of it. 4. Air track reporting officer's position. 5. Chart table. 6. Number 1 'skiatron' table on which the radar picture was projected to facilitate appreciation of the tactical picture for interception control. 7. Number 1 interception control position plan position indicator. 8. Number 2 interception control position plan position indicator. 9. Air teller's position. 10. Number 2 intercept 'skiatron'. 11. Number 2 interception control position. 12. Direction officer's position. (Admiralty, *Manual of Naval Airmanship*, 1949 Edition)

This photograph shows the ADR of a fleet carrier such as *Indomitable* or *Victorious*. It is similar to the accompanying photograph of a light fleet carrier ADR, but viewed from a different perspective. All carriers had slight differences as they were modified at different times to evolving standards. The points numbered are: 13. Fighter state board. 14. Own aircraft state board. 15. Radar state board. 16. General air plot. 17. Ship's heading. 18. Ship's speed. 19. Voice callsign board. 20. Meteorological state board. 21. Clock. 22. Intercept officer's radar plan position indicator. 23. Number 1 interception 'skiatron'. 24. Direction officer's position. 25. 'Skiatron' calibrator unit. 26. Interception officer. 27. Fleet direction officer's position. (Admiralty, *Manual of Naval Airmanship*, 1949 edition)

SM.79. The SM.79s had achieved their only success of the operation by torpedoing *Foresight*, which sank on the following day. When this attack ended *Victorious* recovered the remaining fighters with only seven Fulmars and two Sea Hurricanes left to cover the convoy. The last CAP of the day landed on at 2040 in the dark and a quick appraisal was carried out of the aircraft crowded on *Victorious*' flight deck. Any aircraft that were damaged or could not immediately be made serviceable were pushed over the side, leaving her with six Sea Hurricanes, three Martlets and ten Fulmars ready for operation the next day.

In the US Navy, fighter pilots who accumulated five or more aerial victories were deemed to have achieved 'ace' status. The Admiralty did not recognise the term and shied away from individual publicity for its aircrew but by 1942 the need to make the public more aware of the Fleet Air Arm's achievements led the Admiralty Information Department to encourage press interviews, hence the quotation from Lieutenant Cork. The term ace was used unofficially, however, and on 12 August 1942 three RN pilots scored 'kills' that brought them to unofficial 'ace' status. Lieutenant 'Moose' Martyn of 880 NAS was the first, 'Buster' Hallett of 884 NAS the second and Lieutenant 'Dickie' Cork of 880 NAS the third. Cork continued to score 'kills' as 12 August progressed and his final victory of the day made him the only RN fighter pilot of the war to destroy five or more enemy aircraft in a single day.[20] He was awarded the DSO.

In *Sea Flight*, Hugh Popham described[21] how half *Indomitable*'s fighters were airborne when she was damaged and as they returned from CAP they had to land on *Victorious*:

> They caused a scene of frantic confusion ... only a certain number could be kept on deck ... any that were not fully serviceable or could not quickly be made so were pushed aft and overboard. It took more than an hour to sort things out and then there were, at last, 6 Sea Hurricanes re-fuelled, re-armed and ranged aft ready for take-off.

A torpedo-armed Italian SM.79 flying over a ship on the outer screen as it carries out its attack. (*Author's collection*)

Several members of 880 NAS, including Dickie Cork, joined Popham on *Victorious* and he heard what had happened to the squadron on 12 August from them. Sub Lieutenant Cruikshank had been attacked by a Bf 109 before anyone could save him. Brian Fiddes had been shot down by the fleet's anti-aircraft fire but had ditched successfully and been picked up by the last destroyer in the screen. Most of the others had one or two enemy aircraft to their credit but 'Butch' Judd, the commanding officer, was dead, killed by the rear gunner of an He 111 as he attacked it from astern. Ironically he had impressed on his pilots over and over again that a stern attack was fatal but lack of superior speed, not disobedience to his own instructions, had led to his loss. Popham described him[22] in *Sea Flight* as unsettling in appearance, tall, perhaps 6ft 2in and with a reddish beard and moustache, trimmed after the fashion of the late King George V. The moustache was allowed to run wild and sprang out horizontally from his upper lip, stiff, plentiful and coarse 'like a couple of tarred rope's ends in need of whipping'. His temper was volcanic and his ferocity a matter of legend.

The other commanding officer killed in action on that fateful day was Lieutenant Johnston of 806 NAS. He had radioed to say that he had shot

The dive-bombing attack on *Indomitable*. (*Author's collection*)

down a Ju 88 and was returning to *Indomitable*. An eyewitness described how his Martlet approached the deck...

> too low and too fast. His aircraft's hook caught an arrester wire but 'was torn out of the fuselage and the aeroplane slewed out over the catwalk, a few feet in front of me. As though in slow motion, I watched the pilot, Lieutenant Johnston, try to climb out of the cockpit but the aeroplane turned on its back and fell into the sea. He had been wounded in one of the many air battles.

The RN had lost seven fighters in combat on 12 August – three Fulmars, three Sea Hurricanes and a Martlet – but after the events of the day had been analysed the two carriers' pilots were credited with thirty-eight enemy aircraft destroyed; four by Martlets, nine by Fulmars and twenty-five by Sea Hurricanes. Losses among the fighter squadrons on this day included Lieutenant Commander F E C Judd DSC RN, Sub Lieutenant (A) J I Cruikshank RNVR and Sub Lieutenant (A) H L Cunliffe-Owen RNVR of 880 NAS. No. 801 NAS lost Sub Lieutenant (A) M Hankey RNVR and 800 NAS lost Sub Lieutenant (A) J M Lucas RNVR. No. 806 NAS lost Lieutenant R L Johnston RN and 809 NAS lost Sub Lieutenant (A) C J Evans RNVR and Leading Airman J Stewart. No. 884 NAS lost Lieutenant R A F Churchill RN, Sub Lieutenant (A) J H O'C Nihill RNVR, Sub Lieutenant (A) A Nunn RNVR and Leading Airman W R Reagan.

Between 1850 and 1930 as *Victorious* sorted out her crowded flight deck, two aircraft had to ditch when they ran out of fuel. A final patrol of four Sea Hurricanes was ranged and flown off at 2007. After only half an hour airborne, they were recovered without incident and the day's flying was completed.

The Fleet Air Arm had achieved a notable victory on 12 August. The enemy had held the initiative throughout the day and attacked in great strength with an escort that had always outnumbered the defenders but they had not come close to subduing the exhausted naval pilots until the third attack. By then most of the carrier pilots were flying their third or fourth combat sorties of the day but even then the sixty-one enemy bombers managed to obtain only two really damaging hits on Force Z and they had completely neglected the convoy, the safe passage of which had been the whole purpose of the operation. The enemy's air attacks must, therefore be considered as a tactical failure. In addition to the enemy aircraft shot down by the carriers' fighters, a further nine were claimed as shot down by the fleet's gunfire, making an overall total of forty-seven. These figures accord well with post-war analysis of Italian records, which showed that forty-two Axis aircraft had actually been lost, evenly divided between the Germans and Italians.

The damaged *Indomitable* had been temporarily left behind by Force Z but was gradually able to work up to 22 knots and soon re-joined Syfret's force. Up to this point the convoy had only lost the *Deucalion* and was proceeding to its destination unhindered by anything the enemy was able to do from the air. *Indomitable*'s Captain Troubridge, who had commanded *Furious* during the Norwegian campaign, wrote in his action report:[23]

> So ended a great day... All the pilots were up twice and sometimes three times... they responded to every call. The teamwork between Victorious and Indomitable was one of the outstanding features of a notable day... fighter carriers had proved their worth.

The air battles were over for Force Z and in his own report Lyster wrote that:

> on the approach of our fighters, many of the enemy aircraft jettisoned their bombs and dived away... The sooner the Naval Air Service is equipped with modern high-performance fighter aircraft, the less we

The damage to *Indomitable*'s after lift well and the non-armoured area of deck aft of it. (Author's collection)

The destroyers *Penn*, left, and *Bramham*, right, lashed alongside *Ohio* as she nears Grand Harbour, Valletta. (*Author's collection*)

shall continue to suffer disappointment and the less we shall continue to incur damage to our very valuable ships if they are compelled to operate in waters which are so easily controlled by the enemy shore-based aircraft...I consider that the carrier must be altered to take the fighters; not the fighters altered to fit the carrier...They should be capable of carrying expendable [drop] tanks.

The German Admiral Weichold wrote in Axis Naval Policy and Operations in the Mediterranean[24] that:

The British fighter opposition was so good, even without the Eagle's aircraft, that the Axis planes were denied any major successes in these raids.

An early assessment was made by NAD of the RN fighters' performance during the critical phase of Pedestal on 11/12 August.[25] In this they calculated that a total of sixty embarked fighters were available at dawn on 11 August and on the two days they flew a total of 209 sorties in which there were ninety combats with thirty-nine enemy aircraft shot down and nineteen probably damaged. Against these, eight RN fighters were lost and a further fifteen damaged. NAD further broke these statistics down to show that ten Martlets had been available at dawn on 11 August. These had flown twenty-seven sorties in which there were seven combats that shot down four enemy aircraft and probably damaged three for the loss of one Martlet. There had been thirty-four Sea Hurricanes at the outset, which flew 126 sorties in which there were fifty-six combats, leading to twenty-six enemy aircraft being shot down and a further thirteen probably damaged. Four Sea Hurricanes were lost and thirteen damaged in these two days. There had been sixteen Fulmars at dawn on 11 August. These had flown fifty-six sorties, resulting in twenty-seven combats in which nine enemy aircraft had been shot down and a further three probably damaged. Three Fulmars were lost and two damaged. The figures show that the Sea Hurricanes and Fulmars each flew roughly three-and-a-half sorties per aircraft over the critical period but the Martlets only two-and-a-half. Sea Hurricanes achieved one 'kill' for every two sorties; Martlets one for every one-and-three-quarter sorties and Fulmars one for every three; the latter figure reflecting well on the Fulmar considering its low ceiling and relative obsolescence.

The last hours of the convoy

Force Z steamed west for twenty-four hours and then waited north of Algiers to provide support for Force X after it left the convoy. *Indomitable*, *Rodney* and five destroyers were detached to Gibraltar, arriving on 14 August. Once there, *Indomitable* entered dry dock to have her underwater damage assessed before leaving for Liverpool on 23 August for repairs and a refit that lasted until February 1943.

Burrough took charge of the convoy at 1900 on 12 August but *Nigeria*, and *Cairo* were both hit by torpedoes from a single salvo fired by the Italian submarine *Axum* at 1955 north-east of Bizerta. Burrough transferred his flag to the destroyer *Ashanti* and the damaged *Nigeria* headed west for Gibraltar. *Cairo* could not be salvaged and had to be sunk. These two cruisers had carried the direction officers who were to have controlled fighters from Malta on 13 August and their loss meant that they had to defend the convoy without control. The tanker *Ohio* was also torpedoed but managed to stay with the convoy.[26] Further air attacks took place at dusk on 12 August as the Malta-based fighters returned to their bases and the convoy changed formation from four columns to two to pass through the Skerki Channel. The change and an alteration of course to evade the submarine attack caused the ships to lose their disciplined formation and bunch up and it was at this awkward moment that a group of enemy aircraft attacked out of the dusk. *Empire Hope* and *Clan Ferguson* were sunk and *Brisbane Star* damaged. *Kenya* was hit by a torpedo from the Italian submarine *Alagi* but not badly damaged and remained with the convoy. Syfret sent *Charybdis* and two destroyers back to replace the damaged ships, the convoy rounded Cape Bon at midnight and turned south, keeping close to the Tunisian coast. *Manchester* was hit by torpedoes from Italian MTBs at 0105 on 13 August.[27] She was stopped with all four propeller shafts out of action, three of them permanently. *Pathfinder* and *Somali* took off some of her ship's company but her captain decided that she could not be saved and ordered her to be scuttled. The majority of her ship's company made their way to the Tunisian coast, where they were interned by the Vichy French authorities until after the Allied invasion of North Africa in November.[28] Five merchant ships dropped astern of the main body and were hit; four of them, *Wairangi, Almeria Lykes, Santa Elisa* and probably *Glenorchy*, were sunk between 0315 and 0430.

German bombers returned soon after daylight on 13 August and *Waimarama* was hit and blew up. An enemy aircraft crashed onto *Ohio* after releasing its bomb and by 1050 she was badly disabled, *Rochester Castle* was on fire and *Dorset* hit and stopped. The three remaining undamaged ships drew near to Malta with Spitfires holding off further attempts to attack them. At 1430 the Malta-based minesweepers and motor launches came out to meet *Port Chalmers, Melbourne Star* and the damaged *Rochester Castle*, and they entered Grand Harbour at 1630. *Ohio, Dorset* and *Brisbane Star* were spread out astern of them and desperate efforts were being made to save them. *Ohio* and *Dorset* were hit again in dusk air attacks that sank the latter but the destroyers *Penn* and *Ledbury*, together with the minesweeper *Rye*, stood by *Ohio*. Her Master, Captain Dudley Mason, and his surviving crew never gave up. With the

Ohio, with her upper deck nearly awash, entering Grand Harbour. A tug has replaced *Penn* but *Bramham* is still secured to her port side. (*Author's collection*)

warships secured alongside the tanker as it slowly settled in the water, they fought off repeated air attacks and the three warships continued to tow her towards Grand Harbour, arriving on 15 August, shortly after the damaged *Brisbane Star*. *Ohio*'s upper deck amidships was nearly awash and as she entered the wreck-strewn Grand Harbour, thousands of people lined the ramparts of Baracca, St Angelo and Senglea to cheer her and a band played *Rule Britannia*. As *Penn* cast off her captain called across to Captain Mason, 'I've just had a message from Admiral Burrough, it reads "To *Ohio* – I am proud to have met you."' He added, 'That goes for us too.' Captain Mason, who had not slept for days, replied, 'We're here thanks to you.' He was awarded the George Cross for his bravery and determination. By 22 August 32,000 tons of cargo had been unloaded and removed to comparative safety. *Ohio* was alongside the sunken RFA *Plumleaf* and RFA *Boxall* was used to recover her precious cargo but the enemy made no attempt to interfere with the unloading.

Pedestal was the largest of the resupply convoys to Malta and its successful conclusion allowed offensive operations against Axis logistic supply lines to North Africa to resume in strength at the critical moment before the Battle of El Alamein. In his report to the Admiralty, Syfret wrote that only one enemy torpedo bomber aircraft managed to penetrate the destroyer screen to drop its weapon and praised the merchant ships' determination to press through every form of attack, 'answering every manoeuvring order like a well-trained fleet unit'. This had been a most inspiring sight, 'the memory of their conduct will remain an inspiration to all who were privileged to sail with them'.

Good fighter direction and the large proportion of fighters in the carrier air groups had, he believed, been major factors in the comparative immunity of the convoy during the first three days. On the other hand, he thought that the limited endurance of the Sea Hurricane had been something of an embarrassment, making pilots and direction officers reluctant to intercept enemy formations at any distance from the fleet, the best place to do so before any attack was fully developed. This was a valid point; the Sea Hurricane's Pilot's Notes gave its range on internal fuel as 500nm but the American-designed F4F-4 Martlet had a range of 830nm on internal fuel. The Fulmar fell between the Sea Hurricane and the Martlet at 650nm.

Time and effort had, in Syfret's opinion, been wasted intercepting shadowers in the first two days that turned out to be RAF patrol aircraft that had forgotten to switch on their IFF equipment and he also felt, with hindsight, that attempts to intercept shadowers on 12 August had been wasteful. It would have been better to disregard them and retain more aircraft on CAP and deck alert ready for the inevitable large-scale air attacks that would come later.

Like his predecessors, Syfret had to stress the need for RN fighters of higher performance and added that fighters capable of engaging enemy aircraft at dusk or after dark were urgently needed. He also believed that anti-aircraft fire had clearly acted as a deterrent to enemy torpedo bombers but insufficient aircraft had actually been shot down to fully justify the enormous expenditure of ammunition.

Syfret questioned the number of Albacores included in his force. It would not have been possible to range an Albacore striking force on 11 or 12 August without jeopardising the safety of the fleet and convoy. Such a strike would, in any case, have required a fighter escort and, realistically, none could have been provided. A separate TSR carrier would have been necessary unless the strike was to be carried out at night but even then its preparation would have added to the exhaustion of the handlers prior to the next day's fighter operations. *Argus* had been left out of the operation because of her low speed and, presumably, vulnerability to underwater attack. During Pedestal more aircraft than ever before had been controlled by fighter direction officers and, thanks to a great deal of hard work and preparation by ships' staffs, this had proved remarkably successful. Undoubtedly the RN was the world leader in the relevant equipment, tactics and technique by this stage.

The harsh lesson that inexperienced pilots were vulnerable in a major operation such as Pedestal was accepted by the Admiralty but not easily resolved. Two inexperienced pilots launched on 12 August were shot down on their first contact with the enemy. Even section leaders' average time since leaving the RN Fighter School at RNAS Yeovilton had only been six months but this was inevitable given the shortage of experienced pilots in 1942, both in squadrons and as instructors in the training units. Improvements included the establishment of 'fighter pool' squadrons ashore to give operational experience before new pilots joined embarked squadrons. Plans were also being prepared to establish a School of Air Combat that would train the first generation of air warfare instructors.[29]

The 1SL gave his opinion of Pedestal in a letter to Cunningham in which he wrote: 'We paid a heavy price but personally I think we got out of it lightly considering the risks we had to run and the tremendous concentration of everything...which we had to face.' Stephen Roskill observed in *The War at Sea Volume II*,[30] that the cost had indeed been heavy. 'If ever,' he wrote, 'in the centuries to come students should seek an example of the costliness in war of the failure by a maritime nation to properly defend its overseas bases in time of peace, surely the story of Malta's ordeal in 1941/42 will provide the classic case.' It also emphasised how very wrong those outside the RN had been when they argued against the need for the fleet to have high-performance fighters in its carrier air

Brisbane Star's cargo being unloaded into lighters. (*Author's collection*)

groups in the years before 1939. The Air Ministry's supposed experts and even Winston Churchill had failed to grasp that fleets must be able to fight land-based aircraft and that the RAF, with its own problems to face, would be unable to help when called upon.

The final Spitfire ferry operations

Two further operations, Baritone and Train, were carried out in which *Furious* ferried Spitfires to a position west of Malta. Baritone involved thirty-two Spitfires being flown off; one crashed on take-off and technical defects forced two pilots to bail out, both of whom were subsequently rescued. In Train, twenty-nine out thirty-one Spitfires embarked were flown off, the other two suffering engine defects that prevented them from flying. Small quantities of avgas continued to be ferried to Malta in submarines and other fast warships.

The RN had carried out twenty-five operations to resupply the RAF in Malta with fighters, without which the island could not have survived. Thirty-three carrier sorties, two of them by USS *Wasp*, had embarked a total of 746 fighters, 700 of which had landed safely in Malta between 2 August 1940 and 29 October 1942. One carrier, *Ark Royal*, had been lost.

10

Operation Torch

The Allied landings in Algeria and French Morocco in north-west Africa, designated as Operation Torch,[1] had as their objective an assault by an Allied army that would drive east to match the 8th Army's westward advance out of Egypt and remove Axis forces from North Africa. On 8 November 1942, D-Day for the Torch landings, the RN Mediterranean Station was reorganised into two command areas. Admiral Sir Henry Harwood[2] retained the title of C-in-C Mediterranean and his area of command was bordered to the west by a line drawn across the narrows from Cape Bon to Marittimo. On the same day, Admiral Sir Andrew Cunningham, who had been assisting in the naval planning for Torch in Washington, hoisted his flag as Naval Commander Expeditionary Force, NCEF, and assumed command of the Western Mediterranean area with his headquarters at Gibraltar. At the end of the naval phase of Torch on 20 February 1943, Harwood became C-in-C Levant and Cunningham the C-in-C Mediterranean again.[3] At the same time, the dividing line between the two areas was moved further to the east, roughly to a line drawn between the Tripolitania–Tunisian border and Cape Spartivento on the toe of Italy.

Operation Torch was a considerable undertaking that brought together a broad range of naval and military disciplines[4] but the focus of this chapter is on the part played by British carrier-borne aircraft. These are of particular analytical interest because no similar operation had ever been attempted before. It was also the first time that the American-built escort carriers, CVE, in RN service were used as assault carriers to support amphibious landings beyond the practical radius of action of Allied land-based fighters. The final decision to carry out Torch had taken time and there had been disagreement and argument before it was taken by the Combined US/British Chiefs of Staff in July 1942. This left very little time to make preparations and the effect this caused became apparent in the conduct of air operations.

Avenger with the assault convoy KMS-1 heading towards Algiers. (*Author's collection*)

The Admiralty had decided to rearm most RN fighter squadrons with Sea Hurricane Mark IICs and Seafire Mark IBs or IICs for Torch. The Sea Hurricane IIC was armed with four 20mm cannon, which were far more effective than the eight rifle-calibre 0.303in machine guns of the Mark IIB. The Air Ministry promised to provide forty-five Hurricane IICs and forty-five Spitfire Vs for RN pilot conversion training and airfield dummy deck landings, ADDL, ashore in order to conserve the limited number of Sea Hurricanes and Seafires available for Torch but, in the event, none arrived. Admiral Lyster, Rear Admiral Aircraft Carriers Home Fleet, finally acted on his own initiative and obtained thirty sets of Hurricane IIC wings, which he had fitted to Hurricane IIBs so that pilots could practise the use of their enhanced firepower. Eventually, all the designated squadrons were re-equipped although many pilots had barely achieved the necessary minimum airfield dummy deck landings before they embarked. Most squadrons received their new aircraft in September but 891 NAS only received its Sea Hurricanes in October. The need to give leave to pilots who had taken part in Pedestal had to be factored into squadron work-up plans but, with the exception of 891 NAS embarked in *Dasher*, the remainder were described by Lyster as 'fairly experienced'.[5]

Logistic support for the new fighters fell short of the standard required and was strongly criticised by Lyster after the operation. The Admiralty took the view that in such a hastily organised operation in which the need for secrecy had been rigidly applied his criticism was unwarranted. RAF logistic planning for Torch proved to be equally faulty and the secrecy applied to the location and nature of the operation was clearly a factor. Many other shortcomings were revealed but invaluable lessons were learned that greatly helped future operations. The table below shows the British aircraft carriers and naval air squadrons assigned to Operation Torch and the tasks on which they were to be employed. The RN provided the Centre and Eastern Naval Task Forces; the Western Naval Task Force was provided by the USN. Its carriers and squadrons are listed but not their operations.

Force H – Covering Group

Victorious	Captain H C Bovell RN	
	Flag Rear Admiral A L StG Lyster RA (Air)	
882 NAS	12 Martlet IV	Lieutenant Commander H J F Lane RN
884 NAS	6 Seafire IIC	Lieutenant Commander N G Hallett RN
809 NAS	6 Fulmar FII	Captain R C Hay RM
817 NAS	9 Albacore	Lieutenant Commander N R Corbet-Milward RN
832 NAS	9 Albacore	Lieutenant Commander J Lucas RN

Tasked with twenty-five sorties on CAP over Force H and fighter patrols over Blida airfield on 8 November. Tactical reconnaissance was to be provided in support of land forces on 8 and 9 November and twenty-five bombing sorties were to be flown against Fort Jetée du Nord in Algiers harbour and Fort Dupere St Eugène north-west of Algiers on 8 November. Anti-submarine patrols were to be maintained, night and day, in the vicinity of Force H.

Formidable	Captain A G Talbot RN	
885 NAS	6 Seafire IIC	Lieutenant R H P Carver RN
888 NAS	12 Martlet II	Captain F D G Bird RM
893 NAS	12 Martlet IV	Lieutenant (A) R B Pearson RN
820 NAS	12 Albacore	Lieutenant Commander W Elliott RN

Tasked with 100 sorties on CAP over Force H between 0550 and 1650 on 8, 9 and 10 November together with fighter patrols over Maison Blanche airfield. Bombing sorties were to be flown against Fort d'Estrées on Cape Matilou in conjunction with bombardments by *Rodney*.

Note that both carriers used deck parks to embark more than their original design complement of thirty-six aircraft; both embarked forty-two. At last more replacement aircraft were becoming available from the MAP's expanded production and American Lend-Lease.

Centre Naval; Task Group off Oran

Furious	Captain T O Bulteel RN	
801 NAS	12 Seafire IB	Lieutenant (A) F R A Turnbull DSC RN
807 NAS	12 Seafire IIC	Lieutenant A B Fraser-Harris DSC* RN
822 NAS	9 Albacore, 1 Fulmar	Lieutenant J G A McI Nares RN

Detached from the covering force at midnight 7/8 November. Tasked with a bombing attack on hangars at La Sénia airfield co-ordinated with Seafire strafing attacks on Tafaroui and La Sénia airfields. Fighter sweeps with aircraft from *Dasher* and *Biter*; fighter escort to Albacore bombing sorties on 9 November and tactical reconnaissance by Seafires and the Fulmar.

Biter Captain C Abel-Smith RN
800 NAS 15 Sea Hurricane IIC Lieutenant Commander
J M Bruen RN

Tasked with escorting the bombing force as it attacked La Sénia airfield and providing fighter sweeps in concert with *Furious* and *Dasher*. Fighter patrols over 'Z' Sector and Arzeu harbour. Three Swordfish of 833A NAS had taken passage from the UK in *Biter* to give anti-submarine protection but were disembarked to Gibraltar during the operation. It returned to the UK in *Argus*.

Dasher Commander C N Lentaigne RN
804 NAS 6 Sea Hurricane IIC Lieutenant (A) A J Sewell RNVR
891 NAS 6 Sea Hurricane IIB Lieutenant Commander (A)
M J S Newman RN

Tasked with providing top cover for the La Sénia bombing attack and fighter sweeps with aircraft from *Furious* and *Biter*. Also CAP over 'Z' Sector and Arzeu harbour and tactical reconnaissance in support of ground forces.

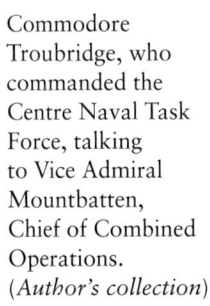

Commodore Troubridge, who commanded the Centre Naval Task Force, talking to Vice Admiral Mountbatten, Chief of Combined Operations. (*Author's collection*)

Eastern Naval Task Force off Algiers

Argus	Captain G T Philip RN	
880 NAS	18 Seafire IIC	Lieutenant Commander (A) W H Martyn RN

Tasked with providing CAP over 'A' and 'B' sectors from dawn to sunset together with *Avenger* and fighter patrols over Blida airfield on 8 and 9 November. CAP over Hatton Beach, Bougie, from dawn to noon on 10 November.

Avenger	Commander A P Colthurst RN	
802 NAS	9 Sea Hurricane IIC	Lieutenant E W T Taylor RN
883 NAS	6 Sea Hurricane IIC	Lieutenant P W V Massey RN

Tasked with providing sixty CAP sorties together with aircraft from *Argus* and to assist *Argus* in supporting landings at Bougie on 10 November. Three Swordfish of 833B NAS had been embarked to give anti-submarine protection on passage from the UK but they were disembarked to Gibraltar during the operation.

USN aircraft carriers operating off the Moroccan coast

Northern Attack Group off Port Lyautey

Sangamon	VGF-26	12 Wildcat
	VGS-26	9 Avenger + 9 Dauntless
Chenango	Ferrying 76 USAAF P-40F Warhawk fighters	

Centre Attack Group off Casablanca

Ranger	VF-9	27 Wildcat
	VF-41	27 Wildcat
	VS-41	18 Dauntless
Suwanee	VGF-27	11 Wildcat
	VGF-28	12 Wildcat (lent from *Chenango*)
	VGS-30	6 Wildcat (fighter flight from *Charger*)
	VGS-27	9 Avenger
Santee	VGF-29	14 Wildcat
	VGS-29	8 Avenger + 9 Dauntless[6]

Force H, under the operational command of Vice Admiral Syfret in the battleship *Duke of York*, was to provide cover against intervention by Italian or Vichy French heavy units and to support the landings at Algiers. Other ships in the force included *Renown*, *Bermuda*, *Argonaut*,

Sirius and a screen of seventeen destroyers. The Centre Naval Task Force comprising seventy warships and thirty-four merchant ships was under the operational command of Commodore T H Troubridge in the landing ship *Largs* and was tasked with supporting the landings at Oran. The Eastern Naval Task Force comprising sixty-seven warships and twenty-five merchant ships was under the operational command of Rear Admiral Sir Harold Burrough in the landing ship *Bulolo* and was tasked with supporting the landings at Algiers and Bougie. Carrier-borne aircraft were also tasked with neutralising the principal Vichy French airfields at Maison Blanche, Blida, Djidjelli, Bone, La Sénia, Tafaroui and La Lourmel. Both *Largs* and *Bulolo* were fitted with extensive radar outfits and operations rooms that included fighter direction facilities and they were used as amphibious command ships.

Torch involved simultaneous assaults on the designated D-Day in the Casablanca area by the Western Task Force, WTF, with exclusively US personnel, ships and aircraft; in the Oran area by the Centre Task Force, CTF, with US military personnel but covered by RN ships and aircraft and in the Algiers/Bougie area by the Eastern Task Force, ETF, with two British Brigade Groups covered by RN ships and aircraft. The landings at Bougie were timed to begin as soon as the Algiers assault had been confirmed as successful and by D-Day +2 if possible. The capture of Djidjelli and Bone airfields to the east of Bougie was an important, but secondary, objective. For the Casablanca, Oran and Algiers assault landings all initial air cover and support, including tactical reconnaissance, Tac-R, for the

Troops with their equipment and vehicles being landed over a beach near Algiers. The soldiers seem to be taking no notice of the small boy who is watching the proceedings at the bottom left of the photograph. (*Author's collection*)

ground troops was to be provided by carrier-borne aircraft until such time as RAF and USAAF squadrons could fly in and establish themselves in captured airfields. For the Bougie, Djidjelli and Bone assaults it was anticipated that the RAF and USAAF aircraft would be available from the outset. Fighter and anti-submarine protection for the naval forces, assault ships and supply ships was, in the first place, to be undertaken by carrier aircraft. Carrier-borne TBR aircraft were to be available, if requested, for the reduction of strong points during the assaults either with or without assistance from bombarding ships.

Because of French sensitivity about the attacks on the French fleet by Force H in 1940 it was thought that American forces would be welcomed more warmly than British in the initial stages and so the British roundels on RN aircraft were overpainted with contemporary American roundels, which had a prominent white star. In some squadrons the words 'Royal Navy' painted on aircraft fuselages above the airframe number were also overpainted to read 'U.S. Navy'. Whether this ruse made any difference to the reaction of French forces on 8 November has never actually been made clear.

The British dockyard, base and airfield at Gibraltar were of pivotal importance to Torch. Both the Allied Force Commander, General Dwight D Eisenhower, and the NCEF had their HQ there and the RAF aircraft assembly facilities at the North Front airfield had been expanded to erect RAF and USAAF aircraft for Torch. Its runway had been extended into Algeciras Bay using material dug out to make tunnels in the Rock of Gibraltar that contained everything from magazines and store complexes to accommodation for thousands of troops.[7] A shore-based Allied air organisation was established with two new commands: the Eastern Air Command, which was largely British, under Air Marshal Sir William Welsh with about 310 aircraft, and a Western Air Command, which became the US 12th Air Force under Major General James Doolittle and had about 730 aircraft.

Initial movements

Advance convoys sailed from the UK to Gibraltar from 2 October and the first assault convoy, KMS 1, sailed on 22 October[8] with *Avenger*, which had three Swordfish of 833 NAS embarked in addition to the fighters to carry out anti-submarine patrols. They disembarked to North Front to fly anti-submarine patrols during the early stages of Torch. *Biter* sailed with convoy KMF 1 with the other three Swordfish of 833 NAS embarked in addition to her fighters. Both CVEs encountered rough weather in the Bay of Biscay and several Swordfish were damaged landing on. The carriers'

Avenger photographed on 26 October 1942 with Swordfish of 833B NAS and Sea Hurricanes of 802 and 803 NAS ranged aft. Note the camouflage scheme continued onto the flight deck from the ship's side. (*Author's collection*)

commanding officers commented on how lively their ships were, even in average sea conditions, and it is indicative that Swordfish, one of the easiest types to deck land, encountered difficulties. The early American-built CVEs soon gained a reputation for their liveliness in any sort of sea, making deck landing difficult for new pilots and batsmen, neither of whom had experienced their peculiarities before. Later US-built CVEs solved the problem by having greater ballast built into their hulls but were too late for Torch.

Argus and *Dasher* arrived in Gibraltar on the morning of 3 November and sailed into the Mediterranean on 5 and 6 November 1942 respectively. *Victorious*, *Formidable* and *Furious* covered the southward passage of the assault convoys. *Furious* called at Gibraltar to refuel and sailed again on 7 November but the other two passed directly through the Straits on the night of 6 November, as did *Biter* and *Avenger*. Convoys KMF 1 and KMS 1 split into four smaller convoys before reaching the Straits of Gibraltar to pass through them at scheduled times. A total of 140 ships had to be passed through within thirty-two-and-a-half hours. In spite of the U-boat threat the convoys were not attacked and no ships were lost. The assault convoys were well inside the Mediterranean by 7 November when the carriers took up their respective positions for the Torch D-Day on 8 November.

Furious, *Biter* and *Dasher* moved to position 'CF' 25nm north of Oran and *Argus* with *Avenger* moved to join Force O 15nm north-north-east of Algiers. The fleet carriers *Victorious* and *Formidable* remained with Force H and steered easterly and westerly courses 15nm to seaward of Force O during the night of 7 November to give cover against hostile surface ships from a position where they could also fly off aircraft at short notice to support the landings at Algiers the next day. Zero hour for the initial landings both at Oran and Algiers was at 0100. At Oran landings were to be carried out in four sectors designated 'R', 'X', 'Y' and 'Z'; the distance between 'R' and 'Z' being 45nm with the city midway between them. At Algiers there were three sectors designated 'A', 'B' and 'C'; 'A' and 'C' being 30nm apart. Each sector was further sub-divided into two or more individual landing beaches. It was expected that the assault on Oran would be the more difficult and this proved to be the case.

The Oran landings by the Centre Task Force

At 0500 local time on the designated D-Day, *Furious*, *Biter* and *Dasher* began flying operations. *Furious* had embarked two US Army liaison officers to help with communications between the carriers' Tac-R aircraft and US troops as they moved ashore. The weather was good with a light wind but visibility, which had been excellent during the dark, moonless night, deteriorated at dawn. By then it was known that the landings were proceeding with little opposition from the Vichy French, who had been taken by surprise. In the pre-dawn twilight *Furious* flew off eight Albacores of 822 NAS, each armed with six 250lb GP bombs fused for instantaneous detonation as the squadron had been briefed to bomb hangars at La Sénia.

A Sea Hurricane of 891 NAS taking off from *Dasher*. Unfortunately the wartime photographer failed to get the whole aircraft into his image but the ship was captured with clarity. (*Author's collection*)

The plan also required them to drop leaflets over Oran encouraging the population to support the Allied cause. *Biter* and *Dasher* flew off six Sea Hurricanes each of 800 and 804 NAS as escort and top cover respectively; the whole strike force taking departure having formed up over *Furious* at 0600.

The Albacores dropped their leaflets first and then climbed to 8,000ft heading towards La Sénia without, initially, encountering any fighter opposition. However, dropping the leaflets first was not a good idea; the Vichy French authorities were alerted and given time to get Dewoitine D.520 fighters from La Sénia airborne before the Albacores reached their target. They were attacked as they began their dives towards the hangars in the north-west corner of the airfield but Dewoitines were, in turn 'bounced' by the escorting fighters. In the ensuing combat five Dewoitines were shot down, one by the TAGs of two separate Albacores and one each by Lieutenant Commander Bruen, Sub Lieutenant (A) B Ritchie RNVR, Sub Lieutenant (A) R L Thompson RNVR and Sub Lieutenant (A) R M Crosley RNVR. Seafires strafed aircraft on the ground at La Sénia and Tafaroui airfields, setting several on fire and damaging others as well as silencing anti-aircraft gun positions and shooting down one Dewoitine.

A range comprising a single Fulmar, Martlets and Albacores with Seafires parked aft of the island on *Victorious* at the beginning of Operation Torch. (*Author's collection*)

The strike was credited with destroying or damaging sixty-nine Vichy aircraft and allowed the assault forces to get ashore at Oran without being attacked from the air.[9] Many of the bombers destroyed on the ground were found by Allied troops to have been armed in preparation for operations against the landing forces. The Albacores suffered considerable anti-aircraft fire as well as the Vichy fighter attacks and 822 NAS' commanding officer, Lieutenant J G A M Nares RN, was shot down in flames and killed together with his pilot, Lieutenant (A) J V Hartley RN and TAG Leading Airman G Dixon. Three others were damaged and forced to land with two pilots and one observer wounded. No. 800 NAS lost a Sea Hurricane and one of *Furious*' Seafires was damaged and forced to land.

Dasher's 804 NAS top cover had failed to see the Dewoitines and played no part in the short combat over the airfield. Captain Bulteel of *Furious*, one of whose squadrons had lost its commanding officer and half its Albacores in the space of a few minutes, felt 804 NAS' failure particularly keenly and commented in his report that the squadron must have been inadequately worked up before joining its ship at the last moment. Whatever the reason, 804 NAS' contribution had not been up to the standard required and its lack of training continued to manifest itself in this unfortunate sortie. All six aircraft could not find *Dasher* on their return and failed to contact *Furious* for assistance, even when they were overhead and could see her. Eventually they flew back to the coast and made forced landings before they ran out of fuel. Only one of the squadron's aircraft managed to return to *Dasher*. No. 822 NAS' dive-bombing attack on the hangars was well executed despite heavy opposition and had caused considerable damage.

Furious' next offensive sortie was a low strafing attack at 0630 on La Sénia and Tafaroui airfields by ten Seafires of 807 NAS, which set fire to two aircraft at the latter, one at the former and damaged others. They were opposed by fighters and heavy anti-aircraft fire, which shot down Lieutenant Commander Fraser-Harris, although he managed to land his aircraft and set fire to it. One Dewoitine was shot down by Sub Lieutenant (A) G C Baldwin RN,[10] the first air victory claimed by a Seafire pilot. For the remainder of 8 November *Furious*' aircraft flew CAP sorties, leaflet drops and Tac-R sorties over roads and airfields as well as answering special requests for information on the situation ashore from Admiral Troubridge in *Largs* or from troops ashore as they moved out of the beachhead. Aircraft from *Biter* and *Dasher*, the latter now with only 891 NAS embarked, flew similar tasks and a CAP over La Sénia, Tafaroui and 'Z' landing sector. The two CVEs often used each other's decks for flying off and landing on aircraft, sometimes because of barrier crashes in

An Albacore of 820 NAS being armed with bombs on *Formidable* prior to a strike. It has the USN-style white star markings backed by a blue circle used during Operation Torch instead of the normal British markings, and the words ROYAL NAVY on the rear fuselage have been painted out and replaced by US NAVY. (*Author's collection*)

Biter and sometimes because pilots had landed by mistake on the wrong carrier since the sister-ships were difficult to tell apart from the air. *Dasher* found herself at one point with no aircraft at all and by the end of the day she only had three Sea Hurricanes of 891 NAS with some of *Biter*'s fighters on board when maintenance was required to get the maximum number of fighters ready for the next day's flying programme.

Landings had not gone entirely to plan but the small airfield at La Lourmel was captured early on 8 November and Tafaroui was taken by noon. This allowed the twenty-four Spitfires of 308 and 309 Squadrons USAAF to land there at 1600 from Gibraltar. Unfortunately three of their aircraft were shot down by a Vichy French fighter CAP, which they had mistakenly identified as RAF Hurricanes. By nightfall the number of USAAF Spitfires at Tafaroui increased to over forty. La Sénia did not surrender until 1600 on 9 November.

Flying by the three aircraft carriers in the Centre Task Force ceased at 1700 on 8 November as daylight faded and recommenced at 0700 on 9 November, D + 1. At dawn *Furious* had nineteen Seafires serviceable, *Biter* had twelve Sea Hurricanes, five of which were in *Dasher*, and *Dasher* had six Sea Hurricanes. *Furious*' first sortie was a sweep by ten Seafires over landing grounds at Mostaganam, Blanche, Relizana and Sidi Bel Abbès. No Vichy aircraft were seen but fires were seen burning around

La Sénia and the oil installation at Perigaux. *Biter* and *Dasher* flew off Sea Hurricanes to CAP over 'Z' sector and Arzeu harbour and these CAP stations were maintained all day without encountering any Vichy aircraft.

Following a request from *Largs*, *Furious* flew off three Albacores led by Lieutenant H A L Tibbets RCNVR at 1241 escorted by four Seafires to bomb Vichy artillery positions, which were expected to hold up the Allied advance. A map reference giving the exact enemy position was passed to the aircraft but when they arrived over the target area at 8,000ft up sun with scattered cloud below them no target could be seen. Tibbets decided, therefore, to bomb the map reference and when Allied ground troops arrived officers inspected the bomb craters and found them to be exactly where the Vichy artillery had been observed but it had obviously been moved before the Albacore attack. This was believed to be the first time that RN aircraft had attacked an unseen target using a map reference passed by a forward air control officer. Tac-R sorties were flown throughout the day by Seafires but little Vichy activity was seen, although they did see USAAF transport aircraft and Spitfires flying into Tafaroui and American Spitfires were encountered supporting their own ground forces.

At 1500 *Furious* flew off three Seafires on a reconnaissance over the St Lucien to Sidi Bel Abbès road, where they found deserted tanks and motor transport but little Vichy movement. When *Dasher* landed on the last Sea Hurricane from the Arzeu CAP at 1700 the carriers' part in the Oran landings ended. *Furious*, *Biter* and *Dasher* headed north at 13 knots until midnight, when the CVEs detached to form their own group. All three arrived in Gibraltar on the evening of 10 November, *Furious* having disembarked 822 NAS to North Front before entering the dockyard. At

Biter and *Avenger* returning from their stations off Oran and Algiers with Sea Hurricanes in a storm range on their flight decks. (*Author's collection*)

noon on 10 November 1942 the Vichy authorities in Oran surrendered the city. *Biter* and *Dasher* sailed for the UK with convoy MKF.1 (X) on 12 November and arrived on the Clyde on 19 November.

During this operation *Furious* had flown seventy-three sorties, sixty-two of them by fighters; *Biter* had flown forty sorties and *Dasher* twenty-eight, a total of 141. Losses, in addition to Lieutenant Commander Nares' Albacore crew, included Sub Lieutenant (A) H Rowland RNVR of 807 NAS. Two pilots were seriously wounded and one observer slightly wounded. Aircraft losses amounted to five Albacores, seven Seafires, twelve Sea Hurricanes and one Fulmar, which had either been shot down, lost over the side landing-on or forced by lack of fuel to land ashore or ditch. Six other Sea Hurricanes were damaged in barrier crashes or other accidents when landing-on, some of them after being damaged by anti-aircraft fire or in air combat. The overall standard of deck landing had not been bad, taking into consideration the light winds encountered throughout the operation and the short working up periods allowed to squadrons only recently re-equipped with new types of aircraft and many pilots straight out of training. The Seafire, used in combat for the first time, had acquitted itself well. At least nine enemy aircraft were shot down in air combat and four more destroyed on the ground in addition to those destroyed and damaged in the attack on La Sénia. Two Sea Hurricane pilots were taken prisoner after forced landings; one managed to escape at his second attempt and the other was handed back when Oran surrendered.

The Algiers landings by the Eastern Task Force

Assault landings near Algiers began at 0100 like those at Oran. There were delays caused by difficulties in locating the landing beaches. Weather conditions were good but an easterly wind at Force 3 to 4 created choppy sea conditions. Only the lee side of assault ships could be used for men to climb down into their landing craft and this added to the delays. In 'C' sector some landings were as much as two hours late but some troops got ashore at 0100 and made good progress.

Argus and *Avenger* operated as part of Force O. *Victorious* and *Formidable* operated further to seaward with Force H, able to provide aircraft for Tac-R, CAP over beaches and airfields or provide strike forces if required to back up bombardments against troublesome strong points. On 7 November the two carriers maintained CAP over the assault force until dusk and then took up their designated positions. At dawn, 0550, on 8 November they flew off fighters to fill CAP stations over 'A', 'B' and 'C' Sectors and Blida airfield. These tasks continued throughout daylight hours until dusk on 9 November.

Armourers loading 250lb bombs under the wings of an 820 NAS Albacore on *Formidable*. (*Author's collection*)

Since the Algiers landings took place nearly 200nm nearer Axis air bases and within 300nm of Sardinia, the probability of interference by enemy aircraft was higher than in the Oran area and *Argus* kept four Seafires at readiness on deck throughout D-Day, although they proved not to be needed. Enemy aircraft were detected on radar after dark and although *Charybdis* opened fire on them, there were no enemy attacks on Force O, landing sectors 'A' and 'B' or Blida on either 8 or 9 November.

Victorious and *Formidable* arrived at their operating area north of Algiers at midnight on 7/8 November. During their eastward passage they had been sighted by a Ju 88 on the afternoon of 6 November and a Vichy French Potez 63. The latter was shot down by a Martlet of 888 NAS shortly before sunset. There were numerous U-boat detections on passage, some of which were attacked by destroyers on the screen without result, but at 1630 on the afternoon of 7 November a large group of enemy aircraft was detected on radar closing from the north-east. The light was bad and so there were no fighters on CAP and an attack by Ju 88s at 1650 was only opposed by gunfire. It lasted until 1720 but only damaged the destroyer *Panther*, causing flooding in several forward compartments but she was able to return to Gibraltar. The carriers and the assault convoys they were covering were untouched.

At 0030 on 8 November *Formidable* flew off three Albacores fitted with smoke generators to screen the landings in 'B' Sector, which were to take place within range of shore batteries behind Jetée du Nord in Algiers harbour. One Albacore strafed a searchlight and destroyed it in a rare use of the type's front gun. The smoke-laying aircraft landed on at 0330 and continuous CAP over Force H began before dawn. The first combat of the day took place an hour later when a Seafire of 885 NAS engaged a Vichy Glen Martin bomber and set its fuselage alight, but it was not seen to crash. *Formidable* flew off a fighter sweep comprising twelve Seafires and Martlets from 885 and 893 NAS to carry out a reconnaissance of Maison Blanche airfield. Their form up in the dark was delayed by bad communications between the squadrons but as they were on the point of taking departure the Martlet flight leader saw the track of a torpedo fired at his carrier by a U-boat. He gave an immediate warning but it fortunately missed ahead of the ship. After this incident the Martlets were held back to augment the CAP over Force H, the Seafires continued to their briefed objective but found Maison Blanche covered by mist, which prevented anything being seen but indicated that the enemy would be unable to use the airfield until it cleared.

By 0700 the landings were achieved and part of Maison Blanche had been seized at 0640 by the US 39th Regimental Combat Team, which had been landed with that objective. Its position was precarious, however, and the Americans were surrounded by hostile Vichy forces. Some fifty Dewoitine fighters were seen lined up ready for take-off but prevented from doing so by mist. An RAF ground party with the officer commanding 322 Wing, whose aircraft were to be flown in later from Gibraltar, was ashore at Ain Taya on the cliffs above 'C' beach. He had with him his interrogation officer, who spoke fluent French, and they drove to the airfield with some of the advance party in a commandeered French Air Force officers' bus, which drove unopposed past French sentries. At 0845 one of two Tac-R Fulmars of *Victorious*' 809 NAS landed at the airfield to find out what was happening and a few minutes later eighteen RAF Hurricanes of 43 Squadron arrived in the overhead after a two-hour flight from Gibraltar. Given the number and variety of Allied advances, Vichy French senior officers surrendered.

The capture of Blida 25nm to the south-west was even more unusual. From twilight 882 NAS Martlets from *Victorious* maintained a four-aircraft CAP over the airfield and had attacked and destroyed two Vichy aircraft seen trying to take off when Lieutenant (A) B H C Nation RN led

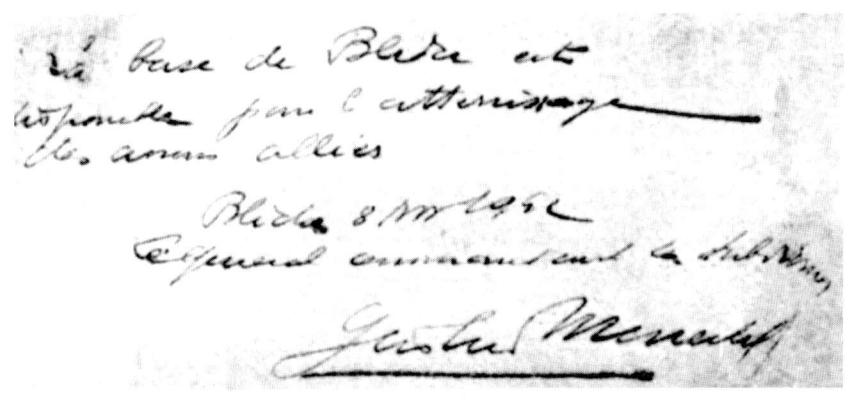

The handwritten surrender document handed to Lieutenant Nation when he landed at Blida airfield in response to waved white flags. It appears to have been written in some haste. (*Author's collection*)

a replacement division to the airfield at 0800. Below him he saw several people on the airfield waving white cloths and after reporting this and assuring the direction officer that he was definitely over Blida because he could see the name painted in large white letters on the ground, he requested and received permission to land. He ordered his division to keep a good watch on the situation and then landed, climbing out of the cockpit with his revolver in hand, though not actually pointed at the men who walked over to greet him. He was given a statement by the airfield commandant, in the presence of a French general, to the effect that Blida was now at the disposal of the Allies to land aircraft.[11] About three hours later Lieutenant Nation was able to hand over command of the airfield to a party of British Commandos, after which he took off and returned to *Victorious*. By 1230 fifty-four RAF Hurricanes and Spitfires had flown into Blida from Gibraltar.

Meanwhile, an air strike was requested by the ETF Commander to silence the fort on the Jetée du Nord, which continued to resist. *Victorious* flew off six Albacores of 832 NAS, each armed with six 250lb SAP bombs to be distributed as a stick at quarter-second intervals. Their attack was made from 7,000ft in a 60 degree dive with release between 2,000 and 1,500ft. Several aircraft actually dived lower than this and their bombs failed to detonate. Nevertheless, the fort was partially destroyed and all its guns silenced. Some anti-aircraft fire was encountered but it only caused splinter damage to a single aircraft.

A similar strike was ordered just after noon against Fort Dupere, north-west of Algiers, which continued to hold out although, by then, most of the city was in Allied hands. For this strike *Victorious* flew off

Lieutenant (A) B H C Nation RN of 882 NAS embarked in *Victorious*; he was the first RN pilot to take the surrender of a hostile force on land. (*Author's collection*)

six Albacores of 817 NAS and two of 832 NAS, each with the same bomb load as the earlier strike. They were led by Lieutenant N R Corbett-Milward RN and on arrival found the target partially obscured by eight-tenths stratocumulus cloud at 2,500ft, which made sighting difficult. They pressed home their attack with determination, however, releasing their bombs in a 45 degree dive from up sun at 1,000ft after first orbiting the fort to confirm that it was the designated target and firing its guns at Allied forces. Most damage was confined to buildings about 300yds from the battery but there were some near misses around the six 7.5in guns themselves. The desired result was achieved and the battery promptly ceased fire. After Algiers surrendered it was found that the morale of the gunners had been considerably affected by the bombing and they had decided to take shelter. The fort Dupere surrendered to Allied troops that evening.

The third call for a strike came later in the afternoon when Admiral Burrough requested a bombardment by the cruiser *Bermuda* backed up by an air strike against Fort d'Estrées on Cape Matifou to the east end of Algiers Bay. *Formidable* flew off six Albacores of 820 NAS briefed to attack after the bombardment, during which *Bermuda*'s Walrus was to spot the fall of shot. Unknown to the Albacores, the fort personnel were in the act of surrendering as they began their attack at 1530. It was later

Biter at flying stations with her funnel and W/T masts lowered. (*Author's collection*)

found by inspection that they had achieved six hits and at least one near miss.

German air attacks on the landing forces gradually increased and by dusk on 8 November there were attacks by up to thirty Ju 88s and He 111s with some torpedo bombers in the vicinity of 'C' Sector but they lost an estimated twelve aircraft to fighters and a further four to anti-aircraft fire. There was some damage to the assault shipping and *Bermuda* claimed to have taken successful avoiding action against a number of torpedoes dropped during the course of the afternoon and evening by aircraft working alone or in pairs.

Victorious' Fulmars flew seven Tac-R sorties for the army, mostly tasked with locating enemy movements within 100nm on roads approaching Algiers. When the Tac-R aircraft, anti-submarine patrol Albacores and CAP fighters had been landed on by the two fleet carriers, flying finished for the day at 1700. *Victorious* had flown fifty-seven sorties with the loss of one Fulmar, forced to ditch after being damaged by anti-aircraft fire. *Formidable* had flown seventy-seven sorties with the loss of one Martlet to anti-aircraft fire and two more damaged landing on. She had also lost a Martlet and an Albacore over the side on 7 November. Overall, however, there were far fewer deck landing accidents among the established squadrons in the big fleet carriers than there were among the newer units in the smaller and unfamiliar CVEs.

As evening on 8 November approached, the ETF Military Commander, General C W Ryder US Army, agreed with the Vichy authorities that Allied troops would occupy Algiers at 1900, ending a successful day's operations. RAF fighters from Gibraltar had arrived promptly at Maison Blanche and Blida but the minimal amounts of fuel they found, together with their lack of ammunition and logistic support, meant that there was little they could do at first. This was the first occasion on which RAF servicing commandos had been deployed and they landed early in 'C' Sector and marched 12 miles to Maison Blanche in three hours to service their aircraft. However, they lacked any form of communication to link them with the tactical force commanders or the Air HQ in Gibraltar, which made it difficult to brief pilots adequately on the tactical picture before their sorties or to control those who actually got airborne. The RN attempted to help overcome this difficulty by flying a Walrus to Maison Blanche to act as a radio link with *Bulolo*. Warning of enemy air attacks and fighter control was conducted through the Walrus and its TAG until the arrival of RAF W/T equipment several days later. By 10 November RAF fighters were finally in a position to take over from the carriers' fighters.

On 9 November *Victorious* and *Formidable* began to launch CAP and anti-submarine patrols at 0545. At 1300 radar detected contacts closing from the north-east and a series of attacks by Ju 88s and He 111s followed, the first serious raids by Axis forces in daylight on Force H during the operation. During the next two hours there were a number of combats,

Fighter pilots of 888 NAS on *Formidable*'s flight deck. (Author's collection)

with both carriers flying off extra fighters when necessary. One Ju 88 and one He 111 were shot down by Lieutenant (A) D M Jerram RNVR and Sub Lieutenant (A) A R Astin RNVR in sections of Martlets from *Formidable* and Sub Lieutenants (A) P D Street and R Tebble RNVR from *Victorious*. A second and heavier air attack developed from the south shortly after 1630 as light began to fail. Fighters were again flown off to meet it but only succeeded in damaging three Ju 88s. *Formidable*'s guns shot one down, however, and the day's total was three enemy aircraft destroyed and three damaged for the loss of one Martlet in a deck landing accident when the last fighters landed on in very bad light amidst intense gunfire from every ship, including their own.

The day 10 November passed uneventfully but CAP and anti-submarine patrols were maintained. The RAF was now established in the Algiers area but had no aircraft suitable for anti-submarine patrol work. Force H therefore disembarked six Walrus amphibians from its cruisers to Maison Blanche airfield for this task. They were subsequently based at the former Air France flying boat terminal at Algiers and from there continued to undertake anti-submarine patrols until the beginning of February 1943 when, after 813 NAS took over their task, three of their aircraft were turned over to the RAF for air-sea rescue duties and the remaining three re-embarked in their cruisers.

On 11 November Force H continued to fly CAP and anti-submarine patrols but while the force was at the western edge of its operating area an aircraft was detected on radar and when intercepted it was identified as a white-painted SM.84 with no markings and it was shot down into the sea. RAF HQ in Gibraltar later reported that a Hudson had failed to return from a patrol. It was a Coastal Command aircraft that must have forgotten to switch on its IFF and had been painted in the command's new, largely white, colour scheme, which had for some reason obliterated its national markings.

Many reports of U-boat activity continued to arrive after 11 November and it was clear that they were now concentrating in the Western Mediterranean. Large anti-submarine search operations were carried out on the nights of 12/13 and 13/14 November by sixteen ASV-fitted Albacores from *Victorious* and *Formidable* to a depth of 100nm to the west and east of Force H. No contacts were gained on the first night but at 0255 on 14 November one of *Formidable*'s Albacores flown by Lieutenant J C N Shrubsole RN, Sub Lieutenant (A) L A Adams RNVR and Leading Airman J J Symonds, gained radar contact and made a very promising attack on a surfaced U-boat, which was illuminated by the destroyer *Ashanti*'s searchlight as the aircraft dived towards it. The

Unable to find *Dasher* after their first Torch mission, all six Sea Hurricanes of 804 NAS had to carry out forced landings ashore when they ran short of fuel. This is one of them, Sea Hurricane IIC JS327, on the beach at St Leu being inspected by curious American soldiers. It has the USN-style white star markings used in Torch and the fin flash has been painted out to conform with USN practice, although the words ROYAL NAVY have been left on the rear fuselage. (*Author's collection*)

decision to attack was complicated by the fact that the aircraft crew did not see the U-boat until they were almost right over it and, since restrictions had been placed on night attacks to avoid the risk of mistaken identity, they had very little time to identify the boat. In spite of this, the depth charges were seen to straddle it but it was assessed that they might have burst too deep to cause severe damage. German records analysed after the war showed that this was *U-431*, which had sunk the destroyers *Martin* on 10 November and *Isaac Sweers* on 13 November. The Albacore attack had actually seriously damaged the boat's batteries together with its engine self-starters and depth indicators. Both engines stopped temporarily but it managed to submerge and eventually reached Pola, via Messina, for extensive repairs. Cunningham considered the Albacore's attack 'deserved much credit'[12] in the circumstances. This had been the first occasion on which continuous day and night anti-submarine patrols were flown by British aircraft carriers.

After sunrise, *Porcupine* with six Albacores escorted by four Martlets from *Formidable* were sent to intercept and attack two U-boats reported earlier as damaged. They only found one, however, *U-595* beached and abandoned near Mostaganem. With the Allies now firmly established in Algeria, Force H's task was complete and it returned to Gibraltar, arriving at 0120 on 15 November having flown anti-submarine patrols until Europa Point was passed. On 18 November *Victorious* sailed for the UK, still flying Admiral Lyster's flag, and on 21 November an Albacore of 817 NAS located, attacked and sank *U-517* with depth charges.

Argus and the landings at Bougie

Bougie is 100nm east of Algiers and Allied landings there on 11 November were confusingly designated Operation Perpetual, a name previously allocated to the ferry operation in which *Ark Royal* had been sunk and which *Argus* had also taken part in. On 10 November *Avenger* had spent a short time off Algiers making repairs to defects in her four Busche-Sulzer diesel engines,[13] a common occurrence in this first batch of US-built CVEs. *Argus* was ordered by Admiral Burrough to provide fighter cover for the Perpetual assault convoys leaving Algiers between 1600 and 1700, despite it only having four serviceable Seafires.

At 1600 on 10 November Force O, including *Argus*, had closed to within 8nm of Algiers ready to cover the Bougie convoy but at 1630 a heavy air attack developed in which both Ju 88s and torpedo bombers took part. *Argus* flew off three Seafires, which could see the enemy aircraft clearly above them but they could not gain height sufficiently quickly to engage them. At 1700 *Argus* was hit on the port after end of the flight deck by a single 500lb bomb during an attack by fifteen

Pilots of 801 NAS pose by one of their Seafire IBs on *Furious* after Operation Torch. The aircraft still has its USN-style markings. (*Author's collection*)

Ju 88s. The explosion wrecked the port main support to the after flight deck overhang, part of the funnel gas discharge system under the flight deck, the after hangar screen, two Seafires in the hangar and two 20mm Oerlikons mounted aft. Four ratings were killed. Near misses caused minor damage to the ship's side and FFO feed tanks, causing a 2 degree list. Notwithstanding her age and the fact that she had been rebuilt as a training carrier rather than for operational duties, *Argus* stood up well to her ordeal and Captain Philip found that she could still steam at her best speed, use full rudder and, most importantly, operate her aircraft. He noted in his report that there seemed to be 'something fatally attractive [to the Germans] in *Argus*' silhouette...a fact noticed on previous occasions with a Malta convoy'. This sentiment was confirmed that night when the tracks of three torpedoes fired at separate times by U-boats were seen to pass under her bridge at various times but not explode. Although her Seafires had not managed to engage the enemy during the afternoon, their presence was probably known for there were no further air attacks on the convoy while it proceeded to Bougie.

The Bougie landings began at dawn on 11 November in moderate beach conditions with some surf and, in spite of earlier warnings to the contrary, they were unopposed. Later in the forenoon all ships were able to use Bougie harbour. With the help of four Sea Hurricanes flown from Algiers by *Avenger*, a continuous beach CAP was managed after dawn in accordance with the programme. Four other Sea Hurricanes failed

A Luftwaffe Ju 88 dives for the clouds with its starboard engine on fire, photographed by the gun-recording camera of a Seafire IIC flown by Sub Lieutenant (A) D G Parker RNVR of 884 NAS from *Victorious* on 10 November 1942 during Operation Torch. (*Author's collection*)

US Army personnel inspecting Seafire MB122, 0-6C of 885 NAS on *Formidable*, anchored in Mers-el-Kébir after Operation Torch. Note that its markings have reverted to the standard British roundels used from late 1942. This aircraft had been reallocated to 885 NAS from 884 NAS in *Victorious* and was actually the Seafire in which Sub Lieutenant Parker damaged a Ju 88 on 10 November. (*Author's collection*)

to locate *Argus* and returned to Algiers. There was no opposition from either Vichy or Axis air forces before noon and after the last section had landed on at the end of its planned period on CAP Force O set heading for Algiers in accordance with previous instructions. The lack of RAF fighters at Djidjelli, however, meant that fighters had to fly 120nm from Algiers to Bougie and they could only spend a few minutes over these landing areas. The troops ashore and the shipping landing their stores and equipment were, therefore, intermittently at the mercy of Axis air forces and the first of several heavy bombing attacks began on the evening of 11 November. Ships and military formations ashore suffered badly but Djidjelli airfield was finally taken on 12 November by paratroops. Even the RAF supply of avgas, sent by road from Bougie, was delayed and Spitfires of 154 Squadron RAF had to be refuelled using innovative methods when they arrived. Fuel was drained out of the half-empty tanks of most of the squadron's aircraft in order to fill some to capacity. Bulk fuel supplies began to arrive at midnight, enabling the unit to fly freely, and it quickly took a toll of the enemy, destroying eleven enemy aircraft during a bombing attack on Bougie on 14 November. By then Force O, which had collected *Avenger* and three fast merchant ships from Algiers, was in Gibraltar. *Argus* and *Avenger* sailed for the UK with convoy MKF.1 on the afternoon of 14 November and carrier-borne operations as part of the assault phase of Torch ended.

Avenger never got back to the UK, however. At 0415 on 15 November she was hit by a single torpedo from *U-155* to the west of Gibraltar. The torpedo penetrated the thin steel hull plating and detonated in the bomb room, causing a massive explosion, after which she broke up and sank in under five minutes, leaving only twelve survivors. Her commanding officer, Commander A P Colthurst RN, was not among them. The subsequent Board of Enquiry found that splinters from the torpedo warhead had detonated bombs and depth charges stowed against the plating of the ship's side. To provide some protection against a similar occurrence the Admiralty gave instructions that a longitudinal bulkhead was to be fitted to all US-built CVEs that would keep weapons 10 to 15ft away from the ship's side. The USN instituted a similar alteration.[14]

While the Bougie landings were still being carried out, another successful landing was carried out even further east at Bone. The Allies now had rather precarious control of a strip stretching roughly 800nm along the North African coast with a far from friendly former Ally 'behind their back' to the south. To their east the first two Axis transports were arriving in Bizerta loaded with German troops for the occupation of Tunisia.

A close-up detail of Martlet AJ108, 0-7K of 888 NAS in *Formidable*. It has the white star markings and the words US Navy have replaced ROYAL NAVY on the after fuselage. Whether these attempts to fool the Vichy French authorities into thinking that Torch was an all-American operation were effective has never been ascertained for certain but the changes do allow the RN aircraft that took part to be dated accurately. (*Author's collection*)

There is no complete record of the number of sorties flown by RN carrier-borne aircraft during Operation Torch but an accurate picture can be constructed from their action reports and ship's narratives, which are available in The National Archive.

Furious flew 62 fighter and 11 other sorties
Biter flew 40 fighter sorties
Dasher flew 28 fighter sorties

Victorious flew 105 fighter and 75 other sorties
Formidable flew 192 fighter and 55 other sorties

Argus flew 74 fighter sorties
Avenger flew 60 fighter sorties

Between them, the carrier fighters shot down eight enemy aircraft and damaged three more during Torch. Fleet gunfire had destroyed twenty-five enemy aircraft and probably fifteen more, with thirty-six estimated as damaged. No figures have been found for Vichy French losses but they were estimated at the time to have exceeded eighty aircraft including those destroyed on the ground at La Sénia.

Admiral Cunningham's opinion of Operation Torch carrier operations
In his report on Torch[15] Cunningham wrote that, taken as a whole, the provision of fighter support over shipping and beaches by carrier-borne aircraft had left little to be desired. He added, however, that it had 'suffered from all the known limitations of carrier aircraft, but was fully effective within these limitations'. The latter statement revealed that it had still not struck him that there was no reason why naval fighters should not be at least as good, or better, than any opposition they were likely to encounter. This was certainly not the view taken by the US and Imperial Japanese Navies and shows that Cunningham's outlook had not kept pace with developments. He should have been arguing the case for the latest, most effective, fighters to be made available to him as soon as possible. Beyond what he considered to be the limitations suffered by all naval aircraft, however, he wrote that: 'in general it is considered that the operations of carrier-borne fighters reflected great credit on the foresight and planning of the Rear Admiral Aircraft Carriers [Rear Admiral Lyster], on the spirit and training of the Fleet Air Arm and the efficiency of the carriers alike…'

Bombing missions by the Albacores had, he felt, suffered from similar limitations but 'in spite of these drawbacks it proved remarkably effective whenever opportunity was given. In particular the dive-bombing of La Sénia aerodrome was most striking not only for its accuracy and effect but also for the extremely gallant and determined manner in which it was pressed home.'

One factor that would have been of particular interest within the Admiralty was the performance of the RNVR aircrew that now formed the bulk of the embarked squadrons as the Fleet Air Arm expanded. Comments about spirit and training were, in all probability, aimed largely at them rather than the core of RN officers who filled the more senior appointments.

Within the Admiralty, NAD made a number of comments about Torch when it studied the various reports. It was felt that the Seafire had acquitted itself satisfactorily as a fleet fighter, although its weak undercarriage counted against it. The early marks had non-folding wings but could be struck down into the hangars of *Furious* and *Argus* with their cruciform-shaped lifts. The small lifts in *Victorious* and *Formidable* meant that Seafires had to be kept on deck using outriggers, limiting the size of squadrons that could be embarked and made the ranging and operation of other aircraft more difficult than it would otherwise have been. The Admiralty informed operational commanders that the Mark III version of the Seafire in development was being built as a naval aircraft from the outset with a stronger undercarriage and folding wings, allowing them to be struck down into the hangars of *Illustrious*-class carriers.

The difficulty of escorting relatively low-speed TBR aircraft with fighters was recognised but NAD admitted that there was no ideal way of doing so. It recommended, therefore, that TBRs should not be used in future for day strikes against targets defended by even mediocre fighter opposition. Bomb-armed fighters were to be used instead. NAD added that the use of obsolescent aircraft such as the Fulmar for Tac-R missions was now unacceptable because they would stand little chance against first-class enemy fighter opposition over the forward edge of the battle area. The Admiralty view was that all naval single-seat fighter squadrons should be given basic training in Army co-operation work and this was immediately set in hand. Pilots on course in the RN Fighter School and all front-line pilots were to be given two weeks intensive training, with more for pilots appointed to squadrons specifically intended for Army co-operation work. It was accepted that dive-bombing by Albacores was accurate and had a significant effect on enemy morale but analysis of the targets after their capture had actually shown that little permanent damage had been inflicted. Notwithstanding Cunningham's positive remarks, the Admiralty view was that the urgency with which naval air squadrons had been re-equipped for Torch had resulted in a serious limitation in the time available for training. This would not have been acceptable against first-class opposition.

The Axis reaction to Operation Torch

The Allies had failed to prevent the rapid movement of German forces into Tunisia by sea and air and, while Vichy French forces might have been expected to react at least as vigorously against German landings as they had against American and British landings further west, they did not. By 10 November some German units had been flown into Tunisia to 'prevent the French from defecting to the Allies'. German E-boats arrived in Tunis on 11 November and the first two troop convoys arrived unopposed on 12 November. These movements were followed by a massive airlift of troops and their equipment as well as the transfer of combat aircraft from Sicily. By 20 November the Luftwaffe had roughly a quarter of its operational aircraft in the Mediterranean based in Tunisia and by the end of the month 12,500 tons of supplies, 150 tanks and 1,900 troops had arrived by sea and a further 15,000 troops had arrived by air. At the same time the Germans seized control of the unoccupied southern part of France, giving rise to fears that warships in Toulon might be seized and used against the Allies. Fortunately the French circumvented this threat

The Prime Minister, Winston Churchill, being greeted by Admiral Lyster on a visit to *Victorious* in October 1942 shortly before she left the Home Fleet to take part in Operation Torch. (*Author's collection*)

by scuttling them at their berths. The Germans did, however, gain control of a number of air bases close to the French Mediterranean coast.

The German moves were just sufficient to block the Allied advance into Tunisia and it was to be another five months before Tunis was eventually taken. Convoys bringing follow-up Allied forces to North Africa began to suffer losses from U-boat and air attacks but the Italian fleet never intervened against them. Force H, which now contained both *Formidable* and *Furious*, was used to cover these convoys by making a series of sweeps to the south of the Balearic Islands and now used Mers-el-Kébir as a forward operating base. On 17 November an 820 NAS Albacore from *Formidable* torpedoed and sank *U-331*, which it found damaged on the surface after a depth charge attack by an RAF Hudson. Increased U-boat activity in the Western Mediterranean led to 700 NAS Walrus anti-submarine patrols in the Algiers area being supplemented by six Swordfish from 813 NAS, which were redeployed to Blida and Tafaroui airfields from Gibraltar. Attractive Axis shipping targets began to appear and the remainder of 813 NAS, commanded by Lieutenant Commander A H Abrams RN, was transferred to Algeria. At first three, and then a total of six, Swordfish armed with torpedoes were moved up from Blida to Bone airfield as a night striking force led by Lieutenant C Hutchinson RN. His pilots lacked experience in night torpedo attack, however, and it was already accepted by the Admiralty that intensive training was needed if squadrons were to achieve decisive results with this type of mission. It was also becoming evident that naval TBR crews could no longer be 'jacks of all trades'. Successful anti-submarine work and strike techniques each required specialists who were not necessarily good at both.

Victory in North Africa

At the end of November Cunningham and Eisenhower moved their expeditionary HQ from Gibraltar to Algiers and it remained there for several months. Apart from the German occupation of southern France and Tunisia, events moved in the Allies' favour. The 8th Army was close to clearing Axis forces from Cyrenaica for the third and last time, allowing Allied air forces to move into coastal airfields and provide cover for Operation Stone Age, a convoy of four ships from Alexandria to Malta that reached the island intact on 20 November with stores, ammunition and avgas. No. 815 NAS provided anti-submarine patrols for the convoy but five RAF aircraft had been lost and the cruiser *Arethusa* damaged by an enemy torpedo aircraft. Also on 20 November, Benghazi was recaptured and the difficult and dangerous task of clearing its harbour began. A continuous stream of supplies could now be convoyed to Malta, which quickly regained its position as a major naval and air base.

With only a small number of aircraft left between them by the end of November, 830 and 828 NAS had been unable to achieve more than occasional sorties against Axis convoys but squadron morale was improved by 'borrowing' Hurricanes from the RAF, with which pilots carried out night intruder missions over enemy airfields in Sicily. A noteworthy success was achieved on 17 November when two Albacore strike aircraft in company with a Wellington flare-dropper torpedoed the 10,000-ton Italian tanker *Guilio Giordani* off Homs in Tripolitania. Left in a sinking condition by two hits, she was finished off by the submarine *Porpoise*, which had witnessed the air attack. This success was especially welcome since Axis forces were desperately short of fuel in North Africa as well as ships with which to transport it.[16]

On 1 December 821 NAS was deployed to Malta with twelve Albacores after its operations in the Western Desert and on 11 December a further five Albacores of 826 NAS were flown to Hal Far from Berka, although a sixth ditched 51nm south-east of Malta. The pilot, Sub Lieutenant (A) J C Manning RNVR, was lost but his observer, Sub Lieutenant N H Kempson RNVR, was found floating in his dinghy on 20 December and rescued.[17] The effect of these reinforcements was immediate. The naval air squadrons based in Malta continued to operate successfully but their indomitable spirit and tactical skill received little attention from press or public. However, a study of their records shows what can be achieved with minimal resources. The German Vice Admiral Weichold wrote in his book *Axis Naval Policy in the Mediterranean 1939 to 1943*[18] that 'enemy torpedo planes were a particularly great danger on moonlit nights and there was no effective means of defence against them'.

During December the Allies sank 68,000 tons of Axis shipping with a further 15,000 tons damaged, roughly 40 per cent of the total sailed. Of the twenty-eight Axis ships sunk, thirteen were by air attack, eight by submarines and five by surface warships. By then 815 NAS' eleven swordfish were operating from Mersa Matruh on day and night anti-submarine patrols; 889 NAS with two Fulmars and twelve Hurricane IICs was operating from both Fuka and Daba on shipping protection duties. No. 701 NAS with six ASV-fitted Walrus was operating from Beirut, Haifa and Lydda on local anti-submarine patrols by day and night but neither 815 nor 701 had any contacts during this period. No. 826 NAS operated twelve Albacores at Berka, near Benghazi, until the night of 11 December. After the six aircraft were flown to Malta the squadron was re-equipped with twelve new longer-range Albacores to form a torpedo striking force against

A Seafire IIC taking off over *Furious*' distinctive, lowered windbreak during operations in the Western Mediterranean in October 1942. (*Author's collection*)

enemy shipping. During December the Albacores and Swordfish in Malta carried out fifty-four anti-shipping sorties armed with torpedoes, fourteen bombing sorties and six minelaying sorties. No. 833 NAS at Gibraltar carried out local anti-submarine search operations until 25 December when it left for the UK in *Argus*. It was replaced by six Walrus sent out from the UK. A Fleet Air Arm Holding Unit at Gibraltar maintained eight Swordfish, five Albacores and nine Seafires as reserve aircraft for naval air squadrons in the Mediterranean theatre. No. 813 NAS had nine Swordfish split between Blida and Bone and three more at Tafaroui, which were redistributed as required. After mid-December those at Bone were used for anti-shipping strikes in the Bizerta area and those at Blida for anti-submarine duties. No. 700 NAS operated six Walrus at Algiers flying boat terminal for anti-submarine patrol and escort duties.

The redoubtable 826 NAS had found no suitable targets for its torpedoes in December so half the squadron relocated to Tamet, where it resumed its long-running task of pathfinding for RAF bombers. From Tamet it advanced with the 8th Army continuously illuminating targets and in one notable action, Albacores dropped flares to illuminate Tripoli harbour while RN MTBs carried out a spirited attack intended to soften it up prior to its occupation on 23 January 1943. In February the pathfinder detachment was relieved by five Albacores from 821 NAS which carried on this important task. No. 826 NAS' two flights were reunited and replaced 813 NAS as an anti-submarine and night anti-shipping strike force, now commanded by Lieutenant R E Bradshaw RN, who had served in the squadron with great distinction since it was first commissioned in 1940. It used Blida as its main base and Bone as a forward operating base. Its most successful strike sortie was carried out from the latter on 17 April 1943 when the Italian merchant ship *Monginevro* was sunk in co-operation with MTBs off Cape Bon. On another less successful occasion when returning from an armed reconnaissance sortie that had found no enemy vessels, an Albacore dropped a flare to identify the coastline only to find that it had inadvertently illuminated a covert British commando raid.

The Afrika Korps was now desperately short of supplies of every kind and Rommel retreated to make a last stand at Gabes in Tunisia. The Italian general staff lost confidence in him and pressed for his dismissal but he was recalled on health grounds before the German collapse. Tunis and Bizerta were occupied by the Allies on 7 May 1943 and on 12 May all organised resistance ceased. General Von Arnim, who had relieved Rommel on 9 March, was captured together with several other generals and about 250,000 German and Italian officers and men.

Vice Admiral A V Willis assumed command of Force H in March and the force continued to be employed as cover for convoys in the Western Mediterranean and in support of anti-shipping operations in the narrows by the smaller Forces K and Q. Up to the end of January both *Furious* and *Formidable* had remained with Force H but then the former returned to the UK for service with the Home Fleet from Gibraltar. CAP was maintained while the force at sea but anti-submarine and surface search sorties predominated.

By 15 May a 200nm long swept channel was established around Cape Bon and Cunningham, who was still CNEF but about to become C-in-C Mediterranean again, was able to inform the Admiralty that passage through the Mediterranean was possible for the first time since the Tiger Convoy almost exactly two years earlier. The need to send convoys to the Middle and Far East on the long route around the Cape was now over, allowing considerable savings in time, the number of merchant ships required and fuel usage. The North African Campaign had seen close co-operation between British armed forces and, latterly, with their new American ally. Naval air squadrons had played a small but critical part in an impressively wide range of operations, few of which had been anticipated or planned for prior to the outbreak of war. It was enormously to the credit of both air and ground crews, many of whom were now RNVR or 'Hostilities Only' personnel, who had only recently joined the RN from all over the Commonwealth, that they had done so. The RN and RN (A) aircrew with which the Fleet Air Arm had begun the war had gained extensive combat experience and were now in command or senior positions afloat and ashore.

11

The Allied invasions of Sicily and Italy in 1943

After victory in North Africa, Churchill and Roosevelt agreed after considerable discussion that the next Allied move should be the invasion of Sicily. Operation Husky would eventually involve 3,000 ships, 160,000 men, 14,000 vehicles, 1,800 guns and over 400 aircraft in assault forces assembled from bases in the UK, USA, Middle East and North Africa. The convoys moving men and material all needed protection against air, surface and sub-surface attack.

The Admiralty took the requirement to train fighter squadrons in Army co-operation tactics very seriously. This 1944 photographs shows pilots of 879 NAS taking a somewhat lighter view during the lunch break in a military firepower demonstration. (*Author's collection*)

Force H

A reinforced Force H under the command of Vice Admiral Sir Algernon Willis flying his flag in the battleship *Nelson* provided cover against any possible sortie by the Italian fleet. It included two fleet carriers and six battleships, some of which were lent from the Home and Mediterranean Fleets, and for several reasons the Force was divided into three divisions. One of these was to was to reinforce the subterfuge that the Allies intended to invade Greece rather than Sicily.[1] As in Torch, the day on which the operation was to start was designated as D-Day. The 1st Division of Force H was based at Mers-el-Kébir near Oran and comprised the flagship *Nelson* with *Rodney* and *Indomitable*. The latter was recently back in action after a refit in Liverpool that had repaired the bomb damage sustained during the Pedestal convoy. She was the flagship of the Rear Admiral Aircraft Carriers, now Rear Admiral C Moody. The 2nd Division was based at Alexandria and comprised the battleships *Warspite* and *Valiant* together with *Formidable*. The 3rd Division based at Gibraltar included the battleships *Howe* and *King George V* but had no carrier.

The carrier air groups for Operation Husky comprised:[2]

Indomitable	Captain G Grantham RN	
807 NAS	12 Seafire LIIC	Lieutenant Commander H M Cox RN
880 NAS	14 Seafire IIC	Lieutenant Commander (A) W H Martyn RN
899 NAS	14 Seafire IIC	Lieutenant Commander R F Walker RN
817 NAS	15 Albacore	Lieutenant Commander N R Corbet-Milward RN

Formidable	Captain A G Talbot RN	
885 NAS	5 Seafire IIC	Lieutenant R H P Carver RN
888 NAS	14 Martlet IV	Captain F D G Bird RM
893 NAS	14 Martlet IV	Lieutenant R B Pearson RN
820 NAS	12 Albacore	Lieutenant Commander J C N Shrubsole RN

Both carriers had increased their aircraft complements with a permanent deck park and *Indomitable* had one larger lift forward that allowed her to strike down Seafire IIs with their non-folding wings into her upper hangar as well as keeping others in a deck park with outriggers. This allowed her to operate three Seafire squadrons. *Formidable* had smaller lifts, which limited her to operating a largely F4F-4 Martlet air group except for one Seafire squadron that was kept in a deck park on outriggers when not

A division of Seafire IICs returning to *Indomitable* after flying a CAP over Force H during Operation Husky. The first aircraft of the relief CAP is lined up for take-off abaft the island with the rest of his division ranged aft. (*Author's collection*)

flying. Despite its weak undercarriage, the Seafire was preferred by the Admiralty over the more robust Martlet because it was the fastest naval fighter in service in 1943. The Seafire IIC was capable of 292 knots at 14,000ft compared with the Martlet IV's 262 knots at 15,000ft.[3]

All three Divisions of Force H played a part in covering Allied convoys as they approached the assault area in south-east Sicily prior to D-Day, which was set for 10 July 1943. Fighter cover could be provided over the beachhead from Malta and a fighter airstrip had been built on Gozo Island by American Army engineers that eased the congestion on the island's other airfields.

The 1st and 3rd Divisions of Force H met off Oran on 5 July, after which they steamed to Algiers and refuelled on 6 July. The 1st Division joined the 2nd Division north of the Gulf of Sirte early on 9 July. During these movements anti-submarine patrols were flown by day and night both by Albacores and shore-based RAF aircraft. Having joined, the two divisions moved north-east to cover convoys from Alexandria and at 1915, soon after sighting an unidentified aircraft thought to have been a shadower, they altered course to simulate an approach to the Greek coast. After dark on 9 July the Force altered course to arrive by dawn on 10 July within easy steaming distance of the Eastern Task Force area off the south-east corner of Italy and so able to cover the landings as well as being ready for bombardment by the battleships if it was requested. The operational planners hoped that Force H would draw the inevitable enemy air attacks away from the landing beaches and so large CAPs were maintained. In the event there was little enemy air activity and by the evening of 11 July there had been no requests for bombardment either. Air reconnaissance showed that the Italian fleet was still in harbour and so the 1st Division of Force H closed Malta and anchored off the breakwater. From then until 17 July the divisions alternated between Sicily and Malta.

On the evening of 15 July the 1st Division left Malta to relieve the 2nd Division. *Indomitable* prepared to fly off a night anti-submarine patrol because command night intentions had stressed the threat of U-boat rather than air attack and at 2230 six Albacores were flown off to search ahead of the force using ASV to a depth of 50nm with a briefed recovery time of 0200 on 16 July. There had been several radar detections of unidentified aircraft, none of them close, and the moon was one day from full at 30 degrees azimuth, visibility was extremely good and the sea calm. Twenty minutes after midnight the force altered course onto 070 degrees on the port leg of a zig-zag and at the same time two ships equipped with Type 273 and one with Type 281 radar detected an unidentified aircraft bearing 057 degrees, at a range of only 8nm. It was tracked in several of the force's operations rooms but none made a report on the air raid reporting net, possibly because restrictions had been placed on the use of VHF R/T. Minutes later an aircraft was seen 2.5nm ahead of the force. Some of *Indomitable*'s Albacores were near the ship at the time but they were all fitted with the reliable Mark III IFF system and the unidentified aircraft was clearly not one of them. There were, however, a number of

Unicorn in 1943 showing the high-sided hull that resulted from her double-hangar design. (*Author's collection*)

Allied aircraft taking part in Operation Husky that night that either had no IFF or had failed to switch it on. At 0025 *Indomitable* was hit by a single torpedo abreast the port boiler room and seconds later an aircraft was heard to open its throttles at the moment it was seen by the gun control positions. The officer of the watch then saw it climbing steeply over the forward part of the flight deck. *Nelson*, one of the three ships to gain the contact on radar, opened fire but was the only ship to do so. *Indomitable* listed to 12.5 degrees but this was quickly corrected by counter-flooding initiated by the engineer officer of the watch.[4] As she was brought level, speed was reduced and the ship turned onto a down moon course to frustrate any further attack. Twenty minutes later she was able to steam at 14 knots, damage having been confined to the port boiler room and its adjacent compartments. P2 pom-pom mounting was also put out of action. Two stoker Petty Officers and five stokers were killed outright but there were no further casualties. The remainder of Force H followed *Indomitable* around and escorted her to Malta, and the six airborne Albacores diverted to the island. Further unidentified aircraft were detected closing the force but were driven off by a sector barrage. *Formidable* was transferred to the 1st Division and *Indomitable* entered

No. 887 NAS pilots photographed in front of one of their Seafire IICs on *Unicorn* in 1943. The original caption identifies them from the left as 'Chips', Dave Olds, Des Viney, Harry Foote, Bill Daubney, David Kirke (commanding officer), Jack Basley, Bill Coleman, 'Duke' Beever, 'Buck' Taylor, Pete Knowler and Tony King. Note the Petty Officer pilot third from the right with his 'wings' on the right sleeve as a branch badge. This rule was never popular and was subsequently changed to allow ratings pilots to wear their wings on the left cuff in the same manner as officers. (*Author's collection*)

Grand Harbour for temporary repairs in HM Dockyard before she sailed on 27 July for Gibraltar. There more work had to be undertaken before she was fit for the passage to Norfolk, Virginia, where arrangements had been made to refit her. RA Aircraft Carriers and her three fighter squadrons were disembarked in Gibraltar on 29 July.[5] On 20 August *Illustrious* arrived in Malta and on 18 August the new carrier *Unicorn*[6] arrived in Gibraltar, both from the UK. Admiral Moody transferred his flag to *Illustrious* on 31 August when she joined Force H.

The damage to *Indomitable* followed a combination of circumstances that should have been avoidable. Willis wrote in his report that the Force had been 'caught napping'[7]. Its attention had been constantly drawn to the need to open fire on any unidentified aircraft in a position that could endanger the fleet, especially at night and, indeed, merchant ships as well as warships off the Sicilian beaches had taken this order so literally that they unfortunately shot down and damaged a number of Allied transport aircraft and gliders approaching their dropping positions, but well off their designated course, during the assault phase. He believed there were three reasons why fire had not been opened.

a) Most of the ships, especially those from the Home Fleet, had not experienced air attack at sea for some time.
b) Four days of immunity from air attack while within comparatively close range of enemy air bases had reduced ships' alertness.
c) The almost continuous presence of friendly aircraft, few of which showed IFF, promoted a false sense of security in the minds of air defence officers. This, in conjunction with the knowledge that some of *Indomitable*'s Albacores were airborne, seemed to have fatally induced uncertainty and hesitancy.

The C-in-C Mediterranean made several comments in his Report 00216/3 dated 11 October 1943. The failure of numerous modern radar sets to pick up the aircraft in sufficient time was, he believed, disappointing. The many interceptions carried out by CAP fighters in daylight on friendly aircraft not showing IFF had led to a sense of false security but he found the failure of ships to open fire inexcusable. An aircraft in a position to menace the fleet must, he emphasised, be engaged unless it had identified itself in the most positive manner. NAD expressed the view, subsequently accepted throughout the Admiralty, that the radar sets fitted in Force H during July 1943 were not ideal for the detection of low-flying aircraft but drew attention to the new Type 277, which would be better able to cope with this difficulty. Nevertheless, the Admiralty shared concern at the evident failure to use the air warning R/T net and other communication systems expressly provided to meet a threat of this kind.

This incident effectively ended active naval air involvement in Operation Husky.

Assault carriers and Army Liaison Sections

The Admiralty appreciated that provision of support for expeditionary forces was a specialised capability that required specialised training[8] and so 807 NAS, equipped with Fulmars, was worked up in the Tac-R role and several Albacore units were trained in the technique of glide bombing against land targets. Seafire and Sea Hurricane squadrons were briefed to include ground strafing in their regular flying practice whilst disembarked. The employment of naval air squadrons during the North African Campaign had confirmed the urgent need for these developments. By early 1943 it was clear that the RN would be required to provide tactical air cover for projected amphibious operations in the Mediterranean that would be beyond the range of shore-based RAF aircraft until airfields could be captured and made operable. In order to do so, RN fighter squadrons would have to counter every type of aircraft in the Axis air forces, including high-performance fighters.

There were not enough fleet carriers to embark squadrons intended for this role and although the new light fleet carriers were being built in large

Attacker. Note the unpainted wooden deck, which has no deck recognition letter. The single catapult forward was seldom used and the after lift, with its greater dimension athwartships, was not easy to manoeuvre aircraft onto or off. (*Author's collection*)

numbers[9] the first would not be ready until late 1944 at the earliest. The Admiralty had no choice, therefore, but to modify CVEs into dedicated assault carriers and it was possible to do so because events in the Battle of the Atlantic were moving in the Allies' favour, with a total of forty-one U-boats sunk in May 1943 alone.[10] A steadily increasing number of CVEs from American shipyards were becoming available for Atlantic operations, allowing the Admiralty to modify four: *Stalker*, *Attacker*, *Battler* and *Hunter*. They had arrived in the UK in early 1943, after which *Stalker* was modified in Chatham Dockyard, *Attacker* and *Battler* in Liverpool and *Hunter* in Dundee.[11] Internal space was altered to provide an air-oriented operations room with advanced fighter direction facilities, an intelligence office and extensive stowage for tactical air maps. Magazines were modified to improve the stowage of bombs, cannon and machine gun ammunition for use by fighter-bombers. The work also brought avgas stowage and pumping arrangements up to RN standards and improved magazine protection in the way agreed after the loss of *Avenger*.

In addition to these ships, the Admiralty directed that a number of fighter squadrons were to be equipped with Seafire LIICs, which had a Merlin 32 engine developing 1,640hp specifically intended for high performance in low-level operations. Unlike the IIC variant,[12] they had four-bladed propellers, could climb to 5,000ft in 1.7 minutes and were capable of 300 knots at that height. They could also be fitted when required with F-24 vertical and oblique cameras, and their pilots were trained in their use in the Tac-R, artillery reconnaissance and spotting roles. Each of these squadrons had their own Army Liaison Section. Other fighter squadrons were trained in fighter-bomber requirements and NAD stipulated that all future naval fighters must be capable of carrying bombs or drop tanks so that they could fulfil the alternative roles of fighter protection or ground attack.

The post of Flag Officer Carrier Training, FOCT, was established on 27 April 1943 to co-ordinate training for the increasing number of aircraft carriers and the diverse roles they were now expected to carry out. Appropriately, the first FOCT was Admiral Sir Lumley Lyster, and to assist him in taking forward the assault role he had his own Army Liaison Section comprising three Army or Royal Marines officers and ten other ranks. A second Liaison Section was formed to work within the staff of the Flag Officer Naval Air Stations, FONAS, to assist him in working up squadrons for the new role and a third in the Admiralty to advise NAD on the required techniques and tactics.

Each assault carrier had its own Army Liaison Section and, ultimately, every carrier had one when it was recognised that carrier air groups might be the only British air assets able to respond to short-notice crises quickly. The cruiser *Royalist*, which was still under construction, was identified as a future CVE flagship and was completed with extensive fighter direction, communications, command and control equipment. Some Army Liaison Sections also included an RAF Intelligence Officer, whose task was the acquisition and dissemination of air intelligence material and the compilation of a tactical picture to be passed to RAF units as they occupied captured airfields ashore and took over from the fleet's fighters.

The invasion of the Italian mainland

At 0600 on 17 August 1943 the last German ferry left Messina evacuating troops as Allied forces entered the town from the west. Allied intelligence had failed to warn that a well-organised German withdrawal was being carried out and insufficient resources had been committed to preventing it.[13] Sicily seems to have fallen more easily than the Allied Chiefs of Staff had thought likely and before firm plans were decided on the next step to be taken. Resistance from the Italian Army had been negligible and the situation in Italy was transformed on 25 July 1943 with the dismissal and arrest of Mussolini.[14] Apparently there had always been a considerable dislike of his Fascist rule in court and military circles and the treatment

Rodney, seen from *Illustrious* in July 1943. She was unable to strike down any of her Seafire IICs because her lifts were too small for them. They had, therefore, to remain in a permanent deck park and are seen here lashed down for heavy weather with cockpit canopies covered and locking bars across their rudders. (*Author's collection*)

of the Italian field army by the Germans after El Alamein had also caused considerable resentment that manifested itself in an unwillingness to fight alongside German forces in Sicily. King Victor Emmanuel III asked Marshal Badoglio to form a new government. He did so but stated that Italy would remain in the war on Germany's side and this led to renewed Allied bombing attacks on railway marshalling yards in Rome and the cities of Milan and Turin on 13 August. Two days later Italian emissaries arrived in Madrid and peace overtures were made to the Allies. The subsequent negotiations were completed in Syracuse on 31 August and the document of surrender was signed on 3 September. One of the Italian terms was that the Germans should be kept in complete ignorance of the armistice, details of which were not to be announced until the Allies saw fit. In the event the surrender was announced at 1830 on 8 September, only hours before the Allied landings at Salerno began on 9 September. The Germans may not have known the whole truth but they certainly suspected that the end of Italian resistance was close at hand and took rapid and effective steps to seize Rome and the country to the north of it, while rushing reinforcements to the Naples area. The German War Diary shows that plans for taking control of Italian ports had been issued as early as 19 August.

The weeks after the enemy withdrawal from Sicily provided a breathing space in which ships and landing craft were refurbished, stored and made ready for the next amphibious operation. The Allies now had options to choose from in their offensive strategy and the first moves against the Italian mainland involved unopposed landings across the Straits of Messina on 3 September. Air cover was provided by RAF and USAAF aircraft from bases in Sicily and assault across the Straits had seemed the most obvious next step but there were many senior officers who believed that they hardly made the best use of the Allied superiority at sea. Alternative plans for an amphibious landing somewhere near Naples designated Operation Avalanche were considered; to the north of Naples, in the Gulf of Naples and in the Gulf of Salerno. Once operations in Sicily were completed on 17 August, the first was discarded. An assault in the Gulf of Naples was considered too hazardous when the strength of the coast defences was considered and so the Gulf of Salerno was accepted as the best option, a decision largely based on the availability of the RN assault carrier task force to protect the beachhead.[15] *Unicorn* was deployed as a light fleet carrier to join the CVEs in a newly designated Force V.

Salerno lay an average of 200nm away from Allied airfields in Sicily and initially the planning staff believed that land-based fighter cover

Seafire IICs of 885 NAS on *Formidable*'s flight deck in early 1943 as she returns to Gibraltar. They could not be struck down into the hangar because of her small lifts and the weathering they suffered in the deck park is obvious. The loss of paint finish combined with the bulky air intake filters would have significantly reduced their optimum performance. (*Author's collection*)

over the assault beaches would be limited. Between them, the RAF and USAAF tactical air forces had over 2,000 fighters in the Mediterranean theatre by then but only thirty-six could be kept on patrol over Salerno at any one time, with Spitfires remaining for only twenty minutes and USAAF Lightnings only forty. The planning staff assessed the provision of the assault CVE task force, Force V, as an essential element to protect the landing beaches against enemy air attack on the designated D-Day, 9 September 1943, and to cover the expeditionary forces as they moved inland until an airfield at Montecorvino could be captured and made usable. This was expected to be on D + 1. In the event the Allied shore-based effort exceeded expectations and the enemy's air reaction fell far below the level estimated.

Force H, still commanded by Admiral Willis, had been intended to provide cover against any move by the Italian fleet but this threat had disappeared with the announcement of the Italian surrender on 8 September. It had also been intended to provide medium level CAP to cover Force V and this became its primary task. Avalanche marked the first use of assault CVEs by the RN to cover an amphibious landing; a tactic that would significantly influence US Navy and Marine Corps operations in the Pacific in the months and years ahead. The RN carrier forces for Operation Avalanche comprised:

Force H

Illustrious	Captain R L B Cunliffe RN	
	Flag Rear Admiral Aircraft Carriers – Rear Admiral C Moody	
894 NAS	10 Seafire IIC	Lieutenant Commander (A) F R A Turnbull DSC RN
878 NAS	14 Martlet IV	Lieutenant Commander (A) M F Fell RN
890 NAS	14 Martlet IV	Lieutenant Commander J W Sleigh DSC RN
810 NAS	12 Barracuda II[16]	Lieutenant Commander (A) A J B Forde RN
Formidable	Rear Admiral A G Talbot[17]	
893 NAS	16 Martlet IV	Lieutenant Commander (A) R B Pearson RN
888 NAS	16 Martlet IV	Major F D G Bird RM
885 NAS	5 Seafire IIC	Lieutenant (A) R H P Carver DSC RN
820 NAS	12 Albacore	Lieutenant Commander J C N Shrubsole RN

Force H also included the battleships *Nelson* (flag), *Rodney*, *Warspite* and *Valiant*.

Force V

Force V was commanded by Rear Admiral Sir Philip Vian, who flew his flag in the cruiser *Euryalus*.

Unicorn	Captain Q D Graham RN	
809 NAS	10 Seafire IIC	Major A J Wright RM
887 NAS	10 Seafire IIC	Lieutenant Commander D W Kirke RN
897 NAS	10 Seafire IIC	Lieutenant Commander (A) W C Simpson DSC RN
818 NAS	3 Swordfish	short detachment only
Stalker	Captain H S Murray-Smith RN	
833 NAS[18]	6 Seafire LIIC	Lieutenant (A) D G Parker RNVR
880 NAS	14 Seafire LIIC	Lieutenant Commander (A) W H Martyn RN

Attacker	Captain W P Shirlay-Rollison RN	
879 NAS	10 Seafire LIIC	Lieutenant Commander (A) R J H Grose RNVR
886 NAS	10 Seafire LIIC	Lieutenant R H L Oliphant RN
Hunter	Captain H H McWilliam RN	
834 NAS[19]	6 Seafire LIIC	Lieutenant (A) F A J Pennington RNZNVR
899 NAS	12 Seafire LIIC	Lieutenant Commander (A) R F Walker RNVR
Battler	Captain F N R Stephenson RN	
807 NAS	9 Seafire LIIC	Lieutenant Commander (A) K Firth RNVR
808 NAS	9 Seafire LIIC	Lieutenant Commander (A) A C Wallace RNVR

Force V also included the cruisers *Scylla* and *Charybdis* and ten Hunt-class destroyers.

Four years after the outbreak of war in 1939 it is interesting to note the number of squadrons commanded by short-service (A) RN and RNVR officers, many of whom had already distinguished themselves and shown their tactical awareness in this new and evolving form of naval warfare as well as outstanding leadership. The use of deck parks now allowed both fleet carriers to operate air groups of about fifty, another indication that earlier, chronic shortages of aircraft were being overcome by Lend-Lease and increased UK production.

Force V's CVEs arrived at Gibraltar from the Clyde in August[20] with Seafire LIICs of three squadrons and two Fighter Flights embarked together with reserve aircraft to re-equip 880 and 899 NAS, which had previously been embarked in *Indomitable*. At the end of August the CVEs sailed with *Unicorn* to conduct flying exercises off Gibraltar, after which they sailed for Malta via Oran. This short period was the only time available for the former *Indomitable* squadrons to carry out deck landing training with their new aircraft but even the 'resident' CVE fighter squadrons had been given very little time for an efficient work up. To make matters worse, the level of pilot experience remained generally low.

Force H sailed at 1600 on the afternoon of 7 September and passed south of Malta to give the impression that it was at sea for exercises. After dark it headed through the Sicilian Channel and thence into the Tyrrhenian Sea to take station in its operating area to the west of Salerno.

The glassy calm sea surface visible in this photograph, taken during operations off Salerno, shows the lack of any natural wind in the area in which Force V had to operate. *Battler*, *Attacker* and *Unicorn* with the flagship *Euryalus* in the background are seen from the deck of another CVE with one of its twin 40mm gun mountings just visible at the bottom right of the picture. (*Author's collection*)

Continuous daylight CAP and anti-submarine patrols were maintained but no enemy opposition was encountered until 2100 on 8 September, when thirty German torpedo bombers attacked the force. Several were engaged by Allied night fighters from Sicily and all met heavy anti-aircraft fire from the warships. Four, possibly six, enemy aircraft were claimed as destroyed and no ships were hit, although *Warspite* and *Formidable* did see torpedoes pass close to them. One of *Formidable*'s 885 NAS Seafires was destroyed on its outrigger by blast from a 4.5in gun as it fired at the enemy aircraft. Several German aircrew from aircraft that had been shot down were rescued from their dinghies and told interrogators that their objective had been the assault convoys. Their attack on Force H had been a mistake. The convoys' progress was not delayed.[21]

As in Torch and Husky, planners had hoped that surprise might be achieved by landings if there was no prior bombardment but its absence was soon keenly felt. The landings began at night in bright moonlight, a time chosen to facilitate a parachute drop but this had been cancelled only hours before it was due to take place. The moonlight helped German gun crews, who had seized the coastal batteries a day earlier, to engage and slow the landing craft. The British assaults in the northern sector had as their initial objectives the capture of the port of Salerno and Montecorvino airfield. The Americans, to the south of the River Sele, aimed to reach and capture the high ground from which enemy fire could be directed onto the coastal plain. Neither objective was achieved.

Fighter direction

At 0550 on 9 September Force H flew off sixteen Martlets, eight for its own CAP and eight to cover Force V's operating area 25nm to the east. The fleet's fighter direction plan was comprehensive and included arrangements for the control and direction of the Force H CAP; the control and direction of fighters protecting Force V; the organisation of Force V's fighter patrols in the assault area and for homing them as necessary during their return flights to their own carriers. Control and direction was also provided for any naval fighter that was required to operate over the landing beaches or the forward edge of the battle area. This was a considerable task and the necessary co-ordination of the various radar pictures, plots and communications nets was beyond the capability of any one ship. They were, therefore, spread among several ships. The controlling ship within Force V was Vian's flagship *Euryalus* in which Lieutenant Commander E D G Lewin RN was the co-ordinating officer. If she was damaged, *Unicorn* was to take over the task. Fighter direction within Force V was the responsibility of *Attacker* with *Battler* as back-up if needed. The remote fighter direction ship operating close to the beaches was *Palomares*, which was to control and direct any naval fighter passed on by Force V's control ship and to act as an R/T conduit with the expeditionary force ashore. She had been fitted out as an aircraft direction ship earlier in 1943 and had Commander C P Coke RN as her direction officer. He was the outstanding fighter direction officer of his generation and had been the chief instructor at the fighter direction school at RNAS Yeovilton from its inception. Another fighter direction ship, *Ulster*

The batsman holds his 'cut' signal as a Seafire IIC catches an early arrester wire in *Indomitable*. (*Author's collection*)

Queen, acted as the back-up. Fighters being passed to Force V for control were directed by *Illustrious* but both fleet carriers were responsible for the direction of their own fighters on CAP. In the fighter control ships, the direction officers and their deputies collected intelligence information, issued instructions for briefings and organised the patrols to be flown. A safety officer[22] vectored out and homed in the fighters. The fighter control and direction ships in Force V shared communication nets with Force H and were also intended to be in touch with the USN headquarters ship *Ancon*, flagship of Admiral Hewitt USN who commanded the Western Naval Task Force, but this net unfortunately failed on D-Day. Other less direct means had to be used. *Ancon* was also the direction ship for all shore-based fighters, which included USAAF Spitfires and Lightnings and RAF Spitfires. Communications with all the ships in Force V except the escort destroyers was on a VHF inter-FDO net but there was only one VHF frequency available for directing Force V fighters to their patrol lines and homing them. This same frequency was also used by the fighter direction ship to direct fighters, with the result that it was congested but seldom actually saturated. It had been intended that *Ulster Queen* should be stationed inshore to control and direct the fighters passed to her by the Force V control ship. However, she was near-missed by a rocket bomb just before the operation and only arrived in time to act as a standby to *Palomares*, which had taken her place at short notice.

Force H flying programme

Two CAP stations were maintained by the fleet carriers at their planned strength of eight aircraft each throughout the thirteen hours from dawn to dusk. The pre-planned programme involved flying off replacement fighters every ninety minutes and landing on every two hours to sustain this effort, which was maintained for three days. It entailed each fleet carrier maintaining eight fighters continuously on patrol with a further eight in the air for half an hour on the eight occasions during which relief operations were carried out in the daily programme. Extra fighters were only flown off on one occasion when an unidentified aircraft, not showing IFF, approached the force. *Illustrious* and *Formidable* managed to conduct all their flying operations while in close proximity to the battleships within the circular destroyer screen but there were occasional problems. Once *Valiant* had to go full astern to avoid hitting *Formidable*, and on the afternoon of 11 September several barrier crashes in *Formidable* and delays caused by returning fighters finding it difficult to locate their carriers in the thickening haze led to the two carriers' flying cycles getting out of phase. It was then very difficult for ships to maintain their position within the force and it became clear that if the fighters had become involved

A replacement four-bladed Seafire LIIC propeller being transferred to *Attacker* from an MTB that had brought it from *Unicorn*. Note the officer taking charge of the evolution holding a megaphone in the sponson at the top of the picture. (*Author's collection*)

in prolonged combat a pre-planned flying programme might not have been workable. The RN still considered that battleships should act as fleet guides upon which all other ships took station but as aircraft carriers had grown in both numbers and importance, this policy was clearly no longer tenable. For those with eyes to see, battleships had already became anti-aircraft escorts for the carriers and the fleet had to manoeuvre in the most efficient way to carry out sustained flying operations, not merely for intermittent launches when ordered to do so by the flag. A carrier should, therefore have been the designated guide with the whole fleet turning together into and out of wind to operate aircraft and the battleships, cruisers and destroyers maintaining their anti-aircraft and anti-submarine dispositions as necessary. The USN was the first to evolve this method of operation in the Pacific during 1944 but it was soon adopted as best practice by the RN and used by the British Pacific Fleet, BPF, in 1945.

On 10 September an Italian SM.79 that had escaped from Milan was intercepted by fighters from Force H and seen to wave a white flag from the cockpit. It was escorted to Malazzo airfield, where it landed.

Illustrious operated a deck park of ten Seafires, which made the aircraft handlers' task difficult but this was alleviated by including two of them in every range of eight fighters to be flown off and keeping the others largely clear of the deck with their tail wheels on outriggers. Late on 11 September *Illustrious* transferred six Seafires to *Unicorn* and *Formidable* transferred two Seafires and six Martlets. This had become necessary because of the reduced number of aircraft left in Force V after a succession of deck landing accidents and was intended to allow it to maintain its own CAP after Force H's withdrawal, which followed at 1900. A further eight Martlets were flown off to *Unicorn* as Force H made its way south to Malta, involving a flight of 250nm. Force H passed surrendered ships of the Italian Navy anchored in St Paul's and St George's Bays as it returned to Malta and Admiral Willis later wrote that with the threat of intervention by an enemy fleet removed, he could have maintained operations off Salerno for another two days if there was no great increase in enemy air activity.

Between 9 and 11 September *Illustrious* achieved 209 deck landings with no barrier crashes, although two Seafires had made heavy landings resulting in damage considered repairable on board. Her aircraft had used 15,200 gallons of avgas out of the ship's total tankage of 50,660 gallons. *Formidable* achieved 214 deck landings but had suffered seven barrier crashes, put down to her pilots only averaging ten hours' flying per month over the preceding nine months. Her aircraft had used 15,600 gallons of avgas out of the same total tankage as *Illustrious*. When the statistics from Avalanche were studied by NAD it was found that up to twelve pilots in each carrier had flown six or more hours in a single day with a further two hours strapped into their cockpits at readiness. The remainder had averaged three hours flying in a single day with two to five hours spent strapped in at readiness.

Clipped-wing Seafire LIICs of 807 and 808 NAS being ranged onto *Battler*'s forward lift from the hangar during Operation Avalanche. (*Author's collection*)

One pilot's view

Hugh Popham was serving in 894 NAS in *Illustrious* with Force H during Operation Avalanche. In his autobiographical *Sea Flight* he described the condition thus:[23]

> ...as patrol succeeded patrol with hardly a rumour of enemy aircraft to break the monotony of cruising round in the thick blue haze we slowly came to the realisation that [the enemy] was not going to play...The [Martlets] did shoot down one shadower but even that had first of all been reported as a 'big bogey', a mistake which fitted snugly into the general pattern of things and provoked Michael Hordern, our fighter direction officer, to a neat impromptu quotation 'Thou wretched, rash, intruding fool, farewell! I took thee for thy better.'...I spent one or two patrols with my number 2 harrying about in the curiously opaque light looking for reputed bogeys but without success. This haze, which was constant throughout the operation, made our routine flights even duller than they would have been for it reduced visibility to a mile or two and from 15 to 20,000ft we could see no glimmer of the land and precious little of the ships directly below us. We might have been a couple of goldfish drifting round in a bowl of thick blue glass for all the reference we appeared to have to the battles rumoured to be raging on that remote shore.

Force V flying programme

Force V sailed from Malta at 1000 on 8 September and passed through the Straits of Messina that night. A number of pyrotechnic displays were seen over mainland Italy and at first they were mistaken for anti-aircraft fire but it was soon appreciated that they represented an outbreak of joy as the Italian population celebrated the BBC announcement, earlier that evening, of the armistice signed by its new government with the Allied powers. The BBC was severely criticised for doing so by the Allied Chiefs of Staff, who had hoped to keep news of the Italian surrender secret until after the Avalanche landings had begun, fearing that premature disclosure might lead to complacency. At first light on 9 September 1943 Force V arrived in its operating area off Salerno where the weather was found to be fine with negligible wind. As the day progressed, however, slant visibility from the air deteriorated in haze. Force V flew off its first Seafires at 0615 on D-Day and then at hourly intervals until the last aircraft landed on at 1930 in the twilight after sunset. Force V had to operate within a designated area 30nm square to the south west of the Isle of Capri, only 30nm from the Seafire patrol lines.

Stalker in Gibraltar before Operation Avalanche with two Martlets on deck among the Seafires of 880 NAS, which were being transferred to the ship after *Indomitable* was damaged. The squadron has clearly not yet completed its re-equipment with Seafire LIICs because five IICs with their three-bladed propellers are visible. Two LIICs, one nearest the camera and one behind the nearest Martlet, have had their wingtips clipped but the appropriate fairings have not yet been fitted. (*Author's collection*)

For the first hour and half after dawn and a similar period before dusk *Unicorn* provided high-level patrols over the beaches, giving cover in the absence of land-based aircraft. The remainder of the seventy-five sorties flown from this ship were in support of the LIIC patrols flown off the four CVEs. The low-level fighters were initially held in the vicinity of Capri controlled by direction officers in *Palomares* and intended to break up any attacks well clear of the beachhead. They were to be relieved by USAAF A-36As, the Allison-engined ground attack version of the better-known P-51A Mustang fighter. Each Seafire mission lasted eighty to eighty-five minutes, of which sixty were spent on patrol. The balance was taken up with the form up and transit to the coast, the return and the period spent waiting to join their own carrier's landing circuit for recovery. The CVEs were limited to four aircraft each for patrols and the larger *Unicorn* to eight, but the pre-planned flying schedule was extremely tight and a high degree of pilot discipline was required to make it work because the tiny area allocated to Force V was far too small to allow five carriers to work together efficiently. Their circuit patterns overlapped dangerously at times but this was Vian's first experience in command of a carrier task force and it is arguable that neither he nor his staff had appreciated the constraints that the operating area imposed on his force and its pilots. An admiral with greater air experience would have demanded a more realistic operating area at the planning stage. By D-Day when the limitation became apparent, it was too late to make changes. Whilst airborne naval aircraft, like those of the RAF and USAAF, came under the operational control of the Commanding General 12th Air Force, Brigadier General House USAAF. He and his staff were embarked in the USS *Ancon* with Admiral Hewitt and so the failure of communications between her and *Palomares* represented a major shortcoming in Allied command and control capability. House's instructions to Force V Seafires were:

1) To maintain a standing low patrol south and west of Capri.
2) To maintain a high patrol over the beaches by *Unicorn*'s Seafires from sunrise to 0745 and from 1810 to sunset, ie during the periods when fighter cover could not be given by aircraft based in Sicily.
3) To maintain a standing high patrol over the low patrol in the Capri area during daylight by *Unicorn*'s Seafires.

The role allotted to Force V's fighters by the 12th Air Force was a distinct disappointment since the pilots had all worked up in the expectation that they would be employed in direct support of the Army as it moved inland from the beaches.[24] In fact, there was very little enemy activity in the Seafire patrol area and so at noon on 9 September the remote fighter direction officer in *Palomares* moved the Seafire IIC patrol lines eastward over the beaches to augment the Sicilian-based fighters. The constant fighter strength over the beaches was then maintained at about twenty carrier-based and thirty-six Sicily-based fighters throughout D-Day. The lack of information from *Ancon* made it difficult for the Force Fighter Controller to fulfil his briefing and sortie planning tasks to best advantage but the limited scale of enemy air activity mitigated this shortcoming.

Force V operated within a circular destroyer screen with *Euryalus* in its centre as the force guide. The five aircraft carriers were dispersed in close formation 2,000yds apart keeping station on the guide, and the whole force was manoeuvred by blue pendant turns onto the designated flying course, DFC, into what little natural wind there was for launches and recoveries, including emergency landings. Pilots had to fly extremely tight finals turns at the end of circuits that overlapped those of adjacent carriers. The hazy conditions made it difficult for pilots to see their carrier's batsman until the very last moment and the close, congested circuit patterns made it difficult for the batsmen themselves to discern their own aircraft until they emerged from the haze on finals. It was fortunate that there were no collisions and the bad visibility also made homing the fighters difficult at the end of their sorties. Despite these problems, Vian reported that flying discipline had remained good, especially when the lack of operational training for the newer pilots was taken into account. All flying operations were controlled from his flagship *Euryalus* and Vian considered his experimental choice of this ship to have been an unqualified success since he was 'free from the noise and distraction inseparable from a carrier's bridge'. After flying off, the fighters formed into their respective high and low patrols and were handed off by the fighter control ship to the fighter direction ship, which took charge of them on their patrol lines until it was time for them to return. They were then given a homing vector provided for them by the fighter control ship and guided back to a waiting position as necessary before joining their various landing circuits.

Enemy air strength in the Mediterranean theatre had been greatly reduced during the spring and summer of 1943 through losses sustained in the Tunisian and Sicilian campaigns, which could not be made good. The surrender of Italy on the day before Operation Avalanche also limited the

A typical assault CVE pilots' briefing room with its comfortable USN-style seats. Note the sign to the right of the door headed 'Have You Got?' It was intended as a last reminder to ensure that pilots had everything they needed from the briefing before they manned their aircraft. (*Author's collection*)

German resources available within range of the assault area but there was still some Luftwaffe reaction, however. Fifteen minutes after first light and thirty minutes after the first Seafires had been flown off, six Ju 88s tried to attack the beaches. Seafires intercepted them but before they could close within firing range the enemy aircraft jettisoned their bombs, turned and fled. The naval fighters had achieved their aim but no enemy aircraft had been destroyed. This attack proved to be one of only a small number by bombers and the enemy mostly relied on hit-and-run attacks by Fw 190 or Bf 109 fighter-bombers, which approached at high speed and very low level. Shortly after noon on 9 September a Seafire patrol intercepted and turned back a raid by a group of more than twelve fighter-bombers that had approached from the north.

The fighter defence of the Salerno beachhead was complicated by the local geography. The high ground behind the beaches and to the north produced heavy clutter on radar screens, which meant that targets over the land could not be detected. The fighter direction ships could not, therefore, detect and intercept enemy aircraft until they had left the coast. Seafire pilots were largely dependent on their own eyes for locating enemy aircraft but with the extensive haze that prevailed throughout the operation visual detection of fast, low-flying attack aircraft was extremely difficult. On many occasions the first warning of a raid was the detonation of enemy bombs around the beachhead. When the last aircraft landed on at dusk on 9 September, Force V had flown 265 sorties, two-and-a-half sorties for every aircraft embarked. It had been a disappointing day for the pilots on patrol because they had not destroyed or damaged any of the enemy aircraft that had been intercepted but on the other hand the aim had been achieved. The Luftwaffe had inflicted no serious damage on the assault shipping or the Army ashore and had turned and fled whenever approached by Seafires. On the ground, however, the British and American troops had not made the advances anticipated and Montecorvino airfield was still being disputed after some of the day's heaviest fighting.

Force V had originally been scheduled to carry out just one definite day and a second probable day of intensive operation but the lack of a shore base meant that the carriers must remain on station for at least the second day. The planning staff had anticipated this and stipulated that Force V must fly 196 sorties on D + 1. An unexpectedly high incidence of deck landing accidents had led to a significant reduction in the number of Seafires available on the second day from 105 to sixty-five but in spite of this the force excelled itself by launching 232 sorties on 10 September, thirty-six more than planned. This was only 12 per cent less than the day before with 40 per cent fewer aircraft. Land-based air cover on D + 1 was reduced by 20 per cent, which made the carrier-borne fighters' contribution all the more valuable. Force V's 232 hours on patrol flown by sixty-five fighters compared most favourably with the 320 hours on patrol over the beachhead flown by the 641 RAF and USAAF fighters based in Sicily.

D + 1, 10 September, was the Seafires' most successful day during Operation Avalanche. More than forty enemy aircraft were driven away from the beachhead in encounters that caused the German fighter-bombers to jettison their bombs and flee before the Seafires could close to within firing range. Without their bombs, both Fw 190s and Bf 109s were faster than either the Seafire IIC or LIIC and because of this there were only ten occasions during the four days of operation on which naval pilots managed to close the range sufficiently for attempted interceptions to be classed as combats. The experience of Sub Lieutenant (A) E J Davies RNVR of 833 NAS was typical. He went to the assistance of a USAAF P-38 flight that had been 'bounced' by Bf 109s at low level. On the appearance of Seafires, however, the enemy fighters made off faster than the Seafires could follow and the frustrated Davies was only able to fire two short bursts at extreme range. An hour and a half before sunset on 10 September a top cover patrol led by Lieutenant Commander W C Simpson DSC RN, the commanding officer of 897 NAS, saw a number of Bf 109s at 12,000ft to the north of Salerno. This proved to be one of the few enemy fighter sweeps encountered by Allied aircraft and, since they were only opposed by Simpson's four Seafires, the German fighters remained to fight. The combat was brief, however, because the Bf 109 pilots employed turning, climb and dive tactics, in which the Seafire's performance was superior. Simpson destroyed a Bf 109, which was seen to explode, and probably another; his wing men damaged two

An 807 NAS Seafire LIIC after a barrier engagement in *Battler*. The engine has broken away from its mountings and avgas is pouring from the main tank; a considerable fire hazard that the flight deck party needed to attack quickly. (*Author's collection*)

others. One Seafire suffered minor damage. Overall, enemy air activity in the area was disappointingly limited and very few combats took place. *Unicorn* flew off a Swordfish of 818 NAS carrying four Seafire pilots squeezed into the rear cockpit, which flew to Castelvetrano airfield in Sicily and picked up four replacement Seafires. Two of them managed to land on *Unicorn* safely but the other pair failed to locate her in the haze and flew to Montecorvino airfield, where they carried out forced landings before being destroyed by enemy artillery fire.

By the end of 10 September Montecorvino was in Allied hands but artillery fire from both sides was passing over it, making it unusable for all practical purposes. During the night US Army engineers managed to level a 1,000yd landing strip across a tomato farm near Paestum, just inland from the American beachhead on the southern shore of Salerno Bay, and it was hoped that this would be ready for dry weather daylight operations by noon on 12 September. It was, therefore, essential that Force V remained in action despite Vian's growing doubts about the viability of his reduced number of aircraft. At dawn on D + 2 Force V had only thirty-nine serviceable Seafires left and the planning staff target for the day's operations, if they were still deemed to be necessary, was to fly 130 sorties. Again, however, Force V exceeded this target and actually flew 160 sorties.[25] In doing so it set a record for carrier aircraft utilisation in the Second World War in terms of sorties flown per serviceable aircraft. The aircraft transferred to Force V from Force H as it withdrew brought *Unicorn*'s air group up to thirty-six aircraft, including eleven of her Seafire IICs that were still serviceable on the morning of D + 3, and these allowed her to fly CAP over the force while the remaining CVE Seafires operated over the beachhead. During its four days in action Force V Seafires claimed one enemy aircraft destroyed, another probably destroyed and four possibles. With the exception of one possible, all these were achieved by *Unicorn*'s Seafire IICs on high patrol.

The Naval Fighter Wing disembarked at Paestum

Flying operations on 12 September began shortly before first light as usual but as the strip at Paestum was announced to be fit for fighter operations from noon only three patrols were launched by Force V, the last of fifty-six sorties landing on at 1000. For the next three hours the maintenance personnel worked as hard as they could to prepare the best of the surviving Seafires for disembarkation to Paestum, where they were to operate until air force fighters could be flown from Sicily to replace them. In the early afternoon of 12 September Lieutenant Commander J C Cockburn RN, the Lieutenant Commander (Flying) of *Stalker*, led two LIICs from his own ship; four from *Attacker* and five each from *Battler* and *Hunter* plus ten IICs from *Unicorn* to Paestum. These twenty-six Seafires constituted an RN fighter wing, which operated under the most primitive conditions for a short period. One aircraft suffered a brake failure on landing and was written off but this was the only casualty. The aircraft had to be refuelled from 5 gallon drums, twenty-three of which were needed for each Seafire, and since the RAF servicing commando was at Montecorvino, pilots had to carry out their own field maintenance and refuelling. None of the Seafires was fitted with dust filters and in the conditions experienced at Paestum this reduced the expectation of life for their Merlin engines dramatically. The only Seafire mission flown from the airstrip on 12 September was a four-aircraft Tac-R search for enemy tanks reported near the area. This intelligence proved false, however, but there were intermittent air attacks and steady artillery bombardment as they spent the night in tents provided by the US Army together with food and blankets. An Italian farmhouse that adjoined the airstrip, together with the livestock it contained, was taken over as a centre of Seafire maintenance activity, described by Lieutenant Commander Cockburn in his action report as 'the first Fleet Air Arm base in Europe'.[26]

The dawn patrol on 13 September consisted of twelve LIICs with four IICs as top cover and it was uneventful until its return to Paestum. In thick haze the Seafires were attacked by a pair of USAAF A-36As, one of which was promptly shot down by the top cover before the mutual misidentification was sorted out. The American Army pilot bailed out and landed unhurt. The Seafires then landed without further incident and the pilots were being debriefed when an irate US Army major in a leather flying jacket and wearing a pair of pearl-handled revolvers in cowboy-style holsters strode up and demanded to know 'which of you Limey sons-of-bitches shot down my goddam idiot number 2?' He was subsequently suitably mollified by the wing. Twenty Seafires flew on the noon patrol, this time entirely without incident, but on landing they discovered that nearly 100 USAAF P-40 Warhawks of the 33rd Fighter Group had arrived and their crews installed in the tented accommodation. Conditions were unsuited to the operation of so many fighters and the naval wing took its aircraft to Asa, another new airstrip just north of the River Sele, where the RAF's 324 Wing had just arrived with its Spitfires. The IICs were not required for the dusk patrol and only eight LIICs participated in what turned out to be another incident-free sortie.

The move to Asa worked out well as an RAF servicing commando was there and it was able to give the Seafires the attention they needed. Eight LIICs flew on the dawn patrol on 14 September and this proved to be the last combat mission flown by RN aircraft during Avalanche. The Spitfire Wing assumed responsibility for the air defence task at noon and Cockburn decided to return to Sicily at once. The twenty-five remaining Seafires took off at 1600 for the RAF airstrip at Falcone on the northeast corner of the island. All aircraft arrived safely and took off again the following morning, 15 September, for Bizerta with a short refuelling stop at Castelvetrano airfield in southern Sicily. By the time they rejoined their ships, the naval wing had flown sixty-six combat sorties in difficult circumstances and although they were exhausted by six days of continuous flying, it was greatly to the pilots' credit that in the course of 132 combat and transit sorties away from their carriers in the most basic and unfamiliar surroundings there had only been one accident and that was attributable to material failure. Their efforts were a fitting finale to the Fleet Air Arm's contribution to Avalanche.

Five pilots are listed as killed during Avalanche in the Fleet Air Arm Roll of Honour. They were Sub Lieutenant (A) M A McKenzie RNVR of 809 NAS in *Unicorn* on 9 September 1943; Sub Lieutenant (A) P B N Prentice RNVR of 886 NAS from *Attacker* on 9 September; Sub Lieutenant (A) J J Urlich RNZNVR of 897 NAS in *Unicorn* on 9 September; Sub Lieutenant E Razzall RNVR of 897 NAS in *Unicorn* on 10 September and Sub Lieutenant (A) G C Mercer RNVR of 880 NAS in *Stalker* on 11

A Seafire beginning its take-off roll from *Stalker* with Admiral Vian's flagship *Euryalus* visible in the background. A visiting Martlet is just visible ranged aft and the calm sea surface shows the absence of any natural wind. (*Author's collection*)

September. Three other pilots were injured and two bailed out. One of the latter, Sub Lieutenant (A) D Cameron RNZNVR of 880 NAS, was forced to bail out over enemy-held territory after an engine failure. He was captured but managed to escape and arrived in Naples shortly after Allied troops entered the city on 1 October.

The situation at Salerno was still critical when the Seafires left and 16 September proved to be a critical day for the defenders with air attacks accompanying counter-attacks on the ground that were only held back with difficulty. Vian was ordered to prepare Force V for further action with thirty-six Martlets transferred from the fleet carriers and thirty Seafires, the most that could be made serviceable in time. However, the German attacks proved to be their final effort and Allied forces advanced out of the beachhead. Vian was informed that Force V was no longer required and it was stood down at Palermo on 20 September.

The Luftwaffe's most notable achievement was the first operational deployment by Kampfgeschwader 100 of remotely controlled glider bombs, the first air-to-surface missiles. These were 3,000lb FX 1400 bombs carried by Dornier Do 17 aircraft and they were used against amphibious shipping and warships on the gun line off Salerno. No RN, RAF or USAAF fighters managed to prevent the release of these weapons, which damaged the US cruisers *Philadelphia* and *Savannah* on 11 September. On 13 September the British cruiser *Uganda*, which was stopped at the time firing at targets ashore, was hit without warning by an aircraft directly overhead at 20,000ft. She had to be towed to Malta for repairs. The destroyers *Nubian* and *Loyal* were both near-missed on the same day and suffered sixteen men killed and seven wounded between them. Last and most serious of all, the battleship *Warspite* was near-missed by two of the new weapons and hit by a third in a boiler room immediately following another attack by ten Fw 190 fighter-bombers. She was towed to Malta through the Messina Strait and arrived on the morning of 18 September. She suffered nine dead and twelve wounded, and was never fully repaired, ending her operational career as a shore bombardment vessel with much-reduced speed and one 15in turret out of action. German FX 1400 bombs also sank the Italian battleship *Roma* as it sailed to surrender but at no time did the Luftwaffe prevent the shore bombardment force from supporting the army ashore.

The Fleet Air Arm contribution to Operation Avalanche reviewed
Carrier-borne aircraft committed to Avalanche carried out the task set for them well, albeit a less-demanding task than they had expected. However, it was achieved at a cost incompatible with the circumstances, especially the limited enemy reaction, and there can be no doubt that

Force V's experience off Salerno was responsible for the bad reputation the Seafire suffered for the remainder of its long career in the RN. Vian, later to command the 1st Aircraft Carrier Squadron in the BPF, was vocal in his condemnation of the type as an embarked fighter. No Seafire had been lost in combat but forty-two had been lost or written off as the result of accidents. In 713 sorties there had been thirty-two catastrophic deck landing accidents in which aircraft had been written off. Four more were lost after engine failure and a further six lost from miscellaneous accidental causes while airborne. Added to these, while landing on their carriers twenty-four Seafires had suffered wrinkling of the rear fuselage that was beyond the limited capacity of the squadron or ship's air engineering staff to repair while attention was focused, rightly, on keeping the serviceable aircraft flying. Seventeen more had suffered undercarriage damage, which was also not repairable because insufficient spare oleos were available on the CVEs. Put simply, every ninth sortie had resulted in the loss of or serious damage to a Seafire, an appalling casualty rate that was never repeated in any other RN operation. Not included in these figures but the most common single

Many broken Seafires were returned to the UK in *Unicorn* after Avalanche for repair or the recovery of reusable components. LR706, seen here, had served with 879 NAS in *Attacker* and was badly damaged on 10 September 1943 when it was flown by Sub Lieutenant (A) R J H Grose RNVR. It shows all three of the major types of damage the type suffered during the Salerno operations; broken propeller tips from 'pecking' nose down on landing, a broken back from a heavy landing and structural damage aft. (*Author's collection*)

cause of temporary Seafire unserviceability was damage to propellers caused by the tips impacting the flight deck, or 'pecking' as aircraft pitched forward on taking a wire or as the pilot raised the tail when taking off. The bottom of the 10.25ft propeller disc[27] of the Seafire LIIC was nearer to the deck than in any other naval fighter and no fewer than fifty-five Seafires suffered broken propellers. Many of the inexperienced pilots embarked in Force V's squadrons lacked the finesse that only hours flown on the type could have given them. A few spare propellers were available in *Unicorn* and while this supply lasted they were ferried from her to the CVEs by the MTBs, which served as the force's air-sea rescue vessels in the waters close inshore and off Capri. The propeller disc could stand some reduction, however, and drastic surgery was suggested by Captain H H McWilliam RN, the Captain of *Hunter*. After consultation with his ship and squadron air engineering officers, he gave instructions that 2in were to be cropped off the blades. No loss of performance or signs of instability became apparent and the availability of *Hunter*'s Seafires improved markedly. The practice became standard among Seafire squadrons and was even continued post-war.

Why were accidental losses so high? Firstly, it would be fair to say that the majority of pilots in the CVE squadrons had too little experience in deck landing the Seafire LIIC, especially in conditions where wind over the deck, WOD, was low. Furthermore, the work up periods that should have got them accustomed to the ship's small flight decks had been too short. This was particularly true of the pilots who had recently transferred from *Indomitable* to the CVEs since they now found themselves operating from decks that were about 30 per cent smaller with considerably less WOD available from ships that were more than 10 knots slower than a fleet carrier. There was one notable exception, however: 834 NAS Fighter Flight commanded by Lieutenant F A J Pennington RNZNVR had been embarked in *Hunter* since 7 July and the experienced Pennington had drilled his pilots relentlessly in deck landing techniques. In consequence, the only issues experienced landing on during Avalanche were four propeller 'peckings', which were quickly repaired. All six of the flight's Seafires were serviceable at noon on 12 September and the lesson to be learnt from this emphasised the one already learnt in Torch. Time must be allowed for squadrons to work up before being committed to operations. Rushing units into service with inadequate preparation to achieve numbers on paper had not produced the desired results.

To add to this lack of experience, CVE recoveries had been made difficult by the lack of wind. Most pilots had carried out their initial deck landing training in the Clyde, where natural wind was seldom absent, even in summer. Many had carried out their training in CVEs just like those in Force V but with no natural wind off Salerno to increase the WOD they were faced with an approach speed, relative to the deck, about 10 to 15 knots greater than any of them had experienced before and this put a strain on pilots, batsmen and undercarriages. Higher relative speed increased the Seafire's tendency to 'float' over the wires when the throttle was closed at the 'cut' signalled by the batsman, making a barrier engagement inevitable if the aircraft was not handled with a finesse few of the new pilots had acquired. If a late wire was caught, higher speed often placed an unacceptable strain on the arrester hook and rear fuselage, and there was only so much of this that the Seafire, adapted from a lightweight design for operation ashore, could stand. *Unicorn* was larger and faster than the CVEs but she had her own problems. The airflow around the island and flight deck was found to produce a violent wind shear over the after round-down in certain wind conditions, which proved to be exactly those encountered off Salerno. The shear caused aircraft to sink rapidly if the batsman and pilot failed to compensate for it. The result was a heavy landing and she suffered twenty-one deck-landing incidents in which Seafires suffered strained or broken undercarriages or wrinkled after fuselages. These could be repaired but not in the time available to Force V off Salerno.[28] A second factor, which received frequent mention in the operational reports, was the poor visibility that accentuated every weakness in homing procedures, circuits and deck landings and the vulnerability of newly qualified pilots.

The policy of flying off a small number of aircraft from every carrier was another problem. It was meant to simplify deck operations in the cramped CVEs but in operation it meant patrols over the beachhead made up with aircraft from several different squadrons. Leaders did not know the pilots flying on their wing and new pilots were unsettled by leaders with whom they were not familiar. Although the squadrons had undergone standardised training before Avalanche, there were inevitable differences and these made the experience of new pilots more harrowing than necessary. Standard operating procedures for squadrons in assault CVEs eventually eased this shortcoming and acted as a focus for the dissemination of hard-won experience. No. 718 NAS, equipped with Seafires, re-formed at RNAS Henstridge, Somerset, in June 1944 specifically to teach pilots amphibious assault techniques using lessons learned in Torch and Avalanche.

Another, cumulative, factor was fatigue among pilots and batsmen as Avalanche progressed, made worse by the lowering of confidence that inevitably followed the high accident rate. The Admiralty deduced from this that a larger number of pilots should be added to the schemes of

Illustrious and *Unicorn* exercise together off Gibraltar prior to Operation Avalanche. Seafires of 894 NAS are parked forward and on outriggers. (*Author's collection*)

complement of squadrons allocated to carry out prolonged or intense operations. Having realised this, however, it took time to implement any change because men also had to be found for new squadrons and carriers. The Admiralty was also forced to recognise that the wartime pilot training 'pipeline' produced men, most of them RNVR, who passed through the system in the shortest time possible. Some of them might have been borderline cases between acceptance or rejection for duty as an operational fighter pilot. In spite of constant refinements to deck landing control and technique, the actual capability of average individuals had, constantly, to be borne in mind.

Radio discipline came in for special comment in the Admiralty's analysis. Inevitably, given the size of the operation and the number of aircraft involved, radio nets were congested but the flag officers of Forces H and Force V found discipline to be generally good. The RAF controller in the USS *Ancon*, on the other hand, wrote adversely in the strongest terms on USAAF procedures. Signals Intelligence, known as 'Y' teams, in the British ships found evidence that the Germans were obtaining useful information from the open use of R/T by Allied aircraft. As in earlier operations, the air operations were complicated by aircraft that blundered into the airspace without showing IFF. These invariably turned out to be Allied aircraft that had forgotten to switch it on.

The most important weakness, however, was the unreasonably small 30nm 'box' within which Force V had to operate. Constant practice improves every pilot's deck landing technique, even in adverse conditions, but with five carriers manoeuvring in close proximity to remain within the allotted sea space a high accident rate would have been likely with any type of aircraft. Force V's 'box' was too small for reasonable operation even if the wind conditions had been good. With no wind and ships having to steam at maximum speed it left no margin for manoeuvre and if a recovery commenced as the carrier neared the edge of the 'box', it had to be completed in some haste. Aircraft that were already short of fuel had no time to wait until the carriers had manoeuvred into a position where they could turn onto the designated flying course again with adequate time and sea room to complete a launch and recovery. Circuits had to be exceptionally tight, overlapped and the poor visibility led to pilots making a late finals turn from a less than ideal position onto carriers that were about to make a drastic alteration of course in order to remain in the operating 'box'. The crash rate rose significantly when there was no wind at all.

Statistics do not tell the whole story, however. The sortie generation rate per serviceable aircraft was an impressive feature of Avalanche that has gone largely unrecognised by historians. In late 1943 two sorties a day by every serviceable aircraft in a carrier was considered exceptional in both the RN and USN. On successive days Force V flew 2.5, 3.6 and then 4.1 sorties per serviceable aircraft. Even the fifty-six sorties flown on the early forenoon of 12 September matched the pre-Avalanche normal for a full day's flying. The effect of this magnificent achievement was that Seafire LIICs flew a total of 516 sorties. The USAAF shared the patrol task with them and had far more A-36As available in Sicily but could only manage 526 sorties, and all of these had only one third of the Seafires' time on task because of the long transit times from their distant bases. Their defensive achievement might appear disappointing with Seafire LIICs involved in only three combats, during which a single Fw 190 was damaged by an 879 NAS aircraft. However, the lack of 'kills' should not detract from the considerable success enjoyed by Seafires in turning back attempted raids, forcing fighter-bombers to jettison their bombs or bomb inaccurately. The object of their patrols was achieved more effectively than would have been the case if they had amassed a string of kills chasing away aircraft that had made successful attacks on the beachhead.

The Avalanche planners had failed to take advantage of the experience gained in Torch and naval aircraft were only tasked for defensive sorties intended to supplement the Allied air forces, although they achieved this to a degree far beyond that which had been originally contemplated. The Seafires of Force V were put in a position of considerable tactical disadvantage, patrolling along fixed defensive lines in an area where radar detection and direction was hampered by the terrain. The LIICs' marginal level speed advantage over bomb-carrying enemy fighters placed the initiative with the latter. If the Seafires had been allocated more wide-ranging offensive patrol areas they might well have caught the fighter-bombers before they began their high-speed approaches. An even more profitable occupation, in view of the strength of enemy resistance, would have been close air support of the ground forces, the role for which the squadrons had actually trained. With their proximity to the forward edge of the battle area and Allied commanders on the ground, the CVEs could have provided support within minutes of a request for assistance, significantly less than the time required to get air support from Sicily. The RN aviators both in the fleet and the Admiralty were fully aware of the missed opportunity and were at pains to ensure that fighters were not tasked in such a limited manner again.

Although its arrival seems perfectly normal, this LIIC on *Hunter* has actually burst its port tyre and will not be able to taxi forward out of the wires quickly. (*Author's collection*)

The two fleet carriers in Force H had flown at a much less intense rate relative to their larger aircraft complements. *Formidable* made no use of her Seafires during the first two days of Avalanche and relied on her Martlets for an average of seventy-two fighter sorties on each day. On 11 September, with a number of Martlets written off or unserviceable for a long period, she launched four Seafire patrols for a total of eight sorties before sending her aircraft to *Unicorn*. *Illustrious* had embarked an unprecedented number of Seafires for her class. Whereas *Victorious* and *Formidable* had operated a maximum of six, four being stowed on outriggers and two parked forward of the island on deck, their sister-ship accepted a permanent deck park of ten LIICs. During flying operations the park could not be allowed to exceed four non-folding aircraft, which had to be continually shuffled up and down the deck, aft for launches and forward for recoveries. During daylight hours *Illustrious* had to keep a pair of Seafires airborne all the time but the ship made things work. No. 894 NAS flew fifty-six sorties during three days off Salerno, the last being delivered to *Unicorn* on 11 September. Of the fifty deck landings on their parent carrier, only two resulted in slight damage, which was repaired within twenty-four hours. The squadron's patrols were uneventful and its pilots had no chance to evaluate in actual combat the new Franks' anti-G suits with which they had been issued for a trial under realistic conditions.

Hugh Popham was one of the pilots who flew wearing a prototype Franks' suit. He said that:

> ...we were the guinea-pigs for a new piece of equipment...a special flying suit, skin-tight, double-skinned and contrived of a remarkably obscene type of pale blue, pimply rubber. Into these rubber combinations we were squeezed and laced like Scarlet O'Hara into her corsets; they were then filled up, like a hot-water bottle, through a nozzle situated well up on one's chest...You may well enquire, as we did when we first saw them, the purpose of these odd garments. It was this. One of the limiting factors in air combat is the fact that the force acting on a pilot when he is pulling out of a dive or doing a very tight turn is a multiplication of the force of gravity which tends to draw blood away from his head with the result that he blacks out. This force is known as G; and the normally healthy pilot blacks out when the force acting on him increases to 2 or 3G.[29] Blacking out itself is momentary and has no other effects; as soon as the turn is relaxed or the pull-out eased, as soon in fact as the G is reduced to the tolerable maximum, one comes to with one's senses unimpaired.

But in dog-fighting where the victory may depend on tightening up the turn as far as possible, and where much of one's time is spent on the grey fringes of blackout, a pilot who is equipped to stand an extra load of G and still remain conscious is obviously at a tremendous advantage. To achieve this, to raise a pilot's G threshold, our pale blue combinations were intended. As the value of G was raised so the water in the suit was forced down and exerted such pressure on one's abdomen that one's blood remained to a great extent where it was and one's threshold was raised to 4 or 5 G. They were given to us to try because there was little likelihood of our being shot down over enemy territory: had the powers-that-be but known it, no secret can ever have been so safe. As a corollary, of course, we had no opportunity of testing them in combat but in dog-fights among ourselves, between one pilot dressed and one undressed, we had no doubts about their efficacy.

Overall, Avalanche was a fruitful testing ground for expanded naval air operations. The principle of operations by a number of squadrons operating a single aircraft type had not proved as successful as had been hoped; not because there was any flaw in the concept of simplified maintenance or logistic support but because the Seafire was not the right type of aircraft at this stage of its development. Even when the principles of assault CVE operations became more firmly established, justifiable prejudice against the Seafire led to its partial replacement by more rugged types such as the later marks of Martlet, renamed Wildcat in January 1944 to align with the USN, and its replacement, the Grumman Hellcat.

Since the planners had only intended Force V to be in action for a maximum of two days, only short-term communications security measures had been set in place. This proved to be a mistake and by D + 2 the Germans were able to jam the fighter direction and homing frequencies, adding to the difficulties of directing and recovering aircraft in the poor visibility. It was also likely that by then the Germans could decode Allied grid references and direct their attacking aircraft clear of the Seafire patrols accordingly. Although these four strenuous days resulted in fewer air combats than expected and fewer enemy aircraft actually destroyed, this was no measure of the results actually achieved by the Fleet Air Arm at Salerno. German broadcasts clearly showed that they regarded the carrier-borne aircraft as a major factor in the Allied assault operations and there can be no doubt that the somewhat feeble efforts made by the Luftwaffe during daylight hours were due to the knowledge that the RN had strong fighter forces available close to the beachhead. The fact that, so far as is known, no serious attempt was made to attack either carrier task force off Salerno by day or night is difficult to explain, except by the assumption that by September 1943 the Luftwaffe lacked the strength, training or resolve to carry out such offensive measures.[30] Avalanche provided the RN with valuable experience that was of great assistance in planning future amphibious operations.

On 6 October 1943 the naval task force to the west of Salerno was stood down and Admiral Cunningham became 1SL following the death in office of Admiral Pound. Admiral Sir John Cunningham became C-in-C Mediterranean ten days later, having been succeeded as C-in-C Levant on 13 October by Admiral Willis. Force H was disbanded on 14 October 1943 after three and a half years of continuous operations based on Gibraltar and by the middle of October all the aircraft carriers that had taken part in Avalanche, with the sole exception of *Battler*, had returned to the UK for refits. *Battler* deployed to the Indian Ocean for duty as a trade protection carrier. For the next eight months there was relatively little Fleet Air Arm activity in the Mediterranean until carriers returned in May 1944 to prepare for Operation Dragoon, the Allied invasion of southern France.

No. 807 NAS' pilots in early 1943. From left to right they are identified on the photograph as Lieutenant (E) R H Webber RN, Sub Lieutenant (A) G Lloyd RNVR, Sub Lieutenant (A) A B C Ford RNVR, Lieutenant Commander A B Fraser-Harris DSC* RN (commanding officer), Lieutenant (A) G C Baldwin DSC RN (senior pilot), Lieutenant de Vaisseau R L Claude FNFL, Sub Lieutenant (A) G R A Darling RNVR, Maitre G Kerlan, Sub Lieutenant (A) G E Pugh RNVR, Sub Lieutenant (A) O R Goodwin RNVR and Maitre F Delery. Note that three pilots are from the Free French Navy serving with the RN. (*Author's collection*)

12

Operation Dragoon

The Anzio landings in February 1944 were supported by Allied aircraft from bases in Italy and so the only aircraft carrier movements in the Mediterranean between September 1943 and June 1944 were by ships on passage to the Eastern Fleet.[1] After Avalanche *Illustrious* returned to the UK for a refit in Birkenhead, which removed the curved, inefficient after round-down and replaced it with an elongated flight deck that allowed more aircraft to be ranged and maintained in a deck park. Her sister-ship *Formidable* was refitted in Belfast before joining the Home Fleet.[2] *Unicorn* returned to Belfast on 20 September to be refitted and completed for her intended role as an aircraft maintenance carrier. *Attacker* returned to Rosyth Dockyard for a more extensive assault carrier conversion, completed in March 1944.[3] *Hunter* arrived at Dundee on 30 September for a refit but her flight deck was damaged as she was taken out of dry dock. Repairs were carried out on the Clyde and she was ready for further service in March 1944. *Stalker* was refitted in Liverpool from 11 October and further assault carrier enhancements were carried out in a Thames shipyard in March 1944 before she returned to service in April 1944. Unlike the other Force V CVEs, *Battler* had disembarked her Seafire squadrons in Gibraltar and replaced them with 834 NAS, a composite unit equipped with Swordfish, Seafires and Martlets. She then sailed through the Suez Canal to join the Eastern Fleet as a trade protection carrier based initially at Bombay.

The Allied plan to invade southern France in 1944
At the 'Quadrant' Conference in Quebec during August 1943, Allied leaders discussed carrying out an assault operation in the Mediterranean to coincide with Operation Neptune, the Allied landings in Normandy, but the idea was only adopted after considerable opposition from Churchill.[4] In December 1943 a preliminary directive was issued by the C-in-C Mediterranean to Vice Admiral H K Hewitt USN, who had been

Emperor with Hellcats of 800 NAS ranged on her flight deck. Note the large deck recognition letter 'E' on the forward part of the flight deck to help pilots identify their own assault carrier within the task group of identical ships when returning from a sortie and short of fuel. The aircraft nearest the island still has 'invasion stripes' from earlier operations in 1944 on its wings and fuselage. (*Author's collection*)

selected as the naval commander of the operation. He had previously commanded the naval task forces in Operations Husky and Avalanche. The new operation was originally designated Operation Anvil but when it was realised that this name might reveal its strategic purpose if the enemy learnt of it, the name was changed to Dragoon.

Preparatory plans for Dragoon proceeded smoothly at a working level but there was continued friction at the highest level. Churchill and the British Chiefs of Staff were firmly of the opinion that diverting forces to southern France from the campaign in Italy would unacceptably weaken the latter. The Americans insisted that it must go ahead, however, and Churchill eventually had little choice but to agree. As planning progressed the Americans realised that there were insufficient landing craft to carry out Dragoon and Neptune, the much larger amphibious assault landings in Normandy. The date 15 August 1944 was selected as D-Day for Dragoon.

Having studied Torch, Husky and Avalanche, the Admiralty made significant changes in the way aircraft carriers were to be worked up prior to operations and then used in action. It had been accepted in April 1943 that with an increasing number of aircraft carriers in a variety of sizes and roles joining the fleet, a Flag Officer with direct responsibility for supervising their work up programmes was required. Admiral Sir Lumley Lyster was, therefore, appointed as Flag Officer Carrier Training, FOCT, with his headquarters initially at Greenock and later at later at Largs on the Ayr coast. In October 1943 Rear Admiral A W La T Bisset hoisted his flag as Rear Admiral Escort Carriers, RAEC, in *Royalist*, the light cruiser that had been specially fitted out as an assault carrier task force command ship. Bisset was closely involved in assembling and then training the assault carrier force that was to be used in Dragoon and, unlike in the earlier operations, he had sufficient time to work up his force and absorb the lessons of past experience.

By mid-February 1944, three of the CVEs from Avalanche, *Hunter*, *Attacker* and *Stalker*, were beginning to work up and in April four more joined them, *Emperor*, *Searcher*, *Pursuer* and *Khedive*. This force, including the command ship *Royalist*, was scheduled for eventual service led by RAEC in the Eastern Fleet but was to take part in Dragoon first. *Emperor*, *Searcher*, *Pursuer* and *Royalist* gained combat experience in Operation Tungsten during April 1944, the Home Fleet's first air attack on the German battleship *Tirpitz* at Kåfjord. *Khedive* only completed her modification to assault carrier standard in May 1944 and her ship's company lacked any combat experience but the CVEs began to operate as a task force and carried out a period of intensive assault training in co-operation with troops in Northern Ireland.

In May 1944 *Hunter*, *Attacker* and *Stalker* sailed with convoy KMS 51, arriving in Gibraltar on 24 May. Once there, a proportion of their squadrons' aircraft were replaced with new Seafire LIIIs. *Stalker* proceeded

Arming 881 NAS' Wildcats with 250lb bombs on *Pursuer*'s flight deck. (*Author's collection*)

A Seafire III of 899 NAS taking off from *Khedive* with a 500lb bomb on its centreline pylon for a dive-bombing attack on German positions in the south of France. (*Author's collection*)

to the eastern Mediterranean, where she carried out work up exercises, while *Hunter* and *Attacker* provided fighter escort for convoys between Gibraltar and Sicily with stops at Oran, Algiers and Naples where troops were gathered for Dragoon. Anti-submarine patrols were flown by three Swordfish from Gibraltar, which were temporarily embarked in *Hunter*.

In June the Seafire squadrons embarked in each of these three CVEs were ordered to disembark eight aircraft each for operations alongside 285, 244 and 7 (South African) Wings of the RAF's Desert Air Force operating on the Italian front at Orviero, flying ground support missions for the 8th Army. These twenty-four aircraft were designated as D Naval Fighter Wing and their pilots were able to gain experience of the latest ground attack techniques and tactics. All their Seafire LIIICs were fitted to carry a drop tank or 500lb bomb on a centreline hardpoint, giving a significant improvement to their operational flexibility. Several others, designated LRIICs and fitted with cameras, were included in the squadrons to fly armed reconnaissance, dive-bombing, fighter escort, Tac-R, artillery spotting and photographic reconnaissance missions, and they did so with great success. D Wing moved forward with the 8th Army and, together with the Spitfire Wings, occupied airstrips at Perugia and Castiglione. It flew a total of 443 sorties and lost only one aircraft to enemy anti-aircraft fire; a second received damage that led to a forced landing near the front line and a third was destroyed on the ground by enemy artillery fire. The wing had one large but largely inconclusive air combat with about thirty Bf 109 and Fw 190 fighters. None of the naval pilots was lost or injured and all gained invaluable experience. On 16 July 1944 D Wing was withdrawn to North Africa for re-embarkation and assault training embarked in their respective CVEs.

The other four RN CVEs arrived in Malta on 25 July. *Khedive* had just completed her work up but *Emperor, Searcher* and *Pursuer* had operated in the Norwegian littoral with the Home Fleet and, most recently, giving fighter protection to anti-submarine escort groups providing seaward protection for the Allied landings in Normandy on 6 June. The Admiralty decided not to concentrate on a single embarked fighter type for Dragoon and the latter three CVEs were equipped with Hellcats and Wildcats.[5] The USN contribution to the first integrated Allied CVE task force comprised the CVEs *Kasaan Bay* and *Tulagi*, both of which operated Hellcats, under Rear Admiral C T Durgin USN, who flew his flag in *Tulagi*. The CVEs formed a task force that was divided into two task groups:

Operation Dragoon 15 to 20 August 1944

Task Force 88

| *Royalist* | Flag Rear Admiral Sir Thomas Troubridge DSO |
| | Captain J G Hewitt DSO RN |

Task Group 88.1   (Rear Admiral Troubridge)

Attacker	Captain H B Farncomb RAN	
879 NAS	24 Seafire LIII and LRIIC	Lieutenant Commander (A) D G Carlisle RNVR
Emperor	Captain T J N Hilken RN	
800 NAS	23 F6F Hellcat 1 Walrus COD	Lieutenant Commander S J Hall RN
Khedive	Captain H J Hayman RN	
899 NAS	26 Seafire LIII	Lieutenant Commander (A) R Howarth RNVR
Searcher	Captain G O C Davies RN	
882 NAS	24 Wildcat V/VI	Lieutenant Commander (A) G R Henderson RNVR
Pursuer	Captain H R Graham RN	
881 NAS	24 Wildcat V/VI	Lieutenant Commander (A) L A Hordern RNVR

The squadrons embarked in TG 88.1 were designated Number 7 Naval Fighter Wing led by Lieutenant Commander M F Fell RN. The CVEs were escorted by the anti-aircraft cruiser *Delhi* and by Captain (D) 24th

Destroyer Flotilla in the destroyer *Troubridge*[6] with five other British and one Greek destroyer.

Task Group 88.2		(Rear Admiral Durgin)
Tulagi	Captain J C Cronin USN – flag Rear Admiral Durgin	
VOF-1	24 F6F Hellcat	Lieutenant Commander W F Pringle USN
Kasaan Bay	Captain B E Grow USN	
VF-74	24 F6F Hellcat	Lieutenant Commander H B Bass USN (Lieutenant H H Basore USN after loss of Lt Cdr Bass)
Hunter	Captain H H McWilliam RN	
807 NAS	24 Seafire LIII and LIIC	Lieutenant (A) G Reece RNZNVR
Stalker	Captain H S Murray-Smith RN	
809 NAS	23 Seafire LIII and LIIC	Lieutenant Commander (A) Eadon RNVR

The RN squadrons embarked in TG 88.2 were designated as Number 4 Naval Fighter Wing led by Lieutenant Commander G C Baldwin DSC RN. The two USN CVEs were of a later design than the US-built British CVEs of the '…*er*' and *Ruler* classes and were slightly faster, capable of 20 rather than 18 knots. The CVEs were escorted by the anti-aircraft cruisers *Caledon* and *Colombo* together with six USN destroyers.

Task force 88 had a total of 216 fighters, all of which were capable of carrying bombs as well as their front guns. *Searcher*, *Pursuer* and *Tulagi* were to provide aircraft to spot the fall of shot during bombardments of inland targets. The two British carriers each had twelve trained pilots and in the USN ship all pilots were suitably trained. *Attacker*, *Khedive* and *Hunter* were designated as standby spotting carriers with eight trained pilots each. Twenty-five Seafires were held in reserve as potential replacements at a temporary RN air facility at Casabianda in Corsica and seven USN Hellcat night-fighters of VF(N)-74 operated from there to give the CVEs night fighter cover. Five USN Avengers operated from Solenzara in Corsica to provide night anti-submarine and carrier-on-board delivery, COD, capabilities.

General Maitland Wilson replaced Eisenhower as Supreme Commander Allied Expeditionary Forces Mediterranean and he ordered Dragoon to begin 0800 on 15 August 1944. The assault was to commence in daylight, putting into practice the lessons learnt at Salerno and Anzio that heavy,

Hunter photographed by one of her 807 NAS Seafires. Note the faded camouflage paint on the flight deck and the deck recognition letter 'H' at the centre of the deck. Neither the size nor the positioning of the letters were standardised at this time. (*Author's collection*)

preliminary air and sea bombardments of the landing zones were vital to the success of initial landings. Despite the time available for planning and work up activities, RAEC and his staff had been committed to operations off Norway and in the Western Approaches. This meant that they had not taken part in the detailed Dragoon air operations planning in Naples and the CVE operating methods that were produced followed USN methods, which differed significantly from those with which the British CVEs had been worked up. The Air Commander designate, Brigadier General G P Saville USAAF, was to issue directions to the two task group commanders, who were then expected to produce detailed flying programmes for the operation of their aircraft. The task forces were given USN-style numbered designations, unlike the earlier lettered designation of British forces up to and including Force V at Salerno. The new method, which used numbered task forces, groups and elements, was used from then on by the RN in the BPF and post-war. The Army and air support communications nets were also configured using USN methods. Another complication occurred on 28 July, shortly after the CVEs had arrived in Malta, when RAEC was taken ill. He was relieved at short notice by Rear Admiral Sir Thomas Troubridge, who had commanded both *Furious* and *Indomitable*. It was a bitter blow for Bisset but Troubridge paid a warm tribute to his achievements in his action reports.

Although the change to USN methods seemed to present problems at first, Troubridge took the sensible decision to overcome any difficulties as they emerged rather than try to seek amendments to a plan that was basically sound, and this pragmatic approach worked well. *Hunter*,

Attacker and *Stalker* joined RAEC's force at Malta on 2 August, followed by the USN carriers. Task Force 88 then carried out extensive exercises prior to sailing on 12 August for the assault area off the French Riviera.

The setting for Operation Dragoon

The eight months available to planners to prepare for Dragoon enabled the experience gained in Torch, Husky and Avalanche to be incorporated. Admiral Hewitt had commanded naval task forces in all three previous operations and had 880 ships under his command for this one. Sardinia and Corsica had been evacuated by the Germans in 1943 and American engineers improved airfields and landing strips on both islands. Overwhelming Allied shore-based air strength had been built up quickly and by mid-August the Allied air forces had 4,000 aircraft available in the region, of which 1,800 were heavy bombers and 1,700 fighters and fighter-bombers, the latter including the naval aircraft in Task Force 88. The Allied navies were virtually unchallenged at sea. Against this, the Luftwaffe only had about fourteen Do 217 bombers able to carry radio-controlled FX 1400 glide bombs, sixty-five Ju 88 torpedo bombers and fifty fighters within striking distance of the assault beaches, numbers significantly less than those predicted by Allied intelligence organisations.

The U-boat threat in the Mediterranean had been practically eliminated, although two boats were known to be operational at Toulon. This satisfactory state of affairs had been made possible by 'swamp' tactics in which close co-operation between Allied aircraft and surface forces had been achieved, keeping U-boats dived with decreasing battery power until they were forced to surface for air and be destroyed.[7] Dragoon started, therefore, under unusually favourable conditions with overwhelming Allied superiority in the air and on the sea, time to effect any necessary changes to a well thought-out plan and with a naval commander who had considerable previous experience of such operations.[8]

Landings were carried out by three US Army divisions over beaches east of Toulon preceded by an airborne divisional assault and French commando raids. The first troops waded ashore at 0800 on 15 August over beaches near Agay and St Raphaël designated Camel Sector; St Maxime designated Delta Sector and Pampelonne and Cavalaire designated Alpha Sector. They were preceded from dawn onwards by heavy air and ship bombardments and the airborne and glider-borne assault included the 2nd Independent Parachute Brigade, the only British troops in the operation.

The CVE task force in action

Each of the two CVE task groups worked independently of the other in an operational area considerably larger than the one allocated for Avalanche. The most northerly point of each area was 30nm south of the coast and at the conclusion of flying every day the whole task force retired to seaward. The two groups were, however, required to keep within visual signalling distance of each other if possible for the transmission of low-grade tactical signals. The CVE's planned tasks were to:

1) provide spotting aircraft for gunfire support ships.
2) provide the maximum persistent fighter protection over the beaches.
3) give persistent close support, bombing and Tac-R support to the assault forces.
4) provide CAP fighters over TF 88 itself.

To meet these tasks a pre-arranged flying programme was issued for the first day's operations and since demands for aircraft were made in advance there was time for detailed pilot briefings. In the first phase of Dragoon detailed missions were allotted to the task groups by the Air Commander, who was embarked in Hewitt's flagship *Catoctin* at first but he moved ashore with his staff as soon as it became practical. As opposition from the German Army weakened the situation became more fluid and he was only able to issue general directions. These were exactly the sort of operations in which carrier air groups excelled and more control was placed on the task group commanders than the original plan had envisaged. Close air

Khedive with deck recognition letters painted on both lifts. (*Author's collection*)

support was soon dispensed with as ground forces moved rapidly forward. The task groups were then allocated areas in the enemy's rear where they could attack targets of opportunity as the task group commanders saw fit. To obtain information about the enemy, task group commanders flew off their own Tac-R missions and fighter-bomber sorties began to predominate. Targets included bridges, aircraft on the ground, rail and motor transport, marshalling yards, railway infrastructure and targets of opportunity located by pilots as they searched large areas at low level. As carrier aircraft attacked targets further and further inland, sometimes up to 120nm from the beaches, the Hellcats of 800 NAS excelled but the Seafires and Wildcats also performed well to the limits of their practical radii of action. The targets they were now attacking were well beyond the reach of Allied fighters based in Corsica that the USAAF had intended to carry out these missions. The ability of carriers to move their aircraft into positions where they dominated enemy movement was seen as a positive benefit by Allied planning staffs who realised, at last, that carrier fighters were not a second-best substitute but the weapons system of choice.

Fighter direction officers in the carrier groups notified the air control ship in the assault area, either HMS *Ulster Queen* or the USS *Catoctin*, of the type of aircraft and the targets for which their pilots had been briefed. The former then took over if the aircraft were on a patrol mission and the latter if the mission was an offensive one. On being called by the leader's aircraft, one of the two ships either confirmed the briefed target or assigned a new one. While in the forward area the mission remained under the control of this ship and on its conclusion it was turned over again to the carrier group's fighter direction officers. Later in Dragoon, after the air commander moved ashore, *Royalist* assumed control of all offensive missions. Within days of the initial landings enemy air activity withered to the point where CAP over the beaches or the task force itself was no longer required.

The first aircraft were flown off at 0555 on D-Day to carry out their pre-planned bombing or strafing missions before setting up CAP stations over the beaches and the task force.[9] The wind remained light all day but even the Seafire squadrons had no problems with deck landing. Problems encountered in Avalanche had been overcome by more thorough training and an operating area with sufficient sea room and circuit space for CVEs to recover their aircraft without having to make constant turns. Conditions ashore were less favourable with low cloud making dive-bombing attacks difficult. Altogether TG 88.1 flew 170 sorties on D-Day, of which thirty-two were bombardment spotting, seventy-six were fighter-bomber, six were reconnaissance, thirty-two were beach CAP and twenty-four force

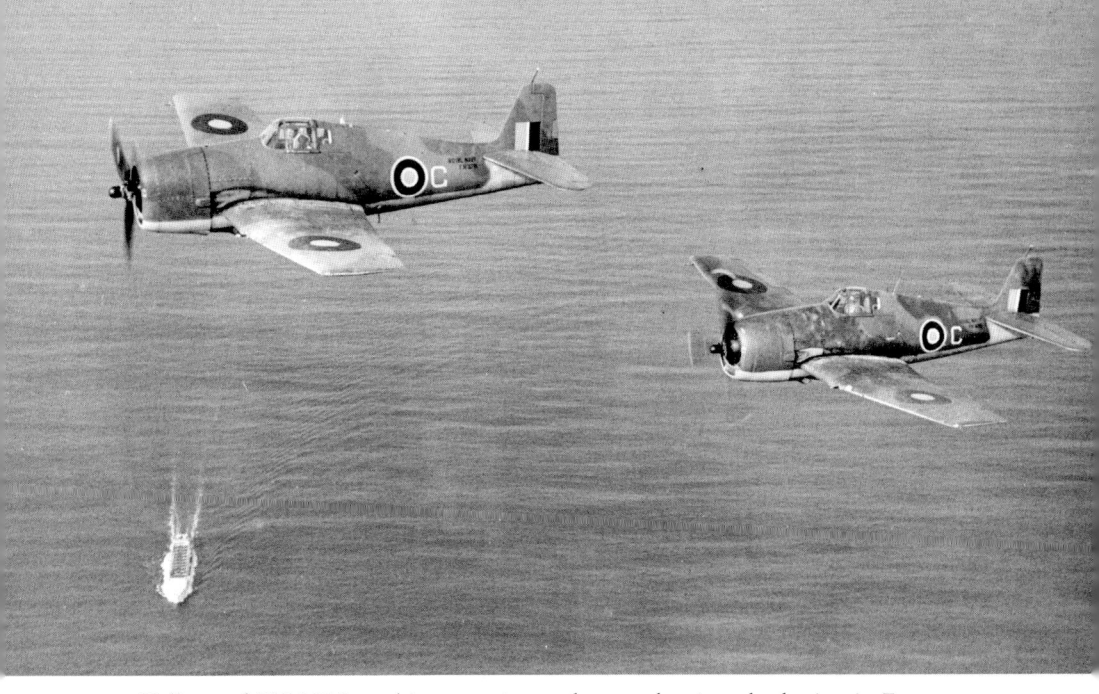

Hellcats of 800 NAS working up prior to the squadron's embarkation in *Emperor* in 1944. The ship below them is a MAC Ship acting as an aircraft ferry with its flight deck loaded with American aircraft bound for the UK. (*Author's collection*)

CAP. No total figures for TG 88.2 appear to have been retained. The last aircraft landed on at 2035 and the task force retired to the south.

During the day each task group had kept in a compact formation near a previously decided datum point and turned into wind together for flying off or landing-on except when only one or two aircraft were involved. On these occasions the carrier left the formation escorted by a single destroyer and manoeuvred as necessary. Admiral Durgin found that the USN carriers' superior speed made it difficult to keep his task group close at high speeds but ways were found to work round this. There was no enemy attack on the CVEs and no enemy fighters were encountered. In general enemy anti-aircraft fire was not heavy. Two of *Pursuer*'s Wildcats had to ditch when they ran out of fuel after failing to locate the force. Both pilots were rescued by a Catalina flying boat at 1250 and it flew them to Ajaccio, where they managed to get hold of transport that took them to Casabianda airfield.[10] A day later they flew two spare aircraft to their ship and landed on at 1700.[11]

The first aircraft was flown off at 0610 on D + 1, with take-offs and recoveries following regularly according to the plan and by sunset TG 88.1 had flown 136 sorties. There were some enemy air attacks on the beaches by fighters with anti-personnel bombs. Radio-controlled bombs were employed in attacks on shipping lying off the beaches but little damage was done by them. The breakdown of missions on D + 1 was fourteen spotting sorties, ten Tac-R, fifty-six fighter-bombing, thirty beach CAP and twenty-six task force CAP. By the end of D + 2 on 17 August, when the assault phase was deemed to be over, 86,575 men, 12,520 vehicles and 46,140 tons of stores had been landed over the beaches with minimal interference from the enemy. On D + 2 aircraft from TG 88.1 flew ninety-two missions, none on spotting, ten Tac-R, thirty-four fighter-bombing, thirty beach CAP and eighteen task force CAP. Less air defence effort was required over the beaches and this function was taken over by shore-based fighters as soon as airstrips were completed by assault engineers on 19 August. Calls for spotting aircraft diminished for a while but increased when the CVEs moved further to the west. On 17 August aircraft from *Emperor* and *Khedive* took part in an attack on an enemy-held fort at Port Cros, which was partially masked by terrain and had held out for three days. They dropped 500lb bombs and the fort surrendered.

The datum point for carrier operations changed every day and on 18 August the CVEs' operating area moved west and closer inshore. On D + 3, aircraft of TG 88.1 flew only eighty-four missions. Eight were spotting, six Tac-R, thirty-six fighter-bombing, sixteen beach CAP and eighteen task force CAP. Missions were flown up the Rhône valley looking for targets and because of the Seafire's short radius of action it was necessary for the carriers to get as close to the coast as possible. Given the Luftwaffe's lack of aggression, the only real danger came from mines, which forced the CVEs to remain to seaward of the 100 fathom line. On 19 August two Hellcats from *Emperor* were over the Rhône estuary returning from an attack on a railway yard when they saw two German E-boats and attacked them with front guns. One was destroyed and the other damaged. On that day TG 88.1 flew 117 missions, eleven spotting, eight Tac-R, sixty fighter-bombing, eight beach CAP and thirty task force CAP. On one of the fighter-bomber sorties a Wildcat of 881 NAS in *Pursuer* flown by Sub Lieutenant (A) R R Banks RNVR was shot down between Orange and Avignon and his report gives a vivid impression of one Fleet Air Arm pilot's participation in Dragoon:

> At 1009 on 19 August, D + 4, White Flight took off to carry out an armed reconnaissance on the roads Arles-Tarascon-Cavaillon-Carpentras, with orders to strafe or bomb any suitable targets. I was flying as White 2. We saw no movement on roads until reaching a large bridge across the river [Rhône] at Orange, where I saw a large tank and small vehicles crossing the bridge. Calling up White Leader to follow me, I dived on the bridge and strafed the tank. I

saw my bullets hitting and the tank burst into flames and crashed off the road.

White Leader then called up for us to strafe the Orange Caritat airfield which was in sight. I followed White Leader and, seeing no aircraft, strafed the control tower. I felt my aircraft being hit by flak [anti-aircraft fire] and the engine began to smoke and failed to respond to the throttle. I was just over the River Rhone with only about 20ft of altitude so I flew down-river about 10ft above the water calling up White leader to say that I was going to ditch. My windscreen was covered with oil and I was losing speed. I flew as far as possible to clear the area and then lowered my flaps and made a pancake landing in the middle of the river, in order to get rid of the aircraft. My nose hit my gunsight, but I was not otherwise injured, and I was able to get clear before the aircraft sank. I was wearing a Franks Flying Suit, but with Mae West inflated, I had no difficulty at all in floating. I let my parachute float down-stream, knowing that it would sink quickly.

The current was very strong and it took me over 10 minutes to reach the east bank. I left the water near some bushes in which I hid whilst I undressed and removed my Franks Flying Suit. I hid the

Wildcat JV406 of 881 NAS photographed seconds after landing on *Pursuer*. It is forward of the lowered barrier in Fly 1 and the marshaller at the port forward edge of the flight deck is giving its pilot the 'brakes on' signal. The pilot is about to select the wing-fold control and handlers have taken hold of the tips to steady them as they move aft into their stowed position alongside the fuselage. Note the large deck recognition letter 'P' under the aircraft and the fact that the wooden flight deck is unpainted. (*Author's collection*)

latter, together with my flying clothing, beneath the root of a tree, after removing my aids from the Mae West, and piled stones over the cavity to conceal it.

I climbed the steep bank, crossed a footpath and hid in the bushes surrounding a field. Some people approached but I lay low and they did not see me. I noticed a farm house across the field, which I approached, hiding in the bushes to observe the situation for some time. Seeing only peasants, I entered the yard, told them I was English and asked for help. They were very good and gave me food and clothing...they took me to an English lady who lived nearby. It was she whom I had seen at the river, apparently where she had been searching for me. (A fisherman had told her that he had seen a plane land in the river.) She had taken a bag containing a first-aid kit, brandy etc. She was very pleased to see me safe and dressed my nose, which by this time was very swollen.

Her French husband fetched a friend who knew the 'Maquis' (French Resistance Movement). This man brought me a complete set of peasant clothes with a large hat to hide my 'English face' and swollen nose. I attempted to recover my flying gear to destroy it but was unable to find the place, so decided that it was well enough hidden. I was told that I had actually landed on an island. There was one bridge across to the east bank, upon which there were many German soldiers. I borrowed my host's bicycle, tied a pitch-fork to the cross-bar and with the Frenchman leading by about 50 metres, we cycled across the bridge, past the soldiers who paid no attention to us. I spent the night at his home nearby, right beside a German barracks.

Next morning, early, we set out by side roads for the hills to the north-east. After cycling about 25 miles, hiding from occasional motor-cycle patrols, we were finally stopped by young men with Sten Guns at a barrier across the road – the Maquis. I identified myself with the epaulettes which I had saved from my uniform and my identity disc. Taking leave of my guide, I was taken by lorry to a Maquis village where I was received with enthusiasm and much food and wine...At noon on the third day of my stay, about 60 Germans attacked the village with tanks and medium guns and the Maquis withdrew into the hills. I went with them. Before very long I met an American advance reconnaissance patrol of 2 jeeps and 3 armoured cars. The officer in charge offered to take me with them and said he could get me further east. I was given a suit of overalls and a rifle and rode in the leading jeep with the officer. After going

A Seafire LIIC of 807 NAS running up prior to take-off. (*Author's collection*)

back to reconnoitre we headed east. I was able to act as interpreter during the journey as none of the Americans spoke French... Next morning I found some US soldiers in the town who took me to their camp for breakfast and then I was taken south to 45th Divisional HQ. From there I got a lift to 6 Corps HQ; no-one could authorise special transport so I found a Major who was travelling south that night to 7th Army HQ at (I think) St Maximin. We drove by night in a jeep and I saw literally hundreds of burnt-out transports (German) on the roadside.

By this time I had put up my epaulettes on my peasant shirt which saved some misunderstanding. I got to the airstrip at Ramatuelle, which became my headquarters from then on. I found a USN Hellcat there which was damaged and tried to contact 'Greyhound' aircraft [collective R/T callsign for aircraft from Pursuer] on the radio without result. I then discovered a Commander Lewin RN with the 12th tactical Air Command near St Tropez who got instructions for me to join my ship at Maddalena as soon as possible. I returned to Ramatuelle and after a hectic day, during which I acted as impromptu airfield control officer, and interpreter for, amongst others, a French General, I got a ride in a French Catalina to Ajaccio. There I persuaded a Fleet Air Arm pilot to fly me to Alghero, Sardinia, in a Swordfish. At Alghero I found the BNO, Lieutenant Frost RNVR, who was most helpful and organised a Walrus aircraft to fly me to Maddalena next morning. It landed me in the harbour near the ship and I was taken on board.[12]

On 20 August TG 88.1 took a break from combat operations to refuel and rest at Maddalena, returning at dawn on 21 August when the group's aircraft flew 114 sorties. Of these six were spotting missions, sixteen Tac-R, seventy-six fighter-bomber, none on beach CAP and only sixteen task force CAP.

Another Fleet Air Arm pilot had an unusual adventure, which began on 21 August. Sub Lieutenant (A) A I B Shaw RNVR flew off *Attacker* in a Seafire of 879 NAS for a ground strafing mission in the Nimes area. Whilst he was diving on an enemy gun emplacement for a third strafing run[13] his engine was hit by anti-aircraft fire and he was forced to bail out. After landing safely he was captured by a German search party but after three days in captivity he escaped by jumping out of a lorry on a dark night with the vehicle moving at speed. He took shelter in a field but awoke the next morning to find that it had been taken over by a German mobile anti-aircraft battery with soldiers all around him. He was returned to his original captors with little enthusiasm on either side.

Shaw found himself moving north as part of the German retreat under the close supervision of two guards. Shrewdly he changed his tactics and began a campaign of persuasion to convince his guards that they would be better off if they surrendered to him. He worked first on a corporal, the older of the two, and convinced him that an Allied prisoner of war camp would be more amenable than a long retreat into Germany under constant air attack. His success was remarkable because the conversation was conducted entirely in German, a language he had only studied in a single year's unenthusiastic tuition at school. He and his two prisoners headed for the Allied lines, clear of German forces and within a week of being shot down he had, by his own initiative and determination, together with not a little luck, regained his freedom to fight again and also delivered two prisoners into Allied hands. He eventually rejoined *Attacker* in Alexandria and was awarded the MBE for his courageous exploit.[14]

On 22 August, TG 88.1 flew 124 missions, of which twenty-two were spotting, eighteen Tac-R, eighty-four fighter-bombing and none on either beach CAP or task force CAP. The following day was the last on which TG 88.1 operated as part of Dragoon and it flew 146 missions, their second highest daily total. Of these, twenty-six were spotting, ten Tac-R, 110 fighter-bombing and again none on either beach CAP or task force CAP. TG 88.1 aircraft had no combats with enemy fighters but did shoot down three Luftwaffe Ju 52 transport aircraft. The group had flown a total of 983 combat sorties with a further forty-seven flown on non-combat missions. Ten aircraft were lost and five of its pilots were killed in action. These were: Sub Lieutenant (A) J G Barrett RNVR on 16 August

Pursuer followed by *Attacker* and *Royalist* after Dragoon. (*Author's collection*)

and Sub Lieutenant (A) D A Cary RCNVR on 18 August, both of 899 NAS from *Khedive*; Sub Lieutenant (A) A Sharpe RNZNVR of 882 NAS from *Searcher* on 19 August; Lieutenant (E) R M Rogers RN on 22 August and Petty Officer W G MacLean on 23 August, both of 800 NAS from *Emperor*. Six other aircraft had to carry out forced landings after being damaged by anti-aircraft fire and their pilots eventually managed to get back to their ships. Twenty-seven aircraft were lost or damaged in non-combat accidents, contributing to a loss rate for all the RN CVEs involved in the operation of nearly 25 per cent.

Records of the two USN CVEs were not passed to the RN and those for the two RN ships in TG 88.2 only list totals, not the number and type of sorties flown on individual days.[15] From the available details it can be seen that TG 88.2 remained in action longer than TG 88.1 and spent two days refuelling in Maddalena on 22 and 23 August. The group finally withdrew from the operation on 27 August. During this period aircraft from the two RN CVEs flew a total of 643 combat sorties, of which 121 were spotting, forty-four were Tac-R, 142 were fighter bombing, sixty-two ground strafing, sixty-eight beach CAP and 206 task force CAP. Taken with TG 88.1's statistics, the task force flew a total of 1,626 combat sorties. The two RN CVEs in TG 88.2 lost seven aircraft and four pilots were killed in action. These were Lieutenant (A) L G Lloyd RNVR on 17 August and Lieutenant E V Speakman RN on 20 August, both of 807 NAS from *Hunter*; Lieutenant (A) C E H Jefferson RNVR and Sub Lieutenant (A) R I MacNamee RNVR, both of 809 NAS from *Stalker*. Eight other aircraft were lost or severely damaged in non-combat accidents. Aircraft from TG 88.2 shot down four enemy bombers on 19 August.

Analysis of Dragoon revealed that there was still scope for improved tactics and better training.[16] Surprisingly, the USN squadrons had no training in fighter-bomber or ground strafing tactics and were unprepared for the unexpectedly high demand for this type of offensive action. They had to learn as they went into action. Even more surprisingly, given the intensive practice that had gone into working up the RN fighter squadrons, a number of RN pilots also lacked awareness of how best to carry out ground strafing attacks. Troubridge even wrote that the low casualty numbers 'were a reflection on the inadequacy of the enemy and not on the skill of our pilots', and he stressed that all pilots must be trained in all forms of assault fighter operations. He found it significant, however, that the RN pilots who had flown with D Wing in Italy prior to Dragoon had derived 'very great benefit from their experience' and were not found wanting. Notwithstanding this criticism, the Air Commander wrote that he was 'agreeably surprised', not only at the unexpectedly [to him] powerful and efficient air support force placed at his disposal, but also by its being capable of 'answering any call at the shortest notice'. Both he and Troubridge remarked on the amount of destruction inflicted on the enemy's communications by naval aircraft as

Wildcats of 882 NAS being ranged on *Searcher*. Interestingly the aircraft on the forward lift is being brought up nose aft and will need to be turned around on deck. Aircraft are usually stowed in the hangar nose forward. (*Author's collection*)

being most impressive and 'proving a not unimportant factor in the rapid advance of the 7th Army from the beachhead'.

Other points noted by RAEC in his report included the conclusion that the Hellcat was markedly superior to the Seafire in every respect. Designed from the outset for carrier operations, it was more rugged, more versatile and had a considerably greater radius of action, roughly 500nm depending on time spent at high power in combat. Even with a 90-gallon drop tank the Seafire's radius was little more than 200nm. Admiral Hewitt commented to RAEC that the Seafire's short endurance meant that the task groups had to turn into wind to operate their aircraft much more frequently than would have been the case in the USN. American Hellcats had also been fitted to carry rocket projectiles, which proved to be the most effective ground attack weapon, and RN fighters were subsequently modified to allow the carriage of four or more 3in rockets on under-wing pylons. Troubridge also commented that, unlike the Seafire operations off Salerno, the light wind that prevailed during the early stages of Dragoon had not presented a problem. In fact, the number of deck landing incidents actually increased later in the operation when the wind rose because pilot fatigue had begun to be a factor. He stated emphatically that better training had overcome the problem.

Seafire NN344, K-O, of 899 NAS catching the last 'trickle' wire on *Khedive*. The rating by the port deck edge has raised his flag to indicate that the aircraft has taken a wire, a signal to the barrier operator to lower the barrier but it obviously came just too late and the aircraft's undercarriage has engaged the barrier as it dropped, albeit at low speed. (*Author's collection*)

It had been found that the largest number of CVEs that could be handled conveniently together in assault operations was four. The experience of fighter direction officers confirmed this and the temporary reduction of TG 88.1 from five carriers to four on one day had noticeably reduced the strain on operations. The largest number of fighter-bomber sorties flown by TG 88.1 was on its last day of operations but the results were disappointing as many targets of opportunity were found to be wrecks left burned out by earlier attacks. RAEC felt that the obvious solution to the lack of skill demonstrated by some pilots was to work up squadrons that specialised only in assault operations but this would inevitably lead to a lack of flexibility in fighter operations. As a compromise he suggested that all fighter pilots should be trained in air combat, dive-bombing and ground strafing; all pilots should be given basic instruction in bombardment spotting and Tac-R techniques and one third of the pilots in each squadron should be fully trained in spotting and Tac-R.

NAD took the view after studying RAEC's report that a commitment to train all fighter pilots in all forms of Army support could be made but the expanded training programme and the extra infrastructure it would require would inevitably take time to create. The Admiralty also took note of environmental issues. None of the CVEs had been fitted with air conditioning and *Emperor*'s aircraft direction room was recorded as averaging 34° Celsius throughout Dragoon, which added to the fatigue

Seafire NF421, K-S, of 899 NAS minutes after a barrier engagement in *Khedive*. Handlers in fire suits have cut down the incipient fire around the engine with portable extinguishers while others move in to clear the wreck from the landing area. (*Author's collection*)

suffered by personnel manning it for extended periods. It was also accepted that officers who had no deputy to relieve them had worked long hours to implement the flying programme and were showing distinct signs of fatigue by the end of the CVE's involvement. Commanders (Air), flight deck officers and their aircraft handlers, batsmen, fighter direction officers, radar plotters and communications personnel had only managed to sleep for about three-and-a-half hours in every twenty-four and the strain of this level of commitment could not be continued indefinitely.

Once Dragoon was fully analysed, the Admiralty recommended that in future assault operations, the maximum continuous flying period for each carrier ought to be three days, after which it should have a brief rest to refuel and refresh key personnel. The rest period should, ideally, be twenty-four hours in harbour or, if this was not possible, clear of the operating area. TG 88.1's break in Maddalena had only amounted to twelve hours once passage time was taken into account. After the initial assault phase, individual pilots should be limited to three hours flying per day and in the advance planning of future assault operations the potential effort should be assessed using this rule. In prolonged operations one task group should be withdrawn as soon as possible after D-Day in order to set up a cycle of three days on station and two days' rest for each group in turn. To maintain the necessary number of sorties, squadrons embarked in assault carriers should include a 50 per cent reserve of trained pilots so that losses could be replaced seamlessly.

Khedive's Seafire IIIs ranged on her flight deck in Grand Harbour, Malta, after Dragoon but before operations in the Aegean. (*Author's collection*)

The British assault carriers following *Khedive* in line astern after Dragoon. (*Author's collection*)

The Admiralty was still not certain about the desirability of having one or more fighter types embarked within a task force, however. Total reliance on the Seafire had been commented upon adversely after Avalanche but the logistic and maintenance support needed to sustain the three different types in Dragoon had shown the problems inherent with the alternative. Realistically, however, given the number of different fighter types that were in service during late 1944 and the expanded calls upon them for fleet carrier operations in the Pacific as well as the Home and East Indies Fleets, it was actually most unlikely that a homogenous force could have been created for assault carrier operations in 1944/45. The adverse comments on the standard of ground strafing were mentioned above but there was some satisfaction that gunnery officers had commented favourably on the high standard of bombardment spotting displayed by fighter pilots. On the other hand, a number of pilots had found difficulty in using the CVE's homing beacons to recover to their ships after long-ranging fighter-bomber sorties. The congested radio nets with large numbers of aircraft airborne had not helped and the Admiralty emphasised the need for fighter pilots to keep their own dead-reckoning navigational plots to help them return to their ships with sufficient fuel for recovery. More training was clearly required in this area.

The use of *Royalist* as RAEC's flagship had not been a success. The Admiralty believed that one of the new light fleet carriers would be ideal as it would have more space for RAEC's staff including a staff bridge and offices, a better aircraft direction room and a flight deck from which its own aircraft could operate as well as acting as a spare deck for the assault CVEs. It would also allow RAEC and his staff to be flown to his other carriers or shore HQ when occasion demanded but none of the twenty-four light fleet carriers on order was complete and the first four were earmarked for the BPF.[17]

Operation Dragoon in summary

The carrier task force had been faced by no significant threat from over, on or under the sea. There were no air combats to disrupt flying programmes and no torpedo or bomber attacks on the fleet. However, Dragoon had brought together a large number of assault carriers and was to be the only occasion on which RN and USN assault CVEs operated together. For most fighter pilots it brought a new and dangerous experience of dive-bombing and ground strafing against sophisticated opposition but there can be little doubt that the naval pilots revelled in their success. Dragoon may, as Churchill feared, have slowed the Italian campaign but it proved to be a triumph of organisation, inter-service and inter-Allied co-operation.

After Dragoon, the Director of the Admiralty's Operational Research Division analysed the flying effort by the seven British CVEs that participated[18] and conclusions were forwarded to all Commanders-in-Chief afloat and to various administrative authorities in the UK and overseas. As a baseline for comparison, the researchers assumed that each CVE carried twenty-five aircraft and had twenty-five pilots available to fly them. They found that the wastage rate had been 3.7 aircraft per 100 sorties and that, realistically, pilot fatigue was likely to limit the carriers' efforts before aircraft wastage, even if it rose as high as six per 100 sorties.

Stalker with Seafires of 809 NAS ranged aft. Note her pennant number, 91, on the hull side. It was not usual for ships larger than destroyers in the RN to have their numbers painted on but since by 1944 there were large numbers of nearly identical American-built CVEs they were displayed as further means of identification. (*Author's collection*)

The latter wastage rate was recommended as the figure for future planning purposes since it took some account of likely air combat losses and less favourable weather than was experienced in Dragoon. They found that both British and American aircraft types had shown high standards of daily serviceability. In achieving its eight days' flying effort, TG 88.1 had not used all its serviceable aircraft on any single day.

If, as RAEC recommended, pilots were to be limited to two sorties per day each at any stage of an operation, a CVE would be likely to be limited to forty sorties a day, reducing on a pro-rata basis as the operation continued. Taking into account aircraft serviceability and wastage, a CVE could be relied upon to fly forty sorties per day for three days and subsequently twenty sorties per day for seven days or thirty sorties a day for six days and subsequently twenty sorties per day for four days. To maintain continuous CAP a CVE would need to have embarked on average three times the number of aircraft to be kept on patrol in order to maintain its effort. Deck landing accidents had accounted for roughly half of the overall aircraft losses, in spite of there being no air opposition and no deck movements on the carriers in calm sea conditions throughout the operation. The deck landing accident rate for the Seafire was high but significantly lower than at Salerno. Significantly, the carriers were able to operate their aircraft out to distances beyond the scope of RAF and USAAF fighters based in Corsica. The assault carrier force had demonstrated the virtues of its mobility and concentration, moving its own logistic support with it for operations at short notice wherever they were needed.

13

The final series of carrier operations in the Mediterranean

On 27 August 1944, three days after they had arrived at Maddalena anchorage, the British CVEs of TG 88.1 were released from any further part in Operation Dragoon. On 29 August they were joined by *Hunter* and *Stalker* from TG 88.2 and the whole force sailed for Alexandria, led by RAEC in *Royalist*. They arrived on 1 September 1944 and, once there, aircraft complements were modified to give a total of twenty in each carrier but retaining the same squadrons with their Seafires, Hellcats and Wildcats as before. Troubridge's CVEs now formed part of a larger organisation designated Task Force 120, within which they became Force A, an interesting mix of British and US force designators. The clearance of enemy strongholds in the Aegean islands was designated Operation Outing and it was to be divided into a series of consecutive phases allowing ships to rest between combat patrols.[1] Initially Force A comprised:

Attacker — Captain H B Farncomb RAN
879 NAS — Lieutenant Commander (A) D G Carlisle SANF(V)
15 Seafire LIIC
5 Seafire LRIIC

Hunter — Captain A D Torlesse RN
807 NAS — Lieutenant Commander (A) L G C Reece RNZNVR
15 Seafire LIII
5 Seafire LRIIC

Stalker — Captain L C Sinker RN
809 NAS — Lieutenant Commander (A) H D B Eadon RNVR
15 Seafire LIII
5 Seafire LRIIC

Khedive   Captain H J Haynes RN
899 NAS   Lieutenant Commander (A) R B Howarth RNVR
20 Seafire LIII

879, 807, 809 and 899 NAS constituted Number 4 Naval Fighter Wing led by Lieutenant Commander (A) G C Baldwin DSC RN.

Emperor   Captain T J N Hilken RN
800 NAS   Lieutenant Commander (A) M F Fell DSO RN
20 Hellcat I

Pursuer   Captain H R Graham RN
881 NAS   Lieutenant Commander (A) L A Hordern DSC RNVR
20 Wildcat VI

Searcher[2]   Captain G O C Davies RN
882 NAS   Lieutenant Commander G R Henderson DSC RNVR[3]
20 Wildcat V

800, 881 and 882 NAS constituted Number 7 Naval Fighter Wing led by Lieutenant Commander M F Fell DSO RN.

For the phases that made up Operation Outing, the Aegean area was deemed to extend as far south as the northern coast of Crete and Force 120 was instructed to interrupt enemy sea and air communications, and to support British landings on the Greek islands and mainland. Put simply, it was to harass the German withdrawal from the region in every possible way. By the autumn of 1944 German forces were in general retreat and in this theatre they were carrying out a massive but controlled withdrawal from Greece and the Aegean islands as the troops that had been stationed there were now needed to defend Germany itself against the Red Army. The background to Outing was complicated, however. The British Government wanted to send troops into Greece to counter Communist partisans who threatened to fill the power vacuum left by the German withdrawal with a government of their own instead of offering their allegiance to the Greek Government in Exile in London. The US Government opposed intervention and refused to be part of it.

   It was clear to the British Chiefs of Staff and their planning teams that there was considerable scope for air and sea attack to disrupt the German withdrawal from the Aegean by a composite force of assault carriers, cruisers and destroyers. The one big obstacle before Outing could begin, however, was the need to clear mines from the various channels between islands. A Special Boat Squadron of the Royal Marines that had been active in the Adriatic was redirected towards the Aegean, where it carried out raiding and strike operations that culminated with landings in the area of Athens in October 1944. British submarines had been active in the Aegean since early 1942.

In early September 1944 the C-in-C Mediterranean ordered Troubridge to take several cruisers and destroyers under his command to form an expanded Force A. Their operation was to comprise a series of phases from 9 September to 15 November 1944 and was to cause considerable disruption to enemy shipping, personnel, railway rolling stock, transport and infrastructure. The once-powerful German Air Force had, by then, almost ceased to be a factor in the region.

For the sake of clarity, each of the five main phases of Operation Outing will be described in its due turn. Between Phases 1 and 2 and again between 2 and 3, at least one assault carrier remained in the operational area to give continuous air reconnaissance.[4] During every phase naval pilots encountered accurate and sometimes intense close-range anti-aircraft fire, particularly in the vicinity of harbours. Yet again, the Hellcat proved its rugged superiority over the Seafire and the latter's liquid-cooled Merlin engine proved particularly vulnerable to damage. Deck landing conditions during Outing proved to be generally good with the exception of only two days on which low visibility precluded all flying operations. On most days there was sufficient natural wind to produce between 20 and 35 knots WOD, which was ideal. During daylight the assault carriers' fighters acted very efficiently as the eyes of the task force, carrying out extensive photographic reconnaissance of the islands, the channels between them, enemy shipping routes and airfields prior to every fighter-bomber strike and shore bombardment. Recent photographs of likely targets were found to be essential, especially if shipping targets needed to be identified before committing aircraft to attack them.

Regrettably, no RFA tankers were available to support Force A by under way replenishment and so the CVEs were used to refuel the cruisers and destroyers. This took advantage of the high FFO storage capacity in the

Admiral Troubridge, when he was captain of *Indomitable*, photographed climbing from the observer's cockpit of a Fulmar after a communications flight. (*Author's collection*)

CVEs; 3,123 tons in the case of an *Attacker*-class ship,⁵ and their own low usage rate gave them an endurance of over 27,000nm at 11 knots. On the other hand, their pumping rate was slow; in fact RAEC described it as 'desperately slow', which meant that some CVEs spent a great deal of time replenishing other warships that would more profitably have been spent operating their aircraft to strike at the enemy. Night replenishments at sea, RAS, were carried out in moonlight twice and on one occasion in daylight when *Attacker* flew off Seafires while replenishing *Royalist*, probably the first time this had been done in the RN. Flying operations while replenishing at sea were to become commonplace after 1945. A constant watch by aircraft and ships was maintained on all the main channels between islands to ensure that enemy minelaying craft did not relay minefields in areas that had been swept. German records examined post-war showed that their minelaying efforts had continued up to mid-October and even later in the approaches to Salonika, with a total of 15,000 mines laid in the Aegean.

Phase 1

On 9 September 1944, RAEC, in *Royalist*, sailed from Alexandria with elements of Force A that included the assault carriers *Hunter*, *Khedive*, *Pursuer*, *Searcher* and the 24th Destroyer Flotilla. Their objective was

to interrupt enemy shipping movements, provide air cover during the occupation of Kithera Island from which the German Army had withdrawn, and to provide cover over the 5th Minesweeping Flotilla as it worked to clear the Kithera Channel north-west of Crete. By 20 September, when this phase ended, the task force had cut off enemy communications with Crete and destroyers had sunk *U-407* south of Milos Island, one of only three U-boats left in the Mediterranean. The remaining two, *U-565* and *U-596*, were sunk by USAAF Liberator heavy bombers in Salamis a few days later.

Khedive and *Searcher* covered the Kithera landings, Operation Aplomb, and protected both the minesweepers and Catalina flying boats that were used to spot mines in the clear Mediterranean water.[6] RAEC and the destroyers made three successful attacks on shipping north of Crete, retiring each dawn through the Kaso Strait covered by aircraft from *Pursuer* and *Hunter*. *Stalker* remained at Alexandria to carry out deck landing training with newly joined replacement pilots but on 15 September *Attacker* and *Emperor* joined the other assault carriers and RAEC led the task force into the Southern Aegean. There, for the next five days, its aircraft carried out reconnaissance sorties over Milos, Kos and Rhodes before attacking shipping and strafing enemy road traffic in Crete as well as spotting for bombardments of Milos. The largest fighter-bomber strike of this phase of the operation took place on 19 September when forty-five aircraft attacked Rhodes harbour. They sank four ships berthed alongside a mole, blew up a mine store and destroyed an anti-aircraft gun emplacement. None of the aircraft was damaged in a successful operation that had achieved complete surprise and overwhelmed the defenders with its weight and precision. The ships sunk had included the 640-ton SS *Pomezia*, a naval ferry and two sailing caïques.

By 20 September further extensive reconnaissance had revealed that there were no other worthwhile targets and Force A returned to Alexandria. Assault carrier fighters had flown a total of 508 sorties with no losses. Eight aircraft had been damaged by anti-aircraft fire but were repairable and four had been damaged in deck landing accidents. The targets destroyed by the whole force included, in addition to *U-407* and the ships sunk in Rhodes, motor vehicles and a Ju 52 transport aircraft on the ground. A number of vessels including two depot ships had been damaged.

Interval followed by Phase 2

In view of Phase 1's success and the urgent need to strike again as soon as possible, Vice Admiral H B Rawlings, the Flag Officer Levant and Mediterranean, FOLEM, ordered RAEC to carry out a second phase at the end of September. In the meantime Troubridge had already sent *Stalker*

Hunter refuelling *Royalist* using the astern method during operations in the Aegean. The buoyant fuel hose is streamed from the starboard after edge of the flight deck. She has Seafires of 807 NAS ranged on deck and many of her ship's company are taking an interest in the proceedings, watching from the after end of the flight deck. The sailor in the foreground on *Royalist* is using semaphore, a secure and reliable means of sending a tactical message over short distances. Although no longer formally taught, it still has its uses in the twenty-first century. (*Author's collection*)

with *Black Prince* (senior officer) and several destroyers into the southern Aegean on 25 September to give air cover to the 5th Minesweeping Flotilla's continued operations. By then these had moved into the important Kinaros Channel, which led into the central and northern Aegean between the islands of Amorgos and Levitha. This small force remained in the operating area until 29 September and in addition to providing cover for the minesweepers, photographic reconnaissance missions were flown over Rhodes, Kos, Syros, Leros and other islands and strike missions were flown against shipping. Spotting aircraft were provided for the bombardment of a German W/T station on Levitha. On the evening of 28 September the ships went to the highest degree of watertight integrity, closed up damage control parties and sailed in line astern through the Kinaros Channel in the central Aegean. Other than submarines, they were the first British warships to do so since the evacuation of Crete in 1941.

On 29 September further cover was provided for the minesweepers and two aircraft carried out a reconnaissance of the Steno Pass between the islands of Andros and Tinos. They located and reported four Siebel ferries, which were found later to have taken shelter in a small bay, where they were attacked by strike aircraft. By then low cloud had become a problem, however, and only one was hit. The rest were subsequently attacked by destroyers' gunfire and set on fire. *Black Prince* bombarded Syros harbour, assisted by air spotting, and the harbour was then attacked by fighter-bombers. In the afternoon a photographic reconnaissance sortie was flown to assess the results of the morning's attacks. When it landed on, *Stalker* set heading for Alexandria. Her aircraft had flown ninety-seven sorties but suffered no losses. Three aircraft had been damaged in deck landing accidents.

RAEC arrived in the operating area in *Royalist* on 30 September with *Attacker*, *Emperor* and *Hunter* and the anti-aircraft cruiser *Colombo* to commence Phase 2 but extensive air reconnaissance found very little enemy activity and the area was devoid of targets. Meanwhile, *Pursuer*, *Searcher* and *Khedive* left Alexandria to return to the UK, where they were to be refitted for assault carrier operations in the Eastern Fleet. Cruisers bombarded the airfields at Maleme[7] and Heraklion in Crete, from where the Germans were flying out troops every night with up to 100 departures by Ju 52 transports.[8] The lack of embarked night fighters was keenly felt as Force A could do nothing to stop this traffic. A W/T station on Levitha and a concentration of small vessels in Portolago harbour in Leros were bombed by sixteen Hellcats of 800 NAS, each of which could carry two 500lb bombs in addition to its full front-gun ammunition. The latter was found to be well protected by anti-aircraft batteries and Force A suffered its first casualty in Operation Outing when Sub Lieutenant (A) K Wilson RNVR was shot down and killed. He had only recently joined the squadron.

Royalist bombarded Milos harbour on 4 October with the aid of spotting aircraft from *Attacker*, while other aircraft looked for targets in reconnaissance sorties flown all over the southern Aegean but they found nothing worth attacking. The Kinaros Channel was still not sufficiently swept to ensure safe passage and RAEC decided against risking his force by moving into the northern Aegean. He decided, therefore, to return to Alexandria with the majority of Force A but detached *Hunter* to give continued cover to the minesweeping operations. While the main part of the force was on passage, further reconnaissance of Santorini, Milos and the north coast of Crete were flown. During the latter sortie a section of 800 NAS from *Emperor*,[9] led by Lieutenant H De Wit RNN, intercepted and attacked a Ju 52 and probably destroyed it as it attempted to land at Maleme. Unfortunately, De Wit's Hellcat suffered damage to its undercarriage from enemy return fire during the combat and he was ordered to divert to Gokova airfield in Turkey 180nm away rather than crash on deck. Nothing was heard of him for several weeks and he was feared to be lost but he managed to return safely to his ship in time to take part in the last phase of Outing. The carriers only flew eighty-two sorties during Phase 2, a reflection on the lack of targets.

Twelve Seafire LIIIs of 899 NAS ranged on *Khedive*'s flight deck being prepared for a strike against shipping in Rhodes harbour. Note the slightly unorthodox way the aircraft are ranged with those on the left of the picture facing aft and having to taxi through 180 degrees to get into the take-off position. This allowed the longest possible deck run, made necessary because the aircraft are all heavy with 250lb bombs loaded on their centreline pylons. The two ratings in the foreground are carrying jury struts that were used to secure the Seafires' wings when they were folded. Nearly all have been removed but one aircraft still has its port wing folded and may still have its jury strut in place. (*Author's collection*)

Interval followed by Phase 3

Hunter was joined on 6 October by *Stalker* and the cruiser *Aurora* from Alexandria on 5 October to maintain a presence. During Phase 2 the aircraft direction ship *Ulster Queen* had directed RAF Beaufighter night fighters from North African bases onto the German transport aircraft flying from Crete and *Royalist* had attempted to do so during Phase 1 but without success. *Ulster Queen* had the more capable Type 277 radar, which gave accurate height information and achieved significantly better results. For eight nights between 28 September and 5 October she took up a datum position 25nm north-east of Cape Spada at dusk and retired to St Nikolo Bay in Kithera Island at dawn. *Ulster Queen* directed fighters into the transport stream and they were able to destroy eighteen Ju 52s, damage a further five and probably destroy two others. Taking into account the large number of enemy transport aircraft actually detected, her commanding officer considered these results 'somewhat meagre' but reconnaissance aircraft from Force A found that by the end of Phase 2 the flow of enemy aircraft out of Maleme had 'been reduced to a mere trickle'.

By 6 October extensive air reconnaissance of the southern Aegean islands including Syros, Naxos, Mykoni, Paros and Leros had still not found any worthwhile targets. Even the airfield at Antimachia on Kos appeared to be deserted and the southern Aegean was clearly no longer worthy of attention. *Hunter*'s aircraft spotted for the bombardment of a

W/T station on Levitha by *Aurora* and after its destruction the cruiser's captain decided to follow this success with a small landing by his Royal Marines detachment to capture the island. A Tac-R mission was flown by a Seafire of 807 NAS to observe and assess enemy movement ashore and reported seeing troops in defensive positions but after looking through his binoculars, the captain decided that the objects seen by the pilot were actually goats. Taking the view that he knew better than an acting Sub Lieutenant RNVR in an aeroplane, he therefore ordered the landing to go ahead but the Marines reported stiff resistance from troops in the interior of the island and returned to the cruiser. Making his report to the captain, the Royal Marines' Detachment Commanding Officer made the point that since goats were unlikely to have mounted an armed resistance, the objects observed must have been German soldiers. The Seafire pilot's skill as a Tac-R specialist was vindicated but the captain's eyesight has to be called into question.

On the morning of 7 October, *Black Prince* (senior officer), *Hunter*, *Stalker* and *Aurora* were led by minesweepers through the Kinaros Channel into the Central Aegean and, once there, they found a number of targets. In the early afternoon twelve fighter-bombers attacked an escorted enemy convoy of three small ships. One of these, estimated at 1,000 tons, was sunk, a caïque damaged and one of the escorts driven aground. One Seafire was hit by anti-aircraft fire and the pilot, Sub Lieutenant (A) D Stewart RNVR, was seen to bail out but unfortunately he was never located. Another pilot, Sub Lieutenant (A) A D Perry RNVR of 809 NAS in *Stalker*, was lost when his Seafire was shot down while attacking motor transport on Kos Island. Later that afternoon a 2,000-ton ship was located and reported near Lemnos. It sank within three minutes of the fighter-bomber attack on it by eight Seafires that quickly followed. The reconnaissance Seafires were airborne on this occasion for two-and-a-half hours and the successful integration of search and strike assets was seldom better demonstrated. In the evening the CVEs detached from the cruisers with Captain Torlesse of *Hunter* as senior officer of the small carrier group. They prepared to operate aircraft on 8 October from datum positions on a line between Strati Island to the north and Tinos to the south.

On arrival at 0730 at a position west of Strati two targets specified by FOLEM were to be attacked but, in the event, one a of these, a destroyer reported to be aground off Kassandra Point, could not be found and the other, a merchant ship stopped in the Gulf of Salonika, was found to be completely wrecked and awash. Outdated intelligence had wasted time and effort since the earliest days of the war and this proved to be yet another example. The rest of the day was spent carrying out extensive reconnaissance of the northern area bounded by Khios in the south,

Parking fighters with their tailwheels on outriggers allowed them to be kept on deck without blocking the runway when other aircraft took off. Although the print is marked, this photograph clearly shows that the whole airframe aft of the main wheels could be outside the edge of the deck. Note the lashing just forward of the tailwheel; securing aircraft on outriggers was not an easy task, especially in bad weather. (*Author's collection*)

Salonika in the north, Velos in the west and Lemnos in the east. Seafires were averaging track distances of 260nm in their ninety-minute searches and the targets they located for immediate attack included a Siebel ferry, a 1,000-ton merchant ship, a small tanker and rolling stock moving on the Volos–Salonika railway at Katerini. The latter led to the first railway strike during Outing. Operations on 9 October followed the same pattern and included anti-shipping strikes in the Petali Channel east of Athens to Mudros Bay in Lemnos. A strike was carried out against three Siebel ferries north of Kassandra in which one was sunk and another left on fire. During this attack 807 NAS suffered another fatality when Sub Lieutenant (A) J A Littler RNVR was hit by anti-aircraft fire and failed to bail out. Early on 10 October the two CVEs were ordered to withdraw. *Stalker* returned directly to Alexandria but *Hunter* flew reconnaissance sorties over Syros and Leros followed by attacks on shipping in harbours, partially with the object of advertising her presence to draw enemy attention away from Phase 3, which had begun on 8 October in the northern Aegean.

The most important lesson learned thus far in Operation Outing was the value of up-to-the-minute intelligence based on photographic evidence, which was used to brief every strike. Intelligence officers used photographs to identify shipping and they also showed the exact locations of anti-aircraft gun defences. Post-strike photographs were used for analysis to give an accurate indication of target destruction. The development of strike operations into the Northern Aegean during the interval between Phases 2 and 3 had been particularly successful. The two CVEs flew 182 sorties; of these *Hunter* flew 102 and *Stalker* eighty. *Hunter* had seventeen aircraft embarked at the start of operations and twenty-four pilots; two aircraft were lost in action with their pilots and one badly damaged. When she withdrew she had ten serviceable aircraft. She had carried out seven RAS operations in which 1,250 tons of FFO were pumped over to other warships. *Stalker* had sixteen aircraft embarked at the start of operations with twenty-two pilots; one aircraft was lost in action with its pilot and three were badly damaged. When she withdrew she had nine serviceable aircraft remaining. She did not carry out any RAS transfers.

On 6 October 1944 Commodore G N Oliver RN relieved Troubridge, the appointment being given the new title Commodore Commanding Escort Carriers, CCEC. He sailed from Alexandria on 8 October to commence Phase 3 in the northern Aegean, flying his broad pennant in *Royalist* with *Emperor* and three destroyers in company. On 1 October Poros Island had been occupied, which was only 30nm south of Athens and later in October this became the forward base for Operation Manna, the assault on the Greek mainland during Phase 4 of Force A's operations.

As Oliver's force transited to the north through the Scarpanto Strait he ordered *Emperor* to fly off aircraft for reconnaissance over northern Crete, Santorini, Milos, Piscopi, Kos, and Leros in the Dodecanese, all of which were still held by the Germans. Shipping was located in Kos and a strike force of eight Hellcats was directed to attack it, sinking several caïques. Instructions were received from FOLEM to remain silent and cease aircraft operations on 10 October while waiting in a position halfway between Khios and Mitylene. *Royalist* searched the southern half of the Gulf of Salonika that night but found no enemy activity. Flying resumed at dawn on 11 October when *Emperor* flew off pairs of armed reconnaissance aircraft from a position north-east of Skyros. As they passed Skyros and the narrow Euripo Channel south-west of Volos they found an enemy ship at Khalkis, attacked it and left it on fire. Unfortunately one Hellcat was hit by anti-aircraft fire and crashed into the sea in flames. Its pilot, Sub Lieutenant (A) G Spencer RNZNVR, was killed. The number of enemy ships located led to a second strike being flown off, this time of twelve Hellcats led by Lieutenant Commander Fell. They sank two E-boats, left a number of caïques on fire and two landing craft hit and stopped in the water. Another flight of four Hellcats, all flown by 800 NAS's Dutch pilots and led by Sub Lieutenant W Saltykoff RNN, located and attacked another two landing craft, which were left on fire with their passengers jumping into the water. A Siebel ferry, three caïques, a tug and an anti-aircraft escort ship were also bombed 'with excellent results'.[10]

In the late afternoon of 11 October two flights totalling eight Hellcats led by Lieutenant J Devitt RNR struck the Khalkis area, sinking two E-boats and observing that some of the ships hit in the morning strikes were still burning. The day's flying ended with a strike against targets on the Larissa to Katerini railway line by four Hellcats led by Fell. They had to fly through severe thunderstorms to reach their objective but destroyed three locomotives and set fire to an ammunition train in which 'the trucks exploded in turn from the centre outwards like an expensive chain of Chinese Crackers'. This had been *Emperor*'s most successful day's operations in Outing; she was ordered to return to Alexandria at 1900 but other targets were attacked while she was on passage. These included Santorini and Rhodes; a W/T station being left on fire at the latter. Some targets had been specified by FOLEM, including an airfield at Calato on Rhodes, but no targets were found and,

Armourers fusing a 250lb bomb slung under the centreline of an 899 NAS Seafire LIII on *Khedive* before a strike against shipping. (*Author's collection*)

again, their absence was put down to stale intelligence. It is surprising that at this late stage of Outing, FOLEM's staff still failed to appreciate that target selection was far more likely to be effective when based on the photographic evidence gathered by Force A's own aircraft.

Before leaving for Alexandria himself, CCEC detailed a destroyer to guard the Kinaros Channel against enemy minelayers. It was his only entrance into the northern Aegean and he intended to return shortly. *Emperor* reached Alexandria at 0800 on 13 October and sailed again with Force A for Phase 4 only eight hours later at 1600, having taken on fuel and stores. During Phase 3 she had flown forty-eight sorties, during which one pilot had been lost but there had been no deck landing accidents. Two aircraft had been damaged but managed to recover on board safely.

Phase 4 and Operation Manna

The landings on the Greek mainland were designated Operation Manna and Phase 4 of Operation Outing was intended to support it. CCEC was in *Royalist* once more and had *Emperor*, *Stalker* and *Attacker* and four destroyers with him. *Hunter* remained at Alexandria. The clearance of mines from the approaches to the Piraeus area delayed Manna but by mid-October all was ready. Force A's original tasking had included beach cover for assault landings, fighter support for the Army as it advanced out of the bridgehead, spotting for ships' bombardment and CAP over the assault shipping as it approached the amphibious area. In the event there was no opposition to the landings; the last German troops had withdrawn from Athens on 12 October, three days prior to Manna's designated D-Day.

While Force A was on passage its carriers carried out what had become the standard reconnaissance along the north coast of Crete from Heraklion to Souda Bay and over Milos, Leros and Santorini islands but found no enemy activity worthy of a strike. After this the force split, with CCEC taking *Emperor* and two destroyers into the northern Aegean while *Attacker* and *Stalker* took up a position south of the Gulf of Athens where their aircraft could cover the landings due to begin at 0530 on 15 October. Once it was learnt that the Germans had withdrawn, a revised plan was implemented in which *Emperor*'s aircraft were to strike from the north at any shipping, road or rail transport being used by the retreating Germans along the line Volos–Khalkis–Skyros while the other two carriers covered the landings from a position 50nm south of the Piraeus. On their arrival, *Attacker* and *Stalker* took it in turns to provide a continuous CAP of four Seafires over Athens until dusk. This task was interrupted for about three hours by severe thunderstorms but at 1110 a Ju 88, probably on a reconnaissance sortie, was detected and intercepted by Seafires of 809 NAS from *Stalker*. After a long chase through cloud it was shot down by Lieutenant D S Ogle RN.

On the morning of 16 October *Stalker* was ordered to join CCEC after flying one CAP mission, leaving *Attacker* to provide any cover requested by the Army. Later in the day *Attacker* was released from covering operations by CS 15, who was in command of the naval aspects of Manna, and she returned to Alexandria at 0930 on 18 October. Once there she was quickly refuelled and restored to sail again on 19 October with *Sirius* and two destroyers for the northern Aegean. Meanwhile, *Emperor* was operating west of Khios and her aircraft carried out strikes against columns of enemy motor transport as they retreated north along the road to Lerissa. These had been detected by her own dawn reconnaissance patrols. Three coasters in Volos were also found and attacked; one of them proved to be an ammunition ship and it exploded, showering the attacking Hellcat with fragments but it still managed to recover safely to the carrier. For the remainder of the day the weather deteriorated and stopped *Emperor* from flying. There was a tragic incident on 17 October, however, when 800 NAS Hellcats mistook British MTBs for enemy E-boats and attacked them,

A Seafire LRIIC of 879 NAS from *Attacker* took this photograph of burning railway flat cars carrying German Army motor transport that had just been strafed and bombed by RN aircraft on 24 October 1944. (*Author's collection*)

killing and wounding a number of men and causing serious damage to two of the boats. Aircraft from 800 and 809 NAS interdicted enemy road and rail communications on 17 and 18 October and *Emperor* took part in a RAS in which 1,343 tons of FFO were pumped across to other warships. On 19 October *Emperor* left the force to return to Alexandria and her aircraft attacked radar installations on Milos while she was on passage.

On 20 October weather conditions in the north were unsuitable for flying but aircraft from *Attacker* flew a strike against Kos airfield and those from *Stalker* attacked Portolago harbour. *Attacker* provided fuel for other warships on 22 October and on both 23 and 24 October Seafires of 879 NAS from *Attacker* struck at enemy rail communications, breaking the line north of Athens in three places. Five trains were hit, thirty wagons destroyed and all rail traffic brought to a standstill. On 25 October *Attacker* anchored at Khios, effectively bringing Phase 4 operations against the Greek mainland to a close. During this phase of the operation four aircraft had been lost, although all their pilots were safely recovered and returned, in due course, to their squadrons. Three of these had carried out forced landings near Mount Olympus[11] and the fourth had ditched. Before she returned to Alexandria on 30 October, *Attacker* flew off aircraft to 'show the flag' to the inhabitants of Mitylene and Lemnos, which was 'very much appreciated'. Both islands were liberated shortly afterwards. Unexpectedly, she was then called upon to provide fighter support for an assault landing on Piscopi Island in the Dodecanese group 95nm to the south, where what was meant to be a lightly opposed landing suffered a harsh reverse after German reinforcements were brought over from Rhodes by night in landing craft. These landing craft were all sunk on the same day by *Attacker*'s fighter-bombers, leaving the German force cut off, but the badly mauled British force had to be withdrawn. The German garrison on Piscopi did not finally surrender until March 1945 and others on Rhodes, Kos and Leros held out in isolation until 8 May 1945, when the war in Europe ended. This incident ended Phase 4 and also marked the end of operations in the Aegean for all the CVEs except *Emperor*. The phase had seen 318 sorties carried out by the three CVEs and, except for the tragic 'blue-on-blue' incident, they had achieved good results in a variety of operations.

Phase 5 and Operation Contempt

Carrier operations in Phase 5 were limited to 800 NAS' contribution from *Emperor* and to the work of a single Swordfish, which was embarked for bombardment spotting duties and to drop leaflets in the hope that they might induce the garrison of the island of Milos to surrender. Several fighter-bomber strikes and cruiser bombardments had been carried out against the island but none of these had the desired effect. *Emperor* sailed on 24 October and carried out deck landing training with the Swordfish,

A Hellcat of 800 NAS, still painted in 'invasion stripes', on *Emperor*'s flight deck photographed off Leros on 3 October 1944. (*Author's collection*)

after which she joined Force B for Operation Contempt, the planned assault on Milos. D-Day for this operation was set for 0830 on 26 October and two Hellcats were flown off as force CAP in good time for this. Eight more Hellcats led by Fell followed with what was described as a 'demonstration flight' over the island; the Swordfish dropped its leaflets urging the enemy to surrender. These were answered by anti-aircraft fire and so the planned bombardments and bombing were commenced. *Aurora* ordered the assault landings to begin and opened fire on an enemy shore battery. As the day progressed the force CAP was constantly relieved and *Emperor*'s air-sea rescue Walrus alternated spotting duties with the Swordfish. Numerous fighter-bomber sorties were flown until the last landed on at dusk.

For the following days *Emperor* settled into a routine of flying off aircraft from dawn to dusk for bombardment spotting, bombing, strafing and force CAP. She also replenished *Aurora* and their escorting destroyers with FFO by both day and night. Her flying effort in Contempt was remarkable and between 26 October and 5 November 1944 she flew a total of 238 Hellcat sorties. The Swordfish and Walrus flew a further twenty-one, making a grand total of 259. The Hellcats dropped a total of 201 500lb bombs; she

The vessel at the top of this picture is a Siebel ferry that has just received a direct hit from a 250lb bomb. A Siebel ferry was a shallow-draft catamaran designed for the German Army and used to move vehicles and equipment across short stretches of water in calm conditions. The lower vessel is a coaster left on fire by an 807 NAS strafing attack. (*Author's collection*)

had only ten left on 29 October and a new outfit had to be brought up for her from Alexandria. Thirty aircraft were damaged by anti-aircraft fire to varying degrees but only one was shot down. Its pilot was recovered by the Walrus. There was only one deck landing accident in which two aircraft were damaged; one ran into the other, ending the ship's run of 401 accident-free landings. The CAP carried out only one interception of a suspected 'bogey' at 10,000ft. The Hellcat pilot directed onto it chased it for many miles through cloud layers only to recognise it as an RAF Mosquito at the last moment before he opened fire. Its pilot had forgotten to switch on his IFF but did so as soon as he saw the Hellcat.

Operation Contempt failed to dislodge the German garrison on Milos and it ended rather ignominiously on 5 November when the British landing parties were taken off without loss during the night. At 1045, after completing nine sorties, *Emperor* set course for Alexandria and Milos remained in German hands until the end of the war in Europe. The captain of *Emperor* compared Contempt with Dragoon in his report, attributing the lack of accidents or pilot fatigue and the low number of aircraft losses in the former to the fact that the pilots could see the carrier even while they were over Milos and therefore had no navigational problems to worry about. The short distance back to the ship had also allowed aircraft that had received serious damage from anti-aircraft fire to return and make safe landings. Good weather on all except two days, a 20 per cent over-bearing of pilots, the absence of air opposition, knowledge after the first few days of the position of anti-aircraft batteries and, above all, confidence in the Hellcat, were also factors that contributed to their success. He noted that new and inexperienced pilots were more vulnerable to short-range anti-aircraft fire but that this was only to be expected.

Phase 5 had one more element, which was carried out between 13 and 15 November 1944. Again *Emperor* was the only carrier but this time she was in company with the battleship *King George V*, on its way to join the BPF, together with the cruisers *Black Prince* and *Aurora*. The intention was to bombard Milos and give *King George V* practice in bombardment techniques. The shoot took place on 14 November with the carrier providing a force CAP of four Hellcats and both the Swordfish and Walrus for spotting duties. After nearly two hours of inconclusive bombardment, *King George V* was engaged by a shore battery at 26,000yds, with one salvo falling only 1,000yds short. Since the battleship was needed urgently as the flagship of the BPF, her commanding officer considered discretion the better part of valour and she moved further out to sea. A Royal Marines Commando was then landed with the aim of capturing a radar station but it was forced to retire empty handed and was re-embarked.

Seafires of Number 4 Naval Fighter Wing, 807, 809, 879 and 899 NAS, disembarked at North Front airfield, Gibraltar, in 1944 waiting to be embarked in their carriers for Operation Outing. There is a mixture of LIIC, LRIIC and LIII variants. (*Author's collection*)

Attacker, *Hunter* and *Stalker* had left Alexandria on 2 November to return to the UK, where they were to give leave before proceeding to the Eastern Fleet. After leaving the Aegean for the last time on 15 November, *Emperor* followed them and arrived in Cardiff on 29 November for a refit. Early in December *Attacker*, *Hunter* and *Stalker* left the UK for the Mediterranean, where they were refitted respectively at Taranto, Malta and Gibraltar; an obvious sign that war had moved on from the Central Mediterranean. Joined by *Emperor* once more, they passed through the Suez Canal to become part of the 21st Aircraft Carrier Squadron initially based at Colombo under Oliver, who was promoted to rear admiral on 5 July 1945, still serving as ACS 21.

The lessons drawn from Operation Outing

The most obvious lesson was not a new one, it was the lack of night fighter capability in the CVEs, a shortcoming shared throughout the RN's carrier air groups. *Ulster Queen* had tried to direct RAF Beaufighters from North Africa onto the stream of German aircraft ferrying troops out of Crete but the distance from their bases at which they were operating had lessened their effectiveness. Carrier-borne fighters operating closer to the scene of action would have had much faster turn-round times and been more effective.[12] Night fighter squadrons, with Fulmars at first and then both Fireflies and Hellcats, began to join the fleet in 1945, just too late for extensive wartime use.

NAD minuted on combat reports that the conditions encountered in Outing were unusual in that the enemy was on the run, there was no significant air threat and little chance of a submarine attack. They felt, however, that even greater damage could have been inflicted on the enemy if the assault carriers had not been tasked with refuelling other warships at sea. The dispersal of Force A to rendezvous with a fleet oiler would, in their opinion, have been a more acceptable alternative and would have allowed more sorties to be flown. The Admiralty also regretted that none of the fighters embarked in the CVEs had been modified to carry 3in rocket projectiles on under-wing rails. Small vessels, railway rolling stock and locomotives together with motor vehicles would have been ideal rocket targets. Work to fit rocket rails to fighters was ongoing but priority had been given to anti-submarine aircraft, which used the same rockets albeit with different warheads. The outstanding performance of the Hellcat compared with the Seafire was also commented upon.

With regard to tactics, the Admiralty emphasised that greater care had to be put into the delineation of bomb lines by troops on the ground so that ground attack pilots could see the position reached by friendly forces. In the area around Athens these had been non-existent. It was vital, even with an enemy in full retreat during unopposed landings, to ensure that pilots knew exactly where friendly forces were. This was especially so if ship to shore communications were imperfect, as they so often were in the early stages of an assault. The value of photographic reconnaissance with intelligence teams in every carrier capable of interpreting the results and briefing strike pilots on their targets was fully appreciated. The Admiralty recognised that the large number of flying hours spent on reconnaissance, both visual and photographic, had paid excellent dividends in locating

The cruiser *Royalist* photographed shortly after her completion in 1943. The transmitting and receiving aerials for her Type 960 long-range, air-warning radar are clearly visible on her fore and main mast-heads. (*Author's collection*)

Seafire LIIIs of 809 NAS from *Stalker* returning to their ship and slotting into the landing pattern flying low and fast down the ship's starboard side. They will break into the circuit in turn fifteen seconds after passing the bow. (*Author's collection*)

targets and concentrations of enemy shipping over an enormous area of sea and land. They also provided FOLEM with a regularly updated picture of the enemy's retreating movements with greater clarity than would otherwise have been possible. Furthermore, it usually gave a more up-to-date and accurate picture than the signalled intelligence reports from other sources upon which FOLEM's staff had relied.

With the final operation against Milos on 14 November 1944, active aircraft carrier operations in the Mediterranean in the Second World War came to an end. Taranto, Matapan, the Malta Convoys, ferrying RAF fighters to Malta, strike operations by RN aircraft from Malta and in North Africa, together with the assault carrier operations carried out with increasing strength from 1942, all bear eloquent witness to the part played by its Fleet Air Arm in the Royal Navy's struggle to control the Mediterranean.

Although never the best deck-landing aircraft, it has to be admitted that the later marks of Seafire were beautiful and effective fighters in flight. (*Author's collection*)

14

Retrospection

The movement of the Mediterranean Fleet from Malta to Alexandria required the retention of Force H at Gibraltar to provide a focus of British power in the Western Mediterranean basin and *Ark Royal*, the RN's newest and most effective carrier, formed a key element of its ability to project power. *Eagle*, the Mediterranean Fleet's carrier in mid-1940, was really too small for fleet work but despite this she did well, especially with the handful of Sea Gladiator fighters that were embarked. The new armoured carrier *Illustrious* brought a complete aviation package with her when she joined Admiral Cunningham's fleet at Alexandria in September 1940. Aircraft carriers are not just mobile runways, they contain logistic support for their aircraft including fuel, weapons, and command and control facilities sufficient to maintain protracted operations. A land-based fighter squadron might be able to fly to a remote airstrip at short notice but it would lack all these important things and would ultimately rely on sea power to provide them.

It has to be said that the RN suffered not only from the lack of priority given to its air component prior to 1937 but also from the ill-considered priorities set by the new Ministry of Aircraft production during 1940 and afterwards. It was starved of new aircraft in 1941 because the MAP failed to recognise the navy's critical need for aircraft to carry out the fleet's wide variety of missions. The fact that *Formidable* had to operate in mid-1941 with an air group far smaller than she was capable of embarking was a poor reflection on the Government's priorities at a critical time. Delays to new aircraft such as the Barracuda and Firefly kept capable aircraft out of front-line squadrons and made the RN largely reliant on American aircraft from 1941 onwards. The cancellation of the Rolls-Royce Exe engine intended for the Barracuda was a particularly severe loss that resulted in the aircraft being under-powered and over two years late when it finally entered service. It could have been a 'game changer' if it had been given the priority it deserved and replaced the Swordfish and Albacore when originally intended. The lack of a high-performance, British-designed carrier fighter was keenly felt throughout the whole war but the Air Ministry had seen no need for such a type when it controlled naval aircraft procurement. The vast production runs ordered for the RAF after the outbreak of war left little room within British industry for aircraft with qualities similar to the USN Hellcat, Avenger and Corsair to be designed and manufactured.[1] Fortunately the appointment of Captain M S Slattery RN as Director of Air Material and Director General Aircraft Development and Production with dual responsibility within

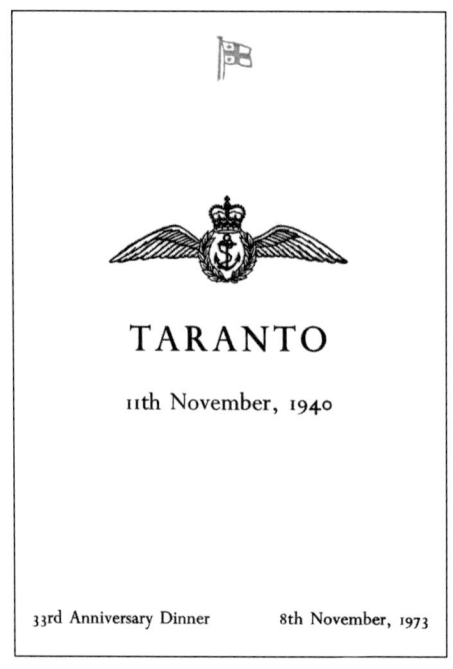

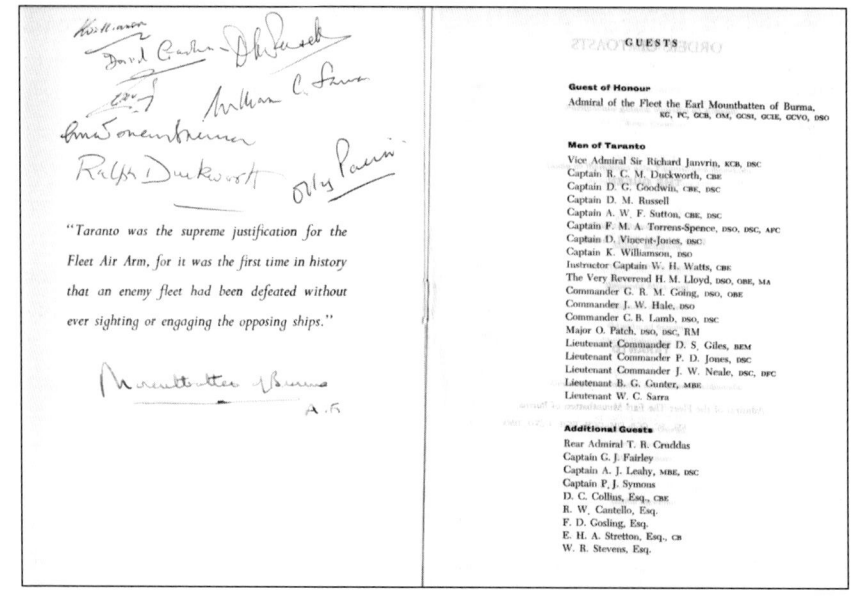

Taranto Anniversary Dinner at RNAS Yeovilton 1973 – outer cover of the menu. (*Jandy Hobbs collection*)

Taranto Anniversary Dinner at RNAS Yeovilton 1973 – inner pages of the menu listing the Men of Taranto present as guests with some of their signatures including that of Admiral Mountbatten, the Guest of Honour. (*Jandy Hobbs collection*)

the Admiralty and as Chief Naval Representative in the MAP improved the situation. He was able to drive forward the development of stopgap fighters such as the Sea Hurricane and Seafire and by 1944 had given the development of new RN aircraft the important status it merited. He even drove forward the development of the venerable Swordfish design to provide radar and rocket-equipped anti-submarine aircraft to defend the North Atlantic convoys. Even so, fighter numbers at the time of the Salerno landings were barely adequate and Forces H and V deployed most of the RN's front-line Seafire force. The need to replace the large number of aircraft lost or damaged was, therefore, of critical importance and was given high priority.

Another problem that the RN had to overcome was the initial RAF distaste for joint or combined operations in which control of their aircraft would be handed to the RN for the time they were airborne. This led to many problems, one of which was illustrated by the refusal to hand over photographs of the Italian fleet in the days before the Taranto strike. Another was the failure to brief aircrew adequately on how to communicate with fighter controllers in warships during the final stages of Malta convoy operations or the important requirement to ensure that IFF was selected on when approaching a task force. In operations from UK bases, both Bomber and Coastal Commands had had to 'borrow' RN observers[2] in 1940 to teach aircrew how to operate with a fleet in action. RAF reconnaissance aircraft in the Mediterranean performed a vital function that had been recognised for some time but even these were of limited value to start with because their reports were communicated through a separate chain of command, not a unified one, and their arrival in the right hands either at sea or ashore took too long. Italian commanders often knew their content before British flag officers because of their ability to decrypt British signal traffic in the early part of the war.

Carrier operations in the Mediterranean give a vivid picture of the Fleet Air Arm's expansion in the years from 1940 to 1944, with growing numbers of young RNVR aircrew from 1941 as the rapidly expanded wartime training scheme produced ever-larger numbers. The largely prewar RN and RN (A) aircrew in the squadrons that attacked Taranto gave way to squadrons largely composed of RNVR aircrew by 1943, with many squadrons commanded by RNVR officers who had gained their experience and skills in action. A number of these transferred to the RN after 1945 and achieved high rank. The reservists had been the 'green' new boys in early 1941 but they learnt quickly as they gathered front-line experience and by 1944 several outstanding RNVR officers were among the Navy's most experienced air warfare experts. The term Fleet Air Arm continued in use throughout the war but the official title of naval aviation, adopted by the Admiralty in 1939, was the Air Branch of the Royal Navy. RN and RNVR officers who were not qualified for ship command had the letter 'A' in the curl of their sleeve lace and referred to themselves as 'Branch Types'.

While aircrew numbers expanded,[3] it should be remembered that many of the staunchest advocates of naval aviation were not pilots at all but executive officers who had commanded aircraft carriers and formed a deep appreciation of what their young aircrew could achieve together with a practical knowledge of their aircraft. Lyster, Boyd and Troubridge could all realistically be described as the driving forces behind their air groups.[4] When he was Flag Officer Air (Home) in 1946, Admiral Boyd introduced the Boyd Trophy, which was presented annually to the aircrew or unit that, in the opinion of the senior RN aviation authority, achieved the finest feat of aviation during the previous year. The trophy itself comprises a silver model of a Fairey Swordfish mounted on a cast brass swordfish and tiered base presented by the Fairey Aviation Company, and for as long as he could, the admiral presented it personally. Sadly the award of the trophy was placed in abeyance after its presentation

Admiral Sir Denis Boyd KCB CBE DSC photographed without a cap or flying helmet in the observer's seat with Rear Admiral Sir Matthew Slattery KBE CB FRAeS behind him in the TAG position. They are strapped into a Swordfish on the flight deck of *Ocean* that was about to carry out the type's last planned take-off from an RN carrier, literally the end of its long operational career in the RN. Unfortunately the pilot was not named on my copy of the photograph. (*Author's collection*)

in 2009 because it was in need of 'repair or replacement'.[5]

Operation Avalanche demonstrated not only that carrier-borne fighters could support the landing of an expeditionary force from the sea but that they might even provide a better, more flexible and adaptive way of doing so. However, the fact was not yet fully appreciated by senior RAF and USAAF officers. On 10 October 1943 Force V's sixty-five Seafires flew 232 hours on task over the beachhead. The RAF and USAAF between them had 641 fighters, ten times Force V's number, at land bases in Sicily with vast quantities of men and material brought into the country to support them. From all of this resource they only flew 320 hours over the beachhead and most of the hours spent airborne were taken up with transit to the operating area. The support of amphibious operations was just one illustration of a growing number of roles and skills created by the Fleet Air Arm since the outbreak of war but which had not been anticipated before 1939. Others included photographic and tactical reconnaissance over land and sea; target marking for the RAF medium bomber force in the North African desert and temporary operations from austere landing grounds ashore. To support these capabilities, methods of mobile logistic support were introduced, such as the mobile air torpedo maintenance unit that backed up the front-line squadrons. As it expanded its own force, the RAF Middle East Air Force learnt the art of co-operation and provided vital air transport for Fleet Air Arm logistics when it was needed. The key points to be taken from the succession of operations that followed the Torch landings were not only that that the carrier aircraft themselves had mobility but that they brought their own logistics with them. They concentrated force at the point at which it was needed at the time it was needed and then moved on to the next area of importance, taking their logistics with them. The RAF had an important role to play of course, but more in the nature of a garrison force intended to operate in one place for a protracted period. Land-based aircraft lacked rapid mobility. It is interesting to observe how inter-service and inter-Allied co-operation improved after Operation Torch, however, showing how the lessons of experience were absorbed.

Admiral Sir Frank Hopkins KCB DSO DSC. (*Author's collection*)

In the series of operations in the Mediterranean I have described, Taranto stands out as the most important. The attack by aircraft from *Illustrious* was, and is, rightly regarded as the battle that provided the first combat demonstration that the aircraft carrier and its aircraft had replaced the battleship to become the dominant factor in warfare.

The Pedestal convoy is another moment in history that deserves to be remembered with pride. The stakes could not have been higher; if it had failed to get through, Malta would have been lost and with it all hope of preventing supplies from reaching the German Afrika Korps. North Africa, Suez and ultimately Middle East oil supplies might have been lost, with all that these disasters would have entailed. But it did get through, largely because of the efforts of the fighter squadrons embarked in the three fleet carriers. Despite their low numbers and obsolescent aircraft, they were right at the scene of action with minimal transit times, the ability to refuel and rearm quickly, and they were flown by pilots who were determined to do their best in a cause they understood only too well. They did as well or better than any fighter force in any arm in history.

The cover provided for the Salerno landings is often portrayed in negative terms because of the number of aircraft damaged in non-combat incidents but there was still much of which the RN can be proud. The weakness of the Seafire as a deck-landing aircraft was compounded by the small operating area inflicted on Force V by the planning staff, the low wind conditions and the decision to operate aircraft in small groups from multiple carriers. Experience was to show how techniques could be improved and losses on this scale were not suffered again. The RN had actually deployed virtually its whole front-line Seafire force to this operation and in addition to the pilots' unfamiliarity with the type it must be remembered that it was new to the air engineering teams as well. It is arguable that the higher sortie generation rates per airframe that were achieved later in Avalanche were actually made possible because the air engineers were able to concentrate on a smaller number of airframes. It was enormously to the Force's credit that it was able to land a naval fighter wing to operate ashore in the final days of the operation. The lessons of how best to use assault carriers were all brought together in the final series of operations in the Aegean. The force was concentrated, achieved battle space dominance when it was needed over both sea and land and then moved on to concentrate in the Indian Ocean a few weeks later in support of Army operations in Burma.

Some aspects of the Mediterranean fighting often described as lessons were not really lessons at all, they were things that were already known but modern warfare had re-emphasised their importance. The Fleet Air

Vice admiral Sir Richard Janvrin KCB DSC standing in the rear cockpit of Swordfish LS326 on 11 July 1969 to salute *Victorious* as she was towed from Portsmouth to the scrapyard at Faslane after her premature withdrawal from service. At the time this aircraft was the last airworthy example of the type. (*Author's collection*)

Arm had always stressed the critical importance of accurate navigation because if an aircraft's crew could not locate their carrier in the open sea they had little choice but to ditch and, probably, drown or die of exposure in a dinghy. In stark contrast the RAF's Bomber Command paid most attention to the pilot's ability to fly his aircraft and very little to its navigation or accurate bomb delivery before the Butt Report of 1942. These differing outlooks explain why 826 NAS' skills proved to be so important in the desert campaign and the growing RAF Middle East bomber force came to rely on them so completely for such a long time. The ability of 830 NAS in Malta to strike at enemy shipping at night from its shattered base at Hal Far in Malta can be traced back to the emphasis placed on night torpedo attack training its senior aircrew such as lieutenant Commander Hopkins had undergone in the late 1930s. It paid off handsomely. More immediately, the RN suffered from the lack of preparation its fighter squadrons suffered from before Operation Torch and the failure of 804 NAS is an example of what can happen all too easily if aircrew are not given time to gain familiarity with their aircraft, ship and mission profiles before an important operation.[6] The Admiralty drew from this the understanding that while numbers give mass, they are not of great value if they are not well trained or prepared. Attempts have been made ever since to make sure that this rule is applied.

Versatility also counted for a great deal. No. 830 NAS was formed out of a training unit with Swordfish that were not prepared for front-line service. Moved to Hal Far in Malta, they were almost bombed into extinction but here the operative word is 'almost'. They never gave up and developed skills in a variety of roles ranging from night torpedo attack, through dive-bombing to visual and radar reconnaissance and flare-dropping. They operated from an airfield that was attacked on a daily basis and the squadron thoroughly earned an imperishable reputation.

The memory of the attack on Taranto has been celebrated every year by the RN and the surviving 'Men of Taranto' were always invited to attend dinners at RN Air Stations and in the wardrooms of carriers.[7] As an example, I illustrate this with the menu card from the 33rd Anniversary Taranto Night Dinner held at RNAS Yeovilton on 8 November 1973, which my wife attended when she was the Captain's Assistant Secretary (Personnel). She managed to obtain the signature of the guest of honour, Admiral of the Fleet the Earl Mountbatten of Burma KG PC GCB OM GCSI GCIE GCVO DSO, and those of eight of the Men of Taranto. Nineteen men who had been present at the battle are listed as guests, of which twelve were aircrew.

Some of the senior officers I have mentioned in earlier pages went on to achieve high rank in the post-war RN after 1945.

Admiral Sir Denis Boyd KCB CBE DSC, who had been the Captain of *Illustrious* at the time of Taranto, became Rear Admiral Aircraft Carriers (Mediterranean) in 1941 and then in the Eastern Fleet in 1942. He was appointed as 5SL/DCNS in 1943 and Admiral (Air) in 1945. In 1946 he became the Commander-in-Chief British Pacific Fleet and retired in 1949. He died in 1965.

Rear Admiral Sir Matthew Slattery KBE CB FRAeS was appointed as Director of Air Material and Director General Naval Aircraft Development and Production with specific instructions to improve the production of aircraft for the RN. Production of the Sea Hurricane and Seafire was forced through on his initiative and by 1945 he was Vice Controller (Air) and Chief of Naval Air Equipment. He retired in 1948 and died in 1990.

Admiral Sir Frank Hopkins KCB DSO DSC followed his command of 830 NAS in Malta with a number appointments, including command of *Ark Royal* in 1956. Promoted to flag rank in 1960, he served as Flag Officer Flying Training in 1960, Flag Officer Aircraft Carriers in 1962, 5SL/DCNAS in 1963 and, finally, as C-in-C Portsmouth in 1966. To his lasting credit he fought hard to prevent the new carrier CVA-01 from being cancelled in 1966 and was 'relegated' to the Portsmouth appointment by the anti-carrier 1SL Admiral Sir Varyl Begg. He retired in 1967 and died in 1990.

Vice Admiral Sir Richard Janvrin KCB DSC, who flew on the attack on Taranto, went on to command *Victorious* in 1959. He became Flag Officer Aircraft Carriers in 1964, 5SL/DCNS in 1966 and Flag Officer Naval Air Command in 1968. He retired in 1971 and died in 1993.

War in the Mediterranean saw the RN make use of aircraft of obsolescent design, albeit still in production, early prototype carriers that were not fully capable of carrying out the tasks required in a modern fleet and CVEs that had to be modified for the assault role because of the lack of fleet carriers. The element of success that stands out above all others, however, is the men who manned them. I have tried to name as many as records allow but regret that there are many that served in the RN Air Branch in the Mediterranean that I have not been able to mention by name. My last photograph is dedicated as a tribute to them all; those that returned and those that will never grow old.

This photograph was obviously posed but it shows three sub lieutenants in their best uniforms and two aircraft handlers in their wind-proof overalls by a Seafire IIC of 899 NAS on *Indomitable*'s flight deck. It was taken in 1943 shortly before Operation Husky. Unusually for the period, the sub lieutenant on the right is in the RNR; note the straight, interwoven rank lace on his sleeve with no 'A' in the curl since he would have been qualified to carry out ship's executive duties. The two sub lieutenants to the left are RNVR (A) officers with their 'wavy' rank lace and an 'A' in the curl. They are wearing standard-issue 1943 Mae Wests, leather flying gloves and are holding their Admiralty-Pattern leather flying helmets, goggles, oxygen masks and their connections. The two chock-men are poised in the position they would adopt when ready to remove the chocks at short notice. (*Author's collection*)

Appendix A

Royal Navy aircraft operated in the Mediterranean Theatre 1940–44

Fairey Swordfish Mark I

Length:	36ft 4in (40ft 11in on floats)
Wingspan:	45ft 6in (17ft 3in folded)
Height:	12ft 10in (14ft 7in on floats)
Maximum weight:	9,250lb
Engine:	One 750hp Bristol Pegasus XXX
Fuel:	Avgas, 155 gallons in main internal tank; 12.5 gallons in internal gravity-fed tank; 60 gallon overload tank could be fitted in rear cockpit; 69 gallon avgas overload tank could be fitted to torpedo crutches
Performance:	Maximum speed in level flight 125 knots
Endurance:	Over four hours at 90 knots on internal tankage
Armament:	One 1,610lb Mark XII torpedo or Type A mine on centreline crutches; up to 1,500lb of bombs or depth charges on centreline and under-wing hard points; one fixed Vickers 0.303in machine gun to right of the pilot's cockpit with 500 rpg and one 0.303in Lewis Mark IIIE or Vickers K gas-operated machine gun on a Fairey high-speed mounting in the rear cockpit with a number of 47-round drums (known as trays); flares

Blackburn Skua Mark II

Length:	35ft 7in
Wingspan:	46ft 2in (15ft 6in folded)
Height:	12ft 6in
Maximum weight:	8,228lb
Engine:	One 890hp Bristol Perseus XII
Fuel:	Avgas, 163 gallons in internal tankage
Performance:	Maximum speed in level flight 198 knots; initial rate of climb 1,580 ft per minute; service ceiling 20,000ft
Endurance:	Four hours twenty minutes at 165 knots
Armament:	One 500lb SAP bomb semi-recessed under the fuselage centreline with ejector arms to swing it clear of the propeller arc on release. Four 0.303in browning machine guns, two in each wing firing clear of the propeller arc, each with 600 rpg.

One Lewis Mark IIIE or Vickers K gas-operated machine gun in the rear cockpit with several 47-round drum magazines. Light series carriers under the wings could each carry four 20lb bombs or flares

Gloster Sea Gladiator

Length:	27ft 5in
Wingspan:	32ft 3in
Height:	10ft 4in
Maximum weight:	5,420lb
Engine:	One 840hp Bristol Mercury IX
Fuel:	Avgas, 83 gallons in internal tankage
Performance:	Maximum speed in level flight 223 knots; initial rate of climb 2,300ft per minute; nine-and-a-half minutes to climb to 20,000ft ceiling
Endurance:	Two hours at 185 knots
Armament: firing	Four Browning 0.303in machine guns, two in the lower wings clear of the propeller arc, each with 400 rpg, two in the cowling forward of the cockpit, each with 600 rpg, firing through the propeller arc with an interrupter mechanism that slowed the rate of fire. With more rounds and a slower rate of fire, the fuselage guns gave more prolonged fire than the wing guns

Fairey Fulmar Mark II

Length:	40ft 2in
Wingspan:	46ft 4.5in (17ft 10in folded)
Height:	14ft
Maximum weight	10,700lb
Engine:	One 1,300hp Rolls-Royce Merlin XXX
Fuel:	Avgas, 155 gallons internal tankage with provision for a 60-gallon overload tank
Performance:	Maximum speed in level flight 216 knots; initial rate of climb 1,200ft per minute; ceiling 26,000ft
Endurance:	Three-and-a-half hours at 200 knots
Armament:	Eight 0.303in Browning machine guns, four in each wing with 500 rpg; provision for two 250lb bombs, one under each wing, seldom used

Fairey Albacore

Length:	39ft 11.75in
Wingspan:	49ft 11.75in (17ft 9in folded)
Height:	12ft 6in
Maximum weight:	12,500lb
Engine:	One 1,085hp Bristol Taurus XII
Fuel:	Avgas, 193 gallons internal tankage
Performance:	Maximum speed in level flight 140 knots; range with a torpedo 800nm; ceiling 15,000ft
Endurance:	Six hours at 100 knots

Armament:	One 1,610 Mark XII torpedo or Type A mine on centreline crutches; three 500lb bombs, one on centreline and one under each wing; six 250lb bombs, three under each wing; four depth charges under wings; flares; one 0.303in Browning machine gun in starboard lower mainplane and one 0.303in Vickers K gun in rear cockpit, the latter with several 47-round drum magazines

Hawker Sea Hurricane Mark IIC

Length:	32ft 3.5in
Wingspan:	40ft
Height:	13ft 3.5in
Maximum weight:	7,800lb
Engine:	One 1,280hp Rolls-Royce Merlin XX
Fuel:	Avgas, two main internal tanks with 34.5 gallons each and an internal reserve tank with 28 gallons
Performance:	Maximum speed in level flight 285 knots; initial rate of climb 2,400 feet per minute; ceiling 35,000ft
Endurance:	Two hours
Armament:	Four 20mm British Hispano cannon, each with 100 rpg, two in each wing firing clear of the propeller arc

Grumman Martlet Mark IV (Wildcat after 1944)

Length:	29ft
Wingspan:	38ft (14ft 4in folded)
Height:	11ft 4in
Maximum weight:	8,762lb
Engine:	One 1,200hp Pratt & Whitney Twin Wasp R-1830-86
Fuel:	Avgas, 144 US gallon internal tankage with provision for one 58-US gallon drop tank under each wing
Performance:	Maximum speed in level flight 280 knots; initial rate of climb 2,000ft per minute; ceiling 34,000ft
Endurance:	Five hours on internal fuel
Armament:	Six 0.5in Colt-Browning M2 machine guns with 240 rpg, three in each wing firing clear of the propeller arc

Supermarine Seafire LIII

Length:	30ft 2.5in
Wingspan:	36ft 10in (14ft folded)
Height:	13ft
Maximum weight:	7,640lb
Engine:	One 1,600hp Rolls-Royce Merlin 55M
Fuel:	Avgas, 85-gallon internal tankage with provision for 30-gallon, 45-gallon or 90-gallon jettisonable tank on centreline
Performance:	Maximum speed in level flight 306 knots; initial rate of climb 4,160ft per minute; ceiling 24,000ft
Endurance:	Three hours with 90 gallon tank fitted
Armament:	Two 20mm British Hispano cannon, each with 120 rpg, one in each wing firing clear of the propeller arc; four 0.303in

Browning machine guns each with 350 rpg, two in each wing outboard of the cannon. Provision for one 500lb or 250lb bomb on centreline pylon

Grumman Hellcat Mark II

Length:	33ft 4in
Wingspan:	42ft 10in (16ft 2in folded)
Height:	14ft 5in
Maximum weight:	13,221lb
Engine:	One 2,000hp Pratt & Whitney Double Wasp R-2800-10
Fuel:	Avgas, 250 US gallon internal tankage comprising two 87.5-gallon main tanks, a 74.5-gallon reserve tank. Provision for a single 150-US gallon drop tank on the fuselage centreline
Performance:	Maximum speed in level flight 330 knots; initial rate of climb 3,650ft per minute; ceiling 35,500ft
Endurance:	Eight hours with drop tank at economical speed
Armament:	Six 0.5in Colt-Browning machine guns with 400 rpg, three in each wing firing clear of the propeller arc; provision for up to two 500lb bombs (plus 3in underwing rockets after 1944)

Data for this appendix has been taken from the author's archive and Captain Eric Brown's *Wings of the Navy*, Jane's Publishing Company, London, 1980 edition.

Appendix B
Royal Navy fighter weapons

Prior to 1940 the Royal Navy had little choice but to use the front guns specified for RAF fighters since these were the only weapons available in the UK. The Air Ministry believed that a high volume of fire from multiple rifle-calibre machine guns would be more effective than a slower rate of fire from fewer weapons of larger calibre. Experience showed this theory to wrong but by the time the MAP was created, production was already on too large a scale to change overnight. Fortunately the USN chose a more effective weapon for fighters such as the Martlet/Wildcat, Hellcat and Corsair and the RN was fortunate to have these in significant numbers after Lend-Lease arrangements made them available.

The 0.303in Browning machine gun used in most British fighters weighed only 25lb, so the total gun installation in a Fulmar, for instance, weighed only 200lb. It had a muzzle velocity of 2,240ft per second and a rate of fire of 1,200 rounds per minute but the weight of each bullet was only 174 grains and it lacked penetrating power, especially after enemy aircraft were fitted with armour around vulnerable points after 1940. Its maximum range was only 300 to 400yds, so fighter pilots had to close in to almost point-blank range in order to achieve the number of hits and penetration required to cause serious damage. As related in the text, this was dangerous, especially against faster aircraft where the fighter could easily be drawn into a stern chase where it was vulnerable to return fire. The explosive 'De Wilde' bullet provided some improvement but not enough to make this a really effective weapon.

The USN weapon of choice was the 0.5in Colt-Browning machine gun, arguably the best fighter weapon of the war. It weighed 64lb and fired either a solid shot, explosive or incendiary round at 850 to 950 rounds per minute. Advantages over the 0.303in Browning included a higher muzzle velocity of 2,900ft per second, which added to the effectiveness of its 710 grain bullets and the fact that it was effective out to as much as 800yds. This was a big advantage in air combat and a battery of four guns in a Fulmar would have weighed 256lb but been far more effective than the eight 0.303in Brownings. The 0.5in Browning was in production in the USA before the Hurricane and Spitfire prototypes had flown, so the Air Ministry choice of a light machine gun armament for them was very much a 'self-inflicted wound' from which it took several years to recover.

Once the inadequacy of the 0.303in Browning was realised, British fighters began to be fitted with the Hispano Mark II 20mm cannon, which was manufactured under licence in the UK and USA. It was capable of firing between 600 and 700 rounds per minute at a muzzle velocity of 2,750ft per second. The gun weighed 99lb but its projectiles weighed twice as much as the 0.5in Browning and the effect of its large explosive bullets could be lethal, few strikes being needed to cause fatal damage to an enemy aircraft.

To illustrate the greater effectiveness of a four-gun 0.5in battery in a Fulmar against eight 0.303in, the Air Armament Department at Whale Island calculated that the energy delivered in one minute by the eight 0.303in guns was 21,047,040 ft lb. The four 0.5in guns would have more than doubled that figure at 45,316,384 ft lb. Taking all the calculations into effect, a hit on an enemy aircraft by a single, solid 0.5in Colt-Browning round would be seven times more damaging than a 0.303in round. An explosive round would be even more effective. Fairey Fulmars modified for the night-fighter role in 1944/45 were fitted with 0.5in Colt-Brownings.

The positioning of front guns in the wings outside the propeller disc after 1936 brought the need to align them accurately with the pilot's gunsight, which was on the aircraft's centreline. The RAF favoured an alignment in which the guns were 'toed in' to converge on a single point 250yds ahead of the aircraft so that they would cause the maximum damage at this point. The Admiralty was never satisfied with the results of this convergent alignment and in late 1940 it devised a pattern intended to fill a cylindrical volume of air with as many bullets as possible as opposed to trying to hit a single point from every gun. Put simply, the guns were aligned to fire in parallel. The results were remarkably effective. In 1941 groups of Fulmars fitted with the two harmonisation systems each shot down thirty-five enemy aircraft but only three Fulmars were shot down by return fire in the group with Admiralty Standard Harmonisation. In contrast, the group with point alignment lost eleven Fulmars to return fire because they had to fire from closer range to achieve their kills and rounds concentrated near the cockpit or engines failed to hit the enemy rear gunners.

For most of the war in the Mediterranean fighter pilots aimed their guns using reflector gun sights fitted as standard. These consisted of small 'black boxes' mounted behind the windshield, above which there was an optically flat glass screen. A simple sight picture was projected onto this from below and the pilot saw a central aiming dot, which represented the line-of-sight axis of the aircraft and its fixed guns. Around the dot was a circle, which represented a 50 knot crossing speed at the ideal firing range and radial lines extending outwards from the dot. To reach a hitting position the fighter pilot aligned his aircraft so that the target was flying towards the central dot, using the radial lines as reference marks so that the enemy reached the appropriate crossing speed circle at the desired range. The pilot had to estimate both range and crossing speed by eye, a skill that could only be learnt with experience, but once fighter pilots acquired it the sight gave the correct deflection or 'aim-off' ahead to allow them to gain hits. The fact that the sight was simple and easy to interpret under combat conditions helped. It was focused at infinity and allowed pilots to concentrate on their targets without having to refocus on 'ring and bead' fitted outside the cockpit. Telescope sights fitted to early production USN fighters had the great disadvantage of reducing the pilot's field of vision to the telescope's eyepiece rather than the wider field of view allowed by the reflector sight, an undesirable feature in a battle space crowded with aircraft. All were replaced with reflector sights in RN aircraft.

This appendix was created from the author's notes from the Air Weapons School at HMS Excellent, Whale Island, and J David Brown's book *Carrier Fighters*, p. 23 et seq.

Appendix C

Aircraft reinforcements flown to Malta from aircraft carriers

Date	Operation	Carrier	Fighters launched/arrived
02.08.40	Hurry	*Argus*	12 Hurricanes/12
17.11.40	White	*Argus*	12 Hurricanes/4
03.04.41	Winch	*Ark Royal*	12 Hurricanes/12
06.06.41	Rocket	*Ark Royal/Furious*	44 Hurricanes/43
14.06.41	Tracer	*Victorious/Ark Royal*	48 Hurricanes/45
27.06.41	Railway I	*Ark Royal*	22 Hurricanes/21
30.06.41	Railway II	*Ark Royal/Furious*	35 Hurricanes*/34
09.09.41	Status I	*Ark Royal*	14 Hurricanes/14
13.09.41	Status II	*Ark Royal/Furious*	46 Hurricanes/45
12.11.41	Perpetual	*Ark Royal/Argus*	37 Hurricanes/34
07.03.42	Spotter	*Eagle*	15 Spitfires/15
21.03.42	Picket I	*Eagle*	9 Spitfires/9
29.03.42	Picket II	*Eagle*	7 Spitfires/7
20.04.42	Calendar	USS *Wasp*	47 Spitfires/46
09.05.42	Bowery	USS *Wasp/Eagle*	64 Spitfires/60
19.05.42	LB	*Eagle/Argus*	17 Spitfires/17
03.06.42	Style	*Eagle*	31 Spitfires/27
09.06.42	Salient	*Eagle*	32 Spitfires/32
15.07.42	Pinpoint	*Eagle*	32 Spitfires/31
21.07.42	Insect	*Eagle*	30 Spitfires/28
11.08.42	Bellows	*Furious*	38 Spitfires/37
17.08.42	Baritone	*Furious*	32 Spitfires/29
29.10.42	Train	*Furious*	31 Spitfires/29

* One Hurricane crashed on take-off from *Furious* and the remaining seven were not flown off because of the accident.

In twenty-five operations spread over twenty-six months, six aircraft carriers ferried 746 fighters to positions from where they could be flown off to Malta. A total of 700 aircraft arrived in Malta but *Ark Royal* was lost on her way back to Gibraltar after Perpetual.

This appendix was put together from data in the appendices in the unpublished *Naval Staff History, the Development of Naval Aviation* 1919–1945 Volume III.

Appendix D

RN and RAF aircraft reinforcements for the Eastern Mediterranean ferried by or flown off aircraft carriers to Takoradi for onward flight across Africa to Egypt

Date	Operation	Carrier	Aircraft launched/arrived
05.09.40	Convoy AP2	Argus	30 RAF Hurricanes/30[1]
27.11.40	Stripe	Furious	34 RAF Hurricanes/33[2]
			3 RN Fulmars/3
08.01.41	Monsoon	Furious	40 RAF Hurricanes/39[3]
			9 RN Fulmars/9
20.03.41	Pageant and Summer	Furious	40 RAF Hurricanes/40
			12 RN Fulmars/12
			6 RN Swordfish/6

In addition to these, a considerable number of RAF aircraft were ferried to Takoradi dismantled in HM aircraft transport ships *Athene* and *Engadine*.

This appendix was put together from data in the appendices in the unpublished *Naval Staff History, the Development of Naval Aviation 1919–1945* Volume III.

Appendix E

Royal Navy planned and actual front-line aircraft strengths 1939–44

Date	Planned number (all types)	Actual number (all types)
09.39	490	232
04.41	746	
09.41	779	
04.42	925	446
06.42	1,789	
12.42	2,689*	560 (approx)
06.43	–	640 (approx)
12.43	–	825 (approx)
07.44	1,800	1,100 (approx)
12.44	1,605	1,300 (approx)

* During 1943 it became clear to Admiralty planners that the RN could not reach this target because it could not expand the number of Fleet Air Arm personnel enough to achieve it. Agreement was, therefore, reached with the Air Ministry that the planned number would be reduced until after the conclusion of the war with Germany. Transfer of pilots and other personnel would then take place in order to bolster naval operations against Japan in the Pacific, during which the RN was to play a larger part than the RAF. Subsequent forecasts of front-line requirements were shorter term and this had the effect of reducing target figures below this figure.

The change in naval warfare during these years is reflected in the fact that in 1940 only 20 per cent of the RN's total front-line aircraft strength were fighters. Of these, 90 per cent were two-seaters and only 10 per cent single-seaters. By early 1945 these numbers had changed dramatically, with fighters making up 62 per cent of the total front-line strength. Of these, over 90 per cent were single-seaters and less than 10 per cent two-seaters. Over half the fighters in 1945 were American types.

This appendix was put together from data in the appendices in the unpublished *Naval Staff History, The Development of Naval Aviation* 1919–1945 Volume III.

Appendix F

Aircraft carrier flight deck, hangar and lift statistics

Ark Royal

Flight deck:	720ft usable × 95ft
Hangars:	upper 568ft × 60ft × 16ft
	lower 452ft × 60ft × 16ft
Lifts:	forward 45ft long × 25ft wide
	centre 45ft long × 22ft wide
	aft 45ft long × 22ft wide
	all capable of lifting 14,000lb with two platforms, aircraft being taken from the flight deck to the upper hangar on one and from the upper to the lower hangar on the other

Eagle

Flight deck:	652ft × 96ft
Hangar:	400ft × 66ft × 20ft 6in
Lifts:	forward 46ft long × 47ft wide
	aft 46ft long × 33ft wide
	both capable of lifting 14,000lb

Illustrious and *Formidable*

Flight deck:	620ft × 95ft
Hangar:	456ft × 62ft × 16ft
Lifts:	forward 45ft long × 22ft wide
	aft 45ft long × 22ft wide
	both capable of lifting 14,000lb

Indomitable

Flight deck:	680ft (extended to 745ft in 1943) × 95ft
Hangars:	upper 416ft × 62ft × 14ft
	lower 168ft × 62ft × 16ft
Lifts:	forward 45ft long × 33ft wide serving upper hangar only
	aft 45ft long × 22ft wide serving both hangars
	both capable of lifting 14,000lb

Khedive (a typical example of the assault carriers)

Flight deck:	450ft × 80ft wood
Hangar:	260ft × 62ft × 18ft
Lifts:	forward 42ft long × 34ft wide
	aft 34ft long × 42ft wide
	both capable of lifting 14,000lb

These figures are taken from my earlier book *British Aircraft Carriers – Design, Development and Service Histories*, Seaforth Publishing, Barnsley, 2013.

Notes

Chapter 1 Introduction
1 Brian Lavery, *Churchill's Navy, the Ships, Men and Organisation 1939–1945* (London, Conway, 2006) p.24. **2** Admiralty, *The Admiralty – A Guide for Newcomers* (London, Admiralty, 1961 Edition) p.15. **3** N A M Rodger, *The Admiralty*, (Lavenham, Terence Dalton Limited, 1979) pp.152, 153. **4** Stephen Roskill, *Churchill and the Admirals* (Barnsley, Pen & Sword Classics, 2004) p.94 et seq. **5** He was a Labour Party MP. **6** Apparently the Admiralty insisted that a combat air patrol of Spitfires should be flown over his state funeral to ensure that the Germans did not take advantage of the gathering to carry out an attack. **7** Admiralty, BR 1806, *Naval War Manual* (London, Admiralty, 1947 edition) p.30 et seq. This was a publication aimed at junior officers to give instruction and guidance in the conduct of naval warfare. The 1947 edition was an expansion of that of 1925 and includes the benefit of experience gained in the Second World War. **8** The others were America & West Indies; Home; Africa; East Indies; China; Australia and New Zealand. **9** American screw threads and spanner sizes differed from those in British-built aircraft and there were numerous other small differences in detail. **10** David Hobbs, *The Dawn of Carrier Strike* (Barnsley, Seaforth Publishing, 2019) Chapter 8, p.117 et seq. **11** The world's first flush-deck carrier, originally completed in 1918. **12** Admiralty, unpublished Naval Staff History *The Development of Naval Aviation 1919–1945*, Volume III (undated) Annexe. A copy is held in the Naval Historical Branch, Portsmouth, and there is a second copy in the author's archive. **13** *Naval Staff History of the Second World War, The Development of Naval Aviation 1919–1945* Volume II (London, Admiralty, 1956) Appendix XII, p.313.

Chapter 2 War spreads to the Mediterranean in 1940
1 *Naval Staff History of the Second World War, The Development of British Naval Aviation 1919–1945* Volume 1 (London, Admiralty, 1954) p.115. **2** See my earlier book *Dawn of Carrier Strike* (Barnsley, Seaforth Publishing, 2019) for detail of Admiral Wells' command of the RN carrier task force off Norway earlier in 1940. **3** Admiralty, CB 3053(1) *Naval Aircraft, Periodical Summary* Number 1, Period ended 20 September 1940 (London, Naval Air Division, October 1940) p.9. **4** Admiralty Letter GO/NAD 134/38 Table 1, dated 7 May 1938. **5** *Naval Staff History*, Volume 1, p.116. **6** CB 3053(1) pp.8–9. **7** J David Brown, *Carrier Operations in World War II*, Volume 1 The Royal Navy (Shepperton, Ian Allan, 1968) p.68. **8** *Naval Staff History*, p.117. **9** Expressed in ACGM 113 dated 13 July 1939. **10** Admiralty, CB 3035 (2) *Naval Aircraft Periodical Summary* Number 2, Period ended 3 February 1941 (London, Naval Air Division, February 1941) Sections 81 and 82, p.14. **11** Ibid., Sections 75 to 79, pp.13–14. **12** A recurring theme from the Norwegian campaign earlier in 1940; see my earlier book *The Dawn of Carrier Strike*. **13** Quoted in the *Naval Staff History*, p.119. **14** The former Alexandria airport. **15** Quoted in the *Naval Staff History*, p.120. **16** *The Dawn of Carrier Strike*, p.17. **17** Donald Macintyre, *The Battle for the Mediterranean* (London, Batsford, 1964) p.19. **18** Peter C Smith, *Eagle's War – The War Diary of an Aircraft Carrier* (Manchester, Crecy Books, 1995) p.7 et seq. **19** The misidentification is not as bad as it seems. The cruisers were 600ft long and the battleship

Cesare only 10ft longer. Superstructures were similar and with ships manoeuvring at high speed firing at the Swordfish it was an easy mistake to make. **20** *The Battle for the Mediterranean*, p.23. **21** Andrew Thomas, *Royal Navy Aces of World War 2* (Oxford, Osprey Publishing 2007) p.89. **22** Captain S W Roskill RN, *The War at Sea* Volume 1 (London, Her Majesty's Stationary Office, 1954) p.299. **23** *Naval Staff History*, p.122. **24** *Naval Staff History*, p.123. **25** Kenneth Poolman, *Night Strike from Malta – 830 Squadron RN and Rommel's Convoys* (London, Jane's Publishing, 1980) p.13 et seq. **26** *Night Strike from Malta*, p.22. **27** Theo Ballance, Lee Howard and Ray Sturtivant, *The Squadrons and Units of the Fleet Air Arm* (Stapleford, Air-Britain Publishing, 2016), pp.193–195. **28** *Naval Staff History*, Note 1, p.225. **29** *Naval Staff History*, Appendix V, p.236. **30** The earlier Hurricanes had been fitted with propellers that could only be selected to course or fine pitch settings by the pilot. **31** Unpublished *Naval Staff History, The Development of British Naval Aviation*, Volume III, Appendix – Summary of RAF Fighter Reinforcements flown to Malta from Aircraft Carriers, Admiralty (London), a copy of which is in the author's archive. **32** John Wellham, *With Naval Wings – The Autobiography of a Fleet Air Arm Pilot in World War II* (Staplehurst, Spellmount, 1995) p.60 et seq. **33** CB 3058 (2) Section 37 et seq p.8. **34** J David Brown, *Warship Losses of World War Two* (London, Arms and Armour Press, 1990) p.36. **35** *Eagle's War*, p.46. **36** CB 3053 (2) Section 42 et seq, p.9. **37** *Warship Losses of World War Two*, p.36. **38** *With Naval Wings*, p.62 et seq. **39** *Fleet Air Arm*, an information leaflet prepared for the Admiralty (London, HMSO, 1943) p.10. **40** Lieutenant Commander Lawrie Phillips TD RD RNR, *The Royal Navy Day by Day* (Stroud, The History Press, 2018), p.486. **41** There is an apocryphal story that Hats was short for 'hands across the sea', indicating the close planning co-operation required between the Mediterranean Fleet and Force H to achieve it, but I have been unable to confirm this. **42** Derek Howse, *Radar at Sea* (Basingstoke, Macmillan Press, 1993) p.63. **43** Ibid., p.62. **44** CB 3053 (2) Section 50 et seq, p.10. **45** Admiralty, CB 3053 (3), *Naval Aircraft periodical Summary Number* 3 (London, Admiralty, period ended 13 July 1941) Sections 36 to 38, p.8. **46** Ibid., Sections 43 to 49, pp.9–10. **47** *Warship losses of World War Two*, p.38. **48** CB 3053 (3), Section 42, p.9. **49** CB 3053 (2) Section 88 et seq, p.15. **50** CB 3053 (2) Section 92 et seq, p.16. **51** *Naval Staff History*, Volume I, p.126. **52** *The Battle for the Mediterranean*, p.24 et seq.

Chapter 3 Operation Judgement – the Taranto Strike
1 Described in my earlier book *The Dawn of Carrier Strike* (Barnsley, Seaforth Publishing, 2019) p.233 et seq. **2** Julian S Corbett, *Drake and the Tudor Navy* (Aldershot, Temple Smith, 1988) p.253. **3** David Hobbs, *The Royal Navy's Air Service in the Great War* (Barnsley, Seaforth Publishing, 2017) p.462. **4** Given the name Cuckoo after 1918. This is believed to reflect the fact that while Sopwith had designed the aircraft, the first production batches were assembled by Blackburn Aircraft under licence in Yorkshire. Another apocryphal story would have it that the name Cuckoo reflected the intention to 'put an egg in someone else's nest', ie to attack an enemy fleet in its harbour. If the latter myth is true it might explain why the name was not adopted in 1918 as it might have revealed the aircraft's true purpose to the enemy before it was ready. **5** This was a very advanced concept for 1918. The idea was eventually adopted in 1945 when Major R C Hay RM fulfilled the role during set-piece strikes against Japanese targets by the British Pacific Fleet. **6** H F King, *Armament of British Aircraft* 1909–1939 (London, Putnam, 1971) p.48 et seq. **7** Ibid., Chapter 17 gives more detail. **8** Stephen Roskill, *Naval Policy Between the Wars*, Volume 2, *The Period of Reluctant Rearmament* 1930–1939 (Barnsley, Seaforth Publishing, 2016) p.264. **9** Don Newton & A Cecil Hampshire, *Taranto* (London, William Kimber, 1959) p.11. **10** Robin Holmes, *The Battle of Heligoland Bight 1939* (London, Grubb Street, 2009). My brief summary is drawn from material in Chapters 3 and 4. **11** Lieutenant Colonel Angelo N Caravaggio, Canadian Forces, Naval War College Review, Summer 2006, Volume 59 Number 3. **12** Admiralty, *Naval Staff History, Second World War, Battle Summary Number* 10, *Operation MB 8 and FAA Attack on Taranto* (London, Admiralty, undated) p.25. **13** Admiral of the Fleet Viscount Cunningham of Hyndhope KT GCB OM DSO, *A*

Sailor's Odyssey (London, Hutchinson & Co., 1951), p.273 et seq. 14 For comparison, the Merlin helicopters in service with the RN in 2020 are twenty-one years old. 15 Wing Commander John A MacBean & Major Arthur S Hogben, *Bombs Gone – The Development and use of British air-dropped weapons from* 1912 *to the present day* (Wellingborough, Patrick Stephens Limited, 1990) p.193 et seq. 16 Kenneth Poolman, *Illustrious* (London, William Kimber, 1955) p.58. 17 Supplement to the London Gazette (London, Published by Authority, Thursday, 24 July 1947) p.3471. 18 Commander Charles Lamb DSO DSC RN, *War in a Stringbag* (London, Cassell & Company, 1977) p.101. 19 The round-down was removed and the flight deck levelled to a position much nearer the stern in wartime refits, allowing many more aircraft to be ranged or parked on deck. The change had no noticeable effect on airflow and the large round-down must be considered one of the weak points of the original design. 20 David Hobbs, *Aircraft Carriers of the Royal and Commonwealth Navies* (London, Greenhill Books, 1996) p.20. 21 *Battle Summary Number* 10, p.31. 22 J David Brown, *Carrier Operations in World War II*, Edited by David Hobbs (Barnsley, Seaforth Publishing, 2009) p.45. 23 37 degrees 43 minutes North, 19 degrees 10 minutes East. 24 Captain Boyd's Report of Proceedings quoted in *The Supplement to the London Gazette*, p.3476. 25 John Wellham, *With Naval Wings* – The Autobiography of a Fleet Air Arm Pilot in World War II (Staplehurst, Spellmount, 1995) p.77 et seq. 26 Vice Admiral B B Schofield CB CBE, *The Attack on Taranto* (Shepperton, Ian Allan, 1973) p.30 et seq. 27 Ibid., p.33. 28 J David Brown, *Carrier Fighters* (London, Macdonald and Jane's, 1975) p.51. 29 Ben Jones, *The Fleet Air Arm in the Second World War Volume 1 1939–1941* (Farnham, Ashgate Publishing for the Navy Records Society, 2012) p.318 et seq. 30 Admiralty, BR 1736 (6) *Naval Staff History of the Second World War – Selected Operations (Mediterranean) 1940 including Battle Summary Number 10 – Operation MB8 and FAA Attack on Taranto* (London, Admiralty, undated) p.42 et seq. 31 *Taranto*, p.48. 32 David Stevens & John Reeve, editors, *The Face of Naval Battle* (Crows Nest NSW, Australia, Allen & Unwin, 2003) – Chapter 7 David Hobbs, *The Aircraft Carrier*, p.127 et seq. 33 *War in a Stringbag*, p.105 et seq. 34 John Wellham, *With Naval Wings* (Staplehurst, Spellmount, 1995) p.87 et seq. 35 Information based on extracts from the report of the Italian Commander-in-Chief afloat to the Chief of Naval Staff after the Swordfish attack, quoted in the *Naval Staff History*, p.83. 36 *Naval Staff History*, p.49. 37 Quoted in *The Fleet Air Arm in the Second World War*, p.326. 38 Note the number of USN battleships refloated and refurbished for further use after the Pearl Harbor strike. 39 *Naval Staff History*, p.46. 40 Enrico Cernuschi and Vincent P O'Hara, Taranto: *The Raid and the Aftermath* contained within *Warship 2010* edited by John Jordan (London, Conway, 2010) p.77 et seq. 41 See my previous book *The Dawn of Carrier Strike* for an account of the Royal Navy's struggles to regain control of and advance its air arm in the period between 1918 and 1937. 42 Donald Macintyre, *The Battle for the Mediterranean* (London, Batsford, 1964) p.38 et seq. 43 *The Attack on Taranto*, p.77. 44 Ibid., p.77. 45 *The Dawn of Carrier Strike*, p.250. 46 Thomas P Lowry & John W G Wellham, *The Attack on Taranto* (Mechanicsburg, PA, Stackpole Books, 1995), p.108. 47 Ibid., p.110. 48 Caravaggio, Naval War College Review Paper. 49 Michael Simpson, editor, *The Cunningham Papers, Selections from the Private and Official Correspondence of Admiral of the Fleet Viscount Cunningham of Hyndhope Volume 1, The Mediterranean Fleet 1939–1942* (Aldershot, Ashgate Publishing, 1999) p.151 et seq. 50 Ibid., p.200. 51 Caravaggio, Naval War College Review paper.

Chapter 4 Fleet operations up to the Battle of Matapan
1 *Naval Staff History*, Volume I, p.136. 2 Ibid., p.137. 3 Admiralty, CB 3053 (3), Naval Aircraft Periodical Summary Number 3, period ended 13 July 1941 (London, Naval Air Division, July 1941), Sections 62 to 64, p.12. 4 Ibid., Section 65, p.13. 5 Which is held in the Naval Historical Branch in Portsmouth. 6 CB 3053 (3), Sections 66 to 68, p.13. 7 Ibid., Sections 72 to 74, p.14. 8 *Naval Staff History*, p.133. 9 Vice Admiral B B Schofield CB CBE, *The Attack on Taranto* (Shepperton, Ian Allan, 1973) p.63. 10 J David Brown, *Carrier Operations in World War* II (Barnsley, Seaforth, 2009), p.47 et seq. 11 Admiral of the Fleet

Viscount Cunningham of Hyndhope KT GCB OM DSO, *A Sailor's Odyssey*, (London, Hutchinson & Co, 1951) p. 303. **12** Designed to defeat bombs of up to 500lb (227.2kg) which, on Air Ministry advice, had been taken at the ship's design stage as the largest likely to be used against warships in the foreseeable future. **13** Quoted in *The Attack on Taranto*, p. 66. **14** Admiralty, Naval Staff History, *The Development of British Naval Aviation 1919–1945*, unpublished Volume III, unpaginated, a draft copy of which is in the author's archive. **15** Mediterranean Fleet War Diary entry for Operation Picket, a copy of which is in the archive of the Naval Historical Branch in Portsmouth. **16** CB 3053 (3) Sections 85 to 89, pp. 16–17. **17** Quoted in the unpublished Volume III of the *Naval Staff History*. **18** This section was compiled from the unpublished Volume III of the *Naval Staff History*, draft p. 42 onwards. **19** CB 3053 (3) Sections 90 to 92, p. 17. **20** CB 3053 (3) Sections 114 to 117, p. 21–22. **21** CB 3053 (3), Sections 114 to 117, p. 21. **22** Quoted on p. 54 of the unpublished Volume III of the *Naval Staff History*. **23** CB 3053 (3) Sections 82 to 84, p. 16. **24** Fleet Air Arm Roll of Honour compiled by Captain F Milner RN and Captain R F Shercliff RN. **25** Shore-based reconnaissance assets would have been operated under fleet orders as a matter of course in the US and Japanese Navies. It is a measure of how far British pre-war defence policy had strayed from reality that Cunningham had to request support from a separate organisation that had its own agenda and priorities. By this stage in the battle it was already too late to seek such aid. **26** Quoted on p. 67 of the unpublished Volume III of the *Naval Staff History*. **27** Quoted on p. 70 of the unpublished Volume III of the *Naval Staff History*. **28** Admiral Iachino, *Gaudo e Matapan*, pp. 130–132, quoted on p. 70 of the unpublished Volume III of the *Naval Staff History*. **29** Quoted on p. 73 of the unpublished Volume III of the *Naval Staff History*. **30** *Dark Seas – The Battle of Cape Matapan* (Plymouth, Britannia Histories of World War II, University of Plymouth press, 2012), p. 91. **31** Quoted on p. 77 of the unpublished Volume III of the *Naval Staff History*.

Chapter 5 Operations in 1941 after the Battle of Matapan
1 Admiralty, CB 3053 (3), Naval Aircraft Periodical Summary Number 3 (London, July 1941) Sections 111 to 113, p. 20. **2** Admiralty, CB 3053 (4), Naval Aircraft Periodical Summary Number 4 (London, December 1941) Sections 156 to 160, p. 28. **3** Letter dated 22 November 1941 from Rear Admiral Aircraft Carriers Mediterranean to the Admiralty quoted in the unpublished Volume III of the *Naval Staff History*. **4** A copy of which is in the Naval Historical Branch in Portsmouth. **5** Quoted on p. 101 of the unpublished Volume III of the *Naval Staff History*. **6** Winston Churchill, *The Second World War* Volume III, *The Grand Alliance* (London, Penguin Books, 2005) p. 218. **7** Quoted on p. 105 of the unpublished Volume III of the *Naval Staff History*. **8** Captain E M Brown CBE DSC AFC RN, *Duels in the Sky – World War II Naval Aircraft in Combat* (Annapolis, Naval Institute Press, 1989) p. 36. **9** Owen Thetford, *British Naval Aircraft* (London, Putnam, 1982 edition) p. 163. **10** Quoted on p. 109 of the unpublished Volume III of the *Naval Staff History*. **11** Quoted on p. 125 of the unpublished Volume III of the *Naval Staff History*. **12** J David Brown, *Warship Losses of World War Two* (London, Arms and Armour Press, Revised Edition, 1995), p. 46. **13** Admiral of the Fleet Viscount Cunningham of Hyndhope KT GCB OM DSO, *A Sailor's Odyssey* (London, Hutchinson, 1951) p. 389. **14** Described in my earlier book *The Dawn of Carrier Strike* (Barnsley, Seaforth Publishing, 2019). **15** Force H letter A0148/41 quoted in the unpublished *Naval Staff History* Volume III in Section 21 on a page that was, unfortunately, not numbered. **16** This 'Holy Grail' of naval fighter requirements has appeared frequently over the decades but is still, in the twenty-first century, incapable of fulfilment. **17** Also quoted in the unpublished *Naval Staff History*, Volume III. **18** The type was not embarked in an operational aircraft carrier until 1947, its protracted development having spanned the whole of the Second World War. **19** Captain E M Brown CBE DSC AFC RN, *Wings of the Navy* (Manchester, Crecy Publishing, 2013) p. 162. **20** 601/563 dated 9 July 1941. **21** A/NAD676/41 dated 8 July 1941. **22** In which Captain Eric Brown served as a sub lieutenant and was awarded the DSC. **23** Barnsley, Seaforth Publishing, 2019. **24** The Short Mayo was a tandem flying boat and seaplane design in which a Short S.20 Mercury seaplane was carried on a trestle fitted on top of a Short S.21 Maia flying boat. The former

could be launched in flight to deliver mail as quickly as possible while the larger flying boat continued to its destination with ten passengers. The combination flew successfully in 1938 and made commercial flights to North America, Egypt and South Africa.

Chapter 6 Disembarked operations by naval air squadrons in 1941
1 There was a shortage of GP bombs, which made it necessary to include some SAP bombs. In its comments on the action reports, NAD commented that the best bomb for use in attacks on destroyers was the SAP with TDO 025 fuses. 2 J David Brown, *Warship Losses of World War Two* (London, Arms and Armour Press, 1995) p.43. 3 This section has been put together from notes in the unpublished Volume III of the *Naval Staff History*. 4 Admiralty, Naval Aircraft Progress Number 3 (London, July 1941) sections 106 to 110, p.20. 5 Admiralty, Naval Aircraft Progress Number 4 (London, December 1941) sections 143 to 147, pp.25–26. 6 David Hobbs, *The Royal Navy's Air Service in the Great War* (Barnsley, Seaforth Publishing, 2017), pp.146–149. 7 Air Chief Marshal Sir Arthur Longmore who had served in the RNAS prior to 1918. 8 He had won the VC serving with the Royal Naval Division in the First World War. 9 Quoted on p.119 in the unpublished Volume III of the *Naval Staff History*. 10 Unpublished *Naval Staff History* Volume III, unnumbered page. 11 The *Naval Staff History* does not make clear how an Australian cavalry unit came to be equipped with a crane in the first place. 12 Unpublished *Naval Staff History* Volume III, unnumbered page. 13 They had not been expected and their arrival caused a further air raid warning to be sounded at the airfield. 14 Unpublished *Naval Staff History* Volume III, unnumbered page. 15 Unpublished *Naval Staff History* Volume III, unnumbered page. 16 Unpublished *Naval Staff History* Volume III, Section 31. 17 Admiral of the Fleet Viscount Cunningham of Hyndhope KT GCB OM DSO, *A Sailor's Odyssey* (London, Hutchinson & Co, 1951) p.416. 18 Unpublished *Naval Staff History* Volume III Section 32. 19 According to the Appendix to a Memorandum from General Rommel to the German Liaison General at HQ Italian Armed Forces in Rome dated 1 September 1941, Rommel himself was interested in the matter. 20 *Warship Losses of World War Two*, p.52. 21 To a lesser extent, apparently, the British did the same. 22 Royal Army Service Corps. 23 No Italian records concerning losses on this day were found post-war to confirm these claims. 24 The day on which Japanese carrier-borne aircraft attacked the US Pacific Fleet at Pearl Harbor and the USA entered the war. 25 USN Bureau of Aeronautics. 26 *Seedie's List of Fleet Air Arm Awards* 1939–1969 (Ripley Registers, 1990) p.44. 27 They could even, possibly, have dated back to the First World War when Maconochie was the largest supplier of tinned rations to the British Army.

Chapter 7 Force H and the reinforcement of Malta
1 Data taken from the unpublished *Naval Staff History*, Volume III, Section 20, no page number. 2 *Fleet Air Arm Roll of Honour*, 2011 Edition, copies of which are held in the Fleet Air Arm archive of the National Museum of the Royal Navy and in the Author's own archive. 3 J David Brown, *Warship Losses of World War Two* (London, Arms and Armour Press, 1995 edition) p.48. 4 Quoted in the unpublished *Naval Staff History*, Section 24. 5 Identification Friend or Foe. 6 Described in Section 27 of the unpublished *Naval Staff History* Volume III. 7 *Fleet Air Arm Roll of Honour*. 8 Described in Section 28 of the unpublished *Naval Staff History* Volume III. 9 Known at the time as Asdic. 10 Brother of His Majesty King George VI. 11 Flag Officer Force H Letter Number 24 dated 18 November 1941, quoted in the unpublished *Naval Staff History* Volume III. 12 David Hobbs, *British Aircraft Carriers – Design, Development and Service Histories*, (Barnsley, Seaforth Publishing, 2013) p.78 et seq. 13 In 1941 the RN Torpedo Branch was responsible for all electrical systems and equipment in HM Ships. 14 When I did my sub lieutenant's course in 1967 the loss of *Ark Royal* was still a major teaching point at the Damage Control School in Portsmouth. A large perspex model of the ship, accurately compartmentalised, with the relevant pipes and pumps was used to show the various ways in which the ship could have been saved. The best, it was explained, would have been to flood the port boiler room while keeping a destroyer alongside to provide power. Thus restored to an even keel she could have been towed into Gibraltar, where there were dry docks large enough to repair her for

NOTES   419

passage to the USA. A package of work on her had already been planned after consultation with the USN. **15** The reports of the Board of Enquiry findings, together with the subsequent Bucknill Report and the papers detailing the court martial of Captain L E H Maund RN, can be found in The National Archive files ADM 156/204, ADM 156/205, ADM 156/206 and ADM 156/203. **16** She was the first large British warship to have a hull structure that was welded rather than riveted in order to keep her weight within Treaty limits. **17** *Naval Staff History*, Volume II, pp. 65–68. **18** Commanding Officer HMS *Argus* C.1884/34 dated 18 January 1942 to Flag Officer Force H. **19** Time on task plus the outbound and inbound flights from North Front. **20** When 812 NAS eventually left North Front to embark in *Argus*, it was considered advisable to continue to employ naval aircraft on anti-submarine patrols from North Front and in May 1942 both 813 and 824 NAS were disembarked from *Eagle* for a similar purpose. **21** Summarised in the unpublished *Naval Staff History* Volume III Section 34. **22** Underlined in original document. **23** This line of thought led to the creation of Mobile Operational Naval Air Bases, MONABS, with the British Pacific Fleet in 1945.

Chapter 8 Operations in North Africa, Malta and with Force H in 1942
1 The material for this part of Chapter 8 was drawn from the unpublished *Naval Staff History* Volume III) Section 35, p. 225. **2** Ray Sturtivant ISO with Mick Burrow, *Fleet Air Arm Aircraft 1939 to 1945* (Tunbridge Wells, Air Britain (Historians), 1995) p. 134. **3** Ibid., p. 134. **4** The cabin of the Albacore was large enough to carry more than the normal crew on non-operational flights such as this one. **5** Held in the Naval Historical Branch in Portsmouth. **6** It did not prove possible from extant records to identify which Allied submarine could have made this attack. It may well have been another U-boat. **7** *U-77* was finally sunk off Cartagena on 28 March 1943 by three RAF Hudsons. **8** She was eventually sunk by an RAAF Hudson on 16 June 1943. **9** Quoted in the unpublished *Naval Staff History* Section 35. **10** The heavy casualties suffered by German parachute forces in Crete may have been a disincentive. Losses against the Malta garrison fighting for their lives in built-up areas and among stone wall-bordered fields would have been considerably heavier. **11** David Hobbs, *British Aircraft Carriers – Design, Development and Histories* (Barnsley, Seaforth Publishing, 2013) p. 54. **12** *Wasp*: 20,500 tons full load; length 741ft 3in; beam 80ft 9in. *Ark Royal*: 27,720 tons full load; length 800ft; beam 94ft 9in. Data from J David Brown, *Aircraft Carriers – WW2 Fact Files* (London, Macdonald and Jane's Publishers, 1977) pp. 42 and 59. **13** CB 3053 (6) Section 136 et seq, pp. 27–31. **14** No doubt including many more tins of Maconochie beef and vegetable rations. **15** Bomber Command's own Pathfinder Force was eventually formed a year later and achieved excellent results. Air Chief Marshal Sir Arthur Harris had become AOC-in-C Bomber Command in February 1942 and one can only presume that he was loath to adopt any idea that seemed to have been evolved by the Fleet Air Arm rather than the RAF. **16** *Wasp* had returned to the USN and demonstrated the enormous reach of carrier air power by being redeployed with her air group to the Pacific. She was torpedoed and sunk by the Japanese submarine *I-19* off Guadalcanal on 15 September 1942. **17** Unpublished *Naval Staff History* Volume III Section 37, handwritten p. 239. **18** Fleet Air Arm Roll of Honour, copies of which are held by the National Museum of the Royal Navy at RNAS Yeovilton and in the author's archive. **19** J David Brown, *Warship Losses of World War Two* (London, Arms and Armour Press, 1995) p. 65. **20** Richard Woodman, *Malta Convoys 1940–1943* (London, John Murray, 2000) p. 337 et seq. **21** And in my experience has still not been adequately resolved in 2019. **22** The practice of early course alteration was later used extensively and effectively in convoys to North Russia. **23** Prime Minister to Mr R J Casey, UK Minister in Cairo; quoted in the unpublished *Naval Staff History* Volume III, Section 38, p. 249. **24** Ibid., p. 250. **25** Copies of which are held in the Naval Historical Branch in Portsmouth and The National Archive at Kew. **26** Quoted in the unpublished *Naval Staff History* Volume III, Section 38, p. 253.

Chapter 9 The Pedestal Convoy
1 Peter Shankland & Anthony Hunter, *Malta Convoy* (London, Collins, 1961) p. 99 et seq. **2** Admiralty, unpublished *Naval Staff History* Volume III, Section 39, pages pencilled in

as 256 onwards. **3** Sister-ship of the ill-fated *Kentucky* lost in the Harpoon convoy. **4** J David Brown, *Carrier Fighters* (London, Macdonald and Jane's, 1975) p. 84 et seq. **5** HQ RAF Middle East Signal to AHQ Mediterranean (Malta) dated 8 August 1942. **6** Quoted in the unpublished *Naval Staff History*, Volume III, pencilled p. 259. **7** *Carrier Fighters*, p. 85. **8** J David Brown, *Warship Losses of World War Two* (London, Arms & Armour Press, 1995) p. 67. **9** David Hobbs, *British Aircraft Carriers, Design, Development and Service Histories* (Barnsley, Seaforth Publishing, 2013) p. 54. **10** Admiralty, CB 3053 (6) Naval Aircraft progress and Operations Periodical Summary Number 6, Period ended 31 December 1942 (London, February 1943) Sections 118–119, pp. 20–23. **11** Unpublished *Naval Staff History* Volume III, pencilled p. 260 et seq. **12** Hugh Popham, *Sea Flight* (London, William Kimber, 1954) p. 127 et seq. **13** The colloquial name given by aircrew to their life-saving waistcoats. They provided buoyancy in the water and had pouches for survival equipment. **14** RN aircraft mechanics responsible for the engine. Riggers were responsible for the airframe. **15** Brevity code for an aircraft's recovery on deck. **16** Figures taken from analysis, post-war, of Italian records. **17** Sunrise was at 0653 local time. **18** Except for Hugh Popham's Sea Hurricane, which had been destroyed. **19** Andrew Thomas, *Royal Navy Aces of World War 2* (Oxford, Osprey Publishing, 2007) p. 37 et seq. **20** His final score when he died in 1944 was eleven confirmed victories. **21** *Sea Flight*, p. 136. **22** *Sea Flight*, p. 59. **23** Quoted in the unpublished *Naval Staff History* Volume III on pencilled p. 265. **24** Quoted in the unpublished *Naval Staff History* Volume III on pencilled p. 266. **25** CB 3053 (6) Section 116 p. 22. **26** Captain S W Roskill DSC RN, *The War at Sea* Volume II (London, Her Majesty's Stationary Office, 1956) pp. 305–307. **27** *Warship Losses of World War Two*, p. 67. **28** A court martial of her captain and senior officers held after their release from internment found that the decision to scuttle the ship had been premature. **29** The school was established at RNAS St Merryn in Cornwall in 1943. AFO 1884/43 described its aim and establishment. **30** p. 308.

Chapter 10 Operation Torch
1 This chapter is based on notes in the unpublished *Naval Staff History* Volume III Section 48. **2** Who had earlier replaced Admiral Sir Andrew Cunningham as C-in-C. **3** He was promoted to Admiral of the Fleet on 21 January 1943. **4** Admiralty, Naval Staff History, *Operation Torch*, BR 1736 (31) (London, Admiralty, Naval Historical Branch, 1948) contains more detail of the wider picture. **5** Rear Admiral (Aircraft Carriers) 306/5 dated 15 November 1942, Appendix II, quoted in the unpublished *Naval Staff History* on an unnumbered page. **6** J David Brown, *Carrier Operations in World War II*, Edited by David Hobbs (Barnsley, Seaforth Publishing, 2009), p. 62. **7** It is possible to drive through the tunnels and I have done so on several occasions, a fascinating experience. **8** Unpublished *Naval Staff History*, Section 49, pencilled p. 297. **9** Admiralty, CB 3053 (6), Naval Aircraft Progress and Operations, Periodical Summary Number 6 (London, February 1943), Section 100 p. 17. **10** A staunch advocate of naval aviation, he rose to the rank of captain after the war and was Director of the Naval Air Warfare Division when the political arguments about the projected new carrier *Queen Elizabeth*, CVA-01, reached their climax in 1966. His stalwart defence of policies that he knew to be right probably cost him his chance of being promoted to admiral. **11** This account of what happened is based on an interview between Barry Nation and J David Brown when the latter was Head of the Naval Historical Branch. **12** Quoted in the unpublished *Naval Staff History*, Volume III, Section 51, pencilled p. 314. **13** David Hobbs, *British Aircraft Carriers – Design, Development and Service Histories* (Barnsley, Seaforth Publishing, 2013), p. 133. **14** Ibid., p. 132. **15** Unpublished *Naval Staff History*, Volume III, Section 52, pencilled p. 322 et seq. **16** Unpublished *Naval Staff History*, Volume III (London, Admiralty), Section 55, p. (typed) 333 et seq. **17** Ray Sturtivant with Mick Burrow, *Fleet Air Arm Aircraft 1939 to 1945*, (Tunbridge Wells, Air-Britain Historians, 1995) p. 139. **18** Unpublished *Naval Staff History*, Volume III handwritten p. 334.

Chapter 11 The Allied invasions of Sicily and Italy in 1943
1 The chapter has used the unpublished *Naval Staff History* Volume III as a reference source, beginning with Section 58 on pencilled p. 345. **2** J David Brown, *Carrier Operations in World*

War II (Barnsley, Seaforth Publishing, 2009) p. 65. 3 Owen Thetford, *British Naval Aircraft since 1912* (London, Putnam, 1982 edition) pp, 333, 214. 4 The hit was on the equivalent side, to port, to that which had crippled *Ark Royal* on 13 November 1941. The prompt action taken shows firstly how much better RN damage control arrangements had become after analysis of the earlier carrier's loss and secondly, on reflection, what could have been done to save *Ark Royal*. The three shaft arrangements of the two ships was similar but obviously the arrangement of funnel uptakes on the starboard side under the island was not such a critical factor in *Indomitable*'s case since she was listing to port. 5 *Indomitable* was out of action until April 1944. 6 Designed as an aircraft maintenance carrier but with full operational facilities as well as the extra hangar and workshop facilities. She was effectively the prototype light fleet carrier. 7 Unpublished *Naval Staff History*, Volume III, pencilled p. 348. 8 Ibid., section 59, pencilled p. 350. 9 The 1942 light fleet carrier building programme was the largest aircraft carrier construction programme in RN history. 10 May 1943 was subsequently taken to be the turning point of the Battle of the Atlantic and its fiftieth anniversary was celebrated in Liverpool during 1993. 11 David Hobbs, *British Aircraft Carriers – Design, Development and Service Histories* (Barnsley, Seaforth Publishing, 2013) p. 139 et seq. 12 All Seafire IICs had three-bladed propellers intended to give the best performance at medium altitude. 13 Captain S W Roskill DSC RN, *The War at Sea*, Volume III Part 1 (London, Her Majesty's Stationary Office, 1960) p. 149 et seq. 14 Admiralty, Battle Summary #37, *The Invasion of Italy – Landing at Salerno – Operation Avalanche* (London, Admiralty, 1946) p. 8 et seq. 15 Admiralty, CB 3053 (8), Naval Aircraft Progress and Operations, Periodical Summary Number 8 for the period ended 31 December 1943 (London, Naval Air Warfare Division, 1944), Section 254 et seq, p. 34 et seq. 16 The first operational Barracuda squadron to be embarked in a carrier. 17 Recently promoted from captain to rear admiral, he remained in command until 22 September 1943. 18 The Fighter Flight of a composite Seafire/Swordfish NAS. 19 As note 18 above. 20 J David Brown, *The Seafire – The Spitfire that went to Sea* (London, Greenhill Books, 1989) p. 46 et seq. 21 Admiralty, CB 3053 (8), p. 34 et seq. 22 Later known as the 'Homer'. 23 Hugh Popham, *Sea Flight*, (London, William Kimber, 1954) p. 175. 24 Admiralty, CB 3053 (8), Section 263, p. 36. 25 *The Seafire*, p. 49 et seq. 26 Unpublished *Naval Staff History* Volume III, Section 66, pencilled p. 366 et seq. 27 The Seafire LIIC had a four-bladed propeller, unlike the IIC's three-bladed unit, in order to gain the maximum engine thrust at low level. Even so, it was not quite as fast as the Seafire IB, which was the fastest naval fighter in the world in 1943. 28 Unpublished *Naval Staff History* Volume III, Section 67, pencilled p. 368. 29 When I flew Hawker Hunters in the 1970s, a later type of anti-G suit enabled me to pull 6 or more G without blacking out. 30 Admiralty, CB 3053 (8), p. 39.

Chapter 12 Operation Dragoon
1 J David Brown, *Carrier Operations in World War II* (Barnsley, Seaforth Publishing, 2009) p. 67. 2 David Hobbs, *British Aircraft Carriers – Design, Development and Service Histories*, (Barnsley, Seaforth Publishing, 2013) pp. 90, 91, 98. 3 Ibid., p. 140 et seq. 4 Admiralty, Unpublished Naval Staff History, *The Development of British Naval Aviation 1919–1945* Volume III (London, Admiralty, undated) Section 68, pencilled p. 373 et seq. 5 The Admiralty changed the RN name of the Grumman F4F from Martlet to Wildcat on 1 January 1944 to give commonality with USN nomenclature and avoid any confusion in joint ventures. The name Wildcat had, in any case, been in everyday use within the RN for over a year. 6 Named after RAEC's illustrious ancestor, who was captain of HMS *Culloden* at the battles of Cape St Vincent and the Nile. Its inclusion in TG 88.1 was fortuitous but appropriate. 7 Between January 1943 and the end of May 1944, U-boats had sunk sixty-nine ships of about 318,000 gross registered tons in the Mediterranean but by August their efforts had petered out. 8 Admiralty, BR 1736(36), Battle Summary Number 43, *Invasion of the South of France* (London, Admiralty 1950). 9 Sunrise was at 0639 on 15 August 1944. Sunset was at 2035. 10 Battle Summary Number 43, p. 34. 11 HMS *Pursuer*, Report of Proceedings, M010202/44 at the National Archive, Kew, p. 3. 12 A copy of Sub Lieutenant Banks' letter is in the author's collection and another in the archive of the Fleet Air Arm Section of the

National Museum of the Royal Navy. **13** Experience taught the lesson that only one firing pass should be made on a strafing attack. Carry out two or more and the enemy gunners are certainly going to get the attacking aircraft's measure and get hits on it. It was drummed into pilots of the BPF in 1945 that a second firing pass was tantamount to suicide. In this instance Sub Lieutenant Shaw was lucky. **14** David Hobbs, *Royal Navy Escort Carriers* (Liskeard, Maritime Books, 2003) p.211. **15** Figures for the RN CVEs that took part in Operation Dragoon sorties were collated post-war from Admiralty records and listed in the unpublished *Naval Staff History* Volume III handwritten p.383. **16** Quoted in the unpublished *Naval Staff History* Volume III, which gives a further reference on the old National Archive cataloguing system as Case 7825. RAEC's Report of Proceedings, on which these paragraphs are based, has as its own reference RAEC A.01762/44 dated 11 September 1944. **17** Five of the 1942-design light fleet carriers, one of them RAN, did operate in the assault carrier role during the Korean War from 1950 to 1953 with considerable success. The Admiralty view of their usefulness was, therefore, entirely correct but too early. **18** AWD 2445/44 in the old National Archive cataloguing system as Case 7825 and quoted in the unpublished *Naval Staff History* Volume III.

Chapter 13 The final series of carrier operations in the Mediterranean
1 Material for this chapter has been researched, partially, from the unpublished *Naval Staff History* Volume III Section 71, p.390 onwards. **2** J David Brown, *Carrier Operations in World War II* (Barnsley, Seaforth Publishing, 2009) p.70, was used to compile the aircraft carriers in Force A and both the type and number of aircraft embarked in them. **3** Theo Ballance, Lee Howard and Ray Sturtivant, *The Squadrons of the Fleet Air Arm* (Stapleford, West Sussex, Air Britain Publishing, 2016); relevant squadron entries were used to compile the names of NAS commanding officers at the beginning of Operation Outing. **4** RAEC's Reports of Proceeding are held at the National Archive at Kew under the old catalogue reference Case 7759. They are quoted in the unpublished *Naval Staff History* Volume III and by notes in the collection of the Naval Historical Branch in Portsmouth. **5** Roughly 75 per cent of the bunker capacity of an *Illustrious* class fleet carrier. **6** A technique that had been used by the RNAS in the First World War. **7** An RN Air Station until it was captured in 1941 during bitter fighting. **8** Each carrying about twenty troops. **9** The Royal Netherlands Navy formed its own Swordfish squadron, 860 NAS, within the Fleet Air Arm but a number of pilots were also flying fighters by 1944, many of them in 800 NAS. Subsequently promoted to Lieutenant Commander, De Wit became the commanding officer of 800 NAS on 20 May 1945. **10** *Emperor*'s Report quoted in the unpublished *Naval Staff History* Volume III, Section 76, pencilled p.404. **11** Described as 'landing in the lap of the Gods' in reports quoted in the unpublished *Naval Staff History*, Volume III, pencilled p.407. **12** For more detailed information about this period, see my earlier book *The Dawn of Carrier Strike* (Barnsley, Seaforth Publishing, 2019).

Chapter 14 Retrospection
1 Over 22,000 Spitfires were manufactured before production ceased. **2** A specialisation the RAF had described as 'unnecessary' in the 1920s. **3** See the table in Chapter 1. **4** This was not something that happened in the RAF, where all senior officers had to be qualified as pilots. **5** I cannot imagine what Admiral Boyd and other officers of the wartime generation would think of this. **6** In my front-line flying days the phrase 'all the Ps' was still in use – Prior Practice Prevents Poor Performance. **7** It used to be said that 'they little realised when they landed on 11 November 1940 that they had earned a free dinner for the rest of their lives'.

Appendix D
1 Disembarked from *Argus* by lighter in Takoradi and assembled ashore. **2** One crashed in sea before reaching Takoradi. **3** One crashed on take-off.

Bibliography

Primary Sources

CB 3307(1), *Naval Staff History of the Second World War, The Development of British Naval Aviation 1919–1945* Volume I, London, Naval Historical Branch, Admiralty, 1954.

CB 3307(2), *Naval Staff History of the Second World War, The Development of British Naval Aviation 1919–1945* Volume II, London, Naval Historical Branch, Admiralty, 1956.

Unpublished, *Naval Staff History of the Second World War, The Development of British Naval Aviation 1919–1945* Volume III, Unpublished notes drafted by the Naval Historical Branch, undated.

BR 1736 (6), *Naval Staff History of the Second World War, Selected Operations (Mediterranean) 1940* – Battle Summary Number 10, *Operation MB 8 and FAA Attack on Taranto*, London, Naval Historical Branch, Admiralty, undated.

Flight Deck, the Admiralty restricted journal on naval aviation matters, Volume I Number 1 August 1944 to Volume II number 5 January 1946, London, Naval Air Division, Admiralty.

CB 3081(27), Battle Summary Number 35, *The Invasion of Sicily Operation – Husky*, London, Naval Historical Branch, Admiralty, 1946.

BR 1736(30), Battle Summary Number 37, *The Invasion of Italy – Landing at Salerno – Operation Avalanche – Naval Operations 9 September 1943*, London, Naval Historical Branch, Admiralty, 1946.

BR 1736(31), Battle Summary Number 38, *Operation Torch – Invasion of North Africa November 1942 to February 1943*, London, Naval Historical Branch, Admiralty, 1948.

BR 1736(35), Battle Summary Number 35, The Battle of Cape Matapan 28 March 1941, London, Naval Historical Branch, Admiralty, 1949.

BR 1736(36), Battle Summary Number 43, *Invasion of the South of France, Operation Dragoon, 15 August 1944*, London, Naval Historical Branch, Admiralty, 1950.

CB 3053(1), *Naval Aircraft Periodical Summary* Number 1, period ended 20 September 1940, London, Naval Air Division, Admiralty, October 1940.

CB 3053(2), *Naval Aircraft Periodical Summary* Number 2, period ended 3 February 1941, London, Naval Air Division, Admiralty, February 1941.

CB 3053(3), *Naval Aircraft Periodical Summary* Number 3, period ended 13 July 1941, London, Naval Air Division, Admiralty, July 1941.

CB 3053(4), *Naval Aircraft Progress and Operations Periodical Summary* Number 4, period ended 25 December 1941, London, Naval Air Division, Admiralty, December 1941.

CB 3052(5), *Naval Aircraft Progress and Operations Periodical Summary* Number 5, period ended 30 June 1942, London, Naval Air Division, Admiralty, June 1942.

CB 3053(6), *Naval Aircraft Progress and Operations Periodical Summary* Number 6, period ended 31 December 1942, London, Naval Air Division, Admiralty, February 1943.

CB 3053(7), *Naval Aircraft Progress and Operations Periodical Summary* Number 7, period ended 30 June 1943, London, Naval Air Division, Admiralty, August 1943.

CB 3053(8), *Naval Aircraft Progress and Operations Periodical Summary* Number 8, period ended 31 December 1943, London, Naval Air Division, Admiralty, February 1944.

CB 3053(9), *Naval Aircraft Progress and Operations Periodical Summary* Number 9, period ended 30 June 1944, London, Naval Air Division, Admiralty, September 1944.
CB 3053(10), *Naval Aircraft Progress and Operations Periodical Summary*, period ended 31 December 1944, London, Naval Air Division, Admiralty, March 1945.
CB 3053(11), *Naval Aircraft Progress and Operations Periodical Summary*, period ended 30 June 1945, London, Naval Air Division, Admiralty, September 1945.
AP(N) 71, *Manual of Naval Airmanship*, London, Admiralty, 1949 edition.
Admiralty, *The Admiralty – A Guide for Newcomers* (London, 1961 edition).
AP(N) 144, *Naval Aircraft Handbook* (London, Admiralty, 1958 edition).

Published Secondary Sources

Andrews, C F & Morgan E B, *Supermarine Aircraft since 1914* (London, Putnam, 1981).
Apps, Michael, Lieutenant Commander, *Send Her Victorious* (London, William Kimber, 1971).
Apps, Michael, Lieutenant Commander, *The Four Ark Royals* (London, William Kimber, 1976).
Bachelor, Len, *Supermarine Seafires (Merlins)*, Aircraft Profile 221 (Windsor, Profile Publications, 1971).
Ballance, Theo with Howard, Lee & Sturtivant, Ray, *The Squadrons and Units of the Fleet Air Arm* (Staplefield, Air-Britain Publishing, 2016).
Brown, D K, *Nelson to Vanguard – Warship Design and Development 1923–1945* (London, Chatham Publishing, 2000).
Brown, Eric M, CBE DSC AFC RN, Captain, *Wings on My Sleeve* (London, Weidenfield & Nicolson, 2006 revised edition).
Brown, Eric M, CBE DSC AFC RN, Captain, *Duels in the Sky – World War II Naval* Aircraft *in Combat* (Annapolis, Naval Institute Press, 1988).
Brown, Eric M, CBE DSC AFC RN, Captain, *Wings of the Navy* (London, Jane's Publishing, 1980).
Brown, Eric M, CBE DSC AFC RN, Captain, *Seafire* – From the Cockpit 13 (Ringshall, Ad Hoc Publications, 2010).
Brown, J David, (Edited by David Hobbs) *Carrier Operations in World War II* (Barnsley, Seaforth Publishing, 2009).
Brown, J David, *HMS Illustrious – Operational History* – Warship Profile 11 (Windsor, Profile Publications, 1971).
Brown, J David, *Supermarine Walrus & Seagull Variants* – Aircraft Profile 224 (Windsor, Profile Publications, 1971).
Brown, J David, *Carrier Air Groups – HMS Eagle* (Windsor, Hylton Lacy Publishers, 1972).
Brown, J David, *HMS Eagle* – Warship Profile 35 (Windsor, Profile Publications, 1973).
Brown, J David, *Fairey Fulmar Marks I & II*, Aircraft Profile 254 (Windsor, Profile Publications, 1973).
Brown, J David, *Carrier Fighters* (London, Macdonald & Jane's, 1975).
Brown, J David, *Aircraft Carriers – WW2 Fact Files* (London, Macdonald & Jane's, 1977).
Brown, J David, *The Seafire* (London, Greenhill Books, 1989 edition).
Brown, J David, *Warship Losses of World War Two* (London, Arms and Armour Press, 1995 edition).
Brown, J David, *The Road to Oran – Anglo-French Naval Relations September 1939–July 1940* (London, Taylor & Francis, 2004).
Cernuschi, Enrico & O'Hara, Vincent P, *Taranto: the Raid and the Aftermath*, a feature article in Warship 2010 (London, Conway, 2010).
Crosley, R, DSC, Commander RN, *They Gave Me a Seafire* (Shrewsbury, Airlife, 1986).
Cunningham, Viscount of Hyndhope, KT GCB OM DSO, Admiral of the Fleet, *A Sailor's Odyssey* (London, Hutchinson, 1951).
Ellis, Paul, *Aircraft of the Royal Navy* (London, Jane's Publishing, 1982).
Foster, David R, DSO DSC* RNVR, *Wings Over the Sea* (Canterbury, Harrop Press, 1990).
Friedman, Norman, *Fighters Over the Fleet* (Barnsley, Seaforth Publishing, 2016).
Friedman, Norman, *British Carrier Aviation* (London, Conway Maritime Press, 1988).
Gardiner, Leslie, *The British Admiralty* (Edinburgh, William Blackwood & Sons, 1968).

Green, William, *Famous Bombers of the Second World War* (London, Macdonald, 1959).
Green, William, *Famous Fighters of the Second World War Second Series* (London, Macdonald, 1962).
Hanson, Norman, *Carrier Pilot* (Cambridge, Patrick Stephens, 1979).
Harrison, W A, *Fairey Swordfish and Albacore* (Marlborough, The Crowood Press, 2002).
Hermon Gill, G, *Royal Australian Navy* Volume One 1939–1942 & Volume Two 1942–1945 (Canberra, Australian War Memorial, 1957 & 1968).
Hezlet, Sir Arthur, KBE CB DSO DSC, Vice Admiral, *Aircraft and Sea Power* (London, Peter Davies, 1970).
Hobbs, David, *Aircraft Carriers of the Royal and Commonwealth Navies* (London, Greenhill Books, 1996).
Hobbs, David, *Royal Navy Escort Carriers* (Liskeard, Maritime Books, 2003).
Hobbs, David, *British Aircraft Carriers – Design, Development and Service Histories* (Barnsley, Seaforth Publishing, 2013).
Hobbs, David, *The Dawn of Carrier Strike* (Barnsley, Seaforth Publishing, 2019).
Holmes, Robin, *The Battle of Heligoland Bight 1939 – The Royal Air Force and the Luftwaffe's Baptism of Fire* (London, Grub Street, 2009).
Horsley, Terence, Lieutenant Commander RNVR, *Find, Fix and Strike – The Story of the Fleet Air Arm* (London, Eyre & Spottiswoode, 1943).
Howse, Derek, *Radar at Sea – The Royal Navy in World War 2* (Basingstoke, Macmillan Press for the Naval Radar Trust, 1993).
Jenkins, C A, Commander, *HMS Furious Part II 1925–1948* – Warship Profile 24 (Windsor, Profile Publications, 1972).
Jones, Ben, Editor, *The Fleet Air Arm in the Second World War* (Farnham, Ashgate Publishing for the Navy Records Society, 2012).
Judd, Donald, *Avenger from the Sky* (London, William Kimber, 1985).
King, H F, *Armament of British Aircraft 1909–1939* (London, Putnam, 1971).
Lamb, Charles, DSO DSC, Commander RN, *War in a Stringbag* (London, Cassell, 1977).
Lavery, Brian, *Churchill's Navy – The Ships, Men and Organisation 1939–1945* (London, Conway, 2006).
Lenton H T & Colledge J J, *Warships of World War II* (Shepperton, Ian Allan, 1968 edition).
The London Gazette, *The Fleet Air Arm Attack on Taranto* (London, Published by Authority, 24 July 1947).
Lowry, Thomas P & Wellham, John W G, *The Attack on Taranto – Blueprint for Pearl Harbor* (Mechanicsburg, Stackpole Books, 1995).
Lyon, David J, *HMS Illustrious – Technical History* – Warship Profile 10 (Windsor, Profile Publications, 1971).
MacBean, John A, Wing Commander & Hogben, Arthur S, Major, *Bombs Gone – The Development and Use of British Air-dropped weapons from 1912 to the Present Day* (Wellingborough, Patrick Stephens Limited, 1990).
Macintyre, Donald, *Fighting Admiral – The Life of Admiral of the Fleet Sir James Somerville GCB GBE DSO* (London, Evans Brothers, 1961).
Macintyre, Donald, *The Battle for the Mediterranean* (London, Batsford, 1964).
Macintyre, Donald, *Wings of Neptune – The Story of Naval Aviation* (London, Peter Davies, 1963).
Mason, Francis K, *The Hawker Hurricane* (London, Macdonald, 1962).
Mason, Francis K, *Hawker Aircraft since 1920* (London, Putnam, 1993 edition).
McCart, Neil, *HMS Victorious 1937–1969* (Cheltenham, Fan Publications, 1998).
McCart, Neil, *Three Ark Royals 1938–1999* (Cheltenham, Fan Publications, 1999).
McCart, Neil, *The Illustrious and Implacable classes of Aircraft Carrier* (Cheltenham, Fan Publications, 2000).
Milner F, Captain RN & Shercliff, R F, Captain RN, *The Fleet Air Arm Roll of Honour*, created in association with the Naval Historical Branch and the Fleet Air Arm Museum, 2011.
Newton, Don & Hampshire, A Cecil, *Taranto* (London, William Kimber, 1959).
O'Hara, Vincent P *Six Victories – North Africa, Malta and the Mediterranean Convoy War November 1941 – March 1942* (Annapolis, Naval Institute Press, 2019).

Pack, S W C, *The Battle of Matapan* (London, Batsford, 1961).
Pack, S W C, *Night Action Off Cape Matapan* (Shepperton, Ian Allan, 1972).
Pack, S W C, *The Battle for Crete* (Shepperton, Ian Allan, 1973).
Pack, S W C, *The Battle of Sirte* (Shepperton, Ian Allan, 1975).
Pack, S W C, *Invasion North Africa 1942* (Shepperton, Ian Allan, 1978).
Payne, Donald, *Swordfish* – From the Cockpit 10 (Ringshall, Ad Hoc Publications, 2008).
Phillips, Lawrie, TD RD, Lieutenant Commander RNR, *The Royal Navy Day by Day* (Stroud, the History Press, 2018 edition).
Poolman, Kenneth, *Illustrious* (London, William Kimber, 1955).
Poolman, Kenneth, *Ark Royal* (London, William Kimber, 1956).
Poolman, Kenneth, *Night Strike from Malta – 830 Squadron and Rommel's Convoys* (London, Jane's Publishing, 1980).
Popham, Hugh, *Sea Flight*, London, William Kimber, 1954).
Popham, Hugh, *Into Wind – A History of British Naval Flying* (London, Hamish Hamilton, 1969).
Reece, Michael, Colonel, *Flying Royal Marines* (Eastney, Royal Marines' Historical Society, 2012).
Reeve, John & Stevens, David, Editors, *The Face of Naval Battle* (Crows Nest NSW, Allen & Unwin, 2003).
Rowe, Anthony, *Seedie's List of Fleet Air Arm Awards 1939–1969* (Chippenham, Ripley Registers, 1990).
Rodger, N A M, *The Admiralty* (Lavenham, Terence Dalton, 1979).
Roskill, Stephen, Captain RN, History of the Second World War – *The War at Sea* Volumes I to Volume III Part II.
Roskill, Stephen, *Naval Policy Between the Wars* Volume I *The Period of Anglo-American Antagonism 1919–1929* (Barnsley, Seaforth Publishing, 2016).
Roskill, Stephen, *Naval Policy Between the Wars* Volume II *The Period of Reluctant Rearmament 1930–1939* (Barnsley, Seaforth Publishing, 2016).
Ross, Andrew T & Sandison James M with a forward by Jack McCaffrie, *A Historical Appreciation of the Contribution of Naval Air Power*, Papers in Australian Maritime Affairs Number 26 (Canberra, Sea Power Centre – Australia, 2008).
Shankland, Peter & Hunter, Anthony, *Malta Convoy* (London, Collins, 1961).
Schofield, B B, Vice Admiral, *The Attack on Taranto* (Shepperton, Ian Allan, 1973).
Smith, Peter C, *Eagle's War* (Crecy Books, 1995).
Smith, Peter C & Walker, Edwin, *The Battles of the Malta Striking Forces* (Shepperton, Ian Allen, 1974).
Stevens, David, Editor, *The Royal Australian Navy in World War II* (Crows Nest, Allen & Unwin, 2005 edition).
Stott, Ian G, *Fairey Swordfish Marks I to IV*, Aircraft Profile 212 (Windsor, profile Publications, undated).
Sturtivant, Ray, *British Naval Aviation* (London, Arms & Armour Press, 1990).
Sturtivant, Ray with Burrow, Mick, *Fleet Air Arm Aircraft 1939 to 1945* (Tunbridge Wells, Air-Britain (Historians), 1995).
Taylor, H A, *Fairey Aircraft since 1915* (London, Putnam, 1974).
Thetford, Owen, *British Naval Aircraft since 1912* (London, Putnam, 1982 edition).
Thomas, Andrew, *Royal Navy Aces of World War 2* (Oxford, Osprey Publishing, 2007).
Till, Geoffrey, *Air Power and the Royal Navy 1914–1945 – a Historical Survey* (London, Jane's Publishing, 1979).
University of Plymouth Press, *Dark Seas – The Battle of Cape Matapan* (Plymouth, 2012).
Vian, Sir Philip, GCB KBE DSO, Admiral of the Fleet, *Action this Day – A War Memoir* (London, Frederick Muller, 1960).
Wellham, John, *With Naval Wings – the Autobiography of a Fleet Air Arm Pilot in World War II* (Staplehurst, Spellmount, 1995).
Woodman, Richard, *Malta Convoys 1940–1943* (London, John Murray (Publishers), 2000).
Woods, Gerard A, *Wings at Sea – A Fleet Air Arm Observer's War 1940–45* (London, Conway Maritime Press, 1985).

Index

Abdiel, HMS 147
Abrams, A H, Lieutenant Commander RN 310
Abruzzi, Italian Cruiser 65, 126, 128
Adams, L A, Sub Lieutenant (A) RNVR 301
Admiralty viii, 1–7, 14, 15, 19, 20, 27, 29–31, 39, 46, 55, 84, 103–105, 110, 121, 122, 129, 140, 147, 150, 158–161, 167, 178, 192, 195, 200, 210, 211, 221, 222, 227, 230, 237, 241, 243, 248, 249, 270, 278, 279, 282, 308, 310, 313, 314, 316, 319–321, 344, 345, 347, 355, 370–373, 393, 397, 398, 401
Airfields
  Ajaccio 361, 365
  Alghero 34, 199, 365
  Bardia 94, 185, 186, 188
  Beirut 237, 311
  Benina 124, 185
  Berka 185, 188, 225, 311
  Blida 283, 285, 286, 294–297, 300, 310, 312
  Bone 286, 310, 312
  Cagliari 33, 34, 41, 45, 196, 201, 265
  Casabianda 356, 361
  Castelvetrano 338, 340
  Castiglione 354
  Catania 32, 96, 147
  Comiso 96, 147
  Derna 185, 188
  Didjelli 286, 305
  El Adem 144, 188, 189, 191, 225, 236
  El Daba 188, 237, 311
  Eleusis 120, 127
  Elmas 41, 45, 104, 262
  Fort Maddalena 181, 186, 191
  Fuka 44, 181, 186, 188, 191, 225, 311
  Gambut 183, 185, 186, 188, 189, 225, 236
  Gazala 183, 185, 186, 188
  Habbaniya 165, 166
  Haifa 172, 175, 237, 311
  Hal Far 28, 31, 32, 113–118, 140, 146, 149, 163, 224, 229, 311, 401, 402
  Heraklion 93, 118, 157, 170, 381
  Hurghada 178, 246
  La Lourmel 286, 292
  La Senia 284, 286, 289–294, 308
  LG 05 236
  LG 104 237
  LG 109 181, 186
  LG 123 181, 186, 187, 189, 191
  LG 128 187
  Lydda 172, 175, 311
  Ma'aten Bagush 34, 35, 37, 38, 43, 178, 181, 182, 185, 186, 188, 190, 191, 225, 226, 236, 237
  Maison Blanche 283, 286, 292, 296, 300, 301
  Maritza 42
  Martuba 183, 185, 188
  Mersa Matruh 44, 175, 180, 181, 239, 311
  Montecorvino 324, 327, 336, 338, 339
  Nicosia 172–175
  North Front 160, 195, 210, 217, 219, 245, 392
  Paestum 338, 339
  Paramythia 120–122, 126
  Ramat David 175
  Shaibah 165, 166, 168, 169
  Sidi-Barrani 34–38, 181, 185, 188, 191, 225, 236
  Sidi Heneish 180, 185, 187, 190, 191
  Sidi-Omar 186
  Sollum 186, 188
  Tafaroui 284, 286, 290–293, 310, 312
  Tmimi 183, 185, 186
  Tobruk 190, 191
Ajax, HMS 43, 81, 126, 147, 173
Alagi, Italian Submarine 276
Albatross, HMS 14
Alexander, A V, First Lord of the Admiralty 4

Alexandria 19, 21, 26, 34, 39, 41, 47, 56, 58, 59, 82, 89, 96, 103, 122, 125, 127, 135, 145–147, 154, 156, 157, 177, 178, 184, 186, 188, 223, 225, 244, 310, 316, 366, 375, 378, 381, 382, 386–389, 391, 392, 395
Alfieri, Italian Destroyer 72, 76, 135
Algiers 200, 239
Allingham, H P, Lieutenant RNR 189
Almeria Lykes, SS 249, 277
Amara 167
Ancon, USS 329, 334, 345
Andrea Doria, Italian Battleship 64, 71, 73, 76, 111
Antelope, HMS 239, 249
Aphis, HMS 190
Aquila, Italian Aircraft Carrier 137
Aquilone, Italian Destroyer 42
Arethusa, HMS 196, 198, 245, 310
Argonaut, HMS 285
Argus, HMS 8, 27–30, 33, 34, 51, 204, 205, 207, 210, 211, 213, 218, 228, 237–241, 249, 250, 252, 254, 279, 284, 285, 288, 289, 294, 295, 303–305, 307, 308, 410
Ark Royal, HMS 7, 11–14, 16–19, 21, 27, 33, 34, 40, 41, 43, 45, 46, 83, 87, 89–92, 95, 104, 106, 110–113, 143, 144, 147–151, 153, 154, 159, 192, 193, 195–208, 210–220, 222, 228, 229, 241, 280, 303, 395, 410, 413
Arnold, G F, Sub Lieutenant 236
Arthey, Leading Torpedoman RN 38
Ash, A H M, Lieutenant RN 169
Ashanti, HMS 249, 276, 301
Ashburner, C, Lieutenant RN 31
Astin, A R, Sub Lieutenant (A) RNVR 189, 301
Athene, HMS 211, 219
Atrope, Italian Submarine 182
Attacker, HMS 320, 321, 326–328, 330, 339, 340, 342, 351, 353, 355, 356, 358, 366, 367, 375, 378, 379, 381, 387–389, 392
Attenborough, N G, Sub Lieutenant (A) RN 112
Augusta 32, 36
Aurora, HMS 185, 210, 382, 383, 390, 391
Australia, HMAS 15
Avenger, HMS 282, 285, 287–289, 293, 294, 303–307, 321
Axum, Italian Submarine 276

Badsworth, HMS 239
Bailey, C P, Sub Lieutenant (A) RN 124

Bailey, R A, Sub Lieutenant (A) RN 66, 84
Baldwin, C P H, Leading Airman RN 165
Baldwin, G C, Lieutenant Commander (A) RN 291, 350, 356, 376
Baleno, Italian Destroyer 73, 76
Balme, D E, Lieutenant 236
Banks, R R, Sub Lieutenant (A) RNVR 362
Bardia 181, 182, 239
Barham, HMS 16, 18, 126, 145, 147, 157, 186
Barker, R P, Sub Lieutenant 236
Barnes, F A, Petty Officer RN 198
Barrett, J G, Sub Lieutenant (A) RNVR 366
Bartolomeo Colleoni, Italian Cruiser 27, 47
Basore, H H, Lieutenant USN 356
Basra 165, 166
Bass, H B, Lieutenant Commander USN 356
Battler, HMS 321, 326–328, 331, 337, 339, 350, 351
Bayly, G W L A, Lieutenant RN 67, 75, 84
Beale, G, Commander RN 40, 127, 128
Beattie, D M, Sub Lieutenant (A) RN 106
Bedouin, HMS 239, 241
Beirut 173, 175
Bell-Davies, R, Rear Admiral 91, 169
Benghazi 22, 42, 124, 152, 185, 188, 224, 225, 310
Bermuda, HMS 285, 298, 299
Berwick, HMS 60, 89
Bibby, R E, Lieutenant (A) RN 132
Bicester, HMS 249
Biddle, J G, Sub Lieutenant (A) RN 194
Bird, F D G, Major RM 283, 315, 325
Birmingham, HMS 245
Bisset, A W la T, Rear Admiral 122, 353, 37
Biter, HMS 284, 287–291, 293, 294, 299, 307
Bizerta 149, 306
Black, A F, Lieutenant Commander RN 119, 177, 178
Blackburn Skua viii, 9, 13, 14, 16, 18, 19, 28, 33, 34, 87, 90, 91, 111, 113, 144, 159, 404
Black Prince, HMS 380, 381, 383, 391
Blankney, HMS 239
Blenkhorn, G L, Petty Officer RN 132
Boddam-Whetham, A P, Lieutenant RN 261
Bolt, A S, Lieutenant Commander RN 133, 134, 176
Bolzano, Italian Cruiser 24, 65, 73, 111, 126
Bomba Bay 36, 38, 43
Bone 31

INDEX

Boosey, S L, Leading Airman 173
Borea, Italian Destroyer 42
Bovell, H C, Captain RN 29, 252, 283
Bowker, D G, Lieutenant RN 199
Bowker, J, Midshipman (A) RN 67
Boxall, RFA 278
Boyd, Sir Denis, Rear Admiral 40, 57, 58, 74, 82, 84, 88, 98, 100, 101, 103, 122, 127, 130, 132, 135, 156, 170, 398, 402
Brabner, R A, Lieutenant Commander (A) RNVR 238, 252, 257, 265
Bradshaw, R E, Lieutenant (A) RN 236, 312
Bramham, HMS 249, 275, 277
Breconshire, HMS 145, 147, 196
Bretagne, FS 10, 12
Brewster Buffalo 119
Bridge, A R M, Captain RN 84
Brindisi 121, 185
Brisbane Star, MV 249, 276–278, 280
Brown, E M 'Winkle', Captain RN 150, 159
Brown, J M, Sub Lieutenant (A) RNVR 225
Brownlee, P, Sub Lieutenant (A) RNVR 259
Bruen, J M, Lieutenant Commander RN 122, 126, 147, 151, 155, 252, 265, 284, 290
Brunt, A, Sub Lieutenant (A) RNZNVR 236
Bryant, R, Sub Lieutenant (A) RNVR 180
Buchanan-Dunlop, D K, Lieutenant Commander RN 252
Bugden, W H, Leading Airman RN 225
Bull, W A, Sub Lieutenant (A) RN 67
Bulolo, HMS 286, 300
Bulteel, T O, Captain RN 252, 283, 291
Burat el Sun 124
Burrough, Sir Harold, Rear Admiral 209, 249, 256, 276, 286, 298, 303
Buscall, J, Sub Lieutenant (A) RNVR 67

Caio Duilio, Italian Battleship 64, 73, 75, 76, 78, 81, 113
Cairo, HMS 239, 241, 249, 276
Calabria 21, 25, 26, 27
Calcutta, HMS 39, 147, 157
Caldecott-Smith, J A, Lieutenant RN 121
Caledon, HMS 356
Cambell, N K, Lieutenant RN 31
Cameron, D, Sub Lieutenant (A) RNZNVR 341
Campioni, I, Italian Admiral 22–26, 46
Cape Spartivento 89, 91, 232
Carducci, Italian Destroyer 72, 76
Carline, G A, Lieutenant RN 67
Carlisle, D G, Lieutenant Commander (A) SANF(V) 355, 375

Carlisle, HMS 147, 157
Carlyle, R, Petty Officer RN 148
Carver, R H P, Lieutenant RN 252, 283, 315, 325
Cary, D A, Sub Lieutenant RCNVR 367
Casey, C R, Sub Lieutenant (A) RNVR 232, 242
Catoctin, USS 359, 360
Cavour, Italian Battleship 22, 64, 70, 71, 73, 78–81, 83, 128, 137
Ceeley, J T D, Sub Lieutenant (A) RNVR 241
Centre Naval Task Force 282, 283, 286, 292
Cephalonia 60, 62, 69
Cesare Battisti, Italian Destroyer 165
Charlier, R S, Sub Lieutenant (A) RN 106
Charlton, P N, Sub Lieutenant (A) RN 189
Charybdis, HMS 230, 239, 249, 277, 295, 326
Cheeseman, N A F, Lieutenant RN 37, 38
Chenango, USS 285
Chevalier Paul, FS 173
Churchill, R A F, Lieutenant RN 263, 273
Churchill, Winston, Prime Minister viii, 4, 10, 107, 146, 245, 280, 309, 314, 351, 352, 373
Clan Ferguson, MV 249, 276
Claude, R L, Lieutenant de Vaisseau FNFL 350
Clifford, E W, Lieutenant RN 67, 74, 75, 102
Clifford, M G W, Lieutenant (A) RN 174
Clook, A G, Sub Lieutenant 236
Cobalto, Italian Submarine 267
Cockburn, J C, Lieutenant Commander RN 338, 339
Cockchafer, HMS 165
Coe, J J C, Sub Lieutenant (A) RN 124
Coke, C P, Commander RN 328
Collins, J S, Captain RAN 27
Collishaw, R, Air Commodore RAF 36
Colombo, HMS 356, 381
Colthurst, A P, Commander RN 285, 306
Commandant Teste, FS 10
Compton, P W, Lieutenant RN 225, 236
Condottieri, Italian Cruiser 91
Cooke, R H, Lieutenant RN 132
Cooper, F, Sub Lieutenant 236
Cooper, Lieutenant Commander USN 180
Corbet-Milward, N R, Lieutenant Commander RN 283, 298, 315
Corbett, J W S, Lieutenant Commander RN 176, 179, 183, 225

Cork, R J, Lieutenant (A) RN 264, 270–272
Coston, F, Petty Officer RN 151
Couch, T, Sub Lieutenant (A) RN 206
Coventry, HMS 39, 147
Cox, H M, Lieutenant Commander RN 315
Cox, Lieutenant RN 187
Coy, G R, Sub Lieutenant (A) RN 168
Crete 58, 87, 93, 105, 118, 124, 126, 127, 134–136, 145, 153–155, 157, 158, 161, 169–171, 177, 185, 191, 223, 225, 243, 376, 379, 380, 387
Cronin, J C, Captain USN 356
Crosley, R M, Sub Lieutenant (A) RNVR 290
Cruikshank, J I, Sub Lieutenant (A) RNVR 272, 273
Cunliffe-Owen, H L, Sub Lieutenant (A) RNVR 273
Cunliffe, R L B, Captain RN 325
Cunningham, Sir John, Admiral 16, 350
Cunningham, Sir Andrew, Admiral of the Fleet 5, 7, 19–21, 23–25, 27, 28, 39, 40, 46, 47, 55, 56, 58, 65, 68, 79, 81–84, 86, 87, 93, 96, 98, 100, 120, 122, 125–131, 133, 135, 137, 152, 163, 173, 176, 178, 237, 279, 281, 302, 307, 308, 310, 313, 350, 395
Cursham, M, Commander RN 194
Curteis, A T B, Vice Admiral 239
Cyprus 172, 173, 175, 176, 184–186

Dakar 14–17, 55
Dalyell-Stead, J, Lieutenant Commander RN 122, 126, 130–132
Danielle Manin, Italian Destroyer 165
Darling, G R A, Sub Lieutenant (A) RNVR 350
Dasher, HMS 282, 284, 288–294, 302, 307
Davies, E J, Sub Lieutenant (A) RNVR 337
Davies, G O C, Captain RN 355, 376
Decoy, HMS 157
Defender, HMS 171
de Gaulle, Charles, French General 16
Delery, F, Maitre FNFL 350
Delhi, HMS 356
Denby, A S, Sub Lieutenant (A) RNVR 210
Denison, G, Sub Lieutenant (A) RN 170, 189
Derna 185, 188
Derwent, HMS 249
Desert Air Force 181, 189, 190, 225, 235, 243, 245, 354
Deucalion, MV 249, 266, 274
Devitt, J, Lieutenant RNR 386

De Wit, H, Lieutenant RNN 381
Dickins, G C, Commander RN 29–31
Dickson, Captain RN 200
Dido, HMS 147, 157
Diggins, H S, Sub Lieutenant (A) RN 189
Dixon, G, Leading Airman RN 291
Dobson, Warrant Officer 236
Dooley, Leading Airman RN 151
Dorset, MV 249, 277
Dorsetshire, HMS 15
Douglas, J S, Lieutenant Commander (A) RN 147, 219
Duncan, J B, Leading Airman RN 241
Dundas, J H, Lieutenant RN 168, 169
Dunkerque, FS 10–13
Dunlop, M M, Lieutenant RN 175
Dunne, I P, Sub Lieutenant 236
Durazzo 121
Durgin, C T, Rear Admiral USN 355, 356, 361
Duthie, H E, Sub Lieutenant (A) RNVR 240

Eadon, H D B, Lieutenant Commander (A) RNVR 356, 375,
Eagle, HMS 7, 19, 20, 23–28, 34–37, 39, 42–45, 55, 57, 58, 61–63, 67, 68, 84, 86, 87, 93, 96, 105, 124, 126, 163, 165, 228, 230, 237–241, 244, 249, 250, 252, 253, 256, 257, 261, 263–265, 275, 395, 410, 413
Eastern Naval Task Force 282, 285, 286, 294
Edinburgh, HMS 196, 205, 209
Edmonson, Midshipman RN 32
Eisenhower, D D, General US Army 287, 310
El Alamein, Battle of 224, 226, 227, 234, 235, 237, 245, 247, 278, 323
Elliott, W, Lieutenant Commander RN 283
Ellis, H M, Lieutenant (A) RN 225
Elwell, Midshipman RN 32
Emerald, HMS 165
Emperor, HMS 352, 353, 355, 361, 362, 367, 370, 376, 379, 381, 385–392
Empire Hope, SS 249, 276
Enterprise, HMS 165
Escapade, HMS 239
Eskimo, HMS 249
Euro, Italian Destroyer 36
Euryalus, HMS 205, 325, 327, 328, 334, 335, 340
Evans, C J, Sub Lieutenant (A) RNVR 273
Evans, C L G, Lieutenant Commander RN 124
Evans, D R B, Leading Airman RN 106

INDEX

Fairey Albacore viii, 8, 9, 56, 122, 124–133, 135, 136, 143, 145–149, 154, 173, 175, 178, 179, 182–185, 187, 190, 191, 210, 225, 228, 230–236, 238–242, 245, 246, 250, 254, 260, 263, 279, 283, 289–299, 301, 302, 307, 308, 310–312, 315–318, 320, 325, 396, 405
Fairey Barracuda 325, 395
Fairey Fulmar viii, 8, 9, 39, 40, 46, 60, 62, 65, 66, 83, 87, 90, 97, 99, 100, 103, 111–113, 118, 119, 122, 123, 125–127, 129, 130, 132, 133, 135.144, 145, 147–151, 153–155, 159–161, 170, 173, 178, 179, 185, 186, 193, 195–198, 200, 202, 204, 206, 208–210, 214, 217–219, 226, 228, 238–240, 242, 256, 257, 261, 263–266, 268, 270, 273, 276, 278, 283, 290, 294, 299, 308, 311, 320, 392, 405
Fairey Swordfish viii, 8, 9, 12–14, 16–19, 21, 23, 24, 28– 39, 41–46, 50, 53–58, 60–64, 66, 69–71, 74, 75, 77, 79, 81, 86–90, 93–95, 97, 99, 104–106, 110–112, 115–122, 126, 127, 129, 130, 132, 133, 136, 138–143, 145, 147, 152, 154, 157, 163–168, 172–176, 185, 186, 191, 192, 194, 197, 199, 201, 202, 204, 206, 208–210, 214, 217–220, 226, 227, 230, 232, 239, 245, 246, 254, 285, 287, 288, 310–312, 325, 338, 351, 354, 365, 389, 390, 398, 401, 402, 404
Falmouth, HMS 165
Farncomb, H B, Captain RAN 355, 375
Fearless, HMS 196
Fell, M F, Lieutenant Commander (A) RN 325, 355, 376, 385, 390
Fiddes, D B M, Lieutenant RN 258, 272
Fiji, HMS 47, 157
Firth, K, Lieutenant Commander (A) RNVR 148, 326
Fiume, Italian Cruiser 24, 64, 73, 76, 126, 135
Folgore, Italian Destroyer 73, 76
Follows, F W, Sub Lieutenant RN 194
Foote, S W, Midshipman (A) RNVR 112
Force A 147, 151, 152, 377, 378, 381, 382, 385, 387, 393
Force B 147, 150, 390
Force D 147
Force F 147, 150, 151, 248, 249
Force H 5, 10–12, 21, 33, 34, 40, 41, 46, 58, 66, 83, 87, 89, 92, 95–97, 104, 105, 107, 109–111, 113–115, 147, 148, 150, 192, 195, 196, 199, 200, 201, 203–205, 209–214, 218, 223, 229, 283, 285, 287, 289, 294, 296, 301, 302, 310, 313, 315–319, 324–332, 338, 345, 348, 395, 397
Force K 185, 210, 211, 313
Force O 289, 294, 295, 303, 305
Force Q 313
Force V 323–329, 331–334, 336–338, 341–347, 349, 357, 397, 399, 400
Force W 230, 231, 241
Force X 196, 197, 209, 239, 248, 249, 254, 276
Force Z 248, 249, 255, 263, 267, 268, 273, 274, 276
Ford, AB C, Sub Lieutenant (A) RNVR 350
Forde, A J B, Lieutenant Commander (A) RN 67, 71, 84, 325
Ford, Sir Wilbraham, Vice Admiral, 79, 104
Foresight, HMS 249, 270
Forester, HMS 196
Formidable, HMS 10, 119, 121–130, 133–137, 145–147, 150–154, 156–158, 171, 283, 288, 289, 292, 294–296, 298–302, 305–308, 310, 313, 315, 318, 324, 325, 327, 329, 331, 348, 251, 395, 413
Fraser-Harris, A B, Lieutenant Commander RN 283, 291, 350
Fulmine, Italian Destroyer 70, 73, 76
Furious, HMS 7, 51, 160, 192–195, 199, 202–204, 249, 250, 252, 256, 257, 280, 283, 288–294, 303, 307, 308, 310, 312, 313, 357, 410
Fury, HMS 249

Gardner, Petty Officer RN 151
Gardner, R E, Lieutenant (A) RNVR 148
Garibaldi, Italian Cruiser 65, 126, 128, 133, 136
Garnett, J N, Lieutenant Commander RN 31, 124, 126, 155
Garside, F R, Captain RN 21
Gavdo Island 126, 127
Genoa 29–31, 81, 104, 110–115
George VI, HM The King 82, 230
Ghurka, HMS 214
Gibraltar 11, 21, 29–31, 33, 40, 41, 46, 89, 96, 104, 105, 110, 114, 144, 147, 150, 153, 160, 192, 193, 195, 196, 198, 200, 201, 203, 210–212, 215, 219, 221, 228, 234, 238, 241, 245, 248, 249, 252, 254, 256, 276, 281, 285, 287, 288, 292, 293, 296, 300, 301, 305, 306, 310, 312, 315, 319, 324, 326, 333, 345, 351, 353, 354, 392, 395
Gibson, D C E F, Lieutenant RN 168
Gick, P D, Lieutenant RN 226, 227

Gioberti, Italian Destroyer 72, 76, 135
Giosue Carducci, Italian Destroyer 135
Giovanni Acerdia, Italian Destroyer 165
Giulio Cesare, Italian Battleship 22, 24, 64, 73, 76, 111
Glasgow, HMS 60
Glenorchy, MV 249, 277
Glorious, HMS 7, 28, 53, 54, 56
Gloster Sea Gladiator 9, 26, 28, 37, 55, 61, 62, 66, 119, 127, 395, 405
Gloucester, HMS 21, 24, 60, 64, 96, 126, 128, 145, 147, 157
Godfrey, Leading Airman RN 148
Going, G R M, Lieutenant RN 63, 64, 67, 74, 75, 84, 86, 100–102
Goodwin, D G, Lieutenant RN 67, 84
Goodwin, O R, Sub Lieutenant (A) RNVR 350
Gorizia, Italian Cruiser 64, 72, 75, 76
Gort, Lord, Governor of Malta 248
Graham, H R, Captain RN 376
Graham, J S, Sub Lieutenant 236
Graham, Q D, Captain RN 325
Grantham, G, Captain RN 315
Grant, K G, Sub Lieutenant (A) RNVR 198
Greenaway, G P, Sub Lieutenant 236
Green, R A F, Sub Lieutenant (A) RN 67
Greenwood, E A, Lieutenant RN 144
Greyhound, HMS 157
Grieve, K G, Lieutenant RN 67
Griffin, R, Sub Lieutenant (A) RNVR 190
Grose, R J H, Lieutenant Commander (A) RNVR 326, 342
Grow, B E, Captain USN 356
Grumman Hellcat viii, 9, 103, 349, 352, 355, 356, 360–362, 365, 369, 375, 377, 381, 385–387, 389–393, 396, 407
Grumman Martlet viii, 8, 9, 103, 160, 162, 175, 176, 180, 186, 190, 229, 260, 265–268, 270, 273, 276, 278, 283, 290, 296, 299, 301, 302, 306, 315, 316, 325, 327, 331–333, 341, 348, 349, 351, 406
Grumman Wildcat 349, 353, 355, 360–363, 368, 375
Gunner, G H, Lieutenant 236

Hale, J W, Lieutenant Commander RN 64, 65, 67, 74, 75, 84
Halifax, G W, Leading Airman RN 112
Hall, E, Petty Officer RN 107
Hall, P A, Lieutenant (A) RN 173
Hall, P R, Lieutenant RN 31, 241
Hall, S J, Lieutenant Commander RN 355
Hallett, A F, Sub Lieutenant (A) RNVR 194

Hallett, N G, Lieutenant Commander RN 252, 265, 266, 270, 283
Halls, G H, Air Mechanic RN 225
Hamilton, R W V, Lieutenant RN 67, 75, 84
Hankey, M, Sub Lieutenant (A) RNVR 273
Hardy, C, Captain RN 239, 243
Harris, S, Sub Lieutenant (A) RNVR 259
Hartley, J V, Lieutenant (A) RN 291
Harwood, Sir Henry, Admiral, 243, 281
Hastings, J F W, Lieutenant RN 264
Hasty, HMS 60
Havock, HMS 60
Hawker Sea Hurricane viii, 9, 103, 160, 162, 203, 219, 238–241, 249, 256–258, 260, 261, 263, 265–271, 273, 276, 278, 282, 284, 285, 288–294, 302, 304, 320, 397, 406
Hay, R C, Captain RM 149, 283
Hayman, H J, Captain RN 355
Haynes, G M, Lieutenant RAN 144
Haynes, H J, Captain RN 376
Hebe, HMS 239
Henderson, G R, Lieutenant Commander (A) RNVR 355, 376
Henley, R S, Lieutenant RN 151, 152
Hereward, HMS 157
Hermes, HMS 7, 14, 15, 165–167, 169
Hermione, HMS 196, 198–201, 203, 205, 209, 216, 245
Hero, HMS 171
Hewitt, H K, Admiral USN 329, 334, 351, 358, 359, 369
Hewitt, J G, Captain RN 355
Hilken, T J N, Captain RN 355, 376
Hill, L S, Lieutenant (A) RNVR 151
Hitler, Adolph 96, 185, 227
Hodgson, J, Sub Lieutenant 236
Holland, C S, Captain RN 12, 106, 110
Hood, HMS 11
Hopkins, F H E, Lieutenant Commander RN 133, 224, 399, 401, 402
Hordern, L A, Lieutenant Commander (A) RNVR 355, 376
Hordern, M, Lieutenant Commander (A) RNVR 332
House, Brigadier General USAAF 334
Howarth, R B, Lieutenant Commander (A) RNVR 355, 376
Howe, HMS 315
Howie, F D, Lieutenant Commander RN 29–32
Humphreys, P, Lieutenant RN 67
Hunter, HMS 321, 326, 339, 343, 347, 353, 354, 356–358, 367, 375, 378–385, 387, 392

INDEX

Hunt, R G, Lieutenant 236
Hutchinson, C, Lieutenant RN 310
Hutchinson, C L, Lieutenant Commander RN 252
Hutton, R M J, Captain RN 249
Huxley, H F, Leading Airman RN 199
Hyde-Thomson, D H, Lieutenant RN 48
Hyperion, HMS 60
Hythe, HMS 239

Iachino, A, Italian Admiral 111, 114, 126, 127, 132, 134, 135, 137, 208
Icarus, HMS 239, 249
Ilex, HMS 60, 174
Illustrious, HMS 8, 27, 39–46, 48, 56–70, 74–76, 82–84, 86, 87, 93, 94, 97–106, 109, 116, 118, 122, 124, 156, 158, 160, 319, 322, 325, 329–332, 345, 348, 351, 395, 400, 413
Imperial, HMS 157
Indomitable, HMS ii, 249, 250, 252, 253, 256–258, 260–263, 265–274, 276, 315–319, 326, 328, 333, 343, 357, 377, 403, 413
Inskip, Sir Thomas, Minister for Defence Co-ordination 7, 20
Intrepid, HMS 249
Iride, Italian Submarine 38
Isaac Sweers, HNMS 302
Isis, HMS 174
Ithuriel, HMS 239, 249, 267

Jago, J de F, Lieutenant Commander RN 118, 121
Janus, HMS 152
Janvrin, H R B, Lieutenant RN 67, 84, 99, 401, 403
Jefferson, C E H, Lieutenant (A) RNVR 367
Jerram, D M, Lieutenant (A) RNVR 301
Jervis, HMS 135
Jewell, C M, Lieutenant (A) RN 199
Johnstone, M, Lieutenant Commander RN 105, 111, 112
Johnston, R L, Lieutenant RN 187, 252, 265, 272, 273
Jones, P D, Sub Lieutenant (A) RN 67, 84
Judd, D M, Sub Lieutenant (A) RNVR 236
Judd, F E C, Lieutenant Commander RN 252, 272, 273
Juno, HMS 134, 157

Kasaan Bay, USS 355, 356
Kashmir, HMS 157
Keighly-Peach, C, Commander RN 19, 26, 37, 163, 164

Keith, A, Sub Lieutenant (A) RN 63
Keith, L K, Lieutenant (A) RN 171
Kelly, HMS 157
Kelvin, HMS 157
Kemp, N McI, Lieutenant RN 66, 71, 102
Kempson, N H, Sub Lieutenant (A) RNVR 311
Kendall, B, Lieutenant Commander RN 150
Kennedy, N, Lieutenant Commander RN 35, 36
Kenya, HMS 205, 239, 249, 276
Kerkenah Bank 115, 118
Kerlan, G, Maitre FNFL 350
Khedive, HMS 353–356, 359, 362, 367, 369–372, 376, 378, 379, 381, 382, 386, 413
Kiggell, L J, Lieutenant (A) RN 67, 69, 76, 77, 84, 134, 135
Kindersley, A T J, Lieutenant RN 198
King, E L S, Vice Admiral, CS15 173, 174
King George V, HMS 315, 391
Kingston, HMS 165
Kipling, HMS 157
Kirke, D W, Lieutenant Commander RN 318, 325
Kithera Channel 118, 119
Knight, R B, Sub Lieutenant RN 107
Kujawiak, Polish Destroyer 239, 242

Laforey, HMS 216, 217, 249, 257
Lamb, C B, Lieutenant (A) RN 62, 67, 69, 76
Lampo, Italian Destroyer 70, 73, 76
Lance, HMS 185, 210
Lane, H J F, Lieutenant Commander RN 283
Langmore, D E, Lieutenant Commander RN 144, 210
Largs, HMS 286, 291, 293
Lashmore, M E, Lieutenant RN 242
Lasson, L E, Leading Airman RN 168
Laurie, S S, Midshipman (A) RNVR 164
Lea, C S C, Lieutenant (A) RN 67, 75, 84
Leander, HMS 93
Leatham, A G, Lieutenant Commander RN 164, 252
Ledbury, HMS 249, 277
Leghorn 104, 111, 115, 200
Legion, HMS 212–216, 219
Leone, Italian Destroyer 163
Leone Pancaldo, Italian Destroyer 36
Leslie, N, Leading Airman RN 225
Lewin, E D G, Lieutenant Commander RN 328
Lewis, J H, Sub Lieutenant (A) RNVR 144
Libeccio, Italian Destroyer 74, 81

433

Lightning, HMS 249
Littler, J A, Sub Lieutenant (A) RNVR 384
Littorio, Italian Battleship 47, 64, 71, 73, 75, 76, 78–81, 85, 244
Lively, HMS 185, 210
Liverpool, HMS 239, 240, 245
Livingstone, C D, Sub Lieutenant (A) RN 194
Lloyd, L G, Lieutenant (A) RNVR 350, 367
Lloyd, O S E, Sub Lieutenant 236
Lockyer, F C, Air Mechanic RN 225
Lookout, HMS 249, 257
Loyal, HMS 341
Lucas, J M, Sub Lieutenant (A) RNVR 273
Lucas, W J, Lieutenant Commander RN 252, 283
Luigi di Savoia, Italian Cruiser 241
Lyle, A V, Lieutenant Commander RN 238
Lyster, Sir Lumley, Vice Admiral 39, 40, 54, 56, 58, 59, 61, 79, 84, 86, 88, 103, 122, 161, 249, 262, 274, 282, 283, 303, 307, 309, 321, 352, 398

Macauley, A S D, Sub Lieutenant (A) RN 66, 71, 84, 173
Mackintosh, L D, Captain RN 54, 252, 257
MacLean, W G, Petty Officer RN 367
MacNamee, R I, Sub Lieutenant (A) RNVR 367
Malaya, HMS 24, 58, 83, 104, 110, 112, 207, 209, 211, 214, 215, 239
Malta 20, 21, 26, 28, 29, 31, 33, 34, 36, 39–41, 46, 47, 58, 59, 62, 64, 68, 79, 86, 89, 94, 96, 100, 101, 104–106, 114–118, 125, 138.140, 142–145, 147, 151, 154, 163, 177, 185, 193, 195–204, 208–213, 223–225, 227–232, 234, 237–239, 241–245, 247–249, 254, 256, 262, 276–278, 280, 310–312, 317, 319, 326, 331, 332, 341, 355, 357, 358, 371, 392, 395, 397, 400–402
Manchester, HMS 89, 91, 196, 198, 249, 277
Manning, J C, Sub Lieutenant (A) RNVR 311
Manxman, HMS 196, 198, 200
Mardel-Ferreira, A, Sub Lieutenant (A) RNVR 67, 102
Marne, HMS 239
Marsh, A E, Captain RM 252
Marsh, A H, Petty Officer RN 37–39
Martin, HMS 302
Martyn, W H, Lieutenant Commander (A) RN 264, 270, 285, 315, 325
Mason, D, Captain MN 277, 278

Massawa 122–124, 126, 163, 165
Massey, P W V, Lieutenant RN 285
Matapan 125, 136–138
Matchless, HMS 239
Maund, L E H, Captain RN 209, 215, 216
Maund, M R, Lieutenant RN 67, 71, 84
McClister, T J, Sub Lieutenant 236
McCloud, H, Leading Airman RN 198
McIntosh, D K, Lieutenant 236
McKenzie, M A, Sub Lieutenant (A) RNVR 340
McWilliam, H H, Captain RN 326, 343, 356
Mediterranean Fleet 5, 6, 10, 19, 21, 27, 39–41, 46, 54, 58, 59, 65, 66, 83, 87, 89, 96, 97, 124–126, 144, 147, 150, 152, 154, 171, 177, 178, 186, 211, 315, 395
Melbourne Star, MV 249, 277
Mercer, G C, Sub Lieutenant (A) RNVR 340
Mers-el-Kebir 10, 11, 14, 305, 310, 315
Middleton, HMS 239
Ministry of Aircraft Production 1, 3, 8, 126, 162, 283, 395, 397
Mobile Airborne Torpedo Maintenance Units 120, 183, 399
Mohawk, HMS 81
Montecuccoli, Italian Cruiser 241
Monte Gargano, Italian Depot Ship 38
Montgomery, B, General, Commander of 8th Army 247
Moody, C, Rear Admiral 315, 319, 325
Morford, W D, Lieutenant (A) RN 67, 74
Muller, D M, Sub Lieutenant (A) RNVR 210
Mundy, N B, Surgeon Lieutenant 236
Murray, J B, Lieutenant (A) RN 67, 74
Murray-Smith, H S, Captain RN 325, 356
Murricane, J D, Sub Lieutenant (A) RNVR 236
Mussolini, Benito, Italian Dictator 10, 53, 322

Naiad, HMS 147, 157
Napier, HMAS 157
Nares, J G A McI, Lieutenant Commander RN 283, 291, 294
Nation, B H NC, Lieutenant (A) RN 296–298
Naval Air Division 3, 12, 13, 15, 18, 28, 55, 60, 139, 159, 166, 200, 231, 275, 308, 319, 321, 331, 370, 393
Naval Air Squadrons
700 186, 237, 310, 312
701 237, 311

718 344
759 40
767 28–31
770 28
775 178
800 34, 90, 113, 144, 159, 252, 263, 273, 284, 291, 352, 355, 360, 361, 367, 376, 381, 387–389
801 238–241, 252, 256, 257, 264, 265, 273, 283, 303
802 19, 28, 160, 285, 288
803 34, 122, 123, 125, 126, 129, 147, 151, 155, 168, 172–174, 177, 180, 181, 186, 187, 189, 190, 225, 226, 288
804 252, 284, 291, 302, 401
805 119, 127, 169, 171, 172, 176 178, 180, 181, 186, 190, 191, 225, 226, 234, 246
806 39, 62, 65, 66, 103, 116, 118, 124, 126, 147, 151, 152, 155, 170, 172, 175, 177, 180, 181, 186, 187, 189, 190, 225, 226, 252, 265, 272, 273
807 144, 147, 148, 194, 198, 205, 206, 218, 219, 238, 239, 241, 283, 291, 294, 315, 320, 326, 331, 337, 350, 356, 357, 365, 367, 375, 376, 380, 383, 384, 390, 392
808 90, 113, 147–149, 159, 194, 198, 205, 206, 217, 326, 331
809 252, 257, 265, 266, 273, 283, 296, 325, 340, 356, 367, 374–376, 383, 387, 388, 392, 394
810 13, 33, 41, 45, 105, 111, 112, 199, 204, 325
812 54, 202, 204, 205, 210, 211, 218–221, 230
813 19, 24, 25, 34, 36, 37, 42, 43, 45, 48, 61, 62, 66, 67, 163, 228, 238, 239, 245, 246, 252, 301, 310, 312
814 15, 55, 165–167
815 39, 41–44, 48, 62, 64, 66, 94, 95, 118–122, 126–128, 134, 137, 164, 169, 171–173, 175, 176, 178, 184–186, 190, 191, 225–227, 231, 246, 310, 311
816 192, 194, 205, 208, 217
817 252, 283, 298, 303, 315
818 33, 45, 112, 192, 325, 338
819 39, 41, 42, 44, 48, 62, 64, 67, 94, 95
820 13, 33, 41, 45, 111, 112, 192, 283, 292, 295, 298, 310, 315, 325
821 184, 225, 226, 235, 236, 238, 241, 245, 247, 311, 312
822 252, 283, 289, 291, 293
823 54
824 19, 24, 25, 35, 36, 42, 44, 45, 48, 62, 67, 163, 228, 239
825 53, 54, 192, 205, 208, 210, 211, 217
826 122, 124–127, 129, 144, 154, 171, 175, 176, 178, 179, 181–186, 190, 191, 225, 226, 235, 236, 239, 240, 245–247, 311, 312, 401
827 252
828 138, 143, 144, 146, 148, 149, 163, 210, 223, 225, 232, 238, 242, 254, 311
829 122, 123, 126, 129, 154, 157, 173, 175, 176
830 31–33, 46, 95, 111, 115–119, 138–140, 142, 143, 145, 163, 197, 210, 223–226, 232, 242, 254, 311, 401, 402
831 252
832 252, 283, 297, 298
833 285, 287, 288, 312, 325, 337
834 326, 343
878 325
879 314, 326, 342, 346, 355, 366, 375, 376, 388, 392
880 202, 203, 252, 258, 263, 264, 270–273, 285, 315, 325, 333, 340, 341
881 353, 355, 362, 363, 376
882 283, 296, 298, 355, 367, 368, 376
883 285
884 252, 263, 265, 271, 273, 283, 304, 305
885 252, 283, 296, 305, 315, 324, 325, 327
886 326, 340
887 318, 325
888 283, 295, 300, 306, 315, 325
889 226, 237, 242, 246, 311, 392
890 325
891 282, 284, 289, 291, 292
893 283, 296, 315, 325
894 325, 332, 345, 348
897 325, 337, 340
899 ii, 315, 326, 354, 355, 367, 369, 370, 376, 382, 386, 403
Naval Fighter Squadron 170, 180, 181, 185, 186, 189–191
Naval Fighter Wing 338, 339
D Naval Fighter Wing 354, 355, 368
4 Naval Fighter Wing 356, 392
7 Naval Fighter Wing 355, 376
Naval Air Stations
  Aboukir 119, 186, 237
  Dekheila 19, 34, 86, 124, 147, 156, 163, 172, 175, 177, 178, 182–186, 188, 225, 231, 234, 236, 237, 245, 246

Fayid 164, 172, 180, 184, 188, 240, 241
Hyeres 28–31
Maleme 118–121, 126–128, 130, 133–137, 170, 172, 381, 382
Nazario Sauro, Italian Destroyer 164
Neale, J W, Sub Lieutenant (A) RN 66, 84, 173
Nelson, HMS 196, 199, 200, 203, 205–208, 249, 250, 315, 318, 325
Nembo, Italian Destroyer 36
Neptune, HMS 28
Neville, C R, Sub Lieutenant 236
Newcastle, HMS 89
Newman, M J S, Lieutenant Commander (A) RN 284
Newson, A C, Captain RM 226
Nichols, G J R, Lieutenant RN 147
Nigeria, HMS 249, 276
Nihill, J H O'C, Sub Lieutenant (A) RNVR 273
Nubian, HMS 81, 135, 157, 341
Nunn, A, Sub Lieutenant (A) RNVR 273
Nuttall, H W, Petty Officer RN 238

Ogle, D S, Lieutenant RN 387
Ohio, SS 249, 254, 275, 277, 278
Oliphant, R H L, Lieutenant RN 326
Oliver, G N, Commodore RN 385, 392
Ondina, Italian Submarine 237
Onslow, HMS 239
Onslow, R F J, Captain RN 14
Onslow, R G, Captain RN 249
Operations
  Aplomb 379
  Avalanche 323, 324, 331, 335, 337, 340–347, 349–352, 358–360, 372, 399
  Baritone 280, 410
  Battleaxe 171, 177
  Bellows 249, 252, 254, 410
  Beserk 250, 253
  Bowery 230, 410
  Calendar 410
  Callboy 143, 210, 211
  Coat 58
  Collar 89
  Contempt 389–391
  Crusader 177, 181, 184, 186, 189
  Demon 121, 145
  Dragoon 351–353, 355, 357–360, 366–369, 371–375, 391
  Dunlop 144, 151
  Excess 96, 100, 104, 105
  Exporter 172, 175, 177
  Grog 110, 115
  Halberd 202, 204, 205, 209

  Harpoon 234, 237, 239, 243, 244, 248, 255
  Hats 40, 41
  Hurry 33, 34, 410
  Husky ii, 314–316, 318, 320, 327, 352, 358
  Insect 410
  Judgement 48, 58, 65, 84, 86, 87
  LB 237, 410
  Lustre 119, 125
  MA 5 21, 22, 26
  MB 8 58, 65, 86
  MC 9 125
  MD 2 145
  MD 3 145
  MD 4 146, 147
  Manna 385–387
  Menace 16, 19
  Mincemeat 200
  Outing 375–377, 381, 384, 386, 392
  Pedestal 234, 248–250, 252–254, 256, 261, 264, 265, 275, 278, 279, 315, 400
  Perpetual I 207, 211, 303, 410
  Perpetual II 219, 410
  Picket I 104, 107–109, 228, 410
  Picket II 228, 410
  Pinpoint 410
  Railway I 193, 410
  Railway II 193, 410
  Result 104, 110
  Rocket 193, 410
  Salient 237, 410
  Splice 193
  Spotter 228, 410
  Status I 203, 410
  Status II 203, 410
  Stone Age 310
  Style 199, 200, 237, 238, 410
  Substance 195, 196, 198, 204
  Tiger 146, 147, 153, 313
  Torch 281, 282, 286, 287, 292, 303, 305, 307–309, 315, 327, 343, 347, 352, 358, 399, 401
  Tracer 192, 193, 410
  Train 280, 410
  Vigorous 234, 237, 243, 244
  White 33, 34, 410
  Winch 144, 410
Oriani, Italian Destroyer 72, 76, 135
Orion, HMS 42, 81, 126, 128, 130, 147, 157
Orwin, W D, Sub Lieutenant 236
Osborn, G M T, Lieutenant RN 132
Ostro, Italian Destroyer 36
O'Sullivan, M H P A, Lieutenant RN 107

P.35, HMS 223, 244
P.38, HMS 223
Pacey, M G, Petty Officer RN 134
Paine, S M, Sub Lieutenant (A) RN 67
Palmer, P E, Sub Lieutenant (A) RNVR 241
Palomares, HMS 328, 329, 333, 334
Pandora, HMS 33
Pangbourne, W J, Lieutenant (A) RNVR 189
Pantelleria Island 97, 197, 209, 232, 233, 238, 254, 255
Pantera, Italian Destroyer 165
Panther, HMS 295
Pares, G M, Lieutenant Commander RN 261
Parker, D G, Lieutenant (A) RNVR 304, 305, 325
Parr, Petty Officer RN 32
Partridge, HMS 239
Patch, O, Captain RM 37–39, 67, 71, 84
Pathfinder, HMS 249, 277
Paton, W N, Lieutenant (A) RNVR 232, 242
Pearson, R B, Lieutenant Commander A) RN 283, 315, 325
Peever, C W R, Lieutenant RN 151
Penelope, HMS 185, 210
Penn, HMS 249, 275, 277, 278
Pennington, F A J, Lieutenant (A) RNZNVR 326, 343
Pennington, F, Lieutenant RN 266
Perkins, E A, Sub Lieutenant (A) RNVR 67, 102
Perry, A D, Sub Lieutenant (A) RNVR 383
Perth, HMAS 126, 147, 155, 157
Philadelphia, USS 341
Philip, G T, Captain RN 239, 252, 285, 304
Phoebe, HMS 147, 173, 249
Phoenix, HMS 22
Plumleaf, RFA 278
Pola, Italian Cruiser 24, 65, 73, 126, 134–136
Pollock, D, Lieutenant RNVR 58, 59
Popham, H, Lieutenant (A) RNVR 258, 266, 271, 272, 332, 348
Porcupine, HMS 302
Porpoise, HMS 311
Porter, L P E, Leading Airman RN 184
Port Chalmers, MV 249, 277
Port Sudan 126, 163, 164
Pound, Sir Dudley, Admiral, First Sea Lord 4, 5, 8, 56, 84, 86, 87, 350
Powell, J F, Sub Lieutenant (A) RN 225
Prentice, P B N, Sub Lieutenant (A) RNVR 340

Pridham-Wippell, H D, Vice Admiral 81, 105, 126–131, 154
Prince of Wales, HMS 205, 206, 208
Pringle, W F, Lieutenant Commander USN 356
Protea, HMSAS 237
Proteus, HMS 33
Provence, FS 10, 12
Pursuer, HMS 353, 355, 356, 361, 363, 367, 376, 378, 379, 381

Queen Elizabeth, HMS 147, 154, 185, 223
Quentin, HMS 249

Ramillies, HMS 83, 89, 91
Ramsay, A R, Lieutenant (A) RN 171
Ranger, USS 285
Rawlings, H B, Vice Admiral 157, 379
Razzall, E, Sub Lieutenant (A) RNVR 340
Reagan, W R, Leading Airman RN 273
Reece, L G C, Lieutenant Commander (A) RNZNVR 356, 375
Renown, HMS 40, 89–91, 95, 104, 110, 112, 113, 147, 148, 150, 192, 196, 199, 200, 230, 285
Resolution, HMS 11, 16
Revett, S L, Sub Lieutenant 236
Rhodes 35, 41, 42, 93, 94, 174, 379, 380, 382, 386
Rice, F C, Petty Officer RN 133
Richardson, H J C, Lieutenant (E) RN 169
Richelieu, FS 14–17, 55
Ritchie, B, Sub Lieutenant (A) RNVR 290
Roberts, HMS 235
Robertson, J, Commander RN 54, 58, 62, 68, 74
Robertson, Pilot Officer RAAF 236
Rochester Castle, MV 249, 277
Rodney, HMS 205, 206, 208, 249, 250, 276, 315, 322, 325
Roe, A J T, Lieutenant Commander RN 242
Rogers, R M, Lieutenant (E) RN 367
Rolfe, H C N, Lieutenant Commander RN 167, 169
Roosevelt, F D, US President 242, 314
Rowland, H, Sub Lieutenant (A) RNVR 294
Rowley, H S, Captain RN 64
Royalist, HMS 322, 353, 355, 360, 367, 372, 375, 378, 380–382, 385, 387, 393
Royall, L A, Sub Lieutenant RN 199
Royal Sovereign, HMS 24, 89
Rudorf, M W, Lieutenant (A) RN 175
Rush, A S, Leading Airman RN 152
Rushbrook, E G N, Captain RN 239, 240

Rushworth-Lund, AJ, Sub Lieutenant (A) RNVR 225
Rye, HMS 239, 277

Salerno 323, 324, 327, 332, 336, 338, 341, 342, 344, 350, 357, 369, 374, 400
Saltykoff, W, Sub Lieutenant RNN 385
Sangamon, USS 285
Santa Elisa, MV 249, 277
Santee, USS 285
Sarra, W C, Sub Lieutenant (A) RN 67, 71, 84
Saunders, Leading Airman RN 225
Saunt, W H G, Lieutenant Commander RN 122, 126, 129, 130, 133, 134, 154
Savage, E G, Lieutenant RN 252, 257
Savannah, USS 341
Saville, G P, Brigadier General USAAF 357
Scarlett, N J, Lieutenant RN 66, 70, 74, 76, 84
Scarpanto 42, 119, 127, 154
Scott, P F, Lieutenant RN 169
Scylla, HMS 326
Searcher, HMS 353, 355, 356, 367, 368, 376, 378, 379, 381
Sedgwick, J L, Lieutenant (E) RN 164
Sergeant, E, Midshipman (A) RNVR 164
Sewell, AJ, Lieutenant (A) RNVR 155, 284
Sharpe, A, Sub Lieutenant (A) RNZNVR 367
Shaw, A I B, Sub Lieutenant (A) RNVR 366
Sheffield, HMS 40, 95, 104, 110, 112, 147
Shirlay-Rollison, W P, Captain RN 326
Shrubsole, J C N, Lieutenant Commander RN 301, 315, 325
Simpson, C P, Sub Lieutenant (A) RN 151
Simpson, W C, Lieutenant Commander (A) RN 325, 337
Sinker, L C, Captain RN 375
Sirius, HMS 249, 253, 286, 387
Skelton, R G, Lieutenant (A) RN 67, 75, 102
Skerki Channel 153, 209, 276
Slattery, Sir Matthew, Admiral 396, 402
Slaughter, H J, Lieutenant RN 67, 75, 84
Sleigh, J W, Lieutenant Commander RN 325
Smeeton, R M, Lieutenant RN 159
Smith, C W B, Lieutenant RN 225
Smith, L W, Leading Airman RN 175
Smith, Midshipman RN 32
Somali, HMS 277
Somerville, M F, Lieutenant RN 148
Somerville, Sir James, Vice Admiral 7, 10, 11, 13, 21, 34, 40, 89–92, 104, 109, 110, 113–115, 147, 149, 159, 160, 192, 194, 195, 198, 200–203, 207–209, 211–214
Souda Bay 58, 87, 118, 128, 135, 145, 153, 154, 169, 171
Southampton, HMS 89, 91, 96
Spalding, G, Sub Lieutenant (A) RNVR 241
Sparke, P D J, Sub Lieutenant (A) RN 66, 71, 151, 152
Sparviero, Italian Aircraft Carrier 137
Speakman, E V, Lieutenant RN 367
Speedy, HMS 239
Spencer, G, Sub Lieutenant (A) RNZNVR 385
Spezia 30, 104, 111, 112, 211, 227
Squadrons
  1 South African AF 180
  46 RAF 296
  73 RAF 180
  84 RAF 126
  113 RAF 126, 182
  148 RAF 116
  154 RAF 305
  203 RAF 163
  211 RAF 120
  233 RAF 255
  252 RAF 147
  274 RAF 180
  308 USAAF 292
  309 USAAF 292
  VF-9 USN 285
  VF-41 USN 285
  VF-74 USN 356
  VF(N)-74 USN 356
  VGF-26 USN 285
  VGF-27 USN 285
  VGF-28 USN 285
  VGF-29 USN 285
  VGS-26 USN 285
  VGS-27 USN 285
  VGS-29 USN 285
  VGS-30 USN 285
  VOF-1 USN 356
  VS-41 USN 285
Stalker, HMS 321, 325, 333, 338, 340, 351, 353, 356, 358, 367, 374, 375, 379, 381–385, 387, 388, 392, 394
Stampalia 45, 93, 94, 119
Stephenson, F N R, Captain RN 326
Stevens, P D T, Sub Lieutenant 236
Stewart, D, Sub Lieutenant (A) RNVR 383
Stewart, J, Leading Airman RN 273
Stovin-Bradford, F, Sub Lieutenant (A) RN 37, 38
Strait of Gibraltar 205, 219, 240
Strait of Otranto 58, 61, 81

Strasbourg, FS 10, 12, 13
Street, P D, Sub Lieutenant (A) RNVR 301
Stuart, HMAS 135
Stuttle, W, Leading Airman RN 225
Suez Canal 39, 103, 122, 124, 157, 171
Supermarine Seafire ii, viii, 9, 103, 160, 282, 283, 285, 290–296, 303– 305, 308, 312, 315, 316, 318, 320–322, 324–326, 328, 330–334, 336–344, 346–349, 351, 353–357, 360, 362, 365, 366, 369–372, 374–378, 382–384, 386, 388, 392–394, 397, 399, 400, 406
Supermarine Seagull V 45
Supermarine Walrus 9, 42, 45, 64, 91, 93, 110, 126, 128, 155, 298, 300, 301, 312, 355, 365, 390
Suthers, S H, Sub Lieutenant (A) RN 164
Sutton, A W F, Lieutenant RN 67, 84, 120, 169–171
Sutton, B F, Sub Lieutenant 236
Suwanee, USS 285
Swayne, H A I, Lieutenant (A) RN 67, 71, 84
Sydney, HMAS 27, 28, 42, 45, 47, 81
Syfret, Sir Neville, Vice Admiral 196, 248, 249, 254–256, 277–279, 285
Symonds, J J, Leading Airman RN 301

Talbot, A G, Rear Admiral RN 283, 315, 325
Taranto viii, 8, 23, 47, 48, 50, 54–58, 61, 62, 64, 66, 68, 69, 71–77, 79, 82–89, 96, 99, 100, 115, 137, 244, 392, 396, 397, 400, 402, 403
Tartar, HMS 249
Tebble, R, Sub Lieutenant (A) RNVR 301
Tembien, Italian Submarine 199
Tempio Cork Forest 200, 201
Thompson, C G, Commander RN 58
Thompson, C H, Leading Airman RN 151
Thompson, R L, Lieutenant (A) RNVR 290
Thompson, Sub Lieutenant RN 31
Thornton, Sub Lieutenant RN 32
Tibbetts, H A L, Lieutenant RCNVR 252, 293
Tickner, L F, Lieutenant RN 241
Tidd, C B, Captain RN 172
Tigre, Italian Destroyer 165
Tillard, R C, Lieutenant Commander RN 147, 148
Tirso Dam 104, 105, 107, 114, 115
Tivy, L R, Lieutenant (A) RN 112
Tobruk 34–36, 44, 144, 171, 177, 180, 181, 186, 188, 227, 236, 237, 246
Torlesse, A D, Captain RN 375, 383

Torrens-Spence, F M A, Lieutenant (RN) 67, 75, 84, 121, 126, 133–135, 137, 178
Touchbourne, P S, Lieutenant (A) RN 151
Trento, Italian Cruiser 65, 73, 75, 81, 111, 126, 244
Trieste, Italian Cruiser 24, 65, 73, 111, 126, 128
Tripoli 33, 94, 95, 115, 116, 138–141, 143–145, 223, 224, 232
Troubridge, HMS 356
Troubridge, Sir Thomas, Rear Admiral 252, 274, 284, 286, 291, 355, 357, 368, 369, 375, 377, 385, 398
Tuck, G S, Commander RN 100, 103
Tulagi, USS 355, 356
Turnbull, F R A, Lieutenant Commander (A) RN 240, 283, 325

U-73 255, 256
U-77 227
U-81 215
U-96 220
U-97 227
U-155 306
U-202 221
U-205 245, 255
U-331 186, 255, 310
U-371 205
U-372 227
U-407 379
U-431 302
U-432 221
U-451 221
U-453 227
U-517 303
U-558 221
U-565 379
U-569 221
U-595 302
U-596 379
U-652 226
Uganda, HMS 341
Ulster Queen, HMS 328, 329, 360, 382, 392
Underwood, J F, Sub Lieutenant (A) RNVR 210
Unicorn, HMS 317, 318, 323, 325, 326, 328, 330, 331, 333, 334, 338–340, 342–345, 348, 351
Upholder, HMS 116, 201
Urlich, J J, Sub Lieutenant (A) RNZNVR 340

Valiant, HMS 11, 27, 39, 40, 58, 97, 105, 126, 135, 145, 147, 180, 185, 223, 315, 325, 329

Vansittart, HMS 249
Vauquelin, FS 174, 175
Vian, Sir Philip, Rear Admiral 325, 334, 335, 338, 340, 341
Victorious, HMS 192, 193, 249, 250, 252, 253, 256, 257, 261–263, 267, 268, 270–272, 283, 288–290, 294, 296, 297, 299–301, 303, 304, 305, 307–309, 348, 401, 403, 410
Vidette, HMS 239
Vincenzo Orsini, Italian Destroyer 165
Vittorio Veneto, Italian Battleship 47, 64, 71, 73, 76, 111, 126, 127, 130–134, 244

Waimarama, SS 249, 277
Wairangi, MV 249, 277
Walker, R F, Lieutenant Commander RN 315, 326
Wallace, A C, Lieutenant Commander (A) RNVR 151, 326
Wall, J A, Sub Lieutenant 236
Walshe, E H, Sub Lieutenant (A) RNVR 144
Walsh, R W M, Sub Lieutenant (A) RNVR 181
Walthal, L E D, Lieutenant RN 252
Wanklin, M D, Lieutenant Commander RN 116
Warspite, HMS 23–26, 28, 40, 58, 97, 105, 126, 130, 133, 134, 136, 145, 147, 157, 315, 325, 327, 341
Wasp, USS 228–231, 247, 280, 410
Waters, Lieutenant RN 31
Waters, W E, Lieutenant Commander RN 204
Watson, J D, Sub Lieutenant 236
Watson, M W, Lieutenant RN 206
Webber, R H, Lieutenant (E) RN 350
Weekes, J R, Sub Lieutenant (A) RN 67, 84
Wellham, J W G, Lieutenant (A) RN 37–39, 63, 67, 75, 77, 84

Wells, Sir Lionel, Vice Admiral 11
Welshman, HMS 231
Westcott, HMS 239, 249
Western Naval Task Force 282, 286
Whitely, E A, Flight Lieutenant RAF 56
Whitworth, A S, Lieutenant RN 132
Wightman, O M, Sub Lieutenant (A) RN 194
Williams, Sub Lieutenant RN 135
Williamson, K W, Lieutenant Commander RN 64–66, 68–70, 74, 79, 84
Willis, A J C, Sub Lieutenant (A) RNVR 189
Willis, Sir Algernon, Vice Admiral 313, 315, 319, 324, 331, 350
Willoughby, G, Commander RN 54
Wilson, K, Sub Lieutenant (A) RNVR 381
Wilton, HMS 249
Wines, Petty Officer 32
Winter, P W, Sub Lieutenant (A) RN 174
Wise, D A, Sub Lieutenant (A) RNVR 173
Wise, P D B, Sub Lieutenant 236
Wishart, HMS 239, 249
Woodley, C J, Midshipman (A) RN 37
Woods, G A L, Lieutenant Commander RN 218, 220, 221
Woods, P R E, Lieutenant (A) RN 180
Wray, A L O, Sub Lieutenant (A) RN 66, 102
Wrestler, HMS 239, 249
Wright, A J, Major RM 325

Yarra, HMAS 165, 167
Yorke, P, Commander RN 137
York, HMS 60, 128, 156

Zara, Italian Cruiser 24, 64, 73, 76, 126, 128, 135
Zeffiro, Italian Destroyer 36
Zetland, HMS 249

By the same author

A Century of Carrier Aviation: The Evolution of Ships and Shipborne Aircraft

The British Pacific Fleet: The Royal Navy's Most Powerful Strike Fleet

British Aircraft Carriers: Design, Development and Service Histories

Warships of The Great War Era: A History in Ship Models

The British Carrier Strike Fleet After 1945

The Royal Navy's Air Service in The Great War

Aircraft Carrier Victorious: Detailed in the Original Builders' Plans

The Dawn of Carrier Strike, and the World of Lieutenant W P Lucy DSO RN

David Hobbs has also written the Naval Aviation section in every edition of the *Seaforth World Naval Review* since it was first published in 2010.